SECRETS

OF THE

VIET CONG

SECRETS
OF THE
VIET CONG

James W. McCoy

HIPPOCRENE BOOKS
New York

For more information, address:
HIPPOCRENE BOOKS, INC.
171 Madison Avenue
New York, NY 10016

ISBN 0-7818-0028-5

Printed in the United States of America

Table of Contents

To Debra Q. McCoy

PART I.

Organization and Control

CHAPTER 1

Chu Luc Maneuver Art

A strange army once held sway over Indochina. To its enemies that army was a phantom force, inscrutable and invincible. For over two decades it beat back the finest troops and equipment that the west could send against it. Inspiring the deepest of fear and hatred, the North Vietnamese Army (NVA), the Chu Luc, proved that warfare doctrines which emphasized human assets and maneuver were superior to the most technologically advanced methods available.

The North Vietnamese Army was infused with a clear understanding of maneuver warfare. That familiarity insured their long string of victories.

However, the western world has never been completely bereft of maneuver savants. The great western maneuver war expert, B. H. Liddell Hart, was one such. Liddell Hart's *Strategy of the Indirection Approach,*[1] compares favorably with Sun Tzus' *Art of War.*[2] The *Art of War* directly influencd Chu Luc maneuver art. Although Liddel Hart never knew of the Chu Luc, his writings also captured the essence of Chu Luc maneuver war campaigning. He called his version of maneuver war, the "Indirect Approach."

If American generals had practiced Liddell Hart's Indirect Approach they might have beaten the North Vietnamese's Sun Tzu approach. Alas, few American generals had read Liddell Hart's book.

Liddell Hart derived some of his understanding of the dislocating and paralyzing effect of the Indirect Approach from researching the operations of the American Civil War general W. T. Sherman. Liddell Hart described that influence in his *Memoirs:* "While the concept of deep strategic penetration by a fast moving armoured force had developed originally in my mind when

3

studying the Mongol campaigns of the thirteenth century, it was through exploring the rival operations of Sherman and Forrest that I came to see more clearly its application against modern mass armies dependent on rail communications for supply. Study of Sherman's campaigns also had a strong influence on other trends in my strategical and tactical thought. Any reader of my subsequent books, in the nineteen-thirties, can see how often I utilized illustrations from Sherman to drive home my points—particularly the value of unexpectedness as the best guarantee of security as well as of rapid progress; the value of flexibility in plan and dispositions, above all by operating on a line which offers and threatens alternative objectives (thus in Sherman's phrase, putting the opponent on the 'horns of a dilemma'); the value of what I termed the 'baited gambit,' to trap the opponent, by combining offensive strategy with defensive tactics, or elastic defense with well-timed riposte; the need to cut down the load of equipment and other impedimenta—as Sherman did in order to develop mobility and flexibility."[3]

Liddell Hart's advocacy of infiltration also paralleled NVA doctrine: "Infiltration would be the basic method, extended much further than it has been, and deployed in subtler ways . . . infiltration which took civil forms rather than open military action . . . devise ways of luring his prospective opponents into giving 'hostages' of some kind, or of intertwining his bases with theirs so that the entanglement became a check on their power of retaliation."[4]

From shaping their thoughts with the ideas of Sun Tzu, the NVA became adept at maneuver war. That skill enabled them to secure and hold the initiative in the Second Indochina War.

The U.S. Pentagon's Office of System Analysis found that the Chu Luc was overwhelmingly dominant in securing the initiative in combat throughout the Vietnam war. A December 1968 report noted: "Three fourths of the battles are at the enemy's choice of time, place, type and duration. CIA notes that less than one percent of nearly two million allied small unit operations conducted in the last two years resulted in contact with the enemy and when ARVN is surveyed, the percentage drops to one tenth of one percent."[5]

The NVA Combat Advantage

North Vietnamese supremo Ho Chi Minh believed that smaller military forces could destroy larger ones: "If the tiger ever stands still, the elephant will crush him with his mighty tusks. But the tiger will not stand still. He will leap upon the back of the elephant, tearing huge chunks from his side, then he will leap back into the dark jungle. And slowly the elephant will bleed to death. Such will be the war in Indochina."[6]

Types of Engagements In Combat Narratives

Type of Engagement	Percentage of Total
1. Hot landing zone. Enemy attacks U.S. troops as they deploy on battlefield.	12.5
2. Organized enemy attack on U.S. static defense perimeter.	30.4
3. VC/NVA ambush or encircle and surprise a moving U.S. unit, using what is evidently a preconceived battle plan.	23.3
4. A moving U.S. unit engages the enemy in a dug-in or fortified position:	
a. The main engagement comes as a surprise to the American tactical commander because the enemy is well concealed and has been alerted by observations of our unit or by engaging apparent stragglers nearby.	12.5
b. The U.S. commander has reasonably accurate knowledge of enemy positions and strength before committing his strength.	5.4
5. U.S. unit ambushes a moving enemy unit.	8.9
6. Chance engagement, both sides surprised.	7.1
TOTAL	100.1%

Source: *The Pentagon Papers: The Senator Gravel Edition* (Boston: Beacon Press, 1971) 4:462.

The reds believed that even the most powerful enemy could always be outmaneuvered. In order to secure such a victory, the NVA always sought to obtain six combat advantages:

- *Initiative:* Setting or changing the terms of battle, by maneuver.
- *Agility:* The ability to act faster than the enemy. Foot mobility usually provides more agility than mechanized mobility.
- *Depth:* The extension of operations in space, time, and resources. Preparing the battlefield and fighting along several avenues of approach, as well as fighting in a nonlinear, "deep battle," deployment, gave depth to the NVA battlefield.
- *Synchronization:* The arrangement of battlefield activities in time, space and purpose to produce maximum combat power at the decisive point. Execu-

tion of this advantage compells the enemy to react to several threats at the same time, thus dispersing his force.

- *Combined Arms:* Striking the enemy with two or more weapons systems, or arms (e.g. infantry and artillery), simultaneously. The orchestration of such multiple strikes forced the enemy, seeking to avoid one arm, to become more vulnerable to another. The combined arms maneuver forces the enemy onto the horns of a dilemma by increasing his physical problems and pulling him apart psychologically.

Contrast the American supporting arms concept which they mistakenly also call "combined arms." That military application consists of striking the enemy with two or more weapons systems, or arms, in sequence, or if simultaneously, in such a way that actions taken to avoid one also protect against the others.

The American concept of combined arms is flawed because it is considered to be an organizational device, not an application of force.

- *Redundant battlefield data sources:* One of the prime requirements for military command, and especially command of maneuver battle forms, is the battle commanders' use of a "directed telescope." According to Martin Van Creveld, a directed telescope enables a battle commander to "direct (a command observation units' focus), at will, at any part of the enemy's forces, the terrain, or his own army in order to bring in information that is not only less structured than that passed on by normal channels but also tailored to meet his momentary (and specific) needs. Ideally, the regular reporting system should tell the commander which questions to ask, and the directed telescope should enable him to answer those questions."[7]

The NVA regularly employed several versions of the directed telescope. For example: "Prior to most important operations, the (NVA) Military Intelligence Agency at the Central Office for South Vietnam dispatched small elite teams, called military intelligence sections, to the battle area to conduct reconnaissance, to act as guides for combat units, and to assist as couriers during the attack . . . the team (sometimes) moved about the objective area for weeks, and sometimes months, before the planned action to study terrain and enemy defenses and to coordinate with local Viet Cong, . . . (it) . . . contacted the Central office for South Vietnam twice each day to relay information that was used to construct the detailed plans for future operations. (And report on current friendly and enemy actions in the objective area)."[8]

NVA MANEUVER FORMS AND CONCEPTS

MANEUVER FORMS

* Gaps and Surfaces
* Recon Pull
* Logistics Cache
* Foot Mobility
* Infiltration
* Narrow Front Penetration
* Combined Arms
* Mission Orders
* Directed Telescope
* Austere/Redundant Communications

DECEPTION

* A and M Type
* Harrassment

INTELLIGENCE

Espionage
Security
Ground Recon
Technical Recon
Penetration

PRIMARY OFFENSIVE METHODS

* Maneuvering Forces Battle
* Ambush
* Power Raid

SECONDARY CONCEPTS

* Advance Detachments
* Hill Traps
* Fortifications Hinge
* Immediate Counterattacks

FIREPOWER CONCEPTS

* Massed Machineguns
* Fire Support as Shock Action
* Standoff Attacks
* Surprise Volley Fire
* Modern Weapons Family
* Ammunition Interchangability
* Fire Tunnels
* Fire Sacks

NVA Deception

The essence of Chu Luc maneuver was diversion, distraction, deception and surprise close assaults. These concepts stemmed from the teachings of Sun Tzu who wrote *The Art of War* in the fourth century B.C. Sun Tzu greatly influenced the Chinese communist dictator Mao Tse Tung who, in turn, influenced Vo Nguyen Giap and the entire NVA hierarchy.

The Chu Luc sought to outmaneuver their enemies by surprising them, decapitating their command echelon, and rapidly striking at their weak points, usually on the flank or rear. Ho Chi Minh emphasized the importance of military mystification to General Giap: "Concerning tactics, practice guerrilla methods: secrecy, speed, initiative (today in the East, tomorrow in the West); appear and disappear by surprise, without leaving a trace."[9]

Understanding deception, Chu Luc leaders knew that their enemies would frequently give themselves away by three categories of indicators: signatures, profiles and patterns. Signatures, such as the cluster of radio aerials of a command unit, are concomitant with the presence of a military unit. Profiles, such as a sudden increase in radio traffic indicating possible displacement, indicate changes in military unit activity. Patterns, such as constant aerial reconnaissance over several landing zones in an area before an imminent airborne operation, stem from military units' tendency to carry out specific tasks in a habitual way.

While they used indicators to discern enemy intentions, the NVA carefully masked or otherwise distorted their own indicators through deceptive measures. They preferred A-Type and M-Type deception measures. A-Type, or ambiguity type, deception seeks to deprive the enemy of indicators and thus cover the battlefield with the "fog of war." An enemy commander, plagued by A-Type deception, is forced to relinquish the initiative since he must either act without a clear understanding of the situation, or delay acting until the situation is clarified.

M-Type, or misleading, deception is both the most difficult to employ and offers the greatest potential for decisive effect. M-Type deception convinces an enemy commander that a falsehood is true. When he acts on the basis of this distorted view of reality he is outmaneuvered.[10]

Indicators Versus Deception

Indicator Types	Deception Types
Signatures	Ambiguity
Profiles	Misleading
Patterns	

Deceptions were always part of Chu Luc planning. They conducted deceptions continuously, sequentially and on several levels simultaneously. At the operation, or major campaign, level NVA deceptions caused the maldeployment of allied forces within corps zones. At the tactical, or battle, level communist deception interfered with allied tactical intelligence and decision cycles. The reds were constantly attempting to provide their enemies with false clues, through several mutually verifying channels, in order that the enemy obtain and defend a false picture of reality.

Deception Confuses the Enemy About:

1. Your true location.
2. The nature, strength and state of your troops and equipment.
3. Your true intentions.
4. The timing and location of your planned maneuvers.
5. Your kowledge of his forces, deployments and/or plans.
6. The degree of success of his own operations.
7. The reliability of his intelligence service.

Every red movement pattern incorporated diversionary and ambiguous features. They would move along several avenues of approach threatening several objectives at the same time. Then a series of attacks would be launched, most of which were feints. Rapidly converging troops from the main forces would then hit the primary target, overrun it, and disperse in several directions.

In the main, the Chu Luc directed their deceptive efforts at enemy information sources. Displayed before those intelligence gathering sources would be one or more of numerous types of military deception.

Sources of Intelligence

Agents
Aerial Reconnaissance
Communications Intercept
Documents
Ground Reconnaissance
Pattern Analysis
Prisoners of War
Radar and other Technological Detectors

Types of NVA Military Deception

- Dissimulation Camouflage: Hide real military facilities and units.
- Simulation Camouflage: Presentation of decoys/simulated targets.
- Feint: Simulated attack preparations and deployment.
- Diversionary Assault: An attack used to divert attention from the main attack.
- Radio Manipulation: Broadcast of false and misleading clues.
- Rumors: Use of political cadres to spread false ideas.
- Media Agents: Use of communist agents of influence in western media to spread deception.
- Political Agents: Use of communist agents of influence in western governments to spread deception and sabotage war efforts.
- Fake Documents: Constructed documents with varying degrees of authenticity to both mislead and mystify the enemy.
- Double Agents: Penetration of enemy command and intelligence agencies with agents loyal to the NVA who spread deceptive data.

The NVA Combat Order

Always security conscious, Chu Luc combat leaders frequently hid their objectives from their own troops until the last possible moment. Fearing enemy spies in their ranks, they conducted pre-battle briefings without identifying the location of the specific battle area: "This kind of briefing, as a rule, always took place before the battle. The drawing of the post which was going to be attacked was hung up in front of the soldiers, but its name was not mentioned. Those who knew Ba Dua could easily recognize it. To Thao (battalion commander) pointed out to the soldiers the various posts in the Ba Dua subsector, enumerated the numerical strength of the unit which guarded each post, and told them about the GVN soldiers' low morale."[11]

The NVA was a maneuver army whose commanders led from the front and employed mission-type orders. Leaving their routine administrative and logistics tasks to a rear service commander, Chu Luc battle leaders carried out their missions from near the point of main effort. From that location they could see and sense the battlefield and respond quickly to developments.

Administrative agencies, such as Rear Services staffs, facilitated attack sequences by carrying out bureaucratic tasks which might distract the battle commander's attention. For example, Rear Services personnel would usually "obtain provisions and ammunition. Rounds of ammunition to be expended by the larger caliber weapons are carefully calculated . . . prepare coffins for the expected number of dead and provide porters for clearing the battlefield, carrying the injured, and collecting captured equipment."[12]

Allied commanders, with their colonels and generals miles behind the front, or in the cloudy heights of helicopter command posts, depended upon both administrative and combat reports to understand the battle. As a result they reacted more slowly. In addition the combat reports were frequently skewed by the emotions of men fighting on the ground, where the atmosphere was very different from that found in a comfortable, air conditioned command post.

Important to NVA leadership methods was the use of mission-type orders. Those orders spelled out the commander's intent and oriented offensive action against the enemy force, not terrain features.

The commander's intent is what he wants to accomplish in relation to the enemy force at hand. Understanding this concept allows subordinate commanders to fight without geographical restrictions, and insures flexibility. Subordinates are freed to seek gaps in the enemy array without worrying about whether they are on top of a prescribed piece of terrain (an objective) by a certain time.

Another effect of this battle philosophy was the tendency to report progress honestly, as either success or failure, by NVA subordinate commanders. As one NVA leader put it: "Finally, when everything is done, the leaders should report to their superiors to put the minds of the latter at rest and to ask for new orders."[13]

American combat officers seemed to be rapidly thwarted during battle. They were usually quickly pinned by NVA fire and they were always requesting assistance to free them up for movement. Their missions always seemed to require outside help, or "support."

The Americans fought toward objectives outlined in Five Paragraph Field Orders. Such orders emphasized terrain objectives and fire support. By their construction, such orders promoted a perception of battle as a frontal, meatgrinding assault, requiring frequent assistance (support) from higher quarters. Many American officers behaved in battle as if they were timid, awkward children, totally dependent upon a daddy who was continuously being telephoned for help.

Comparison of 5 Paragraph and Mission-Type Orders

U.S. 5 Paragraph Field Order	NVA Mission-Type Order
1. Situation: Enemy and friendly forces.	1. Enemy and friendly forces. What the commander wants to accomplish.
2. Mission: Defined as seizure of terrain.	2. Mission related to enemy, not terrain.

THE PARADIGMS OF CHU LUC DECEPTION

"Maskirovka is all types of deception, camouflage and concealment."

The purpose of Maskirovka is surprise

"...given identical forces and other equal
conditions he who outwits the enemy
emerges as the victor..." SOVIET MASKIROVKA
MANUAL, 1944.

"..in warfare one does not inform the foe when an attack will occur." "..one must try to catch the enemy unaware and seize the moment when his troops are scattered ." LENIN

"Surprise is an unexpected action which leads to success."

Surprise is achieved by:

* Maintaining secrecy
* Misleading the enemy
* Swift concentration and regroupment
* Unexpected attacks from unexpected directions
* Destroying enemy reconnaissance assets
* Disguising the main effort with multiple attacks
* Skillful use of terrain, weather, time and season
* Simulations
* Rapid maneuver
* Direction and timing of the main effort
* Employment of new weapons and forms of battle

An enemy is misled by:

* Concealing reality from enemy reconnaissance
* Distorting the appearance of reality
* Executing feints and displaying dummies
* Sound and light discipline
* Radio decption

Chief Devices of Operational Maskirovka

* Demonstrative actions (sometimes in the form of
  offensive operations of comparatively large scale)
* False march maneuvers
* False radio maneuvers
* Hidden regroupment and concentration of forces
* Disinformation-false : rumors, documents, line crossers
* False structures and constructions
* Smoke

Measures essential for achieving Maskirovka

* Secrecy of force deployment and operational intent
* Demonstrative actions which deceive
* Simulations to confuse actual locations and intentions
* Disinformation by technical, document and human means

3. Execution: Scheme of movement. Subordinate missions, given in terms of terrain.
4. Service Support
5. Command and Signal

3. Focus of main effort. Secondary efforts in terms of enemy, not terrain.
4. Same
5. Same

In battle situations, NVA commanders gave brief verbal orders, whenever possible. As one NVA officer recounted: "Communications is an important and necessary task during marches because the orders of the commanders should be known to the troops. Orders should be communicated quickly throughout the ranks to enable the commanders to be in control of the unit at every moment. In issuing orders, the commanders should be careful. The orders should be precise and specific. The commanders should not issue orders at random, one after another, and they should avoid giving long and involved orders."[14]

NVA Operations Order: Short Form

1. Enemy Situation
2. Mission, strength, initial deployment and scheme of maneuver of each friendly element. This segment emphasized the commanders' intent and the point of main effort.
3. Location of unit headquarters.
4. Time of preparation and completion of operation.
5. Report time and method.[15]

After battles, during unit rest periods, NVA staffs would take the time to write out a laborious and lengthy order for the record. Those after-the-fact orders usually violated the tenets of maneuver warfare.

There are some variations in NVA battle order methodology, especially when the order was written up after a battle was over. Some after-the-fact communist orders were as much as five pages long. However, NVA orders never failed to emphasize the prime elements of the maneuver battle.

Example of an NVA Long Form Written Operation Order

A. **Enemy situation**
1. Enemy Situation in Objective Area
2. Area of Activity of Enemy Units
3. General Observations on the enemy

  B. Friendly Situation
    1. General Mission of the Unit (Commanders' intent and main effort)
- Prescribed Objectives
- Area of Activity
- Duration of Activity
- Target of Operations

    2. Combat Guidelines (Coordinating instructions)
    3. Tactics to be Employed (General elaborations on battle methods)
    4. Resolution (Unit pledge regarding victory; motivational propaganda)
      (a) General Resolution of the Unit
      (b) Specific Resolution of Step 1
      (c) Employment of forces

  C. Unit CP location(s)
  D. Rear Services
  E. Time (Precise scheduling of specific maneuvers)[16]

Variant on the NVA Long Form Battle Order

- Description of the terrain of the battle area.
- Deployment of enemy forces.
- Enemy troop strength.
- Three propaganda elements for the record:
  A. Determination of the Battalion (The commanders' intent and a propaganda statement emphasizng that the battalion is determined to carry out its mission.)
  B. Guiding Tactical Principle (A standard statement emphasizing the offensive.)
  C. Tactics (A standard statement emphasizing that the unit will "penetrate the enemy," "surround the enemy." and "fire first.")
- Common mission (A list of reinforcements to the unit.)
- Mission of each company (The identification of main effort units whose operation all other units will support.)
- Missions of the main attacking units and the supporting units (Each main effort units mission and direction of attack is specified. Any extra weapons or troop reinforcement are also indicated for each unit. The secondary attack unit(s) is specified in the same manner as the main effort unit. The base of fire unit is also specified similarly. Detailed target assignments are made to this unit.

- The mission of any assigned *(DDQS)* sappers is detailed.
- Mission of the Forward Communication Element, *Buu Tien* (The Buu Tien was responsible for ensuring continuous unit-wide communications, communications security, and coordination of the operation.)
- Mission of the Reconnaissance Unit (Standard)[17]

To control the maneuver, the NVA employed radios and modern communications gear which existed alongside messengers, signal lights, flags, flares and pyrotechnics as redundant signalling means. Communist units sometimes included a signals table with their battle orders. That table, for example, might define how pyrotechnics and flares would communicate various battle messages.

Example of a Signal Table Extract: Flares and Tracers

Signal Meaning	Flares, Rockets, Tracer Configuration
Friendly troops here	Three illuminating flares
Transfer fire support	One red flare towards target
Cease fire support	One green illuminating flare
Target indication	Tracer rounds in long or short bursts
Pursue enemy	Two red flares
Bypass enemy on right	One green flare
Bypass enemy on left	Two green flares
Enemy position secured	Two green star clusters
Commanders report to me	Two star blue smoke flares[18]

NVA Military Training

Much talk circulated during the Vietnam war about the high state of training of the individual communist infantryman, or *Bo Dai* The NVA was frequently referred to as "a first class armed force of several hundred thousand well trained, well armed, men."[19] In fact, the regular Chu Luc infantry soldier was given the bare rudiments of training.

When new NVA recruits reported to their command, they were sent directly to a regimental or battalion headquarters. There they were assigned to a platoon which trained new recruits under the supervision of the battalion command staff.

The training was carried out in approximately thirty days of intense effort. Sometimes the formal training of Viet Cong (VC) recruits was almost nonexistent. In late 1966, for example, the 514th VC Battalion trained its recruits in only eight days, comprising two days of political indoctrination and six days of military training. "The six days of military training are devoted to . . . drill, firing positions, bayonet thrust, grenade toss."[20]

However, the more common thirty-day schedule included formal training in specific individual infantry skills: "Military training was supposed to include the use and maintenance of weapons; grenade throwing; digging of fortifications; camouflage techniques; movement procedures; individual, cell, and squad tactics in combat; sanitation and preventive medicine; self help measures to be taken against toxic chemicals; discipline; guard and patrol duty; liaison; reconnaissance; POW escort."[21]

Certain minimal skill levels were required of a red infantryman if he was to be useful to his unit. An operational officer of the 5th NVA Division identified five minimum troop training requirements which enabled "a Viet Cong battalion to perform with average effectiveness:

1. Marksmanship and weapons familiarization.
2. Techniques of armored vehicle destruction.
3. Ambush tactics.
4. Surprise attack.
5. Anti-heliborne or paratroop tactics.

Some of these subjects are first taught in the initial training period and then are part of the continuous training program in the battalion."[22]

As their enemies adopted new battle methods and equipment, the Chu Luc made sure that its troops were trained in effective countermeasures. "Recently (summer 1967) the battalion was given indoctrination on how to cope with two tactics of the US 9th Division—the 'butterfly tactic' (buom buom) and the 'chup non' tactic. The butterfly tactic is one in which a small action can turn into a large one. It starts off with a helicopter landing of a small unit to probe the area. If there is an encounter, second helicopter with more troops comes in (and the operation) may rise to a battalion or regiment size for an encirclement. . .

"The chup non tactic means a fast troop landing of a small unit—maybe a platoon—which will hit fast and retreat quickly. There is no set pattern of time and space involved, so that the element of surprise may be gained at any place. This tactic is often used to hit installations or capture cadres."[23]

NVA crew-served weapons, machine guns, recoilless rifle and mortar teams received at least four months of training. That training stressed fire

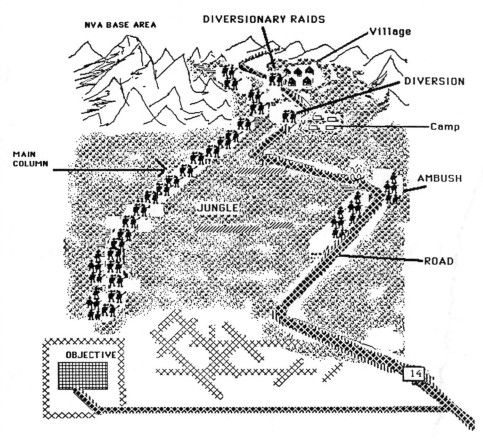

NVA BASE AREA

DIVERSIONARY RAIDS

Village

DIVERSION

Camp

MAIN COLUMN

AMBUSH

JUNGLE

ROAD

OBJECTIVE

14

MANEUVER AND DECEPTION

NVA USE OF DIVERSIONARY ATTACKS
TO DIVERT THEIR ENEMY AWAY FROM
THE MAIN EFFORT

17

support coordination and delivery, firing accuracy, tactical employment, and weapons maintenance.

Much more training time and effort was lavished upon NVA cadres, or leaders. Squad and platoon leaders were trained during three to five months of indoctrination in political (20%) and military (80%) subjects. Leadership concepts, including building unit cohesion and thinking in terms of maneuver warfare were stressed. Psychological attributes such as vigilance and determination were also emphasized.

Advanced military subjects taught to the leaders included: bayonet fighting, camouflage, leap-frog maneuvering, cell (three men) operations, the employment of crew-served weapons, and the techniques of guerrilla and light infantry mobile warfare. The superior training of NVA leaders in maneuver warfare enabled them to achieve success with soldiers whose training was nearly as inadequate as that of U.S. ground troops.

NVA Troop Psychology

NVA troops sometimes exhibited certain traits that marked them as almost animal in their reactions. Assaulting and defending NVA were frequently "hopped up" on heroin and marijuana. Upon numerous occasions, North Vietnamese troops were found chained to their machine guns, recoilless rifles or mortars.

Chu Luc officers were known to commit suicide when captured. "One wounded NVA lieutenant had been left behind during the withdrawal . . . he was packed off to the aid station. He meekly submitted to treatment, but even while his wound was being dressed he swallowed poison and died."[24]

Another badly wounded NVA lieutenant behaved differently: "For more than an hour a dead NVA lieutenant had lain . . . a few feet away. Now incredibly the body was inching down the rear slope so slowly that the motion was barely perceptible. In one hand the 'corpse' clutched a light machine gun, in the other a pistol . . . Lambert made a great leap through the air and pinned the body. . . The (NVA) lieutenant, shot through the shoulder, wounded in both legs, and with most of his penis shot off, still fought back and had to be dragged kicking and screaming up the hill."[25]

Yet, not all Chu Luc officers were as determined to fight to the end: "The NVA captain had taken the precaution to write in chalk on the front of his jacket the word, *officer.* He spoke pretty fair English. His first words were: 'Give me water and then I'll talk.' "[26]

Yet, North Vietnamese close combat ferocity was legendary. Many communist soldiers continued to advance after being wounded several times:

Mucci "saw a large figure loom directly in front of his foxhole . . . realized it was a North Vietnamese . . . He made a football tackle at the man's knees and dragged him down into the foxhole. Mucci had already reached for his machete as he now slashed away at the tall enemy. . . . (another soldier) jumped to help . . . and got a throttling hold on the NVA soldier's neck. Suddenly Mucci's blade broke, leaving half the steel in the man's shoulder. Prunier, maintaining his stranglehold, was now on top of the Vietnamese and bearing down on him with his full weight . . . Mucci had only the man's legs for a target. He fired two bullets into the thighs and the figure went limp . . .

"Figuring he was dead, Mucci and Prunier picked him up out of the foxhole and heaved him toward the outer darkness. The body came down heavily on the back of the (American) aid man . . . (who) . . . grabbed one arm and was astonished to see it swing around in a complete circle; Mucci's machete had cut through the bone and the arm was dangling by flesh alone."

"Later Mucci looked at the ostensible corpse "and saw that the 'dead man,' too, was in motion, pawing his way along using only one arm. That was too much. Having used everything else, Mucci went after him with an entrenching shovel, at last killing the enemy by bashing in his head. It took two or three minutes . . .

"What had once been a fine figure of a man was ornamented with an officer's belt and was carrying a pistol that had remained undrawn, its firing pin broken."[27]

Some NVA soldiers were absolutely fanatical in their devotion: "An enemy soldier wearing a rucksack approached their perimeter with his hands up, yelling in English that he wanted to surrender. A sergeant gestured for the man to enter the perimeter. The man moved forward slowly, yelling 'Chieu Hoi!' over and over again, but when he was about ten meters from the perimeter suddenly lowered his head and charged forward like a bull. Before anyone could respond the man set off a giant claymore mine he had hidden in his rucksack. The NVA soldier disintegrated."[28]

Many NVA soldiers absolutely hated Americans and would do anything to get at them: "The VC also hid the bodies of killed Americans in the tunnels to demoralize their comrades, who regarded it as an absolute priority to retrieve their dead for decent burial at home."[29]

Excerpts from a captured communist unit report provide further evidence of bizarre NVA thought processes:

"Comrades Vi and Vo Dinh Tu got too excited in combat, exposed themselves and got hit . . .

"The corpse of one comrade-in-arms was eaten by dogs and pigs. We must take more care with pigs . . . (during the battle, our troops) substituted bananas and rice gruel for real food for five days."[30]

The pigs which temporarily distressed one group of VC, couldn't disguise the fact that animals were incorporated into red maneuver schemes whenever possible:

"The Charlies came on down the creek bed in strength, grenading as they advanced. It was a bizarre performance, heralded by the mooing and bellowing of about twelve cows that the Congs were herding down the creek to serve as their buffer and shield. The Congs were right in among the cattle, keeping all that beef between them and the bank . . .

"McCorkle was the first man out of his trance. He yelled: 'We gotta kill all those cows; get with it!' and began firing."[31]

The VC/NVA seemed to enjoy using animals and insects against American troops. From time to time they deployed the following "natural" weapons:

- Large rats, some infected with bubonic plague.
- Boxes of scorpions.
- Fierce jungle bees.
- Hornet swarms.
- Centipedes, six inches long.
- Clumps of gigantic poisonous spiders.
- Rabid bats.
- Venomous snakes and boa constrictors.[32]

In 1966, during Operation Thayer-Irving, a highly personalized NVA ambush provided yet another dramatic example of the hatred which the Chu Luc felt for their foe:

"A fresh blood trail on the dirt of the path. It led into the elephant grass. . . . (one American, following the trail, disappeared into the elephant grass). There was a sudden burst of AK-47 fire. He died quickly . . . The VC were gone. They had made a perfect bower by weaving together the overhead elephant grass that hid them perfectly. One pack had been left behind . . . From the flattened grass within the blind (it was obvious that) there had been three Charlies . . . a narrow side trail wound from the rear of the ambush toward the flooding Song Soui Ca . . . the Charlies had carefully plaited the elephant grass that curtained the blind so that the concealment was almost perfect. Hours of work had gone into the preparation. Worthless except for the one object of killing a man at point-blank range . . . a highly personalized deadfall. The thought of it made him shudder."[33]

Like the Japanese army of World War II, communist troops utilized psychological tricks whenever possible. They employed all manner of ruses, decoys and deceptions as part of their operational style, since they were a maneuver army. Some of their distractions were very strange. They laughed maniacally in the darkness, blew whistles, sounded bugles and beat bongo drums.

Communists troops also cursed and threatened their American foes in English. Sometimes groups of red troops would scream taunts in unison, while at other times a single communist soldier would converse with his enemies. After one battle, for example, this exchange was heard: "A voice from a bamboo clump not more than ten meters from the foxhole line shouted, 'Hey, how's your company commander?' . . . One American, not at all jumpy, yelled back, 'Mine's great; how's yours?' The voice replied, 'No good; you just killed him.' "[34]

NVA troops frequently taunted American forces by sarcastically repeating their cries for help or comradeship during combat. During one battle they taunted their enemies by repeating an appeal for assistance: "Sargie, Sargie, come on, you just keep acomin'."[35]

Sometimes red troops infiltrated American units and questioned individual soldiers. A Bo Dai with a Brooklyn accent once asked some sleepy Americans: "Hey, how many honchos do we have out here?" Then, when discovered, he ran from the area yelling: "Hold it! Wait a minute. Be nice now."[36]

One group of North Vietnamese troops yelled derisively as they withdrew: "Hey GIs, we are backing away. But don't worry. We will be back. So don't go yet."[37]

Chu Luc units usually had American radio equipment tuned to the frequencies of the U.S. units operating against them. They used radio monitoring to obtain immediate tactical intelligence, since American radio security procedures were virtually nonexistent. "The NVA monitored this transmission, and reckoning that Alpha Company was no longer worth worrying about, gave undivided attention to the stalling of Charley Company."[38]

The reds also used the radio to deliver spurious orders to American troops and to interfere with attempts to bring in supporting resources or firepower. For example, one American artillery forward observer, Lieutenant Housley, was trying to bring in supporting artillery fire upon enemy targets when he experienced typical NVA radio interference:

"He heard a voice cutting in on his 'freak' (frequency) and saying in perfect English: 'Correction, right four hundred.'

"Housely yelled: 'No, left three hundred, drop one hundred.'

"The other voice said: 'Correction, right four hundred.'

"The (artillery) battery complied."[39]

The communist directed artillery fire came in directly on top of a column

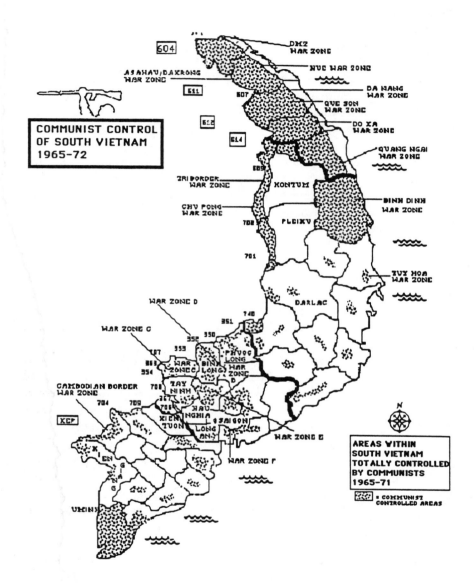

COMMUNIST CONTROL
OF SOUTH VIETNAM
1965-72

AREAS WITHIN
SOUTH VIETNAM
TOTALLY CONTROLLED
BY COMMUNISTS
1965-71

= COMMUNIST
CONTROLLED AREAS

DMZ WAR ZONE
NUC WAR ZONE
DA NANG WAR ZONE
QUE SON WAR ZONE
DO XA WAR ZONE
QUANG NGAI WAR ZONE
BINH DINH WAR ZONE
TUY HOA WAR ZONE

A SHAU/DAXRONG WAR ZONE
TRI BORDER WAR ZONE
CHU PONG WAR ZONE

KONTUM
PLEIKU
DARLAC

WAR ZONE D
WAR ZONE C
CAMBODIAN BORDER WAR ZONE

PHUOC LONG
BINH LONG
WAR ZONE C
WAR ZONE D
TAY NINH
HAU NGHIA
XIEN TUON
SAIGON
LONG AN
WAR ZONE E
WAR ZONE F
UMINH

of American troops. "Then Housley got it: The mystery voice was a Charlie who understood artillery."[40]

During the battle of Hamburger Hill, Colonel Tiger Honeycutt, an American commander with the well-known code name of "Blackjack," received a strange radio message from the Chu Luc. A battalion RTO handed Colonel Honeycutt the handset saying: "Some guy named Pham or something. Says he wants to talk with you. He's using your call sign. Keeps saying Blackjack over and over again . . . Honeycutt took the handset, a voice said, 'Blackjack! Blackjack!'

" 'This is Blackjack. What can I do for you?'

" 'Blackjack, we are going to kill all of your men tomorrow.'

" 'Is that so?'

" 'When you come up the mountain in the morning, Blackjack, we will be waiting for you. All of your men are going to die. Can you hear me Blackjack? All will die?' "[41]

After the ambush at LZ Albany, in the 1965 Ia Drang Battle, NVA troops patrolled the dark battlefield that night. They executed wounded Americans by cramming weapons into the Americans' mouths and blowing their heads off. Numerous American dead were found to have had their hands tied behind their backs before receiving their *coup de grace.*

The NVA were very racist and unit political officers constantly harangued their troops into fevered frenzies of racial hatred towards the Americans. They even awarded medals based upon the numbers of Americans killed by NVA troops. Those medals were called "American Killer Medals": "The Front had decreed that anyone who killed three Americans would automatically receive the Military Medal Class One . . . for six, you earned Class Two, and for nine Americans killed, you would receive a treasured Class Three."[42]

Many NVA soldiers sought to earn their American Killer medals. They got very upset if they were unable to do so. On Hamburger Hill, a number of red troops who felt like failures for not reaching their "American Killer" quota, committed suicide. The group of despondent, suicidal communist troops was found standing in a circle, with their heads bowed, on the top of Hamburger Hill:

"Ten to fifteen rifles crackled at once, and all eight NVA fell . . . they (the American troops) discovered that all the soldiers were dead. To show their willingness to die, four of the men had chained or tied one leg to a tree. All the dead had small cloth patches sewn on the front of their shirts which read: "Kill Americans." On the barkless trees around them, various exhortations had been scribbled. One read: 'Defeat the Americans, here we take a stand.' Another 'The entire nation is watching you. Don't disgrace yourself.' And still another said: 'Stand and fight and not run'" The eight men all belonged to the 29th NVA Infantry Regiment which was known as "The American Killers."[43]

Since that melodrama featured English text, it is obvious that the spectacle was intended to frighten Americans. At the same time, that group suicide exemplified the unforgiving nature of communistic fanaticism, whipped to fever pitch by venemous unit commissars.

Another type of the enemy as fatalistic fanaticism was exhibited during the 1968 Tet Offensive. An American unit broke through a treeline and surprised a huge enemy unit as it was forming up: "No one could believe their eyes. About 250 to 300 NVA were standing in rows, covered with grass from the shoulders up. They were about 30 meters (over 30 yards) away. Some of them waved and yelled 'Hello, GI!'. . . Fire cut into the enemy ranks . . . two soldiers spotted a large enemy group squatting in the grass on their left, ran to that point and killed 16 NVA. It was bewildering; some of the enemy stood straight up and covered their faces with their hands or turned their heads, waiting to be shot. Others began crawling towards the Americans across a dry rice paddy and were killed. Very few of them fired their AK47s. Some of Company C's troops were yelling profanities at the enemy as they fired. Others were laughing and shouting encouragement to their buddies as the enemy fell."[44]

Many weird examples of enemy behavior were recorded during the Vietnam War. One night, in War Zone D, American flares revealed a strange sight:

"The men were 'dazzled by an array of shining objects that seemed to be moving' . . . This dazzling band was about 100 meters wide and six feet tall . . . the troops opened fire with M16s and machineguns. The shining objects began falling . . . The VC had been advancing, each one carrying in front of him a sheet of roofing tin that screened his body wholly."[45]

The roofing tin reflected light but it did not deflect bullets. Even the light-weight M-16 bullets penetrated the tin shield.

The Chu Luc well understood psychological warfare and were adept at its practice. They studied American weaknesses and constantly applied pressure against that weakness.

"The enemy also knew that we placed great emphasis on body count and weapons . . . enemy dead were found and lying by their sides were large tin cans filled with empty cartridge cases . . . The enemy felt that he had won a psychological victory if he could remove his casualties, leaving a sterile battlefield for our men to find, especially if he had inflicted some casualties on us . . . Captured enemy documents revealed that the enemy had been told that as soon as several casualties had been inflicted on U.S. troops in the initial stages of a fortified village action, the U.S. troops would panic and withdraw."[46] That actually happened in many cases.

The NVA presented Americans with many imponderables. Communist behavior during the Vietnam War was certainly eccentric and mysterious. Consider the case of the nine Viet Cong dead women: "Their most startling find—nine dead NVA women soldiers, all bearing arms, the bodies clad in khaki, the close cropped hair almost hidden by berets. In a nearby hooch, nine pigtails hung in a row, possibly for use on ceremonial occasions."[47]

Who were they? What were they doing?

Another bizarre mystery: Who were the strange Viet Cong (?) troops who fought an Australian rifle company near Vung Tau in 1966? "Much superior in fighting ability to any who had been encountered up to that time. This group wore black uniforms and webbing, their packs were black, they had black turbans on their heads and they were armed with automatic weapons."[48]

The NVA were strange, yet behind their behavior lurk many secrets. Many of those secrets are laid bare when the origin of specific NVA behavior is uncovered.

Much North Vietnamese military behavior was borrowed. The Vietcom tried to do everything just like their Soviet and Chinese military mentors. If one seeks the origin of North Vietnamese military behavior one must first research historical military lore, beginning with World War I.

The NVA practice of clearing their dead from the battlefield was not a distinctly Chu Luc adaptation. They copied it from the Soviet army. Curzio Malparte described the World War II Soviet army's habitual evacuation of their battle dead and equipment as "the flight of the dead. They even take their boxes of cartridges with them. . . . (the Soviets) were determined to leave behind no trace of their presence—nothing, in short, that might afford the enemy the smallest clue to their methods of warfare, their tactics, the composition of their units, the nature and function of their weapons . . . It is impressive to arrive at the scene of the struggle, to find that the ground is completely clear and almost unmarked, . . . (with) the inevitable legacy of any battle . . . The Russians leave behind only a handful of dead, scattered here and there about the plain: those who were last to fall, those who remained to cover their comrades' retreat. But they are few in number . . . as though the dead had struggled to their feet, had slowly walked away . . . following unknown paths through the corn fields and the woods . . . it seems that it is the dead themselves who 'clean up' the battlefields . . . (and) disappear forever."[49]

CHAPTER 2

NVA MILITARY ORGANIZATION

In April 1949, the Chu Luc under General Giap commanded 32 regular, and 137 regional, battalions. The strike force had increased to 117 regular battalions and 37 regional battalions by June 1951.

By early 1950, the Vietnamese communist had formed a field army: "after the Chinese Communists had established control over Yunnan and Kwangsi, facilities for the amalgamation of Giap's regiments into divisions began. Working on a pattern of four regiments to a division, Giap was able to form four infantry divisions of over 12,000 men each in the Viet Bac and one in Northern Annam. The divisions in the Viet Bac numbered 304, 308, 312 and 316, while the one in Northern Annam was known as 320 Division."[50] However, some of the divisions were smaller brigade- or task force-sized units until late 1951.

The new Chu Luc under General Giap burst upon the French corps threatening the communists' Chinese bases in the fall of 1950. What the French had considered a guerrilla army revealed itself to be a light infantry force reminiscent of those gaunt scarecrows who marched with Stonewall Jackson in the Valley Campaign. The Viet Minh army was a modern well-trained fighting machine carefully crafted with Chinese assistance:

"The Chinese provided large amounts of artillery and established two practice ranges for the Viet Minh at Tsingi and Longchow. Officers were sent to special staff courses in Southern China, and Chinese advisers and technicians came into the Viet Bac. The regiments came together and exercised as divisions around the Chinese practice ranges. The regimental commanders became highly skilled in the use of the new artillery support, which gave them the strength to overcome a French battalion position. The divisional commanders learned to maneuver their regiments over wide areas so that they could ambush and trap large French columns moving along the roads which linked the main garrison positions."[51]

The maneuver of large units was not practiced by western generals after World War II. Instead they occasionally practiced moving battalions between fortified zones, depending upon map exercises in the mistaken assumption that such limited means could substitute for actual field experience.

The French army, although fortunate to have a high percentage of keen officers, had few who could maneuver large formations off the main highways. As France's expeditionary generalissimo Jean de Lattre de Tassigny fell back into a mobile defensive configuration in the Red River Delta, he realized that the Viet Minh army had disastrously defeated him. However, he probably didn't consider the problem in relation to the cross country maneuver of large formations since he too thought in terms of road-bound task forces and motorized groups.

The red general Giap moved towards the French Red River perimeter with seventy-one infantry battalions, twelve heavy weapons battalions and eight engineer battalions. At first, each Viet infantry battalion had eight hundred men. Later the Viet battalions fielded a "paddy strength" of five to six hundred men.

From 1951, Viet Minh rifle battalions outgunned their French counterparts with superior firepower. The Viet battalion had ten more light machine guns, twice as many submachine guns, and six crew-served antitank/antipersonnel weapons, of which the French had none. Such firepower at the battalion level gave them a similar advantage over the Americans fifteen years later.

Viet Minh versus French Infantry Battalions: 1951–52

Weaponry	Viet Minh	French	Manpower	
Machine guns	30-50	20	3 men per weapon	
Mortars	8, 60mm	8, 60mm & 4, 81mm	6	" " "
Automatic Rifles (BAR)	54	41	1	" " "
Recoilless Rifles, 57mm	3	0	3	" " "
Bazookas	3	0	2	" " "
Submachine guns	200	133	1	" " "
Rifles	200	324	1	" " "
Total Combat Manpower:	Viet Minh-573		French-630	

Source: Fall: *Street Without Joy:* "312 NVA Division-1 light machine gun for every ten men, an automatic rifle for every five and numerous submachineguns, 1952." (70); and Captain Jacques Despuech, *Le Trafic Des Piastres.* French had 2 machine guns per platoon. One battalion—9-12 platoons.

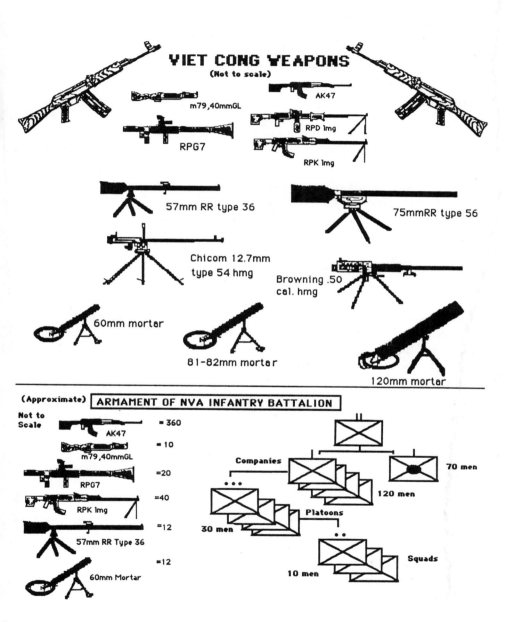

VIET CONG WEAPONS
(Not to scale)

m79,40mmGL

AK47

RPG7

RPD lmg

RPK lmg

57mm RR type 36

75mmRR type 56

Chicom 12.7mm type 54 hmg

Browning .50 cal. hmg

60mm mortar

81-82mm mortar

120mm mortar

(Approximate) | ARMAMENT OF NVA INFANTRY BATTALION

Not to Scale

AK47 = 360

m79,40mmGL = 10

RPG7 = 20

RPK lmg = 40

57mm RR Type 36 = 12

60mm Mortar = 12

Companies

70 men

120 men

Platoons

30 men

Squads

10 men

In early January 1951, Giap surrounded the French outpost at Vinh Yen with the 308th Division, the newly formed 312th division, and a task force which was destined to become the 316th Division. By January 16, five hundred dazed Viet Minh had surrendered. Six thousand other mangled reds littered the Vinh Yen battlefield, many of them fried into crispy critters by French napalm. The retreating Giap had tried to assault French defenses with large scale, "human wave," frontal attacks, a costly tactic which he seldom used.[52]

By March 1951, Giap had formed the 304th, 308th, 312th, 316th and 320th infantry divisions. In addition he controlled several independent infantry regiments including the 42nd, 46th and 50th. he used them in a series of brilliant offensives against the French de Lattre Line around Hanoi.

By 1953, the Chu Luc had added the 325th Infantry Division to its order of battle, which also included six independent regiments and several independent battalions. That forced tied down 190,000 French troops. The Viet red army continued to increase through 1953. "By the middle of 1953 Giap was completing his preparations for mobile warfare . . . He had built up a military organization of some 300,000 men spread throughout Indochina regulars, regional forces and village-level militia. About 60 percent of his strength, including his main striking force, was in the vicinity of the Red River Delta in Northern Vietnam. The striking force, or Chu Luc, consisted of 6 well-armed, battle-tested infantry divisions and an artillery division. In addition the striking force was supported by at least 6 independent regiments in the northern Highlands and Delta."[53]

Among those independent infantry regiments were the 102nd, 148th, 803rd and 108th. Their efforts were complemented by about ten independent infantry battalions. In addition there were such specialized units as the "dreaded 421st Intelligence Battalion of the Viet Minh forces, a special unit of the Communists whose job it was to gather information among the tribesmen about the operations of the French-led (anticommunist) guerrillas."[54]

Against the ill-advised French fortress of Dien Bien Phu, the Viet Minh committed the following units:

- 308th, 312th and 316th infantry divisions
- 57th Infantry Regiment of the 304th Infantry Division
- 148th Independent Infantry Regiment
- 351st Heavy Division.

The Viet Minh sent an army-sized formation against Dien Bien Phu including: eleven infantry regiments, three artillery regiments, one engineer

Viet Minh Divisions At Dien Bien Phu: 1954

Division	Infantry Regiments	Battalions	Div. Commander
308	36, 88, 102		Vuong Thua Vu
312	141, 165, 209	154 Artillery	Le Trong Tan
316	98, 174, 176	812 Heavy Wpns. Co.	Le Quang Ba
304	57	345 Artillery	Hoang Minh Thao
351	151st Engineer, 237rd Heavy Weapons, 45th Artillery, 675th Artillery, 367th Antiaircraft, Field Rocket Unit		Vu Hien

Also present: 148th Independent Infantry Regiment with its 900th, 910th, 920th infantry battalions, 523 Signal Company, & 121 Heavy Weapons Co.[55]

regiment, one antiaircraft regiment and several artillery battalions. The Viet Minh generals with training and experience in moving such large formations, far outnumbered the small number of French generals who had similar experience.

One source claimed that a Viet Minh infantry regiment at Dien Bien Phu controlled three infantry battalions and a weapons battalion composed of 75mm-pack howitzers and/or 120mm mortars. That is erroneous. Nothing larger than 81/82mm mortars was retained at the Viet Minh regimental level. All artillery was concentrated in the 351st Heavy Division.

The 351st Heavy Division, a Soviet-style artillery division, controlled a massive amount of firepower. It was both a breakthrough division and a fire support division.

The Viet Minh 320th and 325th infantry divisions were not at Dien Bien Phu. Neither was the division headquarters, nor three regiments, the 9th, 66th, and 840th, of the 304th Infantry Division.

By late 1954, the Chu Luc included the following units:

The 351st Viet Minh Heavy Division

	Sub Unit	Composition
•	237th Heavy Weapons Regiment:	40 81/82mm mortars
•	45th Artillery Regiment:	24 105mm howitzers
•	675th Artillery Regiment:	18 75mm pack howitzers, 20 120mm mortars
•	367th Antiaircraft Regiment:	20-80 37mm AA guns 50-100 .50 caliber heavy machine guns
•	Field Rocket Unit	12-16 Katyusha multirocket launchers

Tube Total:	42 Artillery;	60 Mortar;	70-180 Flak + Rockets[45]

- 304th, 308th, 312th, 320th, and 325th infantry divisions.
- 316th Infantry division with 98th, 174th and 176th Infantry Regiments, 980th Heavy Weapons Battalion, and one antiaircraft battalion.
- 154th Independent Engineer Regiment.
- 16th Transport Regiment.
- Twenty independent regiments.
- Twenty independent battalions.
- 351st Heavy Division with 151st Engineer Regiment; 34th Artillery Regiment (15, 75mm howitzers and 20, 120mm mortars); 45th Artillery Regiment (36, 105mm howitzers); 237th Artillery Regiment (40, 82mm mortars); 675th Artillery Regiment (24, 75mm Howitzers, 20, 120mm mortars); 367th Antiaircraft Regiment (50, 12.7mm AAMG; 36, 37mm antiaircraft guns; and a Chinese adviser in each gun crew).

The Viet Minh did not concentrate their 120mm mortars or 175mm howitzers in separate regiments, thus simplifying resupply. A possible reason is the fact that 75mm howitzers can provide close-in, direct firepower against close infantry assaults. Pure 120mm mortar units have no close-in defensive capability.

The Chu Luc in the Second Indochina War

The Chu Luc, whether referred to as NVA or VC, had standard tables of organization and equipment. However, unit organization and equipment did vary widely. Naturally such variances affected logistical considerations.

The 3rd NVA Division, also called the Sao Vang or Yellow Star division, sometimes shared its name or number with the neighboring Second NVA

3rd NVA Infantry Division Organization: 1965. II Corps

Unit	Strength	Percentage
Sao Vang Division		
Three regiments	8,134	65.8
Three artillery battalions	1,582	12.8
Transportation battalion	391	3.2
Medical units	546	4.4
Telephone company	126	1.0
Military staff	350	2.8
Political-military school	171	1.4
Recruit training	378	3.1
Special units	623	5.0
Total	12,360	100.0[57]

Division in a successful attempt to confuse their enemy. Its organization, weaponry and strength was representative of most NVA divisions.

A "no-name," division-sized NVA "front" was committed to combat in the South Vietnamese II Corps in 1965. It came directly from North Vietnam and was organized like a Soviet light infantry division, minus the artillery.

NVA Front (Division) Organization: 1965. II Corps

Unit	Strength	Percentage
32 NVA Regiment	2700	22.5
33 NVA Regiment	2700	22.5
66 NVA Regiment	2700	22.5
H-15 Viet Cong Main Force Bn.	500	4.0
120mm Mortar Battalion	400	3.0
14.5 Twin-barreled Flak Bn.	400	3.0
Division Logistics and Services	2700	22.5
Total	12,100	100.0[58]

NVA Divisional Transportation

The Sao Vang Division controlled a number of units which each performed a specific function. The division Rear Services Staff supervised quartermaster, medical, finance and transportation elements.

The quartermaster section was responsible for procurement, storage, maintenance and distribution of weapons and ammunition. The foot mobile 391-man divisional transportation battalion worked with three regimental transportation companies (68 men each) to move those supplies. In effect they could provide the division with 595 porters, if necessary. That porter force could transport at least six tons of supplies fifteen miles a day. Usually, however, division transportation units drafted at least 1,200 civilian porters, capable of moving a total of at least eighteen tons of supplies a day.

The 304th NVA Infantry Division utilized similar portage methods: "Supplies were taken from NVN, through Laos and Cambodia by truck . . . From the Cambodian-Vietnamese border the supplies were taken to Station 4 by bicycle and from there the K19 battalion started its operations . . . The K19 battalion supplied all units of the 304th Division of battalion size or larger on an average of once a month; not on a regularly scheduled date but upon request by each individual unit . . . The K19 Transportation Battalion delivered all types of supplies such as medicine, foodstuffs, and ammunition in addition to evacuating wounded soliders to the hospital."[59]

"For a unit to be supplied by the K19th Battalion it notified the Rear

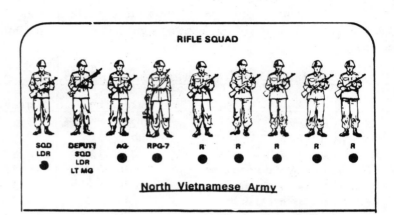

RIFLE SQUAD

| SQD LDR | DEPUTY SQD LDR LT MG | AG | RPG-7 | R | R | R | R | R |

North Vietnamese Army

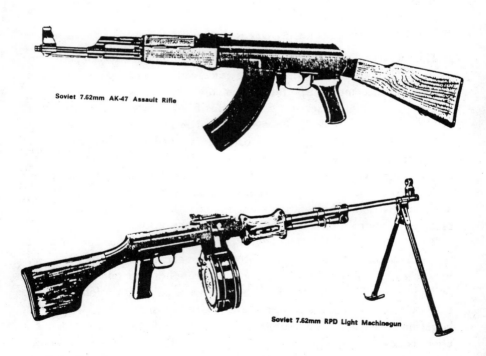

Soviet 7.62mm AK-47 Assault Rifle

Soviet 7.62mm RPD Light Machinegun

Service Officer at the 304th Division Headquarters by messenger except in case of an emergency when the telephone was used. The Rear Service Office would notify K19 battalion which would deliver the necessary supplies."[60]

The NVA transportation system was quite flexible. It offered endless possible combinations of boats, pack animals, porters, bicycles, carts and trucks:

"The weapons battalion had 4 sampans, 2 very large and 2 smaller, which operated 6 times a month. The sampans came into the mooring site at night. The men from the battalion left their mountain camp at 3:00 P.M. and arrived at the road at about 6:00 P.M. My reconnaissance-intelligence platoon had to make the road secure for the carrying party by taking positions at both ends of that portion of the road. The carrying party crossed the road at 6:00 P.M. and arrived at the mooring site at 7:00 P.M., a distance of about 2.5 kilometers. The distance from the road to the camp was about 10 km. The unloading operation was carried out in two hours and at 9:00 P.M. the carrying party would start back with the weapons, due to arrive in camp at 2:00 A.M. The size of the party depended on how many sampans were at the mooring site: if there were 2 large sampans, the entire battalion would come; if there were 2 small sampans, then only 1 or 2 companies would come."[61]

Below division level, there were also rear services organizations. Most NVA support organizations were maintained at the lowest possible establishment in order to prevent a bloated administration and the disproportionate growth of support units in relation to combat units. At their strongest, support units below division level might include the following:

- Regimental Rear Services Organization: "A financial affairs chief; a quartermaster chief, with assistants for food supply and clothing equipment, warehousemen, and tailors; a medical chief, with dispensary and drug storage, and assistants for preventive medicine; an ordnance chief, with ordnance repair stations, warehousemen, and assistants for maintenance and statistics/registration; and a transportation company."[62]
- Battalion Rear Service: "A clothing supply section, a medical officer, an ordnance section, and a transportation platoon."[63]
- Company Rear Services: "A clothing supply cadre, a medic, and an armorer."[64]

NVA Divisional Medical Support

The Sao Vang Division was typically organized to provide full medical services for its troops. Those services were organized as follows:

- Division level: One medical battalion with 546 men organized into four companies and a field hospital. The medical companies could accommodate 80 casualties, while the two dispensaries of the field hospital could care for another 130 casualties. Both field dispensaries carried sufficient total medical supplies to care for 150 casualties.
- Regimental level: One 50-man medical company and one to three surgical teams.
- Battalion level: A medic dispatched from the division.[65]

NVA medical doctrine stated: "Civilian support for evacuation of dead and wounded is assumed to be 20 percent of the battalion strength, on days of combat only."[66]

NVA Divisional Communications

In 1965, all Chu Luc forces reorganized their communications resources and units. The Central Office for South Vietnam (COSVN), Military Region 5, and all division headquarters were assigned a signal battalion. Every regiment received a signal company and every battalion, a signal platoon. By 1966, three area support NVA signal battalions were operating in South Vietnam.

The various NVA units had a variety of signals resources. In 1965, the Sao Vang Division only had a telephone company of 126 men, with 4 percent of divisional personnel assigned to communications duties. At the same time the 7th Viet Cong Battalion had its own communications platoon.[67]

In 1967, the 9th NVA Infantry Division, operating in III Corps, controlled the following distribution of signalmen or communicators:

- 1 divisional 400-man signal battalion.
- 3 regimental 100-man signal companies.
- 9 battalion 35-man signal platoons.
- 1 signal section each in regimental antiaircraft, mortar, and reconnaissance companies.[68]

Usually, NVA division-level communications personnel, including commo-liaison personnel, didn't exceed 4 percent of the total unit strength. The percentage was about the same at battalion level. Such percentage should be compared with the radio operators in American ground combat units, constituting over 20 percent of total unit strength.

The 507th NVA Signal Battalion, with a strength of five hundred men, was organized into six companies: messenger, security, supply, telephone,

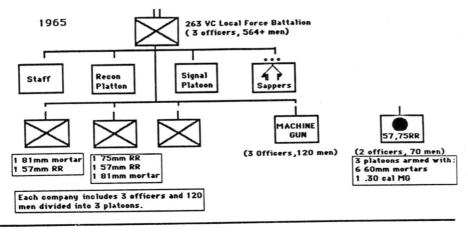

1965

263 VC Local Force Battalion
(3 officers, 564+ men)

Staff

Recon Platton

Signal Platoon

Sappers

1 81mm mortar
1 57mm RR

1 75mm RR
1 57mm RR
1 81mm mortar

MACHINE GUN

(3 Officers, 120 men)

57,75RR

(2 officers, 70 men)
3 platoons armed with:
6 60mm mortars
1 .30 cal MG

Each company includes 3 officers and 120 men divided into 3 platoons.

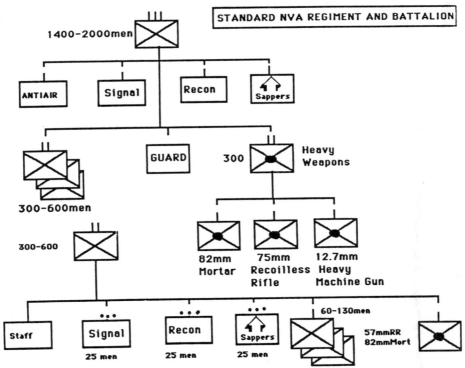

STANDARD NVA REGIMENT AND BATTALION

1400-2000men

ANTIAIR

Signal

Recon

Sappers

GUARD

300

Heavy Weapons

300-600men

300-600

82mm Mortar

75mm Recoilless Rifle

12.7mm Heavy Machine Gun

Staff

Signal
25 men

Recon
25 men

Sappers
25 men

60-130men

57mmRR
82mmMort

transportation and wireless telegraph. The companies frequently operated independently within the II Corps area, supporting various NVA divisions as required.[69]

North Vietnamese Army and Viet Cong Regiments

NVA infantry regiments were capable of powerful mobile offensive action and could simultaneously control several provinces by maneuver warfare. A typical NVA infantry regiment contained three rifle battalions, and seven supporting companies: engineer, transportation, medical, signal, antiaircraft, mortar, and reconnaissance. Sometimes a sapper unit was also attached.

32nd NVA Infantry Regiment Organization: 1965, II Corps

- 334, 635 and 966 infantry battalions. (Four companies each, armed with 57mm recoilless rifles, 10–30 machine guns, 6 M-79 grenade launchers and 3–4 B40 90mm rocket-propelled grenades. RPGs were in short supply in 1965.)
- 1 engineer company
- 1 mortar company
- 1 machine gun company
- 1 antiaircraft company
- 1 75mm recoilless rifle company
- 1 signal company
- 1 transportation/logistics company[70]

Although Chu Luc units were referred to as either NVA or Viet Cong, they

33rd NVA Infantry Regiment Strength: Nov. 1965

1, 2, and 3 Infantry Battalions, each	500 men: total 1500 men
Regimental Mortar Company	120 men
Regimental Recoilless Rifle Company	150 men
Regimental Antiaircraft Company (HMG)	150 men
Regimental Transport Company	150 men
Regimental Signal Company	120 men
Regimental Engineer Company	60 men
Regimental Reconnaissance Company	50 men
Regimental Medical Company	40 men
Regimental Headquarters	70 men
Total	2350 men

3rd NVA (Sao Vang) Divisional Units: 1965

22 NVA Regiment:		1st Co./334 BN/32 NVA Rgt:	1st Plt/3Co/334Bn
Strength:	2372men	117men	31men
82 mm mortar	*14/187		
81 mm mortar	3/10		
60 mm mortar	15/237	3/60	
75 mm RR	10/67		
57 mm RR	3/46		
Bazooka	18/123	3/12	1/4
MG. heavy	6	2/1500	
MG. light	17		
Smg	401	30/9000	3/2700
AR	50	9/4500	3/1500
Rifle	?	38/5700	12/1800
Carbine	33	1	
Pistol	?	4	
Grenade	3593		52

*First number is the total weapons, second number is the basic load[72]

were essentially the same forces. Viet Cong designation actually implied that a unit was less well equipped. Its small arms were more mixed, and it was not organized as a standard Soviet-type unit. A typical VC regiment consisted of two to four rifle battalions and a heavy weapons unit. Such a unit could be armed with mortars, 70mm howitzers, 77mm howitzers, or a mixture of recoilless rifles. It was generally smaller, less well orgaized, and controlled less firepower, than an NVA regiment.

Just as the organization of Viet Cong regiments varied, so did their weaponry and basic loads of ammunition. However, there were some minimal, or average strength profiles which seem to be similar to all VC regiments.

The variation between NVA and Viet Cong unit organization was sometimes marked. For example, the 1st VC Infantry Regiment and the 32nd NVA Infantry Regiment, which both fought in South Vietnam during 1965, were organized differently.

Type Viet Cong Regiment (1400 to 2500 men)

**Three Rifle battalions (each
300–600 men)**

1　Heavy weapons battalion
　or 3 separate heavy
　weapons companies:
1　Mortar company (81mm or
　82mm)
1　Recoilless rifle company
　(75mm, sometime also
　57mm)
1　Machine gun company
　(12.7mm)
1　HQ guard platoon
1　Antiaircraft company
1　Signal company
1　Transportation company
1　Engineer Company
1　Reconnaissance company

Weapon & Ammunition Load, 320 Viet Cong Regiment: 1965

Weapon	No. of weapons	Ammunition rounds	Rounds/weapons
Pistol	56	2,439	44
AA gun	5	3,550	710
12.7mm MG	3	16,160	5,387
12.8 mm MG	2	2,000	1,000
57mm RR	3	45	15
75 mm RR	6	45	8
82mm mortar	5	133	27
81mm mortar	5	133	27
81mm mortar	6	84	14
60mm	15	330	22
B40 rkt launcher	24	76	3
Carbine	42	2,333	56
Other 7.62mm	wpns* 768	113,411	148
Grenades	2,170		

Note: *Includes 63 RPD light machine guns; 16 medium company machine guns; 8 K53 heavy machine guns; 282 AK submachine guns; 339 CKC Rifles[73]

Average Viet Cong Regimental Ammunition Supply

Weapon Type	Rounds	Additional Ammunition
12.7mm MG	700	34 1.2mm bangalore torpedoes
57mm RR	32	6 .15 bangalore torpedoes
75mm RR	11	276 kilograms of TNT
82mm mortar	19	218 concussion grenades
81mm mortar	13	
60mm mortar	13	
B40 rkt launcher	8	
Rifle	50	
Smg	200	
AR	300	
MG	900	
MG.US	500	

1st VC Regiment Organization: 1965. I Corps

- 40, 45, and 60 Infantry Battalions. (Three companies each, armed with machine guns and B40 90mm rocket propelled grenades)
- 1 mortar company, 81mm (12 mortars)
- 1 sapper company
- 1 antiaircraft company (est. 18 : .50 caliber machine guns)
- 1 weapons company (9:75mm and 5:57 mm recoilless rifles)
- 1 signal company
- 1 engineer detachment
- 1 surgical unit.
- 1 transportation/logistics company

Reinforcements for a 1st VC Regiment operation once included: 1 antiaircraft company (est. 12: 12.7mm heavy machine guns and additional German machine guns); Two Mountain artillery batteries, 75mm; One unit of penetration agents/armed service cadre. Three local guerrilla platoons.[75]

NVA and Viet Cong Battalion Organizations

An NVA battalion was a very powerful fighting force. It controlled at least three light infantry companies, sometimes four, and a heavy weapons company. Each rifle company was armed with a minimum of: ten to thirty light (RPD) machine guns, ten antitank (RPG) weapons, four 60mm mortars, three heavy machine guns, and six (US) M-79 grenade launchers. The battalion weapons company usually included: six 82mm mortars (MR), three 75mm recoilless rifles (RR), and three 57mm recoilless rifles.

The six- to seven-hundred-man battalion controlled at least nine rifle platoons with three squads each, and three weapons platoons. Sometimes a sapper platoon, a scout platoon and a few service (i.e. signal, logistics, etc.) platoons were also under battalion command. However, NVA battalions received most of their services from their regiment and usually fought as part of a regiment.

Distinctive Khaki or grass green uniforms were worn by NVA battalions. In 1970, a platoon of dead NVA was described: "They had new green fatigues, pith helmets, full web gear, two canteens, AK47 automatic rifles, and a few SKS carbines. Some had whistles and pistols."[76]

The performance of NVA regulars was superior and they tended to fight as well as Soviet elite troops. They usually operated out of the border areas, war zones, or very well defended strongholds.

Viet Cong battalions were usually less well armed and organized. However, since so many VC battalions operated independently, they were frequently larger than NVA battalions and included more service and logistics platoons. Viet Cong battalions were organized as main forces (regulars), local forces (provincial regulars) and village militia (the only true VC units, since their units were not composed of North Vietnamese).

Frequently individual provinces were divided into two operational areas, one for main force units and one for local units. In joint operations, the main force battalion or a special regimental headquarters controlled all local forces. South Vietnams' Dinh Tuong Province (IV Corps), for example, was frequently the operational area of three VC main force battalions (514th, 261st, and 263rd). In addition the provinces' six districts fielded five VC guerrilla companies.

Viet Cong battalions had three or four rifle companies and a weapons company with three to six hundred personnel. Main force VC battalions wore uniforms, while local force battalions wore a mixture of pajamas, usually black. Main force battalions operated throughout a region, in perhaps several provinces. Local force battalions stayed in one province (state), and local militia, or guerrillas, operated in a district (county).

Typical Viet Cong Battalion

- Three rifle companies (60–130 men each)
- Weapons company (57mm recoilless rifles and 81mm or 82mm mortars)

- Signal, engineer, and reconnaissance platoons (25 men each)
- Battalion headquarters (CO, XO, Political cadre, Bodyguard, Runners)

Typical Independent, VC Regional Force, Battalion Organization

Battalion headquarters	19
Signal platoon	46
Recon sapper platoon	39
Engineer platoon	21
Transport/medical evacuation platoon	30
Combat support company	87
Three infantry companies	405
Total	647 men[77]

Armament: 502 Viet Cong Independent Battalion, 1965

	Organic Military Units				Companies		273 Company			
	Command	Signal	Support	Recon	271	272	1st plt	2nd plt	3rd plt	Recon
Strength	159	43	12	14	148	146	32	32	42	12
57mm RR				3/45*						
60mm										
MR							2	2		2
MG It						4/6000*				
-.30 cal.						(1)				
-Chicom						3/4500*				3
Smg.K50						3/400*				
AR					6/3000*	9/4500*				
-US					(2)	(1)				
-Czech					(4)	(8)	1			
-Chicom							2			
Rifle								8	8	
Carbine			8/800*	9/13500*					4	2
Grenades			40		12					

Notes: * = *number of weapons/rounds of ammo. RR = Recoilless Rifles; MR = Mortars: MG = Machine Guns: S = Submachine guns: AR = Automatic Rifles.*[78]

Weapons/Basic Ammunition Loads, 514th VC Main Force Battalion

Weapon	Basic Load (rounds)	Number	KG/Wpn	Kg/Bn
Machine gun	500	6	50	300
57mm RR	4	6	24	144
60mm MR	24	6	144	864
AR	800	27	3.1	84
Smg	200	30	.8	24
M1 Rifl	250	27	1	27
MAS 36 Rifle	100*	27	8.4	227
Redstock Rifle	100*	162	8.4	1.361
Carbine	300	87	9.2	800
Pistol		9		
Grenades	500 per company	1500	1	1500
Rifle Grenades	2,208	1	2,208	

Total: Basic Load Weight for this provincial battalion: 7,539 kg *Plus 8 rifle grenades per weapon, included in weight of basic load.[79]

Viet Cong infantry battalion headquarters included a battalion commanding officer (CO), a deputy commander (XO), a political officer, messengers and bodyguards. Each company headquarters similarly included a CO, XO and political officer.

Viet Cong battalion reconnaissance platoons were used for actual scouting, unlike U.S. battalion recon platoons. They were also responsible for guidance and cover of moving VC troops.

The VC scouting mission was precisely defined as: "Description and mapping of terrain routes of travel and installations, recommendation of march and withdrawal routes and future campsites, and surveillance of enemy units."[80]

Most VC battalion reconnaissance platoons were connected to their commanders by radio, after 1965. Their political reliability had to be greater than that of typical line infantrymen. The battalion recon unit helped to train a special recon squad in each rifle company in case that company had to operate independently.

Viet Cong companies and platoons used runners to communicate with higher headquarters. Most VC battalion headquarters, which had their own signal platoon, used radio, telephone and messengers to communicate with superior and subordinate units. That communication was carried out in bivouac, movement and battle.

Most VC battalions controlled a sapper platoon of twenty five or thirty sappers organized into eight or nine, three-man cells. Sapper platoon missions included opening paths in enemy barriers, blowing up enemy targets, and covering withdrawals with mines and booby traps.

All VC battalions received logistics support from a regional rear services staff. That staff usually formed a rear services company for each province. It was made up of four twenty-four-man (and women) platoons.[81] The platoons brought forward ammunition and food for combat battalions, and also evacuated the wounded. The rear services company frequently impressed local labor or porters to assist their efforts.

History of Selected Viet Cong Battalions

Many Viet Cong battalions and regiments were formed in South Vietnam's III and IV Corps as part of the expansion of the NVA army that began during 1964. Following is an account of one aspect of those expansion efforts:

"The old T80 Battalion. This organization dated back to 1959, when it was raised in the Mekong Delta and known simply as the 80th Viet Cong Battalion. Later this battalion switched titles and became the 96th Battalion. In 1962, the battalion was relabeled as the T80 Battalion, probably in honor of its original title. By this time it was fighting in the thick U Minh Forest along the western coast of the lowermost Mekong Delta.

"The T70 Battalion was formed in 1962 by taking troops from the older T80 battalion and using them to form another Viet Cong battalion just south of the U Minh Forest zone. The T70 Battalion also benefitted from its sapper experts and other key personnel transferred from other Mekong Delta battalions. In the spring of 1964, both the T70 and T80 Battalions received marching orders to move into Tay Ninh Province northwest of Saigon. Once this journey was completed the T70 Battalion became the 8th Battalion of the 273rd VC Regiment."[82]

In 1960, the Viet Cong 261st Regional Main Force Battalion was composed of only four rifle platoons. By 1963 it was five hundred men strong and its NVA cadres, most of whom had more than a decade of combat experience, controlled six companies. The 261st soon earned a reputation as a highly skilled combat unit.[83]

In 1961, the 514th Viet Cong Provincial Battalion was organized in IV Corps' Dinh Tuong Province, with thirty effectives. It fought a battle and was reinforced to company size. By the following year, after seizing sufficient weaponry, the battalion composed two companies. Each company had three, thirty-man platoons and a recon squad of ten men. A miniscule battalion staff of three men controlled the unit.

A new company was added to the battalion each year thereafter, through

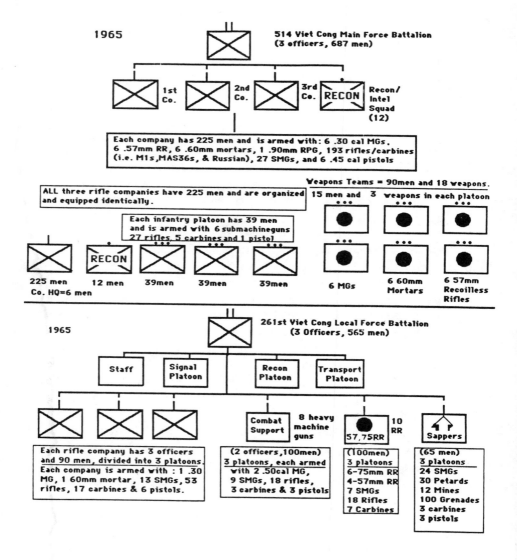

1965

514 Viet Cong Main Force Battalion
(3 officers, 687 men)

1st Co.

2nd Co.

3rd Co.

RECON

Recon/ Intel Squad (12)

Each company has 225 men and is armed with: 6 .30 cal MGs, 6 .57mm RR, 6 .60mm mortars, 1 .90mm RPG, 193 rifles/carbines (i.e. M1s, MAS36s, & Russian), 27 SMGs, and 6 .45 cal pistols

Weapons Teams = 90men and 18 weapons.

ALL three rifle companies have 225 men and are organized and equipped identically.

15 men and 3 weapons in each platoon

Each infantry platoon has 39 men and is armed with 6 submachineguns 27 rifles, 5 carbines and 1 pistol

225 men
Co. HQ=6 men

RECON
12 men

39men

39men

39men

6 MGs

6 60mm Mortars

6 57mm Recoilless Rifles

1965

261st Viet Cong Local Force Battalion
(3 Officers, 565 men)

Staff

Signal Platoon

Recon Platoon

Transport Platoon

Combat Support

8 heavy machine guns

57,75RR

10 RR

Sappers

Each rifle company has 3 officers and 90 men, divided into 3 platoons. Each company is armed with : 1 .30 MG, 1 60mm mortar, 13 SMGs, 53 rifles, 17 carbines & 6 pistols.

(2 officers,100men)
3 platoons, each armed with 2 .50cal MG, 9 SMGs, 18 rifles, 3 carbines & 3 pistols

(100men)
3 platoons
6-75mm RR
4-57mm RR
7 SMGs
18 Rifles
7 Carbines

(65 men)
3 platoons
24 SMGs
30 Petards
12 Mines
100 Grenades
3 carbines
3 pistols

1964. By 1965, the 514th Battalion was organized as follows: "1st Company: 150 men; 2nd Company: 140 men; 3rd Company: 140 men; 4th Company: 80 men; 5th Company: 90 men. Total: 600 men."[84]

The fourth company was armed with thirty machine guns and fifteen recoilless rifles. The fifth company was a special company of diehard communists armed with three 75mm recoilless rifles, as well as machine guns and small arms. A rear services company was used to resupply the five combat companies. Two hundred cadres (leadership and administrative personnel), controlled the battalion.

Until April 1965 the rifle companies operated independently. After that date they were closely controlled by the battalion staff which organized them to be specialists in certain kinds of combat:

- 1st Company: Raids.
- 2nd Company: Attacks on posts.
- 3rd Company: Ambushes.
- 4th Company: Machine gun and antiaircraft unit.
- 5th Company: Recoilless rifle (57mm and 75mm) unit.[85]

In addition, a recon platoon and a signal platoon supported the battalion.

Another source described a far different organization for the 514th Battalion as of spring 1965:

"Battalion 514 comprised five fighting companies, a guard unit of company size for control of supply routes, a self-defense company to protect the Dinh Tuong Province (communist) Party Chapter Committee (to which the battalion is directly responsible), and a special disciplinary company. Leaving aside the three specialized units, four of the five regular companies consisted of three platoons each (the fifth company, a combat or heavy weapons support unit, had two platoons); all the companies were organized on the basis of three squads per platoon and three cells per squad."[86]

In 1963, the Viet Cong 263rd Regional Main Force Battalion was formed into three infantry companies, three combat support companies and three specialized platoons to operate in Kien Hoa Province. In 1964, it fought seven battles and was reassigned to operate in three provinces: Dinh Tuong, Long An, and Hau Nghia.

In late 1964, the battalion was reorganized into three infantry companies, a weapons company, a signal platoon, a recon platoon and a medical squad. It was moved into IV Corps' Duong Minh War Zone and renamed the 711th Battalion. Two of its companies were used as the core necessary to form two new VC battalions, the 707th and 709th. Together the three battalions made up the new Q763rd Viet Cong Infantry Regiment.[87]

The six-hundred-man 711th VC battalion was composed of three rifle companies, a weapons company, and three specialized platoons.

In May 1965, the 263rd VC Battalion was reformed from recruits in Kien Hoa Province. Three months later it had returned to Dinh Tuong where it rapidly gained control of three districts.[88]

"As of December 1965, the 263rd battalion was composed of five companies: three infantry companies and two combat support companies. Companies 1, 2, and 3 were each composed of four platoons, 3 infantry platoons and 1 combat support platoon. Each platoon was composed of three squads; each squad had 3 cells; each cell had 3 members. (However, the combat support platoon had 5 squads.)"[89]

Fragments of NVA/VC Regimental Organizational History

Not much is known of the organization of the Chu Luc regiments which fought in South Vietnam. However, sufficient facts are known for military experts to draw accurate conclusions about the red order of battle. Such inference was necessary during the Second Indochina War because of the dearth of intelligence data.

In 1963, Viet Cong Region 2 headquarters began forming the 1st Dong Thap Regiment. By 1964 that Viet Cong regiment controlled three VC battalions:

• 263rd Dong Thap Battalion
• 265th Dong Thap Battalion
• 261st Regional Main Force Battalion.[90]

In early 1965, the Viet Cong Q763 Regiment was formed with three battalions and stationed in IV Corps' Duong Minh Chau war zone. It composed three battalions:

• 707th VC Battalion
• 709th VC Battalion
• 711th VC Battalion.

The Q763rd VC Regiment was still in action in 1967.[91]

On December 22, 1964 the 273rd VC Regiment, under Colonel Chin Hien, was activated outside of Saigon. Operating from its initial headquarters in the Boi Loi woods, the powerful regiment controlled three battalions, one weapons battalion, and nine supporting companies. It was organized as follows:

"The first two battalions, the T80 and T70 battalions, arrived in Tay Ninh Province during July and August 1964. They were joined by a third battalion, the 263rd Dong Thap, during December. At that time these three battalions were redesignated as the 7th, 8th, and 9th Battalions of the 273 VC Regiment respectively. The regiment contained those three infantry battalions, plus one artillery battalion (10th), and nine separate 'K-series' companies . . . The regiment was now fully assembled and ready to fight . . . It was clear from the outset that this regiment was controlled by the North Vietnamese and supplied with foreign arms from around the globe . . . The 273rd VC Regiment was a fully trained, modern tactical formation led by experienced infantry combat experts fresh from North Vietnam and by proven guerrilla commanders. Regimental soldiers were clothed in standard khaki-green uniforms with full web gear. They were equipped with the latest ammunition and weapons from the Soviet and Chinese factories. The men carried AK-47 rifles capable of full automatic fire. Individual equipment included sacks stuffed with Chinese-manufactured grenades and chest-mounted ammunition pouches full of Russian-supplied rifle magazines. Many elements had heavy machine guns, towed artillery, rocket propelled grenades and sophisticated demolitions devices."[92]

273rd Viet Cong Regiment, III Corps, 1965

- 7, 8, and 9 Infantry Battalions
- 10 Artillery Battalion
- K16 Sapper Company
- K17 Assault Infantry Company
- K18 Antiaircraft Machine Gun Company
- K19 Engineer Company
- K20 Signal Company
- K21 Reconnaissance Company
- K22 Transportation Company
- K23 Medical Company
- K24 Convalescent Company 93

The 273rd VC Regiment was one of three combat infantry regiments assigned to the new 9th Viet Cong Infantry Division raised in III Corps, near Saigon, in 1965. It joined a wave of new NVA divisions formed in South Vietnam's I, II and III corps that year.

CHAPTER 3

Chu Luc Logistics

The first priority of all NVA military planning was logistics. During the Second Indochina War, the Chu Luc needed food, water, clothing, equipment, ammunition, weapons, spare parts and other supplies, in order to fight. All of the skirmishes, battles and campaigns of the North Vietnamese/VietCong army were decided by the availability of those necessities.

Local "Viet Cong" taxation of South Vietnams' peasantry provided food. Small caches of ammunition would support limited action. However, both sources together would not support even medium-sized campaigns involving one or more NVA divisions. Such operations required either tens of thousands of porters and major supply assets moving along behind the combat units, or major logistics dumps feeding supplies into prepared battlefields. The supplies in those dumps, usually located in major border bases and war zones, came down the Ho Chi Minh Trail[94] from North Vietnam and the communist bloc nations.

The preparation of a foot mobile army for major campaigning is very slow. Two to three months are required to build up to a battle. Prepared battlefield supply dumps soon became depleted, as fighting combat troops use up ammunition and spares. Those troops have to be resupplied.

Yet the very strength of the NVA's primitive logistics system also contained its vulnerability:

"Giap's only means of moving large amounts of supplies was by coolies and ox carts, and his ammunition and food crawled across the countryside at three miles an hour and arrived piece by piece, mostly in thirty-three pound lots. Skillful planning and a careful build up beforehand could make this system adequate for fighting a large battle at any one particular point, but it was too inflexible to permit a sudden shift of the point of thrust over any appreciable distance. Thus, once Giap had begun an attack in one locality, he was unable to exploit French weakness arising elsewhere as more French reserves were committed to battle."[95]

However, lest the effect of General Giap's supposed inflexibility be overstated, a comparative perspective must be considered. American forces during the Second Indochina War, in spite of their helicopters and other technogear, were even slower and less flexible than the foot mobile Viets in battle. They could only move large numbers of troops long distances if they were operating out of range of enemy troops. They took as long, or longer, to build up for offensives. For example, the American company-sized Son Tay Raid into North Vietnam, in the early 1970s, required months of planning and preparation. Mechanized and technological equipment *did not* increase either American flexibility or mobility.

As long as the NVA held the initiative and could control its logistics network without fear of serious ground disruption, it could maintain its momentum. However, if NVA supply depots had been continually hit by allied ground forces, the whole Chu Luc machine would have become paralyzed.

Sudden, unexpected main force incursions into war zone logistics complexes would have easily dislocated the NVA. Chu Luc counteraction would have been awkward at best. Small communist forces, carrying out holding actions, would have to delay the attacking enemy until NVA main force regiments and divisions could be deployed. Those main force units could not be deployed until the NVA Logistics Service had mobilized its porter transport system and moved supplies into the area.

An invading allied force would have to remain in a central war zone-interdicting position for three to six months in order to affect the Chu Luc. By converting such a central position into an allied base for offensive action into neighboring red war zones, total area interdiction of the communist war effort would have been achieved.

The slowness of the logistics-driven Chu Luc battle system impaired its operations. That slowness also limited the flexibility of any NVA combat forces attempting to operate at significant distances from the huge communist logistics centers along the Ho Chi Minh Trail in Laos and Cambodia.

General Vo Nguyen Giap, the NVA's main leader during most of the Indochinese wars, harbored no doubt about the importance of logistics: "the supply of food and munitions was a factor as important as that of tactics; logistics constantly posed problems as urgent as those posed by the armed

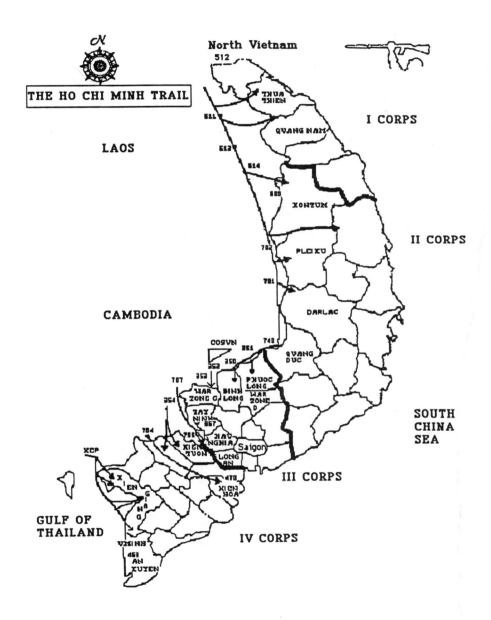

THE HO CHI MINH TRAIL

North Vietnam

LAOS

I CORPS

II CORPS

CAMBODIA

SOUTH
CHINA
SEA

Saigon

III CORPS

GULF OF
THAILAND

IV CORPS

struggle. . . Thousands of bicycles from the towns [also] carried food and munitions to the front, hundreds of sampans of all sizes, hundreds of thousands of bamboo rafts crossed rapids and cascades, day and night hundreds of thousands of volunteers crossed the passes and forded the rivers."[96]

That supply system was certainly vulnerable, but not from the air. It was vulnerable from the ground. Attacks upon the enemy supply lines would have won the wars in Indochina.

Chu Luc Logistics Organization

The Indochinese wars cannot be understood without understanding the Chu Luc logistics system. The system operated along the Ho Chi Minh Trail in Laos and Cambodia just like it did within North Vietnam.

Within South Vietnam, where the North Vietnamese invading army was frequently called the "Viet Cong," the Chu Luc logistics system operated differently from the more sophisticated Ho Chi Minh Trail West. Within South Vietnam, the red supply system could be characterized as follows:

- Logistical storage areas were numerous and well dispersed.
- Very large supply dumps were found only within heavily defended war zones.
- Numerous supply routes, frequently referred to as infiltration routes, ran everywhere, in every direction, using every possible mode of transport.
- The communists relied upon forcibly recruited civilian slave labor for transportation, construction, food production, ordnance activities, evacuation of wounded, and purchase of miscellaneous supplies.
- Since the local NVA never represented more than 2 or 3 percent of the total population in South Vietnam, they had to be sure that sufficient armed men were available to control their civilian forced labor.
- There was always a high ratio of civilian laborers to communist troops except during peak labor periods of rice production.
- Oxcarts, pack animals, elephants and sampans were used for logistical transport. In addition, the NVA ran thousands of trucks along the Ho Chi Minh Trail, inside and outside of South Vietnam.

The most essential element of communist operations was unpaid civilian (corvée) labor. The Viet Cong/North Vietnamese troops who occupied large parts of South Vietnam from 1965 to 1975, were very careful managers of that manpower resource. Their entire logistics service system was organized around impressed porter transport.

In most cases, the communist Central Office for South Vietnam (COSVN, NVA/Viet Cong), usually headquartered in Cambodia, directed NVA operations within South Vietnam. COSVN controlled three agencies which were responsible for Viet Cong logistics: 1. Finance and Economic 2. Rear Services 3. Frontline Supply.[97]

The three agencies had overlapping and interrelated functions. Their efforts had to be closely controlled and coordinated at all times.

All the money behind NVA operations was controlled by the Finance and Economic Section (FES). The FES dealt primarily with political and civilian aspects of the war, but its extortionate methods of fundraising provided sufficient capitol for the purchase, production, storage and issue of certain types of military supplies used by the reds.

The Rear Services Organization (RSO) was a massive web of supply bureaucracies, or as the reds called them, "committees." Every communist political echelon and military unit included representatives of the RSO. In addition, the RSO controlled the Rear Services Group, an organization with area responsibility for military support. That group controlled logistics units, ranging in size from 300 to 3,000 men, who worked to support NVA main forces (usually regiments and divisions).

Rear Services Group units operated manufacturing programs, ordnance and repair workshops, and medical facilities in their areas. In addition, they purchased, transported, stored and distributed large quantities of all types of supplies, including food.

The Frontline Supply Council, established in 1965, was explained in a captured enemy document: "Through the direct leadership of the Party Headquarters, all echelons take charge of supplying recruits, civilian laborers, food, money and necessary facilities for main force troops in the battlefield . . . inspire the people, organize and send all the human and material resources contributed by the people to the units and the battlefield, strengthen the people by urging them to increase agricultural production, practice economy to the limit."[98]

The Frontline Supply Councils, also known as the Organizational Weapon, were divided into four subsections: Recruiting, Civilian Labor Management, Food Supply, and Burial. The efforts of these subsections were focused upon South Vietnamese villages, which were collections of small hamlets.

The Recruiting subsection recruited new soldiers for the NVA from the sixteen- to thirty-five-year-old age groups. Each village was expected to send one to two platoons (30–60 men) a month to NVA main force units.

All civilians between the ages of thirty-six and forty-five were organized

NVA LOGISTICS PLANNING DATA

Truck Column :
One hundred 2.5 ton trucks
Speed :45 miles per hour

Horse Cart Column:
Four Columns of five horse carts each.
Each horse cart carries 473 pounds,
twelve miles per day.
A horse cart column carries 2365 pounds.

Ox Cart Column:
Six columns of five ox carts each.
Each ox cart carries 770 pounds,
twelve miles per day.
An Ox cart column carries 3850 pounds.

Bicycle Column:
Sixty columns of fifty transport bikes each.
Each transport bike carries 150 pounds,
twelve miles per day.
A Bicycle column carries 7500 pounds.

Porter Column:
Ten columns of one hundred men each.
Each porter carries 30 pounds,
nine miles a day.
A Porter column carries 3000 pounds.

Total Portage In A One-Way Trip, For Each Type Of Transport Resource :
Horse Carts : Four Coumns X 2365 = 9460 pounds.
Ox Carts : Six Columns X 3850 = 23,100 pounds.
Transport Bicycles : Sixty Columns X 7500 = 450,000 pounds.
Porters : Ten Columns X 3000 = 30.000 pounds.
Trucks : One Column X 3000 = 300,000 pounds.

Approximate Length of All units in Column For Each Type of Transport :
Truck : One mile
Horse Cart : One eight of a mile
Ox Cart : One eight of a mile
Transport Bicycles : Three to Four miles
Porters : One to two miles.

into platoons subordinate to the Civilian Labor Management subsection. Depending upon requirements, some of those platoons were impressed for three to six months' service at the front lines, away from their homes. All other platoons of forced labor were organized into squads for local labor.

Each squad was usually expected to maintain four hammocks, four carrying poles and, if near trafficable waterways, four sampans (including two motorized sampans). Each village was required to mobilize from one to three labor platoons. Most platoons also included a few assigned communist party activist youths, and a medic.[99]

A Food Supply subsection committee was located in each village, with a cell assigned to each hamlet. They encouraged the production of more vegetables to feed the troops. In addition, they required each family to hide, in reserve, one to three *gia* (a gia is a bushel of 40 liters, equivalent to 19 kilograms or 42 pounds of unmilled paddy rice) to feed communist troops when they came through the area.

The Burial subsection, usually composed of the families of cadre and soldiers, buried the communist dead brought back from battlefields. Members of that subsection also indoctrinated families of the dead.

Portage Along the Ho Chi Minh Trail

The numerous NVA logistics and transportation regiments deployed along the Ho Chi Minh Trail within Laos and Cambodia were usually empoyed in four platoons; each company was composed of 100–150 men. A regiment might control as many as eighteen way stations along the trail.

Each station, usually spaced twelve kilometers apart along the trail, might have a quota requirement of 50 kilograms, or 110 pounds, per man, of supplies transhipped per day. Each company had to transport an average of 3 metric tons a day, including 1.8 tons of rice, foodstuffs and medicine. The other 1.2 tons consisted of weapons and ammunition. "Each station had many storehouses. Station 12 had rice storehouses, each containing eight tons of rice. Weapons and ammunition were placed under racks of branches and leaves. About 1–1.5 tons of weapons and ammunition were stored in Station 12. Station 13 was organized in the same way."[101]

Porter companies on the trail might carry 30–33 kilograms (60–73 pounds) of supplies per trip load. Their rate of march was usually 3 kilometers an hour over rough terrain. Some porters carried as much as 45 kilograms (99 pounds). Others had more reasonable ambitions: "There was a very high competitive spirit to break the record and some comrades went so far as to carry up to 75 kilograms (165 pounds) in order to get sick afterward because they hoped to be allowed to return to the north. (Their hope was not realized.)"[102]

In early 1965, the 10th NVA Transportation Battalion carried the initial supply load for the 18th NVA Infantry Regiment infiltrating down the Ho Chi Minh Trail into II Corps' Binh Dinh Province. Traveling from March to May 1965, the 10th Transportation Battalion was supposed to be absorbed by the 18th Regiment after it had reached its destination. In the meantime, there was a huge amount of supplies to be transported: "The battalion counted 300 soldiers, 82 of them women. Though some small carts and bicycles were used, the bulk of the supply was loaded on backs. Each 'cargadore' carried 10 kilograms, or more than 22 pounds, of fighting supplies, such as 81 or 82mm shells and recoilless rifle rounds. On departure, each man would carry a seven day supply of rice, which weighed five kilograms. The permitted daily ration was three fourths of a kilogram."[103]

Forced Labor: Construction

There were three types of corvée labor: porterages, construction and special assignment. If the slave labor was paid at all, the wages were a pittance, confiscated from the citizenry by local communist tax collectors. All that the forced labor could count on was food and water, issued under the watchful eyes of armed communist guards.

The availability of labor resources within an NVA controlled area varied with population density, age distribution and the intensity of combat. However, the reds didn't hesitate to shanghai forced labor under any conditions.

Each NVA battalion usually cooked its own food, with one man per cell spending, on the average, an hour per day on the task. Such activity consumed about 2 percent of the battalion effort per day.

The production of food was usually left to the local populace. In rice-rich areas like the delta, food was easily obtained since farmers needed only about 5 percent of their crop for their own consumption. A typical communist battalion could be supplied with rice by thirty-one farmers. Another ten farmers could grow all the manioc and corn needed by the battalion. Most VC/NVA battalions also regularly assigned about a squad of their own men to farming chores. They preferred confiscation to manual labor, however.

Forced labor assignments varied from a village requirement of three to five days per month, to as long as six months away from home. The numbers of laborers forced into communist service within a specific province or district also varied. In some areas, forty people might be mobilized at one time, or as much as two to four hundred might be mobilized. Entire villages of several thousand people were impressed for fortification construction, too.

As the main force NVA battalions and regiments wandered across South Vietnam for years, they developed habits. Every province was criss-crossed with their road systems. Those road systems connected communist war zones, strongholds, minibases and campsites.

The red military road system insured both NVA mobility and control, necessary since the red units were vastly outnumbered by the populace. For example, the 514th VC Battalion, with a strength of 693 men, amounted to less than 1 percent of the population it controlled within its base/campsite (nomad) area.

Yet such units confiscated information, recruits, food, land and labor from the South Vietnamese peasants whenever they wanted to. For example: "it has been the practice of the 514th to send many women to the market, each to buy a small quantity of rice, so as not to indicate the battalion's presence (or imminent presence) in the area."[104]

South Vietnamese peasants usually submitted to forced labor. They accepted that duty because it exempted them from military obligations or fines for not volunteering: "In the villagers' eyes being drafted by the Front was considered equivalent to being killed on the battlefield. Experience has shown that many of those who have joined the Front units have not come back. Therefore they thought it better to work on transportation than to be led away to a military unit."[105]

The reds were very systematic about extracting labor from the populace. The communist cadre in Binh Ba Village, Phuoc Tuy Province, required the following labor assignments: "Everyone in the village had to do three months' labor a year. All the young men had to do labor in battlefields, carrying wounded and ammunition; 7–20 day missions. Men under 45 and single females transported rice and goods, but not in battle. Men over 45 worked on the destruction of roads."[106]

Construction projects varied too. Some villages were required to dig tunnel networks, in a year or more of intense effort. Others were required to work periodically on nearby tunnels or fortifications, over longer stretches of time. Construction workers usually put in an eleven-hour day.

A thousand or more people might work for months, building a fortified camp or village. The extensive defensive system required for village fortification could include bunkers, trenches, pit traps, booby traps, tunnels and secret trenches for hiding and retreating. Even bunker building required a lot of work: "underground bunkers were two and one half meters high, three meters wide and three meters long. The ceilings were usually made of tree

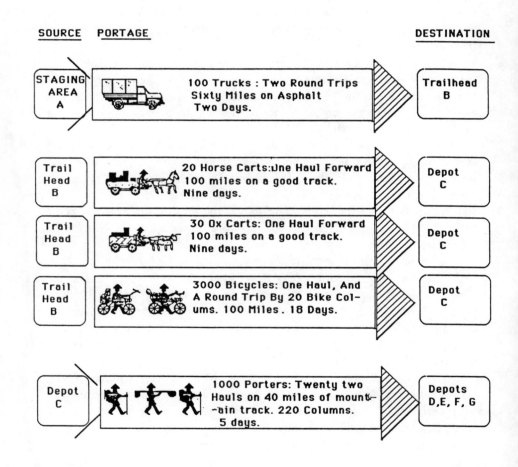

NVA MOVEMENT OF SUPPLIES FROM STAGING AREA A TO DEPOT G : 200 MILES

SOURCE PORTAGE   DESTINATION

STAGING AREA A | 100 Trucks : Two Round Trips Sixty Miles on Asphalt Two Days. | Trailhead B

Trail Head B | 20 Horse Carts:One Haul Forward 100 miles on a good track. Nine days. | Depot C

Trail Head B | 30 Ox Carts: One Haul Forward 100 miles on a good track. Nine days. | Depot C

Trail Head B | 3000 Bicycles: One Haul, And A Round Trip By 20 Bike Col-ums. 100 Miles. 18 Days. | Depot C

Depot C | 1000 Porters: Twenty two Hauls on 40 miles of mount--ain track. 220 Columns. 5 days. | Depots D,E, F, G logs, reinforced vertically under a sand clay cover two meters thick. Bamboo pipes provided ventilation and light."[107]

In An Xuyen Province, all villagers had to work ten to twenty days a month digging trenches, mining roads, digging canals and traps, and building fortified villages. Some of their villages were fortified with concrete. [108]

Construction gangs, known as "assault labor groups," had been known to clear a ten-kilometer trail, one meter wide, in one day. Of course they needed at least four hundred men to accomplish such a feat. [109]

Roads for transporting heavy weapons had to be three meters wide, flat surfaced, with trenches and foxholes dug along both sides. One NVA road, six kilometers long, was completed in three months with 250 slaves working 22,500 man days. The communists also used 1,200 blasting caps and 540 kilograms of explosives to build the road. [110]

Many villages were responsible for maintaining the communist controlled roads and bridges in their area. In emergencies, the roads were upgraded by mobilizing entire communities as well as bringing in additional labor from outside.

Typical Monthly Support Requirements: 514th VC Battalion

| Activity: | Manpower Contribution | | | | Civilian |
	Battalion	Other mil.	Civilian	Total	Support Factor
Cooking	14			14	
Food Raising	7		34	41	.05
Medical care	9	40		49	
Medical Evac.			9	9	.01
Construction			35-350	35-350	.05-.50
Communications	21	7		28	
Food Porterage			22	22	.03
Ordnance Work (8 sites)			49	49	.07
Ammunition Porterage			13	13	.02
Total	51	47	166 to 477	260-575	.23-.68[111]

Forced Labor: Porters

Civilian porters usually worked part of the night and all day too, for a total of fifteen hours at a stretch. They usually rested one full day out of every ten days of labor. However, some porter units would only make one trip a day, carrying supplies from a base to a storage cache.

The 514 VC Battalion found that it could always mobilize all the porters it needed. The most porters it ever impressed from the local populace was 567, distributed as follows:

- 377 to carry one basic load of battalion ammunition.
- 52 to carry a two-day supply of rice.
- 138 to aid in evacuating dead and wounded. "Civilian support for dead and wounded evacuation was usually twenty percent of the battalion strength, on days of combat only."[112]

Before an NVA unit mobilized coolie porters, it had to engage in detailed planning. The four elements involved were organization, schedule, control and protection.

Every porter unit had to be formed, oriented and equipped. Then the porters had to be told where to report. Upon arrival at a porter staging area, communist guards would be assigned to control and protect the porters: "District authorities will see to it that rice and other foodstuffs are available at the assembly areas. Laborers will have to bring their personal effects such as hammocks, nylon sheets, mosquito nets, blankets, sandals, clothes, medicine, latern, rice pouches, mess kits, and dry rations. Each squad will furnish three hill hocks, five pickaxes and two cooking pots.

"The Corridor Section is in charge of the corridors going in from north to south and also from one region to another. This is very important because, without it, all units would get lost in the immense forest."[113]

Porters could cover an average of fifty kilometers a day, and thirty to forty kilometers if they traveled all night. Every porter unit was closely guarded, with an average of one guard for every five porters.

When moving arms and ammunition, more communist troops were assigned for supervision. For example, one seventy-man porter unit carrying mortar rounds, machine gun ammunition and rice, had eighty armed guards. Another unit reported a similar ratio: "When we went to get ammunition we needed at most eight civilian porters and ten guerrillas to protect them. Each porter would carry two rifles or 1,000 rifle cartridges [an exaggeration, 1000 rounds weighs too much for one man to carry]. It took us two days and one night to cover on foot a distance of over 50 kilometers. We had to pass by two staging points."[114]

A South Vietnamese teenager, who was tricked into attending a communist "educational meeting" and then forced into an ammuniton carrying detail, was able to observe and report NVA porter control procedures. He reported that his porter unit carried thirty boxes of ammunition and the rice needed to feed all the porters, guards and administrative personnel in the march group. They marched for seventeen nights, with five days of rest, carrying roughly 780 kilograms of ammunition and 1,180 kilograms of rice. They were fed from way station supplies during rest halts.

"After being captured . . . led to Phuoc Chi . . . stayed there for 3 days. . . noted the presence of approximately sixty male youths from 20–30 years old . . . natives of different districts in Bien Hoa Province. The following day these youths were formed . . . into 6 ten-man squads. Squad leaders and assistant squad leaders were Front cadre [communist politruks]. In addition to the 60 male youths there were 9 female youths who did the cooking and a 50-man Front platoon equipped with 1 machine gun, three automatic rifles, and . . . rifles and submachine guns.

"After one day of movement through the forest the group arrived in Ba Ria and halted . . . for 2 days. Subject's squad was ordered to transport three .80 x .50 x .50 meter boxes of ammunition of between 24 and 26 kilograms each . . . was told that other squads transported the same type boxes and they were of a total of 30 . . . Trip to Gioc Moi lasted approximately 12 days since the boxes were heavy and the group moved at night to avoid airstrikes."[115]

Another Viet Cong prisoner described coolie recruitment: "Some 30–50 people had been recruited as coolies to transport ammunition boxes to my village. Then the same number of coolies were recruited in my village for transport to the next village, and so on. These ammunition boxes were made of tin and weighed 15–40 kilograms each. Each coolie carried one box according to his physical strength. This corvée was carried on at irregular periods of time, usually every 5–7 days. The village guerrilla unit was responsible for recruitment of coolies. As a rule he was informed 2 hours in advance of each arrival of ammunition. The guerilla squad leader sent his man to call on the people's houses to recruit coolies, who are assembled at a selected place at night, prior to the arrival of the ammunition. The coolies were generally escorted by a platoon."[116]

Porter Capabilities

Each porter could carry 20–30 kilograms (44 to 66 pounds).
Each porter ate an average of one liter of rice per day.
Typical load A-Three artillery shells plus ten liters of rice.
Typical load B-Nine to thirteen liters of rice.[117]

Porters were important to communist logistics throughout South Vietnam. The U.S. Army identified primary NVA transportation modes by Corps Tactical Zone:

I: Porters, some sampans and elephants.
II: Porters, some oxcarts and sampan.
III: More than half by sampan and oxcart, the rest by porters.
IV: Watercraft, some porters and oxcarts. [118]

However, the above list is misleading since it fails to mention communist truck traffic. The U.S. military was loathe to admit that the enemy ran truck convoys within South Vietnam. Trucks were regularly used as supply vehicles, usually at night, and on shorter road segments. One enemy defector described the vehicles of his Front, which was located within South Vietnam: "The Front had trucks, fuel, and even an M113 [U.S. armored personnel carrier] they had captured. They used it for rice transportation. *In the jungle there were real roads,* but people would not believe it." [119]

The weather greatly affected logistics. During the rainy season, only animals and porters could make headway since even pack bicycles mired down in the mud.

Porter Support Factors

Careful calculation was needed to plan the porterage of supplies. Various formulas have been used to calculate the number of porters required to transport a specific number of supplies. Each formula is based on averages and assumes smoothly functioning plans and schedules and controlled execution.

In a study of the 514th VC Battalion, it was found that their average civilian support requirements were predicated upon two factors: (1) the average distance to logistics sites and (2) the average consumption of supplies.

In any one forty-day time frame, the 514th VC Battalion could draw porter support from twenty different villages. By careful planning, requirements could be established in relationship to supply caches contiguous to local villages and VC campsites.

Each combat engagement of NVA troops lasted about one day and consumed at least one-half of their basic load of ammunition (e.g. the standard amount of ammunition kept on hand for each weapon or weapon type). Sufficient porters had to be on hand to carry that ammunition.

To carry in one of the 514th Battalion's basic ammunition loads, "one lift required three hundred and seventy seven porters [7,539 kilograms of total basic load/ 20 kilograms per porter]. To carry an entire two day battalion supply of rice in one lift required fifty two porters. That calculation was computed as follows:

$$\underline{693 \text{ men} \times .75 \text{ kg/day} \times 2 \text{ days}} \quad 20 \text{ kg/porter}$$

The Rand corporation has composed a formula assuming that each porter can carry 20 kilograms, 24 kilometers a day. The number of porters required for a given task can be calculated by inserting known figures into the formula, $N = 2 \text{ SD/pV}$, where

N is the number of porters required.
S is the supply rate in kilograms per day.
D is the one-way distance to a storage site.
p is the porter payload.
V is the average distance traveled daily.[121]

If each man in the 514th Viet Cong Battalion ate 750 grams of rice per day, then the entire unit ate 518 kilograms ($693 \times .75 = 518$ kg). "The value of N [the number of porters necessary to carry that food] is ($2 \times 518 \times 10.2$ / (20×24), or a requirement of 22 porters per day.[122]

It is also possible to calculate the number of porters necessary to replenish ammunition expended at the rate of one basic load per month. First, it must be realized that one month's basic ammunition load for a typical Viet Cong battalion weighed 7,539 kilograms. At a rate of expenditure of one basic ammo per month, porter requirements could be computed using the above formula: "S is 7,539/30 or 2,513 kilograms/day and N is 13 porters per basic load per month."[123] The key factor in that calculation was the distance to storage sites. For short distances, fewer porters were required.

Other formulas are slightly different. For example: "A consumption of 1.65 lb/day (750 g) was used. 'Average' porterage involves a payload of 50 lb and a daily round-trip distance of 30 kilometers. 'Difficult' porterage involves reduced values: 40 lb and 10 km. This would be for some combination of difficult terrain, poor visibility, and delays due to GVN control or harassment."[124]

Securing Food for NVA Troops

Local and main force NVA troop units periodically moved to alternate campsites, minibases, or strongholds within their operational areas. Those movements were undertaken for two reasons: (1) security, (2) area control.

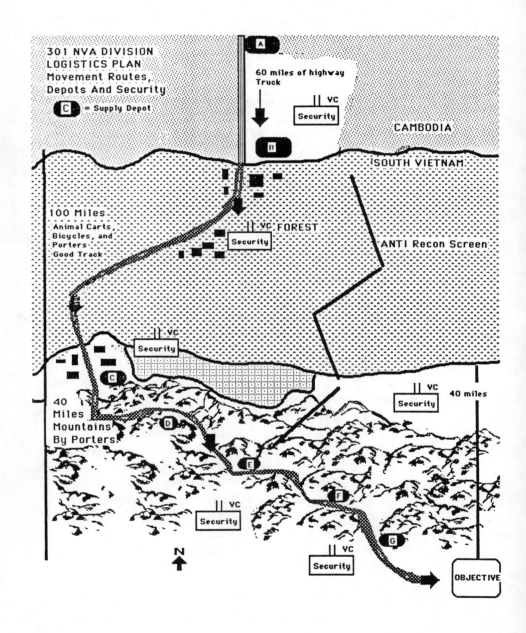

301 NVA DIVISION
LOGISTICS PLAN
Movement Routes,
Depots And Security

C = Supply Depot

A

60 miles of highway
Truck

B

VC
Security

CAMBODIA

SOUTH VIETNAM

100 Miles
Animal Carts,
Bicycles, and
Porters
Good Track

VC FOREST
Security

ANTI Recon Screen

VC
Security

C

VC
Security

40 miles

40
Miles
Mountains
By Porters

D

E

F

VC
Security

G

N

VC
Security

OBJECTIVE

66

In addition, the movement of communist troops facilitated a more even-handed confiscation of area food stuffs. Since the reds preferred to obtain their rice supplies locally, they commonly took food from the peasantry of each area which they traversed. The distribution of the burden was thus spread more evenly.

Much surplus rice was usually available in the agricultural areas of South Vietnam. For example, farmers in Dinh Tuong Province villages controlled by the 514th VC Battalion enjoyed a surplus of nearly 20,000 kilograms per day.[125] Since the 514th VC battalion only needed 500 kilograms of rice a day, even large deficits in peasant agricultural production would not present a problem.

However, since rice kept so well, everybody hoarded it. Some over-zealous communist rice tax collectors, dreaming of huge rice stockpiles, collected ten times as much as they should have. Such measures inevitably caused the local people to demand payment for subsequent levies.

If the people began charging for food, combat troops got nervous. Chu Luc food purchase allowances were rarely adequate: "a 10-man squad received a total sum of 70 piasters. Rice cost 7 piasters a liter in liberated areas. The squad had to spend 52 piasters on rice and thus had only 18 piasters to buy food for ten persons. What could they buy for 18 piasters? In fact, we only had bean sauce or bean curd to eat with rice. Very often we scattered to look for vegetables to supplement our diet."[126]

Inflated rice levies, population movements and disruptions caused by battles, restricted rice supplies in some locales. Such restrictions caused the NVA to set up depots which were replenished from outside the area. A member of the 261st VC Battalion described the effect of one food shortage crisis in 1965:

"Many people . . . left and the supply of food is more difficult . . . the Front has had to set up quartermaster depots and every time the battalion goes there, it draws a ration for the soldiers. Every time a ration is received from a depot we usually have to get enough to last each person three days, and the battalion has to figure the movement so that after three days we can pick up another supply at another depot . . . the Front has put out instructions to the village to stockpile rice for the use of the units."[127]

Securing Ammunition for NVA Troop Units

Ammunition expenditures by NVA troop units were carefully calculated. While preparing the battlefield before a fight, the reds always cached some ammunition.

Battles typically consumed massive amounts of supply resources, including tons of heavy ammunition. After the battle against an NVA infantry regiment near Plei Me, South Vietnam, in late 1965, Americans picked up the following communist arms and ammunition in the battle area:

"Chinese copies of individual weapons, including AK assault rifles 903
Chinese 12.7mm heavy machine guns 23
Chinese . . . . . light machine guns . . (Degyarev and model 58,7.62) 52
82mm mortars 10
57 mm and 75 mm recoilless rifles 13
Chinese 40 mm rocket launchers (RPG) 3
7.62mm ammunition (rounds) 120,000
82mm mortar ammunition (rounds) 59
40mm rocket ammunition (rounds) 54
12.7mm heavy machine gun ammunition (rounds) . . . . 1,200 . . . . . ."[128]

Some communist units were required to cache their ammunition in villages near potential battle areas. Before a battle, the local Rear Services unit reassembled the cached ammunition for use: "some of it is specifically sent to a village to be held in reserve until the unit has a battle in that area, at which time it will be available for use. The 261st Battalion has sent ammunition to almost all the villages."[129]

Resupply of ammunition to recently engaged units usually occurred shortly after a battle. Battalion subunits would rendezvous at prescribed ammunition storage sites for replenishment. "I don't know where our ammunition came from. I only know that before a battle, ammo was stored in a preselected place. After fighting the entire battalion had to go there to obtain fresh munitions to replace those used during the fight."[130]

The 514th VC Battalion was usually resupplied with ammunition within one day after a battle: "Usually it took the 514th Battalion one day to be resupplied with ammunition after an attack, because the Rear Services unit always had everything ready for this. Only in the case of surprise attacks by the GVN [South Vietnamese troops] for example, in cases where the battalion or the company had to fight against a GVN sweep operation was the supply of ammunition delayed, because the Rear Services unit didn't have ammunition ready to resupply it. In this case, it took the unit from two to six days to be resupplied with ammunition. For example, during a sweep operation defense in Hung Thanh My Village in Chau Thanh District in either August or September 1963, my company used up 40 percent of our ammunition. After the battle it took us up to four days to be resupplied with ammunition."[131]

Ammunition caches were part of the resupply system. Some units attempted to hedge against emergencies by hoarding some of their ammunition. "The reason . . . is that experience has shown that if a company runs out of ammunition, it will be three or four days before they get a new supply, and if during that time they have to beat off an ARVN sweep operation they could be at a severe disadvantage. As a result, the company commanders usually hide ammunition for their own protection."[132]

Chu Luc Supply Purchases and Confiscations

The Chu Luc freqently supplied its troop units from U.S. logistics coffers. Many of the NVA supplies were obtained by ransacking abandoned allied bases or operational areas.

Supplies were also purchased from South Vietnamese merchants and soldiers: "Before the ARVNs abandoned the encampment at Henderson Trail, we had given them 36,000 Bouncing Betty mines. When they came back there were 36,000 60mm Bouncing Betty mines missing. The VC just came right in and picked them up, and we had to go out and find them one at a time. Meaning, BOOM . . ."[133]

The COSVN logistics unit, Rear Services Group 83, regularly purchased U.S. goods on the open market in the Saigon-Cholon area. Group 83 purchasing agents regularly acquired and shipped out of the area medical, ordnance, engineer, quartermaster, office equipment, radio, camera, and fuel supplies.

"From October, 1965 to April, 1966 the following supply items were purchased in Saigon and shipped into nearby NVA war zones:

- 33,200 liters of gasoline.
- 3,040 liters of lubrication oil.
- 232 twenty-liter cans of kerosene.
- 123 cans of asphalt.
- 46,802 meters of cloth
- 800 meters of canvas.
- 150 kilograms of grease.
- 37,760 meters of parachute cord.
- 20 recording tapes.
- 44,444 meters of plastic material.
- 2,443 PRC 10 dry batteries.
- 70 PRC 6 dry batteries.
- 3,910 regular size dry batteries.
- 112 flashlights.

- 35,880 meters of electric wire.
- 31,267 sheets of tin.
- 860 pickmattocks.
- 1,181 machetes.
- 1 refrigerator.
- 2 typewriters."[134]

Every day, hundreds of Chinese and South Vietnamese merchants gathered at Tay Ninh, near the Cambodian border. There they sold goods to the NVA. The VC paid top dollar for salt, cloth, tobacco, fat, kerosene, batteries, electric wire, rubber and typewriters.

In Phuoc Tuy Province, the Australians laid a minefield of M16 "Bouncing Betty" mines, which they called "jumping jacks." The Viet Cong promptly dug the mines up, losing thirty men in the process. When asked how the VC were able to do that, the Australians replied: "In fact, the necessary patrolling was not carried out, and many of the approximately 31,000 mines laid were removed."[135] The VC then used the M16 mines against the Australians, causing several hundred casualties.

The Chu Luc emphasized looting battlefields, or confiscating the spoils left after a battle. In fact, it was part of their doctrine to recover all the supplies and equipment that they could grab. They were especially interested in capturing signals equipment: "Captured communications equipment was the highest-quality gear in the communist inventory. Units often entered battle with special squads whose only assignment was to capture radios. Some agents specialized in stealing equipment directly from warehouses. By mid-1966 the village and hamlet radio program had lost 1,324 radios to the Viet Cong. When American units began arriving in the mid-1960s, their new PRC-25 voice radios became prime targets for the Viet Cong warehouse thieves. First priority for issue of those valuable radios went to the Viet Cong (NVA) units monitoring American communications, but by the early 1970s, so many PRC-25s had been captured that the radio was standard in most enemy line units."[136]

Why didn't American generals try to prevent the possible enemy confiscation of American radios and signals equipment? Why couldn't a miniature command detonated mine have been embedded inside each radio? Such high explosive "signals" could have been detonated by aircraft flying over the jungle.

Chu Luc Logistics Planning for a Military Operation

When an NVA general began planning a campaign, he had to consider a variety of factors. After picking out a target or objective area and devising a scheme of maneuver, including deceptions and diversions, he had to calculate the operation's logistical requirements. That is when the real brain work began.

Working from detailed maps of all the relevant terrain, the NVA general commanding an operation would first consider these factors:

- Combat forces available and their locations.
- Combat and labor support forces available and their locations.
- Distance to the objective area.
- Routes to the objective area.
- Logistics transport resources (i.e. vehicles, carts, bicycles, porters), including unit types and numbers.
- Supply depots available en route to the objective area, and their current stock of supplies.
- Troop consumption rate versus transport capabilities.
- Transport column payloads versus march rates.

The end product of such considerations would be a detailed logistics transport movement plan.

It would all began when the commander of his staff consulted the Chu Luc Logistics Handbook. In that book would be found data norms on relevant operational/ logistics subjects.

Typical NVA Logistics Norm Categories

Roadways—The types of roads encountered during the operation and the speed they can be traversed by the type of logistics transport traveling over them. If the commander determines to use several avenues of approach, sound thinking, he must apply his calculations to all roadways.

Engineer Support—The necessity, due to road conditions, to dispatch engineer road repair on mine clearing teams along the prescribed route(s) ahead of the main force and logistics columns.

March Rates—The amount of ground which each unit can cover, based on terrain to be encountered, every twenty-four hours.

Consumption Rates—The amount of rations and ammunition consumed per man per day, both en route and in combat. Porter consumption of food would have to be factored into his calculation.

Carrying Capabilities—The number of pounds each logistics transport unit could carry and the distance they could carry those supplies every day.

Weights—What various types of supplies weigh[1]

14.5-MM AA HEAVY MACHINE GUNS
ZPU-1, ZPU-2, AND ZPU-4

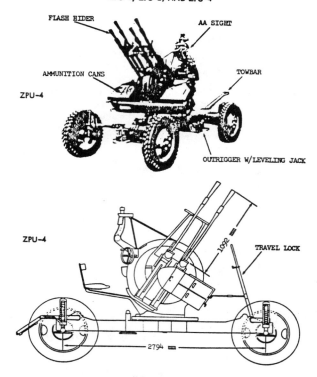

FLASH HIDER

AA SIGHT

AMMUNITION CANS

TOWBAR

ZPU-4

OUTRIGGER W/LEVELING JACK

ZPU-4

1092

TRAVEL LOCK

2794

12.7-MM DShK
HEAVY MACHINE GUNS M38, M38/46

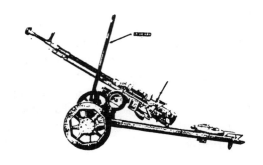

A Notional Example: The 301st NVA Division's Logistics Plan

General Nguyen Than Son of the 301st NVA Infantry Division has been given the mission of attacking an enemy base, as part of a multi-division dry weather "Blossoming Lotus" Campaign. That campaign will take place in South Vietnam's II Corps. General Son's unit will have to travel two hundred miles from his cantonment/staging area along the Ho Chi Minh Trail, to the objective area.

For the operation, General Son will command an infantry division reinforced by engineer, flak and labor units, code named the B-10 Front.

Troops of the B-10 Front

301st NVA Infantry Division	10,000 men in 3 infantry regiments,
1 Artillery Regiment (75mm)	1,140 men,
1 Antiaircraft Battalion	200 men (12.7mm machine guns),
1 Engineer battalion	1,500 men including labor,
1 Artillery labor battalion	1,084 men towing guns and carrying one basic load of ammo.
Total	13,924 men, inclu. 12,340 combatants.

As General Son and his staff consider the problems which must be solved in projecting the reinforced 301st Division 200 miles to a battle area, they rapidly inventory their available lift capacity. That lift capacity consists of all resources available to transport supplies. Each category of transport (lift capacity) resource has three characteristics: the weight of supplies that it can carry, its march rate and what type of terrain it can negotiate.

Transport Resources for B-10 Front's Operation Blossoming Lotus

- one hundred two-and-one-half ton trucks for transport within Cambodia to the South Vietnamese border, sixty miles away.
- sixty ox carts.
- twenty horse carts.
- three thousand bicycles rigged for supply hauling.
- porters as required, secured from villages en route.

A map study reveals that the best approach route for the 301st NVA Division requires the traverse of 200 miles of intervening terrain. That route is divided into the following avenues of approach:

- Hard surfaced, all weather road: Sixty miles.
- Good track: One hundred miles.
- Mountain trail: Forty miles.

The various transport resources are limited according to the type of roadway that they can negotiate.

Roadways Trafficable For Transport Resources

- Hard surfaced, all weather road: All transport resources.
- Good track: Trucks would damage the track. Besides, the Chu Luc high command made trucks available for use only on hard surfaced roadways. Animal carts, bicycles, and porters travel on tracks.
- Mountain trail: Only porters can negotiate the mountain trails available to the 301st Division. Most mountain trails, however, are negotiable by bicycle transporters.

The next step required in the logistics planning process was to determine the required movement serials between all operational staging and replenishment areas. General Son's supplies will first be transported by trucks from his staging area at Location A, to the trailhead at Location B, sixty miles away. From Trailhead B, the NVA supplies will have to be transported 100 miles to Depot C.

From Depot C, the reinforced 301st NVA Division will pass, en route to its objective area, four depots located approximately ten miles apart. The four depots are stocked with the following tonnage of rice for the use of the 301st Division:

Depot D	100 tons	*Depot F*	50 tons
Depot E	60 tons	*Depot G*	50 tons

Depot G is located ten miles from the objective area. There are ammunition cache sites within the battlefield zone which Depot G borders.

General Son decides to schedule his scheme of maneuver allowing twenty days for his approach march, five days for assault/follow-up operations, and five days for withdrawal. He plans to disperse his unit into nearby war zones rather than attempt to withdraw it into Cambodia after the operation. During those thirty operational days the 301st Division will cover a minimum of 200 route miles one way, since the distances covered are not in a straight line.

The NVA general plans to use the assigned truck fleet to move his supplies to the trailhead at Location B. From Trailhead B, animal carts, bicycles and porters will move the supplies 100 miles into Depot C. After Depot C is reached, only porters can be used across the mountainous terrain routes which pass by Depots D, E, and F on the way to the objective area. The distance from Depot C to the last route depot short of the objective area is forty miles.

General Son is required to calculate not only the consumption of supplies by combat troops during the battle. He must also calculate what will be consumed by all participants throughout the entire operation.

Norms were available to NVA logistics planners which had been derived from careful recording of actual troop consumption patterns during a variety of operations. Those recordings were translated into extrapolated norms and then tested in new operations. If the norms proved to be sufficient as planning tools, they were retained. Examples of such norms were the consumption of: 1.76 pounds of food and .88 pounds of ammunition per combatant, per day.

Calculated Logistics Requirements: 30 Days

Rations: 12,340 men at 1.76 per man × 30 days =	651,552 lbs
Ammo: 12,340 men at .88 per man × 30 days =	325,776 lbs
Spare Weapons: (6% of total ammo usage) =	20,000 lbs
Miscellaneous Spares: (6% of total ammo usage) =	20,000 lbs
Explosives: (5% of the total ammo usage) =	15,000 lbs
Medical Supplies: (.03% of total ration usage) =	2,000 lbs

Total = 518 tons − 210 tons of en route food = 308 tons to transport.[137]

Now the NVA logistics planners must balance what will be consumed during the operation against their own transportation capabilities. The supplies must then be broken down into loads which are assigned to the various means of transport. The central factor in such assignment is the carrying capacity of each transport unit.

Planning Data: Consumption Rates vs Carrying Capabilities

Consumption Rates: (lbs per man, per day) *Rations*-1.76; *Ammo*-.88
Carrying Capabilities: (Type of transport and march rate)
Horse Cart: 473 lb at 12.4 miles per day.
Ox carts: 770 lbs at 12 miles per day.
Bicycles: 150 lbs at 12 miles per day.
Porters: Flat terrain-55 lb of food or 50 lb of other supplies, 15.5 miles per day; Mountain-30 lb at 9 miles per day.
Combat troops: Each man carries 8 days rations in a food tube.[138]

General Son realizes that his logistics staff, reinforced by corps headquarters, must calculate other factors relevant to the movement of his reinforced division. The transport units must be controlled by the assignment of assembly areas and by dividing them into movement columns, or serials to facilitate management. Each column's transport capability in pounds and march distance per day must also be considered.

Movement Columns or Serials: Payload vs March Rate

Horse cart columns: Five carts carrying 2365 pounds each in four columns a day. Horse carts cover twelve and 4/10 miles a day.

Ox cart columns: Five carts carrying 3850 pounds each in six columns a day. Ox carts travel twelve miles a day.

Porter Columns: One hundred men carrying 3000 pounds each in ten columns. Porter columns travel nine mountain miles a day.

Bicycle Columns: Fifty bicycles carrying 7500 pounds each in sixty columns. Bicycle columns travel twelve miles per day.

The trucks, animal carts, bicycle pushers and porters required for movement of the 301st NVA Division's supplies would probably exceed 28,000 men. In addition around 1,000 men of the Logistics Service would be required to organize, guide and control the transport columns. The Logistics Service also has to supervise labor squads, route maintenance and depot facilities.

The ratio of combat troops to logistics troops, or tooth to tail ratio, during Blossoming Lotus, would be approximately 12,340: 30,000, or a logistics-to-combat ratio of 1 to 2.5. That ratio is higher than one would expect for a foot-mobile force. However, NVA support-to-combat ratios were not as high as the approximately twelve-to-one, tooth to tail, ratios common in U.S. Army and Marine Corps units.

NVA staff officers must also plan for route maintenance of the fragile mountainous tracks to be traversed. Usually one day in seven was set aside for route maintenance and improvement by attached engineers.[139] Deletion of that track maintenance from the operational scheme would save four or five days, but it would ruin the route for withdrawal. If he had to, General Son would take that chance and arrange to withdraw over alternate routes.

The invasion route(s) would also have to be secured from ground attack. Village militia could provide security along the way, but the division might have to send advance detachments composed of engineer and infantry troops two days ahead of the main body. In any event, at least four to five regional

Viet Cong battalions would be required to set up an anti-recon screen in front of the division's approach corridor.

Marching NVA infantry could easily cover fifteen to twenty miles a day on hard surfaced roadway and good track. They could cover at least ten miles a day on mountain track. Therefore the foot marching 301st Division could easily reach its objective area in fifteen days. However, the more laborious movement of logistics transport and the artillery regiment slows down the actual divisional march rate.

General Son's staff came up with a typical movement plan for logistics. It was divided into stages according to depot location

Operation Blossoming Lotus Movement Stages

Stage A—Staging area A to Trailhead B, by two round trips of the 100 two and one-half ton trucks. Consuming two nights, the trucks could easily cover the sixty mile stretch of road to the border. In their last trip, the trucks could transport the artillery regiment and antiaircraft battalion as well as a few infantry and engineer companies of the advance detachment in their excess trucks. From Trailhead B there are 140 miles and twenty-eight operational days remaining.

Stage B—This stage requires the transit of 100 miles of good track by animal carts and bicycles from Trailhead B to Depot C. One trip forward by horse cart, ox cart, and bicycle would move forward 241 tons of supplies. A round trip by twenty bicycle columns could move up the remainder of the supplies. This leg of the journey would require eighteen days. So far, twenty days and 160 miles have elapsed. If forty five columns of porters were used in Stage B, nine days could have been saved.

The combat troop units, starting eight days later than the supply columns, have now covered 145 miles.

Stage C—The last forty miles of mountain tracks includes one rice depot every ten miles (Depots D, E, F, and G), and ends ten miles short of the objective area. It will take 22,000 porters to carry 308 tons of supplies to forward supply dumps within ten miles of the objective area. That number of porters could transport 330 tons of supplies in two hundred and twenty, 100-man, columns. It would take them five days.

The total movement time to the objective area would require twenty five days, leaving five days to attack and withdraw. If porters had been used at Stage B, four extra days would have been saved, leaving nine operational days.

In this situation, General Son discovers that he has insufficient resources to mount the envisioned operation. If he decides to employ porters during Stage B, he will be able to launch the operation.

Twelve major data and decision categories were required for planning each Chu Luc operation:

- Scheme of maneuver.
- Available troops.
- Determination of relevant logistics norms categories.
- Transport resources available.
- Avenues of approach.
- Route trafficability versus transport resources.
- Depot locations and stockage.
- Unit logistics requirements.
- Unit supply consumption rate versus transport asset capability.
- Transport movement serials: Payload versus march rate.
- Security screening of the movement to contact.
- Movement stages.

Chu Luc major offensive operations required a lot of planning effort, including some redundancy and excessive supply stockpiling. They also required the mobilization of massive human resources and the expenditure of a lot of time.

CHAPTER 4

Command, Control and Resupply

The Chu Luc had an excellent maneuver doctrine, which was complemented by superlative command and control techniques. North Vietnamese Army commanders had what the French called *courage de tete,* the boldness to trust their own decision making. NVA troops were disciplined within a framework of motivation which exploited their unique psychology. Like the Roman army of twenty centuries earlier, the Chu Luc had "the stability and iron discipline (which) made tactical flexibility and the exercise of initiative at the lowest level possible."[140]

The Chu Luc system of command/control was, like the Roman legions, based upon "standardized tactical drill coupled with a deployment that gave commanders at the lowest levels the means, as well as the opportunity, of exercising their own initiative and supporting each other . . . Also of great importance was the standardized repertoire of tactical movements carried out by various units."[141]

NVA commanders, relieved from distraction by non-combat considerations, were reinforced by yet another command factor. They were not in direct charge of any subordinate unit or administrative responsibilities. Not being in direct command of a subordinate unit located in the headquarters area, freed Chu Luc combat leaders from focus upon nonessentials and facilitated their ability to move about and see the battlefield. The NVA commanders' subsequent grasp of reality encouraged a valuing of initiative. As a result, North Vietnamese combat leaders enjoyed a "diffusion of authority throughout the army (which) . . . greatly reduce(d) the need for detailed control."[142]

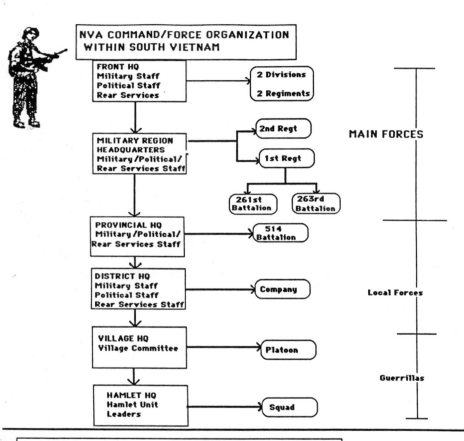

NVA COMMAND/FORCE ORGANIZATION WITHIN SOUTH VIETNAM

FRONT HQ
Military Staff
Political Staff
Rear Services

→ 2 Divisions
2 Regiments

MILITARY REGION
HEADQUARTERS
Military /Political/
Rear Services Staff

→ 2nd Regt
1st Regt

261st Battalion   263rd Battalion

PROVINCIAL HQ
Military /Political/
Rear Services Staff

→ 514 Battalion

DISTRICT HQ
Military Staff
Political Staff
Rear Services Staff

→ Company

VILLAGE HQ
Village Committee

→ Platoon

HAMLET HQ
Hamlet Unit Leaders

→ Squad

MAIN FORCES

Local Forces

Guerrillas

BA LONG PROVINCE VC MILITARY ORGANIZATION : 1970

Battalions: D440 and D445 | Provincial Units |
Companies: C4, C41, C25 ,C1 | District Units |
Platoons: K44, C70, 206, 205, C610, Vung Tau | 2 District and 4 Village Units |

CHAU DUC DISTRICT VC MILITARY ORGANIZATION :1970

C41 Company : | District |
7 | Village | Platoons

NOTE: Cahu Duc District was subordinate to Ba Long Province

80

Like the Grande Armée of Napoleon, the NVA "radically decentralize(d) the conduct of operations in the field and spread them over hundreds, later even thousands of square miles of territory."[143]

The reds also realized that in addition to their usual redundant means of communication they required "directed telescopes." "A commander needs . .a kind of *directed telescope* . . . which he can direct at will at any part of the enemy's forces, the terrain, or his own army in order to bring in information that is not only less structured than that passed on by normal channels but also tailored to meet his momentary (and specific) needs."[144]

Special teams equipped with radios and providing their own security accompanied important NVA operations. These teams communicated directly to NVA headquarters, reporting all they saw and heard. They were the NVA's directed telescopes.

Communist warlords realized that, even in modern times, orders are still communicated at "an average speed of five and one half miles an hour, a speed that (has) hardly changed for millennia."[145]

Like the Grande Armée, the Chu Luc could "in a twenty-four-hour period . . . issue . . . three separate movement orders and . . . have those orders carried out. This is a figure that present day armies, for all their telecommunications equipment, can barely equal and certainly not improve upon."[146]

Chu Luc command and control was reinforced by a unique communist system of unit cellular control and surveillance which some called the "Tripod." The Tripod was composed of three elements: the line, the cadre and the cell. The line was whatever propaganda the communist high command was pushing.

The cadre was "any soldier or civilian with the rank of assistant squad leader (or its equivalent) or above."[147] In every red unit there were two military leaders at every level from squad on up. Two political leaders supplemented that leadership at platoon level and above.

The cell was the three-man basic group of soldiers or other communist-controlled operatives. That cell had one leader who was either a communist or an aspirant.

The cells, like those of the human body, made up every communist military body. The 514th VC Battalion, for example, "was structurally an integration of one hundred twenty six cells."[148]

In order to make the Tripod effective the reds had to insure that they had absolute control and surveillance down to the lowest level. Control was exercised by giving orders, supervising the execution of those orders, and the daily exercise of party indoctrination and control.

FIRST CORPS ZONE

INCLUDES:

Infiltration Routes: Roads, trails, tracks and waterways running west-east and north-south.

Allied Units/Bases: DMZ, Dong Ha, Quang Tri, Hue, Phu Bai, Danang, Chu Lai
1, 2 ARVN Divisions; 1,3 US Marine Divisions; 2 MarBde(ROK); 23 US Infantry Division

Red Units Stationed There: DMZ/Laotian Front- 325C, 304, 324, 316,320, 308-NVA Divisions
NVA/VC battalions-22 803, 68 Artillery, 164 Artillery-NVA Regiments

Hue Front-95,6,66,24,4,5-NVA Regiments. 1Prov,328 VC Regiments

DaNang/Queson Front-2 NVA Division.368 Artillery,102,141,31,90-NVA Regiments.1 VC Rgt.

Quang Tin/Chu Lai Front-36 NVA Regiment

Quang Ngai Front-401,18,21-NVA Regiments. 2 VC Regiment.

Strategic Sanctuary Zone	Operational Border Zone	Tactical Zone	Battle Zones
Laotian Sanctuary Bases: 604, 612, 613	Border Bases: 611, 607, 614 ,512	Stronghold Bases: Street Without Joy. Khe Sahn, DMZ, Ashau DaKrong, Que Son ,Do Xa, Batanga Peninsula 101,114,127,112, 128, 124 ,117,119, 121,116,100.	Battle Fronts: DMZ, Hue, Queson/ Danang, Chu Lai, Quang Ngai

SECOND CORPS ZONE

INCLUDES:

Infiltration Routes: Same as First Corps
Allied Bases/Units: 22,23 ARVN Infantry Divisions. Capitol,9 ROK Infantry Divisions, US 1 Cav,4 Infantry Divisions, 173,1/101 Brigades Pleiku, AnKhe, Qui Nhon, Nha Trang, Tuy Hoa, Phan Rang,Cam Rahn Bay

Red Units Stationed There: Triborder Front-1 ,B3 Front NVA Divisions
24, 2 NVA Regiments
Binh Dinh Front- 3 NVA Division
Route 1 Coastal Front-320 NVA Regiment
Tuy Hoa Front-95 NVA Regiment

Strategic Sanctuary Zone	Operational Zone	Tactical Zone	Battle Zone
Cambodian Sanctuarys: Lines from Base 613	Border Bases: 609,702,701, 740	Stronghold Bases: Binh Dinh,229, 226,202,236, 238,252,251, 203, Entire Border area Chu Pong	Fronts: Binh Dinh, Triborder, Route 1 AnKhe/14, Tuy Hoa/ Hub

One form of that control exercise was the self-criticism group. Daily, each cell got together and criticized its own performance, focusing upon deficits which had to be corrected. Individuals were pressured to inform on their comrades if the comrades were not forthcoming with a confession.

Once any weaknesses were identified and the guilty party chastised, a program of re-education was instituted to help the malefactor "grow." In reality the group criticism device was used to enforce conformity with communist orders and the "line," or latest influence/propaganda effort. The groups rapidly taught soldiers to express no outward signs of dissatisfaction with the red regime or its policies. Criticism was limited to problems which interferred with the implementation of communist aims.

Communist Battalion Leadership

Unit	Number of Units	Military Cadres	Political Cadres
Squad	39	78	—
Platoon	14	28	28
Company	5	10	10
Battalion	1	3	2
Totals		119	40[149]

In capitalist societies man is frequently considered to be, and treated like, a machine. In communist societies, man is a slave! Slaves require special handling. Many overseers are required for slave management. That is why there was usually one communist cadre for every 2.6 soldiers.

Within Chu Luc battalions and higher headquarters was a system which the Chinese communists called "dual leadership." The military commander made all military decisions, while the political commander made all political decisions, and maintained unit morale. Each category of decision was precisely defined.

Every red unit included a communist party parastructure or parallel hierarchy. Controlled by the unit's top commissar, or political officer, a communist party committee met regularly. The unit military commander was only a member of that governing committee.

Every party member in every unit belonged to the unit's local communist party organization, itself a paramilitary political construct. That communist party actually ran the military or political unit because it "set forth policy lines and operational plans that are carried out by the command staff . . ."

Of course, subordinate units received their instructions from higher head-quarters. Upon receiving an operational order from higher headquarters, the military command staff planned its implementation. Then the political committee examined the plan and made the decisions. However, the structure was flexible. One guiding litany was frequently repeated: "Commanders can take appropriate measures when immediate decisions must be taken."[150]

To inspire thoroughness, each NVA combat leader was conditioned to review a mental checklist before deciding upon a combat plan. That checklist included a systematic consideration of the common factors of combat: "How strong is the enemy? How do we fight him? Where? When? What means do we have at our disposal to knock down the enemy opposition? How is secrecy maintained? How would the enemy oppose us? How would we react? What will we do when the enemy is destroyed—should we advance or pull out, where and how?"[151]

Chu Luc Organization for Area Command

The NVA divided all of Indochina into military Fronts or army commands. The Fronts were territorial headquarters responsible for troops and real estate in a prescribed area.

All Chu Luc military units were under command of either an army or territorial headquarters. An army headquarters usually commanded at least two divisions and several regiments. Regional headquarters, with two exceptions, controlled regiments. Provincial headquarters usually controlled battalions. District headquarters controlled companies, villages controlled platoons and hamlets controlled squads.

Logistics or Rear Services were usually organized by regional headquarters. In Region 2, for example, three elements carried out rear service functions under a main headquarters. Those services functions included the supply of ammunition, medicine, food, clothing, money, transport, depots, worksites and weapons.

Provincial and local rear services were independent from those rear services supporting NVA and main forces. One such provincial service unit, the 509th Rear Services Company in Dinh Tuong Province, fielded four platoons in 1965. The platoons, composed of males and females, transported ammunition and other supplies as well as evacuating battlefield wounded. They press-ganged local peasants into servitude to those functions whenever necessary.

NVA Battle Organizations

The NVA organized its forces within South Vietnam into North Vietnamese Army forces, regular (main) forces, provincial (local) forces, and village guerrillas. Each type of organization had different equipment, organi-

THIRD CORPS ZONE

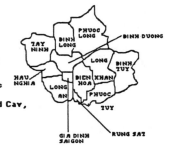

INCLUDES:

<u>Infiltration Routes</u>: Roads, trails, waterways going west-east and
north-south.

<u>Allied Bases/Units</u>: Saigon, Bien Hoa, Cu Chi, Phuoc Vinh, Xuan Loc
Vung Tau.
5, 25,10 ARVN Divisions. 1, 25,US Infantry Divisions. 11 Armd Cav,
199, 1 Australian Bdes. Thai Infantry Division

<u>Red Units Stationed There</u>: 5,9 VC Divisions. 7 NVA Division.
3 NVA Division (5/66 only). 274, 275, 95C NVA Regiments.

Strategic Sanctuary Zone	Operational Border Zone	Tactical Zone	Battle Zone
Sanctuary Bases: 712, 711, 714	Border Bases: 351, 350, 352, 708, 353, 363, 707, 354, 706, 713, 367	Stronghold Bases: ThanhDien Forest,War Zones C,D,E,F Iron Triangle, Trapezoid, HoBoWood Filhol Plan.,LongNguyen Sec. Zone, BoiLoi Woods, Hat Oich, May Tao, Minh Than Plan.,Michelin Plan.,Minh Danh Secret Zone, LongHai Hills, Dinh Hills, Rung Sat, CourtenauPlan CauDinh Jungle, 355, 356, 359, 302,303, 372.	Fronts: War Zone C War Zone D War Zone E War Zone F Angel Wings/ Parrot Beak

FOURTH CORPS ZONE

INCLUDES:

<u>Infiltration Routes</u>: By sea, waterways, roads, trails, and
paths going north-south,south-north and
west-east.

<u>Allied Units/Bases</u>: My Tho, Sadec, Bac Lieu.
7, 9, 25 ARVN Divisions. US 9 Infantry Division.

<u>Red Units Stationed There</u>: 18B, 261, 262 NVA Regiments.
DT1 VC Regiment.
22 NVA and VC battalions

Strategic Sanctuary Zone	Operational Border Zone	Tactical Zone	Battle Zone
Sanctuary Bases: 714, 715, KEP	Border Bases: 709, 704	Stronghold Bases: 400, 470, 490, 487, 483, 482. Cam Son, That Son, Hot Hoa, Phu Thanh, Plain of Reeds, Chuong Thien.	Fronts: Long An, Cam Son, U Minh, Cambodian Border.

zation, training, weapons and missions. Main force units were only slightly less well equipped than North Vietnamese Army forces. Regular NVA troops were differentiated from main forces by their khaki or bright green uniforms, and greater unit integrity. In addition, they tended to fight as part of larger formations.

Chu Luc Front or Army Headquarters lay at the apex of a regional command pyramid:

"Army Headquarters controls two divisions and two regiments. With the exception of Military Regions 5 and 6, the Region Headquarters usually controls regiments; Province Headquarters controls one or two battalions, and a District Headquarters controls a company. A village controlled by the Viet Cong usually has a platoon, and a hamlet has a squad of guerrillas."[152]

Army Headquarters and Region Headquarters controlled main forces. Main force battalions were usually distinguished from local forces by the wearing of khaki, black, blue or green uniforms, newer model weapons, better training, and heavier caliber crew-served weapons. Main forces could operate throughout a region encompassing several provinces (states).

Province and District Headquarters controlled local forces. Local forces were not as well organized and equipped as main forces. They operated within defined provincial or district (county) boundaries. Local forces conducted raids, ambushes and harassing operations. To maintain unity of effort there was full cooperation between local and main forces. Local forces supported main forces by providing intelligence, combat and logistics support, impressed labor and guides. During operations, local forces provided security for regular forces and covered main force withdrawals with delaying actions. It was also the mission of local forces to prepare battlefields with intelligence data, mobilization of slave labor, and caching of weapons, food and ammunition. In addition they provided battlefield surveillance, policed the battlefield, conducted diversions and carried out any other tasks required by main forces.

Unlike their main force counterparts, guerrilla units were not bound by fixed organizational criteria. Their configuration depended upon what was available locally. Village and District Headquarters controlled guerrilla companies and platoons. Guerrillas operated in the vicinity of their homes.

NVA Communications and Command/Control

In order to control even foot mobile forces, strong modern communications are necessary. The NVA had such communications at the unit level. In fact, operations orders usually included information specifically oriented towards message traffic and signals. One captured NVA operations order mentioned a Buu Tien, a battalion forward communications element, and its' mission: "Mission of the Forward Communications Element (Buu Tien): its mission is to ensure communication from one end of the battalion to the other, and to maintain good communication between the Battalion Command Staff and the various companies.

—The PRC10 (captured American radio) should keep the call signs secret.

—This outfit is also in charge of coordinating the unit's maneuvers (Van Dong)."[153]

NVA units had signal platoons at battalion level, signal companies at regimental level and signal battalions at division level. The signal battalions were always triangular and usually had a radio company, a wire or telephone company and a messenger company. At lower levels there were more messengers than radio-telephone operators and fewer still radios. Whatever the organization, the availability of American, Chinese and Soviet equipment determined the actual signal capability of a unit. However, all battalions and major supporting weapons were tied into higher headquarters by radio from 1966 onwards. After that time, most NVA companies were tied into battalion headquarters by telephone too.

NVA communicators were expected to serve the command and control requirements of their superiors by executing standard operations in support of specific missions. As an attack force left its staging area all communication was carried out by messengers. Upon occupation of attack positions, telephone nets were linked from the commander to each subordinate unit and to supporting weapons units. Messengers were utilized throughout an attack. If secured objectives were to be held for any length of time, wiremen set up telephone nets on the objective.

Ambush positions required installation of a switchboard to a telephone net linking the ambush position, observation posts and supporting weapons to the commander. If the wiremen had not finished the net when the enemy passed into the kill zone, the ambush was usually not initiated.

After an ambush or attack began, NVA signalmen could use radios. Then encrypted voice transmissions were broadcast over captured PRC-10 FM portable radios or Chinese Communist 71 or K-63 radios. Low powered, portable AM sets were used at lower tactical levels.

Communications with higher headquarters was carried out by Morse code, using model 71s or K-63s. For greater distances Chinese Communist radios model 102 fifteen watt AM radios were used. NVA radio operators were more highly trained than American radio men. Nearly all of them could transmit twenty words a minute in Morse code.

If NVA units were forced to withdraw, the signal unit had to retrieve or destroy all wire. They were told to reassemble at designated rally points if separated from their units. During withdrawals no radios were used, as messengers again dominated battlefield communications.

In certain situations the reds found that they couldn't use messengers, radio or wire communications. At that time they switched to audiovisual signals and codes. For example, radio operators might tap coded messages on a radio microphone. Pyrotechnics, such as various colored flares, and blinking flashlights were used to communicate messages. Bugles, whistles and the beating of drums frequently signaled attacks and withdrawals.

The first priority of NVA signal operations was not communications, but security. Professional cryptographers, handpicked and intensively trained communist party members, were assigned to every NVA regiment and province. They were kept separate from radio operators in order to prevent radio operators from gaining any knowledge of unencoded classified information. They practiced two rules of operation: 1. Limited access. 2. Compartmentalization. Those two rules worked directly against one of any military units most critical signals security problems, radio operator carelessness.

Another important aspect of red signal security was careful and overbearing supervision by signal officers. NVA signal officers were constantly devising new codes and eliminating old ones. Those signal officers enforced numerous communications transmission rules including:

1. No unencrypted transmissions.
2. Utilize encrypted Morse code whenever possible.
3. Utilize courier messengers instead of electronic transmissions whenever possible.
4. Keep transmission time as brief as possible.
5. All signal operating instructions were communicated verbally to radio operators who copied them into their own notebooks. Then the notebooks were inspected by signal officers. Those instructions included extracts, from general instructions, which only pertained to the individual operator.
6. Prosigns or international procedural jargon were mandatory in the transmission of signals. This shortened transmission time.
7. Transmitters were located away from their superior headquarters to thwart American homing equipment. [154]

Radio deception was used to distract American direction-finding units. In addition, radios were shut off when aircraft or other vehicles, possibly con-

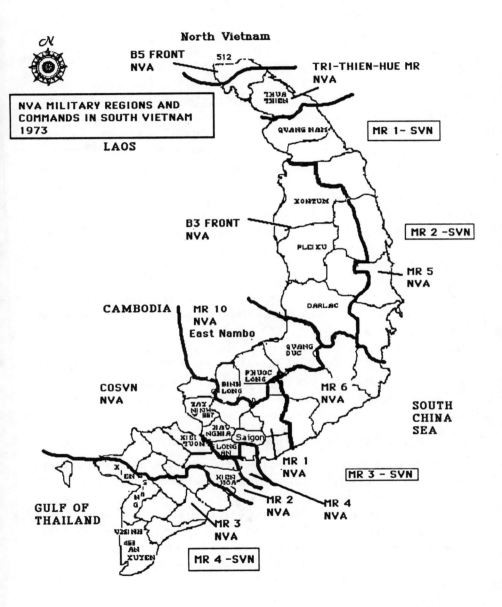

North Vietnam

B5 FRONT NVA

512

TRI-THIEN-HUE MR NVA

THUA THIEN

QUANG NAM

MR 1- SVN

NVA MILITARY REGIONS AND COMMANDS IN SOUTH VIETNAM 1973

LAOS

XONTUM

MR 2 -SVN

B3 FRONT NVA

PLEIKU

MR 5 NVA

CAMBODIA

MR 10 NVA East Nambo

DARLAC

QUANG DUC

PHUOC LONG

BINH LONG

COSVN NVA

TAY NINH BET

MR 6 NVA

HAU NGHIA

Saigon

SOUTH CHINA SEA

KIEN TUON

LONG AN

MR 1 NVA

MR 3 - SVN

X I EN G I A N G

KIEN HOA

GULF OF THAILAND

MR 2 NVA

MR 4 NVA

MR 3 NVA

UMINH BEP AN XUYEN

MR 4 -SVN

89

taining direction finding equipment, appeared in the transmission facility area.

Every Viet Cong signalman carried with him a notebook called the "recipe book." That book contained a comprehensive list of every action they had to perform. NVA signal officers frequently updated the recipe book and tested signalmen on its contents.[155] Before an operation the NVA radiomen anticipated and rehearsed every action that they might be required to perform. That rehearsal was usually guided by the recipe book.

All communist radio transmissions were precisely scheduled. That was necessary for security reasons as well as to conserve resources and maintain control. NVA radios were turned on for the briefest periods possible and operated at the lowest possible power output. Concise messages in specially devised and coded communications jargon sped up the process. Every signalman had to follow a precise monitored transmission schedule called a "sked."[156] That sked required transmissions only at certain times of the day. Messages were passed during those specific times and then contact was broken. Any deviation from the schedule, "breaking sked," was a serious breach of discipline requiring harsh punishment. Every sked and relevant frequency was copied by hand into the operator's personal notebook.

"The Viet Cong used three types of radio nets in consonance: a traffic net, a CQ net, and a watch net . . . CQ and traffic nets . . . had planned skeds; the watch net was used in emergencies only. Most communications was done sequentially . . . the Viet Cong normally communicated with each subordinate station at different times and on separate frequencies."[157]

Communist military messages were usually one-way transmissions. There was no need for prolonged give-and-take communications conversations.

NVA Unit Supply Depots and Consumption Patterns

During the Korean War each Chinese Communist infantry division consumed fifty tons of supplies daily. When quiet prevailed along the front, the Chinese "stockpiled (much supplies) against future operations."[158]

NVA divisions consumed large amounts of rice and ammunition during the Second Indochinese War. Unit rice consumption forced them to begin storing their own rice in numerous depots in late 1965. The Sao Vang Division, in 1965, consumed 460 metric tons of rice every fifty days (i.e. 650 grams per man/12,360 men), yet they stored 650 metric tons in depots, with 400 tons stored in the largest depot.[159]

Many smaller rice caches were stored in civilian homes, along river banks and in other unlikely locations. "In Kontum, the Front recommended that caches contain two to three tons of rice, and that villagers who stock Viet

Cong rice in their homes maintain about thirty bushels."[160] Some red units always purchased some of their food items: "some units in the Mekong Delta area purchased most of their rice from villagers. . . Others in Quang Ngai . . . purchased none of their rice; and still others in Binh Dinh . . . bought fish, fruit and meat but not rice."[161]

The 261st VC Battalion in rice-rich Dinh Tuong Province usually purchased its rice instead of carrying it:

"Rice was always purchased from the inhabitants of villages where the battalion settled. We stayed in a village only from one to four days each time, but when we left a village it was to move to another. We settled in a forest only when we prepared to attack a GVN post near it. In this case we brought along rice bought from the inhabitants of the village we left the day before."[162]

Although the local populace remained the main source of food supplies, commanders tried to hedge their bets. The Sao Vang Division issued its regiments thirty day rice rations to be replenished when half consumed. The regiments stored one third of the rice in regimental depots and two thirds in civilian houses. Each village and hamlet in Binh Dinh thus became an NVA depot. As the regiments moved along their habitual axis of advance, they replenished from their rice depots along the way. Such measures allowed each fighter to maintain his prescribed rice tube of seven days' worth of emergency reserve.

The 22nd NVA Infantry Regiment, operating in the Binh Dinh War Zone, exhibited typical NVA food resupply methods:

"The regiment was well fed. It had an abundance of rice, more than enough to feed every individual sufficiently for more than three months, provided its two 50 ton caches were not overrun. Phuc had never seen the caches, but he had been told they were somewhere in the area . . . the possibility of destruction had haunted many of the soldiers. So as a reserve, to put down these fears, each battalion had started its own special rice cache of five tons or so. . ."[163]

Larger rice depots were hidden in rugged terrain near populated areas. They were also stored in fortified strongholds and war zones. Food was never far from communist units. The reds placed great emphasis on feeding their troops through the depot system. The depots kept in Long Khan Province by the 5th NVA Infantry Division were extensive:

"All supply for the military was from money or supplies received by the rear services from the Front Finance and Economic Section. For this reason, storage facilities were not normally maintained in excess of that required for 30–60 days.

"The individuals' rice ration was normally brought up to the seven-day individual supply every few days. . . . there are two types of depots: those depots which are maintained by Front Finance and Economic Sections for normal use and those which are reserve depots for use in support of campaigns. An average district would have approximately 20 tons depending on whether or not the district produced an average or large amount of rice. In addition . . . the district would maintain 30–40 tons as a strategic reserve for campaigns.

"For military units the Rear Services Headquarters serving a particular area also maintains temporary strategic depots (reserves) . . . there are thousands of tons of reserve rice supplies in scattered strategic depots.

"Normally, regiments and divisions did not maintain reserves for the entire regiment or division, but strictly maintained temporary rice depots for their headquarters. Normally, temporary reserve depots contained anything from a few days' to a sixty-day supply of rice. A battalion usually kept the same amount for the entire battalion."[164]

Naturally, consumption rates for rations and ammunition was carefully monitored and recorded by NVA leaders. Various units reported a variety of consumption rates. The 3rd Infantry Regiment of the 1st NVA Infantry Division, located in NVA Military Region 5 in 1965, ate around two hundred thousand cans of rice a month. Assuming a regimental strength of 2700 men, they ate an average of two to three, one-third liter, cans of rice per man, per day.[165] The NVA attempted to specify standard daily consumption rates. Such rates were based upon extrapolated averages of troop food consumption patterns.

Allowed Daily Consumption Rates

Mountains—infantry in bivouac, 500 grams of rice plus 500 grams of seasoning; infantry in movement and combat, 750 grams of rice; artillery troops in bivouac, 750 grams; artillery in movement and combat, 875 grams.

Lowlands—infantry in bivouac, 700 grams of rice; infantry in movement and combat, 750 grams of rice; artillery troops same as above. Allocations-2 kilograms of meat per month and 300 grams of vegetables daily.[166]

The installation of prescribed consumption patterns led to standardized ration issues. For example, one 77-man VC infantry company was allowed a monthly issue of 6,752 cans of rice, 152 cans of salt and $4,848 piasters for food purchasing. Eventually prescribed ration stockage guidelines were issued.

Prescribed Stocks

"Soldiers should have at all times in their individual packs seven days of rice supply (two days of roasted rice, five days of normal rice). Regiments must have 10 to 13 days supply, to be replenished when nearly consumed. Upon movement the regiment should return (sic) its depot with the remaining rice to the division or region sub-rear service. The division or region sub-rear service must have 30 days of supply for all forces operating in their areas of jurisdiction (excluding regimental and individual rice packs) with emphasis on the area where mobile forces are likely to operate. Dispensaries and hospitals must have 60 days of supply. Salt is collected in the (weight) ratio of 22/1 in the lowlands and 20/1 in the mountainous area. Wastage should be kept below three percent for a duration of six months."

"(1) Each battalion should remain a prestock of rice for a seven day supply and of dry food for a 30-day supply at all times; (2) each regiment should at all times maintain a prestock of rice for a 20 to 30 day supply and of salt for a two month supply; (3) company size and smaller units attached to the regiment will receive their rice and salt supplies from the regiment; (4) the permanent civilian laborers will receive rice and food supply from the units in which they serve after the prescribed period of self-supporting. The individual daily ration is three cans of rice and two piasters of food allowance; (5) for the procurement and storage of meat, salted fish, sugar, milk, etc., the forward supply sections of the concerned regiments are to coordinate with the local finance economy."[167]

NVA Ordnance Expenditure and Resupply Factors

The 22nd NVA Infantry Regiment, in II Corps' Binh Dinh Province, followed typical ammunition replenishment procedures:

"Every three months the transportation company drew ammo from the division caches and completed distribution right down to the individual soldier. Because there had been no serious fighting for longer than that, the regiment had more than it could carry on march."[168]

Most NVA units were in combat once a month or less. Each battle was decided by the communists' rate of ammunition expenditure, measured in basic loads per weapon. NVA units used up "one-half to two-thirds of their

Soviet 7.62mm SKS Carbine

Soviet 7.62mm RP-46 Light Machinegun

Soviet 7.62mm AK-47 Assault Rifle

Soviet 7.62mm RPD Light Machinegun

basic loads in any one engagement, since it was an established Viet Cong tactic to break off before expending too much ammunition."[169] If an NVA unit fought at a maximum intensity, almost daily, it would consume ten basic loads per month. It was calculated that .88 forced labor civilian ordnance workers were required, per soldier, to reload ammunition of .50 caliber or smaller, and to make grenades.[170]

How likely was it that a Viet Cong unit would run out of ammunition during a battle?

"[the] Viet Cong soldier rarely runs out of ammunition while fighting; the duration of the battle is probably predetermined by his ammunition supply. When attacking, he saves enough ammunition to cover his withdrawal, if necessary. A unit might run out of ammunition if attacked by surprise by a superior GVN unit, in which case, if hand-to-hand fighting were impossible, rifles might be buried or destroyed before withdrawing. One regional force unit allocated 20 shells for each 81mm mortar. When half of this was used, a one-month trip through forest and mountain was required for resupply."[171]

Most NVA battalions were resupplied with ammunition on the day following a fight. To wait much longer was too dangerous. In rare cases it took two to six days for resupply. If that happened, communist units, or portions of them, would withdraw toward their deep supply bases, or simply disperse.

Communist commanders issued directives specifying the handling of basic loads and resupply: "(Regarding) Ammunition for small arms, and grenades. Units were to carry enough supplies to fight for the day, replacements were to be made during the night. (Mortar and 57mm recoilless rifle ammunition, and antitank grenades.) Units were to carry at least one-third of their basic load during movement. Rear Services was to replace expenditures within the same day."[172]

Average Viet Cong Basic Ammunition Loads/Expenditures

Ammunition	Basic Load (rounds)
Rifle	70
Carbine	120
LMG/assault rifle	390
12.7mm heavy MG	500-600
57mm recoilless rifle	4
40mm grenade launcher	5
60mm mortar	24
81/82mm mortar	15[173]

Viet Cong Unit Weapons: Basic Loads (Rounds)

Weapon	Province unit	District unit	Village unit
57mm RR	20	-	-
81mm mortar	20	-	-
60mm mortar	20	15	-
US heavy MG	1000	600	-
Maxim heavy MG	100	600	-
German Co. MG	1000	600	-
US AR	1000	300	250
US assault rifle	400	60	40
Smg	80	50	40
K50 Smg	300	50	100
K44 rifle	80	50	30.[174]

Examples: Basic Load and Ammo Expenditure Data

60th VC Battalion attack on Ba Gia. Basic load per weapon :
AR-500 rounds; Smg-90 rounds; Carbine-60 rounds; K44 rifle-50 rounds.

Quang Ngai Province. 38th Battalion (Main Force) basic loads:
Rifle-40-50 rounds; AR-500-600 rounds; Carbine-100 rounds; Smg-200-250 rds.

In attack on ARVN Hamlet. 80th Battalion carried:
MG-600 rounds; AR-300-400 rounds; Smg-200 rounds; Rifle-100 rounds.

Binh Dinh Province. 97th Battalion. basic loads;
MG-600 rounds; AR-450 rounds; Smg-150 rounds; K44 Rifle-80 rounds.

Viet Cong Company: Weapons and Ammunition Carried:

2-12.7mm Russian heavy MGs	1,530 rounds (18 boxes)
2-12.7mm US heavy MGs	945 rounds
3-K53 MGs	1500 rounds
18 CKC rifles	350 rounds
2-K50 Smgs	400 rounds

Antiaircraft Company: Basic Load

Weapon/Basic Load	Rounds to be used per contact
CKC Rifle/80	20
Smg/120	50
RR/5	2
12.7mm heavy MG/400	300
MG.K53/750	200[175]

CHAPTER 5

Espionage and Security

The allies never understood the Chu Luc during the Second Indochina War, but the Chu Luc knew most of the secrets and plans of the allies. Most of that information imbalance was caused by the allied reliance upon technological, instead of human, intelligence resources. However, there were numerous other reasons as well:

"No high-level permanent (U.S.) institution was created to analyze enemy strategic thinking . . . No one, in or out of government, ever produced a history of PAVN (People's Army of Vietnam, also known as Chu Luc or North Vietnamese Army or Viet Cong), a PAVN guide, or any other full-scale study of PAVN and PLAF. No significant biographical studies of enemy leaders were done . . . The number of analysts working on the Viet Cong (NLF or Chu Luc) could be numbererd on the fingers of one hand, and they started years after the organization was formed. One can search the voluminous Pentagon Papers in vain for extended discussion of the other side, any discussion at all. Unlike earlier wars in which research and analysis were both extensive and esoteric . . . in Vietnam we allocated hardly any resources. Much tactical intelligence was generated that could have been exploited but wasn't . . . politics of the Politburo was hardly touched . . .

"(Such oversights were) a manifestation of . . . arrogance. When . . . Robert McNamara wanted to know what Ho Chi Minh would think about a matter . . . he would interview himself, asking what he would think if he were Ho Chi Minh. Having answered the question, he would proceed on that basis, only later to discover that Ho Chi Minh, being Ho Chi Minh, had not shared his opinion."[176]

Why did such fallacious, sophomoric reasoning occur? Was it because the Chu Luc employed an aspect of intelligence which the United States Armed Forces didn't discover until the mid-1980s, deception? Some observers thought so: "we were deliberately misled, presented by the (North Vietnamese) enemy with a strategy that was not what it seemed to be nor as officially portrayed. More correctly, we allowed ourselves to be misled."[177]

Those "darn North Vietnamese sure were cunning," they fought a war without following any silly rules! They kept the allies from learning their secrets, while penetrating allied headquarters where they obtained access to allied secrets at their source.

American Traitors

So many millions of pounds of bombs and artillery shells were dumped on the Indochinese landscape by American forces, yet they injured so few communists. The NVA seemed to outsmart the allies at every turn. They were especially adept at avoiding every operation and springing every trap. They even found it easy to sidestep B-52 carpet bombing.

Communist avoidance of B-52 "arc light" sorties mystified allied officers. How could the reds know? The bombers flew so high they couldn't be seen or heard! Yet the reds knew when the bombers were coming. But, how?

American losses in Vietnam can be attributed to three basic reasons: (1) American mistakes. (2) North Vietnamese penetration of American military intelligence units and secrets: tactically, operationally, strategically and world wide. (3) North Vietnamese protection of their own secrets at all levels.

Starting from the top, penetration of American military secrets was caused by two things: (1) American mistakes. (2) American traitors who revealed intelligence and strategical secrets to the reds.

American mistakes really started multiplying during World War II: "The North Vietnamese . . . had lots of . . . code equipment—much of it U.S.-made and given to the Soviets in World War II."[177] Later the Vietnamese communists repaid Soviet generosity by reciprocal exchanges of the latest American equipment: "In the next few years the Soviets also obtained secret communications gear from their Vietnamese allies . . . Vietnam placed considerable communications equipment in Soviet hands, as did several crashed American aircraft and the South Vietnamese command posts that fell into communist hands."[179]

Unbelievable mistakes were made by the American intelligence establishment at all levels during the Vietnam War. Within U.S. tactical intelligence units, for example, intelligence operational incompetence was traceable to basic errors repeated at higher levels. Major Grinalds, a US Marine intel-

Central Research Agency: Staff Divisions

- Administration
- Technical (false ID and documents)
- Communications
- Training
- Protection (counterespionage)
- Collection a.) B-36; b.) Battlefield A-Cambodia, Battlefield B-Laos, Battlefield C-Laos; c.) International (America, Asia, France) d.) Long range special espionage nets; e.) MR or Front MIAs.

COSVN Intelligence and Security Units

- **COSVN Security Agency**
  Internal Reconnaissance Section: K25 Detention Camp, K35 Camp Security-Maintain and insure security in communist controlled areas of Cambodia and South Vietnam.
  External Reconnaissance Section: Operate espionage nets, direct assassinations, and obtain security reports.
  Protection Section: Protection Regiment No. 180. Protect headquarters (bodyguard and area security); protect infiltration corridors of the Ho Chi Minh Trail.

- **COSVN Military Intelligence Agency**: B2
  Administrative Division
  Reconnaissance Division: D46 Ground Reconnaissance Battalion
  D4 Technical Reconnaissance Battalion
  Security Division: MIA Communications Battalion
  Intelligence (Collection) Division:

- **COSVN Security Zones**: D1 Zone-Immediate HQ security; D2 Zone-area security. (D1 and D2 Battalions of 180th Protection Regiment)

Local Security Zone Organization
  Outer Zone-All movement of strangers checked.

  Intermediate Zone-Zone of restricted stranger movement, in which every displacement or activity by the local populace is tightly controlled.

  Inner Zone-limited access alowed only to people with official business.

Communist Party Espionage/Counterespionage Apparatus (def/off)
  Hamlet: 2 security agents.
  Village: Security cell under village security chief. (powers=guard, identification, detection, investigation, assassination)
  District: Unit-area surveillance, situation (enemy and friendly) reports, counterespionage).

ligence officer and graduate of military Vietnamese language schools, revealed why he couldn't actually perform his role as intelligence interrogator:

"I could ask: 'Where's the head?'; 'I'd like a cup of coffee.'; 'How are your
children?' Things like that. But to actually get in and interrogate a . . .
captured NVA or VC—unless he were really willing and trying to give me
information—was a very difficult thing. The same thing is true of every other
American interpreter or linguist I saw."[180]

In his book *About Face,* Colonel David Hackworth described how U.S.
officers would pretend, in front of higher commanders, to converse with
Vietnamese. One officer would count rapidly from one to ten, in Vietnamese,
and back again several times as he tricked his commanders into believing he
was able to communicate with Vietnamese.[181] The willingness of American
officers to compromise their integrity directly affected intelligence gathering,
which cannot take place without a central core of human centered trust.

By 1968, the communists had obtained a complete set of machine-keylist
cryptographic systems from American traitors and their own penetration
efforts. The American military knew about the 1960s hemorrhage of secrets,
but: "Incredibly, the machine-keylist cryptographic system of 1968 was still
in use in 1980. Keylists still were the key to the code machines on board the
Nimitz and the code machines on every U.S. warship, on every U.S. military
base, and in every U.S. intelligence communications center in the world."[182]

The Soviets and North Vietnamese read American military ciphers
throughout the most crucial years of the Second Indochina War. Benefitting
from an American secrets hemorrhage which constituted "an unmitigated
disaster of measureless dimensions,"[183] the Chu Luc knew, ahead of time,
when and where American B-52s and ground forces would strike.

Since the John Walker spy ring had enabled the NVA to "read American
cyphers since 1968,"[184] much damage was done to America, not the least of
which was defeat in the Second Indochinese War: "Both Secretary of the Navy
John Lehman and Admiral Studeman have stated that communications
compromises caused by Walker may have cost American lives in Vietnam
. . . they could have been 'responsible for ineffective air strikes, downed
aircraft, abandoned targets, and infantry losses.' "[185]

The work of American traitors decisively influenced the outcome of the
Vietnam War. But there was collateral damage too, such as "the unveiling of
virtually all navy secrets contributed significantly to the development of the
modern Soviet navy and the diminution of the U.S. technological lead in
important spheres."[186] There are too many traitors to even list, but here are
several brief examples:

"Ronald L. Humphrey, State Department foreign service career officer who gave classified documents to David Truong, an agent of the communist government of Vietnam."[187]

"David Truong, the son of a leading Vietnamese antagonist of the Thieu government, had been involved in U.S. antiwar activities for many years; and, even after being convicted of espionage, he still speaks for Communist groups in this country.[188]

"Dai Kiem Tran, a research physicist at the Naval Research Laboratory in Washington with secret clearance, was (finally) identified in 1983 as a (long term) Vietnamese intelligence officer. The Navy said he resigned from the laboratory "and took employment with a private company after his security clearance had been turned down."[189]

Between 1969 and 1973 the (communist nations of the world, including North Vietnam) trained and supported a broad spectrum of revolutionary violence-prone radicals in the United States with equipment, money and safe haven.[190]

B-36 Penetration

In 1975, the Saigon bureau chief of United Press International reported some "surprising" facts:

"A chief translator and interpreter for the CIA is now a province chief and wears the insignia of a VC/NVA lieutenant colonel. A military police officer worked years inside the RVN intelligence apparatus while waiting for the enemy to win. A chief surveyor who drew up plans for allied ammunition storage sites and military bases is currently a member of the PRG."[191]

In other words, certain members of the new communist government of Vietnam formerly served as allied intelligence operatives. Perhaps the allied intelligence effort was actually controlled by the NVA during the Second Indochina War? North Vietnamese intelligence found it suspiciously easy to penetrate, influence, and loot all echelons of American and allied intelligence, military, and diplomatic circles.

Some sources "estimated that a network of at least 30,000 (communist) agents was operating inside South Vietnam. About 20,000 agents were thought to be ARVN (South Vietnames Army) officers and senior noncommissioned officers who tried to recruit for their cause, carried out assassinations, and generally made arrangements for 'inactivity' on the battlefield. The second group, consisting of about 7,000 agents, concentrated upon sabotage and had infiltrated the police and all government services, as well as the ARVN, while the more selected and highly trained 3,000 had penetrated the intelligence services of the US military forces in SVN, the

CIA, the ARVN, police, government, religious and political parties. Despite this information which had been gathered by the CIA, none of these alleged agents had been identified, nor had any arrests been made, which indicated a high degree of general SVN tacit complicity . . . The vast all-embracing intelligence network enabled the NLF to have advanced warning of military operations against it, and knowledge of the allies' strategic thinking and their future intentions."[192]

Using every artifice from sex and drugs to family connections, the reds penetrated deeply into allied secrets as they gained influence in one allied intelligence agency after another. The first major allied intelligence agency to become a North Vietnamese asset was South Vietnam's CIA-trained Central Intelligence Organization (CIO): "CIA was handicapped in obtaining intelligence on North Vietnam and its forces in the south. One reason lay in . . . agency errors . . . That meant the South Vietnamese would have to shoulder most of the intelligence-gathering responsibility. The South Vietnamese, however, failed totally, and by 1967, it was clear to the CIA that there was no hope that their allies could gather even the most elementary intelligence on the North Vietnamese."[193]

The American CIA was already in a self-imposed bind because: (1) Very few CIA officers assigned to Vietnam actually spoke the language. (2) The average one-year tour of duty was too short to develop any understanding of Vietnamese thought patterns, much less "develop the necessary intuitive grasp of the enemy's military and political behavior."[194] (3) Total reliance was placed upon South Vietnamese intelligence and police agencies for information.

The CIA became very nervous as it tried to find out why the South Vietnamese were so incompetent. They were worried about the magnitude of the American intelligence failure in Vietnam and its relationship to their failure to secure a competent indigenous intelligence system:

"The magnitude of the failure led some CIA officials to conclude that the South Vietnamese CIO and other security operations might have been thoroughly penetrated by one of the Vietnam War's most mysterious organizations, Unit B-36 (the North Vietnamese intelligence service within South Vietnam). Next to nothing was known about this organization, but early in 1967, CIA officials in Saigon discovered that a South Vietnamese CIO agent was actually a double for B-36. The agent had confessed his role for the North Vietnamese, and began to tell an incredible story about North Vietnamese penetration of the highest levels of South Vietnam's (and America's) government and security agencies.

The agent's revelations were so alarming that a special CIA unit, codenamed Operation Projectile, decided to take a close look at those revelations and discover just how deeply the South Vietnamese had been penetrated. Very deeply, as it turned out. The communists had infiltrated the astounding total of 30,000 agents into the South Vietnamese security and government apparatus, including the two chief political advisers to South Vietnamese Premier Nguyen Van Thieu. The depth of the penetrations shocked the CIA (which also discovered that most of the indigenous Vietnamese on its payroll were B-36 agents) and the agency cut off virtually all contacts with its South Vietnamese counterparts. From now on, the Americans decided, they would go it alone."[195]

However, the CIA was also riddled with traitors and incompetents, which caused it to fail too. Up until the last days of South Vietnam freedom, the CIA performed as if it too were penetrated and controlled by B-36:

"The CIA's last action had been to miss completely the impending North Vietnamese offensive. Having cut themselves off from their South Vietnamese CIO counterparts, they tried to wade through a mountain of communications intercepts, captured documents, and other raw intelligence, only to find this often-contradictory mass provided no answers. There were no human-intelligence assets anywhere to tell them of North Vietnamese plans, there were no assets anywhere in the jungles to tip them off about North Vietnamese troop movements, and none of their remaining South Vietnamese assets . . . gave them a single clue about the impending disaster."[196]

It seemed that no American organization was immune to B-36 penetration. In July 1969, Colonel Robert B. Rheault, then commanding officer of the 5th Special Forces Group (Airborne), six officers of an intelligence detachment temporarily assigned to Special Forces, and a Special Forces sergeant, were all arrested by order of General Abrams. They were accused of murdering a North Vietnamese double agent. Although the B-36 agent's treachery had caused several Green Beret deaths, General Abrams saw the situation as an opportunity to destroy the Special Forces, which he hated. Abrams' revenge against a pet hate, was more important than the elimination of a dangerous enemy double agent who had caused American defeats and deaths.[197]

Allied counter-espionage, security and counter-intelligence assets were either nonexistent or incompetent too. They never even slowed down B-36 penetrations. So many intelligence leaks flowed constantly into enemy hands, that they constituted a veritable flood of information. Following are some examples:

"In 1958, a lieutenant working for ARVN G-1 General Staff was found AWOL. He was responsible for processing ARVN strength reports. An investigation discovered that . . . he fled North Vietnam with other refugees in 1954 . . . he had . . . returned to Hanoi."

"In 1962, a young and brilliant signal officer earmarked for an assignment in COMINT was extradited from the U.S. where he was attending a computer course related to decrypment work. He was a . . . planted agent in South Vietnam since his school days in Hanoi . . . in Saigon he was watched over by a communist cadre, his own stepfather, . . . an ARVN warrant officer. Also arrested with him was his brother-in-law, a communist agent, . . . serving as an ARVN lieutenant and English instructor."

In 1963, "ARVN forces seized from the enemy a copy of the entire RVN Economic and Strategic Hamlet Plan . . . an investigation failed to determine when and where the document had been stolen."

"During the 1968 Tet offensive, a note booklet was discovered on the corpse of a communist intelligence cadre in Hue. In this booklet there was a long list of important RVN personalities, complete with their addresses, professions, vehicles, habits, etc. Even minor details were found carefully noted, if deemed relevant. On a certain official, it was noted, for example, that he always carried a pistol for self-defense but the pistol was usually put away in the glove compartment of his car."

"A captured VC document in III Corps (in 1969) was another shocker. It listed Americans and Vietnamese working at CICV and CDEC (American military intelligence offices) and even included drawings of the interiors of the two buildings . . . In 1970, . . . forces in MR-3 captured . . . a copy of the (ARVN) JGS Combined Campaign Plan (AB-44) in which important directives were given to Corps for the implementation of the GVN pacification and rural development program. After an investigation, it was found that the plan had been sold by a major working at J-3, JGS for 250,000 piasters, of which he had received 100,000."

Also "in 1970, a communist cadre disclosed that he was completely conversant with the RVN-US negotiating platform and objectives in the Paris talks thanks to a source close to a member of the RVN delegation . . ."

"One of the most important . . . espionage cases was the Huynh Van Trong affair, unearthed in 1971. He was a trusted aide working in the office of the (SVN) presidential political assistant. To help his penetration, a communist cadre recommended him to a Catholic bishop who enjoyed a close relationship with President Thieu. Operating under a preconceived plan . . . he soon earned complete trust from his superiors. In his capacity, he was tasked to write situation analyses and estimates."[198]

"In . . . 1973, communist sappers in coordination with planted (penetra-

NORTH VIETNAMESE INTELLIGENCE

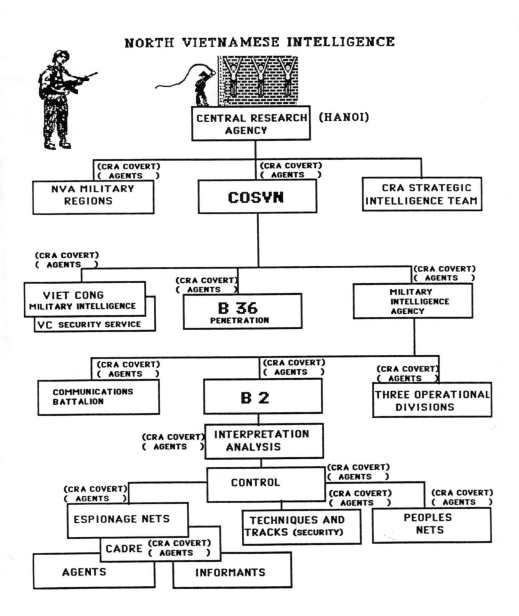

CENTRAL RESEARCH AGENCY (HANOI)

(CRA COVERT) (AGENTS)

NVA MILITARY REGIONS

(CRA COVERT) (AGENTS)

COSYN

CRA STRATEGIC INTELLIGENCE TEAM

(CRA COVERT) (AGENTS)

VIET CONG MILITARY INTELLIGENCE

VC SECURITY SERVICE

(CRA COVERT) (AGENTS)

B 36 PENETRATION

(CRA COVERT) (AGENTS)

MILITARY INTELLIGENCE AGENCY

(CRA COVERT) (AGENTS)

COMMUNICATIONS BATTALION

(CRA COVERT) (AGENTS)

B 2

(CRA COVERT) (AGENTS)

THREE OPERATIONAL DIVISIONS

(CRA COVERT) (AGENTS)

INTERPRETATION ANALYSIS

CONTROL

(CRA COVERT) (AGENTS)

(CRA COVERT) (AGENTS)

ESPIONAGE NETS

(CRA COVERT) (AGENTS)

TECHNIQUES AND TRACKS (SECURITY)

(CRA COVERT) (AGENTS)

PEOPLES NETS

CADRE (CRA COVERT) (AGENTS)

AGENTS

INFORMANTS

tion) agents succeeded in blowing up the Shell fuel storage plant at Nha Be."[199]

In 1974, a "communist messenger was apprehended at Cu Chi . . . some microfilms were found concealed in his merchandise. Among the microfilms seized, there was a photocopy of a report by the Joint Senate-Lower House Defense Committee filed after an inspection tour of MR-2. The report contained detailed information on the friendly situation, enemy capabilities and policy and the difficulties and requirements of MR-2 (II Corps). Another microfilm revealed a photocopy of the enemy order of battle strength in South Vietnam. The investigation of the Senate-Lower House report did not bring about any result because of the constraints imposed by congressional immunity."[200]

Such penetration successes continued up until the very end of the war. Agents of B-36 must have smirked with pleasure as they rang down the final curtain on South Vietnam in 1975. The unit's penetration agents greatly influenced the outcome of the war. They didn't forget a final gesture of contempt. "In March 1975 . . . South Vietnam's military headquarters, trying to get its forces organized to fight a massive North Vietnamese offensive, found itself unable to locate the communist forces. The headquarters battle maps were all wrong: they showed incorrect locations for just about every major North Vietnamese unit, and as a result, South Vietnamese military intelligence could not tell unit commanders where the enemy was.

"It was a development that caused a great deal of anger, mostly directed at Sergeant Le E. Tang, a young intelligence clerk who was responsible for preparing accurate battle maps. His infuriated superiors announced their intention to beat Sergeant Tang to a pulp, but he was nowhere to be found. He finally reappeared two months later, on the morning of May 2, (1975) when he walked into the headquarters—in a North Vietnamese uniform. Captain Le E. Tang of the North Vietnamese Army Intelligence Unit B-36 had arrived to claim the building in the name of his victorious army."[201]

NVA Intelligence Doctrine and Unit B-2

The communists relied upon human assets for intelligence gathering while the United States relied upon technology: "Based more on human than technological resources, North Vietnam's intelligence system was conceived within the conceptual framework of a people's war and came to be known as Peoples' Intelligence."[202]

The communists clearly understood the structure, purpose, relationships and procedures required to obtain intelligence "as North Vietnam saw it, there was no distinction between military intelligence and political intelligence. Situation assessments or estimates, therefore, were highly synthesized works that took into account every consideration, every aspect of the war. Structurally there was no discrimination either, since in North Vietnam there existed no separate military and political collection agencies as was the case in South Vietnam."[203] . . . where "the Viet Cong/North Vietnamese Army system to collect and process tactical intelligence information illustrated the maturity and expertise gained during the Indochina War. The apparatus was a blend of the simple and complex. Although quite a few agencies had to do with intelligence, counterintelligence and internal security, there was no sign of unsure direction or bureaucratic bickering. The setup on the contrary featured direct command lines, well-defined functions, and a closely controlled information flow. Consequently, the VC/NVA commanders who planned and conducted combat operations . . . could generally count on competent intelligence support."[204]

North Vietnam's Central Research Agency (CRA) was the major intelligence collecting agency serving North Vietnam, world wide.

The "top echelon was in Hanoi. There the Central Research Directorate (a Ministry of Defense agency) exercised supreme control over the VC Military Intelligence Service (VCMIS), which was nominally under the Central Office for South Vietnam. The VC Security Service (VCSS), the counter-intelligence arm, was organized along the same lines. Though technically an organ of the COSVN, the VCSS took its orders from the Ministry of Public Security in Hanoi. Within the Republic of Vietnam the VCMIS and VCSS paralleled VC district, province, and region administrative structures. At each of those levels, both services were also linked with and responsive to the corresponding echelon of the Peoples' Revolutionary Party. This was standard practice in the Communist world to insure Party supremacy."[205] However, as a maneuver oriented war-making state, North Vietnam decentralized its intelligence gathering. There were intelligence gathering units deployed everywhere as part of every political, communist party, and military unit or activity.

Every communist military front deployed against South Vietnam, B-3 Front, MR 5, MR 6, MR 10, MR Thi-Thien-Hue and COSVN, controlled its own Military Intelligence Agency (MIA). Each MIA operated as a decentralized entity, passing information to CRA, but operating independently unless CRA directly intervened. At the same time, CRA agents worked within each MIA and reported directly to Hanoi. Hanoi also operated separate, independent CRA nets parallel to B-26 and MIA nets.

The Central Research Agency indirectly controlled such units as B-26 and

B-2 (MIA) too. Upon the arrival of CRA's strategic intelligence units, dispatched directly from Hanoi, MIAs subordinated every other consideration to their support.

Every North Vietnamese-serving intelligence agent, staff section, and unit was assigned several different code names and code numbers. The code names and numbers were frequently changed or transferred to other operatives or units in order to confuse enemy order of battle specialists.

Most communist espionage activity against allied headquarters was concentrated within South Vietnam's II and III Corps areas, South Vietnam's largest cities, and especially Saigon. In South Vietnam's III and IV Corps, as well as the communist controlled Cambodian areas (including Krek, Svey Rieng, Prey Veng, Kompong Cham, etc.), COSVN's Military Intelligence Agency (MIA) ran the show. A regional command, code-named B-2, subordinate to COSVN's MIA, collected and processed COSVN area intelligence data.

The Military Intelligence Agency controlled three types of units: temporary task forces, military units, and staff sections. Temporary task forces were organized and utilized to the limits of their utility and then were either reorganized, merged with a permanent organization or disbanded.

B-2 was supported by a communications battalion and eleven staff sections: Enemy Situation Study, Cadre and Organization, Ground Reconnaissance, Technical Reconnaissance, People's Intelligence Nets, Espionage, Techniques and Tracks, Rear Service, Training and Crypto. The eleven staffs were further subdivided into four operational divisions. [206]

MIA's Four Operational Divisions

Administrative Division: Cadre and Organization Section; Law Enforcement Section; Rear Services Section; and Training Section. This division controlled the notorious prisoner detention camp, codenamed K55, with its "Ward Number 3" underground punishment cells for uncooperative prisoners. The administrative division also operated a dispensary and separate recovery center.

Reconnaissance Division: Ground Reconnaissance Section and Technical Reconnaissance Section.

Security Division: Crypto Section; Military Intelligence Agency Communications Battalion; and Techniques and Tracks Section.

Intelligence Division: Enemy Situation and Study Section; Espionage Section: and the Peoples Intelligence Nets Section. [207]

The Enemy Situation Study Section, or the "S Section", was B-2s' nerve center. All information despatched from the Central Research Agency (CRA), COSVN and other headquarters passed through this section. Intelligence estimates and reports were produced by S Section intelligence controllers who analyzed and interpreted all intelligence data collected by intelligence operatives functioning at all political and military levels within South Vietnam.

Espionage Agent Nets

The Espionage Section, or "Control I," exercised control over agent nets. In addition to managing agent nets, Control I reviewed all agent reports before forwarding them to S Section.

The MIA supervised 200 agents in III and IV Corps alone. They were completely outfitted with plenty of conscience money, top pay, identity papers and vehicles such as cars, motorcycles and speedboats. Their mission was to collect, "tactical information and political and military information of strategic characteristics."[208] They carried out all kinds of intelligence coups. For example, their nets enabled Viet Cong artillery spotters to take up positions within allied bases and from there, direct the fire of NVA standoff attack units.[209] Air bases such as Tan Son Nhut and Binh Tuy were favorite targets of such activity.

The intelligence gathering units of NVA espionage seemed to operate as part of three specific but overlapping systems: "One made use of local VC/ NVA cadre to report information upchannel through the district, provincial and regional military hierarchy. Another specialized in recruiting South Vietnamese who held sensitive positions in Allied installations. The third system used informants living in villages and hamlets near target bases."[210] In addition, the local Viet Cong infrastructure operated nets of South Vietnamese who worked on U.S. and allied bases. That gold mine of data furnished all the information necessary to plan standoff attacks by mortars, rockets and artillery as well as NVA infantry raids.

At the center of NVA espionage efforts were their "in-place" cadre subordinate to Hanoi Control, "The cadres' job was to maintain contact with the local VC infrastructure (VCI, the shadow government that directed the insurgency and competed with the legal RVN government for control of the people) . . . enlist informants from the workers on Allied installations, and to send intelligence data to the (Hanoi) control group. Allegedly from 1 to 4 in-place cadres were inserted in the vicinity of every Allied . . . base within the Republic of Vietnam.

"An in-place cadre first established himself in the community as a legal resident with lawful employment. He next secured from the VCI prospects as informants. Usually these were known to the VCI as Viet Cong sympathizers or relatives of VC members. Any number might be chosen in a deliberate effort to develop informants in the maximum number of base activities. A maid employed in officer . . . billets was in a position to acquire information on troop strength, unit designations, and the construction or location of buildings, bunkers, or defenses. With a better grasp of English she might also get details on casualties, troop movements, and offensive or defensive operations. Grasscutters working in or around the flight line, bomb dump, fuel storage, and base perimeter could report the number of aircraft and their parking areas; the position and size of munition and supply stockpiles; the type and location of weapon emplacements, barriers, and minefields; and the siting of powerplants, communications centers, and command posts."[211]

The South Vietnamese government was riddled with traitors who pretended that their careless handling of state secrets were merely necessary side effects of discourse in a free nation. Some misguided South Vietnamese politicos actually celebrated that carelessness: "the GVN felt compelled to duplicate the Western democratic way of life in national affairs, even its errors and weaknesses."[212] Similarly, security considerations were frequently dismissed with rationales such as references to the "impossibility to keep operational preparations under wraps."[213]

Saigon became a schizoid counter-espionage mother lode created by warped American ideas of fair play and distorted into suicidal openness by traitors and the naive: "it was known that governmental agencies were generally careless and peremptory in safeguarding classified documents and papers. A crypto clerk in the Ministry of Foreign Affairs was once found working on his encrypted messages in an open office in the presence of visitors. The loss or pilferage of documents, therefore, went unnoticed and even if it was discovered, there were chances it would not be reported. A utility man might by chance obtain old files and documents and sell them for a profit. In one instance it was discovered, also by chance, that classified papers by stacks were used by street vendors to wrap food and sandwiches."[214]

The South Vietnamese Army (ARVN), penetrated and influenced by over 20,000 enemy agents,[215] was also a treasure trove of intelligence data for the reds. As soon as any ARVN unit geared up for an operation, the details became street talk. Whenever tactical air and reconnaissance flights over a target area were suspended, the word got out that a B-52 strike was on the way. In one case the information was more directly conveyed to NVA agents when "an ARVN corps commander was notified in advance of B-52 flights. The corps commander felt it his duty to notify his division commanders who in turn notified their subordinates down the channels with the end result that at battalion level, notification was communicated among units by messages in the clear."[216]

Much intelligence data was secured from informants who, unlike penetration agents engaged in sabotaging allied operations, provided information from within allied headquarters. "Informants as a rule were organized into 2 or 3 man teams with one member acting as agent net chief. The latter received information from the others and relayed it to in-place cadre. New targets for intelligence collection and other instructions flowed to all net members through this same channel. The net chief and the cadre met off base, generally after work and in one another's home. But in time of danger, to escape counterintelligence detection, it was not unusual to communicate by couriers who were family members."[217]

In 1969, one such informant, an ARVN officer working in the intelligence section of South Vietnam's Joint General Staff (riddled with informants and penetration agents), provided a windfall of data on the Tan Son Nhut Air Base. Among the data he provided was "strength figures on . . . security units . . . and National Police elements. . .; the number of tanks operated by RVNAF security troops; the number and location of on base artillery pieces and antiaircraft emplacements; and a count of parked aircraft by model designation . . . descriptions of the perimeter fence complex, minefields, and bunker positions . . . grid coordinates of all allied units committed to base defense."[218]

NVA espionage assets furnished advance warning of U.S. artillery and air strikes. Early in the war, the NVA were using French maps to plot the coordinates of anticipated American fire support. Map incompatibility resulted in errors. The reds soon began to redress that problem, and in early 1966, when the NVA began to seek American maps, "the Police Chief of Dong Ha City reported that the VC/NVA were advertising an offer of $10,000 piasters ($85) for each American-made map of RVN areas delivered to them."[219] Soon the NVA had as many American maps as they needed because they mobilized agent nets throughout South Vietnam to obtain them. American maps were acquired everywhere. For example "the discovery of 13 U.S. maps of Quang Tri Province in a trash dump near Dong Ha Air Base . . . (prompted) the VC/NVA . . . (to order) . . . their informants to hunt for official documents in dumps and other disposal areas."[220]

As streams of information flowed west toward B-2 headquarters, some of it had already been used. Any intelligence information which passed through a subordinate NVA headquarters, and was perishable enough to be out of date before it reached the MIA or an intervening headquarters, was supposed to be acted upon without hesitation. That important North Vietnamese intelligence doctrine guaranteed that timely and locally useful intelligence served its immediate customers, the people that its time-constrained revelations affected in real time.

The Techniques and Tracks Section, a counter-espionage or security organization, also supported the Intelligence Division. It "produced false identification papers and documents intended for use in GVN controlled areas or in Cambodia."[221]

People's Intelligence Nets

Intelligence nets made up of untrained agents or informants located within South Vietnam were called People's Intelligence Nets. A special section organized and managed the People's Nets received their reports and conveyed any possibly useful intelligence information to the S Section.

Every South Vietnam citizen was theoretically an intelligence agent working for the North Vietnamese. "The people's intelligence system reached down to every household and encompassed the entire social stratification. Its basic method of information gathering was reporting . . . in the areas completely under communist control, reporting was directed toward counterintelligence and unusual happenings while in contested areas both intelligence collection and counterintelligence. . ."[222] In essence every Indochinese citizen was supposed to report every observed allied activity to a communist official.

The reds preferred to recruit women, children and old people into their people's nets because draft age young men were subjected to identity checks. When they found out that American troop units were on the way to Vietnam, people's intelligence net managers "initiated a program of agent training whereby women were taught English and prepared to apply for jobs in American agencies and organizations. To give credence and a good cover, the communists subsequently managed to have them attend GVN-run English classes."[223]

Some People's Nets apparently carried out paramilitary duties as well as espionage. In 1969, prisoner of war interrogations and captured documents described an espionage school conducted by the Military Intelligence Agency in Cambodia. "The students attending the courses were very young male and female teenagers, the vast majority of whom were residents of Saigon. Training emphasis for the males has been on demolitions training with a projected assignment to a sapper/sabotage unit. For the females, the emphasis has been upon English language training. The female is also being taught to draw pictures of military installations. Once she has gained employment on an installation, she will select targets and then be prepared to lead the sapper/sabotage elements to it. The reason given for emphasis on youth was that U.S. military personnel are extremely relaxed and friendly when dealing with young girls and are known to allow some freedom to move about U.S. installations without guards."[224]

The vast pool of agents controlled by People's nets afforded opportunities for developing many new communist intelligence agents. Such a large pool of informants was bound to spawn a greater than average number of agents with a flair, or personal gift, for intelligence.

Not all communist Military Intelligence Agency activities were classifiable as espionage missions. The Press Section of COSVN completed a press analysis report for MIA, gleaned from Saigon's newspapers every day. Those newspapers provided information on South Vietnamese military, political, economic and diplomatic activities. Such information had some minimal value when cross referenced with harder intelligence.

NVA Security and Counter-Espionage

The North Vietnamese hierarchy was never penetrated by allied intelligence during the Second Indochinese War. There were two reasons for that situation: (1) The allies were too inept and unprofessional. (2) The communist security and counter-espionage apparatus was too tight. As a result, the allies had to depend on tactical communications intelligence and airborne direction-finding for their paltry intelligence data base.

Communist MIA security directors depended on the Techniques and Tracks Section for counter-espionage. Any traitors that were detected were first interrogated and then turned or exterminated. The closely managed Crypto Section encoded and decoded most messages. Reconnaissance unit messages as well as those of other MIA divisions were handled by that section.[225]

Parallel to military security units were security functions controlled by the communist party at each level of its hierarchy. In the same way, military intelligence was part of the "staff organization at each tactical echelon."[226]

At NVA front level, a communications battalion served as part of the security effort. It was usually composed of three radio companies, one express messenger company mounted on Honda motorcycles, one repair unit and one training school. Its transmission sked included twice daily communication with subordinate military intelligence assets.

A favorite security measure employed by all North Vietnamese Units, military, intelligence and political, was the use of cover designations. Frequently one of those cover designations would include the word, "shop," for

NVA MILITARY INTELLIGENCE STRUCTURE WITHIN SOUTH VIETNAM, 1965

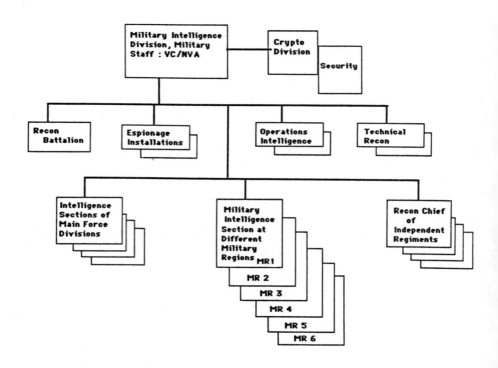

example, "Shop 32." It was a long term communist tradition to use the shop designation. "Shop" was used as a cover designation for the first Bolshevik workers organizations formed in Moscow in the early 1900s. [227]

The proliferation of cover designations was disliked by allied intelligence as one frustrated American military intelligence analyst disclosed: "The enemy did not label his units as conveniently as we would have liked. For every name that we relied on, such as the 38th VC Local Force Battalion, there might be several AKAs ('also known as') or cover designations. The 38th was also called Nghien Doan; Labor Union 38; Shop 38; 83rd Battalion; Worksite 83; Thi Xa 38; 803rd; 504th; Cong Ty 38; and the 48th Battalion. A source could refer to any one of these AKAs and our analyst had to decide if he was reading about a brand new unit or one we already had listed. The enemy's intent, of course, was to confuse us and reduce the risks from capture of documents or soldiers." [228] At the central American military intelligence center in Saigon a special AKA file was also retained: "The section 'NVA/VC Unit AKAs and Cover Designations' was one of the most useful and important sections of the summary." [229]

People's Intelligence Net Security Efforts

Every Vietnamese citizen was supposed to be a security agent who gave warning of allied approaches. For example, surprise appearances of allied troop units in or near a hamlet might be given away by peasants making a lot of noise, or shining lights at night. To ensure that no citizen was giving away any communist secrets, the party instituted a double control system of internal observation and monitoring. That surveillance system was based on housing units, where wardens watched other residents. Trade and professional organizations were also used as security organizations, where other informants also watched their peers.

The reds sought to eliminate the possibility of South Vietnamese planted agents volunteering for communist intelligence service. As a security measure, the communists excluded certain categories of people from their People's Nets, reserving them for the agents of B-2 or B-36. The categories excluded from People's Nets included: "1. those employed by any RVN governmental or police agency; 2. those who were pro-GVN; 3. those who were active in religious organizations; 4. those who bore a hatred towards communism for personal reasons; 5. those who had been convicted or indicted by the communists; 6. those former communist personnel who had been detained and released by GVN after cooperating with it; 7. and finally, ralliers." [230]

Communications Security

Using both airborne and ground based equipment, the allies constantly sought to intercept and triangulate communist communications transmissions. All types of American military units were involved in that effort: "Marine radio technicians listened to enemy messages and tried to fix the location of transmitter sites. They made an average of 2,000 to 3,000 radio direction fixes each month (in 1970)."[231]

The communists were not strangers to foiling such intercept attempts. Their tactical communications codes usually proved impossible to break by even the huge National Security Agency computers. The codes which *were* broken, were invariably decoded at least three weeks too late. "The North Vietnamese were being exceedingly clever. They changed codes every four hours or sooner. They sent a massive amount of transmissions—Chairman Mao's little red book, speeches by Ho Chi Minh, tracts, manuals, pages from newspapers, anything—in the midst of which was an important coded message, or part of one, for the message might be sent part in one code, part in others. Those acres of NSA computers were inundated and overmatched, running behind. And three weeks in a war situation was considered an eternity."[232]

Once again the U.S. technological intelligence effort, a last resort adopted because of human asset management incompetence and disinterest, was stymied. The usual paramilitary solutions were grasped at, as various American intelligence units launched "a series of raids on North Vietnamese communications bunkers in the demilitarized zone, hoping to find code books and other materials to speed up the decoding process. The raids failed to locate useful material."[233]

The North Vietnamese always correctly handled communications security. For example, they permitted unencrypted transmissions only on news/propaganda broadcasts. Red radio operators were closely trained and tightly controlled by communications security directives. The American prima donna syndrome, was not tolerated in the Chu Luc.

In communications as in other operational realms, young partially trained American technicians, ego-inflated by the praise of instructors who falsely described their short training as "the best in the world," invariably developed attitude problems. Driven by a mixture of inflated egos, overcharged hormones, institutional tolerance of indiscipline, selfishness, and antagonism toward authority, many American technical prima donnas relied upon immature judgement to misinterpret directions. They usually despised security procedures, viewing themselves as "exceptional" persons who could skew the rules at will.

Rapid personnel transfers and short job tenure caused the American military to think that anyone in Vietnam with six months experience at anything was a "real expert" who could "improve the system." Since American technicians were too inexperienced and hyperactive to really improve the system, their shortcuts only ruined it. North Vietnamese signalmen's close attention to detail, which included painstaking planning, closely controlled rehearsals, and precise execution was anathema to the American style.

Communist communications leaders avoided using electrical transmission when couriers were available. "Any information transmitted by radio had to be protected even if it was no longer classified, lest an enemy discover it in an unencrypted form and break signal codes by comparing the text of encrypted and unencrypted communications."[234]

Unlike the loose American system, red communications operations were structured so that it was impossible for NVA radio operators to enter nets in which they did not belong. At COSVN, for example, communications codes, calls signs and frequency assignments were individually distributed to every communications technician separately. They were following a security procedure known as the cut out device, unknown to the American side.

Every NVA regiment and every South Vietnamese province was assigned cryptology teams. Members of such teams were reliable communists who had received careful and intensive training. NVA cryptologists were separated from other communicators in a successful effort to restrict access to important cryptographic material. This compartmentalization security device precluded the inadvertent transmission of classified information in the clear by careless radio operators.

In order to preclude enemy efforts to intercept a particular NVA station by continually monitoring a single frequency, transmissions skeds and frequencies were varied continuously. To cut down on transmission times, the reds employed prosigns, or shorter procedural words, to communicate longer strings of communication.

To prevent American airborne detectors from homing in on signals emitted by radio transmissions the reds: (1) located transmitters as far from supporting headquarters as possible; (2) shut off radios when airborne direction finding aircraft were in the area.

The hardest communications net to control is voice radio. Voice radio can function with poorly trained operators, and is usually a great source of communications security breaches. In American units, with twenty percent

of their total strength being radio operators, the problem was nearly unmanageable. Conversely, strong supervision by communist leaders, combined with cryptology and sound operational procedures, achieved security
success for the reds.

The South Vietnamese, earnest mimics of American habits, were simultaneously unable to penetrate communist communications security, and prey
for red penetration and disruption efforts: "the enemy greatly increased his
interference and jamming of our radio communications. Several frequencies
were so badly jammed that communications became impossible. In many
instances, enemy radio operators argued and exchanged insults with ours.
Those heated verbal exchanges occurred most frequently when the enemy
intensified his attacks. . . To return the courtesy, our operators also intercepted and jammed enemy radio frequencies . . . (our) operators overheard a
female voice giving combat orders. . . South Vietnamese units did not make
enough effort to safeguard radio communications security, often using the
most rudimentary of self devised code systems."[235]

CHAPTER 6

Reconnaissance

The Chu Luc conducted three types of reconnaissance operations: ground reconnaissance, technical reconnaissance and counter reconnaissance. Considered an elite, NVA recon troops were the only communist troop issued with camouflaged uniforms. Ground reconnaissance was carried out by a variety of units ranging from teams to regiments in size. Such units were responsible for scouting enemy deployment, organization and equipment, with special attention to any gaps or weak points in the enemy array. They scoured battlefields prior to, and during campaigns, seeking information.

Prior to launching a military operation, recon units were despatchd by higher headquarters to scout the terrain and enemy situation within the objective area. They were seeking information which the reds called "situation research."

Elements of situation research included: "enemy, local population, and probable impact of military action on the political situation. Concerning the enemy, research efforts focused on his order of battle, strength, forces, organization, equipment, disposition, defenses, morale, habits, commanders and reinforcements. Concerning the local population, the research task was to find out the attitude of the people towards the communists, toward the RVN, the kind of popular support that might be expected, and the probable impact of the campaign on the populace. Reconnaissance on terrain was aimed at collecting the same information that every tactical commander needed to know to plan and coordinate his fire and maneuver with accuracy and to make judicious use of firepower on each type of target."[236]

Reconnaissance Units

Chu Luc infantry were prepared for combat in a one month training period and elite sappers were trained for six months. NVA reconnaissance troops were usually trained for much longer periods of time. According to Second Lieutenant Nguyen Van Thong, Platoon Leader, Reconnaissance Company, 320th Infantry Regiment, 1st NVA Infantry Division, "some NVA reconnaissance units were trained for as much as eighteen months."[237] Stressing visual perception techniques, each reconnaissance trainee was given at least three months of instruction on observation and patrolling. Training emphasis was then focused upon movement, penetration of defensive lines, noise and light discipline, camouflage, map and compass reading, tracking and reports preparation.

The Chu Luc utilized many training exercises to provide practical experience for their scout trainees. In practicing the penetration of defended perimeters for example, trainees operated out of realistic mockups complete with obstacles. They alternated roles as penetrators and defenders.

Another captured NVA recon officer described NVA reconnaissance training: "We are taught and given training on sand tables about American defensive perimeters in general. We have much training on how to disarm mines. The claymore is the easiest. We have received lots of training on disarming four or five particular mines. One is the small plastic antipersonnel stepmine. The second is the claymore and the third the ground and tripflares. We also were trained in the one that has either the push or pull firing device in the safety pin hole. I have never seen one of my men blown up while disarming a mine and have only seen two of my men step on mines and neither of those mines exploded . . . [Perimeter defense penetration] . . . In training we have a man lie on the wire and run over him, but we never do this in combat operations."[238]

Every NVA combat unit, from company through front or army level, controlled a reconnaissance unit. Every communist front, including COSVN, controlled one or more ground recon battalions and numerous detachments. In the Viet Cong Local Forces (LF), controlled by provincial or district communist party committees, one reconnaissance squad of twelve men was assigned to every LF company and battalion. Recon platoons or companies were assigned to the rare LF regiment. Main Force (MF) units, controlled by NVA front or regional headquarters, such as COSVN, were assigned a reconnaissance platoon for each battalion. Each MF regiment was assigned a recon company and so was each division. There were also regional reconnaissance companies: "In addition to organic reconnaissance units, a regional reconnaissance company operates in conjunction with the 261st and 263rd battalions of Military Region 2. The company reports to the battalion command staff but is not organic to the battalion."[239]

COSVN, an NVA front headquarters, controlled the D46 Ground Reconnaissance Battalion which had a strength of four hundred men organized into three companies and Section 7. Section 7 controlled three organic detachments of seventeen men each, which were targeted against III Corps' Suoi Vang, Cau Khoi, and Suoi Da areas, as well as Trang Sup Airfield in Tay Ninh Province.[240] Ground Reconnaissance Section 7 also supervised ten reconnaissance detachments each commanded by a company or battalion commander. Those ten detachments were targeted against Cu Chi (Hau Nghia Province), Phu Hoa (Binh Duong Province), Ben Cat (Binh Duong Province), An Loc and Loc Ninh (Binh Long province), Boi Loi (Tay Ninh Province), and Ba Ra (Phuoc Long Province). In addition, one detachment was targeted against each of three other provinces: Phuoc Tuy, Bien Hoa and Long Khan.

Most NVA reconnaissance battalions were smaller than the D46 Battalion. They ranged in size from 150 to 300 men.

Selected Reconnaissance Battalions Identified: 1972

Unit	Strength	Unit	Strength
18th NVA Recon	250 men	32d NVA Recon	150 men
11th NVA Recon	200 men	42d VC Recon	150 men[241]

Ground Reconnaissance Doctrine

The Chu Luc essentially conducted six categories of attacks against enemy units: standoff attacks by mortars, artillery or rockets, mine and booby trap screens along enemy routes and positions, ambushes, close assaults by battalions and regiments, sapper raids, and sabotage. Recon troops provided data which could be used to carry out all of those attack categories.

Reconnaissance by fire, a favorite method of American recon troops, was not used by NVA recon units, who practiced stealth and observation to gather data. Reconnaissance by fire was employed by Viet Cong local troops and NVA regulars, in tactical situations. Small unit probes, sniping and harassing fires were used as recon by fire to elicit enemy counteraction. Such probes deliberately sought to attract attention and reaction as a method of revealing enemy weapons and troop positions.

NVA recon troops were guided by two main principles: (1) Scouting is a concrete behavior which must obtain data through human sensory apparatus. In other words, recon should deal with what could be "seen by the eyes and touched by the hands."[242] (2) Scouting is an on-going process that must be repeated several times with each mission's findings cross-checked and double-checked against the discoveries of other scouting offorts.

A captured enemy document outlined NVA reconnaissance imperatives: "before mounting any attack, you must learn the exact number of enemy troops and their armanent . . . (and) all you can about the commander . . . You should also study the morale of the enemy soldiers, the locations of their strongpoints . . . and heavy weapons emplacements, and the organization of their forces . . . identify enemy units by number or name. Find out the equipment of each unit, the fire power of which it is capable."[243] The document also stressed the need to identify any enemy radios or telephone indicators. In addition, approach and withdrawal routes were described as being especially important.

Chu Luc reconnaissance units usually reconnoitered point targets, geographical areas, or avenues of approach. They were also used to track enemy troop units. NVA scouts employed a number of methods of collecting information from mobile or fixed positions, including:

1. Strategic inquiries: This rare form of reconnaissance was carried out by strategic recon teams answerable to major NVA headquarters such as the Central Research Agency. It usually involved cloak and dagger type assignments such as "abduction of enemy troops and seizure of documents if required."[244]

2. Political inquiries: "Probes among the local populace; contacts with local party and government representatives who were usually supported by local sources such as people's agent nets, security agents and informants; (contact with) . . . military intelligence personnel disguised as local inhabitants or the local inhabitants themselves who lived near or within the target area."[245]

3. Combat reconnaissance: "During an offensive campaign, reconnaissance cells operated in conjunction with combat troops on the battlefield. Their mission was to keep track of developments in the enemy situation, his movements, reinforcements and supply activities, and to assess the results of shelling, attacks or raids."[246]

One South Vietnamese officer claimed that NVA reconnaissance troops were used in non-recon, hunter/killer roles, just like American reconnaissance troops. He also claimed that the NVA mimicked other common American and ARVN misuses of recon troops, including wasting scouts as messengers, security troops and forward observers: "Reconnaissance units also assisted in the routing of information and messages by establishing field telephone lines between the command post and combat units. More recent tasks performed by reconnaissance cells included combined activities with artillery forward observers to assist them in adjusting fire on target."[247] Clearly the officer was mirror-imaging, since NVA reconnaissance units never deviated from their scout roles. It was the secret of their success. The ARVN officer's warped assertions demonstrate how historical facts can be distorted by individuals conditioned to view other people as mirror images of themselves.

Ground Reconnaissance Operations

NVA recon operations usually unfolded in a patterned sequence. North Vietnamese reconnaisance officer Thong described the first phase of that sequence: "When we arrive at the reconnaissance objective, we usually establish an observation post approximately one or two hours distance from the objective. Next we dispatch small teams (two or three men) to move in as close to the objective as possible. If we possibly can, we try to penetrate and enter the objective area to determine the exact enemy strength and location. We try to locate and count the number of heavy weapons such as 105mm howitzers and 81mm mortars. If we are successful and are not detected we withdraw using the same route."[248]

NVA recon units did not normally establish observation posts, in non mountainous terrain, two to three hours from an objective area. They might have set up a rear rally point or mission headquarters there, but not an observation post. Thong was either misinterpreted or he used the wrong descriptive terminology.

A unique mountain observation post was discovered in 1967, near Nha Trang in II Corps' Khanh Hoa Province. "The (ARVN) rangers came upon a recently abandoned VC/NVA campsite in the Dong Ha Mountains about 6 kilometers southwest of the (Nha Trang Air) base. Among the camp's structures was an observation platform that commanded the entire Nha Trang area. From here with minimum effort and risk, it was possible to map the air base in detail and to observe air traffic and troop activities."[249]

Thong was more accurate when he described the ease with which American perimeters were penetrated by red scouts: "All U.S. defensive positions are very easy to get through. I can say that I have never encountered a tough one in my experience. We just crawl slowly through the wire, cutting the bottom strands. In case we are detected while inside the camp and must make a hasty withdrawal, we use wood planks or ladders if available and go over the top of the wire."[250]

Usually NVA scouting activities were conducted by small squads of twelve men divided into four cells of three men each. One cell member observed and recorded data while being covered by his two cell mates.

NVA RECONNAISSANCE UNITS

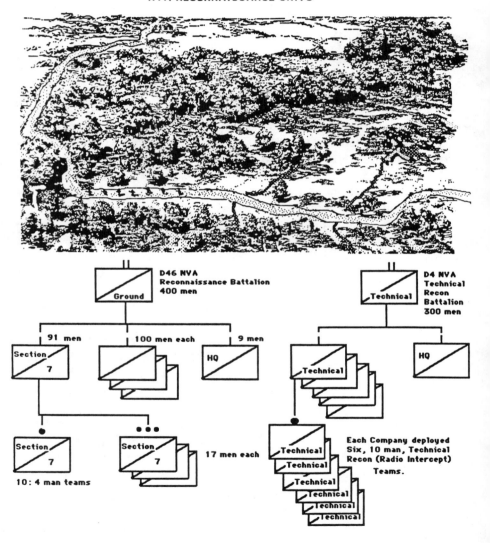

D46 NVA
Reconnaissance Battalion
400 men

Ground

91 men

Section 7

100 men each

HQ

9 men

Section 7

10: 4 man teams

Section 7

17 men each

D4 NVA
Technical Recon
Battalion
300 men

Technical

Technical

HQ

Technical
Technical
Technical
Technical
Technical
Technical

Each Company deployed Six, 10 man, Technical Recon (Radio Intercept) Teams.

The first priority in a recon mission was a detailed investigation of the terrain in the vicinity of an objective area. Particular attention was focused upon roads and other avenues of approach as well as potential landing zones. "When we got orders from the battalion's command to obtain information on a certain GVN post, we sent out half of our recon platoon. This small detachment was always accompanied by two officers from the battalion's staff. Usually we arrived at the neighboring hamlets of the post late in the afternoon and we at once set about finding the local guerrillas and cadres to ask them everything they knew about the strength, armament, and defense works of the post. We always took care to try to know what inhabitants maintained close relations with the troops in the post so we could arrest them just before the attack.

"At night, our detachments broke into three groups to converge on the post from three different sides in order to check the accuracy of information thus far obtained on the terrain features and the post defense system. Sometimes when information on the post armament turned out to be inadequate, someone had to get inside the post itself. It was only after obtaining all possible data that the staff officers accompanying us worked out a sketch plan of the post with details of the defense system, heavy weapons emplacements (mortars, machine guns) and the posts' environment."[251]

The location and distance to nearby enemy troop units was also plotted. Then the immediate terrain around the objective area was intensely scrutinized from camouflaged and covered avenues of approach and withdrawal, assembly areas, crew served weapons positions and other friendly deployment possibilities. That's the way it happened at Khe Sahn in 1968, when "an NVA recon unit had been tracing all the avenues of approach into the combat base. Apparently, in the gear left behind were maps showing the approach routes into the base and the hill outposts. The routes provided that long columns of troops could move off the trails if they were discovered and bombed by aircraft, so the troops wouldn't be exposed to the aircraft in long, easy-to-hit columns."[252]

The daily routine of the enemy residing in the objective area was also noted, particularly guard post locations and times when guards were changed. Enemy patrol routines, and habitual supply procedures, as well as sleeping and eating times, were also observed and recorded.

NVA scout units paid close attention to obstacles in the objective area including the structural pattern, height, length and depth of barbed wire. Other facts were recorded as well: "the location and specifics of minefields, bunkers, and emplaced weapons. Other considerations were how firepower was combined with obstacles, and any obstructions that blocked the view from the interior of the base . . . every effort was made to learn the reaction time of artillery support, the likelihood of helicopter and tactical air support and the strength and response time of reserve forces."[253]

After several scouts of an objective area, a scaled down sand table would be prepared depicting the main features of the enemy position. That sand table would be used for planning purposes and pre-attack rehearsals. A last minute reconnaissance would be conducted shortly before an attack was launched in order to detect any last minute changes in the objective area.

Mistakes could cost a lot of lives and the communist cadres realized that accurate reconnaissance could insure success: "A reconnaissance team's failure to estimate correctly the strength of a post led to a serious defeat. The Sao Vang Division attacked an ARVN camp in My Loc Village, Binh Dinh Province in September of 1966. A regiment was stationed at the post rather than the estimated battalion size force. A dawn counterattack by the GVN routed the Viet Cong forces."[254]

The commander of the attacking unit would usually conduct a personal reconnaissance of the objective area. In many cases a battalion or regimental commander and his primary subordinate officers would accompany recon patrols to the objective area at least once before an attack was launched: "before the 514th's attack on the Tan Thuan Binh post on 8 June 1964, two investigations were made. In early May 1964, the battalion commanding staff and some of the 514th reconnaissance agents, in coordination with the Cai Lay District (communist party) Executive Committee investigated the terrain of the post. Then in late May the battalion commander and a battalion reconnaissance team reconnoitered the terrain again and made a chart of the post. The chart showed fortified works, walls, moats, barbed wire fences and mine fields."[255]

Frequently, attacks on important targets like air bases might require a long period of reconnaissance. The December, 1966 sapper raid on Tan Son Nhut Air Base was preceded by a two-month prestrike reconnaissance carried out by a seven-man team, which consisted of two cells and a squad leader.[256]

In some cases reconnaissance information on a target area would prove to be too insufficient or unreliable. In that case, the Chu Luc would dispatch special recon or sapper recon teams on a penetration mission. Such missions were carried out by three man cells clad in loin cloths or shorts, and camouflaged in keeping with the terrain found in the objective area. For penetrating particularly difficult barriers, recon agents carried special equipment including:

1. An automatic weapon.
2. A set of wirecutters.

3. One knife or bayonet.
4. A sharp metal rod to probe for mines.
5. Bamboo sticks to prop up barbed wire.
6. A quantity of small pins to disarm mine fuzes.[257]

A recon agent from the 261st Viet Cong Battalion described one such penetration: "Once I got into the middle of Cai Be post where the district chief's office was. It was fifteen days prior to the attack and take-over of the post by our battalion. I was accompanied by two comrades armed with submachine guns to protect me in case my presence was discovered while I was near the post entrance. I was then wearing pants only and had in my belt a pair of pincers, a knife, and a grenade. At one hundred meters from the post I started crawling and quietly approached the post entrance with the two comrades following me. At twenty meters from the post, my comrades halted while I crawled on.

"At the post entrance there was a barbed wire barricade on which hung two grenades. Behind the barricade stood a guard. I made my way between the barricade and the stakes holding up the barbed wire fence. I waited in the dark for the moment when the guard lit a cigarette. I passed two meters away from him and sneaked through the entrance. On that occasion I was unable to find out where the munitions depot was but I did discover the positions of two machine guns and the radio room, I got out at the back of the post by cutting my way through the barbed wire."[258]

On some occasions NVA agents within allied installations were utilized to provide information or gain entry. Some units placed great emphasis upon using such spies: "If the Front decided to destroy the post where a Front spy was living, we had to first ask his family to come to the post to call him back to the village to receive instructions. In general, the Front only launched an attack at the moment this spy was on sentry duty at night. We then used a conventional secret signal to let him know that we were ready to attack. The signal which was most often used was to turn on a flashlight three times and the spy replied by three strokes of his lighter. We acknowledge reception of his reply by turning the flashlight on once more and then we sneaked into the post. The spy would let us come into the post before opening fire. I noticed that the GVN had lost many posts because the Front had spies to help it."[259]

A penetration of Bien Hoa Air Base by a ten-man recon squad was detected in May, 1967. The squad belonged to C-238 Sapper Company, a "reconnaissance sapper" unit believed responsible for successful attacks in 1966 and 1967 against the U.S. Army Long Binh Ammunition Depot. The recon effort began from a recon base, or harbor, far from the air base: "When the squad arrived at a point four hours from the air base, . . . the . . . cell members separated from the squad and began their final approach to the target. Each man left behind all clothing except small camouflaged briefs and a head cover made of nylon. They were provided with a submachine gun, one .45-cal pistol, and a Soviet handgrenade and were permitted to study a base map created from photos snapped from nearby Buu Long Mountain. Their orders were to count the cargo aircraft on the west parking ramp, and to find out the contents of a number of 200-liter barrels in the same area."[260]

An NVA reconnaissance penetration of Tan Son Nhut Air Base in 1966, correctly identified "a point to infiltrate the perimeter and cut three wire fences without detection. It also accurately assessed infiltration cover afforded by excavation work, fixed the positions of aircraft parking areas, and traced out routes for undetected access to three munitions bunkers."[261]

When recon troops were following an American unit moving through the brush, their real work usually didn't begin until the American unit moved into its night laager, or night defensive position. At that time a recon unit, under the cloak of darkness, would move forward scouting avenues of approach. Scouts would encircle the perimeter in steadily smaller circles, searching for American listening posts and machine gun positions. As they came near the edge of the enemy perimeter they would begin checking for flares and mines.

If the American unit was unusually disciplined, noise and grenading would be used to provoke fire. A prime objective had to be realized, the enemy must reveal his positions. After enemy positions were detected, recon units would take pieces of cloth painted with luminous arrows and tie them to trees. The arrows would point toward the enemy positions and the luminescence would face away from the enemy.

An assault line, or final line of departure, would be carefully selected near the enemy perimeter. Securing one end in the vicinity of the assault line, communications wire would be unrolled by the NVA scouts, along avenues of approach leading away from the enemy perimeter. The commo wire would be played out into selected assembly areas, usually in gullies or ravines safe from direct fire. Assault squads, guided into the assembly areas by recon troops, would arrive later. At the appointed time, those attack squads would slither toward the enemy, guided by the communications wire, as they moved directly into jump off positions, along the assault line, twenty to thirty meters short of the enemy perimeter.

In I Corps, the U.S. Marines found many instances of recon participation in NVA night attacks: "two (NVA) infantry battalions had hammered into Bravo Company. Black communications wire was also found around Bravo's perimeter. It had been unreeled during the night as guides so the NVA infantrymen leaving their treeline could navigate forward in the dark. Some strands ran straight across those lines to indicate staging points for the various NVA units; a final strand marked the line of departure . . . It was the black communications wire that the NVA had strung, the guides for the NVA infantrymen as they crept in the dark towards the Marines. Bodies were clustered stiffly along the guides, some of the dead NVA still clutching the wire . . ."[262]

Technical Reconnaissance

Technical reconnaissance units essentially employed modern communications equipment to collect information through radio communications intercept. It was part of a Chu Luc electronic warfare triple threat. The reds practiced communications jamming, imitative deception and intercept operations, which they called technical reconnaissance.

Jamming was used to deprive enemy units of communications by disturbing their transmissions. When jamming stations were placed near a target they became capable of completely overriding a target frequency. Simple jamming techniques were employed including: "play with the dials, whistle, make noise or simulate sounds."[263] Humming, special screeching jam-tapes and musical recordings were also used as jamming devices.

In an attempt to deceive the allies, the NVA would utilize imitative deception, which consisted of entering an American or South Vietnamese radio net posing as an authentic allied station. NVA radio operators transmitted messages on the same frequency and used the same language as their enemy. Success or failure in the deception depended upon whether or not the message receiver used authentication codes to challenge the validity of Viet Cong deceivers. Also, Viet Cong deceptions tended to work better when a rapid response by a receiving station was required.

The reds transmitted deceptive orders for troop movements, artillery fire direction, and air strikes. At Da Nang Airbase, red infiltrators killed a guard and then announced in English over the guard's unsecured telephone, that the far end of the base was being attacked. That distraction drew American reaction troops away from the enemy objective area which the reds then assaulted, inflicting over $15 million of damage.[264]

Other imitative deceptions worked well too: "Entering fire control or air support nets, they would request a halt to fire that was hitting their positions or even call in fire on American or South Vietnamese positions. Helicopter pilots who rarely employed authentication codes, sometimes found themselves drawn into traps by false radio messages or smoke grenades, the latter a means by which ground troops marked their locations for helicopters. The

Viet Cong used smoke grenades both to ambush helicopters and to divert American and South Vietnamese fire. For the Viet Cong, visual signals had the additional virtue that using them required no fluency in English."[265]

Another typical NVA radio deception was used during unit movements to cover the displacement of headquarters. A moving headquarters would leave its old station in its last position. That station would continue transmitting until a few weeks after the moving unit had established itself in a new headquarters location.

Communications intelligence units collected information through radio communications intercept. Technical reconnaissance or intercept was the most important communist electronic warfare technique and it was impossible to detect.

In the early 1950s, the French first discovered that the Viet Minh were listening to their transmissions. The Chu Luc continued to strengthen their ability to conduct technical reconnaissance. In the early 1960s, NVA strategic technical reconnaissance calls were deployed to South Vietnam where they began to intercept high-level South Vietnamese military communications.

Technical Reconnaissance Units

In 1963, a number of strategic technical reconnaissance cells were formed into the 47th NVA Technical Reconnaissance Battalion which was subordinate to COSVN.[266] Local Viet Cong units monitored ARVN logistics nets to choose easy ambush targets. Captured ARVN GRC-9 radios were used to monitor South Vietnamese unit transmissions. From the beginning, NVA technical recon within South Vietnam was crowned with much success.

In 1964, tactical and strategical technical reconnaissance units from the top down to provincial and regimental units were formed. Every military regional headquarters and front was assigned a technical recon platoon. COSVN received a new technical reconnaissance battalion in 1965. COSVN's Technical Reconnaissance (TR) Battalion, code named D4, was organized into five companies.[267] The 300-man battalion fielded thirty technical reconnaissance teams in III Corps. Each team had a strength varying according to its mission. The TR battalion was charged with intercepting enemy communications to collect information. It was also assigned secondary missions to jam enemy radio transmissions and conduct imitative communications.

In September 1966, D4 reported that it was able to exploit 7,745 messages out of a total of 7,793 intercepted, an incredible success rate of ninety nine and four tenths percent. D4's TR teams were equipped with Red Chinese radio sets, such as models 71B and 102E. In addition they operated many captured allied sets including the AN/PRC-10, AN/PRC-25, AN/PRC-6, AN/GRC-9, SCR-300, AN/VRC-3, SCR-694 and many others.[268]

By 1966, the Viet Cong had deployed technical recon cells to the district level throughout South Vietnam. There were 1,500 regular NVA specialists operating within South Vietnam by 1967. COSVN's TR battalion, drained by numerous cadre detachments, was dissolved and an elite new 4,000 man Technical Reconnaissance and Intelligence Division was created.[269]

Technical Reconnaissance Operations

The NVA went to great lengths to shield its technical recon assets from discovery. They realized how very important their intercept activities were to the war effort.

Communications intercept methods are quite simple: "In this technique the intercept operator simply tuned his receiver to the target station's frequency, and copied the traffic by hand or recorder. The intercept station never transmitted on this frequency, because strange signals might lead the target station to take evasive action. Of course, the success of intercept operations varied with the degree to which the target stations adhered to communications security. Results also hinged on the location of the intercept station. It had to be close to a target station using a short range radio, chiefly the FM (frequency modulation) kind. An AM (amplitude modulation) radio could be intercepted at a greater distance. Moreover, weak or intermittent AM signals could be partially compensated for by a highly sensitive receiver."[270]

COSVN's Military Intelligence Agency commonly dispatched small elite TR teams to battle areas prior to major operations. Each three man team included a specially trained TR operative. The team stayed in the battle area for weeks, or even months, transmitting twice daily messages to COSVN. The messages covered facts about the local terrain, friendly and enemy situations, and other factors used by COSVN to complete detailed offensive preparations and plans. The teams also coordinated with local NVA forces, acted as guides for combat units and assisted as couriers during the attack. Back at COSVN, the MIA communications assets used a motorcycle messenger detachment to convoy intelligence received from the field to relevant staff sections. Those COSVN staff sections were located in War Zone C.

In 1969, members of the U.S. 1st Infantry Division's 1st Brigade overran a camp and captured twelve members of Technical Reconnaissance Unit A3. Also captured were their unit logs and equipment and 1,400 handwritten copies of voice transmissions. The small team had been monitoring voice and

Morse code traffic of American and South Vietnamese units operating around Saigon for several years. The A3 unit had intercepted everything transmitted in Subregion 1 with a set of simple but well maintained radios including "two captured PRC-25s and one captured PRC-77 for monitoring FM voice traffic, and one Chinese communist R-139 receiver and seven small commercial transistor radios for monitoring AM Morse traffic. With precisely engineered antennas the intercept operators were employing the equipment at far beyond its normal range limitations."[271]

The Unit A3 logs, containing entire texts of numerous American messages, provided a gold mine of embarrassing information about intelligence data obtained from careless American radio transmissions. The reds knew more about allied communications than most allied signals experts: "They even knew the voice characteristics and communications habits of many of the radio operators working in the area. After following the American nets for several years—a continuity most US signal officer on a one year tour never enjoyed—the Viet Cong intercept operators had discerned various exploitable patterns. Having heard the confusion on American and South Vietnamese nets when frequencies and call signs were changed, they learned to adjust to new Signal Operating instructions more quickly than the communicators in the nets. Knowing each unit had a limited block of frequencies for switching among its nets, when Signal Operating Instructions were changed the intercept operators would simply monitor each frequency in a division's assignment block for recognizable voices and then begin reconstructing the net. Sometimes their American adversaries, in attempting to reorganize the nets quickly, would make the intercept teams adjustment easier by giving the frequencies and call signs in the clear to confused radio operators.

"Since radios were used extensively to coordinate the planning and conduct of joint ground and air operations, the A3 unit focused on air nets both as lucrative sources of operational intelligence and as keys to reconstructing other nets. Working against the 1st Cavalry Division, for example, the Viet Cong listened each evening to transmissions of the 11th Aviation Group, the division's helicopter support unit, to learn which units would be airlifted into battle the following day and *what their destinations would be*. During those nightly warning orders to the pilots, even the command frequencies of the supported ground units were passed by a simple frequency designation code which the Viet Cong broke in the first week of its use. Undoubtedly *many air assault landings were ambushed using intelligence gathered from the nighty reports*.

"The Viet Cong turned their attention to other divisional nets (as well). The Air Liaison Net, on which medical and special aviation support was arranged, still *operated in the clear* to give stations without security equipment an opportunity to request assistance. The most fertile source of all was the Air Warning Net; it broadcast information concerning air strikes, artillery barrages, and impending enemy attacks to every fire base and to all aircraft flying in the area. *Besides receiving prior warning of maneuver and fire support plans, the Viet Cong also learned from the Air Warning Net whether their own attack plans had been compromised and whether American and South Vietnamese units were being alerted. Even more important was advance warning of pending strikes by B-52s.* After monitoring a B-52 warning, the Viet Cong knew that they had between ten and twenty minutes in which to dispatch a courier to a nearby radio station and send warnings to other Viet Cong units in the area before huge 750-pound bombs rained from the sky."[272]

Unit A3 was discovered by American infantry. However, there were numerous other redundant technical recon units which remained undetected. They helped the NVA win the war.

As time passed the Chu Luc committed more English linguists against the allies: "Rather than simply adding to the total body of communications intelligence, the intercept of American communications dramatically improved the quality of the effort against the South Vietnamese. Information monitored on American nets supplemented and confirmed information obtained from South Vietnamese nets. To pit American and South Vietnamese communicators against each other, Viet Cong cryptologists also caused suspicion between the two allied forces. Exploiting parallel nets of U.S. advisers and their South Vietnamese counterparts, where one net might be encrypted and the other insecure, technical reconnaissance agents reconstructed entire coding systems by comparing encrypted and plain text traffic. Although high-level operations codes were never broken, the two front attack on communications aided the Viet Cong in breaking the low level codes used by South Vietnamese prior to 1969 and in more easily understanding the simplistic, unauthorized codes often used by ingenious, but naive, Americans who thought that they could fool their adversaries by cloaking sensitive information in uniquely American references."[273]

Counter Reconnaissance

The NVA was very particular about foiling allied reconnaissance efforts. Several methods were used to defeat allied recon units, including:

1. Landing zone and trail watchers.
2. Trackers.
3. Counter reconnaissance screens.
4. Special counter-reconnaissance units.

In the bush, the enemy stationed landing zone watchers near areas where American helicopters might land. Trail watchers were assigned trails to observe, along with any traffic moving along them. Stream crossing points were also closely observed. Once an allied recon party was detected, it was followed and its position continuously communicated by a simple rifle fire code. At the same time, runners summoned nearby NVA troop units to converge on the allied force from all directions.

American forces moving in the bush were frequently tracked by NVA scout teams. After American forces departed one of their temporary harbor or fire base sites, enemy trackers would search it for scraps of intelligence. The reds had no problem trailing American units since they always left a clear trail. However, good trackers could read a lot of information from the faintest trail left by small recon patrols. For example "footprints . . . say a lot about who is using (a trail), how much equipment they are carrying, and their speed. Deeply embedded footprints mean troops are carrying a lot of equipment; footprints that have the toes deeply embedded mean they're moving quickly. We couldn't see any footprints, but a trail that wide with hardly any vegetation growing on it meant the trail was used quite frequently."[274]

All major NVA bases, war zones, installations, routes and units were surrounded by counter-reconnaissance screens. That picket of infantry troops intensely patrolled the bush seeking enemy recon units to destroy or drive back. When NVA units moved, they were similarly preceded by counter-recon screens providing security for the maneuver.

The only allied ground units that worried the security conscious NVA were Long Range Reconnaissance Patrol Units (LRRPS or Lurps). Lurps which concentrated on ambushing and other offensive missions were no problem for the reds. They feared those Lurp units which sought only to locate and report NVA units, routes and bases. As a result, the Chu Luc created numerous anti-recon units.

In their strategically critical A Shau/Dakrong War Zone the communists deployed a counter-reconnaissance battalion composed of Counter-Reconnaissance Companies 11A and 11B. Those camouflaged units were equipped with the latest recon and communications intercept equipment as well as dogs and trackers. Their mission was to locate and pursue unto death all allied Lurps found in their area.[275]

In addition smaller counter recon units were organized by the reds: "It was occasionally confirmed through captured documents and prisoner interrogations that many enemy units established bounties on LRRPs. Most often this was in the way of cash paid in amounts as high as the equivalent of $1,000— the same bounty for killing a U.S. colonel.

"On at least one occasion, the NVA trained and sent south a special team with the specific mission of countering the recon men. Interestingly the team was composed of six men—just like its prey. In this case, however, the hunter became the hunted. In February 1972 a patrol of H Company ambushed the NVA counter-LRRP team. Among the documents captured was one detailing the NVA team's mission and a picture of the six men taken in the North holding their country's flag. According to the documents, they would each receive a small rice farm for killing or capturing an entire LRRP team."[276]

Several NVA scouts retired to small rice farms after the war.

CHAPTER 7

Nomading and Mobility

The NVA forces which grasped for control of South Vietnam throughout the decades of the 1950s and 1960s placed top priority on their own survival. They meant to fight only where and when they wanted to fight. In most cases they avoided battles, since they were more intent upon organizing the terrain and population of the specific province they were assigned to control. As a result, Chu Luc units spent little time in combat: "The average Viet Cong soldier operating in the Central Highlands or in the Mekong Delta fights only one or at most two days out of 30. His weapon and ammunition requirements are therefore significantly lower."[277]

Within the provinces of South Vietnam, the Chu Luc organized its milieu by establishing supply dumps, military routes, supplementary units, fortified strongholds and systems of confiscation from the populace. At the same time the communists worked on influencing the population to furnish them with their intelligence, manpower, food, ordnance, and other needs.

The reds realized that if the South Vietnamese army could concentrate against one of their units, that unit might be annihilated. Such occasions had to be avoided at all costs.

In addition to avoiding destruction, Chu Luc forces strove to seize the initiative. The key to both objectives was information. The first rule was that information on the whereabouts of NVA forces must be denied to the enemy. If that failed, the NVA must be able to defend itself to the maximum extent possible. If defensive efforts proved insufficient, and they would if the slothful South Vietnamese were allowed to build up local superiority, then safe withdrawal would become necessary. Safe withdrawal necessitated the continuous preparation of multiple, disguised, escape routes including, but not limited to, tunnel systems.

Viet Minh Mobility Lessons

When General Vo Nguyen Giap selected his first major base in Vietnam, the Viet Bac, he made certain that it possessed those geographical characteristics which facilitated the survival of the Viet Minh forces operating within its borders. Located in a rugged, jungled, hilly region, eighty miles north of the French headquarters at Hanoi, the Viet Bac met all criteria for a light infantry base. With a radius of approximately fifty miles, the region consisted of high ridges dissected by steep valleys. It was honeycombed with bomb-proof caves, camouflaged by heavy vegetative growth. Two other factors of the area combined to reduce the mobility of invading mechanized-dependent military forces: (1) The weather (2) The lack of roads.

The weather was always important in Vietnam. It frequently helped the communists by providing them with huge operational lulls, or spells of safety, during which their western enemies were reluctant to operate:

"To mount offensive operations on a large scale during the southwest monsoon (May to November) was almost impossible for an army which depended to any extent on mechanical transport and air power. Once May 1947 had passed without a French attack in the Viet Bac, Giap was able to be almost certain he had another five months for preparations before he had to worry about Valluy's (the French commander) intentions."[278]

The ruggedness of the Viet Bac terrain also protected the red bases: "Roads and bridges were few while streams and rivers abounded . . . Foot tracks . . . linked each settlement . . . there were almost no roads which could take wheeled vehicles . . . cart tracks winding through narrow valleys which could be dominated by a small ambush party."[279]

Only two roads even came near the periphery of the red base area. The Clear River-Song Gam waterway provided some limited access too. In addition, the geography of the Viet Bac facilitated the establishment of early warning systems and multiple escape routes: "the Viet Minh could afford to concentrate their defenses on a few lines of approach only, and they could have ample warning of a French thrust by virtue of the great depth of the area in which they were based. Once an alert had been given, there were many suitable refuge areas to which . . . an army . . . could flee with small risk of pursuit."[280]

The task of any French force invading the Viet Bac was complicated by the French dependence on machines and roads. That machine/road dependence directly affected French planning. Although the French objective was to

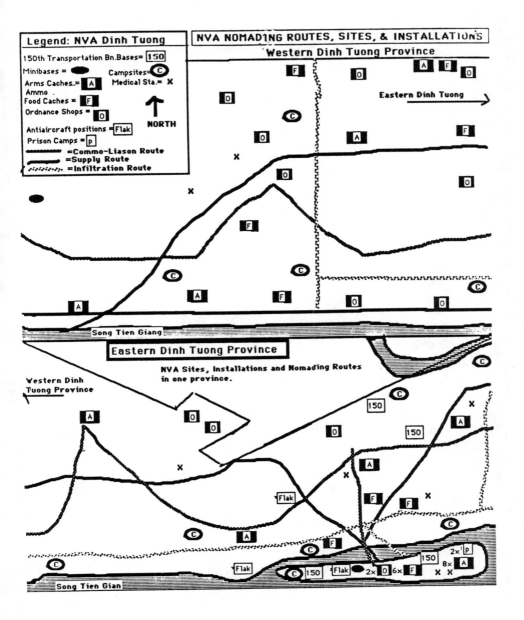

NVA NOMADING ROUTES, SITES, & INSTALLATIONS
Western Dinh Tuong Province

Legend: NVA Dinh Tuong

150th Transportation Bn.Bases = 150
Minibases = ●   Campsites = Ⓒ
Arms Caches = A   Medical Sta. = X
Ammo
Food Caches = F
Ordnance Shops = O
Antiaircraft positions = Flak
Prison Camps = P

NORTH

~~~~~~~ =Commo-Liason Route
———— =Supply Route
⌇⌇⌇⌇⌇ =Infiltration Route

Eastern Dinh Tuong

Song Tien Giang

Eastern Dinh Tuong Province

NVA Sites, Installations and Nomading Routes in one province.

Western Dinh
Tuong Province

150

2x P
8x A

2x 6x

Song Tien Gian

locate and defeat a force of 60,000 reds, the fact that the communists were maneuvering in an area of nearly inaccessible (by French standards) 7,500 square miles, worried the French more. The French refused to create the foot-mobile force which the situation demanded.

The mobility principles first noted by the Viet Minh in the Viet Bac Base in 1947 remained useful against the Chu Luc's enemies straight through 1975. The fact that western armies would not organize foot-mobile mountain infantry units, in corps strength, and commit them against the red base areas, marked them as losers from the beginning. The Viet Minh were given a gift of mobility which was reserved exclusively for their benefit. Thus Giaps' Viet Bac obfuscated center of gravity and interior lines enabled him to speedily switch troops during his maneuver phases.[281]

General Giap knew that he only had to contend with French troops constrained by obvious terrain characteristics. In apparent servitude to Viet Minh maneuver, Giap's enemies always insisted upon:

1. Tailoring operations so that the fullest use could be made of mechanized/technological equipment, whether that equipment was necessary or not.
2. Prefering to fight along the best roads or avenues of approach available.
3. Refusing to commit large formations, of three or more divisions, of foot-mobile troops to the bush for extended, three or more month, campaigns.
4. Ignoring the supreme importance of red base areas and logistics infrastructure.
5. Fighting essentially defensive wars.
6. Refusing to train their generals in maneuvering large multi-divisional forces in the bush.
7. Refusing to adapt their forces to the milieu in which they fought. (The true definition of intelligence is the ability to adapt.)

The Viet Minh devised a battle timetable, made imperative by their foot mobility, which modeled the phrased regroupment and maneuver of combat forces. That timetable broke down three phrases: movement, reconnaissance and assault.

Standard Viet Minh Battle Time-Table

1. Three weeks of moving troops into the battle area.
2. Six to ten days for the reconnaissance phase.
3. The assault phase lasting several days.[282]

At the battle of Dien Bien Phu, General Giap concentrated four and one-third divisions. His unit battle movement timetable unfolded as follows:

1. Movement phase—six weeks.
2. Reconnaissance phase—one hundred days.
3. Assault phase—fifty seven days.[283]

When Giap decided to fight for the Dien Bien Phu Valley, he set into motion the foot-mobile concentration of his forces. First he ordered the 316th Division, the closest to Dien Bien Phu, to threaten Lai Chau and advance south on Route 191. Then he ordered the 308th, 312th and 351st (Heavy) Divisions westward out of their Phu Tho-Yen Bay-Thai Nguyen base areas in late November, 1953. Those units then began an over 200-mile march westward toward Dien Bien Phu.[284] In early December, 1953 the 304th NVA Division sent its 57th Regiment on a 250-mile march northwestward from south Annam. All of the red units were moving at a rate of fifteen to twenty miles a day.

As the NVA units converged on Dien Bien Phu, they followed the area roads and routes:

- 316th Division south along Route 191.
- 351st Heavy Division southwest along Route 19.
- 308th, 312th, and 57/304th north along Routes 191 and 192.[285]

The reds moved with impunity. No sizable French foot-mobile forces interdicted their passage or struck at their supply lines.

Oddly, the French forgot their own emphasis on light infantry operations. Although two French battalions of foot-mobile Tai mountain tribesmen kept the mountains between the Red and Black Rivers clean of Viet Minh in 1947, their success was ignored. Also ignored by the French and Americans were such lessons as "the 5,000 members of the GCMAs (French led guerrillas) operating in western Tonkin and north-eastern Laos during the Dien Bien Phu battle immobilized up to fourteen Viet Minh battalions for a cost of 200 tons of supplies per month while the 15,000 men in the Dien Bien Phu fortifications engaged twenty-eight battalions at a cost of 200 tons of supplies per day. However, . . . the GCMAs were not permitted to make any serious attack on the vital supply routes between the Viet Bac and Dien Bien Phu, but how many security forces were required to prevent such attacks will never be known."[286]

A few Viet Minh battalions probably sufficed to contain the GCMA threat. The French didn't really understand the importance of attacking enemy supply lines with ground forces.

There are several aspects to mobility, the first of which is organization of

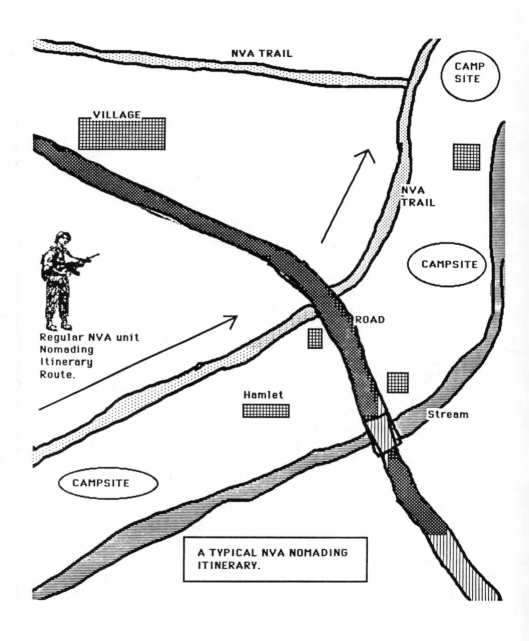

A TYPICAL NVA NOMADING ITINERARY.

the theater of war. The NVA decided to carve up South Vietnam into several subdivisions which would enhance their operational and strategic mobility: "Covering all the mountain, Central Highlands and coastal regions from the DMZ down into the lowlands approaching Saigon, the enemy divided this part of the country alone into four theaters of operation: Quangtri-Thuathien, Central Trungbo Theater, Western Plateaux Theater and South Trungbo Theater. The fifth zone, Eastern Nambo, and the sixth, Mekong River Delta Theater, encompassing the remainder of the southern part of the country from Saigon to the Ca Mau peninsula, which extends into the Gulf of Siam.

"Why has this made the Viet Cong as mobile as the Americans with all their machines? Consider IV Corps' responsibility. The distance from the Ca Mau peninsula to Saigon is around 200 miles. For the same area the Viet Cong have two separate commands, so that regular troops operating in the Eastern Nambo Theater are probably no more than fifty to seventy miles from a battle site—only a few hours by bicycle. The men of IV Corps, with a much larger area of responsibility, must diffuse their strength more, and by the law of averages, are always further away, at any given time, from a place of battle."[287]

The Chu Luc never forgot their Viet Minh mobility lessons, as they proved time and again during their war against the Americans. In August and September 1966, the U.S. 1st Cavalry Division was hunting for the 18B and 66th NVA Infantry Regiments which had recently engaged them along the Cambodian border's Chu Pong War Zone. Suddenly, elements of those two regiments, along with the 32nd NVA Regiment, were discovered 120 miles to the west, near coastal Tuy Hoa. The Americans were shocked at the foot-mobile speed demonstrated by the NVA as they moved large combat units so far, so quickly: "It was mighty unkind of 18B and the 66th and a mean trick to play . . . (1st Cav) . . . people were wearing out their jungle boots to no good end, threshing out the unpeopled Buon Blech range . . . and all the time the little stinkers had sideslipped . . . by the distance that an NVA soldier can conquer in approximately one week" . . . Not only was the . . . 18B Regiment massing, maneuvering, and mooching in the Trung Luong Valley, but so were the NVA 32nd and 66th Regiments, or at least their major elements."[288]

The Commo-Liaison System

In the mid-1950s the Viet Cong established Chu Luc communications-liaison (commo-liaison) missions throughout South Vietnam and the Ho Chi Minh Trail system. Commo-liaison troops were responsible for guiding communist leaders through every region of Indochina. In 1963 the commo-liaison units were placed under party control.

Regional commo-liaison stations had been established throughout Indochina by 1965. Each station was manned by seven to forty men. The personnel assigned to those stations served as guides for all manner of traffic, including the movement of troops, cadres, weapons, ammunition and other supplies. In addition, each station carried out mail delivery and moved at least a ton of material, including: money, medicines, radios, photographic equipment, medical supplies and Viet Cong propaganda, on each trip.[289]

Soon, every province in South Vietnam had its own communist commo-liaison platoon of twenty to thirty-five people. That platoon controlled a network of cells charged with postal, transportation, administrative, propaganda, training and security guard duties. Eventually provincial commo-liaison platoons established commo-liaison squads in every district and commo-liaison cells (three people each) in every village.[290]

Commo-liaison routes were maintained by part-time agents who lived among the population. They managed stations located eight hours march apart. Supplies and personnel were constantly moved between the stations. Sometimes the stations were operated out of people's homes for a month or more. However, most stations were separate, permanent installations. Commo-liaison stations opened South Vietnam to communist control, like the American mountain men opened up the West to pioneer farmers. In Kien Hoa, for example, commo-liaison units established secret storage areas, movement skeds and road crossing points, an imperative infrastructure for mobility enhancement and area control.

Cunning Chu Luc commanders noted the effectiveness of commo-liaison operations. Commo-liaison routes and stations provided operational data and models which were later developed into the military nomad system.

The Nomad System

A system of fortified installations connected by multiple routes enabled NVA units to meet all of their area control and survival needs. NVA units, which operated as battalions until 1965, could move along those controlled routes, periodically mooring in safe fortified harbors. By adopting that nomading system they could maintain their mobility and if they were surprised, they could defend themselves better from a system of fortified villages and camps.

Even regular NVA infantry regiments, subordinate to full strength divisions, utilized nomading principles. For example, the 22nd NVA Infantry Regiment of the 3rd NVA Infantry Division, headquartered in II Corps' Binh

Dinh War Zone, followed the nomading system: "The battalions were separately deployed, each some distance from the others. It was their practice to spend five to seven days at base camp and then relocate forces, although remaining in the general area."[291]

Special communications systems were also maintained in support of the nomading movement system: "It was standard operating procedure that the regiment talked with the battalions four times each day and the battalions called regiment as many times. Not even Phuc was permitted to know the appointed minutes at which this clock had to be punched. It was a secret within the signals."[292]

One principle of nomading was borrowed from infiltration methods. Larger units organized for movement in smaller groups. Regular Chu Luc regiments, like the 22nd NVA Regiment, were accustomed to moving in battalion and smaller sections.[293]

The nomading system facilitated population control by siting routes, camps and fortifications so that they threatened contiguous civilian living areas. Civilians living near or within the nomading zones were forced to finance, supply and work for the red units controlling those zones. The NVA forced indigenous Indochinese civilians to build and maintain the nomad zones. Press-ganged civilians built roads, fortifications, tunnels, and food caches. The peasantry also manufactured explosives and weaponry while providing military manpower, porterage and information.

The reds had most South Vietnamese provinces organized into nomading zones by 1964. For example, Dinh Tuong Province had 124 villages organized into the nomading system. Each village ranged in population from 1,800 to 17,000, with the average village harboring 5,500 souls. Dinh Tuong Province was controlled by a few NVA battalions which never represented more than two percent of the total populace. Those few NVA battalions were never driven out either. In fact the red units defeated locally assigned ARVN divisions and the powerful U.S. 9th Infantry Division's Riverine Brigade. The NVA battalions in Dinh Tuong Province controlled their areas by nomadding.

Communist Campsites

Viet Cong units eventually established a pervasive nomading system, complete with standard operating procedures, which insured high mobility. The system also insured that once located, red units would be difficult to destroy. If surprised, the reds would fight from prepared defensive positions and withdraw at night.

Each South Vietnamese village usually was composed of approximately seven smaller population groupings, called hamlets. Each hamlet usually included about one hundred families and could accommodate one Viet Cong battalion. NVA battalions dominated that web of hamlets with fortified installations which they called "campsites." Eventually each South Vietnamese province became dotted with an archipelago of NVA campsites. Several red units and their transport/logistics service units would remain in constant motion between the sites. They always traveled on the same trails. Yet, since several routes connected each site, the reds usually didn't settle upon one habitual avenue of approach.

Usually, at least one NVA regiment controlled each province. That regiment was normally composed of three battalions of main force troops, consisting of two regional force and one provincial force battalions. The provincial force battalion was usually the best combat unit.

NVA/VC battalions operated independently, moving along their own routes and using their own campsites. Each battalion usually controlled a network of approximately twenty to twenty-five campsites, usually located in one specific sector of a province.

Campsites were selected according to three geographical criteria:

1. Defensibility—Each site had to be geographically positioned so that it offered suitable potential for defense, and several covered routes of withdrawal.
2. Cover—Each site had to be undetectable from the air and masked by foliage which enhanced its camouflage.
3. Distance—The camp must not be more than fourteen hours, or one night's march, from one or more other camp sites.[294]

Many sites in every South Vietnamese province easily met those criteria. Although some campsite criteria were occasionally overlooked, no compromise was made with the criteria of campsite defensibility, which were rigidly observed.

Campsite Defensive Imperatives

1. Withdrawal routes—The several routes out of a campsite must not be impeded by rivers or highways.
2. Surrounding area—Campsite perimeters must be surrounded by terrain offering the minimum cover to advancing enemy troops.
3. Defensibility—Hamlets and villages surrounding the campsite must be sited favorably for defensive operations.

Chu Luc campsite and fortified area requirements were similar to the ground configurations preferred by U.S. military forces. American ground commanders commonly assessed terrain for: Observation, fields of fire, cover and concealment, obstacles and avenues of approach.

Potential enemy avenues of approach into the vicinity of campsites were closely scrutinized. The NVA preferred that their campsites be surrounded by open fields or paddies. They avoided villages surrounded by high ricefields, berms or dikes, graveyards or trees. Such terrain features could provide cover to advancing enemy troops.

For vegetative camouflage, the Viet Cong preferred that large trees, not mangrove shrubs, conceal their campsites. To shield a battalion camp, a forested region, with an area of at least five kilometers by one-half kilometer, was sought. A regimental camp required four times that amount of cover.

Campsite Forest Cover Requirements	
Unit	Area Coverage in Kilometers
Company	$1.4 \times .20$
Battalion	$5 \times .50$
Regiment	20×2^{295}

Although each NVA battalion controlled its own camp network, detachments sometimes occupied other unit's campsites. NVA battalions also had favorite campsites, or campsite complexes, where they stayed longer. Such "permanent" campsite complexes might be occupied for as long as three or more months. No one campsite would be occupied that long, but a unit might move among three or four campsites within a small geographical area for a prolonged period.

Since the Chu Luc was a maneuver army, it decentralized its command structure. Commanders of battalions, and lower level units, were frequently given mission orders with the specific plan of execution left up to them. Within the provinces of South Vietnam, the usual mission order was area control. The nomading system was the vehicle. However, the movement sked, or itinerary, was left up to the unit commander. As a result, red battalions were in constant, apparently random, flux. Nomading units periodically interrupted their movements for supply replenishment, the exercise of population control, or in reaction to an ARVN sweep.

Remarkably, NVA battalions controlling South Vietnamese provinces didn't spend much time fighting. Since their own survival depended upon area control, they spent most of their time controlling the real estate around them. They might not fight more than once or twice a year, after very careful preparation. Each battle was followed by drawn out after-action critiques. Only incursions by ARVN troops seemed to interfere with the red's nomadic, area-control lifestyle. The Chu Luc's routes, supply caches, campsites, mini-bases, strongholds and war zones had to be protected. As long as they were inviolate, there was no need to fight.

Most campsites were within one night's march of four to seven other sites. Communist leaders usually randomly selected their next campsite, or at least made such choices in an unpredictable fashion. Even trusted junior officers couldn't guess where their commander planned to move next. One assistant platoon leader of the 514th Battalion claimed that he could only guess which of several campsites was the next likely harbor: "For instance, if while being stationed in Binh Ninh, we got shelled during the day, I could guess that we were moving to one of these three villages: Quan Long, Thanh Binh or My Tinh An. To know for sure which of them would be our next campsite I had to wait until we began to move. Then seeing the direction my unit takes, I would know where we were going."[296]

It is clear that the above mentioned platoon leader was referring to an area with relatively fewer trail and campsite options. In those areas covered with a veritable web of trails and sites, even the direction of movement was no indicator of destination. A platoon leader of the 262nd VC Battalion described the movement flexibility which occurred in those areas where larger numbers of campsites and radial avenues of approach were located: "There are no fixed regulations for moving. Because it had to avoid strafings and shellings, the battalion lately has reconnoitered and used new roads. The short or long marches don't follow any fixed regulations either. Sometimes the battalion reaches a village at night and leaves it for another village at 4 AM . . ."[297]

Although the NVA battalion commander could decide which camp to move to next, frequently on a random basis, his route choices were less flexible. South Vietnamese Army defensive positions and camps, as well as contiguous road and canal locations, shaped route selection. The shortest path between two campsites usually was not taken, since the necessity to avoid some area of high trafficability or government control/observation might require a more lengthy bypass.

Roads and canals had to be crossed by the red units and, because of security requirements, crossing points were few. In many cases such crossing points were used so exclusively and habitually by red units that they constituted a vulnerability of some dimension: "The 514th battalion had its own route to follow when it has to move, and especially some fixed crossing points on Highway 4. For instance, whenever this battalion has to go through Binh Phu or Binh An village. On the stretch of road between Cai Lay and Long Dinh districts, it has to go through Nhi Qui Village. So far it has always stayed inside Nhi Qui until it came to the highway and crossed."[298]

Road and canal crossings were selected with as much care as possible. Local guerrillas and village youth frequently outposted, guided, and secured such crossings.

Another obstacle in battalion movement was experienced when South Vietnamese posts were encountered. Such areas caused time-consuming detours: "It took my unit about 4 hours . . . because we have to make a detour to avoid passing by the Than Nhut military post. This GVN post is manned by one platoon of Civil Guards and one platoon of Popular Force soldiers."[299]

Unit Movement Methods

Many Viet Cong units became rather complacent about their nomading operations. However, the majority adhered to experience-based doctrinal guidelines for nomading operations. When a communist battalion commander planned a unit move, he had to consider several relevant factors including:

1. Reconnaissance of the route and objective area.
2. Security of the route and objective area.
3. Preparation of the objective area (i.e. the presence of nearby food/ammo caches, or preliminary organization for victual confiscation from nearby villages).
4. Movement formation.
5. Road, canal and other danger area crossings required.
6. Enemy presence and activity within the objective route area.
7. Security and secrecy methods to be employed.

Viet Cong nomading regulations and standard operating procedures required that units not stay longer than specified periods in various types of campsites. Permanent bases were to be inhabited for not more than seven days at a time. Regular campsites were to be evacuated within four days, although they might be visited as much as five times within the same month. In contested areas, campsites were to be moved every three days or sooner.

Twenty-four hours before a battalion move, a reconnaissance element would be dispatched along the avenue of approach to the objective area. That reconnaissance element, led by battalion reconnaissance assets, included a liaison party composed of food supply coordinators and representatives from battalion and company headquarters.[300] Communist district and village cadre would be contacted by the liaison party to arrange housing and provision for the battalion. Local communications-liaison personnel, experts on local route conditions, were also contacted.

To insure secrecy, unit moves always took place at night. The battalion would usually move out after four PM, expecting to bed down at its destination after midnight, and before daybreak. Companies received their march orders verbally, only an hour or two before they were to move out. Everything was then gathered up and the current campsite area was checked to ensure that it remained camouflaged and undetectable from the air. All fortifications were left undisturbed since they were frequently reused.

The Approach March

After necessary arrangements had been made, the VC unit was ready to move. Moving in a battalion column of companies, the red battalion would jump off toward their new campsite. About one half kilometer ahead of the column moved a long-range recon element composed of commo-liaison personnel or local militia. Two hundred meters behind them was a battalion reconnaissance-intelligence team.

Marching as the column's advance guard would be two rifle companies and the battalion command staff. Following them in order would be the combat support company and/or a heavy weapons company, at the finger tips of battalion headquarters. Next in column would be a rifle company, minus one platoon which would be following the battalion column as a rear guard. The battalion column would usually stretch in one file, four to eight kilometers in length, along the approach route.[301]

Marching in single file, each man would maintain two to four meters separation from every other man. In daylight, that separation would be increased to five to ten meters between each man. Platoons were usually separated by fifty meters, and companies marched one hundred meters apart.

Daylight movement required heavy camouflage, especially appropriate when crossing open areas, which were avoided as much as possible in any case. Daylight routes were always chosen through the most vegetated areas available.

Danger areas, especially road and canal crossings, were approached with elaborate precaution. For road crossings, a special battlegroup was organized. That battlegroup was composed of a recon team, an infantry platoon and two road security squads. The road security squads, usually armed with RPG antitank weapons, took up positions to the left and right of the crossing site, where they set up to defend against enemy armored vehicles. The rifle platoon then established a shallow bridgehead on the opposite side of the road, while the recon unit patrolled deeply to insure area security.

If the coast was clear, the battalion began to cross the road rapidly. The entire crossing procedure usually required two to three hours of time. Viet Cong battalions usually crossed roads and canals at the same points every time. That habit, although never exploited by allied forces, jeopardized the crossing operation.

Actions in the Objective Area

As the battalion moved into its bivouac objective area, liaison personnel assigned units to housing or shelter, usually one squad per "hootch." Heavy weapons were placed in the center of the bivouac area, near battalion headquarters. Recoilless rifles and light machine guns were distributed along likely enemy areas of approach, among perimeter rifle companies. An outpost line of friendly guerrillas or self-defense militia was usually deployed around the battalion bivouac area, which was also outposted with close-in battalion security posts.

After the first night in the new bivouac area, the battalion coordinated its defensive plans for the area with local militia or other units. Contingency plans and withdrawal routes were rehearsed and the area was intensely patrolled.

An anti-recon screen of local units was thrown out along all likely avenues of approach into the bivouac area. That screen had several purposes including:

1. Provide early warning of approaching enemy.
2. Destroy enemy reconnaissance assets.
3. Monitor and shape enemy movement.
4. Delay enemy movement.
5. Locate and scout enemy campsites.
6. Surround enemy campsites with an anti-recon screen.
7. Guide Main Force units into night attack positions around the enemy site.

The Nomading system worked very well.

Route Markers

In order to facilitate efficient traffic along their infiltration, nomad, commo-liaison and other routes, the NVA instituted a system of road, trail and route markers. Many of those markers were similar to those utilized by American Indians in centuries past. Included in that repertoire of signs and symbols were:

1. Military symbols.
2. Map and topographic symbols.
3. Mine and booby trap signs or indicators.
4. Instructional signs.
5. Trail information signs.
6. Trail indicators.
7. Enemy position indicators.

If allied troops had been trained to operate along enemy routes they would have been more effective. If they had been taught to read NVA road and trail markers, they might have won the war.

ROCKS OR STONES	THIS IS THE TRAIL	TURN RIGHT	WARNING! OR CACHE
DISKS ON TREES	TURN LEFT	TO	FROM
TUFTS OF GRASS	THIS IS THE TRAIL	TURN RIGHT	WARNING! OR CACHE
CLOTH STREAMERS	THIS	MARKS THE	TRAIL
LAKE AND RIVER MARKERS	EMBARKED HERE	DIRECTION TAKEN	UNKNOWN DESTINATION
SPECIAL CODE BLAZES	MEANINGS	DEVISED BY TRAIL	BLAZERS

American Indian trial signs and markers illustrated in:
Living Like Indians by A.A. MacFarlan, Berranger Books, NY 1961

153

VIET CONG/NVA INSTRUCTIONAL TRAIL SIGNS

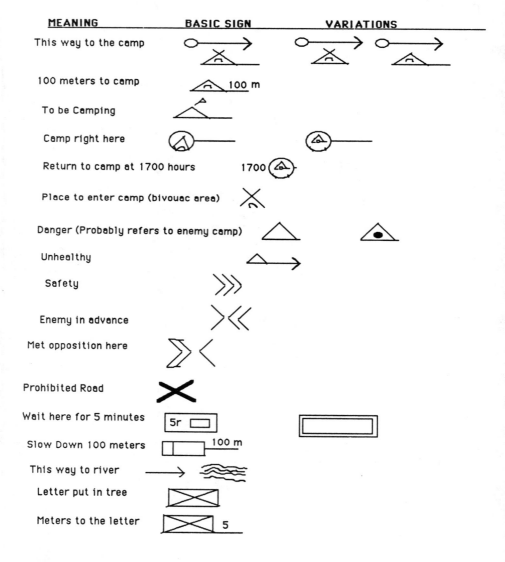

MEANING	BASIC SIGN	VARIATIONS
This way to the camp		
100 meters to camp	100 m	
To be Camping		
Camp right here		
Return to camp at 1700 hours	1700	
Place to enter camp (bivouac area)		
Danger (Probably refers to enemy camp)		
Unhealthy		
Safety		
Enemy in advance		
Met opposition here		
Prohibited Road		
Wait here for 5 minutes	5r	
Slow Down 100 meters	100 m	
This way to river		
Letter put in tree		
Meters to the letter	5	

VIET CONG INSTRUCTIONAL TRAIL SIGNS

These signs gave NVA/VC, units and individuals, valuable information regarding trail trafficability, area amenities, even speed limits. The signs were usually drawn on pieces of wood, shaved trees, or with stones or sticks arranged into meaningful patterns.

MEANING	BASIC SIGN	VARIATIONS
Walking Mark		
To Start		
Follow This Way		
Quickly		
Slowly		
Return		
Turn Left		
Turn Right		
To Cross Obstacle		
Well Water		
Divide Into Two Groups		
Unite Into One Group		
Return Back To Camp		

VIET CONG TRAIL SIGNS III

Pointed towards
spike trap.

The end of a vine wrapped around a stump,
pointed towards a spike trap.

A tripod of sticks tied together indicated a nearby spike trap.

Mine   Stick

A stick, shaved flat on one side, approximately 1/2 meter
in length, was stuck in the graound at a 45 degree angle
with the flat portion of the stick facing skyward. That
stick indicated a mine located forward and on line with
the point where the flat side of the stick entered the
ground.

VIET CONG TRAIL MARKERS

Four stakes were used to pass information about enemy patrols and their
equipment. The bark was shaved from one side of each wooden stake
leaving the white wood exposed. On the exposed side, marks were made
which gave information about the enemy patrol, when decoded. The stakes
were sharpened at one end and stuck into the ground. The length of the
stake remaining above ground was from ten to twelve inches.

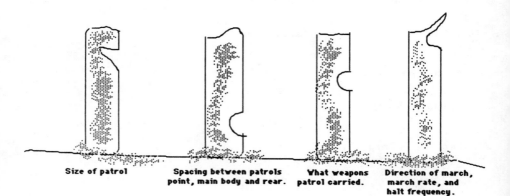

Size of patrol   Spacing between patrols   What weapons   Direction of march,
                   point, main body and rear.   patrol carried.   march rate, and
                                                                      halt frequency.

VIET CONG TRAIL SIGNS IV

ENEMY POSITION INDICATORS

Forked stick, upright with another stick in the fork. The stick in the fork pointed towards an enemy position.

Forked stake, "V" pointed towards enemy position.

Split tree stump. The "V" pointed towards an enemy artillery position.

Tree stump with a stick wedged in it indicated nearby enemy mortar position.

VIET CONG TRAIL DIRECTION MARKERS

These markers indicated that a specific trail served the VC/NVA as well as providing information about the trail.

Three bamboo strips, 3' long, one strip placed diagonally on the others.

Gray diamond shaped rock, 6" by 3".

Three bamboo strips placed parallel on a 12" diameter bamboo circle. This sign was placed about 1 foot off the ground in a bush.

A 6" circle having a 2.5" strip of bamboo with the arrow head pointing in the direction of movement.

Three strips of 3' long bamboo placed parallel, in a circle, with the center bamboo strip having an arrow head.

Five parallel bamboo strips, 3' long, with one diagonal bamboo strip.

157

VIET CONG MINE AND BOOBY TRAP TRAIL SIGNS

A stick or length of bamboo broken at right angles and placed on a
road or trail indicated that VC mines are booby traps were 200-400
meters ahead.

Sticks or bamboo

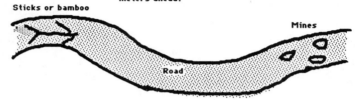

A stick or length of bamboo lying parallel to a trail or road could
indicate that the area is mine and booby trap free.

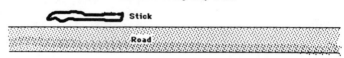

Three sticks or stones, one on each side of the road and one in the
center means DO NOT USE THE ROAD.

Prior to ambushing vehicles on a road, the Viet Cong sometimes build
mounds of dirt up to 2 meters high along the shoulder of the road.
They then rig booby traps or lay mines in these mounds so that when
vehicles are stopped during the ambush, the troops will attept to use
the mounds as cover, setting off the mines.

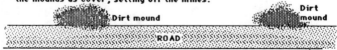

A bow and arrow trap indicator, placed 10 meters in front of the trap,
consisted of a forked stick 5 feet high, with a pole resting in the fork
and pointing towards the trap. 25 meters beyond the trap was a, usually
2 feet high, stump indicator with four wedges driven into it. The end of
a vine wrapped around the stump pointed towards the aroow trap.

VIET CONG MINE AND BOOBY TRAP TRAIL SIGNS II

A paper marker weighted with a rock or a wooden sign attached to a tree indicated there was an ex--plosive device nearby.

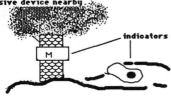

indicators

Tufts of grass ties in knots, in a square pattern indicated a mine in the square.

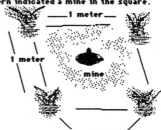

1 meter

1 meter

mine

Tufts of tied grass.

An arrow fastened at the top of a 1 meter high post pointed towards a mined area. The feather end of the arrow pointed towards the safe area. Such arrows were gerally removed at the approach of enemy troops.

A stick placed in the fork of another stick, pointed towards a mined area.

1 meter

Mines

Bamboo

Bamboo sticks arranged in a "V" or "U" shape indicated a punji trap nearby.

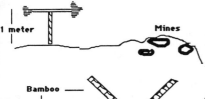

A thorn branch lying on the ground in a half circle indicated a nearby explosive device,

Three sticks tied together to form a tripod were placed directly over a spike trap and were re-moved at the approach of enemies.

Tree

Paper marker

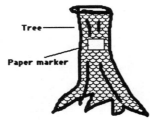

A paper marker attached to a tree, indicated that a mine was nearby.

PART II.

Battle Art

CHAPTER 8

Offensive Maneuver

For over three years the U.S. Marines tried to control I Corps' An Hoa Valley War Zone, twenty-six miles south of Da Nang, but they always failed. The best they could do was to maintain a "combat base" at An Hoa, from where the besieged marine battalions were sometimes able to launch tactical stabs into "injun country."

That An Hoa base required constant resupply. The Marine 11th Motor Battalion ran one or more, up to fifty truck, supply convoys south out of Da Nang to the fire base daily. Six miles north of An Hoa those convoys had to cross the Song Thu Bon River, which was not bridged until 1969. Three or more hours were required to cross a convoy over the river on a motorized pontoon barge. That slow crossing provided an excellent target for NVA artillery.

In March 1969 a Navy Mobile Construction, or Seabee, Battalion was assigned to build a bridge over the crossing site to be known as Liberty Bridge. Movie goers who viewed the John Wayne World War II movie *Fighting Seabees,* received accurate information about the purpose and organization of Seabee Battalions. The well-armed Seabee construction battalions, were able to defend themselves while being engaged in construction tasks, and fight offensively too. There were twelve or more Seabee battalions floating around South Vietnam's I Corps, at any one time from 1965 to 1972.

In spite of the fact that Seabee battalions were armed and trained for combat, line Marine battalions were always assigned to protect them. A Marine battalion, the 1st Battalion of the 5th Regiment and an artillery battery (D/2/11, armed with eight 105mm howitzers), were assigned to protect the Seabee battalion which was building the Liberty Bridge.

A fire support base was built on an elongated hill, straddling the road to An Hoa, south of the bridge site. The small fire base had all the usual amenities of a marine fire base including a chapel, mess hall, three barracks, a motor pool, and several ammunition and supply dumps. There were around twenty-five buildings in the small base, not counting bunkers.[302]

The fire base afforded excellent observation and dominating fields of fire over the open terrain around the river crossing site. The marines deployed the artillery battery and the infantry battalion's 81mm mortar platoon on the west side of the road which pierced the center of the fire base. The marine battalion's command post was located on the east side of the road.

A number of bunker positions were constructed in front of each 105mm howitzer parapet, overlooking all avenues of approach into the position. Those bunkers masked all howitzer direct fire close-in capability, except for howitzer parapet number six. In addition, the artillery battery position was surrounded with seven strands of triple concertina, about five feet high, spaced ten meters apart. Over one thousand trip flares and masses of tanglefoot barbed wire were dispersed between each concertina line and throughout the barbed wire barrier.

The 1/5 infantry battalion had placed small "killer teams" in defensive positions in a northwest arc, four to five hundred meters out from the artillery battery. They had neglected, however, to outpost the obvious enemy assembly area located in a treeline about three hundred yards south to southeast of the fire base's perimeter.

One 1/5 company was dug in on the north side of the river to protect the Seabee battalion. The rest of the marine infantry battalion was dug in on the south side of the bridge defending its headquarters. No counterattack unit was ever designated within marine fortified positions.

At 1:40 AM on the morning of March 19, 1969 an NVA night attack hit the marine position north of the river. Bedlam ensued. Nervous marine gunners began firing in support of the position across the river, and all attention was focused toward the north. Members of the artillery battery who were supposed to be manning bunker defensive positions on the south and southwest sectors, withdrew from their bunkers.

Taking advantage of the confused fireworks and light show, an NVA battalion stealthily approached from the south-southwest. Sapper cells rapidly cut their way through the barbed wire with rubberized wirecutters. When the trip wires were cut, being pull-type, the tension was released negating any danger of detonation. However, the NVA unit cut very few wires at all, penetrating the barrier by stealth and skill. Although the NVA battalion had moved across open terrain illuminated by the fire and parachute flares, it was not spotted by the defending marines.

Suddenly the communists unleashed a whirlwind of rocket, mortar and bangalore torpedo fire at two perimeter penetration points: "The NVA sappers and infantry, following the mortar barrage in trace, effected a two-fold penetration of the battery perimeter. Hurling ChiCom grenades and firing short busts from AK-47/50 assault rifles, the enemy penetrated from the south and southwest and quickly engaged the Marines occupying the parapets of howitzers 8 and 7 . . . a substantial number of NVA, with satchel charges, small arms, and two ChiCom flame throwers . . . (were inside the southwest perimeter sector in a flash) . . .

"The NVA initially possessed the upper hand, with their subsequent movements quick and frenzied. Casualties among the Marine cannoneers were numerous. The NVA methodically 'flamed' three personnel bunkers and the battery's gravest concern, . . . was enemy flame throwers exploitation of the artillery ammunition bunkers . . ."[303] At the same time, an NVA platoon, armed with flamethrowers, penetrated the infantry battalion command post (CP) area from the southeast. That platoon began to systematically "flame" toward the marine CP.

As suddenly as it began, the enemy battalion withdrew. Losing less than one company equivalent, the NVA unit was able to rapidly disappear. The shocked marine defenders claimed that they had defeated a major enemy attempt to destroy the two fortified camps. They insisted that the enemy "had planned one of two options upon initiating the action:

- Effect linkup, neutralize the defenders, and upon withdrawal, destroy the artillery weapons and ammunition bunkers in place, therefore indirectly supporting a possible ground attack against the bridge complex.
- Effect linkup, neutralize the defenders, and direct the artillery weapons upon the bridge complex itself, supporting a possible ground attack designed to neutralize the bridge construction efforts and to destroy the pontoon barge."[304]

The marines were wrong. They had been victimized by one of the three primary Chu Luc offensive tactics, the power raid. If the assault had been a major effort, the NVA would have sent more troops against the reinforced regimental-sized marine/Seabee force.

The sparse vegetation in the area was insufficient for the concealment of an NVA regimental sized assault force. In addition, there was the problem of withdrawing from the area at daybreak under a hellfire of marine artillery and air bombardment. A battalion could get away, a regiment might lose a lot of men.

In any case, the NVA operation was a power raid, which might have been exploited according to the two option possibilities outlined by the marines, if the attack had been launched earlier and if the marines had caved in quicker. The NVA didn't commit enough resources to the battle for it to qualify for anything more than a battalion power raid.

NVA Offensive Doctrine: Encapsulated

From his beginnings as the Viet Minh generalissimo, General Giap, the North Vietnamese commander, had been a model combat commander. "Giap's mind was able to select the crucially important strategic factors, deduce that he had sufficient strength to undertake the operation and to outline the fundamental concept of the development of the battle . . ."[305]

Giap was always guided by clarity of thinking and nonlinear problem solving ability. Yet he also adhered to fundamental principles of war, which he once characterized as follows: "we resolutely chose the other tactic: to strike surely and advance surely. In taking this correct decision, we strictly followed this fundamental principal of the conduct of a revolutionary war; strike to win, strike only when success is certain; if it is not, then don't strike."[306]

The NVA was an offensive entity, oriented toward fast moving, hard striking war. Giap and his minions were guided by the military thoughts of Sun Tzu who believed that, "Supreme excellence consists in breaking the enemy's resistance without fighting. Thus the highest form of generalship is to baulk the enemy's plans; the next best is to prevent the junction of the enemy's forces; the next in order is to attack the enemy's army in the field; the worst policy of all is to besiege walled cities."[307]

Chu Luc offensive maneuver doctrine was guided by three bedrock success factors, three primary offensive methods, "One Slow" and "Four Fasts" (discussed elsewhere), and several "strike" tactical methods. In addition, the Chu Luc launched other types of offensive actions as well, including:

- Close, or breakthrough, assaults.
- Standoff attacks.
- Hill traps.
- Forward detachment operations, like the Blossoming Lotus.

The three NVA bedrock offensive success factors were composed of: (1) five battle principles, (2) accurate and up-to-date intelligence, and (3) deliberate standardized assault planning.

The Five Battle Principles

1. *Speed of movement:* To achieve speed the NVA practiced rapid concentration; rapid deployment from march columns; movement and assaults at night; pursuit without thought of reorganization; and fast withdrawals. They also traveled light and were willing to shed everything but their weapons in order to move faster.
2. *Surprise:* To surprise their enemies, the NVA integrated deception into every operation. In addition to moving and fighting under the cloak of darkness, NVA units launched multi-leveled diversions in support of even battalion operations. Those diversions could occur at strategic, operational and several tactical levels simultaneously. Infiltration was used whenever possible.
3. *Undermine enemy morale:* The NVA purposely created a myth of invincibility. Their sanctuaries and base camps, already deemed inviolate, were further characterized by the NVA as impregnable. Their troop units, refusing to fight unless they thought they could win, purposely circulated exaggerated legends about their fighting prowess. Even their removal of casualties from battlefields left doubt in the minds of their enemy that many Chu Luc troops were hurt in combat.
4. *Security:* All battlefields were prepared in advance if possible. Counter-reconnaissance screens around NVA units, bases, routes and installations fought to cover their locations and movements.
5. *Collaboration with the local populace:* To conserve energy, manpower and other resources, the local populace, viewed by the communists as draft animals, was employed in operations whenever possible.

In order to fight, fully accurate and up to date intelligence information was always necessary. Reconnaissance preceded all operations and the primary skills of recon were constantly emphasized. Particular emphasis was focused upon: direction and distance determination, noise analysis, triangulation methods, ambush siting and terrain diagnosis.

The NVA emphasized that every attack must include five provisions: combative spirit, timing, planning, preparation and avenues of retreat (along both the march route and in the battle area). Although every battle action was planned and rehearsed separately and deliberately, the NVA did employ standardized assault planning.

NVA Standardized Assault Planning Principles

- *Reconnaissance:* Study the target for its routine and weakness. Study the terrain for approach and withdrawal routes, assembly areas, support weapons emplacements, enemy reinforcement routes or landing zones, enemy gaps for exploitation by the three standard attack devices: the main effort, secondary and diversionary attacks.
- *Preparations:* Plan for logistics, movement, deception, three attack devices and withdrawal. Conduct rehearsals and pep talks.
- *Infiltration:* Move to target area in smaller units. Slip smaller friendly units into the enemy defensive area through gaps.
- *Night Attack:* No preparatory fires, attack near or later than midnight. Use sappers or other troops to open at least two lanes through enemy barriers. Launch at least a three pronged attack: 1. the feint, one-tenth of the assault force was used for this, and then reverted to unit reserve. 2. secondary attack(s) utilizing two tenths of the assault force. 3. the main effort, utilizing seven-tenths of the assault force, supported by heavy weapons in the same proportion. Supporting weapons fire commences as the attack is launched.
- *Assault organization:* The *Support group* fires machine guns, mortars, antitank rockets and recoilless rifles toward at least two breakthrough areas. This group also supports the main effort, engages point targets and covers the withdrawal. *Breach group,* This unit must clear two or more assault lanes through the enemy defensive barrier with wire cutters, bangalore torpedoes and satchel charges. *Shock group,* This main effort force advances through the breakthrough lanes into close assault against enemy personnel. *Reserve group* exploits success and covers the withdrawal. (The NVA usually maintained too small a reserve. They felt that most of their combat power could be safely expanded by the shock group, since *fighting at night provided extra measures of surprise and security.*)

The Ambush Primary Offensive Maneuver

The main NVA offensive maneuver was the ambush, a maneuver which traps an enemy force within an annihilating kill zone. Ambushes cannot usually be carried out unless at least three informational prerequisites are known: (1) The target's route and direction. (2) The target's troop and weapon strength. (3) The approximate enemy time of passage through the ambush site.

An NVA ambush site was selected along an enemy avenue of approach. It was placed under continuous surveillance while the surrounding terrain was being studied. The surrounding terrain was analyzed from both the enemy and friendly standpoints.

The Chu Luc preferred an ambush site which:

1. Permitted concealed ambusher movement into and out of the ambush area.
2. Provided cover and concealment.
3. Facilitated deployment and maneuver.
4. Provided suitable sites for crew-served supporting weapons.
5. Permitted the establishment of camouflaged observation posts in all necessary directions.
6. Provided a position from where the enemy avenue of approach might be enfiladed by fire.
7. Provided a flank from which the enemy column may be close assaulted without requiring the traverse of open ground.
8. Could be organized to obstruct or constrict enemy counter maneuver.

From the enemy side of the coin the terrain had to provide the element of surprise. The route into the ambush site should:

1. Not be so obvious that the enemy will bombard the area or attack it rather than traverse it in column.
2. Be similar to several other areas along the route.
3. Not be the first possible ambush site along the route.
4. Constrict enemy counter action.
5. Impede enemy mutual support.
6. Facilitate enemy fragmentation by road curves.
7. Obstruct the use of supporting weapons.
8. Cause the enemy column to slow down.

There are few perfect ambush sites. Some of them can be improved by the construction of obstacles, barriers and minefields. By burying a 250 pound command-detonated bomb in the center of a road, an ambushing unit can covert a site which offers sparse cover near a route, into an adequate ambush site. When the bomb is detonated by one cell concealed in sparse cover, the resulting shock and devastation might permit an NVA battalion to advance behind smoke cover across a kilometer of open space into close combat with an enemy who cannot react fast enough because of the explosion's shock effect.

The NVA always scouted the enemy avenue of approach, or route, into the ambush area. They even developed a set of route reconnaissance procedures.

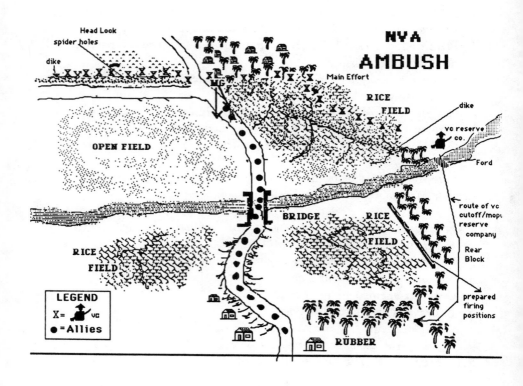

A MANEUVERING AMBUSH IN POSITION

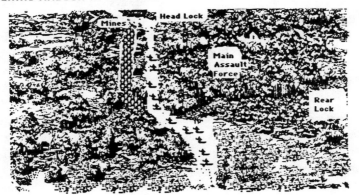

Route Reconnaissance Procedures

"The procedure involved in reconnoitering a road requires that the recon cadres observe topography relative to the road axis. They note high points, trees, jungle, cultivated fields, rivers, and streams up to three meters (sic) along both sides of the road. With respect to the road itself, the recon cadres make observations as to whether the surface of the road is wide or narrow; made of dirt, stone or asphalt; curved or straight; rough or smooth. They also notice if the road was built by cutting or filling. It was also necessary to observe the population's movement patterns in the area. In addition, reconnaissance cadres must obtain intelligence on the routes of convoys and GVN forces escorting the convoy. If possible, the cadre always tried to learn the patrol method, strength of patrol force, and the command level. In order to obtain the necessary information they often had to construct an observation station on a high but safe point with good visibility of the target. They destroy the observation point and camouflage the remains when it is abandoned."[308]

After a site was selected, a plan was drawn up for the ambush. The first three considerations were actions to be taken: prior to opening fire, upon opening fire and during withdrawal. Then enemy surprise counteractions were considered and contingency solutions devised.

Logistics considerations were carefully scrutinized and weapons ammunition supply was planned. Any necessary caching of supplies or ammunition within the battle area was also planned.

In many areas, NVA troops, who were involved in relatively few battles each year, had time to prepare several battlefield sites and fortified villages. Some of those prepared battlefields were earmarked as ambush sites. If the site was already prepared it might include pre-dug fortifications and tunnel systems.

Secrecy, security and deception was always emphasized during the planning process. Any feints or lures that were appropriate were fitted into the scheme of maneuver. Security screens were thrown out, and roundabout approach marches to the ambush site were planned. Camouflage along the route to the ambush site and in the site itself was also planned for.

Any coordinated maneuvers, such as a delaying force, preliminary assaults in other areas, or the mining or destruction of contiguous areas were also considered. For example, a series of assaults, bridge demolitions and mine laying incidents might have been carried out during a lengthy time period preceding an ambush. Such demolitions and mine attacks were frequently calculated to impede trafficability over alternate routes and channel enemy traffic over a supposedly more "secure" route where the ambush site was located.

The "shape" of the ambush was also established during planning. That shape depended upon the terrain, the objective, the amount of friendly forces available and the nature of the enemy forces. The preferred shape was the L Ambush, with an enfilading element firing down the length of the enemy column, and a linear element firing into the flank of the enemy column.

Ambush Shapes

L	Ambush	Linear Ambush	Maneuvering Ambush
Z	Ambush	Sequenced Ambush	Quick Ambush

During the planning phase, the scheme of maneuver was devised, incorporating the five components of an ambush operation: command posts, observation posts, the lead blocking element, the main assault element and the rear blocking element. Other factors such as extra maneuver elements, supporting weapons positions, obstacles and minefields were not always considered.

Ambush Elements

Command posts: The ambush commander established command posts which provided observation of the kill zone, and communications with the various ambush elements. At least two redundant communications systems linked the command posts with the various elements. Some command posts also doubled as observation posts. Field telephones usually interconnected all ambush elements.

Observation posts: Those posts were deployed for maximum observation of the battlefield and to facilitate early warning. In addition, multiple observation posts facilitated the transmission of reports to the ambush commander. Usually one main observation post and several secondary ones were established. They were intended to detect the enemy and report his movements in a timely fashion. Runners and other redundant communications means were used to report enemy movement, formations, deployment during the battle, reinforcement and routes of withdrawal.

Lead blocking element: That element "uses sudden firepower to inflict casualties upon the enemy and disorganize his formation, forcing him to halt or concentrate. The lead blocking element provides the main assault element with an opportunity to close in or begin the attack. When the main assault element begins to encircle and split the enemy, the lead blocking element coordinates with the main assault element."[309]

Main assault element: That unit's mission "is to split up the enemy and destroy his main force. It usually deploys along the flank of the enemy formation, it may account for sixty to seventy percent of the entire strength of the ambushing unit and will be reinforced with antitank weapons (recoilless rifles, bazookas) and antipersonnel mines."[310]

Rear blocking element: "usually makes up ten to twenty percent of the ambushing force. Its mission varies with the enemy situation. If the entire enemy force moves into the ambush site, the rear-blocking element attacks from the rear. If the rear of an enemy column stays out, the rear-blocking element has the mission of cutting it off. Part of it neutralizes the enemy and (the remainder) protects the flank of the main assault element."[311]

Close surveillance of the ambush site and surrounding area was maintained prior to its occupation. Any indication that a planned NVA ambush was detected could have caused a change of plans.

After a plan was devised, sand table rehearsals were carried out before the unit moved into proximity to the ambush site. The sand table rehearsal was skipped if all unit cadres participated in the recon and understood their missions. No sand table rehearsal was used for small, simple ambushes.

The NVA ambush unit moved into an assembly area, usually located in a covered and concealed position near the long axis of the ambush site. A few outposts were then dispatched to reconnoiter the area and provide early warning of surprise enemy movements. At dawn, a final inspection was made of the site and the surrounding terrain. Then the ambush unit waited until it was notified to occupy the ambush site. That occupation might not take place until the very last possible moment.

Maneuvering Forces Battle: Primary Offensive Maneuver

In order to enjoy the advantage of fortified areas and bases within South Vietnam the NVA created the Maneuvering Forces Battle (MFB), an abbreviated form of the Soviet Deep Battle concept. The MFB was fought within prepared battlefields sited ten to fifteen miles from a stronghold area containing NVA forces. At least two prepared battle sites were usually established as MFB areas.

Area reconnaissance screens and small unit patrols formed the first line of the MFB. Upon the sighting of an enemy force within the MFB battle zone, which could cover fifty square miles, the enemy was closely monitored as reports were steadily forwarded to provincial communist leadership or the command element of major area NVA combat formations.

If the command echelon made a rapid decision to destroy the encroaching enemy, an NVA advanced detachment, already on the way, would engage the force. Then the enemy force would be maneuvered into one of the prepared battlefields and destroyed.

The Maneuvering Force Battle required the sequenced interplay of:

1. Prepared battlefields.
2. Area surveillance units.
3. An advance detachment.
4. Main force troops of maneuver.
5. A battle of annihilation involving all four of the above.

The Maneuvering Forces Battle: Prepared Battlefield

Near an NVA base or bivouac area, two or three potential battlefields were usually selected for preparation as MFB areas. One of the battle areas was usually "designated as primary and used as the basis for detailed study of the coordination and deployment of the various units."[312] The battle areas were located contiguous to the communists' area movement pattern or itinerary.

Tentative operational schemes were drawn up and every battle area was surveyed and mapped. Specific attention was devoted to identifying and mapping all possible friendly and enemy, covert and overt, routes of approach and withdrawal.

Logistics caches were prepared within the battle areas or their inclusion in the scheme of maneuver was specified. Local civilian labor was earmarked for transport and the evacuation of casualties and loot. If logistics were not cached in the area, maneuvering units would move out with a basic load, expecting rear services elements to organize resupply missions to be executed within twenty-four to forty-eight hours.

On some occasions, NVA units would begin preparing a primary designated battleground during the first night that they arrived in a new bivouac area. Their documents have specified that such "prepared terrain" required "building trenches, bunkers, and heavy weapons emplacements; planting

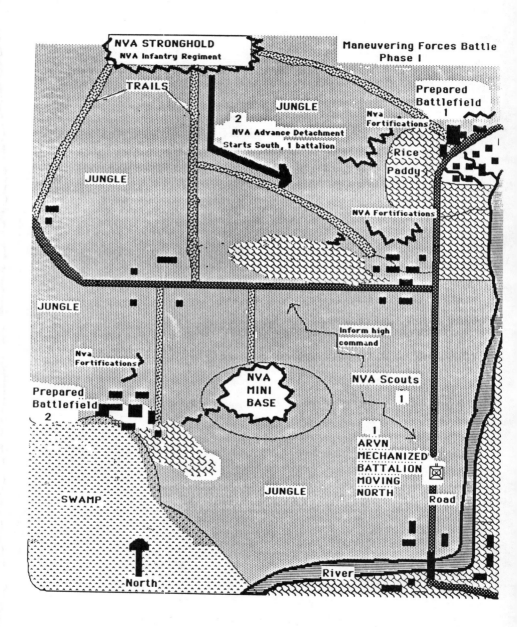

NVA STRONGHOLD
NVA Infantry Regiment

Maneuvering Forces Battle
Phase I

TRAILS

JUNGLE

2
NVA Advance Detachment
Starts South, 1 battalion

Prepared
Battlefield
1

Nva
Fortifications

Rice
Paddy

JUNGLE

NVA Fortifications

JUNGLE

Inform high
command

Nva
Fortifications

NVA
MINI
BASE

NVA Scouts

1

Prepared
Battlefield
2

1
ARVN
MECHANIZED
BATTALION
MOVING
NORTH

SWAMP

JUNGLE

Road

North

River

mines and booby traps; and preparing concealed, secure routes for battlefield mobility and subsequent withdrawal."[313]

When an enemy unit was detected within a battle area, NVA commanders or the local party committee, were notified. Then either command element began deciding whether or not to attack the enemy. Only if the "go" signal was given for an attack, was the MFB process put into motion. In the meantime, the enemy force would be placed under constant surveillance. One Viet Cong reconnaissance operative described how his reconnaissance squad carried out that surveillance:

"We stop when we are about 300 or 500 meters from the advancing unit. At that distance we can see what the ARVN soldiers are doing. We retreat while they advance and we always keep the same distance from them. Our squad will then be split into three cells. The first cell stays 300 meters from the enemy, the second cell 100 meters farther, and the third 100 meters from the second. The last two cells will remain still while the first cell pulls back. When the first cell meets the second cell, the reconnaissance unit becomes the second cell. The first cell will hurry back and take a position 100 meters from the third cell waiting for their turn to come up again. One of them will have to run fast to the command staff and report the situation. This being done, he will have to come back to his cell at once. The same procedure must be followed by the second cell, and then by the third, and that is why the battalion command staff, although at a distance, could be constantly informed of the ARVN soldiers' moves."[314]

If the command element decided to attack the enemy force, an advanced detachment composed of ten to thirty percent of the total available NVA maneuvering force, moved out immediately. The fast-moving, lightly equipped forward detachment was required to have sufficient combat capability to contain the target enemy unit in a predetermined area. The NVA command echelon directing the MFB rapidly established a forward command post (CP) which moved behind the advanced detachment. The main CP, located in the communist stronghold, was in constant contact with the forward CP.

The main command post was located near the base of departure, along with the main effort force, throughout the battle. Some documents have compared the NVA base of departure to a U.S. attack position or line of departure. However, the base of departure was the bivouac area where the main force was located. From there, various detachments received assignments, organized for combat, and advanced to the battlefield. When the main effort force moved forward, so did the command elements located at the base of departure.

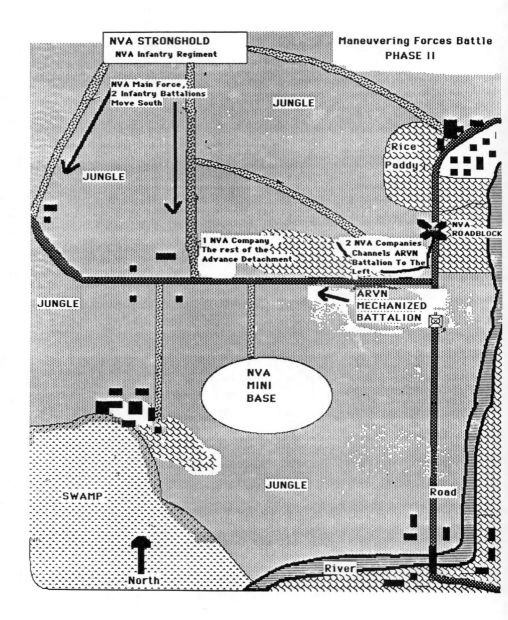

NVA STRONGHOLD
NVA Infantry Regiment

Maneuvering Forces Battle
PHASE II

JUNGLE

NVA Main Force,
2 Infantry Battalions
Move South

JUNGLE

Rice
Paddy

NVA
ROADBLOCK

1 NVA Company
The rest of the
Advance Detachment

2 NVA Companies
Channels ARVN
Battalion To The
Left

JUNGLE

ARVN
MECHANIZED
BATTALION

NVA
MINI
BASE

SWAMP

JUNGLE

Road

North

River

178

As the events of the MFB proceeded, the command element needed time to organize and begin operations. The advance detachment provided that time, enabling the NVA unit leadership to rapidly prepare for battle and move toward the sound of the guns.

The Chu Luc required the advance detachment to "intercept, attrit, and bait the enemy into an anticipated area, while our main force maneuvers from a concealed staging area to close in, attack, and destroy the enemy."[315]

The advance detachment had to hold the enemy force until the main force arrived. One document mentioned a phenomenal advance rate for the main effort force, "the distance is approximately 15 kilometers and is supposed to be traversed at the rate of 7 kilometers per hour."[316] Another Viet Cong document stated that the detachment must force "the enemy into a disadvantageous area almost in consistence with the battle plan."[317]

The advance detachment was usually assigned several missions:

1. Engage the enemy and seek to force him onto the defensive.
2. Report continuously on enemy movements.
3. Engage the enemy for at least three hours unless the main effort force was very close to the battle area.
4. Maneuver the enemy unit toward the designated battle area.
5. Participate in the battle of annihilation.

During Operation Attleboro in 1966, an American force was fixed by a communist advanced detachment. That force was using a prepared bunker line to fix the Americans. The NVA maneuver was described as follows: "It was steady and rhythmic: They were chanting directions to one another as they moved from bunker to bunker within the tree line. Hardison followed the beat, also. The VC were deploying more people around the clearing and the fire intensified in an ever-widening circle."[318]

As the main effort force moved toward the designated battleground, antiaircraft elements were deployed along the route, with one third moving and two thirds in firing positions at all time. The flak unit performed that maneuver in a leap frog fashion.

One or more NVA units were usually dispatched from the main body to distract allied attention away from the main force. For example, smoky fires might be lit or smoke grenades detonated, to attract enemy aircraft away from the battle area.

The NVA main effort force moved from its base of departure in columns along one to three avenues of approach. The most concealed routes would be preferred, especially treelines and overgrown waterways banks.

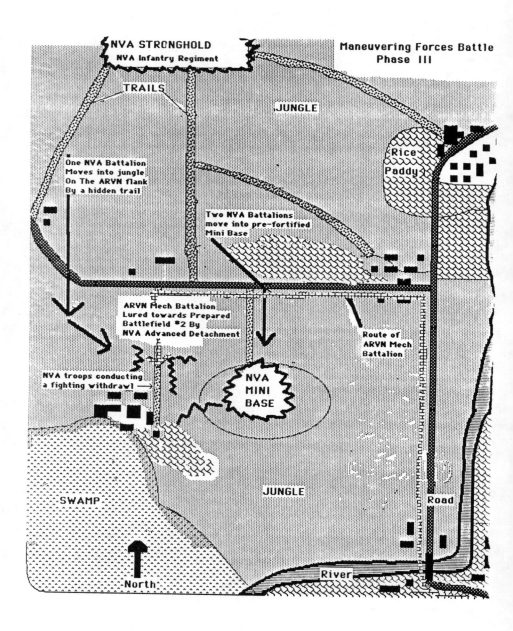

NVA STRONGHOLD
NVA Infantry Regiment

Maneuvering Forces Battle
Phase III

TRAILS

JUNGLE

Rice Paddy

One NVA Battalion
Moves into jungle
On The ARVN flank
By a hidden trail

Two NVA Battalions
move into pre-fortified
Mini Base

ARVN Mech Battalion
Lured towards Prepared
Battlefield #2 By
NVA Advanced Detachment

Route of
ARVN Mech
Battalion

NVA troops conducting
a fighting withdrawl →

NVA
MINI
BASE

SWAMP

JUNGLE

Road

North

River

180

Upon reaching the enemy force, the main effort maneuvered along one flank and shook out its deployment. The first unit that made contact with the enemy force became the advanced detachment which attempted to "front lock" the enemy by fixing him. Recoilless rifle teams would rapidly move to cover avenues of approach or threatening enemy armor. Mortars and other supporting weapons would move into position. Antiaircraft weapons would be positioned to simultaneously protect the main CP and support the main assault element.

Simultaneously a deep flanking unit, the rear blocking element, would swing wide grasping for the enemy rear. The main assault element, the main effort of the attack, would move up to the rear or flank of the front lock.

"When the rear blocking element occupies its assigned positions, the entire battalion opens fire. Battalion mortar fire is first concentrated to help the rear blocking element seize its area. Then it is switched to aid the main assault element. As the battle proceeds, mortars are attached to or accompany the infantry of the main assault element to provide against targets of opportunity."[319] The main assault element then maneuvered forward, passing to the flank of the advanced detachment. Only about one-tenth of the NVA force would be held back as a reserve.

During Operation Abilene, a search and destroy operation carried out by the U.S. 1st Infantry Division in Phuoc Tuy and Long Khan Provinces, the Americans were looking for the Viet Cong D-800 Battalion. On April 11, 1966 Charlie Company of the 2nd Battalion of the 16th Infantry Regiment stumbled into a prepared battlefield next to D-800s' base camp. They were met with the "chung, chung of two .50 caliber and pat, pat, pat of eight .30 caliber machine guns from outside of the company perimeter.

"D-800 had moved its heavy weapons out of the nearby base camp and placed them all around Charlie Company's steadily shrinking circle. Machine gun bullets, especially .50 caliber, are lethal not only because they come in streams but also because they are heavy and cut through bush and branches without losing accuracy or killing power. Two .30 caliber and one .50 caliber were slamming rounds into the 3d and 4th platoons on the company's northwest point; a second .50 caliber and a .30 caliber were firing into 2d platoon holding the northeast quadrant of the perimeter, and two .30 calibers were raking 1st Platoon in the southeast quadrant."[320]

Charlie company was destroyed in a classical NVA Maneuvering Force Battle.

The Power Raid: Primary Offensive Maneuver

The power raid was an NVA narrow front assault conducted against enemy installations, defensive perimeters or base camps. It usually involved at least one battalion.

The NVA power raid unfolded in several phases:

- Reconnaissance: Inside and outside of the target. Consultation and coordination with NVA agents within the objective.
- Preparations and planning: Logistics, movement, security, deployment, ambushes, assault, mop up and withdrawal.
- Movement into the objective area.
- Deployment: Ambush units deployed in sites targeted against relief troops. Deployment of penetration, support and shock units.
- Assault: Penetration, supporting fires and the assault.
- Mop up: Finish off opposition and loot spoils of battle.
- Withdrawal: Escape enemy aerial and artillery counteraction.

Recon units spent some time studying the target and its surroundings. They gathered information on enemy troops, the terrain, avenues of approach and potential deployment areas. They were expected to abide by meticulous guidelines. For example, recon data secured for an assault on an allied fire base might require them to "make a separate report on each side of the post from outside to the center. For example: Approaching the post from the east, we will find an open area, then a bamboo fence, barbed wire fence No.3, ditch No.2, a spike field at big ditch No.3 adjacent to the earth wall, search lights, earth wall with moat behind it, earth wall at barracks, post yard, and blockhouse. Remember to clearly note down the size of each thing and space between the obstacle and the fortification. This will be useful to each separate attacking column . . .

"Alarm methods and signals . . .

"Patrol regulations, guards inside the post, guard strength, watch tours, guard rotation at the watch house, search light and flare procedures, alarm regulations, weaknesses in the guard, the direction of the enemy's primary defenses. A study is made of the number of available infantry reinforcements, their routes of advance, and their reaction time. Careful study is given to possible sites for ambush of reinforcements."[321]

A "post chart" was usually made up for each fire base objective. That chart described fortified works, bunkers, mine fields, walls, moats, barbed wire obstacles and patrol routes.

In many instances, NVA recon parties penetrated the inside of the objective area either overtly, disguised as someone who had a right to be there, or covertly, at night. Such reconnaissance was intended to identify areas not observable from outside the enemy works. Special attention was given to housing areas, communications centers, ammunition dumps, crew-served weapons emplacements and the command post.

Coordination was also effected with red agents working inside of the target area or posing as members of enemy armed forces. Attacks were synchronized, whenever possible, with NVA agent guard duty schedules.

"If the front decided to destroy a post where a front spy was living, we had first to ask his family to come to the post to call him back to the village to receive instructions. In general, the front only launched an attack at the moment this spy was on sentry duty at night. We then used a conventional secret signal to let him know that we were ready to attack. The signal which was most often used was to turn on a flashlight three times and the spy replied by three strokes of his lighter. We acknowledged reception of his reply by turning the flashlight on once more and then we sneaked into the post. The spy would let us come into the post before opening fire. I noticed that the GVN had lost many posts because the front had spies to help it."[322]

After the reconnaissance data was collected and processed the planning and preparation phase began: "We usually carried out an attack operation only when we had obtained reliable information as to the number of enemy troops, their weapons and their position. And we always ensured that we were absolutely superior in numbers before starting the attack. If not, we preferred to avoid any contact with the enemy."[323]

The plans/preparations phase was divided into several components including: Standard logistics preparation; labor mobilization and coordination activities; Secrecy, deception and movement planning; The scheme of maneuver, including the assault, and any necessary ambushes; and Rehearsals.

Standard Logistics Preparations

Assembling food and ammunition; planning for resupply efforts; Mobilizing porters for supply-transport, clearing the battlefield, securing dead and wounded, and collecting captured booty; Preparing cache sites for captured booty; Establishing casualty clearing and burial facilities; Coordination with local logistics personnel, village militia, agents and party members. Reviewing routes and resource locations contiguous to those routes.

Standard Secrecy, Deception and Movement Planning

Initially inform only leaders concerning the objective and routes; Designate one or more units as diversionary troops and assign them

deception missions in support of the assault; Obscure the unit destination by: moving along circuitous and indirect avenues of approach;
disguising the movement to appear as routine, by conducting the
movement within the confines of the network of unit campsites and
bases; Near the objective, use guides to facilitate fast night movement.

"My unit was stationed at Long Tien village at that time. We moved at
4:30 PM but, as usual, I did not know what our destination was. We arrived
at the battlefield at 11 PM and began to dig foxholes at once. I knew that we
were going to fight but I did not know the name of the post then standing in
front of me with all its electric lights sparkling all around it. I then recalled
that on the previous days, all the platoon leaders of my company had
attended special sessions held by my company commander, and I understood
that they had gathered to learn about the plan of attack. And I realized they
had kept it a secret from the squad leaders."[324]

"After the terrain and regular moves of the GVN battalion had been
reconnoitered, the 514th battalion then camping in Tam Binh set out toward
Long Tien. Tam Binh was very close to Long Tien but, to fool the GVN
spies, the battalion first came to My Long village and came into Long Tien
only on the second night . . . Tam Binh-My Long is on the camp network
(and the movement appeared routine)."[325]

Components of the Scheme of Maneuver

Division of the assault force into four elements: penetration, support,
shock and ambush; Identification of assembly areas and approach/
withdrawal routes; Schedule/timing; Designation of specific targets;
Designation of signals for attack/withdrawal contingencies.

"(The) Attack was generally launched upon completion of sand table
training (rehearsals). If the attack was not launched, the plan was considered
as disclosed and cancelled . . ."[326]

"When the 261st battalion attacked a post and if its position was not
revealed, it was almost sure that it would come out a victor because it always
applied a great number of soldiers and weapons against weak defenders."[327]

Power assaults were always launched during the hours of darkness, usually
at midnight or later. The NVA wanted to be able to withdraw under the
cloak of darkness.

Upon reaching the objective area, the main assault force moved into an
objective assembly area, while the ambushing force moved to ambush sites
along pre-selected enemy avenues of approach:

"In the attack on Tan Thuan post, two of the three companies of the 514th battalion were allocated to the interception of reinforcements. Sometimes the main objective is the destruction of the reinforcements and the encirclement or harassment of posts is sometimes only a trick to lure reinforcements into ambush . . ."[328]

After dark, crew-served supporting weapons were moved into position and the assault began. No preparatory fires were used in order to retain the element of surprise, as a penetration or sapper unit stealthily crept toward the enemy defensive obstacle line. The penetration element rapidly cut one or more lanes through the enemy barriers and penetrated inside the enemy position. Upon hearing explosions set off by the penetrating element inside the enemy lines, the shock (main assault) force ran forward. They dashed through the lanes cut by the penetrating element, firing from the hip. At the same time mortars and other supporting fires opened up on designated enemy targets and in support of the shock element.

"By this reason we must find every way to concentrate our strength, fire power, and efforts to annihilate the enemy main body first, then we exterminate his remaining elements. However, this main body is usually the strongest element of the enemy. Thus we have to take advantage of the *enemy gap and weak points* to exterminate his main body. For example, to attack a post, we will take advantage of the darkness and carelessness of the enemy sentries to send our sappers deep into the enemy area and attack his command post or field artillery, then open the way for guerrillas to assault and harass his defense system at the beginning.

"I noticed that, in an attack against a GVN post, the very first thing the Front did was try to destroy the telephone of the post or its telephone lines. In the attack against the Nha Tho La post, the primary mission of the recoilless rifles and B-40s was to destroy the means of communications of the post to prevent it from calling in relief troops."[329]

Throughout Indochina the fury of the power raid swept irresistibly forward.

CHAPTER 9

NVA Defensive Maneuver

Everywhere in Indochina the Chu Luc built their fortresses and fortified zones. In answer to American aerial and artillery superiority, vast labyrinths of tunneled and bunkered defense lines crisscrossed every type of terrain. Mountains and lowlands alike were transformed into impregnable bastions similar to the huge fortified zones found only on the Eastern Front in World War II.

American troops were usually overwhelmed by the professionally complex enemy defensive array. An American airborne officer who had fought near Dak To described his perplexity: "The enemy defenders would hold their fire until we were right on top of them—then open up. All of the enemy positions were low silhouette bunker-type for automatic weapons and spider-trap foxholes for riflemen. These positions were so well concealed that you couldn't get an exact fit on a machine gun that was firing from just ten meters away."[330]

A lieutenant from the U.S. 25th Infantry Division was equally dumbfounded by enemy defenses: "We didn't have fields of fire because of the thick vegetation; the Cong got around this problem by pre-cutting small tunnels through the underbrush. These fire lanes were cleverly concealed and gave his machine guns excellent grazing fire; you couldn't see the lanes until you were almost in them. The only thing we could do was dig in, so we scraped out holes and there we sat facing Charlie for three days while his buzz saw ripped away.

"All of the enemy fortifications had firing slits so small that it was impossible to toss a grenade inside. The firing slits were just a few inches above the ground and on all sides of the bunker. They were firing from 360 degrees and each bunker was mutually supporting. The enemy had stay behinds to our rear and flanks. These guys sniped at us with rifle grenades and sniper fire."[331]

Although the Chu Luc essentially was an offensive fighting machine, it was also adept at defensive maneuver. So well attuned to the defensive arts was the NVA, that they riddled all of Indochina with their fortified positions and villages.

"Beneath each hut are deep, heavily reinforced bunkers to be used as air raid positions and fighting positions. Under the entire village, an ingenious tunnel network has been carved out by men who burrowed like moles deep into the earth. Large enough for a man to walk upright, these tunnels allow the enemy to reinforce any threatened sector . . . quickly and with relative impunity from artillery and tactical air fires."[332]

Fortified base camps ringed with deeply dug bunker lines were invariably found everywhere, even in the deepest jungle, where "he built his fortified base camps and located his bunkers on ridges and in the heads of draws, in hopes that a U.S. platoon or company would blunder into the area. The enemy habitually emplaced his fighting positions to fire down a valley or ridge."[333]

In every rural base camp and campsite, extensive fortifications were found: "His base camp area is completely sealed by fortified positions, intercon-nected by tunnels and communications trenches. . . All of the enemy's defensive positions are cleverly camouflaged and blend in perfectly with the jungle background."[334]

Although the NVA did have a unique approach to defensive warfare it was radically different from the western view. In fact Chu Luc defenses constantly confounded professional American military officers:

"These fortified positions are not established in any set pattern. Many of the positions I have seen were not tactically sound and appeared to be a disorganized series of fortifications, not unlike a mole colony. But, then, many things that the enemy does in Vietnam are tactically difficult to understand. I have found positions dug into saddles between hills, on military crests of hills, deep in almost inaccessible draws, and on ridges leading into high ground. At times the positions would be part of a continuous defensive complex surrounding a base camp; other positions would be found scattered about in isolated, indefensible locations."[335]

Fortified Villages

In June 1966 the NVA fought several battles in and around Truong Luong village near coastal Tuy Hoa. They chose to fight a defensive battle from that village because of the strength of its fortifications and "the maneuver advantage deriving from its tunnel system."[336]

The NVA controlled village, one of dozens in the Tuy Hoa area, was laid out like so many other red fortified villages:

"The fortified village's main defensive positions incorporate the textbook principles and are models of well balanced, integrated defensive positions. Firing bunkers—waiting for the unwary in patches of bamboo, in tree lines, in hollowed out anthills, and in the bottoms of hedgerow walls—are connected by deep zigzag trenches which permit the defenders to withdraw or reinforce quickly and easily. Superbly concealed, these firing positions are fronted by gardens of razor sharp punji stakes and numerous booby traps. Early warning outposts are well to the front and along likely avenues of approach; one man observation posts are hidden in trees throughout the village."[337]

"Truong Luong was served by one of the most extensive tunnel systems anywhere in the country."[338] That system afforded the NVA defense of the area great advantages. They could move from one firing point to another without exposure to harm. The strong tunnel construction also made them bomb proof shelters as well.

An American platoon was caught in the open on the outskirts of Trung Long and decimated by interlocking fire from three innocent looking hay stacks. "The killing fire that had downed Second Platoon had come from under the haystacks. They were mere camouflage, topping off three *concrete* bunkers, fixed with fire slots, armed with light machine guns, and equipped with field telephones. Not one thing in the field had indicated the existence of a military position anywhere nearby. The ground had not been tramped over; the grass was not beaten down. Not one foxhole marred the surface. The appearance of innocence had deceived the platoon completely."[339]

Highly sophisticated NVA concrete fortifications were not rare in Vietnam, as one American Army officer revealed: "In the Iron Triangle, I have seen reinforced concrete pill boxes with heavy machineguns mounted on rails. The machinegun could be easily moved on its tracks to fire from any point along the thirty foot aperture. These particular positions were also supported by tactical wire and antipersonnel minefields."[340]

The NVA preferred to fight from fortified villages and habitually occupied them during their movement sequence within communist controlled areas. They used them as safe harbors for rest, and as staging areas.

Communist units didn't have to fight if they didn't want to. They could easily hide in their invisible tunnel systems. A captured NVA captain described one manifestation of that option: "My battalion was hiding in a village near Bong Son when a U.S. patrol passed within 100 meters. We were prepared to fight should they enter the village, but they passed on. It was my regiment's rule to never fight Americans except only after careful preparation."[341]

The fortified villages were easy to occupy and defend. The NVA simply manned the defenses already prepared by forced peasant labor. One American observer spoke in awe of the communist fortified villages:

"One of the enemy's favorite battlegrounds was the fortified village. This usually consisted of several hamlets prepared with extensive fighting positions, trenchworks, connected tunnels, and spider holes. The fighting bunkers often had five to seven feet of overhead cover and could take a direct hit from a 155mm howitzer round. The bunkers were placed to cover avenues of approach and were interspersed throughout the village, with tunnels connecting the bunkers and trenches, thereby allowing the enemy to disappear and reappear firing from another location. Trees, shrubs and even the earth itself were reshaped to conceal these positions.

"At first glance, there seemed to be no logic or method to these defensive works. But upon closer investigation, one could find an intricate, well-planned defensive position that took advantage of existing cover and concealment, natural barriers and avenues of approach into and within the village.

"The enemy elected to use a hamlet or a village as a battleground for one or more reasons:

- He expected to inflict enough casualties on U.S. troops during the attack to justify his making a stand.
- The village offered the enemy a labor source to prepare the fortifications.
- In the open valleys and coastal lowlands, the villages concealed a great deal of natural cover and concealment.
- The hamlets in a village were usually spread out and their arrangement offered many avenues of escape.

The enemy's usual plan of battle followed the same pattern: . . . opening fire, usually 15 to 25 meters . . . hugging tactics . . . to get U.S. soldiers so closely engaged that they could not effectively use artillery and tactical air support.

- The enemy felt that if he inflicted several casualties in his initial burst, the U.S. troops would become involved in trying to get the wounded back to the rear for evacuation. . . (becoming) easy targets. . .
- Another facet of his battle plan was to fight viciously until dark; then, using the cover of darkness, he escaped by using one of his many preplan-

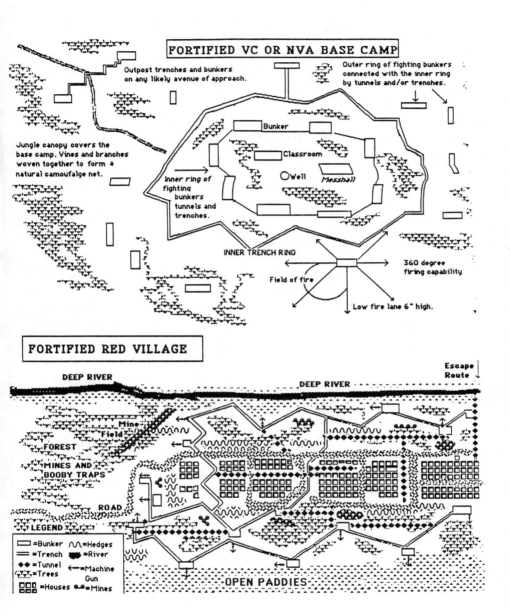

FORTIFIED VC OR NVA BASE CAMP

Outpost trenches and bunkers on any likely avenue of approach.

Outer ring of fighting bunkers connected with the inner ring by tunnels and/or trenches.

Jungle canopy covers the base camp. Vines and branches woven together to form a natural camoufalge net.

Bunker

Classroom

Well

Messhall

Inner ring of fighting bunkers tunnels and trenches.

INNER TRENCH RING

Field of fire

360 degree firing capability

Low fire lane 6" high.

FORTIFIED RED VILLAGE

Escape Route

DEEP RIVER

DEEP RIVER

Mine Field

FOREST

MINES AND BOOBY TRAPS

ROAD

LEGEND

▭ =Bunker	∧∧=Hedges		
= =Trench	▓=River		
◆◆ =Tunnel	←=Machine		
⊻⊻=Trees	Gun		
▦▦=Houses	•○=Mines		

OPEN PADDIES

191

ned escape routes, carrying off his dead and wounded, their weapons, and even empty cartridges."[342]

When American troops attacked Phu Huu 2, near II Corps' Landing Zone Bird, in 1966, they were rapidly pinned to the ground, dazed and bleeding, their objective transformed from fighting to cutting losses, evacuating wounded and bugging out. General S.L.A. Marshall described the situation as follows: "It is a situation that too frequently occurs in the Vietnam fighting. The forward element, losing men and becoming pinned down, compromises the position of all others. What has started out as an attack, loses all forms and deteriorates into a costly rescue act."[343]

Defensive Maneuver and Battlefield Mobility

The Chu Luc adopted defensive measures only as a prelude to the offensive. Realizing that wars are won only by offensive action, NVA defensive efforts were actually maneuvers made to retain battlefield mobility and the initiative. Viet Cong Strategist were very emphatic about mobility:

"Only highly mobile troops and firepower in counteroperation defense can ensure timely reinforcement to units that are in danger. They can also aid units that are being annihilated by enemy aircraft and artillery and, when necessary, can concentrate forces to conduct mobile attacks, ambushes, or raids against an enemy element."[344]

Prepared battlefields with shelters and defensive positions along routes and in unexpected areas, facilitated mobility. Foot-mobile troops could weave in and out of protected areas which functioned like turtle shells, offering both protection and cover.

Allied sweeps sporadically rolled through NVA controlled areas. The awkwardness and rigidity of those sweeps enabled the reds to perfect their mobility enhancing defensive tactics by practicing them against an amateurish enemy. The sweeps were easy to predict because the allies invariably telegraphed their punches by indicators which the NVA dutifully listed:

"a. Making use of informers to collect information, spies to conduct investigations, and Special Forces personnel to arrest people and seize documents.

b. The conduct of air reconnaissance, placement of diversionary troops, and spreading false news.

c. Conferences between command echelons and local authorities to formulate plans.

d. Restriction of the soldiers' movements, blockage of roads in preparation for the operation. Harassment by aircraft in those areas bordering the location where the sweep will be conducted."[345]

Nor did the reds have to worry about facing large enemy forces. The allies usually sent small units against them, operating in abbreviated time frames:

"The (GVN) force participating in a raid is usually not very large in order to ensure its mobility and preserve secrecy. It consists of one or two battalions only, heliborne to the battlefield to attack one of our companies. The operation lasts two or three hours."[346]

Defensive Maneuvering

When allied troops entered a communist operational area they would usually encounter NVA troops conducting mobile reconnaissance and defensive operations. Such maneuvers sometimes required a wide fighting style with a battalion spread out over a potential battlefield 5 kilometers long.[347] A widely spaced communist defensive battle deployment might require attacking forces to spread out over thirteen or more kilometers. Yet a battalion can only cover so much ground: "it was impossible to seal off a pocket in an airtight fashion as long as the battalion had to hold more than 1500 yards of ground."[348]

If the above calculation is true, it would require nine battalions to cover thirteen kilometers, if each held 1,550 yards (1,372 meters). In any case, it was usually impossible for allied forces to concentrate a division (nine battalions) around an area within twenty-four hours of cornering a red unit. In fact there is no record of any allied unit piling onto an area with nine or more battalions within twenty-four hours. The allies were slowed down in their mobility by the troop deployment time factors required to fight a technological, helicopter centered, war. Any "cornered" communist units would thus enjoy a day or two of rich opportunity to exploit gaps in the allied cordon and to cause casualties. Then they would escape, laughing all the way to the river bank.

Communist campsites and base areas were carefully chosen to avoid constrictions on mobility. The terrain was carefully surveyed to determine its military characteristics.

Viet Cong Campsite Terrain Imperatives

• Campsites must be selected which provide both favorable defensive locales and several avenues of escape.

- Very detailed maps must be drawn of the surrounding terrain indicating every possible path that can be used.
- All concealed tunnels, trenches and hides interconnected with defended areas must also be mapped.
- Night movement routes must be chosen with different criteria than day routes.

By organizing the terrain, the reds were able to fend off most incursions into their habitat.

"The counter sweep operation site was within our base. As it has long been liberated, the people's movement was high and combat villages had been established (specifically, fencing in the village, digging air-raid shelters along the village roads, along creeks and in the people's houses, and digging trenches against M113 APCs). The village guerrilla force was relatively strong and the people were experienced in countering sweep-operation and avoiding enemy aircraft and artillery."[349]

When surprised or forced to fight in a fortified area or village, Viet Cong troops would usually fight all day and exfiltrate at night. After slipping through the enemy lines, they would rendezvous in a safe rallying area. However, communist troops might not withdraw from a fortified village for several days if they thought that by staying longer they could cause more enemy casualties and still get away.

"If attacked during the occupation of these positions, he will fight a determined and tenacious defense while the main body withdraws along previously selected escape routes. After the main body has safely withdrawn and all supplies and equipment have been evacuated, the delaying force will then give up the fight and break contact."[350]

Reconnaissance stay-behind parties and communist agents, located outside the enemy cordon around a defended communist fortified area, maintained communications with the "surrounded" NVA unit. Closely reconnoitering the allied dispositions, the outside recon troops reported the possible routes of escape through the allied lines to their comrades "trapped" inside.[351]

"The secret withdrawing action requires an investigation by the reconnaissance men. They should have a firm knowledge about the open slots through which we can move out and also the point of assembly. At this time, a deceiving combat element should be left behind and should be the last to move out. In this connection, it is necessary to make a calculation on the route: rivers, canals, and times. We will usually withdraw during the night after an element has encountered the enemy during the day."[352]

Communist troops frequently elected to counterattack the enemy which

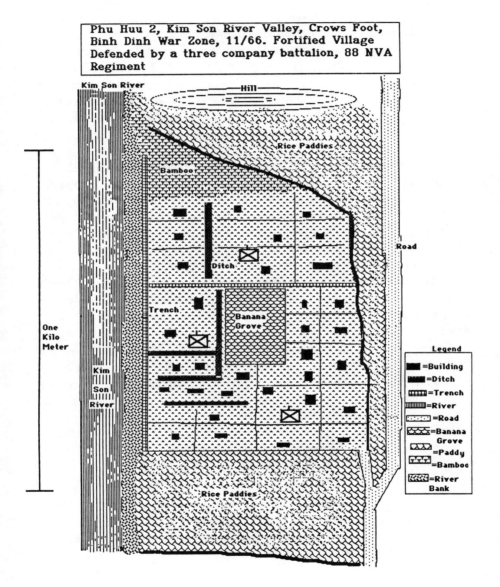

Phu Huu 2, Kim Son River Valley, Crows Foot, Binh Dinh War Zone, 11/66. Fortified Village Defended by a three company battalion, 88 NVA Regiment

Kim Son River

Hill

Rice Paddies

Bamboo

Road

Ditch

Trench

Banana Grove

One Kilo Meter

Kim Son River

Legend

■ =Building
▨ =Ditch
▥ =Trench
▦ =River
⋯ =Road
▩ =Banana Grove
⋀⋀ =Paddy
⋎⋎ =Bamboo
▨ =River Bank

Rice Paddies

supposedly had them trapped. In the dead of night, Chu Luc *Bo Dai* (infantry) would stealthily creep forward through the surrounding host and, upon signal, sweep forward in a powerful and shocking surprise attack against an enemy night bivouac.

"Usually enemy sweep operations last a few days with several elements moving toward the pre-determined concentration point. Consequently, the enemy usually has to bivouac on open fields at night. The distance between various units varies with the size of the unit. Their fortifications are very simple. The enemy usually takes advantage of natural terrain and encamps in a close formation. . . The enemy morale, fear of being attacked and the poor organization of his artillery support are objective factors very favorable for our raid.

"Enemy weaknesses can often be found within their cantonments. During the day, the enemy circulates in disorder without regard to any formation. At night their troops gather in sections. However, their firepower has become restricted and their artillery and mechanized equipment lose their effectiveness. Therefore, we should get information on the enemy situation and organize a raid on their bivouacs, especially their command post and artillery or mechanized equipment section, in order to acquire easy gains.

"A raid on the enemy bivouac should be organized with light units, which can make a secret approach in a short period of time and then suddenly open fire. A deep thrust is made into the center to separate the enemy troops for annihilation.

"During the countersweep a raid does not require careful preparation. It is necessary to act quickly in a short time, and to organize *strong raiding arrows* which must have a factor of bravery in fighting, and can assault hastily and fiercely. We would lose excellent opportunities to destroy the enemy if we desire to be well prepared and well equipped before launching a raid on an enemy bivouac. We need to develop the techniques of raiding during the enemy operation, in order to disrupt the enemy."[353]

Defensive Deployments

NVA defensive areas always included mines, booby traps and other obstacles. The reds frequently incorporated natural obstacles such as waterways, including ditches, canals and dikes, into their defenses. They sought to channel enemy troops and vehicles into pre-selected killing grounds. Such defenses impeded the maneuver of mechanized vehicles. Enemy defensive positions were always modern and well planned too.

"The enemy occupies these defensive positions much like a U.S. unit. An outpost line is established several hundred meters to the front; coupled with trail watchers and local patrolling, this line provides early warning.

"The positions are mutually supporting, extend in great depth, and are virtually impossible to locate because of the heavy jungle vegetation and the expertise of the enemy in camouflage."[354]

To prevent unnecessary losses, the communists kept the precise location of their fortifications secret. They camouflaged them expertly, exploiting the very size of their base area for greater concealment:

"Next to Hoa My is Binh Ninh campsite. This campsite is regarded as a very good one. The site is large and is covered with dense foliage too. The width of the campsite gives us a special advantage; it confuses the GVN artillery about where to shell."[355]

To further obscure their locations, the NVA constructed dummy positions as a deception measure:

"Recently, enemy artillery shelling and strikes have been relentlessly conducted against our routes, combat fortifications, sites of repeated attacks by friendly forces, frequently used assembly areas such as road junctions and intersections, . . . uncamouflaged trenches, etc.

"To prevent the enemy from bombarding the villages, we must use deception by setting up dummy troop locations in little frequented areas, far away from roads and hamlets. These dummy positions must be camouflaged but not thoroughly enough to make it impossible for the enemy to see them. A dummy anti-aircraft position will be set up 200 or 300 meters away in order to attract the enemy fire and avoid his destruction of villages and hamlets."[356]

L and V Shaped Fortifications

When digging in a fortified area, the reds shaped their fortifications like a capital letter L. That shape, which made crossfires much easier, was constructed in two mutually supporting trench lines connected to bunkers.

"As matters stand, the Front soldiers can shoot at the advancing column of attackers and force them to withdraw and when the enemy withdraws to shell the defenders, the latter can take refuge in the covered portion of the trench and therefore remain unharmed. If the enemy stops shelling to launch a new assault, the Front's soldiers once again move to the embrasure of the trench to fight."[357]

The L shaped fortification provided a rational method of preserving defending troops for counteraction in the face of enemy artillery bombardment and set piece assaults. Such fortifications allowed defenders to avoid punishing supporting fires, recoil before determined enemy attacks, and then spring back at the enemy before he had time to consolidate his gains. The system was very similar to defensive tactics pioneered by the German Army.

Imperatives of L Shaped Fortified Systems

- Individual trenches 1.2 meters long, 1.2 meters deep and .4 meters wide.
- An embankment of earth with firing slits or embrasures to be placed in front of each trench.
- A bunker built at right angles to each trench. It is one meter long with an earthen roof forty centimeters thick reinforced with banana tree trunks.
- Such fortifications must be built by troops in an unfortified area if they plan to remain there for at least a day.
- The separation between the two lines of fortification depends upon the width of the defended area, the terrain, and the vegetation. If the defended area is very narrow the lines may have to be built only fifty meters apart.
- If width is not a constraint, the separation between the two trenchlines must be large enough to prevent an enemy who has captured the first trenchline from seeing the second line. If heavy underbrush exists between the two lines they can be located nearer each other.
- No mines or booby traps are placed between the two lines.
- L shaped systems can be thrown up in one or two hours of battalion efforts.

The second line of fortifications, connected to the first line at both flanks, had several purposes including:

1. A fortified fallback position if defending troops were forced from the first line.
2. An assembly area for staging counterattacks.
3. A surprise ambush to be triggered from the trenchline against a pursuing enemy.
4. Flanking trenchline connections to get behind the enemy, who advances after capturing the first line. In that way the NVA could take him in the rear, or decapitate him by destroying his command element.

"The second line of trenches has great utility. If the Front soldiers are driven out of the first line of trenches they can withdraw to the second line and once again take advantage of prepared fortifications to continue to fight. Since the GVN soldiers do not have any fortifications to their advantage they would be easily pushed back against their first effort, and immediately after the withdrawal of the enemy, the Front soldiers would be ordered to come back to the first line of trenches."[358]

By covering the connecting flank trenches with earth and vegetation, thereby converting them into tunnels of approach, surprise flanking maneuvers would be enhanced. However, such usage would make flanking fire from those approaches impossible.

When artillery and aerial bombardment began to impact in the area of the L System, NVA troops would either seek shelter in bomb proof dugouts or withdraw to the second trenchline. Or the Bo Dai might shelter in the bunkers hidden in nearby hamlets, emerging to occupy the L System in time to meet the enemy assault. NVA troops were expected to occupy their firing positions when the enemy preparatory bombardment lifted. One Viet Cong battalion commander orchestrated his counter measures as follows:

"The main objective of enemy bombardments and shellings was the fortification line outside the village. When the enemy shelled and bombarded for a second time, the battalion conjectured that the enemy might land troops to conduct a sweep operation. It ordered detachments deployed at fortification lines outside the village to withdraw to the edge of the village to avoid enemy preparatory fire or troops landing right on the line."[359]

Another NVA defensive system was encountered near the Tae River and Plei Me Valley in 1965. That defensive deployment pattern was called the V System.

"More than 150 well-concealed fighting positions had been dug just inside the tree line along this V-shaped line of resistance. At the center of the V was a large open field, large enough to accommodate a dozen or so helicopters at one time. At the apex of the V were the bulk of the automatic weapons, sited to bring grazing fire across the clearing. The battalion commander deployed two companies into the lines of the V, and placed one platoon of the third company in a position where it would swing the door shut on the open end of the V, driving the attacking enemy force deeper into the trap. Two other platoons were placed in reserve and for local security. . . The fourth company, the weapons company, armed with four 82mm mortar tubes and five recoilless rifles, two 75mm and three 57mm, was positioned where it could bring fire upon the clearing. All fighting positions were, of course, well dug in and superbly camouflaged."[360]

The Soviets called such a position a "fire sack."[361]

NVA FORTIFICATIONS

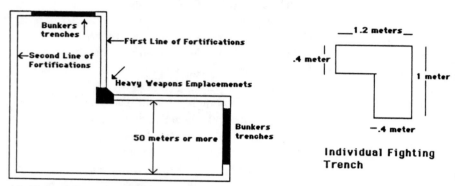

Bunkers trenches

First Line of Fortifications

Second Line of Fortifications

Heavy Weapons Emplacemenets

50 meters or more

Bunkers trenches

L Shaped Fortification

1.2 meters
.4 meter
1 meter
.4 meter

Individual Fighting Trench

Kieng or Tripod Defense In Depth

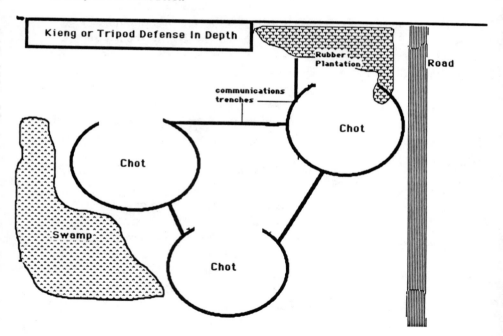

Rubber Plantation

Road

communications trenches

Chot

Chot

Chot

Swamp

Allied Operations Against NVA Fortified Areas

In April, 1968 the 3rd Battalion of the 26th U.S. Marine Regiment was helilifted onto Hill 881 South just outside the Khe Sahn perimeter. Close-in patrolling indicated that enemy fortifications extended to within 300 meters of Hill 881 South's defensive wire. Extensive marine bombardment of that intervening terrain forced an enemy withdrawal.

Now the marines turned their attention to Hill 881 North where an NVA battalion was dug in. That enemy battalion fortified area included bunkered strongpoints outposting Hill 881 North and numerous supporting weapons emplacements. The marines worried that their battalion attack would have to face 12.7mm heavy machine guns, 120mm mortars and 122mm/140mm rockets. They knew that Chu Luc 130mm and 152mm artillery, firing from Laos, had registered on all avenues of approach to Hill 881 North.

Attacking due north with all three rifle companies on line, two of the marine companies were temporarily pinned by an enemy outpost line on two ridge fingers in front of their main position. However, the fact that they were using sufficient troops for flanking leverage enabled the marines to envelope the outpost line and drive on towards their primary objective.

Some enemy units maneuvered to occupy reverse slope positions on the northern slope. One NVA company maneuvered forward on the southern slope of Hill 881 North to trap a marine company advancing toward it. That maneuver was spotted by the marine base of fire on Hill 881 South and blasted with hundreds of rounds of direct, 106mm recoilless rifle, fire. Enemy counter suppression fire with 122mm rockets failed as an enemy counter attack by fire was blunted.

Suddenly the enemy broke contact. The NVA left only 106 bodies on the battlefield.[362]

By May of 1969, I Corps' An Hoa Combat Base had been garrisoned by the 5th Marine Regiment for nearly four years. Yet that location, only twenty-five miles southwest of Da Nang, where the 1st Marine Division was deployed with a two-division sized force, was totally controlled by the Chu Luc. The An Hoa Base remained under siege, controlled by a "mortar belt" from which enemy troops ceaselessly pinned down the marines.

Nearby Charlie Ridge, home base for the 31st and 141st NVA Regiments, dominated the area which the marines called the Arizona Territory. The seven miles long by four miles wide Arizona Territory, a flatland just north of the An Hoa Base literally swarmed with red troops. For example, between April 22 and May 9, 1969 reported sightings in the northern part of the Arizona Territory included:

- The 31st NVA Regiment.
- Six battalion sized NVA forces.
- Ten platoon sized NVA forces.
- An NVA 122mm rocket unit.[363]

The Marines decided to send the better part of two marine battalions into Northern Arizona. There, they expected to encounter, as described in Marine operations order jargon, "Two NVA battalions, possibly 7th and 8th Bns of the 90th Regt. Estimated Bn strength approx 350 men armed with AK, SKS, 82mm mortars, 60mm mortars and B-40 rockets."[364]

The marines elected to use the familiar "hammer and anvil method," discredited as an offensive method in World War II. One marine battalion would attempt to drive fleeing NVA into another marine battalion "blocking force." Marine commanders described their operation in dramatic terms: "the success of the operation depended on the ability of the assaulting and blocking forces to keep the enemy off balance and disorganized. This would cause his resistance to be limited to fragmented, stimulus-response type reactions, with the stimuli being provided by the Marine field commanders. If the enemy had been able to anticipate the Marines intentions prior to first light on the first morning, he would have evacuated the area or dug in and put up a well-organized defensive action or counterttacked."[365]

Unleashing a sustained hurricane of supporting drum fire, the marine battalions awkwardly launched their three day raid. The reds fought a delaying battle, losing less than a company's worth of men. There is evidence that major parts of the 36th and 141st NVA Regiments were in the area and escaped the marine "trap," preferring to avoid the tremendous weight of supporting bombardment thrown into the area. NVA trenchlines and bomb proofed shelters, found everywhere in the area, protected red troops from being more severely punished by the marine bombardment. Arizona remained a Chu Luc stronghold area.

NVA Defense in Depth Along Constricted Terrain

On certain occasions, the NVA was able to set up defensive deployments in great depth along constricted enemy avenues of approach. Since allied forces insisted upon employing company size forces to find the enemy, the allies unilaterally eliminated sufficient troop strength for flanking maneuvers. Once a company was deployed there were insufficient troops remaining for any sort of offensive maneuver.

After contact with the NVA was made by an allied company, it would curl into a defensive perimeter and call down the hellfire of abundant American fire support. If the Americans decided to reinforce that isolated company, they always used piecemeal reinforcement, preferably with units whose commanders were not acquainted.

American generals were hypnotized by the "task force concept," a method of military organization which they misinterpreted and misapplied. Task forces were conceived as temporary expedients only used by veteran armies with superior training, leadership and doctrine. Neither the U.S. Army nor Marines qualified on that score.

The task force expedient was supposed to be employed for some good reason and every effort was supposed to be made to include troops who had worked together before. Professional armies which utilized task forces always returned to use of the established order of battle, using companies and battalions assigned to the same regiment, as soon as possible. They realized that normal operations were best served by units and commanders who knew each other and could work together. Joint experience built up a military-style, familial cohesion and unified, force-multiplying morale.

American generals, being managerial oriented, considered men and units to be nothing more than interchangeable machine parts. The misunderstood task force concept seemed to advance that idea. American generals preferred troops who were all cogs in a bureaucratic green machine.

American Army and Marine commanders were constantly detaching, attaching and otherwise jumbling their troop units. That crazy quilt pattern of strangers mixing with strangers only multiplied the ills caused by the bankrupt individual replacement policy.

Marine Colonel Peatross attributed the limited success of his 7th Marine Regiment directly to its short term avoidance of some aspects of the task force concept. He claimed that the 7th Marines had two advantages over most other U.S. regiments in Vietnam: "It had one regimental commander and no changes in the battalion commanders, and these units were always to-gether."[366]

What was universally achieved by American ground forces in Vietnam was a mass lowering of all units to the lowest common denominator. A paralysis of command and function was the end result which, as a self-imposed handicap, constantly impeded American maneuver efforts.

Some few professional American military officers despised and resisted the task force insanity. Marine Colonel Leon N. Utter was one of those profes-sionals:

"Platoons, companies and battalions are **not** interchangeable parts of identical machines. . . As a battalion commander, I frequently was directed to provide a platoon or a company to someone else's headquarters for

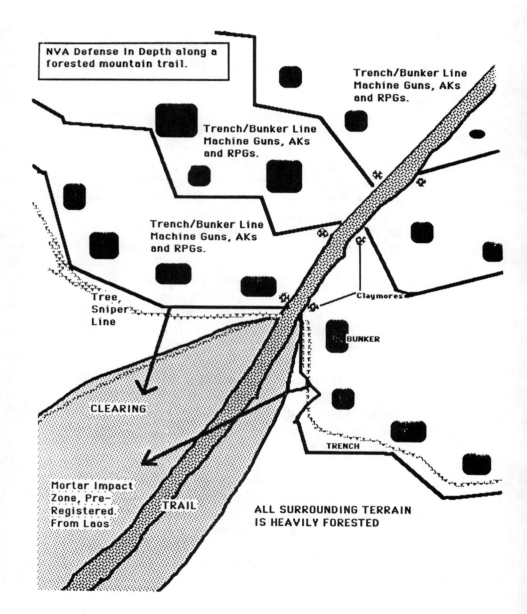

NVA Defense In Depth along a forested mountain trail.

Trench/Bunker Line Machine Guns, AKs and RPGs.

Trench/Bunker Line Machine Guns, AKs and RPGs.

Trench/Bunker Line Machine Guns, AKs and RPGs.

Tree, Sniper Line

Claymores

BUNKER

CLEARING

TRENCH

Mortar Impact Zone, Pre-Registered. From Laos.

TRAIL

ALL SURROUNDING TERRAIN IS HEAVILY FORESTED

204

operations. My answer was invariably, 'Assign me the mission and let me take my own people!' While this required the replacement of 'my own people' on the line (all marine battalions were dug in defending some frontline during most of the war) — we went to the field as 2/7. We **knew** each other, how to **communicate**; we had our common experiences and lessons learned and mistakes made; we could anticipate one another. While we frequently distressed administrators and logisticians by wanting to fight as a unit, it is my not-too-humble opinion that our tactical successes proved, repeatedly the validity of the concept and justification of the effort."[367]

Yet the task force concept prevailed in Vietnam and if isolated rifle companies in contact were reinforced, it was usually by strangers. Naturally caution dominated such unit mixtures and hardly any of the very necessary flanking maneuvers were ever carried out.

American attacks were launched by advancing frontally until pinned down, then retreating into defensive perimeters. Another American habit was to stop everything and rescue all wounded and dead under fire. The next day, the pattern would be renewed.

In mountainous or constricted terrain, like Hamburger Hill, American units would advance and be thrown back along the same enemy defended trail, time after time. American leaders insisted upon reinforcing failure, certain that their fire support would win the day.

The NVA saw those American weaknesses and exploited them. Red battalions fighting in heavily vegetated overgrown terrain, would defend one or two avenues of approach in great depth. Dozens of bunkers, mutually supporting and interconnected with trenches, would be deployed about a mile deep along a mountain or jungle trail. The reds didn't bother spreading out in a typical battalion defensive frontage, they didn't have to. All of the American assault power would be concentrated along the narrow lane through which they advanced.

The reds knew they they were fighting an attrition-oriented enemy. Such an enemy is too dumb to maneuver and too clumsy to win.

NVA Obstacle Doctrine

NVA doctrine seemed to favor a modern approach to obstacle employment which was characterized by the integration of battlefield obstacles/barriers, minefields, direct fire and indirect fire. All Chu Luc tactical obstacles could be fitted into a barrier categorization by function. Each barrier was intended to disrupt, turn, fix and/or block enemy passage.

Disrupting obstacles were deployed as limited frontage, quick and easily breachable barriers, set up to slow enemy units. They were usually covered by indirect fire and sometimes direct fire as well.

Huge Chinese claymores or other command detonated devices were frequently employed by the NVA to disrupt allied approach marches. If the level of disruption within the enemy ranks appeared high enough to the observing NVA, they immediately assaulted their paralyzed enemies.

As American troops moved cautiously along heavily mined avenues of approach in the vicinity of their base camps, they were entering defensive battle zones which restricted their mobility. Frequently they would encounter both a psychological and an actual barrier. The psychological barrier was brought about by fear of mines, the actual barriers were those easier avenues of approach seeded with minefields.

Turning obstacles were used to channel enemy formations into killing or entrapment areas. In Vietnam such barriers were usually natural ones: waterways, village hedgerows, or open areas. Movement to avoid a known danger area has the same turning effect as a wall of pointed stakes (abbatis).

Fixing obstacles were established to slow an allied force before a line of massed fire. In mountainous terrain, some avenues of approach were organized as fixing barriers by the communists. American units pausing before such barriers would be subjected to 120mm mortar barrages. Some NVA fortified villages also established fixing obstacles. However, they were usually battered down by American supporting fires.

Blocking obstacles, designed to stop an enemy force in front of an obvious defensive complex, are more common to European battlefields. The combination of complex barriers and supporting fires required by blocking obstacles, were rarely established by the NVA since such defensive arrays are the least subtle of all. Although such obstacles require some time to breach, they also assist in the detection of defensive schemes of maneuver. The NVA never planned on holding terrain long enough to justify such efforts.

Urban Defensive Fighting Methods:
After January 1968

NVA urban fighting methods were similar to their other combat sequences. First they infiltrated advance detachments, and supplies into the urban area where both elements were deployed in scattered hides and a few fortified bridgeheads. Then unit leaders and recon units scrutinized targets, pinpointed assembly areas and selected supporting weapons positions.

Large NVA units would suddenly strike toward objectives within an urban area, totally surprising the allies. Those main force units either attacked from bridgeheads previously seized by advance detachments or infiltrated in small units, assembling near their objectives just prior to the attack.

Leading the attacks would be small teams of special purpose advance detachment troops. They were usually targeted against enemy communications and headquarters. Larger units would assault allied bases, defended areas and other strategically important objectives.

The NVA thoroughly prepared for each offensive action and possible contingency. American marines, searching NVA troops killed in Hue in 1968, were surprised by a particularly ruthless example of communist battle preparation: "they found packets of what looked like white sugar. It was heroin. They found syringes, matches, bent spoons with scorch marks on the bottom; like a bunch of urban junkies. The NVA always fought professionally, . . . couldn't figure why some of them would go into combat too stoned to know they were about to be blown away. . . . He finally came up with the answer. They knew they were going to die."[368]

The primary form of NVA urban combat was defensive, even if it was preceded by an attack. Usually the surprise and shock of NVA urban operations paralyzed the allies for a period of time. The reds used that period to consolidate their control by preparing sections of the city for defense. In the meantime sapper and infantry units blocked roads leading into the area, destroying as many bridges as possible so that enemy efforts to introduce tanks into the fighting would be impeded.

First the reds would insure that their supply lines entering the urban area, usually from the west, were well protected. They used those routes continuously during the battle: "The North Vietnamese moved—unharmed—throughout the night, carrying their dead and wounded out, and supplies in."[369]

The reds immediately fortified brick or stone buildings which offered enfilading fields of fire straight down city streets. One such defended area was the strongly built treasury building in Hue:

"The treasury was built like a treasury is supposed to be: two stories high with a loft; thick concrete construction, an eight foot wall around the tree dotted courtyard."[370]

Whenever possible, communists troops established strongpoints in multistoried buildings surrounded by courtyards and stone or brick walls. Radiating out from such buildings, in every direction, would be red sniper teams commanding the streets from upper level firing positions. Within his strongpoints, the Chu Luc organized from the top down, placing forward observers, snipers and antiaircraft weapons on roofs and top floors. Automatic weapons would be placed on the lower floor to command surrounding avenues of approach. Individual communist infantrymen, armed with RPGs and AK47s, would dig individual spider holes around the courtyards. Firing ports or slits would be knocked in walls or stone fences, enabling the defenders to fire in all directions. "The walls (of the NVA position) were two foot thick concrete and had little bunker style firing slits in them."[371]

At least one communist platoon would be sheltered by each fortified strongpoint. Together with three other mutually supporting strongpoints, the reds would form an urban "chot" or "horseshoe block."

Large, well-constructed city buildings, and their ruins, were easily converted into fortresses. When the NVA fortified Hue's Thua Thien provincial capitol building they had a natural fort: "The capitol building itself was a large, two-story construction of French design; the top floor was a good vantage point for the NVA to fire from into the street. The capitol compound was surrounded by an eight foot high wall with firing slits at the top."[372]

The Imperial Palace's ancient Citadel was an even better fort, and was strongly defended by the NVA: "two North Vietnamese battalions (were) inside the Citadel, and a third to the west keeping the enemy supply lines open . . . (each Citadel wall was) approximately 2,500 yards long, twenty feet high and varied in width from fifty to two hundred feet."[373]

The Citadel was an excellent choice as a long term defensive position. The heavily built up urbanized terrain encircling it also seemed naturally to form a fortified zone: "There was row after row of one-story, thick walled, masonry houses jammed together, wth only narrow streets and alleys, too narrow for a tank or Ontos to maneuver in effectively. There were courtyard walls around most of the houses, big mature trees and hedgerows; it was hard to see anything clearly past twenty five yards. The northeast wall on their left flank was made of brick and filled with earth, rising in terraces and parapets, dotted with trees and brush. The NVA had had two weeks to prepare . . . and the Citadel environment suited them well. They dug their spider holes along the walls and hedgerows, put snipers in the lofts and windows, dug in tight atop the wall; they had literally hundreds of naturally camouflaged, mutually supporting, fortified positions. A small number of well placed soldiers with automatic weapons could tie up an entire company.

"Across the moat of the northeast wall, the North Vietnamese held several four and five story buildings, allowing them to cover the top of the wall by fire. . . Enemy mortars were set up inside the palace, NVA riflemen could fire down . . . from the top of the walls."[374]

Siting their profusion of light and heavy machine guns for grazing fires, NVA gunners would control roads from several blocks away. They sited

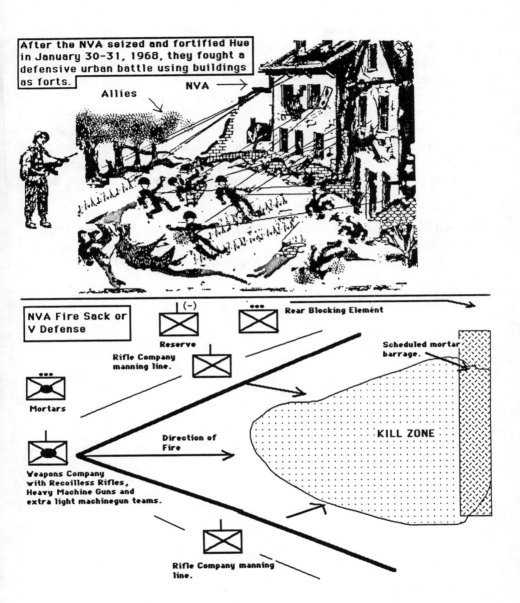

After the NVA seized and fortified Hue in January 30-31, 1968, they fought a defensive urban battle using buildings as forts.

Allies

NVA

NVA Fire Sack or V Defense

(-)

Reserve

Rear Blocking Element

Rifle Company manning line.

Mortars

Scheduled mortar barrage.

KILL ZONE

Direction of Fire

Weapons Company with Recoilless Rifles, Heavy Machine Guns and extra light machinegun teams.

Rifle Company manning line.

weapons for both flanking and enfilade fire down streets, which provided excellent fields of fire.

Once attacking American troops got a foothold in a defended enemy building, the reds would immediately retreat to a nearby building. From the next building they would fight another defensive battle. In this way, they could extract a terrible price in blood from attackers, still retain the advantage of fortified cover, and hold their troop units together longer.

The reds defended many urban streets in South Vietnam by lining them with bunkers constructed out of local material and rubble. NVA recoilless rifle and RPG gunners would fire from such positions, knocking down walls and fences as necessary. If American or allied units attempted to obscure their movements across streets with smoke, the reds knew what to do. They fired into the smoke.

The communists used few counterattacks in urban fighting. They preferred a gradual delaying action which moved their units back toward their escape/resuppy routes. Before final annihilation, they hoped to retreat through the portals offering their last remaining escape gates.

CHAPTER 10

Chu Luc Strike Tactics

North Vietnamese Army forces were truly professional. The intellectual imperatives of their sound combat doctrine requires sufficient objectivity to evaluate mistakes and the mental flexibility necessary for the modification of their methods when necessary.

General William Westmoreland, the former MACV commander, attempted to understand the Chu Luc. After much study he finally reached a partial understanding of NVA military methodology. From the American "war manager" perspective, there was no understanding of operational art. That is why Westmoreland focused only upon the tactical aspects of NVA maneuver art.

"His appreciation of how the North Vietnamese Army operated went something like this after one year of being at grips with the problem:

1. At the tactical level this opponent is a capable planner who organizes offensive operations in four successive steps.
2. The plan itself will always accentuate deception or the staging of an entrapment.
3. His intelligence stems primarily from comprehensive reconnaissance of the chosen battleground and forces adjacent to it.
4. He will usually prepare the battlefield, moving up and caching ammunition and other supply; while that goes on, the hitting forces rehearse the attack, using sand tables, mockups and similar ground in the training exercise.
5. If while that preparation goes on, as a result of counter intelligence, his

over-all maneuver can be divined, parried or blocked, he will have to start all over again.

6. Because of his set-piece approach to operations, he is hurt far more by spoiling attacks than is an average, conventional opponent in war."[375]

General Westmoreland's understanding of basic NVA tactical principles was on target. If he had also understood maneuver and operational art, he would probably have devised a more complete battle scheme. Maneuver ideas are not taught at either Harvard University or U.S. military schools. Westmoreland's selection of the spoiling attack as a counter to NVA maneuver exemplifies the deficit of imagination caused by a lack of maneuver orientation.

Spoiling attacks were capable of dislocating the enemy only if that dislocation was exploited with offensive pursuit. American generals conducted spoiling attacks as strictly defensive raids, attempting to only delay their own inevitable defeat. The blame for such military malfeasance cannot be placed upon a general like Westmoreland who was one of the best. He understood pursuit but did not properly institutionalize it within the American forces in Vietnam.

Colonel David Hackworth reported one exchange which proved that General Westmoreland understood the value of pursuit. The exchange also demonstrated the dearth of military imagination which characterized most of Westy's subordinates.

"(General Westmoreland said), 'Well done, Major' and then added, 'Now you've just got to pursue, pursue, pursue!' "Pursue? I thought . . . Did he really mean he wanted us to charge into the woods and get our asses torn apart by the enemy's inevitable delaying screen of snipers and booby traps?"[376]

Applying their principles of offensive battle, "One Slow, Four Quick" (explained in other chapters), communist units carried out a variety of maneuvers including ambushes, raids, harassments, maneuvering force battles, standoff attacks and power raids. Sniper fire, booby traps, grenades, mortars, machine guns, recoilless rifles, medieval mantraps and minefields were all familiar communist warmaking tools in Vietnam. However, NVA units were not always totally professional: "On the trail, or during any movement in which they have no reason to suspect the near presence of a U.S. or allied force, they are incessant chatterers and otherwise noisy."[377] The Chu Luc was composed of human beings, after all.

NVA Versus American Infantry Tactics

Chu Luc officers didn't think linearly, like American engineers. They leaped immediately to pinpoint central problems. One captured NVA officer demonstrated this facility when he critiqued American troops:

"The U.S. soldier is very poor when moving through the terrain. The American infantry units are weak, their firepower is poor and their equipment is poor. An example of this is that an American unit cannot take or destroy a machinegun position in a properly prepared bunker except by calling for air or artillery; however, the NVA can destroy any American bunker with its B40 or B41 (RPG) rockets."[378]

Another Delta-based NVA cadre described U.S. troop vulnerabilities in a more sneering tone as "inability to adapt to the climate; low morale of the *'Little Lord Fauntleroys;'* excessive size of the average U.S. soldiers which make them good targets as well as cumbersome operators in rice paddies; difficulties of supply."[379]

The NVA also benefitted from habitual American mindsets: "The Americans became over dependent upon their supporting firepower, much as in the Second World War or Korea . . . it is possible that a more aggressive, better armed and trained American infantry could have achieved more results and fewer losses."[380]

Besides being plagued with inadequate doctrine and insufficient small unit armament, American officers found it hard to properly orient their troops to the Chu Luc. One American I Corps battalion journal entry lamented that deficiency in 1970:

"Training in the small unit tactics of fire and maneuver, and fire and movement needs to be stressed. Even though this battalion has constantly stressed these tactics, it was learned from this action, that units cannot be over-trained (a constant worry of American officers?); and not until the basics become automatic reactions, do units even begin to be proficient. Individual soldiers seem to believe that this war is drastically different from past conflicts. This is true in some technical aspects, but the small unit tactics have not changed in the slightest."[381]

It should be noted however, that the American army in Vietnam, for all of its technology, was a near clone of the American army which crossed the Atlantic Ocean to "fight the Hun," in 1917. Although by 1917, the German Army was fielding infantry platoons armed with flame throwers, rifle grenades and light mortars, the U.S. Army still clung to eighteenth century military concepts. American troops attacked German positions frontally in waves of four ranks, just like they did in the Civil War.

The 1917 American Army began the traditional American disdain for the machine gun. While eleven-man German rifle squads armed with light machine guns mowed down their opposition in windrows, Pershing's officers in 1917 claimed that the machine gun was not important and that fire superiority could be achieved with riflemen. American generals harbored the same sentiments during the Vietnam War. Yet, the American Army was not then, or at any time since, blessed with even an average number of expert riflemen. Instead its troops included a majority of abysmal rifle shots.

The U.S. Army in 1917 also preferred huge divisions to smaller ones. Like the American Army in Vietnam, the 1917 American Army knew that "they did not have the officers to direct a larger number of reasonably sized units."[382]

The U.S. Army did have huge staffs in 1917, like they did in Vietnam. The American 1st Army in France in 1917 had a staff of 600 officers and 2,000 enlisted men, which was about the size of a division staff in Vietnam.

In Vietnam and in 1917, the American command had no loyalty to units, dismembering whole divisions at will to provide individual replacements. There was no thought of rotation of whole units either.

There were Vietnam style shirkers in 1917 too. Over 100,000 American AWOLs slunk about the rear avoiding combat in 1917.

American rifle companies were the same size in both wars. Circa 1917 rifle companies were 250 men strong. In 1965, the marine and army companies that landed in Vietnam had 205 to 250 men each.

By 1917, the Germans had long abandoned the practice of "attacking on line, with flanks anchored to the advance of neighboring unit and confined to boundaries drawn on terrain maps."[383] Yet the U.S. Army practiced those tactics in both France and Vietnam.

Although the Chu Luc fought military amateurs who were burdened with antiquated approaches to warfare, NVA military art was both modern and imaginative. The NVA was a unique military force in many ways. When considering its tactical and operational level art, another broad category of considerations should also be addressed: Chu Luc tactical innovations, or strike tactics.

Chu Luc Strike Strategems

American General S.L.A. Marshall described both Chu Luc professionalism and its effects upon allied troops:

"The enemy was scouting, measuring, and plotting the countryside. He had every possible landing zone tabbed and taped and he knew where to set his mortars to zero in on them. We were literally engaging the Charlies on the maneuver ground where they did their training exercises. Our average

Combat Frontage

Unit	Mixed Terrain	Jungle Terrain
Squad	70-80meters	10 meters
Platoon	250 meters	15-30 meters
Company	750 meters	40-250 meters
Battalion	2200 meters	300-900 meters

Battle Opposition

Unit	Men	Weapons	Base of Fire	Reserve	Maneuver Units
US Co	158	6 MG, 24GL	2-3 platoons	1-2 platoons	-------
US BN	632	24 MG 96GL	2-3 companies	1company	-------
NVA BN	4-500	30-40MG, 10GL, 20RPG, 6-12RR, 6-12 MR	Weapons Company and 1-2 Squads	1-2 Platoons	3 companies

When an NVA battalion met a US battalion or, more commonly, a US company
(90% of the time) the NVA battalion initiated the combat (88% of the time).
Using the weapons company, several rifle squads and 2-5 machine guns, the
NVA battalion pinned the US force along a narrow frontage. Indirect fire from
the Chu Luc's 60mm battalion mortars reinforced that pinning action.
Then the NVA maneuver units begin to move against the US flanks and rear.

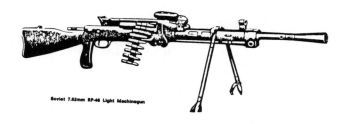

Soviet 7.62mm RP-46 Light Machinegun

HOW NVA INFANTRY OUTGUNNED US INFANTRY

Standard US Infantry Battalion, Modified in Vietnam

Units	Men	7.62MG	90mmRR	81mmMR	40mmGL	RIF	OTHER
HQ Co	147	2	---	----	8	149	---
A Co	158	6	3	3	24	158	---
B Co	Same						
C Co	Same						
D Co	Same						
E Co	96				6	96	12 Flame * Throwers & 4 4.2 MR
Total	632Inf	24 MG	12RR*	12 MR*	96GL		

* = Too heavy to carry into the field, left in base camp.

NVA Infantry Battalion

Unit	Men	MG	RR	MR	GL	RPG
1-4 Co	120men each	9-10ea.	--	---	2-3ea	5ea
WpnsCo	70 men	----	6-12*	6-12*	----	---
Total	480 Inf	30-40MG	6-12RR	6-12MR	8-12GL	20RPG

215

line infantry unit was almost as foreign to this countryside as a first astronaut landing on the moon." . . .held nothing good for our side except in the most extraordinary circumstances where sheer luck or some fluke made things break our way. . ."[384]

The essence of Chu Luc strike tactics was their imaginative creation of military strategems. One NVA strategem that always seemed to work, was their "human bait" ambush lure.

"This was part of the lure, the beginning of entrapment, a trick that the Congs use time and again, to create the impression that there is game to be sought somewhere in the background, but no immediate danger palpable and present. It will make troops hurry on, and out of rushing comes carelessness . . .

"The enemy will deploy the live bodies of his own men as decoys to lure our troops forward and set them up before a hastily contrived ambush or well concealed but fortified position . . . live decoys are used at such short range and so fully exposed to our fire as to create a better than even prospect that their lives will be forfeit . . .

"If you come upon a jungle clearing and see two or three or even one enemy soldier with backs turned, or you are moving fairly in the open, and you see a few NVA or VC moving at a distance with backs turned, never facing about, watch out! The chances are very good that you are being led into a trap.

"Whenever the (NVA) enemy makes his presence obvious and conspicuous, whether during movement or in a stationary and seeming unguarded posture, it is time to be wary and ask the question: 'Is this the beginning of some design of his own, intended to suck us in by making us believe that we are about to snare him?' "[385]

NVA Small Unit Organization and Tactics

The Chu Luc fought from a flexible organizational structure for their infantry forces. Although they usually conducted operations at the battalion, regimental, divisional and corps level, some explanation of how their smaller units fought is important.

The rifle squad was composed of three cells, totaling nine men. It was supposed to include a squad leader, one RPG (antitank weapon), a light machine gun manned by the assistant squad leader, and six riflemen armed with AK-47s.

Three rifle squads made up an NVA platoon. In addition, some platoons were armed with a couple of M79 grenade launchers, which were directly under the platoon leader's control. Platoons and lower elements hardly ever fought independently since their size made them easy to overrun.

North Vietnamese rifle companies were composed of three or four rifle platoons and some crew-served weapons teams. The company commander usually controlled four 60mm mortar crews and two light, medium or heavy machine gun crews.

Vietcon mortars typically fired at enemy firing position targets at under 600 meters range. Their minimum range was 200 meters and they could fire fifteen rounds a minute. Mortar crews advanced behind attacking NVA infantry at a maximum distance of 200 meters so that coordinating communications, by visual or messenger means, would be facilitated.

Communist heavy machine guns opened fire on targets at under 800 meters. They fired from platoon flanks or through gaps deliberately left within attacking formations.

NVA battalions usually controlled three or four rifle companies, several service elements of various types, and a heavy weapons contingent. A typical battalion heavy weapons unit included four 81mm or 82mm mortars, two or three 57mm recoilless rifles and two or three heavy machine guns. That weapons company was served by a unit of porters forcibly recruited from the local peasantry.

NVA battalions usually attempted to pin down their enemy with the firepower of their heavy weapons company and one or two rifle platoons. By extending their battlelines to the right and left, they attempted to spread the enemy defensive line as wide as possible, while keeping it fixed in position.

Two communist rifle companies would probe on both enemy flanks, searching for a gap, or weak spot. Simultaneously one rifle platoon would stage a diversionary attack before withdrawing into battalion reserve. In the meantime, battalion sapper/recon elements might flank deeply behind the enemy front line seeking the enemy headquarters for decapitation. Explosions and firefights within the enemy defensive area would sometimes signal the initiation of an NVA main effort assault.

Once one or more gaps, as near to enemy flanks as possible, were found within the enemy front by red infantry probes, then two main effort rifle companies would plunge into them. Supporting fires would be massed opposite the two primary penetration efforts, initially. As soon as one thrust proved more successful, it became the main effort and all resources, save those used to pin enemy secondary frontage, would be mobilized to support it.

NVA SMALL UNIT TACTICS

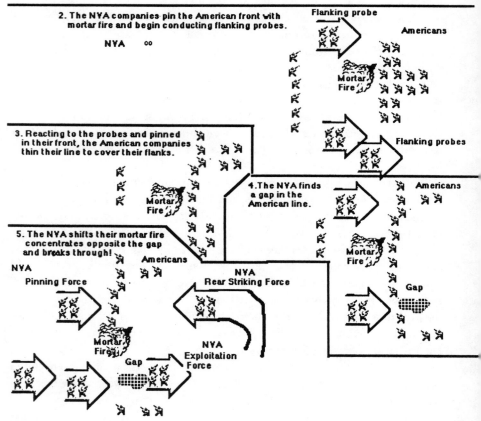

1. Two NVA infantry companies encounter two American rifle companies, and deploy into a battle line

NVA co   Americans

2. The NVA companies pin the American front with mortar fire and begin conducting flanking probes.

NVA   co

Flanking probe

Americans

Mortar Fire

3. Reacting to the probes and pinned in their front, the American companies thin their line to cover their flanks.

Mortar Fire

Flanking probes

4. The NVA finds a gap in the American line.

Americans

Mortar Fire

Gap

5. The NVA shifts their mortar fire concentrates opposite the gap and breaks through!

NVA

Pinning Force

Americans

NVA
Rear Striking Force

Mortar Fire

Gap

NVA
Exploitation
Force

Gap

If the NVA battalion failed to envelop enemy flanks and destroy them, it would attempt to withdraw before enemy fire support assets could be massed against it. The reserve platoon, and maybe one company, would act as rear guard.

When making a conventional infantry-only assault, NVA units followed a patterned sequence. They began advancing with a slow walk, spread out in skirmish line. As they advanced, they accelerated to a fast walk. At seventy-five meters from the enemy line they broke into a dead run, firing from the hip and screaming as they approached. Their supporting mortar fire was timed to begin impacting on the enemy frontline as the red skirmishers reached fifty meters from the enemy line. Then red infantry followed their mortars on in.

If enemy assaults ejected an NVA unit from a position or simply drove the unit back, the communists immediately sought to regain the initiative. Chu Luc forces would launch an immediate counterattack to regain the initiative whenever necessary. Calling their immediate counterattack the "rubber band tactic,"[386] communist troops would sometimes withdraw far enough to obtain maneuver room before launching their counterstroke.

The RPG, ostensibly an antitank weapon, was used as a squad assault weapon by the communists. It was frequently fired directly at personnel or into trees in order to shower the enemy with shrapnel. The firepower of the RPG and light machine gun, frequently employed in tandem at the squad level, completely suppressed American counteraction.

The RPG antitank rocket was unexcelled as a bunker buster and antitank weapon. No hand-held American antitank weapon came close to it in efficiency, firepower or utility. In fact the American counterpart to the RPG, the LAW, was a liability to its user:

"At the Battle of An Loc, during the 1972 Spring offensive in Vietnam, one Russian built light tank absorbed seven LAW hits before being knocked out. Russian built medium tanks proved invulnerable to the LAW from the front, and the South Vietnamese paratroopers had to go back to the deadly game of tank stalking, often popping up out of sewers to LAW Russian built tanks from the rear. The South Vietnamese were so dissatisfied with the LAW that they requested Bazookas be airdropped to them."[387]

The Americans had nothing comparable to the NVA's battalion level 57mm, or heavier, recoilless rifles either. While it is true that American battalions were sometimes equipped with 90mm recoilless rifles, that assignment was not standard.

NVA Machine Gun Employment

Chu Luc units frequently gained fire superiority over larger American units. The secret of that superiority rested in their application of machine gun fire. Each NVA battalion deployed as many machine guns as it could, for a total of thirty or forty light machine guns per battalion.

The Chu Luc also realized that the machine gun is the primary infantry weapon. At the squad level, where communist troops maintained at least one light machine gun, American units were outgunned. At NVA platoon could commit three or four light machine guns, supplemented by RPGs, to a firefight. This firepower could easily pin an American company equipped with only six light machine guns.

Naturally, tactical firepower disadvantages caused American troops to become even more dependent upon supporting weapons. "American infantry became reliant not on their own firepower, but on that of supporting weapons, mortars, machine guns, artillery, and air strikes. This, unfortunately ended up, in many cases, in over reliance upon outside firepower.

"Yet the Americans still would not learn the vital point, that the essence of the infantry lies in its machine guns. The American Army infantry squad did not have in Vietnam (and does not have, when operating dismounted today) a light machine gun. The Army apparently still feels that sufficient automatic firepower can be achieved by using two M-16s per squad as automatic firepower, keeping the rest as semi-automatic weapons. The lessons of the last thirty years still have not penetrated into the Pentagon. Without a squad light machine gun, the American infantry squad still must rely on outside firepower. They lack the close range firepower of enemies armed with sub machine guns and assault rifles (souped up, long range SMGs, of which the Russian AK-47 is most notable)."[388] During the Vietnam War, Americans, and their allies who accepted American doctrine, faced the reds with one third to one half less machine guns.

American employment of machine guns was retarded by two, uniquely American, conceptual and perceptual distortions:

1. The machine gun was viewed as a defensive weapon, best used along a final protective fire line. A constant feature of every American infantry action was the holding back of machine guns in order to employ them later as part of an inevitable defensive perimeter.
2. The standard American infantry command "guns up,"[389] was not a call for light infantry howitzers to be advanced. Rather it was a summons forward of machine guns from the platoon machine gun pool. There the

platoon's two machine guns were retained, in the same manner as light supporting artillery.

NVA rifle squads used their light machine gun to rapidly obtain fire superiority over American platoons, quickly pinning them to the ground and fixing them in position. From being pinned, American troops recoiled into defensive perimeters, screaming for fire support. In that way, they lost both the fire fight and the initiative. That is how the scarcity of American machine guns forced them to become more dependent upon fire support.

The red rifle squad was usually armed with the *Ruchnoi Pulyemet Degtyarova* (RPD) light machine gun, which weighed only sixteen pounds. The American M-60 weighed twenty-three or more pounds without the tripod. ". . with a rate of fire of seven hundred rounds per minute, (the RPD) was far better than any comparable weapon produced by the U.S."[390]

The Chu Luc actually deployed more firepower on the front line where it counted. As a result, the communists won most of the fire fights.

Important Crewed Weapons and Machine Gun Fire Concepts

- *Grazing Fire:* Fire in which the center of the cone of fire hits the waist of a standing man and does not rise over one meter above the surface of the ground. (The NVA tried to hit the ankles.) Grazing fire is delivered parallel to the surface of the ground. Grazing fire range is 500 meters or less.
- *Plunging Fire:* Fire in which the danger space is practically confined to a beaten zone. Plunging fire is obtained when firing from high ground to low ground, when firing into abruptly rising ground, and when firing at long ranges. (Machine guns can be used as indirect fire weapons.)
- *Dead Space:* Any area within the maximum range of a weapon which cannot be covered by fire from a position because of intervening obstacles, the nature of the ground, characteristics of trajectory, or the mechanical limitations of elevating and depressing the tube.
- *Defiladed Area:* The protection from hostile ground observation and fire provided by an obstacle such as a hill, ridge, or bank.
- *Enfilade Fire:* The most desirable class of fire with respect to the target. It makes maximum use of the beaten zone/rectangle of dispersion, thus providing the most effective distribution of hits on the target.

- *Final Protective Fire:* Fire from a machine gun whose elevation and direction are predetermined and fixed. The gunner fires and waits for the target to walk into the fire stream. It is fired at grazing fire range, and usually from a flank across an avenue of approach where it overlaps with fire from the opposite flank.

Final protective machine gun fires are very effective. A man who runs 100 yards in 13.6 seconds, moves at the rate of 6.7 meters per second. If a skirmish line of 100 men attempt to run at that speed, across a machine gun's final protective line, thirty of them will be hit. It will only take fifty-four rounds of ammunition to knock down thirty percent of the attacks.

If four machine guns are firing two overlapping final protective lines, the results would be different. At least 93 of the men, running at least 6.7 meters a second, would *not* make it through that overlapping fire. It should be remembered that: "Compared with other weapons in terms of cost and effectiveness, the machine gun stands in a class of its own."[391]

NVA Antitank Methods

Communist antitank techniques were sophisticated applications employing all available weapons and materials. Recoilless rifles and RPGs, the NVA's primary antitank weapons, were not only perfectly suited to the military requirements of the Chu Luc, but also superior to allied infantry antitank weaponry.

Chu Luc commanders were well aware of armored fighting vehicle weaknesses, such as "dead space." Dead space is the fire free zone surrounding an armored vehicle where machine guns cannot be sufficiently depressed to engage close personnel targets.

Red tank killers also understood that bundles of grenades placed on the thinner top and engine compartments of allied tanks would immobilize them. Antitank mines, satchel charges, demolition blocks, flame throwers (tanks will burn easily since they are invariably covered with a napalm like mixture of oil, fuel and dirt), and command-detonated, 250 pound bombs were also utilized against allied armored fighting vehicles.

RPG2 and RPG7 antitank rockets were frequently fired at allied vehicles from less than fifty meters away. They were highly lethal, as one American tank commander admitted: "Although many measures to defeat these weapons (RPGs) were tried, no adequate means was ever found."[392]

Antitank weapons were used against allied vehicles during vehicular ambushes. The first and last vehicles in the column would be destroyed, thus

ANTITANK LAUNCHER RPG-2

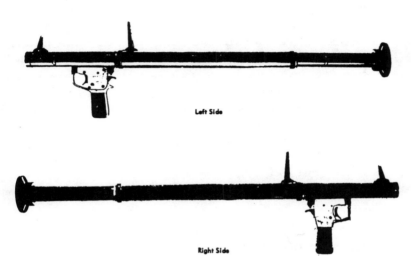

Left Side

Right Side

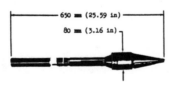

650 mm (25.59 in)

80 mm (3.16 in)

HEAT Grenade PG-2

blocking the road and trapping the column. NVA troops would then throw grenades into the vehicles from positions only three meters from the road.

When American M-113 armored personnel carriers (APCs) were introduced into South Vietnam in the early 1960s, the Viet Cong used crude countermeasures. They dug huge holes, called "elephant traps," in the roads and camouflaged them. Occasionally an M-113 would fall into such holes, which were dug to its exact dimensions. The reds would then finish off the APC crew with grenades and small arms. However, the NVA constantly perfected its antitank tactics: "In 1965 the Viet Cong published a comprehensive and fairly accurate training document entitled *Attack on M113 APC.* This document listed characteristics of the APC; organization, equipment, and strength of mechanized units; tactics used by APC units; methods of attacking an APC; and some training techniques. Included were instructions for using the new antitank weapons. In the spring of 1963 the Viet Cong had begun to use recoilless rifles with 57mm high explosive antitank rounds, and the number of hits on M113s had increased dramatically by the fall of 1963. Although the rounds often penetrated, they did not usually destroy the M113."[393]

The reds found that their 12.7mm heavy machine gun fire easily penetrated American APCs. The highly flammable, aluminum APCs went up like torches when they caught fire.

NVA Anti-Airmobile Operations

The allied helicopter threat presented the reds with a new challenge. Calling upon both Soviet advisers and Algerians who had fought against a French helicopter war in North Africa, the NVA rapidly developed an anti-airmobile doctrine. That doctrine consisted of the following optional elements:

- Ringing potential landing zones with prepared fortifications and rigging it with obstacles.
- Fighting against the helicopters with missiles, flak and heavy machine guns.
- Fighting airmobile troops as they landed.
- Maneuvering against airmobile troops after they moved off their landing zones.

The first Chu Luc anti-airmobile tactical priority was to place potential landing zones (LZs) under surveillance and/or prepare fortified positions encircling the open area. Then the LZs were rigged with obstacles, including mines, trip devices and wires, punji stakes, punji pits and devices to hurl grenades to achieve airbursts.

Poles were also erected on LZs, including some with explosives attached, to disable any chopper attempting a landing. Explosive devices were also rigged to be detonated by the downwash of rotary blades.

Landing Zone obstacles also had another purpose. They forced the allies to "prep" the landing zones with artillery and air strikes. Naturally such preparation eliminated the element of surprise.

The reds refrained from attacking enemy aircraft conducting LZ prep fires, in order to prevent unnecessary casualties to themselves. If they fired at helicopters, poorly armed troop transport craft were their favorite targets.

If the NVA units in the area felt strong enough, they would engage every enemy unit from the beginning of the airmobile operation. However, they realized that it was better to wait until allied troops, clumped up on the open terrain of landing zones, offered more lucrative targets. The reds frequently close assaulted recently landed allied troop formations in order to avoid the heat of retaliatory fire support.

In the early sixties, an American helicopter returned to base with a huge arrow through its fuselage. That arrow, fired by some type of catapult device, only marked the lower limits of weaponry, ranging to shoulder fired missiles, deployed by the NVA in their relentless destruction of thousands of U.S. helicopters during the Second Indochina War.[394]

The reds used massed infantry small arms fire to bring down the highly vulnerable and fragile helicopters from their earliest appearance on the battlefield. Soon, however, the Bo Dai began to practice antiaircraft tactics with heavy machine guns deployed in two gun batteries. One would fire and the other would remain silent. If an allied aircraft dove on the revealed gun, the hidden gun would conduct a surprise fire assault. Such weapons were camouflaged and dug into fortified weapons pits. Some flak weapons were hidden in caves or underground, surfacing only to fire quick bursts at lucrative targets. Communist gunners were taught how to lead the helicopters and how to hit their vulnerable points. Mockups of helicopters, moved by strings and pulleys, were used in training.

NVA units, harbored in stronghold base areas, developed antihelicopter schemes of maneuver against potential nearby landing zones. First, they identified all potential helicopter landing zones within the immediate vicinity (one hour's march, about five kilometers). Then they identified landing zones up to three hours' march (fifteen kilometers) away. If the identified landing zones did not overlap the control area of any other Chu Luc forces, they were selected for contingency planning. The targeted LZs were categorized as "immediate" (one hour's march) and "distant" (three hours' march) targets.

The next step was to ensure that trails led from the vicinity of the stronghold fortified area to each landing zone. NVA doctrine required that at least one of those trails would not be observable from the air. Highly camouflaged, covert traffic trails leading to target LZs were newly constructed if necessary.

Potential enemy night laager, or night defensive, positions were identified on the terrain. Red strike positions and ambush areas were sited in relationship to those potential allied harbor locations. The NVA knew that American troops would probably continue to move away from their LZs until late afternoon.

Typically, American troops moved two to seven kilometers from their LZs to night defensive positions, depending on whether they used trails or not. Usually an allied unit would begin to bed down in a defensive perimeter in the early afternoon.

NVA ambush sites were selected along trails or avenues of approach leading toward locations where allied troops might harbor in laagers or defended bases, after dark. Most of those sites were fortified ahead of time.

Strike positions, assembly areas contiguous to one or more enemy landing zones and/or potential night defensive position, were also selected during anti-airmobile contingency planning. Both ambush sites and strike positions were fortified. Although landing zone perimeters were usually fortified, not all landing zones would be rigged with obstacles.

Red antiaircraft weapons and mortars might be cached near LZs ready for instant deployment. Mortars would usually be preregistered on LZ targets as well as nearby ambush sites.

Landing zone/trail watchers might be assigned to observe distant landing zones. Landing zones in the immediate area were usually detectable by normal communist stronghold security measures and patrols.

Antihelicopter Preparations

- Identification of potential immediate and distant landing zones.
- Identification of overt and covert routes to landing zones.
- Identification of potential enemy night defensive positions.
- Selection of strike positions and ambush sites.
- Time and distance from all points recorded.
- Rally points designated for NVA troops separated from their units.
- Fortification of landing zones, ambush sites and strike positions.

- Rigging of obstacles on selected LZs.
- Selection of antiaircraft sites covering LZs.
- Selection of mortar sites covering LZs and ambush areas.
- Caching of weapons and ammunition.
- Double-checking to ensure that all tunnel systems are functioning.
- Preregistration of mortars on targets and corrections to fire control and fire control data.
- Assignment of LZ/trail watchers.
- Analysis of stronghold security measures to ensure that immediate LZs are covered by patrols and/or trail watchers.

NVA command staffs prepared a series of battle maps clearly marked with all of the above information. Map preparation would be followed by rehearsals of various contingencies. Each plan was be based on a scheme of maneuver directed against each separate landing zone.[395]

When an allied airmobile LZ preparation began, the NVA antihelicopter maneuver was initiated as the Chu Luc base area commander began to process a series of command decisions. First a decision was made whether to attack the allied force on the landing zone or away from the landing zone. The NVA commander also might decide later to cut off the landing force from the LZ. Such a decision would be based on whether or not a small LZ defense force remained on the landing zone.

A communist scout element would follow the allied unit from the time it left the LZ. That unit would closely observe the allied unit, count it, inventory its firepower and equipment and note its tactical procedures. Compass azimuths and map studies would be utilized to predict the probable route and potential night defensive positions (NDP) of the enemy. As soon as the scout unit detected and reported the march rate of the allied unit, the NVA commander would attempt to predict enemy intentions and began to make maneuver decisions.

Operational Anti-Airmobile Maneuvers

- The dispatch of an ambush force to a site along the enemy march route.
- The use of an intervention force to slow down or channel the allied movement, or lure it into an ambush.
- When and where the mortar fire might be employed.
- Whether or not a power raid might be used against the enemy night laager.
- Whether to avoid main force contact entirely.

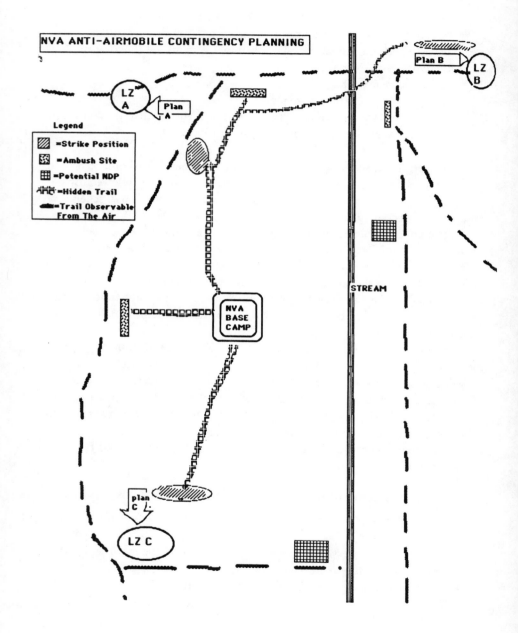

NVA ANTI-AIRMOBILE CONTINGENCY PLANNING

Plan B

LZ B

LZ A

Plan A

Legend
= Strike Position
= Ambush Site
= Potential NDP
= Hidden Trail
= Trail Observable From The Air

NVA BASE CAMP

STREAM

plan C

LZ C

228

- Whether to evacuate the stronghold and occupy a secret strike position or tunnel hideout.

All of the above decision options were based on the factors endemic to the situation. The enemy LZ location, enemy force correlates, direction, and rate of march were also important.

NVA Anti-Airmobile Command
Decision Contingencies

- Seek or avoid a fight.
- Fight on or off the LZ.
- Evacuate stronghold.
- Use intervention unit and for what purpose.
- Deployment in ambush site(s) or strike position(s).
- What deception maneuvers to employ.
- Use flak or mortars against LZ, ambush area or NDP

If an attack was scheduled against the allied Night Defensive Position (NDP), red reconnaissance units would come to the fore. Communist scouts were required not only to report the enemy NDP locations, but also gauge its deployment and prepare the area for a night assault.

As soon as the enemy occupied a NDP, NVA recon units would begin scouting its perimeter. They would be looking for mines, flares, crew-served weapons positions, listening/observation posts, and command posts. Recon parties would attempt to observe the NDP in daylight and after dark. After the NDP was thoroughly scouted, NVA recon troops began to probe it to determine the level of discipline of the allied unit and to locate any unaccounted for weaponry. Grenades or fire crackers might be thrown at the perimeter or the recon troops might adopt a total stealth posture to deny the enemy any indication of their presence.

If a decision was made to assault the enemy perimeter, night assembly areas, approach routes and supporting weapons positions had to be designated by recon elements, if those sites were not already preselected. Then the positions had to be marked for night detection and guides assigned to move friendly troops into the sites.

Beginning short of the enemy perimeter, an attack line, twenty to thirty meters from the allied perimeter, was marked. Then, communications wire was laid away from the attack line toward a night assault assembly area. The commo wire would be used as a guide wire for assault files to hold onto in their approach to the assault line. The wire would be unraveled all the way to the night assembly position which would, preferably, be sheltered from enemy fire support bombardment and direct fires.

Luminous arrows and tape, facing away from the enemy and undetectable, might be attached to trees as supplementary guides for movement. To ensure that squad integrity was maintained, a small luminescent patch might be attached to the rear of each soldier's head gear.

NVA recon troops would meet the night assault force and guide them into the night assembly area. Upon arrival at the night assault assembly area, final coordination and sub unit organization would be affected as the communist attack unit prepared to move out. Guided by scouts and following each other in file, NVA penetration units would lead main assault parties forward to the attack line. Advancing NVA assault files would maintain direction by sliding along the previously laid communications wire all the way to its tied-off point at the attack line near the enemy perimeter.

When the attack line was reached, the main shock units would spread out in skirmish line while penetration units infiltrated the enemy perimeter. At a designated signal, the shock units would rush forward determined to link up with infiltrated penetration units already inside the enemy perimeter.

Firing from the hip and screaming insults, the attack force would go in. Within a manner of minutes, they would either be retreating, dead, fighting for their lives, or leering triumphantly over the corpses of their enemies.

NVA Tactical Innovations

Several interesting tactical innovations or modification to their own strike tactic doctrine were made by the Chu Luc during the Vietnam War. Among those innovations were:

- The "American Annihilation" perimeter.
- Antipacification tactics.
- The rubber band tactic.
- The Chot defensive position.
- The Triangle or Tripod defensive formation.
- Fire tunnels.

When the short-lived U.S. 9th Infantry Division base was established at Dong Tam in Binh Duc, the communists were alarmed. They were worried that American assaults would interdict the Delta's role as a manpower and rice supplier to red bases in South Vietnam's II Corps and III Corps areas.

The NVA immediately mobilized an adaptive tactical response to impede

7.62-MM LIGHT MACHINE GUN
DEGTYAREV (RPD)

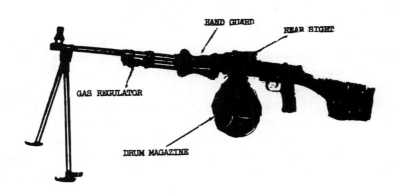

HAND GUARD

REAR SIGHT

GAS REGULATOR

DRUM MAGAZINE

103.7 cm

U.S. operations and secure enemy controlled areas. They called their adaptation the "American Annihilation" perimeter, an encirclement concept borrowed from the Chinese.

Three concentric defensive perimeters were to be established around major American bases. Those perimeters were intended to "create a tight encirclement of the Dong Tam Base of the Americans in Bunh Duc and, at the same time, prevent the ARVN and its allies from raiding or conducting large operations into the surrounding villages."[396]

Aggressive allied incursions into those areas would threaten highly vulnerable NVA supply and liaison routes. In addition, the local political and logistics support structure of what the reds referred to as the "20/7 Zone,"[397] of Dinh Tuong Province, would be jeopardized by allied assaults.

The first communist step was to decentralize demolition units as they began to train large numbers of women in mine laying and booby trapping. They then set up the three concentric perimeters, with the first perimeter immediately surrounding the Dong Tam Base. The second and third successive perimeters circled through outlying village belts. Small demolition teams began to create a maze of spike pits and grenade traps along the concentric perimeters around the base. Regional cadre were sent to control the first perimeter while the other two were controlled by district cadre. It was an all out defensive effort to restrict allied offensive maneuver.

By April 1967, supplementary organizations called "Counter-pacification Committees," were also deployed along the perimeters. The purposes of the committees included: "consolidate the weakened guerrilla forces . . . provide more energetic support of the battlefield . . . attack roads and build roadblocks . . . bolster the morale of the guerrillas."[398]

The triple perimeter scheme worked more effectively than people realized at the time. Within a year, the U.S. 9th Division's Riverine Brigade was withdrawn from the Delta.

The Antipacification Tactic (APT) was a companion to the American Annihilation Perimeter in the IV Corps area. It had the same purpose. The APT technique was motivated by fear that the allies had finally wised up and were going to deploy strong aggressive main effort offensives. They also feared the aggressive small unit raids carried out by the U.S. 9th Infantry Division, one of the best divisions in South Vietnam.

"The (U.S.) 'chup non' (net) tactic means a fast troop landing of a small unit—maybe a platoon—which will hit fast and retreat quickly. There is no set pattern of time or space involved, so that the element of surprise may be gained at any place. This tactic . . . is very effective."[399]

"We met with very strong enemy units that were ten times stronger than we are. Therefore we dared not resist their operations. If we stood against them, we would have been completely eliminated . . . our areas of control have been encroached on and reduced in size."[400]

The APT was designed to exploit "two elements of basic weakness in the U.S. capabilities in the Delta . . . (1) the inevitable dispersion of forces . . . (2) the inextricable connection between search and destroy and the pacification tasks. If one failed the other would also be doomed to failure."[401]

NVA main force battalions were directed to avoid head on collisions with American units. Instead they were to "strike in relatively undefended areas, and force the opposing troops to spread themselves thin."[402]

The 261st VC Main Force Battalion was directed to force U.S. troops in Long An Province to disperse their units:

"We had our plans of attacks but not in Long An itself. We would attack the district towns and force the enemy to spread its forces which otherwise would be used to pacify the province alone. When the enemy was forced to spread its forces thin, we would move in to destroy them . . . Even though the GVN was going to pacify Long An Province, the Front was not going to mass its forces in Long An to fight back. If the Front forces did that it would become a war with a definite front line and not a guerrilla war."[403]

The Viet Cong hoped to gain the initiative after first dispersing enemy troops in packets which could be defeated in detail. At the same time they sought to place enemy bases under siege. These efforts were also timed to complement the forthcoming Tet Offensive of January, 1968, which was only months away. That is why the Viet Cong Delta hierarchy received such strong encouragement:

"The incoming force will be dispersed as were other U.S. troops in other theaters of war, thereby weakening itself and providing favorable conditions for the three categories of troops of the Liberation Armed Forces to annihilate its (U.S.) forces . . ."[404]

The "rubber band tactic," was what the NVA called their immediate counterattack from one trenchline to another. They used that tactic when countering allied sweep operations:

"This tactic helps the platoon leaders to keep control and command the fighters during the battle, and prevents the Front soldiers from being disbanded by the first successful assault from the ARVN. It also helps us to resist until darkness comes and, at that time, we can withdraw from the battlefield in safety. Experience has also proved that, thanks to it, we have usually resisted successfully and have inflicted heavy casualties upon the ARVN so far."[405]

The NVA frequently referred to various defensive position configurations as "Chots." Chot, in revolutionary jargon referred to "a small group of men who are committed to defend a particular position at all costs, a kingpin that cannot be jarred loose."[406] During the defense of Dinh Cuong Hill in Quang Nam, the NVA deployed cell-sized Chots. The Chots were to be defended to the bitter end. A poem was taken off one NVA corpse which read:

"As long as I have breath, This chot will not be lost."[407]

During the 1972 offensive, the 209th Infantry Regiment of the 7th NVA Infantry Division established in-depth fortified blocking positions near III Corps' Tau O. Those blocking positions, which the NVA called "Chots," were composed of A-shaped underground shelters. The shelters were configured in a horseshoe shape with multiple outlets assigned to each company. "Every three days, the platoon which manned the position was rotated so that the enemy continually enjoyed a supply of fresh troops."[408]

The 209th NVA Regiment's Chot positions were further organized into a large triangular defensive pattern which the NVA called "Kieng" (tripod). Tripods were sited for mutual protection and fire support. A communications trench connected the tripods to a rubber plantation to the north of Tau O. The very deep defensive zone was laid parallel to Route 13, along a railroad bed, and centered on the deep swamps fed by the Tau O stream.

At the small unit level, "Charlie" consistently demonstrated combat prowess. The NVA cleared fire tunnels a few inches above the ground, which led straight into central killing fields. American troops caught in those kill zones would have their legs knocked out from under them by machine gun fire. The red bullet stream would then blow their heads off as they plummeted to the ground. Fire tunnels were also used by NVA sharpshooters. In one action, NVA sharpshooters accounted for six dead and sixteen wounded Americans in quick succession:

"They had set up foxholes and positions off to one side of the trail. As the point man came up they shot him. They couldn't see much of the killing zone because of the heavy vegetation, but the field of fire was cleared so low that they originally shot everybody in the legs that came into it. As people would come into it to help a wounded person . . . they would get shot in the legs. Then once they were down, they had one sniper that would either shoot them in the head or back."[409]

The NVA also experimented with daring ambush innovations. In 1962, a South Vietnamese Self Defense Corps squad was destroyed in a Viet Cong triangular ambush. The ARVN squad was allowed to enter a kill zone where fire was poured upon it from three directions. It is not known how the reds were able to avoid hitting each other during the fusillade of fire. Since the

VIET CONG BATTALIONS: 1965

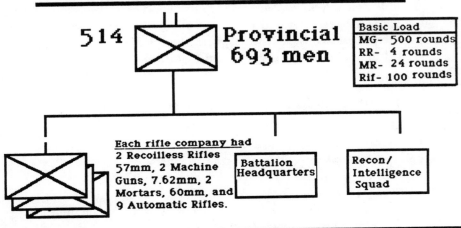

514 Provincial 693 men

Basic Load	
MG-	500 rounds
RR-	4 rounds
MR-	24 rounds
Rif-	100 rounds

Each rifle company had 2 Recoilless Rifles 57mm, 2 Machine Guns, 7.62mm, 2 Mortars, 60mm, and 9 Automatic Rifles.

Battalion Headquarters

Recon/ Intelligence Squad

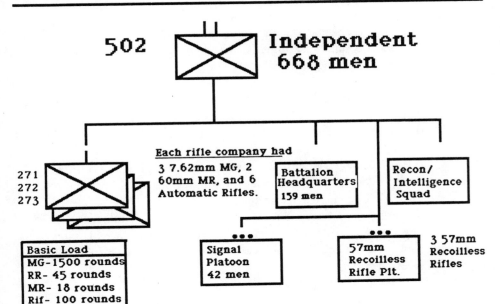

502 Independent 668 men

271
272
273

Each rifle company had 3 7.62mm MG, 2 60mm MR, and 6 Automatic Rifles.

Battalion Headquarters 159 men

Recon/ Intelligence Squad

Basic Load	
MG-1500 rounds	
RR- 45 rounds	
MR- 18 rounds	
Rif- 100 rounds	

Signal Platoon 42 men

57mm Recoilless Rifle Plt.

3 57mm Recoilless Rifles

triangular ambush was rarely used thereafter, it is likely that some communist ambushers actually shot their own men.[410]

NVA Strike Tactics Indicators

Before a unit attacks or defends, it must take certain preparatory steps. Depending on the strength of that unit's security precautions, certain of those steps may be observed by an enemy who is thereby forewarned. Those steps are called indicators. During the Second Indochina War, the U.S. military identified numerous indicators of NVA offensive operational intentions.

Possible Indicators of NVA Offensive Operations

a. Systematic assassination and abduction of government officials.

b. Abduction of young men.

c. Increased sabotage activities in a particular area.

d. Sudden absence or increase of guerrilla activity.

e. Sudden absence or increase of civilian population in an area.

f. Shortage of a particular type of supply, e.g. weapons, ammunition, medical supplies, footgear, etc.

g. Demonstrations by minority groups.

h. Increased propaganda in a certain area.

i. The local population, to include children, in a particular area will not talk or associate with U.S. forces or ARVN /forces. (Dual indicator with control.)

j. Concentration of local watercraft or other types of mobility, especially if an attempt has been made to conceal them.

k. High rate of defection of regular and paramilitary forces of South Vietnam.

l. Visits in villages, towns, etc., by strange women, men or children.

m. Disappearance of suspected insurgents who normally spend all of their time in one particular area.

n. Friendly attack of guerrilla secure area, supply dump, or the capture of guerrilla personnel of great value to the guerrilla force.

o. Low VC morale. Guerrilla leaders use the attack as a vehicle to boost morale.

p. Increased reconnaissance activity.

q. Increased radio activity.

r. Massing of VC forces.

s. Change in location of VC headquarters, medical facilities, and other supporting activities.

t. The occurrence of national or religious holidays.

u. Birthdays of guerrillas or sponsoring power key personnel and/or leaders.

The above list is incomplete. Other possible indicators identified during the Vietnam War included: (1) If the VC began to build coffins and dig graves, an attack may be indicated. (2) Preparing battlefields by pre-caching ammunition was frequently an attack indicator. (3) If much chipped bark was found at shoulder level on trees along trails, the enemy was probably portering crew-served weapons into the area. (4) If enemy troops were encountered in the bush wearing rucksacks they were probably a long way from their base areas. (5) If enemy troops were encountered in the bush without rucksacks, their base was probably nearby. (6) The fresh fecal count of an enemy latrine gave some indication of the number of troops who used it. Each fresh stool sample found on the ground was multiplied by twenty as a rough estimate of the number of troops in a unit. However, that estimate was made only if other spoor in the area indicated a large number of enemy troops. After all, *one* bear does defecate in the woods. (7) Warm soft stools indicated that the enemy was within several hours of the stool location. (8) Crusty stools were at least twenty-four hours old. (9) Hard stools were at least five days old. (10) Eight or more multicolored strands of communications wire running along a trail or open area indicated the presence of an enemy regiment in the area. (11) The presence of a nearby enemy large base camp was indicated when three geographical characteristics were found near each other: triple canopy jungle, an excellent water supply and a large enemy trail complex. (13) An enemy listening or guard hut usually faced away from the area it was protecting. (14) Clear water upstream and mud clouded water downstream indicated an enemy crossing, very recently.

Many other enemy indicators were provided by reading tracks and trail spoor. In addition, the enemy also used a system of coded trail signs to convey messages. Astute allied scouts only had to decode those trail signs to understand much about local enemy usage of the trail complex. (See also, Chapter 5).

NVA infantry battalions and larger formations usually left signs of their passage, no matter how careful they were. However, the signs deteriorated so fast that if they were observed, they were probably fresh:

"From my own experience I know that the battalion (261st VC) usually leaves behind traces of its passage. In the rainy season it is even easier to find these traces. The heavy weapons units in particular leave a train through the rice fields. In the dry season the grass is crushed and the battalion leaves a 2 meter wide path through the grass . . . The battalion often travels along trails. If you see the stubble along the sides of a trail you know that a unit has gone by. It should also be remembered that the movement regulations are strongly oriented towards avoiding artillery, for example, in the Plain of Reeds, a path that lies out of artillery range is always chosen."[412]

CHAPTER 11

Close Assault Power Raids

War Zones C and D, part of the enemy fortified belt which stretched hundreds of square miles in an arc to the north and west of Saigon, were never conquered during the Second Indochinese War. The War Zone Front remained an inviolate sanctuary where whole communist divisions maneuvered to strike targets in South Vietnam's III and IV Corps.

For years, the American high command tied down dozens of American and South Vietnamese battalions in defensive positions along the War Zone Front, yet the communists never relinquished control of War Zones C and D during the Vietnam War.

In March, 1967, Special Forces Detachment A-334 opened a border surveillance camp deep in the War Zone C province of Binh Long, at Tong Le Chon. By early August, 1967, elements of the 165th North Vietnamese Army (NVA) Regiment were completing their preparation of the battlefield for a power raid against the camp.

The camp was defended by three Special Forces trained Indochinese irregular units: two Mike Forces (560 veteran mercenaries) and a 200 man CIDG (Civilian Irregular Defense Group) unit. The camp defenders were not doing a very good job of securing their perimeter. On the night of the assault no listening posts or ambush security positions were manned. Half the claymores in the camp's protective minefield were neutralized because CIDG personnel had used their explosive compounds as fuel for cooking fires.

Around midnight on August 7, mortar fire began to fall upon the

239

southeastern portion of the camp. Communist sappers had already begun to clear and mark lanes through the barbed wire.

During the next hour and a half, the mortar fire intensified. The supply tent and the fuel storage area were ignited as smoke billowed throughout the camp. Special Forces advisors frantically called for artillery support and helicopter gunships, which soon joined the fray. At 0122 hours, enemy supporting fires were switched to targets inside the camp, scoring a direct hit on the Special Forces command bunker. North Vietnamese infantry surged through lanes cut in the southeastern perimeter wire. The red infantry were following behind elite sapper troops armed with satchel charges, B-40 rocket launchers and bangalore torpedoes. The wire had been cut with large American wire cutters and the lanes marked with white rags.

As one of the CIDG platoons surrendered, red shock units swept into the camp's inner perimeter. Suddenly the camp's mortar dump exploded, vaporizing the lead elements of the attackers and throwing the rest into confusion. That detonation saved the day, as a Mike Force counterattack drove the stunned communists back out of the camp.[413]

Although the battle of Tong Le Chon was lauded as an American victory, it was nearly a total defeat. Utilizing expertise gained assaulting hundreds of strongpoints and perimeters, the North Vietnamese had broken into a fortified camp defended by a reinforced battalion-equivalent (nearly 800 men). Their violent night assault, following a one and one half hour mortar bombardment, unfolded like clockwork.

Several months later at Khe Sahn, an NVA company actually broke into the base area, through a perimeter defended by three marine battalions.[414] Many American defenders were overrun in their fortified firebases, grim witnesses to the violent irresistibility of VC-NVA breakthrough operations.

Invariably, VC/NVA breakthrough operations caught the allies by surprise. In most cases allied defenders were unaware of communist presence until it was too late. Sometimes they could hear red fire support elements digging weapons positions within fifty to one hundred yards of their perimeter, just before an attack. They didn't realize that those sounds meant that enemy sappers had already begun to infiltrate and neutralize their base's barbed wire and mined approaches, along a narrow front.

Base camp defenders usually realized they were under attack only after heavy direct and indirect suppressive fires began to hit specific targets along, and inside of, the defensive perimeter. Mortar, recoilless rifle, and machine gun fire was directed against selected bunkers and other defensive works. Other mortar fire fell on the interior of the position, discouraging deployment toward the threatened sector.

Supporting fires provided cover for a small breaching detachment, usually composed of elite sapper troops, which systematically breached all mine and wire barriers with wirecutters and/or bangalore torpedoes. Cutting narrow lanes in the defensive barrier, the sappers moved rapidly toward the nearest bunker or firing position, whose fire could command the breach. They destroyed bunkers with B-40 rockets, satchel charges and grenades.

Following on the heels of the sappers was the main VC assault force, running forward firing from the hip, straight for assigned objectives. Sometimes the shock troops threw smoke pots in front of them to mask their movements as they rushed forward.

Chu Luc Offensive Doctrine

Although the NVA were capable of launching attacks much faster than their opponents, they believed in controlling as many battle variables as possible. Their offensives tended to be more thoroughly planned than American operations because they were foot mobile. They were guided by their sequence of combat known as "One Slow, Four Quick"[415] when planning all offensive operations.

During the first step of their battle sequence, "prepare slowly," the VC took deliberate care to insure that their intelligence on the target base camp or installation was up to date and their planning was thorough. They did not usually undertake any mission unless it had an excellent chance of succeeding.

The VC commander began by carefully evaluating the enemy situation and the terrain, utilizing the latest intelligence data. Then he followed his map reconnaissance with a visit to the objective area to make an on-site investigation of the target. He paid particular attention to routes to and from his objective area.

When he returned to his secure base area, the NVA commander organized his tactical units and prepared an elaborate, by American standards, rehearsal. Terrain similar to that found around his objective area was chosen and elaborate mockups of the target were constructed on it. The commander and his unit would then rehearse every aspect and possible contingency of the forthcoming power raid operation.

Nothing was left out, from caching ammunition and other supplies in the battle area, to planning for disposal of the dead and wounded. Sand tables and stake and string replicas of the target were used during the rehearsals, which might last from three to thirty days, depending on the defensive strength of the target.

At the end of practice, every communist soldier knew his role in the assault. The VC also took careful pains to fully inform every soldier about why the assault was being undertaken and how it contributed to the overall war effort.

Usually the battlefield that encompassed the target area was one that had already been carefully reconnoitered and otherwise prepared, months before the offensive action began. All the communist commander usually had to do was update himself on the current status of the target area. For example, he might verify that tunnels to be used for the approach march and withdrawal were still available, that firing positions for the support element were still tenable, and that local guides, well-informed on the current status of the target defenses, would be waiting at designated rendezvous points.

When all was ready, the "four quick" steps of the execution phase began. Since the battlefield had been prepared during the "One Slow" step, the Viet Cong attack force began to "advance quickly," from their sanctuary to staging areas near the objective. During that advance, diversionary attacks usually took place to attract enemy attention elsewhere. Anti-recon screens protected the advancing unit from discovery.

The VC tried to minimize their exposure time by frequently utilizing underground tunnels during the approach march. Hundreds of such tunnels stretched along the war zone front, surrounding and penetrating many American base camps.

The NVA attack began with a preliminary barrage of direct and indirect fires which was used to stun the enemy and suppress his reactions while elite sappers cut lanes through defensive obstacles. Within an hour or two, the VC attacking force would begin to "assault quickly," attacking along narrow lanes cleared through the wire and minefields, deep into the enemy held position.

Whether the assault was a victory or defeat, the VC unit began to "Mop up Quickly", by grabbing everything of value and removing it, including weapons and ammunition. A specified unit also evacuated all wounded and dead if possible.

As soon as the mop up phase drew near completion, the attacking unit would begin to "Withdraw Quickly". Moving over planned withdrawal routes, covered by rear guard ambushes, the VC unit would head for the nearest underground tunnel complex or sanctuary area.

If enemy reaction threatened to annihilate the attackers, the communists would break off the assault. The NVA unit would disperse into smaller elements and attempt to exfiltrate the battle area in several directions.

When attacking an enemy post or fire base, the NVA was guided by a specific power raid doctrine. That doctrine was a maneuver doctrine.

Power Raid Doctrine

1. The attacking force had to be superior to the defending force. "When the 261st Battalion attacked a post and if its position was not revealed, it was almost sure that it would come out a victor because it always applied a great number of soldiers and weapons against weak defenders."[416]
2. The assault force concentrated its power along one attack axis.
3. Surprise was valued over supporting fire.
4. The main effort was concentrated against enemy weak points: "we must find every way to concentrate our strength, fire power, and efforts to annihilate the enemy main body first, then we exterminate his remaining elements.

   However, this main body is usually the strongest element of the enemy. Thus, we have *to take advantage of the enemy gap and weak points to exterminate his main body.*"[417]

The Chu Luc believed in hand to hand combat and never hesitated to engage in close combat. They wanted their enemies to know and fear their willingness to close assault.

American troops especially dreaded hand to hand combat and, their officers tried to protect them from it. One American "Lessons Learned Report" quite emphatically explained the American reaction to NVA close assaults:

"We must make imaginative and constant use of our tremendous fire support advantage to *kill the PAVN enemy before he gets so close that we must fight him on his terms.* This includes heavy use of the M-79 and even hand grenades to *hold him out* so that artillery, TAC Air, and aerial rocket artillery can work on him."[418]

Although the typical North Vietnamese soldier was smaller than the average American girl, his willingness to fight in close combat provoked fear in his enemies.

The Breakthrough Assault

The NVA/VC assault force was usually given a detailed battle order by their unit commander. The shock force was broken down into sub-units with each one assigned a specific task. Special care was taken to explain redundant means of communications. Coded sequence firing of crew-served weapons, pyrotechnics, tracers, and whistles were preferred signalling devices.

Most attacks were undertaken at dark to impede the technologically strong Americans' use of their fire support and mobility assets.

The power raid assault force usually included two elements: (1) an attack force which was further divided into three offensive elements (breach, shock, and reserve) and two supporting elements (fire support and porters); (2) an ambush force whose mission was to destroy relief columns. In many cases the ambush element was larger and had the primary mission.

The fire support element included all direct and indirect fire weapons such as mortars, rockets, recoilless rifles, and heavy machine guns. Those weapons were used to suppress enemy reaction, interdict movement toward the breakthrough area and destroy point targets. A small part of the fire support element was always detailed to act as a diversionary force by drawing attention to itself and away from the main breakthrough area.

The main effort of the supporting fire was directed against point targets in the enemy camp, including machine guns, mortar emplacements, command posts, communications and ammunition dumps. The VC did not use their supporting weapons to "soften up" their objective area. They realized that preparatory fires sacrificed surprise. They valued surprise more highly than the suppressive effects of prolonged bombardment. That is why most VC fire support did not begin until just before the shock element went in.

The other supporting element consisted of carrying parties charged with clearing the battlefield during the mop up phase. This unit was composed of support personnel, as well as locally impressed civilian porters. They some-times went into action while the battle was still raging.

The breach group was usually composed of sappers armed with explosives and B-40 rockets. They began to surreptitiously clear and mark paths through the enemy wire and minefields before the attack started. Their mission was to get the shock group through the enemy mine/wire belt.

If the breach group was discovered before it had time to clear paths through enemy obstacles, all fire support weapons would cover it until the breaching mission was accomplished. After paths were cleared through the enemy defensive belt, the breach group would lead the charge forward and assist in destroying specified targets.

Sappers of the breach group usually had two missions: (1) prepare open-ings in the barbed-wire and mine fields for the main assault unit(s) (2) blow up specified targets inside the enemy base. In many situations, the firing of sapper demolitions, placed on important targets within the enemy perim-eter, signaled the initiation of the shock assault.

The shock group was the main assault force and usually included eighty to ninety percent of the total force. This element would attack from at least two directions, with the main assault party attacking down the lane cleared

NVA BREAKTHROUGH ASSAULTS

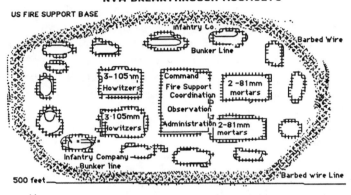

US FIRE SUPPORT BASE

Infantry Co.

Barbed Wire

Bunker Line

3-105mm Howitzers

Command Fire Support Coordination

Observation

Administration

2-81mm mortars

3-105mm Howitzers

2-81mm mortars

Infantry Company Bunker line

Barbed wire Line

500 feet

11

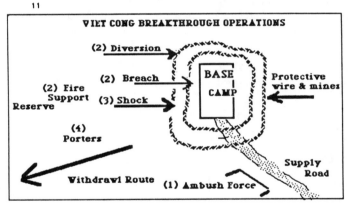

VIET CONG BREAKTHROUGH OPERATIONS

(2) Diversion

(2) Breach

BASE CAMP

Protective wire & mines

(2) Fire Support Reserve

(3) Shock

(4) Porters

Supply Road

Withdrawl Route   (1) Ambush Force

VIET CONG/NORTH VIETNAMESE ARMY COMBAT SEQUENCE

One Slow (Preparation)	Four Fasts ⟶			
	Movement	Attack	Mop Up	Withdrawl
🚶🚶🚶🚶 🚶🚶🚶	🚶🚶🚶🚶🚶🚶🚶	🚶🚶🚶🚶	🚶🚶🚶🚶	🚶🚶🚶🚶🚶

245

through obstacles by the sappers. If no lane through the enemy barrier was cleared, the shock force would have to clear its own.

The shock force would advance swiftly, firing and throwing grenades and satchel charges on the run. After the enemy defensive perimeter was penetrated, sub-units of the shock group would peel off in all directions, attacking pre-designated targets with demolitions and direct fire.

The attack would reach its climax as the shock unit violently drove home its assault. Every man and weapon was dedicated to making this element succeed. Yet, the VC commander was prepared to withdraw the shock element and his whole force, if any change in the battle situation convinced him that he was risking failure or annihilation.

Shortly before the shock element launched its attack a reserve element might launch a diversionary attack and then withdraw to its reserve position. That reserve element was used by the VC to exploit enemy weak points or to reinforce success, it was never supposed to be used to attack a part of the enemy line that was too strong for the shock troops to break into. Frequently the reserve force was used as a rear guard to protect other withdrawing assault elements. In some cases the reserve unit was too small to be of much value, or even nonexistent.

VC breakthrough operations were beautiful ballets of violence. Each step was painstakingly choreographed to ensure success. The offensive spirit and lust for close combat which was displayed on such occasions proved time after time that technology and firepower could never defeat fast-maneuvering, hard-striking, foot-mobile shock troops.

Power Raids Versus Conventional Assaults

Although NVA conventional assaults usually followed the same maneuver rules as power raids and used similar tactics, there were distinct difference. Conventional assaults were usually undertaken to hold terrain for a longer period of time. The briefer power raid was thus easily differentiated from a conventional assault.

In some cases breakthrough assaults were undertaken by larger attacking formations. "At Tan Son Nhut the VC/NVA committed one sapper and four infantry battalions and at Bien Hoa two infantry battalions and one reinforced infantry company."[419] In such cases the NVA intention was usually to seize and hold an objective, at least temporarily.

Naturally, the commitment of larger units in power raids required staging the assault from longer distances: "the units that engaged Tan Son Nhut, Bien Hoa, and other objectives in the Saigon area made formal tactical marches over set routes and through prepared base camps. They were held in assembly areas 9 to 12 hours marching distance from their targets until time for the coordinated assault. One prisoner at Bien Hoa placed the VC/NVA staging area at 29 kilometers, a 9 hour march due east of the air base. Upon arrival, they immediately cut through the perimeter fences and attacked the base. Except to avoid detection on approach, these forces (unlike the stealthy sappers) moved openly against their targets, preceded or accompanied by supporting fires. The main attacks at both bases were supplemented by secondary ones."[420] There seems to be two errors in the above quotation: (1) It seems hardly conceivable that an advancing NVA unit would proceed at an approximately three kilometers an hour march rate, in an approach march over such a prolonged distance. (2) Larger NVA attack units usually attempted to obtain the element of surprise by avoiding preliminary supporting fires.

Chu Luc conventional assaults were similar to western assault methods and frequently incorporated a complex scheme of preparatory fires. A captured NVA officer, Lieutenant La Thanh Tonc, described a planned conventional assault upon U.S. Marine outposts around Khe Sahn:

"Hill 881N is presently surrounded. There is a company of sappers presently deployed in the general area of 881N. This sapper company will be . . . used against Hill 861.

"Once Hill 861 has fallen, the general attack against the Khe Sahn Combat Base will begin. This will consist of a reinforced regimental size force from the direction of Lang Hoan Tap by way of Hill 861, where they will link up with the occupying force there. Once linked up, Khe Sahn Combat Base will begin receiving heavy artillery fire and rockets from unknown positions, but from a northwesterly direction. When this occurs, the first regiment will move to assault positions under cover of fire. One mortar platoon east of Hill 1015 will cover the Marine heavy weapons on Hill 950."[421]

When the U.S. Marines at Khe Sahn realized that the NVA units besieging them were using conventional large-unit assault methods, they became more able to predict enemy behavior. They referred to their doctrinal handbooks on conventional Soviet-style assaults which implied that communist tactical deployments always unfolded in the same patterns, for example:

"Enemy doctrine calls for an attacking force to move to its assault position in echelons, make a last minute reconnaissance, and attack in waves. If this was indeed a regiment, then the force would probably be disposed in a regimental column, battalions in line one behind the other . . . a large force, moving at two kilometers per hour (NVA rate of march in darkness and mist—more doctrine) . . . Enemy attack doctrine usually positions the reserve battalion directly behind the assault unit."[422]

Yet, the NVA did not closely follow Soviet doctrine at Khe Sahn. Their modifications thwarted the U.S. Marine attempt at mirror imaging. U.S. military mirror-imagining frequently caused American officers to erroneously assume that their own lock-step approach to battle was similar to communist approaches.

The Power Raid on LZ Bird

In December, 1966 two American artillery batteries and a weak (sixty-five man) company of infantry were dug in on Landing Zone (LZ) Bird. LZ Bird was located in the II Corps' Binh Dinh War Zone. Bird was dug in along the flat bank of the Kim Son River in the NVA Crow's Foot Stronghold, just east of Phu Huu 2 village. The area was the usual stomping ground of the 18th NVA Infantry Regiment, then refitting.[423]

A shallow trench encircled the American position which depended upon the river bank for part of its security, although it was dominated by surrounding hills. Each of the twelve (six 105mm and six 155mm) howitzers emplaced at Bird, had an individual encircling trench dug around it. In addition each sandbagged howitzer parapet was protected by a fighting bunker. Each howitzer position also included a protective bunker for sleeping and an ammunition bunker.

Around the battery positions, the American infantry company deployed into fourteen machine gun positions covering 550 meters of fighting frontage. There was approximately forty yards between each machine gun. Half of the infantry company manned the machine guns, the rest were spread out in small squad lots.

In addition to being insufficient in infantry protection, Bird was not properly fortified. There were no wire barricades, no interlocking fields of fire, no claymores, no minefields, no trip flares and no detection sensors. The few amateurishly rigged mines and flares put in by the infantry company shouldn't be counted.

The 3rd NVA Infantry Division decided to dispatch its 22nd Infantry Regiment to destroy LZ Bird.

22nd NVA Infantry Regiment: December, 1966

- Three rifle battalions (7, 8, 9). Each battalion controlled three rifle companies, each of which had four 60mm mortars and two heavy machine guns assigned to it. Each company had three or four rifle platoons which included one or two M79 grenade launchers and three rifle squads. Each rifle squad was composed of nine men armed with one light machine gun, three AK-47 rifles, three SKS carbines and grenades.

- One recoilless rifle company with six (DKZ) 75mm and six (DKZ) 57mm recoilless rifles.
- One transportation company of one hundred (including seventy women) porters.
- A signal company equipped with four 15 watt radios, four 2 watt radios, one switchboard, ten field telephones, ten captured and PRC-25 light field radios. This signal equipment tied all battalion and companies to the regimental headquarters. They carried out a commo sked of four daily transmissions.
- A surgical element and mobile hospital with one hundred personnel (including sixty women).[424]

On December 16, 1966 the 22nd NVA Regiment's commander, Major Tin Phuong, received a map overlay of his objective, an attack order to be executed by December 23, 1966, and 250 replacements. Major Phuong's assault was timed to occur so that he could withdraw his regiment safely from attack during the American scheduled "Christmas Truce." He knew that the celebrating Americans would be reluctant to pursue his withdrawing host during their holidays. The regiment left immediately and on December 23, 1966 its battalions, which had infiltrated by three separate routes, closed on the regimental staging area north of Bird. Each NVA battalion was assigned an objective according to the mission-type order schemata.

22nd NVA Regiment: Battalion Missions

- 7th Infantry Battalion: Establish two ambushes on likely American withdrawl routes. Collect weapons, POWs and war trophies.
- 8th Infantry Battalion: Wipe out American infantry company.
- 9th Infantry Battalion, with one seven man sapper unit assigned from division headquarters: Destroy the twelve artillery pieces.[425]

Each battalion then assigned specific objectives to its companies and platoons.

Obviously, Major Phuong made a mistake. He did not provide for overwhelming force against the enemy. The 7th Battalion was left hanging. He should have deployed the 7th Infantry Battalion, in company elements, as a reserve to exploit any success by the main effort.

On December 24, 1966 the 1st Cavalry Division G-2 (division intelligence officer), in a rare stroke of professionalism, "concluded that a communist force was assembling in significant numbers in a staging area 4,500 meters southeast of LZ Bird; he guessed it was the 22nd Regiment."[426] At 7 AM on December 26, an artillery barrage was fired into the area. "However, the barraging was too far off line even to be rated a near-miss. So the 22nd Regiment remained unhurt, and its men came on strong, most of them outfitted with helmets, knapsacks, boots, entrenching tools, and sheath knives, besides firearms."[427]

After dark on December 26, 1966, the 8th and 9th Battalions surrounded Landing Zone Bird. "The 8th Battalion was responsible for the northeastern flank of their line next to the hill mass. The 9th Battalion blocked to the southeast . . . these dispositions in a semicircle closed all escape routes. 'The forward line of 8th Battalion,' said Phuc, 'was within 12 meters of your perimeter for the next six hours.'

"There was much work to be done. By 2200 [10 PM], wire had been laid just outside of Bird so that the battalions were in contact with one another as well as with the command. Two 81-mm. mortars were emplaced on the foothills to the northeast, within 400 meters of Bird; there were only five rounds per tube. Two 75-DKZ recoilless rifles were positioned 300 yards from the perimeter under direct command by Major Phuong. Each battalion had two 57-mm. DKZs, two 60mm. mortars, two heavy machine guns and one light machine gun, . . . positioned to bear on the camp . . . These arrangements were completed one hour before midnight."[428]

22nd NVA Regiment Fire Support Plan

Diversionary Fire Support: Two groups—A. Two heavy machine guns. B. Two machine guns. *Target:* right side of objective area.

Secondary Attack: Covered by: two recoilless rifles, two 660mm mortars and 1 M-60 machine gun. *Target:* Left side of objective.

Main Thrust: Covered by 81mm mortar battery, 60mm mortar battery, two M79s, two M60 machine guns and recoilless rifles. *Target:* North central objective area.

The attack jumped off at 0105 and the 8th and 9th Battalions immediately broke into the battery position in four locations. The two major penetrations of the American perimeter, involving nearly a battalion each of NVA troops, occurred in the southeast and northeast corners. The North Vietnamese were chanting: "Die GI, die GI, die GI. Yankee, you die tonight! Yankee, go home! What you do now, GI?"[429]

American resistance immediately collapsed. In one platoon bunker two wounded and four unwounded Americans were discovered hiding. They told the officer who found them, "There's no real fight going on out there."[430]

Suddenly, however, the cohesion of the NVA began to break down as they looted American Christmas goodies. They became distracted and fragmented, fighting as individual squads and cells. Then the NVA battlefield evacuation unit arrived and began clearing out red bodies.

One of the 22nd Regiment's battalions still sat idle. The 7th Battalion was dug into an ambush position south of Bird. They were deployed along a sandbar paralleling a treeline.

The fight inside the perimeter of Bird degenerated into a melee. Soon American airpower began to arrive. They blasted enemy crew-served weapons positions and the 7th Battalion's ambush position. Realizing that with the dawn would come overwhelming aerial support, Major Phuong decided to withdraw his regiment.

The withdrawal signal was sounded and the 22nd NVA Regiment retreated, after losing one-third of its troops or the equivalent of more than one battalion dead. "Among other fighting supplies, they abandoned on the battlefield eight satchel charges, seven Bangalore torpedoes, 250 hand grenades, three cases of rifle grenades, 25 81mm mortar rounds, 30 60mm mortar rounds, and 20 B-40 rockets."[431]

The Power Raid at Dong Tre

In June 1966, American Special Forces officers began to receive intelligence information that several enemy regimental equivalents were approaching Dong Tre near II Corps' coastal Tuy Hoa. Dong Tre, a fortified Special Forces base, had the inappropriate mission of securing a main road connecting the base with La Hai, another fortified base camp. Three kilometers north of Dong Tre, on the west flank of the road, were three hills, spread out over four kilometers, and commanding an expanse of open plain. The hills were held by one platoon of indigenous troops each, leaving another CIDG company to garrison Dong Tre.

On the night of June 18, 1966 four explosions were heard from the direction of the hills. Suddenly the area was lit up by green star clusters and gun fire. One of the platoon commanders called in saying: "Under full attack, grenades, satchel charges, machine guns. Running out of ammunition. We got many bodies stacked up."[432] Then the radio went silent.

Worried that the attack on the hills was an ambush lure, the defenders of Dong Tre stayed put. The next day most of the hill defenders arrived at the base, lying about their heroism. In fact they had been attacked while

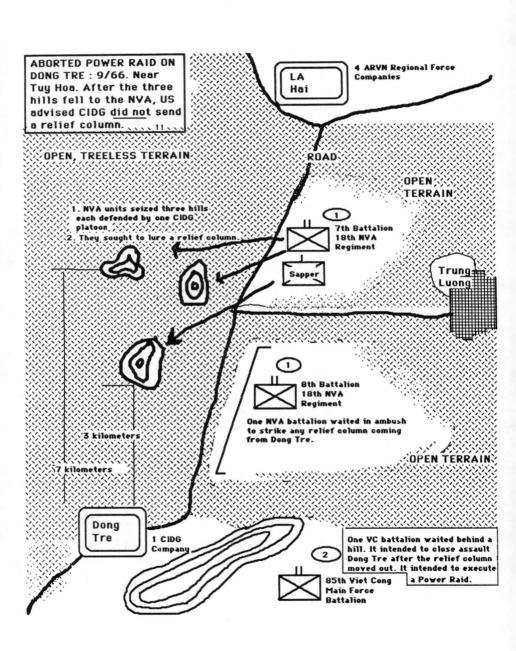

ABORTED POWER RAID ON DONG TRE : 9/66. Near Tuy Hoa. After the three hills fell to the NVA, US advised CIDG did <u>not</u> send a relief column. 11

LA Hai — 4 ARVN Regional Force Companies

OPEN, TREELESS TERRAIN

ROAD

OPEN TERRAIN

1. NVA units seized three hills each defended by one CIDG platoon.
2. They sought to lure a relief column.

1 — 7th Battalion 18th NVA Regiment

Sapper

Trung Luong

1 — 8th Battalion 18th NVA Regiment

One NVA battalion waited in ambush to strike any relief column coming from Dong Tre.

OPEN TERRAIN

3 kilometers

7 kilometers

Dong Tre — 1 CIDG Company

One VC battalion waited behind a hill. It intended to close assault Dong Tre after the relief column moved out. It intended to execute a Power Raid.

2 — 85th Viet Cong Main Force Battalion

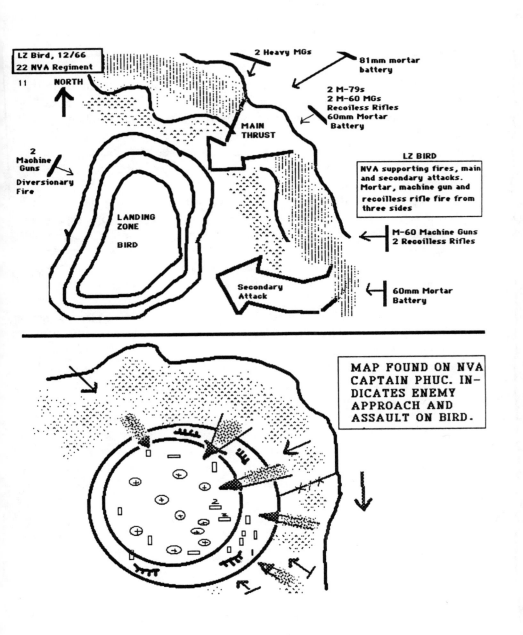

LZ Bird, 12/66
22 NVA Regiment

11

NORTH

2 Heavy MGs

81mm mortar
battery

2 M-79s
2 M-60 MGs
Recoiless Rifles
60mm Mortar
Battery

MAIN
THRUST

2
Machine
Guns

Diversionary
Fire

LZ BIRD

NVA supporting fires, main
and secondary attacks.
Mortar, machine gun and
recoilless rifle fire from
three sides

LANDING
ZONE

BIRD

M-60 Machine Guns
2 Recoilless Rifles

Secondary
Attack

60mm Mortar
Battery

MAP FOUND ON NVA
CAPTAIN PHUC. IN-
DICATES ENEMY
APPROACH AND
ASSAULT ON BIRD.

sleeping. Most of the CIDG troops had run away in their loin cloths, abandoning the hill positions without a fight.

The NVA had carried out a strong close assault power raid. The 7th Battalion of the 18th NVA assaulted and secured the three hills in order to draw a relief column toward them. Each hill was close assaulted by one NVA company, led by two sapper squads. They encountered no resistance as the cowardly defenders hastily fled. The green star clusters were communist signals that the hills were in the hands of the NVA.

Dug in along the side of the road to the hills was the 8th Battalion of the 18th NVA Regiment. Its mission was to slaughter any rescue force. Hiding behind a hill directly to the south of Dong Tre was the 85th Viet Cong Main Force Battalion. The 85th was primed to close assault Dong Tre, seizing it after the relief force marched out.

A two company allied relief force approached the enemy held hills later that morning. They were fought by NVA rear guards defending each hill with about a platoon. The NVA were screaming, "Keep coming Americans! We got you! We show you real fight!"[433]

Driven off by air power, the reds left no bodies behind. Even their tracks had been scruffed out. Later a small mass grave with eighteen bodies was found.

The NVA had decided to retire when they realized that their plan was not going to work. They had left a company of the 7th Battalion, 18th NVA Regiment behind as a rear guard.

Later the surprised Americans learned that the Dong Tre battle was only the "first gambit in the setting of a very large trap."[434] An NVA battlefield had been prepared with nearby Trung Luong as its centerpiece. The communists hoped to catch American forces in the area and annihilate them either by ambushes, defense of fortified areas or in power breakthrough assaults.

Two battalions each of the 18th and 66th NVA regiments were joined by the 85th VC Main Force Battalion in the operation. It was an operational size, five battalion battle scenario.

CHAPTER 12

NVA Ambushes

On July 28, 1967 the 3rd U.S. Marine Division sent the 2nd Battalion, 9th Marines on a spoiling attack into the Demilitarized Zone (DMZ) which separated North and South Vietnam. The battalion was reinforced with a tank platoon, three ontos assault vehicles, three amtracs and engineers. The marine unit, with its reinforcements, five companies and two command groups, was twice as big as any Army battalion. In fact the reinforced marine battalion, with over 1,200 men, dwarfed a Viet Cong regiment.

The marine battalion traveled north up Route 606 toward the DMZ, with one company (200 men) providing security on either flank. The area that they were traversing south of the Ben Hai River was an NVA stronghold and fortified zone. Although the surrounding terrain was famous for being good tank country, the column restricted itself to a road lined with thick vegetation.

When the battalion reached the river, it turned around and started back over the same road, Route 606. At 1115 hours, a 250 pound bomb, buried in the road, was command detonated. North Vietnamese soldiers then opened fire against the column with machine guns, 60mm and 82mm mortars, and RPG anti-tank rockets.

A running battle began, as the enemy quickly fragmented the marine column into company-sized segments. By nightfall the marines were pinned down in five or six perimeters, fighting desperately to protect and evacuate casualties. On the next day, after the enemy suddenly broke off the running fight, the marines found that they had lost 275 men and most of their vehicles.[435]

253

A few weeks earlier, Bravo Company of the 1st Battalion, 9th Marines had been nearly wiped out in the same vicinity. The 1/9 suffered over 250 casualties while rescuing the twenty-seven surviving members of Bravo Company who were able to walk out of that trap. A North Vietnamese Army maneuvering ambush had been used to pin, close assault and fragment the shocked and reeling marine units.[436]

Emphasizing surprise, the VC had been known to lie in ambush undetected for periods in excess of ten days. Their ambushes would usually be set up along avenues of approach including roads, trails and streams. They also chose unpredictable or unexpected places including locations close to friendly bases.

Preparing a Chu Luc Ambush

In preparing for am ambush, the NVA adhered to their sequence of combat known as "one slow and four fasts:" Slow Preparation, Fast Advance, Fast Assault, Fast Mop Up, and Fast Withdrawal.

Chu Luc operations were planned in detail and based on careful reconnaissance and up-to-date intelligence. Enemy force patterns were studied in detail. When collecting intelligence for ambushes, the NVA wanted to know their enemy's route and direction of movement, troop and weapon strength, and approximate time of passage through the ambush site.

Detailed rehearsals, including the use of mockups, sandtable exercises, and similar terrain simulations were used when preparing for the ambush. During the rehearsal, particular attention was paid to three phases of combat: actions prior to opening fire, actions upon opening fire, and withdrawal from the battle area.

Once a plan was made and rehearsed, the NVA seemed reluctant to depart from it. Being careful, not inflexible, they were very cautious and attempted to determine the size, disposition and direction of movement of their opponent before engaging him. They would rather let an opportunity slip by than act hastily without proper intelligence and preparation.

The communists realized that their carefully planned operations depended upon a predictable enemy. Any unpredictable element insinuated into the situation could cause a mission abort. The NVA lived by the motto, "Fight and run away. Live to fight another day."

Each red ambush site was carefully selected according to clearly defined criteria. The first requirement was for cover and concealment which would allow both secret movement into the ambush site and withdrawal from it. In addition, positions had to be available for establishing early warning observation posts and heavy weapons emplacements.

VIET CONG AMBUSHES

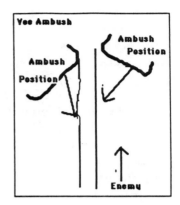

Yee Ambush

Ambush Position

Ambush Position

Enemy

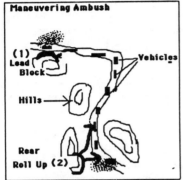

Maneuvering Ambush

(1) Lead Block

Vehicles

Hills

Rear Roll Up (2)

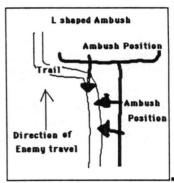

L shaped Ambush

Ambush Position

Trail

Ambush Position

Direction of Enemy travel

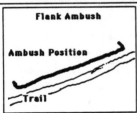

Flank Ambush

Ambush Position

Trail

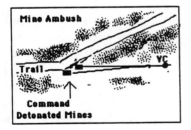

Mine Ambush

Trail

VC

Command Detonated Mines

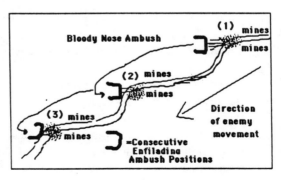

Bloody Nose Ambush

(1) mines

mines

(2) mines

mines

(3) mines

mines

Direction of enemy movement

=Consecutive Enfilading Ambush Positions

255

The terrain surrounding the ambush site was of key importance. Nearly as important as preventing detection of the ambushing unit, was the requirement for sufficient concealed avenues for maneuver-favoring encirclement of the ambushed enemy.

The ambush area terrain had to permit the deployment of at least three primary NVA ambush elements: The lead blocking element, the main element, and the rear blocking element. Some ambushes deployed other elements as well.

The NVA preferred a kill zone commanded by their ambush position, which enabled them to channel the enemy, prevent deployment and impede the use of heavy support weapons. A column of enemy troops crammed into a roadway with little maneuver room was the ideal situation.

If possible, the VC prepared the battlefield, both in the vicinity of the ambush and further away. In the vicinity of the ambush site they carefully marked pathways which would be used to maneuver their units for close assault.

Unlike American units, which remained in the ambush position until they withdrew from the battlefield, the VC planned to move part of their ambush force, after the ambush had been sprung, to strike the enemy in close combat. They were eager to close with and destroy the enemy, realizing that even ambushed troops are hardly ever totally annihilated by fire.

The ambush battlefield was also prepared by digging graves along the avenue(s) of withdrawal. Ammunition caches were pre-positioned as necessary. In addition, crew-served weapons emplacements might be pre-selected and fields of fire laid out. If applicable, mortar firing positions and ammo supply points were designated and all potential targets within range mapped and plotted.

In many cases bunker positions, complete with overhead cover, were prepared in the ambush zone. In some cases unit hides were prepared from which the ambush elements would move into their firing positions at the last minute.

Further away from the site, supporting efforts might be planned, including diversionary attacks and troop movements to lure targeted enemy forces into or away from the kill zone. Maneuvers associated with a major ambush might take place over geographical areas dozens of square miles wide and deep. Baited traps and ruses were often used, such as attacks designed to lure reaction or reserve forces toward or away from prepared ambush positions. Retreat might be feigned to draw an enemy force into an ambush.

Ambushes were usually timed to occur just before dark in order to thwart allied aircraft and artillery by depriving them of daylight conditions. Such timing could be brought about by using small units to delay an approaching enemy column until it advanced into the killing ground of the main ambush at the proper time. The VC referred to actions associated with preparing the battlefield as "creating conditions for the ambush."[437]

Secrecy was preserved at all times. A surveillance unit was assigned to keep the ambush site under close surveillance before it was occupied. The unit provided warning if allied forces discovered any trace of the ambush or prepared ambush positions of its own.

The NVA devoted great attention to security during movement into the ambush site. Scouts were usually deployed in observation of the route to the ambush position and on the site itself to insure against surprise. Movement into the ambush position was undertaken to avoid inhabited areas and take maximum advantage of concealment.

Organization of the Ambush Position

The reds always strove for three standard advantages in their defensive actions, maneuver battles and ambushes: prepared battle plans, terrain of their own choosing, and the combat power multiplier effect realized by fighting from previously prepared fortifications.

When deploying into an ambush site, the NVA first occupied several observation posts (OPs), placed to detect the enemy as early as possible and provide early warning to the unit commander. Usually one main OP and several secondary OPs were set up. Each OP was tied into the command element by at least two separate, redundant, communications means, for example, a runner and a radio. The OPs were located so that they could observe enemy movement into the ambush, routes of reinforcement and withdrawal, and maneuver options. Frequently the OPs were reinforced to squad outpost size and served as flank security.

In addition to the observation posts, the ambush was organized into a command element, a rear blocking element, a close assault element and a lead blocking element. Other elements might also be included if the situation demanded it, such as a sniper screen along a nearby avenue of approach to delay enemy reinforcement.

Failure to set up proper OPs and flank security was usually costly to communist ambushers. In 1965, two local VC, or guerrilla, platoons totaling about fifty men, tried to ambush an ARVN ranger company. Noticing that the ranger company always used the same route during its road clearing mission, the VC had set up a linear ambush along the edge of a clearing. The clearing was located along the edge of jungle where the ranger road-clearing operation ran through a rubber plantation.

The ambush position was 200 meters from the road and offered unimpeded observation and fields of fire. However, the VC failed to establish OPs or flanking security elements.

When the ranger company approached the ambush site, the reds discovered the ARVN unit had adopted a new formation. The company commander advanced one platoon through the rubber plantation on the left side of the road, and the rest of the company along the right side of the road. As the right hand ARVN column neared the clearing where the VC ambush lay, the ARVN commander ordered his advanced platoon to swing around the clearing through the jungle. That move hit the VC ambush on its left flank and a fire fight began.

When contact began, the ARVN company commander swung his other right column platoon to the right. That maneuver toward the rear of the VC ambush force, which was now engaging his advance platoon, jeopardized the VC rear. Simultaneously, the ARVN commander ordered his platoon on the left side of the road to move into a skirmish line opposite the enemy-held clearing.

The plucky Viet Cong counterattacked the two ARVN platoons which were attempting to envelop their left flank. They held their own for about thirty minutes.

When ARVN mortar fire began impacting in the area the reds began a precipitate withdrawal. They hadn't forgotten to select a covered and concealed line of retreat through the jungle to the south. The VC left only seven bodies behind.[438]

Ambush Types

A VC force of any size, from squad to division, could execute an ambush. Smaller units usually didn't have enough troops to stage a complete five element ambush. They simply set up one of the preferred ambush types and avoided close assaulting the enemy. The NVA favored eight types of ambushes: Mine, Bloody Nose, Flank, L, Maneuver, Vee, Triangle and Zee.

The Mine ambush depended up command-detonated mines triggered by hidden VC who held a detonating device connected to the demolition by electrical wires. Mine ambush kill zones might also include punji traps or other homemade traps, land mines and natural obstacles. However, the ambush was always triggered by electrically detonating a mine, when enemy troops moved within the mine's killing range (usually forty yards or less).

The Bloody Nose ambush was used by small Viet Cong units against larger enemy forces as a means of harassment, delay, and disruption. By positioning the ambush to enfilade an avenue of approach, the VC obtained a greater result. Minefields, man traps, and booby traps were placed along both sides of the trail and perpendicular to it. As the enemy unit came under fire and attempted to maneuver right or left to close with the ambushers, casualties would be inflicted by the protective barriers. As soon as the ambushing element realized that the enemy had advanced into, and taken casualties from, the mine/trap line, the ambushers withdrew to another pre-selected site where they might repeat the maneuver.

The Flank or Linear ambush was one of the simplest to set up and operate, and was most commonly used by the NVA. It was also easy to get into and away from quickly. The ambush position was laid parallel to the target area. Mines or other obstacles were placed on the other side of the ambush. Upon command, fire was brought to bear on the kill zone from multiple, overlapping firing positions. The linear ambush pumped bullets into the flank of a surprised enemy column.[439]

The L ambush included the best aspects of both the Bloody Nose and Linear ambush. The short end, or base, of the L was positioned so that at least one machine gun could fire straight down the kill zone, enfilading it. Parallel to the kill zone and tied into the L was a second, flanking ambush. That ambush was harder to control than the Linear ambush, which is why the VC usually tried to place it on the outside of a curving roadway.

The L ambush could provide its own security protection as well. The base of the L might be placed along either flank of the ambush position, not to fire into the kill zone, but to ambush enemy units who were attempting to flank the main ambush position along obvious avenues of approach.[440]

In some situations the enemy located a reserve unit in line with the vertical bar of the L, forming a T ambush. After the ambush was sprung, the enemy maneuvered his reserves to block the enemy line of withdrawal. The reserves either close assaulted the Americans or set up another ambush along the first stream or trail crossing to the immediate rear of the kill zone.[441]

The Maneuvering ambush was usually directed against a road bound column of vehicles. The NVA usually sprung it out of high ground, near a bend in the road which allowed cover and longer fields of fire for automatic weapons. Weapons opened fire from positions within forty yards of the road, or less.

A road bend was included in the kill zone so that the end of the column was out of sight of the head of the column when the ambush was sprung. Interruption of a column's front-to-rear line of sight increased the chances that the head and tail of an ambushed column would split apart and try to fight separately.

VIET CONG AMBUSHES

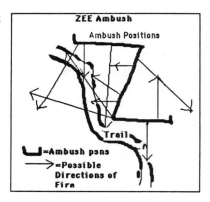

ZEE Ambush

Ambush Positions

Trail

�”=Ambush psns
⟶=Possible
Directions of
Fire

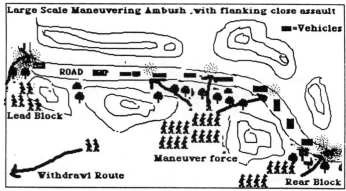

Large Scale Maneuvering Ambush , with flanking close assault

■=Vehicles

ROAD

Lead Block

Maneuver force

Withdrawl Route

Rear Block

MANEUVERING AMBUSH

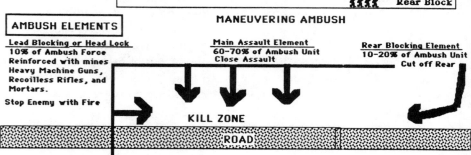

AMBUSH ELEMENTS

Lead Blocking or Head Lock
10% of Ambush Force
Reinforced with mines
Heavy Machine Guns,
Recoilless Rifles, and
Mortars.

Stop Enemy with Fire

Main Assault Element
60-70% of Ambush Unit
Close Assault

Rear Blocking Element
10-20% of Ambush Unit
Cut off Rear

KILL ZONE

ROAD

The Maneuvering ambush was initiated by a small NVA element striking the head of an enemy column and stopping it by fire. Then the communist main body would attack the column from the rear and/or flank, fragmenting it and rolling it up. The two strikes were timed close enough together so that the target column was engaged from both ends before it could deploy and face toward either danger.

The Vee ambush, positioned with its open mouth toward the enemy advance, was a favorite of the Viet Cong. It was used in fairly open terrain and jungle. The ambushers, in good concealment along the legs of the vee, would creep close to the trail after the enemy point had passed. The Vee ambush was virtually undetectable by enemy point or flank security until at least a portion of the target force was in the kill zone. Red bushwhackers could also direct enfilading fire down the enemy axis of advance, and interlocking fire from each leg across the vee. The Vee lent itself to the use of controlled mines, booby traps and fougasse.[442]

The Zee ambush, usually laid along a road, was both effective and confusing to the unit being ambushed. The VC usually planned this complicated ambush, and dug their low bunkers along the kill zone, months prior to the ambush. The Zee was usually occupied after word was received that an enemy battalion or larger unit would be using the road which passed through the ambush site.

The long end of the Zee ambush was located on one side of a road or trail enabling the ambushers to employ both enfilading fire and flanking fire. It was also placed to neutralize attempts to flank the ambush from nearly every direction.[443] NVA units deployed along the two short ends of the Zee could fire in either direction. The Zee was dangerous to ambushers because ambush elements sometimes fired into each other by mistake.

In January 1965, the 514th Viet Cong Battalion decided to exploit a habitual ARVN battalion's road movement by ambushing the unit. Although the VC didn't know the ARVN's exact time of departure, they decided to ambush the ARVN battalion after it left its base at Bau Dua, Long Tien.

Leaving their Tam Binh campsite, the 514th VC Battalion marched for two nights, taking a circuitous route. The reds entered their ambush position at 0100 hours on the second night.

At 1300 hours of the next day, the ARVN unit left its base and embarked upon its usual itinerary. Opening the ambush, the 514th's second company hit the ARVN front and headlocked it. Then the first company assaulted the ARVN flank, fragmenting the column. The third company forced the rear of the South Vietnamese column back toward its base and then swung right, joining the second company in an encirclement of the forward ARVN company. Within forty-five minutes, the forward South Vietnamese company was annihilated and, after mopping up the battlefield, the 514th VC Battalion rapidly withdrew.[444]

The Battle of Annihilation

On certain occasions the Chu Luc would have to "shape" an enemy into an ambush. That shaping effort might involve a lure or delaying maneuver:

"In La Nga ambush battle, if we had allowed the enemy to move freely, as usual, the convoy would have entered the ambush site too early, permitting enemy aircraft and artillery to intervene when the first shots were fired, causing us much trouble. The Command Committee was very flexible. It sent some cells out to delay the enemy step by step, slowing down his advance, wearing him down and making him underestimate friendly forces. Not until 4:30 P.M. did the convoy fall into the main ambush site, where it was annihilated. Enemy aircraft and artillery did not have enough time to intervene as darkness set in."[445]

Under the right conditions, the NVA would spring a full-scale, five element ambush. The three primary elements of such an ambush were the lead blocking element, the main assault force and the rear blocking element.

The lead blocking element, usually ten percent of the total enemy force, had but one mission. They were to stop the enemy unit by inflicting as much casualties and disorganization upon him as possible. "The opponent's lead element must be halted at any cost. The lead elements usually have very strong firepower; therefore they are firmly and strongly engaged in combat. In order to affect the trick, bridges and roads must be sabotaged, obstructions must be set, or equipment must be damaged in order to force the whole convoy to stop."[446]

Fire tunnels, carefully disguised firelanes with cover, were usually sighted so that both enfilading and converging fire could be poured into the kill zone. Maximum firepower would be generated by the lead block against the front of the enemy, stunning, and stalling him. In a battalion-sized ambush, the lead blocking force would consist of a platoon reinforced by mines, one or two recoilless rifles, one or two heavy machine guns and 60mm or 82mm mortars.

The rear blocking element, ten to twenty percent of the total Viet Cong force, was targeted against the rear of the enemy column. If the entire enemy force was trapped within the kill zone, the rear blocking element attacked its rear "and cooperated with the battalion main force with heavy weapons such as the 51mm and 60mm mortars, and recoilless rifles firing at long range to wear down the rear element of the opponent."[447]

If the rear of the enemy column was not caught in the ambush, the rear-block unit would move to cut off the enemy rear from the rest of the column. The rear block protected the flank and rear of the close assault force and coordinated its actions with that main maneuver element. If possible, the rear block would simultaneously neutralize the enemy rear while cooperating with the close assault force in an envelopment of that part of the enemy column trapped in the kill zone.

Sixty to eighty percent of the NVA ambushing unit was deployed as the close assault or main maneuvering element. That element massed to the flank of the enemy formation's line of march and was committed after the lead and rear blocks went into action. Reinforced with mines, anti-tank weapons, machine guns, and flame throwers, the close assault element struck the enemy column when it was most organized. In some cases, part of the maneuvering element was held out as a reserve and later employed as a rear guard during the withdrawal phase.

Attacking from several directions near the center of the enemy column, and firing from the hip, the close assault element engaged the survivors of the initial firefight in hand-to-hand combat. The close assault element was charged with annihilating the enemy force by close combat and shock action.

The NVA attackers sought to fragment the enemy column and defeat it in detail within the killing zone. Each enemy fragment was then surrounded and wiped out.

Maneuvering Ambush

Lead blocking element: **Facilitates main assault force's opportunity to close assault. Coordinates with main assault force and covers flank.**
Main assault force: **Splits the enemy unit with close assaults. Attacks from the flank and encircles fragmented enemy.**
Rear blocking element: **Attacks the rear of entire enemy force in kill zone. Cuts off portions of enemy column rear which do not enter the kill zone. Protects flank of main assault force.**

The ambush commander, directing the battle from an OP near the staging area for the close assault element, sometimes chose not to commit it. Instead he might decide to use it to reinforce the fires of the other two elements, or to carry out some other mission.

If at any time, the situation deteriorated to the point that a sizeable number of the ambushing unit was in danger of being itself annihilated, the commander signaled a withdrawal of some, or all, of his forces using a

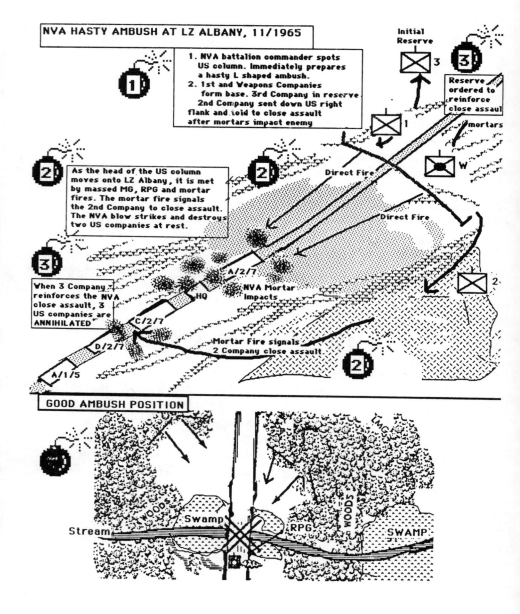

NVA HASTY AMBUSH AT LZ ALBANY, 11/1965

(1) 1. NVA battalion commander spots US column. Immediately prepares a hasty L shaped ambush.
2. 1st and Weapons Companies form base. 3rd Company in reserve. 2nd Company sent down US right flank and told to close assault after mortars impact enemy

Initial Reserve

(3) Reserve ordered to reinforce close assault

mortars

Direct Fire

Direct Fire

(2) As the head of the US column moves onto LZ Albany, it is met by massed MG, RPG and mortar fires. The mortar fire signals the 2nd Company to close assault. The NVA blow strikes and destroys two US companies at rest.

A/2/7

NVA Mortar Impacts

(3) When 3 Company reinforces the NVA close assault, 3 US companies are ANNIHILATED

HQ

C/2/7

D/2/7

A/1/5

Mortar Fire signals 2 Company close assault.

(2)

GOOD AMBUSH POSITION

WOODS

Swamp

Stream

RPG

WOODS

SWAMP

MG

combination of flares, whistles, bugles, and/or voice commands. The withdrawal itself was sometimes used as a vehicle for laying additional deliberate or hasty ambushes of delay or annihilation.

The Mop Up

If the close assault unit successfully executed its mission by destroying the enemy main force, the battlefield was rapidly mopped up. A pre-designated element of the ambushing unit removed all friendly dead, wounded and weapons. Members of the close assault force simultaneously looted the enemy dead of weapons, ammunition and documents. Prisoners were either sped along the withdrawal route(s) or executed on the spot. If a sizable amount of loot was seized, other pre-designated elements carried it off.

A fast withdrawal over pre-selected routes then began. NVA rear guards, consisting of ten to twenty percent of the ambush unit, sought to cover the withdrawal by delaying actions such as sniping and Bloody Nose ambushes.

The dead were buried in pre-dug graves along with the withdrawal routes if time was available. Some NVA corpses usually were booby-trapped.

If necessary, the ambushing unit could divide itself into numerous small units which then exfiltrated the area in various directions. The red unit later rendezvoused at a pre-designated location, according to a predetermined time schedule.

By the time large American conventional units began arriving in Vietnam, the reds had perfected their ambush methods. Their success could be measured by the numbers of allied corpses rotting in thousands of kill zones.

Ambushes During the Tay Nguyen Campaign

As NVA Brigadier General Chu Huy Man maneuvered his Front across Pleiku province during Operation Tay Nguyen in the summer and fall of 1965, his 32nd NVA Infantry Regiment carried out two major ambushes. In August 1965, the 32nd NVA Regiment ambushed an ARVN armored column along Route 19 seven kilometers east of Duc Co, near II Corps' Triborder War Zone. One 32nd Regiment battalion had enfircled Duc Co to lure a rescue force over Route 19. The other two battalions were poised in ambush to exploit that lure. Deployed along the six-kilometer ambush site were the 32nd NVA Regiment battalions reinforced with some crew-served weapons teams. They were deployed in an L shaped ambush.

The ambush began with a small NVA base of fire element locking the head of the ARVN armored column. Then a two-company pincers attack split the ARVN task force into two parts. A rear blocking company assault pinned the rear of the South Vietnamese column, immobilizing it. It looked like NVA Colonel Dinh Khan's regiment had won the battle. However, the ARVN armored force was too strong and, with the help of American air power, beat off the NVA attack. The 32nd Regiment had made a big mistake, launching an ambush in open terrain against an armored force which could maneuver off the road.[448]

In October 1965, the same lure tactic was tried again. This time the 33rd NVA Regiment had Plei Me surrounded and the entire 32nd Regiment was deployed in a huge ambush ten kilometers north of the town waiting to hit another ARVN armored rescue column. The Plei Me ambush site was more appropriate than the one used in August, its vegetation constricting armored movement off the road. The ambushing battalions were deployed along a site which included a sharp reverse S curve dominating a seven kilometer straight stretch of Route 5.

The reds set up a giant L ambush with the 635th Battalion reinforced by the regimental 75mm recoilless rifle company, dug in on two hills south of the first curve. Along the western edge of the road the 344th Battalion was spread along a two kilometer frontage. Although the battalion occupied three small hills its frontage was too great.

The 966th Battalion, reinforced by the regimental antiaircraft company, was hidden in a reserve position two kilometers west of the ambush area. It would be used against any airmobile intervention in the area or as reinforcement for the other two battalions.

Finally, the slow ARVN armored column arrived and, after directing airstrikes against the suspected positions occupied by the 635th and 344th NVA Battalions, moved into the kill zone. At that time, both communist battalions opened fire and locked the head of the column. The ARVN return fire was so intense that after two hours the 635th Battalion had to be pulled back. Then the 344th Battalion hit the supply vehicles which had parked in the ARVN rear. Soon gas and ammo trucks were exploding everywhere. The 344th close assaulted and seized two 105mm howitzers. However, American airpower drove the 344th back off the road.

That night the reserve 966th Battalion hit the ARVN force with three company column attacks from the north. Enemy tank and air firepower drove the 966th back into the woods, the repulse signaling the 32nd Regiment to begin an immediate withdrawal, leaving a small covering force behind. The regiment lost all three battalion commanders, two of them killed, during the Plei Me ambush. Half of its infantry strength was also destroyed, along with most of its crew-served weapons. The depleted regiment headed southwest toward its base in the Chu Pong Mountains War Zone, along the Cambodian border, twenty kilometers away.[449]

The Hasty Ambush at LZ Albany

On November 16, 1965 the weary 2nd Battalion of the 7th U.S. Cavalry Regiment trudged in a long column toward LZ Albany. LZ Albany was located in the Ia Drang Valley, scene of a recent battle involving the U.S. 1st Cavalry and two regiments of NVA troops. The 2/7 was under command of an inexperienced personnel officer who marched his command across the open scrub terrain in a loose one-column wedge formation. He had no security patrols out in any direction.[450]

In the early afternoon the U.S. troops captured two enemy soldiers, part of the flank security for the 8th Battalion of the 66th NVA Infantry Regiment. That capture did not alert the Americans to any immediate danger. However, NVA scouts had already warned the red battalion commander of the American column's approach.

Since the NVA battalion had also been on the march and not expecting to run into any American units, the NVA commander was forced to stage a hasty L shaped ambush. Rapidly setting up his mortars, he ordered his lead rifle company to dash down the long axis of the American column along the right. That approach would keep the red unit out of the American line of sight, since a screen of trees was between the company and the American column, one hundred meters away. The rifle company commander was told to close assault the American column after the NVA mortar barrage subsided.

Placing another company in skirmish line along the edge of a clearing astride the Americans' direction of march, the NVA commander that placed his reserve company to the northwest of the kill zone. Most of the NVA troops still had their packs on.

The NVA commander only had about twenty minutes to prepare, which was not enough time to dig in. The communists rapidly deployed along the base of trees and ant hills, preparing camouflage from whatever was near.

When an American company staggered into the open kill zone, it was hit with mortar and small arms fire. Sending two squads into the trees as snipers, the NVA company hit the American column's right flank in a close assault. That attack fragmented the U.S. battalion into several groups of desperate, confused men. Then the NVA commander realized that he had attacked an American battalion, not a company-sized unit. That realization caused him to reinforce his flanking close assault company with his reserve company.

In the meantime, the American battalion commander, Colonel McDade, lost self-control and the U.S. battalion was decapitated.[451] The American units formed small perimeters everywhere as the NVA cut them down in piles. The battle raged over a thousand meter front surrounding and engulfing the panicked Americans.

"The noise was deafening, and in the confusion GIs began firing on each other. A sergeant who was at the center of the column remembered that 'suddenly everyone around me was getting hit and dying. I could hear screams all around me, all over the place.' The North Vietnamese were 'all around us, jumping out of trees and charging out of bushes.' Shouting 'Kill GI son of a bitch' in English, they rushed the panic-stricken Americans and engaged them in deadly hand-to-hand combat.

"All afternoon, an American participant remembered, there were 'smoke, artillery, screaming, moaning, fear, bullets, blood, and little yellow men running around screeching with glee when they found one of us alive, or screaming and moaning with fear when they ran into a grenade or bullet.'

"One company caught in the middle of the ambush suffered 93 percent casualties . . . The scene along the river resembled the 'devil's butcher shop,' . . . with 'blood and mess' all over the place, dead snipers hanging from trees, and grotesque piles of as many as twenty tangled bodies. The ground was 'sticky with blood' and a journalist who visited the battlefield reported that it was impossible to walk twenty paces without stepping on a corpse. There were stories of horrible North Vietnamese atrocities. A few Americans shot themselves to avoid capture, and significant numbers of GIs were apparently killed by friendly fire."[452]

That night the few survivors clinging to life in scattered perimeters heard the enemy killing American wounded. They heard Americans scream, "No, no . . . please," and then a gunshot. The NVA troops were seeking glory as "American Killers."[453]

Although there is no question that the American 2/7 Battalion was almost completely wiped out, the 1st Cavalary Division denied it. Instead, they claimed to have destroyed the 8th NVA Battalion of the 66th Regiment. As evidence of their victory, the Americans presented 212 rifles, thirty-nine light machine guns, three heavy machine guns, six 82mm mortars and six RPGs.[454] They claimed to have picked up those weapons, abandoned by a retreating enemy, on the battlefield. It is doubtful that any NVA battalion would lose thirty-nine out of its forty-plus light machine guns without being totally destroyed. However, the North Vietnamese 8th Battalion *did* withdraw in good order, before daylight of the second day. They left the field of gore in American hands.

Ambush of Task Force Prong

In late 1966, an American-led battalion of Montagnard "strikers" was hunting the NVA in II Corps' Plei Trap Valley area. The three-company force was called Task Force Prong.

The 6th Battalion of the 33rd NVA Infantry Regiment lay in an L shaped ambush along the route of Task Force Prong. Deployed across the base of the L was the 1st Company of the 6th Battalion. Echeloned along the banks of a winding stream, running northwest from the ambush position, was the rest of the battalion waiting to pounce on the Task Force's rear.

When the head of the long allied column entered a clearing, the point spied an NVA soldier standing thirty meters away. A full clip of bullets was fired into the impassive NVA soldier. The red corpse had been a human lure who was supposed to draw the allied force into the clearing, which was an ambush kill zone.

The ambush was prematurely sprung when a few excited NVA ambushers loosed off several shots. As the "Yard" column hit the ground, ten communist automatic weapons swept the clearing, mowing down rows of elephant grass. None of the allied column had been caught inside the kill zone.

Demonstrating a rare aggressiveness, the Americans tried to swing a company in a wide left hook to the enemy flank. That maneuver caused the enemy to react similarly. Both sides then began extending simultaneously to the east, probing for each other's open flank. The enemy rear blocking element sent only a small number of troops towards the allied rear.

Suddenly a machine gun opened up from the rear of the allied column. Fearing encirclement, the Americans called in fire support along both sides of the trail. Under that covering fire, the allied force withdrew to the west.[455]

After the Americans withdrew, the reds broke contact to escape the artillery bombardment. Evidently, the ambushing force had become rattled and was unable to carry out its ambush scheme. Several factors probably caused the abrupt communist withdrawal:

1. Pressure initation of the ambush which resulted in the entire allied force being able to avoid the kill zone.
2. Demonstrated American willingness and ability to maneuver.
3. The rapid arrival of American supporting fires.
4. The size of the allied column. It had sufficient manpower to carry out flanking maneuvers while holding a base of fire.

If the remaining two companies of the communist battalion had maneuvered rapidly along the west side of the trail, they could have probably struck a telling blow against the strung out allied column. By close assaulting the column, the reds could have fragmented it into several parts. Such fragmentation would have probably destroyed the column's cohesion while complicating allied fire support efforts.

CHAPTER 13

Chu Luc Sappers

In June, 1965 the Marine base at Da Nang, South Vietnam was guarded by most of the 3rd Marine Division. Numerous battalions were dug into a line of mines, bunkers and barbed wire which encircled the Da Nang airfield. Beyond that line, marine units conducted hundreds of ambushes and patrols daily, across the flat, open terrain surrounding the airbase. Day and night, nervous marine gunners poured thousands of rounds of "harassing and interdicting" artillery fires into suspected enemy locations. Numerous highly sophisticated fighter/bomber aircraft, complemented by dozens of aerial reconnaissance aircraft, patrolled the area day and night. The marines bragged about their operational statistics and impenetrable defenses.

Yet, on July 1, 1965 a small party of Viet Cong sappers penetrated three perimeter fence lines undetected, and reached the Da Nang aircraft parking ramp. There they destroyed nearly a hundred million dollars worth of aircraft including three C-130 transport planes and three F-102 fighter/bombers. Using demolition charges and hand grenades they also damaged three more F-102s. The sappers were not driven out, they withdrew after they had exhausted their explosives, with the loss of only one man.[456]

Another Viet Cong sapper battalion of over ninety men, attacked Da Nang's Marble Mountain helicopter base on October 27–28, 1965. Colonel Thomas O'Conner, the Marine MAG-16 commander, told this tale:

"I woke to the sound of explosions shortly after midnight . . . arriving at the command post I received a phone call from General McCutcheon. He warned me that the airfields at Chu Lai had been attacked and to be on the

271

alert. I told him . . . we had also been under attack for about fifteen minutes.

"Helicopters were burning all over . . . VMO-2 was practically wiped out. . . . they (the VC) destroyed 19 helicopters and damaged 35, 11 of them severely . . . the destruction of the helicopters at Marble Mountain resulted in a 43 percent loss of helicopter mobility and put a crimp in division plans for several months thereafter."[457]

Marine statistics regarding their patrol coverage around Da Nang and other bases only demonstrated their inability to detect intruding enemy sappers or infantry. "In October 1965, the 3d Marine Division units at all three enclaves (then occupied) conducted 2,877 patrols and 1,061 ambushes which resulted in seventy contacts with the enemy. In December, the division reported a total of 9,698 offensive operations which resulted in 510 contacts."[458]

What did it all mean? The marines were conducting thousands of operations with about two percent "contacts," and no battles. Yet the enemy was moving whole battalions into marine fortified bases at will.

In March, 1969 a reinforced marine battalion was dug in defending Liberty Bridge, near the Arizona Stronghold in South Vietnam's northern I Corps. Passing through five marine outposts and numerous night ambushes, NVA sappers penetrated multiple defensive barriers of wire and mines, in seven places. They did not set off any of the 300 tripflares and anti-intrusion devices emplaced around the perimeter. Totally surprised and paralyzed marine defenders were attacked at close quarters with flamethrowers, explosives, and small arms fire.[459]

On March 21, 1971 red sappers penetrated the well defended American Vandegrift logistics base, then supporting Operation Lam Son 719. The sappers' morning attack detonated 10,000 gallons of aviation fuel and shut down the base for awhile.[460]

The Sapper Phenomenon

From their earliest beginnings, the NVA realized that small advance detachments could save casualties while facilitating victory by enhancing the shock of combat. The NVA found that sapper spearheads could pave the way for power raids or breakthrough assaults and also reduce casualties to the main body. By infiltrating, or penetrating, enemy defenses before a main assault force, and then attacking from within the enemy array, the enemy would be forced to fight in two directions simultaneously. Or, if the penetration force was acting independently, their sudden appearance within a fortified position terrorized the defenders and dislocated their counteraction.

The Chu Luc Sapper Corps began in 1946 when "the Viet Minh imaginatively employed professional thieves with special skills and such competencies as martial arts, swimming, climbing and housebreaking, to penetrate French installations and bases and steal weapons, ammunition, explosives, documents, or carry out assassinations or sabotage."[461]

North Vietnamese leadership was well pleased with the results of sapper action. Ho Chi Minh delivered an address to the headquarters of the 305th Sapper Group and the March, 1967 graduating class of the North Vietnamese Sapper Training School. His speech profusely praised sapper methods and success. One of his statements, "Sapper action is a special action which requires special methods and special skills to perform,"[462] became the official motto of every major communist sapper unit.

Who were these sappers, these Oriental supermen? Why were they feared so much by allied army and marine troops?

Actually sappers were not supermen. In fact most of them were trained for less than a year (six times as long as the NVA regular infantryman's one month of training). Their fame grew because they utilized that training to defeat defending American forces a thousand times their size. Such victories were more a reflection of the lack of motivation, demoralization and amateurism of American troops, than they were of sapper proficiency. Against a professional army, the sappers would have floundered.

Sapper success depended on the training, experience, determination and, most of all, focused concentration of the sapper unit and its leaders. Sappers approached their military art with serious dedication and controlled application.

Conversely, American conscripts, alien to the warrior life, spent a considerable amount of their Vietnam duty time separating and distracting themselves from military activity. The misguided American high command reinforced such escapism by offering a wide variety of diversions, from liquor to pizza, in dozens of base camps. American youths, drunk on alcohol, drugs, boredom and homesickness, were hardly interested in concentrating on war fighting.

It was the American approach to war which created the myth of sapper elitism, not the excellence of sapper performance. While it is true that sappers could penetrate any American perimeter, they were much less successful in penetrating Australian or Korean perimeters.

Late in the war, communist sappers who had defected to the allied side staged demonstrations at large American bases and major headquarters. As beer drinking American brass stared in wonder, sappers demonstrated how they could penetrate the numerous wire fences surrounding Long Binh Base in only ten minutes. Their stealth, absolute concentration and complete body involvement was anathema to the American lifestyle represented by the observers.

In 1973, the South Vietnamese sent noncommissioned officer instructors from Quang Trung Training Center to a sapper course conducted by ex-NVA sappers. The red sappers demonstrated how they could break through several barbed wire fences in less than ten minutes. That high speed penetration was most appealing to the ARVN students. Yet there is no record of them ever applying the lessons.

Why didn't American "combat" engineers practice any methods similar to the sapper techniques? American "combat" engineer units weren't interested in such training because they really didn't consider themselves to be combatants. United States combat engineers viewed themselves as builders and emphasized the construction aspect of military engineering.

Refusal to utilize available, heavily armed, combat engineers as assault pioneers deprived the allied forces of five division equivalents of combat troops during the Vietnam war. At one time there were nearly fifty American engineer battalions, including five Marine and fourteen Navy Seabee battalions, deployed in Vietnam. Most of those units were known as "combat," not construction, engineer battalions. Allied engineer units were usually deployed far from combat. Most allied engineer troops were used to build and maintain numerous roads and luxurious bases. They built many swimming pools and pizza parlors.

American engineers actually had to be protected by combat units although they were heavily armed with tanks, machine guns, flame throwers and demolitions. The bizarre de-emphasis of combat by American engineers magnified the performance of communist combat engineers, the sappers. The reds better understood that combat engineering has its place in warfare. NVA construction engineers were kept separate from combat sappers.

Sapper Training

Aspirant NVA sappers came from all walks of life. Preference was given to "poor farmers and those with natural aggressiveness and keen senses, especially of sight and sound."[463] Sapper trainees, who included within their number both volunteers and honor graduates from basic military training courses, received six months of basic training.

NVA officers had a rougher go of it: "Officers volunteers were stripped of rank during training . . . enlisted candidates commonly received promotions when training commenced."[464]

The Chu Luc emphasized specialized training as very important to sapper

SAPPER TRAINING COURSE

	HOURS
1. Explosives: Xit Dit, black powder, TNT; Safety, Explosives in mines	:48
2. Wiring and Electric Power: Electricity-measurement, sources; Types of Wiring; Protecting Wire.	:120
3. Reconnaissance: Principles; Organization of a Scout Team; Scouting- airfields, bases, routes, ports, docks, and bivouacs.	:48
4. Camouflage: Methods; Individual Movement; Lighting.	:72
5. Overcoming Obstacles With Explosives: Barbed wire, trenches, mine fields; Bangalore torpedoes; Assault planning.	:120
6. Penetration of Enemy Positions: Night Training.	:144
7. Coordination Among Sapper Cells: Formations; Weapons and Explosive Preparations; Assault operations	:72
8. Overcoming Natural And Artificial Obstacles:Mud; deep water; ditches; dry leaves; lime; sand; grass; Using ladders and planks to negotiate barbed wire obstacles.	:168
9. Ambushing:	:216
10. Power raiding:	:24
11. Close assault:	:24
12. General Review:	:72
13. Final Test:	:48

TOTAL NUMBER OF HOURS OF INSTRUCTION: 1176 Hours; 49 Days

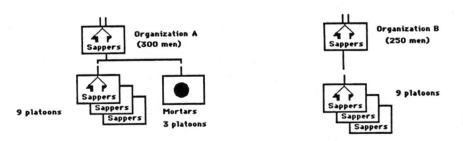

Organization A (300 men) — Sappers — 9 platoons — Sappers, Sappers, Sappers — Mortars 3 platoons

Organization B (250 men) — Sappers — Sappers, Sappers, Sappers — 9 platoons

275

performance. They reinforced that idea with assignment of elite status "to make both cadre and soldiers aware that to serve in the special sapper arm is a great honor and although this is a new arm, it already has a victorious background."[465]

Sapper combat training consisted of pure assault pioneer course work. They were taught reconnaissance techniques, barrier and defense penetration, assault tactics, stealth, demolitions, and the destruction of: barriers, installations, logistics facilities and munitions dumps.

Sapper training itself was not extraordinary, the maneuver execution and discipline of sapper units made the difference:

"A basic phase of sapper training covered reconnaissance techniques and skills such as land navigation, negotiating natural and manmade obstacles, observation, penetration, and withdrawal. Next came intensive drill in assault tactics based on the 3-man cell, a tactical organization concept highly esteemed and widely applied by the VC/NVA. According to official doctrine the 3-man cell, due to 'its close organization and its close inner command and control structure,' was uniquely fitted for day or night, offensive or defensive, and independent or coordinated operations. However, when employed in combination 'the capabilities and qualities of each cell in relation to other cells' required the combat effectiveness of the overall organization. Instructors were warned that 'the organization of cells is different from the organization of squads, platoons, and companies as employed in infantry.'

"Because the explosive charge was the key to sapper effectiveness and because survival might well depend on competence with this weapon, demolition training was exhaustive. Sappers were taught to recognize, arm, and disarm conventional explosives as well as those of local manufacture. Instructions included the characteristics and uses of detonators; the characteristics, properties, maintenance, and force of all available explosives; and the quantity and position of explosives required to destroy fences, buildings, bunkers, aircraft, fuel tanks, and munitions. Sappers were also instructed on the details of allied mines, flares, and booby traps, which they were taught to disarm, and convert to their own uses. In short, the trained sappers were specialists in the employment of explosive charges."[466]

In Dinh Tuong Province, a Sapper and Special Action Staff set up a sapper training school. The coursework was typical sapper fare:

"The course lasted for three months. Trainees numbered about two platoons. Troops were first taught how to avoid making noises while walking in various kinds of terrain such as flooded or muddy rice fields, that took us about a fortnight.

"They spent the remaining two and one-half months in practice. Phat Da

Pagoda was used as a mockup military post. Troops practiced impending attacks on military posts by trying to sneak near to it to lay mines. A team played the role of GVN soldiers who guarded the post. They had to discover our operation, and we had to practice until we were able to reach the walls of the pagoda unnoticed and blow up some small dynamite sticks which had little destructive power when exploded."[467]

Sapper training varied in duration and content. Courses could last from three to six months. One course covered "the use and function of the rifle . . . (1) the use and handling of various types of explosives (TNT, Beta Mines, Bangalore Torpedoes). (2) the wiring of mines, (3) methods of hiding batteries both on land and in water, (4) repair of mines, (5) evading mine sweepers and detection, (6) observation and reconnaissance techniques.

"Key sapper cadres are given further training that includes theory of guerrilla war, the principles of electricity, military topography, map making and reading, battlefield observation, development of combat play, and combat and battlefield reporting.

"Training is also given in crossing all types of terrain. Techniques of infiltration, camouflage, and reconnaissance must also be a part of the sapper's knowledge. The offensive tactics the sapper learns are broken down into separate instructions for attacking boats, bridges, airfields, vehicles, outposts, blockhouses, and enemy troops."[468]

Sapper Objectives

The NVA Sapper Corps was an assault engineer combat arm trained to oppose a greater force with lesser strength, and to move in complete silence. Their primary mission was to erode the strength of South Vietnamese and allied forces by carrying out special missions. Usually preceded by infiltration/penetration, those special missions included: target destruction, command decapitation, sabotage, reconnaissance, close combat, ambush warfare and spearheading attacks.

"—Demolish war materials and strategic and tactical objectives.
—Penetrate and destroy command facilities, outposts, billets, service bases, supply bases, signal centers, radar stations and military schools.
—Penetrate and sabotage defense firms and factories of military value.
—Reconnoiter and conduct battlefield preparation for the infantry.
—Secure bridgeheads to pave the way for infantry advance.

—Support infantry operations during offensive and defensive cam-
paigns.
—Forestall enemy mop-up operations.
—Mounting ambushes and counterambushes."[469]

Many sapper raids were independent operations, without participation by
infantry or other forces. However, there were six primary ways that North
Vietnamese Army (NVA) sappers could be utilized:

* Penetration assaults without infantry.
* Support of infantry assaults.
* Penetration assaults with infantry support.
* Urban terrorism, sabotage, and propaganda action.
* Naval sapping against shipping and bridges.
* Mechanized sappers trained to seize and instantly employ enemy mecha-
nized equipment.[470]

Most Chu Luc Military Regions controlled at least one sapper battalion,
early in the war. Sappers from that battalion were regularly attached to
regional battalions for special operations. Few real sapper troops were organic
to regional or provincial Viet Cong Main Force battalions. However, the
NVA Sapper Corps was constantly expanded. "From 1969 onward . . .
COSVN converted several infantry battalions to sapper battalions and gave
sapper training to all infantry units."[471]

Naval Sappers

There were two kinds of sappers, surface sappers and naval sappers, and
two kinds of underwater activities, mining and frogman attacks. Late in the
Vietnam War, the miniscule NVA naval sapper force successfully sunk many
allied ships and barges. Although the naval sapper effort was but a fraction of
the ground sapping effort, 189 underwater operations were initiated in the
first nine months of 1970, with a thirty-eight percent success rate for
mining, and a fifty-five percent success rate for frogman attacks. Among the
naval successes were:

* Destruction of the USS *Krishna*.
* Eradication of ARVN Naval Headquarters 225 in An Xuyen.
* The detonation of three barges carrying over 300 tons of ammunition in the
Saigon River on March 5, 1972.
* The burning of the Nha Be gasoline depot on December 2, 1973.[472]

Many special countertactics were tried to foil naval sappers. "Against underwater sappers, the most common defense for ships consisted of spotlights to illuminate the surface of the water and searchlights to sweep the banks. Another method called for throwing grenades around the ships' hulls, but this was expensive.

"Among other defenses tried was sinking a high-intensity light in a ball deep below the surface but this proved ineffective since the light did not radiate far enough. Less costly and more effective ways included frequent river patrols on sampans, mine clearing by small craft dragging hooked steel cables, and periodic engine idling to hamper frogmen with the turning propeller."[473]

Bridges had to be protected from North Vietnamese naval combat swimmer sappers. Wire mesh was deployed around bridge supports to impede sapper sabotage attempts. Wire nets were spread upstream about 100 meters from the bridge on floats to stop drifting mines, frogmen and especially water hyacinths which were frequently used by sappers for concealment. Troops would fire at approach hyacinths as a precautionary measure.[474] "To combat frogmen-sappers at Cam Rahn Bay, live electric wires were trailed in the water, and dolphins were used as well as U.S. Navy frogmen to detect sappers."[475]

U.S. Navy Seabees built a bridge at Dong Ha specifically tailored to prevent attacks by sappers. To protect the bridge the Seabees "rigged a six foot chain link fence on the river side of the abutment. A Y-shaped yoke at the top of the fence held three rolls of concertina wire, which were partially extended in spring semi-coils. The concertina pressed against the bottom of the stringers, leaving no clear access to the bridge's underside without extensive wire cutting. The old type of concertina was studded with thousands of steel barbs to puncture and tear anyone trying to work through it. . . . German steel tape was worse. Small razor sharp blades of metal would slash a person foolhardy enough to take it on."[476]

Sapper Infantry

The communist ground sapper effort was a hundred times as active as the naval effort and even more successful. That is why the communists, always eager to exploit success, began to increase the number of their sapper battalions in 1969 by converting several infantry battalions. Later, some sapper training was provided to all infantry units.

Sappers were occasionally used as advanced detachments spearheading infantry raiding parties. In May 1969 an NVA rifle company crossed east over the Trung Pham River from Laos into South Vietnam's A Shau War Zone.

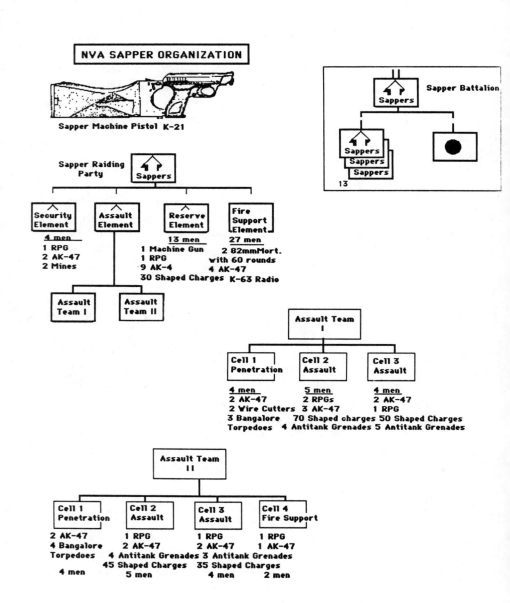

NVA SAPPER ORGANIZATION

Sapper Machine Pistol K-21

Sapper Battalion

Sappers

Sappers
Sappers
Sappers

13

Sapper Raiding Party

Sappers

Security Element
4 men
1 RPG
2 AK-47
2 Mines

Assault Element

Reserve Element
13 men
1 Machine Gun
1 RPG
9 AK-4
30 Shaped Charges

Fire Support Element
27 men
2 82mmMort.
with 60 rounds
4 AK-47
K-63 Radio

Assault Team I

Assault Team II

Assault Team I

Cell 1 Penetration
4 men
2 AK-47
2 Wire Cutters
3 Bangalore
Torpedoes

Cell 2 Assault
5 men
2 RPGs
3 AK-47
70 Shaped charges
4 Antitank Grenades

Cell 3 Assault
4 men
2 AK-47
1 RPG
50 Shaped Charges
5 Antitank Grenades

Assault Team II

Cell 1 Penetration
2 AK-47
4 Bangalore
Torpedoes
4 men

Cell 2 Assault
1 RPG
2 AK-47
4 Antitank Grenades
45 Shaped Charges
5 men

Cell 3 Assault
1 RPG
2 AK-47
3 Antitank Grenades
35 Shaped Charges
4 men

Cell 4 Fire Support
1 RPG
1 AK-47
2 men

Leading that company's night approach was a platoon of sappers carrying approximately eight light satchel charges apiece. As the sappers entered a draw they seemed to sense the American platoon lying in ambush there. Since they didn't know where the Americans were deployed, the sappers began flinging satchel charges to their front and flanks. After ten charges were thrown, the Americans answered with showers of grenade and M-79 fire.

For the next five hours the sappers flung around eighty satchel charges toward suspected American positions and were not deterred by aerial bombardment from Shadow gunships, AC-119G fixed-wing jets and Cobra gunships. In the surreal half light of echoing explosions, the sappers never gave up until near dawn, when they collected their dead and made an orderly withdrawal back into Laos. They always withdrew before dawn in order to avoid allied air power, whose efficiency increased in the daylight hours.[477]

The Sapper Raiding Party

Every NVA sapper operation was tailored to the needs of the situation, which caused sapper organizations to vary in size and composition. The basic sapper battalion was composed of four or five companies. Each company contained three fifteen- to twenty-man platoons, each split into two squads. Each squad was further subdivided into three-man cells.

A sapper raiding party, organized to attack without infantry support, consisted of a security element, an assault element, a fire support element and a reserve element.

The security element was the smallest element of the raiding party and seldom exceeded one reinforced cell. Its task was to keep allied reinforcements from entering the battle area. Direct fire weapons such as RPG-2s and RPG-7s (rocket-propelled grenades), M79 grenade launchers and directional mines enabled the security cell to carry out its mission.

Reserve elements, usually a reinforced infantry squad, were formed only under unusual circumstances and furnished close-in support and assistance where required. Reserve elements were armed with machine guns, rocket-propelled grenades, AK-47 assault rifles and explosive charges.

The indirect fire support element was included in most attacks. It provided general indirect fire support for the raiding party and was composed of several weapons crew cells protected by a security cell. Fire support elements never used mortars heavier than 60mm or 82mm, and usually the former. Rarely were more than two mortars committed to a single raid.

The mission of the indirect fire support element was to mask any noise made by sapper penetration units and suppress enemy reaction and movement within the target area. In addition they were supposed to distract enemy attention away from that sector of the perimeter where the assault element was operating.

The key component of the sapper raiding party was the assault element composed of two or more "arrows" (assault teams).[478] Each arrow was responsible for moving along a single approach route to the target. There were normally three types of cells in each arrow: shock, penetration, and direct fire support. Most of the demolitions material was carried by the assault arrows.

Sometimes cells were even broken up so that the arrows could be tailored exactly to overcome the peculiar characteristics of a specific perimeter defense. In lieu of explosive charges, a penetration cell might carry wirecutters, bangalore torpedoes, stakes, tape, cloth strips and probing devices. It might also dispense with AK-47s and drop one man from the cell.

A direct fire support cell might use rocket-propelled grenades instead of demolitions and also vary in unit size. However, every effort was made to preserve cell unit integrity in the shock arrows, whose only mission was to destroy enemy troops.

Preparations for the Sapper Raid

Sapper unit commanders made personal reconnaissance of enemy targets. They secured every scrap of intelligence available on the target from: numerous agents within allied bases, tunnel observers who kept the target under constant surveillance from both outside and inside the base perimeter, and radio intercept intelligence. Sapper commanders were primarily interested in the size, disposition, strength and weaknesses of enemy base defenses, during the reconnaissance phase.

After the latest intelligence data was analyzed and compared to the sapper leader's reconnaissance findings, he developed a plan of attack. That plan defined approach, infiltration and withdrawal routes, fire support positions, the priority of targets, and organization of the raiding party.

A primary consideration was whether or not the raiding party could approach the target overland, or actually go under it. Whenever possible, the communists utilized their extensive labyrinth of subterranean tunnels which surrounded and penetrated nearly every allied base. The sapper leader specified the size, composition, and armament of every unit in the assault force. Great effort was expended on ensuring that every man knew his element's mission and the mission of other elements.

Then the rehearsals began, as each man was fully acquainted with his task and the tasks of each subunit. Full use was made of maps, diagrams, mockups, sand tables and terrain similar to that found in the target area and its environs. The dry runs, or rehearsals, were vital to the success of the mission and could require from three days to three months of practice.

Sapper attack plans were usually complicated and required mutual support from a variety of cooperating units. Failure of any part of the plan would jeopardize the whole operation. Each sapper, and sapper subunit, was expected to know his role in the operation so completely that he could act independently after the attack began. Once the attack started, the commander would not be able to use a radio to call in fire support and rescuers if the arrows were "pinned" or otherwise stymied. They had to fight forward without whining for assistance.

Iron discipline was required to maintain proper determination and morale within sapper units. Sapper company commanders usually warned their subordinates that anyone endangering the mission's success would be shot on the spot.

In February 1969, a wounded sapper taken prisoner by Phu Cat Air Base security, had been shot by his commander and left behind. The prisoner had triggered a trip flare while trying to penetrate a perimeter fence, and thereby endangered the mission.[479]

Sapper tactics, in attacks without infantry, were designed to eliminate the need for fire support and thwart the massive fire support commanded by allied units. The soldierly virtues of secrecy, stealth, surprise and maneuver replaced fire superiority. Diversions, feints, and deep thrusts into the bowels of enemy bases, combined with simultaneous attacks on several targets, confused defenders and scattered their fire support.

The Sapper Raid on Fire Support Base Airborne

In April, 1969 the U.S. 101st Airborne Division built Fire Base Airborne on a ridge running parallel to the A Shau Valley floor. A two-gun 81mm mortar platoon, utilized for night illumination and close-in fires, was emplaced on a small knoll near, and fifty meters above, an American artillery position on the north end of the ridge. A battalion of three howitzer batteries was emplaced on the edge of the ridge in three positions within the 200 meters long and twenty-five meters wide firebase. The batteries were placed in line and separated from each other by 50 to 70 meters.

All of the American positions were surrounded by foxholes and single strand concertina barbed wire. An airborne infantry company provided security for the battery.

The 6th NVA Infantry Regiment, which had commanded the special NVA assault division during the Battle of Hue, was headquartered in caves on Doi Thang Mountain, two and one-half kilometers to the west of Fire Base

Airborne. On the night of May 12, 1969, the 6th Regiment dispatched a battalion—sized assault unit to take the firebase. Leading the assault was a forty-six man company of the K12 Sapper Battalion, which had fought so well the year before during the Hue Campaign. An 82mm mortar battery and rifle companies 3 and 4 of the 806th NVA Battalion were also part of the assault battalion.

At around two in the morning, the operation having been delayed by some glitch, sapper cells armed only with wire cutters and a few thin strands of bamboo approached the American perimeter. Other sapper cells came toward the artillery position from the north and northeast. Still another group of sapper cells approached the knoll position from the north, east and northwest. Their eyes fixed in cobra concentration, the sapper penetration cells slithered up to the wire and began undulating through the barbed wire. As trip flares were discovered, their strikers were tied down with strands of bamboo.

After all flares along an avenue of penetration had been neutralized, the sappers started back toward their entry point cutting gaps in the wire. All three rows of barbed wire were penetrated and six assault avenue gaps opened in them by 3 AM. Then the sappers picked up satchel charges and automatic weapons and began to penetrate the wire toward their objectives inside the American firebase.

At 3:12 AM, a mortar barrage opened which quickly detonated one of the artillery position's ammunition dumps and threw the base into pandemonium. After three minutes of pinpoint fire, a red mortar barrage was marched back and forth over the main position. Then the American mortar position on the knoll was hit with thirty rounds, as the air was filled with a swarm of RPG rockets fired at point targets from all around the firebase.

By then, sapper cells were inside the perimeter, flinging satchel charges into bunkers and shooting their occupants. Some sappers were firing RPG rockets at point blank range. The air was filled with the screams of the dying. The fifteen sapper cells seemed to be everywhere. Some sapper cells threw satchel charges from the inside of the artillery position outward. Others threw them from outside of the knoll position, inward.

Suddenly steel-helmeted North Vietnamese infantry platoons, following sapper cell spearheads, and firing from the hip, began dashing through the wire gaps. The spearhead sappers were also throwing grenades and satchel charges in all directions as the fragmented American defense force reeled in confusion and pain.

The American defenders began to counterattack in isolated uncoordinated fire teams as the sappers overran the bunkers along the north side of the perimeter. Setting up machine guns inside the American main position, the communists began to spray the foreground. Enemy bases of fire outside the perimeter continued to direct flurries of RPG fire at pinpoint targets. Sappers were everywhere gunning down American troops and flinging satchel charges.

As American aerial fire support began to enter the battle, enemy efforts intensified. However, at daybreak the reds withdrew rapidly, leaving behind thirty-nine bodies. If the NVA had attacked earlier in the night, they would have taken Fire Base Airborne.[480]

Sapper Raid Tactics

Sapper penetration cells began their operations at dusk because it took a long time to penetrate base camp defenses. Sappers often took six to seven hours to cover the last 200 meters to the objective. Modern defensive barriers with their maze of barbed wire and other obstacles require special penetration procedures. "When breaching a wire obstacle, the sapper uses bamboo poles to raise it, mats to crawl over it, or wire cutters to go through it. If . . . the defensive wire cannot be breached by one of these methods, it may be blown apart with bangalore torpedoes or small charges of plastic explosive."[481]

At one army installation, a sapper cell devoted over eight painstaking hours in an undetected stealthy penetration. They spent most of that time moving across the last 100 meters of the perimeter and through the wire of the barrier belt.[482]

Painstaking application of proven penetration methods was the hallmark of the sapper: "Such a penetration was usually carried out by a single cell of three men clad only in loin cloths or shorts and camouflaged with mud. Their standard gear was an automatic weapon, one set of wirecutters, a single knife or bayonet, a sharp metal rod to probe for mines, bamboo sticks to prop up barbed wire, and a quantity of small pins to disarm mine fuses.

"One cell member stayed outside the perimeter while the other two penetrated. The lead man propped up the wire with bamboo sticks then disarmed the mines. His partner followed him under the wire and removed the props. Crawling meticulously to escape detection, each used hands and feet to probe the ground for wire that might reveal mines, bobby traps, tripflares, or other warning devices. After examining the base, the men withdrew by the same route, with the lead man repropping the wire, the second man removing the props and rearming the mines. Wirecutters were a last resort because the intent was to avoid all trace of entry. Having completed withdrawal, all cell members met at a prearranged location to prepare their report for the commander."[483]

Diversionary attacks, feints and other ruses were frequently coordinated to distract defender attention away from the area selected for sapper penetration. One standard sapper tactic employed the fire support element to disguise the raid as a standoff attack, so that defenders would take cover in their bunkers and leave the base perimeter unguarded.

Slowly but surely, penetration cells would mark a path through the obstacle barrier for following assault cells and infantry troops. Usually two or more arrows, led by their penetration cells, advanced into the enemy defensive perimeter under cover of darkness. Wirecutters were used whenever possible as lanes were cut through the wire, and mines, tripflares and anti-intrusion devices nullified.

If necessary, the penetration cell would employ bangalore torpedoes, long tubular explosive charges, run under or through obstacles, and detonated to blow a way through the barrier. Sappers tried to avoid use of bangalore torpedoes if possible so as to avoid attracting attention to their penetration lanes through the enemy barrier field. They might use them if discovered or to rapidly penetrate the final barrier. If forced to employ bangalore torpedoes, sappers sometimes threw satchel charges or fuzed demolition blocks to attract attention away from the bangalores and make the defenders think that errant mortar rounds were impacting in the area.

If the penetrating sapper force was prematurely discovered or pinned, assault cells would use RPGs, rocket-propelled grenades, to suppress the defenders and try to ram the assault through at high speed. Sappers who were prematurely detected by enemy defenders began throwing explosive charges in all directions, attempting to blast through the perimeter and assault the interior of the target before they were annihilated themselves.

If assault arrows could not overcome opposition, they would retreat rapidly. Otherwise they would drive ruthlessly forward without regard for casualties or their flanks. Neither the security of their rear nor their own escape concerned them until the mission was accomplished or a withdrawal was ordered.

Once the perimeter was penetrated or the raid detected, the sappers moved at top speed to their targets in an attempt to complete the mission in thirty minutes or less. Demolition charges would be placed on key targets while satchel charges and rocket-propelled grenades would be fired in all directions to suppress reaction. After attaining their objective, the sappers withdrew through their lanes in the perimeter. Fire support and/or reserve elements covered the withdrawal.

All elements of the raiding party then moved to a rallying site, normally

NVA SAPPER ASSAULT ARRAY

ASSAULT UNITS

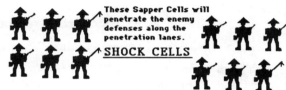

Penetration lanes

Enemy Barbed Wire and other obstacles

Sapper Machine Pistol K-21

These Sapper cells will open gaps in the enemy line.

PENETRATION CELLS

Bangalore Torpedoes

Satchel Charges

DIRECT FIRE SUPPORT

These Sapper Cells will suppress Enemy counteraction with direct firepower.

These Sapper Cells will penetrate the enemy defenses along the penetration lanes.

SHOCK CELLS

SUPPORT UNITS

These Sapper Cells will protect the flanks ans with-drawl routes of the assault force.

SECURITY

SECURITY

RESERVE

This Sapper Unit will be used to exploit an opportunity or success. It may also be used to cover the withdrawl.

This Sapper Unit will suppress enemy counteraction with indirect fire.

INDIRECT FIRE SUPPORT

the same place as the assembly area. Then the sappers rapidly regrouped and quickly returned to their base camp. They tried to use subterranean tunnels as withdrawal routes whenever possible. Most sapper raids succeeded.

General Vo Nguyen Giap once claimed, ". . . regardless of how strongly the U.S. or puppet troops are defended, they can easily be destroyed by our crack special combat troops with their special combat abilities."[484] He was praising the effectiveness of his sappers.

During the Second Indochinese War, the number of enemy sapper battalions was constantly increased as COSVN converted several infantry battalions to sapper battalions and gave sapper training to all infantry units. In 1969, there were thirty-nine sapper battalions. In 1970, the total number of sapper units increased to sixty-five sapper battalions, the equivalent of seven sapper divisions.

NVA Sapper Order of Battle, 1973

NVA/VC Sappers in South Vietnam's MR 1: 1/73.

NVA B-5 Front, Quang Tri Province
Sapper: 126th Naval Sapper Group (500)*; DMZ Sapper Group (5 Bns, 1500). 15th Sapper (200)
NVA Military Region Tri Thien
7th Sapper (200)
NVA Front-7, Quang Tri Province
Battalions: 810th Sapper (250).
NVA MR 5, Quang Nam and Quang Tin Provinces
Regts, Sapper: 45th (550); 5th (1,000).
NVA Front-4
Quang Nam, Misc. Bns: 89th NVA Sapper (200); 91st NVA Sapper (200); 471st NVA Sapper (150);
Quang Ngai, 70th VC Sapper (150);

NVA/VC Sappers in South Vietnam's MR 2: 1/73

NVA B-3 Front
Regiments: 400th Sapper (800).
Misc Bns: Kontum (P) Bns: 406th NVA Sapper (150).
Gia Lai(P) Bns: 408th VC Sapper (200).
Dar Lac (P) Bns: 401st NVA Sapper (200).
NVA MR 5

405th NVA Sapper Bn (150).
Phu Yen (P) NVA Bns: 14th Sapper (150)
Khanh Hoa (P) Bns: 7th NVA Sapper (200); 407th NVA Sapper (200); Khanh Hoa VC Sapper (200).

NVA/VC Sappers in South Vietnam's MR 3:1/73

All Under COSVN
429th Sapper Command HQ (400); 29th Sapper Regt (600); Sapper Bns: 7, 8, 9, 10, 11, 12, 16 (1,400).
Separate Sapper Bns, NVA: 89th (150); 268th (150); 4th (150) 6th (150); 7th (150); 211th (150).
Separate Sapper Bns. VC: 10th (100); 12th (150).

NVA/VC Sappers in South Vietnam's MR 4:1/73

COSVN
Regts: 44 Sapper
VC MR 2
Misc Bns: 207th Sapper (100)
NVA Sapper Bns: 267B (100); 281st (200).
VC MR 3
VC Sapper Bns: 2012D (150): 2014th (150).
* = the number of men in each unit, is in parenthesis.

Sapper Stealth

South Vietnamese outpost defenders tried to use farm animals to detect enemy sappers. They deployed packs of dogs, geese and ducks on the outer perimeter of their defenses because such creatures are known to give the alarm at the approach of strangers, or anyone else.

Undeterred by such naturalist approaches, NVA sappers used several innovative methods to fool the animals. Dogs were foiled when sappers lay in the night dew long enough to erase their strong human scent. Then the animals were calmly approached and either petted or fed poisoned/tranquilized food.

Ducks and geese, deathly afraid of snakes, were neutralized by first rubbing green onions on the sapper's body. Green onions smelled like snakes and frightened the birds.

Sometimes sappers attached a blackened water potato to the end of a walking stick and dangled it toward the birds. Thinking they saw a snake, the geese or ducks froze into terrified immobility, and would not dare make a sound.[486]

Anti-sapper Barriers

Other perimeter defenses easily breached by sappers included minefields, noise making devices, booby traps, barbed wire and fortifications. Sensors, search lights and flares were effective anti-sapper weapons. However, sensor effectiveness was limited since they had to be periodically replaced and were frequently defective.

Fences were important in defending against sappers. Sometimes white-painted sheet iron fences were used to replace wire mesh fences since they were more difficult to cut.

In some areas the allied defense perimeter was either totally concreted or bordered by concrete paths. Area vegetation, killed by herbicides, also made the sappers' job more difficult. Usually a 200 meter wide corridor was cleared around every base perimeter. Beyond that perimeter, farming was permitted.[487]

At the U.S. Long Binh Base, two illumination systems were utilized as defense against sappers. Both the inner and outer sides of fences were illuminated.[488]

Every base included patrol routes both inside and outside of its perimeter. Eventually those routes became the centerpiece for more effective barriers. The South Vietnamese were relatively more successful at building anti-sapper barriers than the Americans. Their perimeter barriers showed more understanding of sapper vulnerability:

"In addition to the regular barbed wire fence, a barrier made of corrugated tin and chain links was erected along the patrol route . . . The cutting of tin and chain links was difficult, time consuming and noisy. Experience showed that it took ten to fifteen minutes to cut a hole wide enough to let one person crawl through. As the fence was built on the inner side of the patrol route, the Communist sappers attempting to penetrate it had to sit or lie on the flat patrol route and could be easily detected by the guards. The fence was also whitewashed to provide contrast with shadows at night.

"Electric lights along the patrol route were beamed on the tin fence instead of the barbed wire. This was required since the wire often became hidden in tall grass which reduced the sentries' observation.

"As a result of better barriers the number of successful penetrations by communist sappers dropped from forty three percent in 1972 to five percent in 1974 and zero percent in 1975 (the year South Vietnam fell to the

Communists). The total number of communist sappers killed during those attempts also . . . (increased)."[489]

Sapper raids did a lot of damage. From 1972 to 1975, years of minimal sapper anti-installation assaults, numerous attacks were made against allied ammunition depots.

Sapper Attacks Against Ammunition Depots

Year	Sapper Attempts	Sapper Penetrations	% Success
1972	37	16	43
1973	15	3	20
1974	21	1	5
1975	2	0	0[490]

Sapper Attacks By Fire Against Ammunition Depots

Year	Fire Attacks	Number of Hits	Percent of Hits
1972	13	3	23
1973	10	1	10
1974	21	0	0
1975	7	0	0

Sapper Casualties Versus Ammunition Destroyed

Year	Tonnage	Value $ US Million	Sappers Killed
1972	23,903	54,245	16
1973	5,851	11,032	13
1974	5,875	7,724	27
1975	0	0	0

CHAPTER 14

Hill Trap Maneuvers

Sometime in 1966, the North Vietnamese Army began developing a new doctrinal modification which was called the "Hill Trap" maneuver. The Hill Trap maneuver sought to exploit known battle habits of American troops by drawing them into a mountainous killing ground where a defense in depth, combined with standoff bombardment and rear attacks, would likely annihilate them.

Hills and mountains in each of South Vietnam's four corps areas were prepared as battlefields. Huge numbers of conscripted laborers were marched into NVA mountain stronghold areas where they dug bunkers, trench lines and tunnel complexes. Most of the work was concentrated in I Corps with its strategic A Shau/Da Krong War Zone (west of Hue), and II Corps with its strategic Triborder (west of Dak To) and Chu Pong, War Zones.

To ensure that their preparations were not impeded, NVA troops occupied the A Shau Valley in early 1966 and established strong anti-recon screens to the west. The same procedure was followed between the Triborder Zone and Dak To.[493]

Preparation of the two mountain battlefield areas probably began in May, 1966. Thousands of laborers were required to carry out the engineering feats required to convert two areas into huge, 900 to 1,000 square mile, bridgeheads thrusting deep into South Vietnam. Where were the U.S. units charged with defending those border areas while all of the communist fortification building was going on?

Two reinforced U.S. Marine divisions lay doggo along the coast only thirty miles from A Shau. Three major U.S. Army units, the 4th Infantry Division,

1st Cavalry Division and 173rd Airborne Brigade were based even closer to the Dak To area.

Where were the American reconnaissance screens? Where were major reconnaissance in force units reacting to discoveries by those screens? Why had the Americans become afraid of these two enemy stronghold areas so soon?

The malfeasance and timidity of American generals allowed the NVA to precisely prepare battlefields for execution of the Hill Trap maneuver.

The Dak To Battle

Early in 1966, allied intelligence reports consistently indicated a strong NVA buildup in the Triborder area. Two NVA infantry divisions, the 1st and 10th, were supposedly preparing for action under the B-3 Front's command. However, the U.S. 4th Infantry Division didn't begin scouting the Dak To area, opposite the B-3 Front's headquarters and staging area, until April 1967.[494]

The U.S. 4th Division had been rapidly intimidated by skirmishes with the NVA further south along the Cambodian border, near the Ia Drang River. In May 1967, the K4 and K5 Battalions of the 32nd NVA Regiment, and elements of the 66th and 95B NVA Regiments, had been encountered there.[495]

NVA attacks began to flare up near the Cambodian border. In June 1967 the NVA began rocket attacks on Pleiku. In July 1967, elements of the 66th NVA Regiment whipped the U.S. 1/12 Infantry Battalion near Duc Co. Later in July, another 4th Infantry Division unit encountered the 32nd NVA Regiment south of Duc Co. Both of those NVA regiments had fought in the historic Ia Drang campaign, in the same area, only six months previously. Now they controlled the border around the Chu Pong War Zone.[496]

The 6th Battalion of the 24th NVA Infantry Regiment, appeared near Dak To on June 22, 1967. The 24th, which had recently battered the 1st Brigade of the U.S. 101st Airborne Division, was hunting for bear. In a bloody battle along a jungled ridgeline, the 6th Battalion destroyed one company of the 2/503rd U.S. Airborne Battalion, leaving seventy-six dead paratroopers crumpled on the forest floor.[497]

In August 1967 ARVN troops fought the 2nd Battalion of the 174th NVA Infantry Regiment near Dak To. In early November the 4/503rd U.S. Airborne Battalion suffered severe casualties when assaulting an NVA bunker line near Dak To.[498]

NVA battlefield preparations, supported from the Triborder War Zone in South Vietnam's II Corps, extended over a 900 square mile rectangle encompassing Dak To. The northern side of the rectangle extended fifty miles eastward, and ten miles north of Dak To, from the border intersection of Laos, Cambodia and South Vietnam (the Triborder). The southern side of the rectangle extended fifty-five miles eastward from the Cambodia border and thirty miles south of Dak To. Both sides of the rectangle were eventually extended beyond Dak To, twenty to thirty miles to the east on the other side of South Vietnam's Route 14, which linked Dak To to Kontum City.[499]

In mid-1966, the 24th NVA Infantry Regiment moved into the mountainous area twenty miles due northeast of Dak To. The 24th Regiment began to occupy fortified battlegrounds centered around Hill 1416. That position theatened the key Route 14/Route 512 road junction west of Dak To. Under extreme pressure the 24th would follow escape routes to the northwest, away from the Cambodian border.

Directly ten miles south of Dak To began the fortified battle zone to be controlled by the 32nd NVA Infantry Regiment. The 32nd would occupy a series of fortified mountain redoubts twenty miles wide and twenty miles deep. Primary 32nd Regiment defensive areas were concentrated around Hills 1262 and 1338. Fortifications were also established along the projected NVA line of retreat, following a watercourse, southwestward toward the Cambodian border. Fortified Hill 1030 formed the hinge of that escape route.

Only ten miles west of the Triborder Zone, and less than ten miles south of Ben Het, was another fortified area. The 66th NVA Infantry Regiment and the 40th NVA Artillery Regiment would be dug in there along a ten mile fortified mountain front centered on Hill 823.

Five miles south of that position was the prepared battlefield of the 174th NVA Infantry Regiment. The 174th Regiment's defensive area was centered on Hill 875, five miles due west of the Cambodia border.[500]

As the commander of the U.S. 4th Infantry Division, General Peers, later wrote: "The enemy had prepared the battlefield well. Nearly every key terrain feature was heavily fortified with elaborate bunker and trench complexes. He had moved quantities of supplies and ammunition into the area. He was prepared to stay."[501]

Where was the 4th Division during all of those preparations? The commander of the 4th U.S. Division and his ARVN counterparts learned in early 1967, that the NVA was maneuvering far west of the Cambodian border. However, General Peers didn't attempt to maneuver against them. He outposted the environs of Dak To with five or six companies from his division, intending to use battalions from the 173rd Airborne Brigade for most of the real fighting. The timidity of the 4th Division became nakedly blatant.

The 1967–1968 Winter–Spring Campaign in II Corps

The B-3 Front which controlled the Triborder and Chu Pong War Zones launched the 1967–1968 Winter–Spring Campaign with a confident assumption of victory. In the II Corps area, the following Chu Luc objectives soon became obvious:

- Draw allied troops into the Triborder area where some of their elements could be annihilated. If the campaign went awry, NVA troops could rapidly withdraw out of harm's way into the Cambodian or Laotian sanctuaries.
- Practice the Hill Trap Maneuver in the prepared battlefields.
- Coordinate the campaign with other NVA initiatives.

For the campaign around Dak To, the 1st NVA Infantry Division was allocated units which had been in combat for over a year in 1967, including:

- 32nd NVA infantry regiment (1337 men).
- 66th NVA Infantry Regiment (1335 men).
- 24th NVA Infantry Regiment (1620 men).
- 174th NVA Infantry Regiment (2000 men).
- 40th NVA Artillery Regiment (800 men, estimated). This regiment controlled one 120mm heavy mortar battalion and two 122mm rocket battalions.[502]

The 1st NVA Infantry "Division" controlled approximately 7,000 combatants, or the equivalent of seven U.S. Marine battalions. The division was spread out along 900 square miles of jungled terrain. Their fortified mountain redoubts were too far apart to mutually support each other. The road into the Triborder Stronghold was wide open.

So what did the Americans do? Instead of threatening the red base and drawing red units down to defend it, the Americans set up fire bases and began attacking whatever fortified positions they could find.

In early November, 1967 the U.S. 4/503rd Airborne Battalion with 500 men, fought small elements of the 66th NVA Regiment on Hill 823. As was the habit of most 173rd Airborne Brigade subordinate commanders, the 4/503rd battalion commander, Lieutenant Colonel Johnson, did not accompany his battalion into battle. Colonel Johnson sent one of his staff officers to command the battalion in battle, while he managed from the "rear command post," or swooped overhead in a helicopter.[503] That behavior was common among American battalion commanders in Vietnam. However, battalion commanders in the elite 1st Cavalry Division usually deployed on the ground with their units.[504]

In mid-November, 1967 the 2/503rd Battalion was told that the 174th NVA Infantry Regiment was covering the withdrawal of the "beaten" 32nd and 66th NVA Regiments. The 174th was dug in on Hill 875, five kilometers east of the Cambodian border (only a half-hour's walk to safety) and twelve kilometers southeast of the Triborder Zone.[505]

The Trap on Hill 875

Arriving at the foot of Hill 875, two rifle companies of the 2/503rd Battalion lined up abreast facing the objective area. Hill 875 was thick with vegetation and tall trees. Its steep slopes were covered with mixed bamboo and scrub brush.

The American companies meant to advance up the gradual, 100 meter wide ridgeline leading toward the top of the hill. If the enemy was there, they would use bombs and artillery shells to beat him down.

The two assault companies were fighting side by side but independently, there being no overall commander of the three companies on the ground with them. When the three companies jumped off in their assault, their battalion commander was not with them. He was leading from the deep rear.

The three rifle companies were expected to meet the enemy, curl into a defensive perimeter and watch while air and artillery "bombed hell out of them Charlies." Then the Americans would simply occupy the smoking charnel house of enemy dead. It didn't work that way.

As the two assaulting American rifle companies advanced, they were rapidly pinned down by an enemy bunker line defended by the 2nd Battalion of the 174th Regiment. The aggressive NVA troops soon left their fortified lines and began close assaulting the American companies. The reds were well trained and thirsting for blood: "The NVA attackers were well camouflaged, their faces painted black and their weapons wrapped in burlap. Machine guns, rifle grenades, mortars, and well placed snipers riddled the paratroopers of the two lead companies."[506]

Behind the front line, the American reserve company chopped a landing zone (LZ) out of the foliage and set up a string of outposts covering the rear. Then two platoons from the company began ferrying wounded from the frontline back to the LZ.

Observing that American company around the LZ were the two other 174th NVA Regiment battalions, preparing to execute a Hill Trap maneuver. Their Hill Trap Maneuver probably included the following steps:

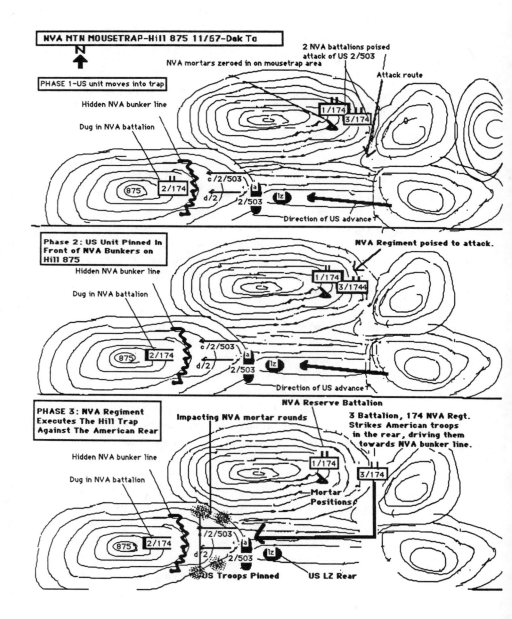

NVA MTN MOUSETRAP-Hill 875 11/67-Dak To

N

2 NVA battalions poised attack of US 2/503

NVA mortars zeroed in on mousetrap area

Attack route

PHASE 1-US unit moves into trap

Hidden NVA bunker line

Dug in NVA battalion

1/174
3/174

875   2/174

c/2/503

d/2/   a
2/503   1z

Direction of US advance

Phase 2: US Unit Pinned in Front of NVA Bunkers on Hill 875

NVA Regiment poised to attack.

Hidden NVA bunker line

Dug in NVA battalion

1/174
3/1744

875   2/174

c/2/503

d/2/   a
2/503   1z

Direction of US advance

PHASE 3: NVA Regiment Executes The Hill Trap Against The American Rear

Impacting NVA mortar rounds

NVA Reserve Battalion

3 Battalion, 174 NVA Regt. Strikes American troops in the rear, driving them towards NVA bunker line.

Hidden NVA bunker line

Dug in NVA battalion

1/174

3/174

Mortar Positions

875   2/174

/2/503

d/2/   a
2/503   1z

US Troops Pinned   US LZ Rear

1. Pin the American assault force on Hill 875 before the defenses of the 2/174th NVA, causing as much casualties as possible. After several hours of that battle the American reserve company would be spread thin carrying casualties and protecting the rear.
2. At the right moment, bombard the American reserve company with a deployed mortar platoon and then hit it with the 1st Battalion of the 174th NVA Regiment. The 1st Battalion would then drive through the enemy reserve company and into the rear of the enemy forces pinned on Hill 875.
3. The 3rd Battalion 174th NVA Regiment, deployed behind a hill nearby, would be committed if the enemy defense began to totter.
4. Otherwise the 3rd Battalion would either strike the enemy perimeter from another direction or cover the withdrawal of the 1st and 2nd Battalions.

Four hours after the battle began, the NVA 1/174th Battalion struck the American rear guard company. "Waves of screaming North Vietnamese Army regulars charged through the position in such force that two platoons simply evaporated. Now split and under fierce assault, the battalion's reserve was in immediate danger of being overrun as well. Most of the paratroopers were already dead when the six-man command group was completely wiped out in hand-to-hand combat."[507]

The force of the red assault drove remnants of the reserve company up the hill and into the rear of the other two companies. The NVA were shrieking, "Now you Chieu Hoi, GI!"[508] as the American perimeter was surrounded and pounded for the next twenty-four hours, until relieved by the 4/503rd Battalion. The American perimeter barely survived in spite of the terrific amount of bombs and shells raining down onto NVA positions all around it.

Suddenly-nervous American pilots accidentally dropped a bomb on the U.S. perimeter on Hill 875. That bomb killed forty-two men and wounded forty-five, destroying one American paratrooper company with one American 250 pound bomb. If the reds had not been pinned at the moment by other bombs dropping on them, they would have destroyed the Americans.

When the 4/503rd Battalion tried to attack up the hill to relieve its surrounded comrades, the reds volley-fired RPG rockets and machine guns into their faces at point blank range. Mortar shells impacted all over the American lines, as the reds constantly struck the flanks and rear of the battalion. Only massive artillery and aerial bombardment saved the 4/503rd as it reeled back down the mountain, joining its sister unit in defeat. Now two decimated paratroop battalions littered the slopes of Hill 875.

That night the 174th NVA Regiment slipped away and crossed over into Cambodia without further losses. Then, and only then, were the Americans able to advance under their fire support umbrella and "capture the hill."

Sorting Out the Mess

The American troops who attacked Hill 875 were a heroic lot, they "stomped their feet . . . yelled, chanted, and cursed at the NVA as they attacked. Some sang paratrooper songs."[509] But too many died. Both the 2/503rd and its rescuer the 4/503rd, were effectively destroyed as combat battalions.

Both battalions fought alone, without their battalion commanders. They were committed piecemeal and fought defensively. They never executed or attempted any outflanking or rear seeking maneuvers. Too few troops were committed to allow maneuvering in any event. A maneuver force must have a pivot, or base of fire, to maneuver around. There were no troops left over for that, after the small American units spread out in their thin perimeters.

Neither was there any demonstrated American knowledge of how to maneuver. Also missing was the will to maneuver, exemplified by the failure of both American battalion commanders to share the pain and share the glory, by joining their comrades on the ground, facing the enemy.

If the two paratroop battalions had been NVA, a regimental headquarters would have also been on the ground with them. NVA doctrine required a regimental headquarters to be with any collection of two or more of its subordinate battalions.

The aggressive troops of the 174th NVA Infantry Regiment won the Hill 875 fight. They had prepared for it, "all NVA soldiers appeared in good health, were well turned out and excellently equipped . . . the readiness of the equipment was most impressive. Every item of the hundreds of captured NVA packs—sweaters, mosquito nets, rice rolls, and ammunition—was brand new. Mortars and rocket launchers bore manufacture dates of 1967 . . . the 174th Regiment had been completely equipped with new clothing and equipment before crossing into South Vietnam."[510]

Yet the NVA battalions weren't able to successfully complete the Hill Trap Maneuver all the way to annihilation of the American force. The red units had advanced too slowly.

It was the fortified bunker and trench lines which gave the enemy their pivot base around which they could maneuver: "the NVA's well prepared defenses were able to withstand USAF strikes for so long. Crossed logs and thick earth cover made them immune to anything less than a lucky direct hit from a 500 pound bomb or 105mm shell. Detection was almost impossible as the bunkers had been built well before the events of November 1967 and the undergrowth had grown back giving the enemy the advantage of full concealment.

"The NVA troops had prepared a complex defensive system on Hill 875 several months earlier. The natural growth had time to repair the scars of constructing the system on interconnecting trenches, bunkers, and tunnels. It was a formidable natural fortress, manned by fresh and full strength units supported by similar ones in nearby mortar range.

"Overhead cover of the NVA fighting positions were a combination of logs and dirt. Bunkers were flush with the ground. Most had short tunnels leading outward in the rear or from connecting trenches. Bunkers were sited for mutual support and interlocking fire, deadly against attackers."[511]

When the two 173rd Airborne Brigade battalions left Hill 875, they were skeleton commands. Companies had only twenty or so effectives and platoons were reduced to six or seven men, yet the American high command heralded the battle as a victory and denied that two paratroop battalions had been wiped out in the four day struggle for Hill 875. In truth, the 173rd Airborne Brigade was gutted during the Dak To battles. It was never deployed as a complete combat unit again.

There was a cover-up of the true extent of paratroop casualties during the Dak To Battle of Hill 875. One intelligence officer investigated the casualties of Dak To during the war. He visited the 519th Supply Depot near Saigon where the personal effects of American dead were shipped to their next of kin. Although only three hundred American dead were officially admitted, the 519th "processed some seven hundred boxes of personal effects."[512] undoubtedly from victims of the Hill 875 fight, in one week. It caused the American intelligence officer to wonder:

"Could we have lost as many, or more, men than had the NVA during those twenty days? Had most of the American dead from Dak To been added to the KIA count for Operation MacArthur which had gone on for weeks, and would for several more, and which covered much more area than just Dak To? The dead would ultimately be reported, but spread out so you wouldn't notice all those bodies on a couple of hills during another of our 'victories.' "[513]

Hill Trap on Hamburger Hill

By 1969, the communists had controlled the A Shau Valley War Zone for several years. They had mobilized thousands of South Vietnamese peasants as road builders, tunnellers and fortification builders. As a result, the mountains surrounding the valley were riddled with hundreds of miles of tunneled fortifications protecting thousands of supply bunkers, depots, parks and dumps.

Most of the mountains surrounding the A Shau Valley had at least three lines of bunkers girdling them. The bunkers were mostly two-man affairs, but numerous larger ones could be found as well. A number of the bunkers were of the A-frame type. Most NVA bunkers were interconnected with tunnels and fighting trenches, and sited for mutual support. The communists dug grenade sumps into the bunker floors. Any grenades tossed into the bunkers could be kicked into the sumps where they would harmlessly explode without harming the bunker occupants. Concussion grenades were sometimes used to overcome that problem.

Trails and other avenues of approach up the mountains were defended in depth with multiple bunkered trenchlines and sniper positions. Indirect fire support was ranged in on most A Shau mountain trails and other avenues of approach/assembly. NVA heavy mortar, cannon and rocket batteries fired from emplacements inside sacrosanct Laos.

Dong Ap Bia, later known as Hamburger Hill, was defended by the 29th NVA, "American Killer," Infantry Regiment with its 6th, 7th, and 8th Infantry Battalions. The full strength regiment had brought its light machine guns, RPGs, light mortars and heavy 12.7mm machine guns with it. Other crew-served weapons, including recoilless rifles and 82mm mortars, were left in Laos just a few miles away. Fire support for the 29th was provided by heavy 120mm mortar and artillery batteries safely dug into Laotian battery sites. The red artillery already had all likely avenues of approach zeroed in.[514]

The 29th, with between 1,200 and 1,800 men, was a "lean, mean fighting machine." It occupied positions on Dong Ap Bia that had been carefully dug during thousands of man hours of effort. Several rows of ground level bunkers girdled the mountain from its midpoint and across its military and topographical crests. The bunkers were dug in at ground level, sited at the business end of fire tunnels, and connected with covered and tunneled fighting trenches. Each position was mutually supported by other positions on either flank.

Each defense line was sited in depth, with its greatest depth layered along approach trails. Those trail sectors were enfiladed with firing positions at ground level and each commanding contour level up. That "fire stack" extended to the tops of 100-foot trees along the way, where many red snipers perched. The snipers were deployed in swarms because their positions were so high above the ground that they were safe from the predictable thousands of rounds of rocket, bomb and artillery shell fire which would be directed there.

Being professional soldiers, Chu Luc commanders took careful note of the terrain compartments found along the slopes of the mountains. They had walked the ground with detailed maps in one hand looking at their positions from the American perspective, which they knew so well. They carefully examined every place where American troops could shelter from fire, in areas known as dead space. Where their bunker lines were insufficient to rake the foreground with fire, they set up flaking clusters of saliented bunker positions. Fire from those positions could hit the dead space, or ground which had been in defilade.

Chu Luc Organization of Mountain Terrain

- **Avenues of approach:** Trails, streambeds, ridgelines or spurs leading on a gradual slope, up-hill. Defended in depth with bunker lines. Any terrain outcroppings providing salients which could deliver flanking or enfilading fire along those approaches were turned into fortified bunker strongpoints.
- **Draws:** Stream beds or other declivities between two promontories. Used as avenues of approach to seek rear or flanking attack positions. Draws are key elements of the Hill Trap Maneuver.
- **Saddles:** Lower areas between two higher areas. Ambushes set up in saddles to hit the enemy as he came down-hill into the lower area. Bunkers containing 12.7mm heavy machine guns as well as light machine guns and RPGs were common in saddle positions.
- **Reverse Slopes:** Areas on the opposide side of a mountain from where an enemy is attacking. Such positions can't be hit by artillery and can strike enemy troops as they are skylined coming over the topographical crest. The reds on Dong Ap Bia didn't employ reverse slope positions.
- **Slopes:** Areas extending at the same relative contour level, all the way around the mountain. Defense lines were constructed all around the mountain in some cases. However, the lines tended to "peter out" about one hundred and fifty yards on either side of avenues of approach.

The reds attempted to convince the Americans that their defenses were the same all around the mountain by deceptions, such as building three rows of hundreds of irregular fires all around the mountain at night. However, their fire sacks, or V system defenses, were not continuous. Large units, deployed with widely probing columns, could have got behind the enemy lines.

From the standpoint of the communist defenders the best approach route for the attacking Americans would be up the west slope of the mountain. The Americans could be hit easily by mortar and artillery batteries firing from Laos. If the Americans came up on the east face of the mountain, the red artillery couldn't have done much damage.

An American approach up the west face also had a great disadvantage for the red defenders. Such an approach placed the Americans between the red positions on Dong Ap Bia and their primary resupply, reinforcement and escape routes. Those routes consisted of a camouflaged improved road and several trails running eastward out of Laos, across the Trung Pham River and through the large eastwest draws southwest of Hill 900.

The NVA escape route ran down the west face of the mountain, through the saddle between Hill 900 and 916, and out the western draw into Laos. The reds planned alternate supply/reinforcement routes which swung laterally in arcs to the left and right of their defenses, if the Americans interdicted their primary lines of communications. They were not worried because they knew several truths about American troops:

1. American units were deployed in such small numbers that they could not simultaneously carry out two widely disparate missions without exposing themselves to defeat in detail.
2. A large proportion of any deployed American force was assigned to defend their landing zone which dissipated strength and provided another vulnerable point for the reds to threaten.
3. American troops tended to ignore enemy lines of communications being fixated on enemy defenses.

The reds were amazed and happy to discover that during their defense of Hamburger Hill, the Americans never completely interdicted their primary supply route. Every night, red troops and porter convoys were shuttled back and forth from the mountain defenses to the Laotian sanctuaries, right under the noses of the American troops.

The Chu Luc prepared Hamburger Hill for a long siege and intended to fight there until the build-up of American supporting weapons forced a withdrawal. Their prepared mountain battlefield was described as being "honeycombed with deep tunnels interconnected with a giant hospital, regimental CP, and numerous storage areas."[515]

Three or more communist battalion command bunker were dug into the slopes of Hamburger Hill, in addition to the regimental command post bunker. One such bunker was described by Americans as "a large command bunker, probably a battalion headquarters . . . equipped with field tele-

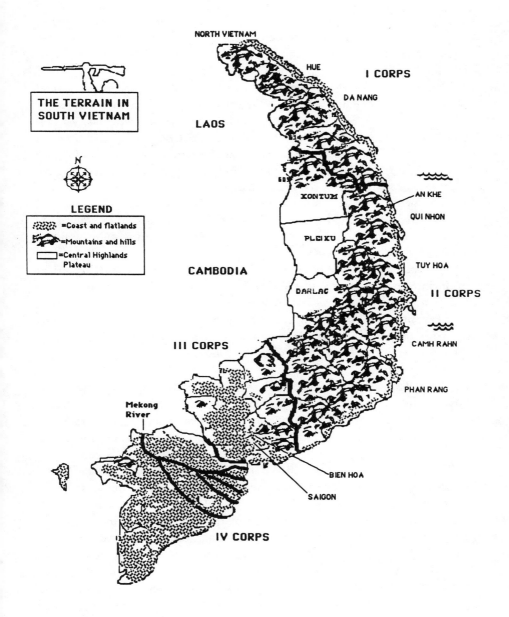

THE TERRAIN IN SOUTH VIETNAM

N

LEGEND
=Coast and flatlands
=Mountains and hills
=Central Highlands Plateau

NORTH VIETNAM

HUE

I CORPS

DA NANG

LAOS

KONTUM

AN KHE

QUI NHON

PLEIKU

TUY HOA

CAMBODIA

DARLAC

II CORPS

III CORPS

CAMH RAHN

PHAN RANG

Mekong River

BIEN HOA

SAIGON

IV CORPS

phones, detailed maps of the mountain and northern A Shau, and large quantities of ammunition."[516]

Although the reds began cooking up a three or four day supply of rice, preparing for a long fight, they were contemptuous of the Americans. They planned to kill Americans as long as possible, and they didn't care who knew it.

The reds had all their ammunition and food already cached in several places on the mountain." In the (NVA) storage areas . . . (American troops eventually) uncovered 152 individual and 25 crew-served weapons, 75,000 rounds of ammunition, thousands of mortar and RPG rounds and over ten tons of rice."[517] That meant that they didn't have to be burdened with heavy rucksacks, like the comfort conscious Americans. As a result the red infantry had greater mobility than the Americans.

The enemy defense lines included huge Chinese claymore directional mines which were sited to enfilade trails. Those mines were command-detonated into the face of American columns which were then close assaulted while still in a state of shock.

Approximately twelve to eighteen 100–125 man NVA companies lurked in the bunkers, trenches and spider holes of Dong Ap Bia, ready to execute a combination of fire and close assault maneuver against the hated American "Lord Fauntleroys." Exercising excellent fire discipline, they would only open fire with weapons that had clear targets. Then as the Americans deployed, they would raise their crescendo of fire to volleys of RPGs and long bursts of machine gun fire.

The RPGs, originally intended as very effective, reusable individual infantry antitank weapons, were used as antipersonnel weapons on Hamburger Hill. They replaced direct firing recoilless rifles and even mortars, which enabled red units to move even faster. Every red squad on Dong Ap Bia seemed to have one or two RPGs and at least one light machine gun.

The red troops remained hidden in their camouflaged positions until their targets were at point blank range. Then they would pop up and loose bursts of fire into their enemies' faces.

Another defensive method employed by the reds on Dong Ap Bia was the close assault counterattack. They were very aggressive and were constantly seeking opportunities to use flanking draws as avenues of approach to get behind American troops.

On countless occasions, red troops would leave their defense lines and charge down on the Americans. On such occasions one red force (fixing force) would come straight at the Americans, dodging from tree to tree and firing from the hip. One or more other red assault groups (flanking force) would be dashing against the American flanks. The idea was to envelop and destroy the Americans.

Triggers For An NVA Counterattack

1. A slackening of American resolve or infantry fire.
2. American confusion, for example, just after a claymore mine was detonated in the midst of an American unit.
3. When American units began to withdraw.
4. After American fire support aircraft or helicopter left the scene.

If the reds even sensed, and they did have excellent military sensory apparatus, confusion or an American withdrawal, they came out shooting. At first they would start coming out of their holes in twos and threes, and then in groups of five and six. Soon squads and platoons would join the assault. Sometimes whole red companies would sweep through the American line.

The 29th Regiment was tough. Its troops were imbued with the offensive spirit and they attacked whenever possible. One enemy company counterattack exemplified the offensive spirit of the 29th: "Firing RPGs and flinging satchel charges, (the communist troops) swept right through the (American) platoon, *then turned around and charged through it again. . . .* the fighting was close and savage, with many men shooting NVA soldiers from only a few feet away."[518]

American Command Incompetence

American leadership during the battle of Hamburger Hill was hardly competent. U.S. commanders knew what they were up against on the second day after the first American paratroop battalion arrived on the scene. The Americans discovered the enemy resupply roads and trails leading west out of Laos straight up the mountain, but they didn't interdict them. They discovered, from captured documents, that they were facing an entire NVA regiment, but they didn't reinforce.

After the first two days of attacking piecemeal, when American units were decimated, they knew that the reds were stronger, well dug in and ready, "in two hours they (Charlie Company) had lost their first sergeant, two of three platoon leaders, the company executive officer, two platoon sergeants and forty enlisted men."[519]

Colonel Honeycutt, the battalion commander of the "Rakkasans," who did most of the fighting, told his brigade commander that more troops were needed, several times. Any soldier with a lick of sense knew that sending one battalion at a time up the mountain was wasteful.

Lieutenant Frank Boccia, who commanded a rifle platoon during the battle, understood the situation better than most American generals: "we should have brought in a couple of more battalions, even an entire brigade. On the 14th, we hit that hill with a full battalion and an unbelievable amount of firepower, and the NVA brushed us off the way you would a fly. At that point General Zias should have brought up a full brigade. It should have been obvious we were facing a full regiment. Military history is filled with commanders wasting their strength piecemeal, and that's exactly what Zias did . . . the evidence is overwhelming that he failed in his primary function as an infantry commander; which is you fulfill your mission with all available means and keep your losses at a minimum."[520]

American troops were most certainly poorly led during the Vietnam War. Senator Stephen Young of Ohio described the problem with great accuracy: "Our generals in Vietnam acted as if they had never studied Lee and Jackson's strategy. Instead they flung our paratroopers piecemeal in frontal assaults. Instead of seeking to surround the enemy and seeking to assault the hill from the sides and the front simultaneously, there was just one frontal assault after another, killing our boys who went up Hamburger Hill."[521]

There is evidence that the Brigade commander of the "Apache Snow Operation" against Hamburger Hill realized that with two or more battalions moving simultaneously up the mountain, the reds could not easily concentrate against one or the other. Carrying out maneuvers based on an understanding of that simple military fact could have thwarted the enemy's consistent locally superior troop concentrations against strung out American forces. Yet the Americans never lined up even two battalions abreast. Instead the Brigade commander ordered Colonel Honeycutt of the 3/187, after several days of debilitating struggle, to "move his two companies forward until they made contact, and then have them continue advancing until they were exerting maximum pressure on the enemy's defenses. They were not however to become decisively engaged."[522] Such an order sounds more like some diplomatic nicety than a combat command.

Colonel Honeycutt was part of the problem. He used his special status as one of General Westmoreland's favorites to influence his commander to let him continue attacking frontally and piecemeal after his unit had already been played out. "As before, the main thrust of the Rakkasan attack would be against the western face of the mountain with Charlie Company attacking up the main ridge and Alpha Company up the large southern one."[523]

That attack was carried out by overburdened troops, some "carrying two 50-pound rucksacks, his machine gun, and ten belts of ammo and . . . near the point of complete physical collapse."[524]

Instead of moving fresh battalions into the fray, the incompetent American brigade leadership used the ineffective individual replacement method and soon the combat battalions on the scene were busy "processing replacements shuttled in from Camp Evans—the replacements were not infantrymen but cooks, truck drivers, and other rear-area men."[525]

The Hill Trap Maneuver on Hamburger Hill

The 29th Regiment utilized variations of the Hill Trap maneuver several times during the Hamburger Hill fight. Yet they never used several companies or even a battalion in the decisive manner that the 174th NVA Regiment had carried out the maneuver at Dak To.

The similarities between Dak To and Hamburger Hill were not lost on Colonel Honeycutt, who told his Brigade commander, Colonel Joe Conroy, early in the battle, "The 506th has got to get their asses in gear and get involved in this fight. *This is a goddamn Dak To battle,* and we're fighting it with a fucking battalion."[526]

Colonel Honeycutt also seemed to be familiar with the Hill Trap maneuver. Once when he was told that a large group of enemy soldiers were observed slipping down from Dong Ap Bia and into the draw which flanked his command post, Honeycutt said, "Those bastards are gonna try and get down in that draw. They figure we won't be able to spot them in the morning fog, and when the companies move up to their assault positions, they'll move right in behind them. Then when the fog burns off, they're gonna climb out of the draw, get on the ridges, and hit the companies in the rear."[527]

Colonel Honeycutt alerted the rifle company that was guarding his battalion command post (one fourth of his total strength) and deployed them along the draw where the infiltrating NVA company was poised. After a while, movement up the slopes of the draw was heard: "The NVA infantry in the draw, thinking that Alpha and Bravo were in their assault positions started moving up towards the ridges. They thought they were moving into the rear of the companies, but instead walked right into a wall of rifle and machine gun fire."[528]

On several other occasions the 29th Regiment used part of its forces to execute some variation of the Hill Trap. One infiltrating force was sent against an American landing zone near the battalion command post. The reds "used a draw to get in close to the LZ and then hit it with an infantry platoon."[529]

Several attempts were made to cut off American units by using draws as avenues of approach: "the NVA moved into the draw in an attempt to cut off the platoon . . . ten to fifteen enemy soldiers moving on-line, came out of the draw, their AKs barking."[530]

On at least one occasion the Hill Trap maneuver was used as part of a general counterattack by one NVA battalion: "the NVA launched a counterattack . . . Enemy infantry swarmed down from the top of the mountain and began maneuvering against the front of the platoon. Another group of enemy soldiers slipped down from Hill 937 and began pouring enfilading fire into the platoon's left flank. And still another group, which had hidden in the large draw during the attack, moved out of it and began shooting into the platoon's rear."[531]

The Use of Maneuver by American Forces

The enemy defense lines didn't have to be battered by two weeks of artillery and air bombardment. The guns of the battleship *New Jersey,* firing locomotive shaped sixteen inch shells from dozens of miles away in the South China Sea, were not needed. The enemy lines could have been outflanked and taken in the rear.

If several battalions had been used in the assault their frontage and ability to probe the enemy defenses would have been appropriate. If all battalion commanders were on the ground with all four companies on the line, gaps could have been discovered in the enemy defense. American reserve battalion columns could have penetrated those gaps and rolled up the enemy lines from the rear. But the American brigade commanders just couldn't bring themselves to set up a regimental headquarters a few hundred yards behind a battle line, even if a couple of rifle companies were dug in around that command post as security.

Four American and/or allied battalions could have been distributed as follows:

1. One battalion cutting the enemy lines of communications and defending the nearby regimental CP.
2. Two battalions probing the enemy lines for gaps.
3. One battalion deployed in eight two-platoon columns, read to mass against any gaps discovered.

The 1st Battalion, 506th Airborne Regiment, which also fought on Hamburger Hill, proved that maneuver warfare worked. Although only one of their companys, A/1/506, did much maneuvering, their results proved the concept. "Not wanting to risk a costly frontal assault on the bunkers, Lieutenant Burney (Commanding officer Alpha Company 1/506) ordered (two of his subordinate platoon leaders) . . . to lead their platoons up a draw to the south of the ridge and try to get in behind the bunkers. Once they

HAMBURGER HILL Ap Bia Mountain, A Shau Valley, Vietnam, Hill 937
May 10-21,1969
3/187, 3Bde, 101 Abn Division versus 29 NVA Regiment: 6,7,&8 Bns
Joined on 19/5/69 by: 2/3 Arvn, 2/501, and 1/506

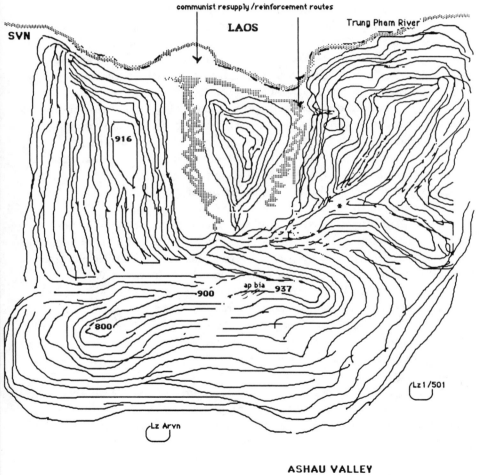

West

N.

communist resupply /reinforcement routes

LAOS

Trung Phem River

SVN

916

ap bia
900   937

800

Lz 1 /501

Lz Arvn

ASHAU VALLEY

were above the bunkers, Leisure's job was to set up a defensive perimeter facing Hill 900, while Schmitz and his men swept down on the bunkers from the rear.

"Lieutenant Burney's decision to hit the enemy from the rear proved to be a wise one. There were enemy bunkers, trenches, and spider holes all up and down the ridge, and Schmitz's men had a field day cleaning them out with grenades and rifle fire. Within thirty seconds, they destroyed ten bunkers, killed about fifteen enemy soldiers, and linked up with Lieutenant Burney and the rest of the company."[532]

It must have been a truly gratifying experience to see American troops actually attacking an enemy bunker line from the rear: "he calmly took out a grenade and flipped it in the back entrance. A second after the explosion, he jumped down into the bunker and opened up with his pistol, then jumped back out and moved to the next one. There he did the same, flipped in a grenade, then went in shooting. Out again, he took two or three steps down the ridge, located a third bunker, and fragged it also. Rather than jumping in this time, he lowered his head in and pumped five or six shots into the enemy soldier inside. Skaggs was moving down to the fourth bunker when the NVA soldier inside, suspecting what was happening above him, started crawling out the back entrance. The NVA was bringing up his AK to fire, but Skaggs, rather than seeking cover, jumped up on a log above the startled man and shot him in the head twice."[533]

Yet such efforts occurred in only one isolated sector of the battlefield. In most areas it was "hey diddle diddle, attack up the middle." Piecemeal attacks were launched in the same direction, repeatedly, like Russian troops assaulting German Army defenses on the East Front in World War II.

Perhaps Senator Young was right? Maybe the only way to get American colonels and generals into a maneuver frame of mind is to force them into combat: "let us hope that General Wright will personally lead that assault and be in the forefront of the brave GIs to take part in it, and encourage them with his display of leadership and bravery. I suggest that (General) Melvin Zias . . . be assigned to accompany him."[534]

Nine days and five hours of combat were required to take Hamburger Hill. It was a clumsy effort marked by total American dependence on airpower and artillery support. Although the commander of the assault, General Zias, publicly decried the overuse of such instruments: "I don't know how many wars we have to go through to convince people that aerial bombardment alone cannot do the job."[535]

Did General Zias' admirable offensive spirit toward Hamburger Hill have some reason for being? Did it have some relationship to victory? His reasons for attacking Dong Ap Bia seemed to have no relation to a campaign of numerous maneuvers dedicated to victory! Instead, General Zias offered a bureaucratic, linear engineering rationale for the attack on Dong Ap Bia. "That's where the enemy was, and that was where I attacked him. If I find the enemy on any other hills in the A Shau, I assure you I'll attack him there also."[536]

After realizing that the massing American air and artillery support was attriting his personnel at an increasing rate, the commander of the 29th NVA Regiment decided to extract his command. But he held them in their positions as long as possible in order to kill more Americans. Only when the first American assault parties reached the topographical crest of Dong Ap Bia, did the order go out for withdrawal. At that time, most enemy troops infiltrated into and through the advancing allied units and headed for the Laotian border on the other side.

A few days later, the victorious Americans used a bulldozer to open up a road along a large ridge leading from the valley floor to the top of the mountain. A number of tanks and APCs drove up that road and formed a perimeter around the top of the mountain. On June 5, 1969 Hamburger Hill was abandoned to the communists. They now had a new road to use during their reoccupation of the terrain. By June 17, more than 1,000 NVA had reoccupied the mountain. Some people think that the unit which reoccupied the mountain was the 29th NVA Regiment, the "American Killers!"

CHAPTER 15

Standoff Attacks

From the earliest beginnings of the Chu Luc, communist military cadres were painfully aware of the importance of fire support. Although their form of mobile war forced the reds to value mobility above weight of metal, they seemed to understand that mobility was more important in any case.

The most common method of attack by the NVA was not the infantry assault, but the safer, simpler, cheaper and more effective standoff attack. Standoff attacks have been adequately defined as that attack which used "A weapon . . . launched at a distance sufficient to allow the attacking personnel to evade defensive fire from the target area."[537]

NVA weaponry which met that criterion fell into several categories:

- *Direct fire:* Essentially 57mm and 75mm recoilless rifles. These weapons could not evade defensive fire unless they sniped a few rounds and then ceased firing in order to "run like hell."
- *Mobile mortars:* Only 60mm mortars were light enough to be evacuated with their crews after firing a few rounds. Heavier 81mm and 82mm mortars were pre-sited in emplacements aimed at specific targets which did not move (e.g. an air base). Ammunition was brought in by a crew and rapidly fired. Then the crew hid the mortar and fled on foot. In many cases mortars would be spotted by allied aircraft and destroyed before they fired off their basic load.
- *Man-transportable rockets:* Very effective standoff weapons.
- *Pack Howitzers:* Light weight 70mm and 75mm howitzers which had to be

transported by pack animals. When American airpower became pervasive and redundant, these NVA weapons disappeared from the battlefield.

• *Heavy artillery, mortars and rockets:* Usually fired from Laos, Cambodia or North Vietnam. Mobile "nebelwerfer" type rocket trucks, with racks of rocket launchers mounted on the truck bed, were encountered during the Khe Sahn siege.

• *Mines and booby traps:* Purists will argue with this category. However, it does fit the definition of a standoff weapon, and most of its explosive power was donated by the Americans to their enemies, who used it to kill about 10,000 Americans and maim 50,000 more.

The prime attribute of standoff weaponry was superior mobility. "Despite all their differences all VC/NVA mortar, recoilless rifle, and rocket units shared one key attribute-superior mobility. All weapons and munitions could be man-packed to just about any launch location. When circumstances permitted the use of waterways, oxcarts, bicycles, or trucks, mobility was further increased, the requirements for porters decreased, and weapon effectiveness markedly increased."[538]

Pack Howitzers, Mortars, and Recoilless Rifles

Chu Luc infantry regiments had both 81mm/82mm mortar companies and 75mm recoilless rifle companies. Their subordinate battalions were also armed with 60mm mortars, some 81/82mm mortars and a few 57mm recoilless rifles.

NVA Regimental Recoilless Rifle (RR) Company

100 men divided into 3 platoons and 9 squads
Weapons: 6 75mm RR and 4 57mm; or 9 75mm RR or 57mm RRs.
75mm RR squads contained 10 men, 47mm squads contained 6.

NVA Regimental Mortar Company

100–120 men divided into 3 platoons and 9 squads
Weapons: 9 81mm or 82mm Mortars; or 6 81/82mm Mortars and 3 57mm or 75mm RRs. Each squad contained 10–12 men

NVA Regimental Heavy Machine Gun/AntiAircraft Company

100–150 men divided into three platoons with 8 to 10 squads.
Weapons: 12.7mm Soviet HMG or .50 caliber U.S. HMG.
Each squad contained 10 to 15 men.

NVA Infantry Battalion Weapons Company

300–400 men divided into 3–4 platoons and 9–12 squads.
Weapons: 3–6 60mm/81mm/82mm Mortars; 3 57mmRR; 3 75mm RR
Each squad contained 6–10 men

Weapons Logistics Requirements

Weapon	Rate of Fire	Basic Load	Porters per Weapon	
MG	230–300 rpm	500–1,000	*A.4	*B.4
75mm RR	10 rpm	4–9	A.15	B.6
57mm RR	10 rpm	4–15	A.10	B.9
60mm MR	2–6 rpm	20–24	A.10	B.5–6
81/82mm MR	2–6 rpm	12–20	A.20	B.4–7

Note: MG = machine gun; RR = Recoilless Rifle; MR = Mortar. *A = Number of porters required to carry weapon. *B = Number of porters required to carry basic load.

Recoilless rifles were usually fired from the flanks of NVA units or from high points offering concealment and longer fields of fire. The recoilless rifle which had the best mobility was also the lightest one, the 57mm. The 57mm recoilless rifle weighed about fifty-five pounds and could be fired from the shoulder, or it could be afixed to a sixty pound machine gun tripod for more accurate firing. Its maximum effective range was about 1500 yards and it could destroy point targets, although it had little effect on armored fighting vehicles.

The longer range 75mm recoilless rifle weighed about 105 pounds and had to be carried by two or more people. It fired high explosive rounds to a maximum range of 7,300 yards and HEAT shells to an effective range of 875 yards. As a standoff weapon, attackers needed luck to survive firing the heavier 77mm recoilless rifle. However, it could knock out tanks.

Pack howitzers were only used by the NVA in areas where American airpower couldn't intervene within forty minutes. By 1966, there was no location in the South Vietnamese theater of war that fit that criterion.

The Chinese 70mm howitzer weighed nearly four times the 81/82mm mortar, had less explosive power and yet had about the same range. Therefore it was not an adequate standoff weapon.

Both the 81mm (132 pounds) and 82mm (123 pounds) weighed over 100 awkward pounds when fully assembled, but they were able to hit targets more than two miles away. When the medium mortar was fired, the crew had to drop the rounds in rapidly and then move. Counter battery fire by enemy aircraft was just too effective. It took some time to break this mortar down into three or four man-sized carrying loads.

The 60mm mortar, weighing only forty-five pounds assembled for firing was an ideal standoff weapon. A crew could fire it, and then pick it up and run with it. Its nearly two kilometer maximum range, and ninety meter minimum range, also made it an ideal infantry support weapon.

When the NVA established a mortar position they usually formed a semicircle of aiming stakes twenty to thirty meters in front of the tube position. The mortar position was a hole dug one and seven-tenths of a meter deep and two meters in diameter. It was camouflaged with only the mortar tube fire path uncovered during firing. Standoff mortars were frequently sited near inhabited places so that their crews could seek refuge there after getting off a few shots. Usually mortars were sited to fire along the long axis of targets in order to take advantage of their small deflection error (dispersion of the impact of their shells within the target area). Mortar positions were frequently linked to headquarers by communications wire.

The discovery of a recently evacuated NVA mortar position was described by S. L. A. Marshall: "He discovered the base plate for the 81mm mortar, the indentations made by recent, repeated recoil. In pockets under a brick-red earth bank he found the black plaster plugs, a fuse box and the canisters that went with the mortar . . . (nearby) . . . he picked up a piece of enemy commo wire."[539]

During the 1968 siege of Khe Sahn, standoff mortar bombardment was a key factor in Chu Luc planning. An enemy defector revealed a portion of the assault plan and the integration of mortar fires:

"Once Hill 861 has fallen, the general attack against the Khe Sahn Combat Base will begin. This will consist of a reinforced regimental-size force. . . . One *mortar platoon* on the northeast side of Hill 1015 will cover

NVA Pack Howitzers

Weapon	Caliber	Wt/Lbs	#Loads	Range
ChiCom Howitzer	70mm	468	3 pack animal	2.8km
US Pack Howitzer	75mm	1270	8–9 pack animal	8.7km

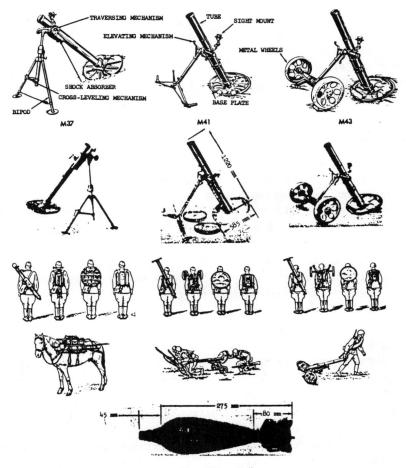

82-mm HE Mortar Shell

the Marine heavy weapons on Hill 950. One *mortar platoon* will begin 82mm mortar barrage on parked helicopters and the airstrip. Each of the *mortar platoons* has one 12.7mm aircraft gun platoon in their adjacent area to cover them from counter air attack."[540]

Two to six mortars made up an NVA mortar platoon.

NVA Mortars and Recoilless Rifles

Weapon	Weight	Range
57mm Recoilless Rifle	55 pounds	1500 yards
75mm Recoilless Rifle	107 pounds	7300 yards
60mm Mortar	45 pounds	98–2188 yards
81mm Mortar	132 pounds	2 miles
82mm Mortar	123 pounds	2 miles

Standoff Rocket Bombardment

In 1966, rockets began to dominate over mortars as standoff weapons. They were light-weight and could be more flexibly employed. Their salvo fire capability, and explosive power, increased the red standoff threat. That threat was further enhanced by the fact that the peak standoff range of the 120mm mortar, 5,700 meters, was doubled by the range of the 122mm rocket, 11,000 meters.

Usually mortar and recoilless rifle units operated separately from rocket units, but sometimes they worked together in varying combinations. If they were used as part of the same standoff attack, they were fired sequentially in this order: 1. Rockets. 2. Mortars 3. Recoilless Rifles 4. RPGs and machine guns.

Rockets and mortars fired on area targets such as ammo dumps, aircraft parking areas, fuel dumps and troop cantonments. Recoilless rifles and the other direct firing weapons hit point targets such as bunkers, weapons positions and communications centers.

Prior to a standoff attack, intelligence agents and recon units scrutinized the target and visited it at least three times. ". . . Normally, the rocket company commander(s) performed a last reconnaissance before the final decision and the attack preparation."[541]

Each point target within the target area was precisely identified. Then standoff weapons resources were allocated to it. After that, an operational plan was drawn up which included the date and time each of the following actions was to occur:

1. Identification of firing position.
2. Pre-positioning of munitions.
3. Approach and withdrawal route selection and reconnaissance.
4. Site survey preparations.
5. Movement of weapons and crews into position and preparation of weapons for firing.
6. Movement of forward observers to target area. Commence firing.
7. Cease firing and withdrawal.[542]

Security was rigidly maintained and weapons crews were not informed of any details of the operation ahead of time. They were guided to the sites and given firing instructions just prior to opening fire.

Rocket accuracy depended on precise firing data calculations utilizing such instruments as theodolites and transits. On the afternoon before the attack on the following day, a rocket survey team arrived at the rocket site, staked it out and aligned the rocket positions. They decided on the position, azimuth direction and firing elevation of every launcher or rocket, and prepared aiming stakes. They decided which launching mode, whether ramps, pits or improvised stick tripods was necessary, as well.

That night, rocket launch crews arrived at the rocket launch sites armed with tools such as picks, shovels and machetes. First a trail from the rocket storage point was laid out and the hidden rockets inventoried. Then the individual rocket launch sites were aligned with the aiming stakes and double checked against survey party calculations. Then the rocket launch pits were dug, the launch system wired for firing, and the rockets were loaded into position.

Each group of six rockets was located twenty meters from the other rocket groups. Within each firing battery, rockets were individually spaced ten meters apart. Such preparations normally required three hours of effort.

Then the rocket crews began transporting the rockets from their storage sites which were rarely located more than five kilometers, or one and one-half hours travel time away. The camouflaged storage points were usually hidden in areas of copious vegetation. Storage points were frequently located in tunnels, thickets, graveyards, and hamlets. They were also hidden along the banks of rivers, streams, and canals. Camouflaged rocket storage points were usually sited near infiltration trails from supply bases.

The rockets in every hidden storage cache had been brought down the Ho Chi Minh Trail to supply dumps along the borders of Laos and Cambodia. Later, porter columns transported the rockets into smaller dumps located in

NVA war zones and major strongholds, inside of South Vietnam. From those locations, the rockets were pre-positioned near their launch sites, five to thirty days before they were used.

A U.S. Marine rifle company discovered a rocket launching site near Khe Sahn: "About twenty meters in front of us, in a lightly wooded area on the side of the hill we had been approaching, were a dozen or so long black objects, right out in the open. Each was about seven feet long and about fifteen inches in diameter. They were obviously 122mm rocket launchers. Beside each launcher was a line of long stakes with vines wound around them. It was easy to see the NVA rocketmen could erect the stakes and vines as bipods to support the rocket tubes at angles from which the rockets could strike the Khe Sahn Combat Base, which was directly at our backs, though miles away.

"We found three 122mm rocket warheads, aiming stakes, fuses, and fuse boxes in among the launchers, each with Chinese markings. It was difficult to tell if the rocket site had ever been used, for we found no telltale burn marks from rocket ignitions. However, bark had been burned from several of the trees, so it was possible that the site had been used.

"The launchers were manufactured, of course, but they were stabilized on bipods constructed of wooden poles cut in the forest, pounded into the ground, and tied off with jungle vines. Neat!

"After we crossed the next hill behind the rocket hill we walked along a ridgeline until we came to . . . a small bunker complex . . . it was a small medical facility . . . this extensive network of trails and fighting, living and even medical bunkers had been abandoned . . . with no terrain features except an unmapped enemy trail to guide us. I could not see any of the hills of other prominent terrain features that showed on my map."[543]

Chu Luc rocket units were organized into regiments, all of whose rockets could be fired from improvised launchers. Each regiment contained a headquarters company, a signal and reconnaissance company and three rocket battalions. Each rocket battalion included a headquarters company and three rocket companies.

NVA Rocket Companies

Rocket Co.	# of Launchers	# of Rockets	Wt kg	Launcher Wt/kg	Range
107mm	12	24	19	248/12tubes	6– 8km
122mm	6	18	46	54.9each	3–11km
140mm	16	16	41	10each	1–10km

*km = kilometer   kg = kilogram

In large standoff attacks, infantry weapons units protected the rocket sites. The potential reaction time and firepower of enemy counter action by fixed-wing aircraft, helicopters, and artillery determined how long rocket attacks lasted. However, rocket attacks usually lasted two to twenty minutes depending on the availability of antiaircraft protection for the launch sites, the size of the assault force and ammunition availability. As the war progressed, rocket attacks increased in ferocity and duration: "the next morning, several hundred 122mm rockets lifted off from the slopes of 881 North and impacted in the Khe Sahn Combat Base. The now famous 77-day siege of Khe Sahn had begun: over 5000 rockets would be fired from the 881 North complex during the next eleven weeks."[545]

The NVA usually fired rockets in salvos of three, six, twelve, and eighteen rockets. On some occasions a regiment might fire thirty-six rockets at once. If counterfire reaction was slow, fire adjustment was made after the first two or three registration rounds. Forward observers, near the target area, called in launch data corrections to the rocket commanders by radio or field telephone. There were also frequent malfunctions of the rocketry: "In the February 1967 attack on Da Nang Air Base, one hundred and thirty 140mm rockets were emplaced at a single site. But due to malfunctions only 66 were successfully launched with 56 striking the air base, eight hitting an adjacent village and two falling outside the target area."[546]

Allied countermeasures exploited rocket exhaust trails, clearly visible as far as 300 meters from ignition to burn out points, as aids to locating firing positions. To solve that problem, the reds began utilizing hit-and-run rocket raids. NVA rocket troops learned that they must follow certain rocket raid rules if they were to survive.

Rules for Hit-and-Run Rocket Raids

- No more than five rounds fired in twenty minutes from any single tripod launcher.
- No more than two salvos fired in ten minutes from improvised launchers.
- Crews and equipment vacate launch sites within five minutes of launch.
- Exfiltrate speedily along preplanned routes to staging areas after the launch.

Another rocket firing method, calculated to confuse allied counter-

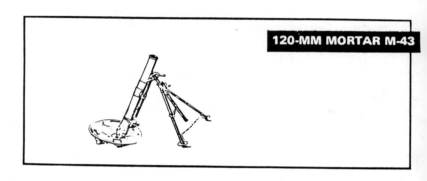

120-MM MORTAR M-43

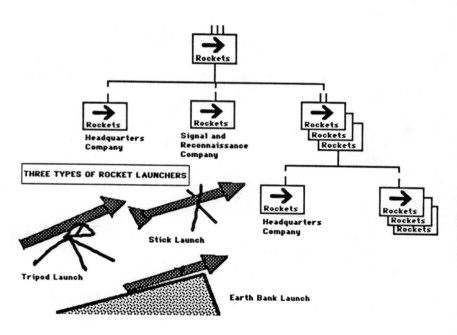

Rockets

Rockets
Headquarters
Company

Rockets
Signal and
Reconnaissance
Company

Rockets
Rockets
Rockets

Rockets
Headquarters
Company

Rockets
Rockets
Rockets

THREE TYPES OF ROCKET LAUNCHERS

Tripod Launch

Stick Launch

Earth Bank Launch

measures, included "attacking . . . from two or more launch sites, either simultaneously or in alternating salvos."[547]

The Rocket Belts

In 1966, the NVA began firing rockets at I Corps' Da Nang, DMZ defense bases, and other targets of importance throughout South Vietnam. From positions six to twelve kilometers southwest of Da Nang, across the Cau Do River, many exhaust trails followed salvo after salvo of rockets fired at the port city. The U.S. Marine reaction to the rocket threat was most dramatic.

The marines began calling the terrain, forming a crust five kilometers to twelve kilometers wide, surrounding each of their coastal enclaves, "rocket belts." Thousands of marine aircraft and infantry patrols were supposedly directed against the rocket belt areas. They were told to find and destroy enemy rocket sites within range of marine bases.

By mid 1967, it was obvious that the marines could not handle the Da Nang rocket belt problem: "(the 1st Marine Division) repositioned firing batteries so that by July (1967) at least two batteries covered each part of the DaNang TAOR. Observation aircraft flew constant patrols over the rocket belt. Additionally artillerymen manned strategically located observation posts throughout the belt, but the threat persisted."[548]

The marines discovered that the reds were firing four types of rockets out of the rocket belts towards marine bases: 107mm, 122mm, 140mm and "Garbage Cans."

NVA Rocket Characteristics

107mm Rockets: A spin-stabilized, barrage rocket of Chinese communist manufacture equipped with a high explosive, fragmentation warhead. This rocket was employed against both point and area targets. One man could easily transport the complete round, rocket and fuse. The lightest of the rockets, it could be introduced into otherwise inaccessible launch sites. The 107, with an effective range of 6–8 kilometers, could be fired from launch tubes, earth banks, bamboo frames or improvised crossed sticks.

122mm Rockets: This Soviet rocket possessed the longest range, three to eleven kilometers, of any of the rockets fired at the allies. A fin-stabilized weapon with more destructive power than any others, this rocket was lethal within a 163 square meter burst area. Although the use of launch tubes ensured greater accuracy, the 122 could be fired from improvised launch sites with a range of three to eleven kilometers.

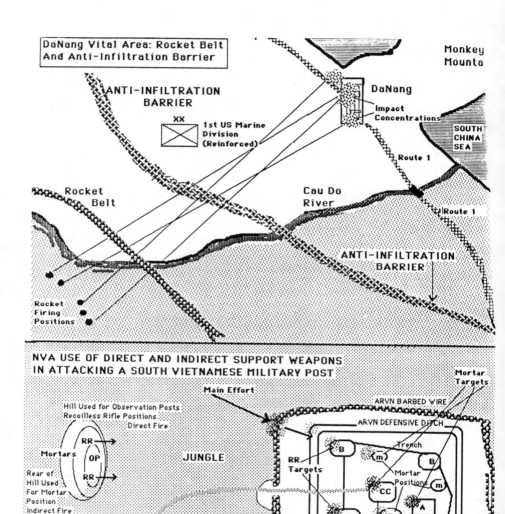

DaNang Vital Area: Rocket Belt
And Anti-Infiltration Barrier

ANTI-INFILTRATION
BARRIER

Monkey
Mounta

DaNang

XX   1st US Marine
Division
(Reinforced)

Impact
Concentrations

SOUTH
CHINA
SEA

Route 1

Rocket
Belt

Cau Do
River

Route 1

ANTI-INFILTRATION
BARRIER

Rocket
Firing
Positions

NVA USE OF DIRECT AND INDIRECT SUPPORT WEAPONS
IN ATTACKING A SOUTH VIETNAMESE MILITARY POST

Main Effort

Mortar
Targets

ARVN BARBED WIRE

Hill Used for Observation Posts
Recoilless Rifle Positions
Direct Fire

ARVN DEFENSIVE DITCH

RR

Mortars

OP

JUNGLE

RR
Targets

B

Trench

(m)

B

Mortar
Positions

(m)

RR

Rear of
Hill Used
For Mortar
Position
Indirect Fire

CC

A

Supply Road

B

(m)

Ammo
Dump

B

Bunker

Command/commo

Diversionary Attacks

326

140mmm Rocket: With a lethal area of 140 square meters the Soviet 140 was more useful against material targets. Very easy to deploy, it could be fired from a board-mounted tube or earth mounds. With an effective range of one to eleven kilometers the fin-stabilized 140 could be fired close to its target.

Garbage Can Rocket: Sometimes the NVA launched short range 107mm or 122mm rockets with oversized warheads containing twelve to ninety kilograms of explosive. "Garbage can" rockets were very inaccurate but they could be fired from earth mounds.

As time passed and the rocket threat never diminished, the marines began to dig in more and more troops around Da Nang. Soon the entire 1st Marine Division, the size of an infantry corps, was defending one city, Da Nang. That dug in, reinforced marine division was a great waste of offensive maneuver unit manpower and weaponry.

1st Marine Division Units Defending Da Nang 1966–1971

- 1st, 5th, 7th, and 26th Marine Infantry Regiments.
- 11th Marine Artillery Regiment, heavily reinforced.
- 1st Reconnaissance Battalion.
- 1st Tank Battalion and 1st Antitank Battalion.
- Engineer and numerous other supporting battalions.
- Military police battalions.
- Several CAC battalions
- Numerous fixed-wing aircraft and helicopter squadrons.
- Navy warships and carriers in the South China Sea.
- A Hawk antiaircraft battalion.[549]

By 1969, the marines were desperate: "enemy rocket, mortar, and ground assault teams persisted in attacks against allied installations and population centers (in the DaNang area) while planting mines and boobytraps, gathering food and tribute, and maintaining an unrelenting campaign of terrorism against the civilian population."[550]

By 1970, the marine defenders of Da Nang had been reinforced with numerous allied battalions. A force of fifty-four allied battalion were deployed to defend against rocket attacks and other red incursions, including:

- 2nd ROK (Republic of Korea) Marine Brigade with four infantry battalions.

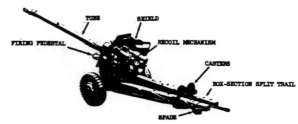

MUZZLE BRAKE

TUBE   SHIELD

FIRING PEDESTAL   RECOIL MECHANISM

CASTERS

BOX-SECTION SPLIT TRAIL

SPADE

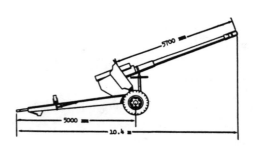

5700 mm

5000 mm

10.4 m

57 mm

545 mm

122 mm

784 mm

145 mm

~122-mm HE Round~

- 51st ARVN Infantry Regiment with four infantry battalions.
- 1st ARVN Ranger Group with three infantry battalions.
- 1st ARVN Armored Brigade with three mechanized battalions.
- 17th ARVN Armored Cavalry Squadron (mechanized battalion).
- Fifty-two ARVN Regional Force Companies (18 battalions).
- 177 ARVN Popular Force Platoons (15 battalions).
- 3,000 ARVN National Police (six battalions).[551]

The allied units were spread out in a vast semicircle outside the marine defended area which they called the Da Nang Vital Area: "With the division as its defensive shield, the city of DaNang, the airfield to the west of it, and Tien Sha Peninsula and Marble Mountain Air Facility to the east of it constituted the DaNang Vital Area. . . Beyond the (Marine DaNang) defense command lay the Rocket Belt."[552]

The six division equivalent allied force defending Da Nang, added to the marine units in Quang Nam Province, brought the total of units defending the Da Nang Vital Area to over eight division equivalents. An army was tied up defending "a series of concentric belts centering on DaNang"[553] against about 7,000 NVA, including one or two rocket regiments. The defenders outnumbered the attackers by about twenty to one.

The marines tried everything to keep the NVA out of Da Nang. After resisting the establishment of an anti-infiltration barrier across the DMZ, which they claimed would erode the marine offensive spirit, they built one around Da Nang. In June 1968, the 1st Marine Division began building the Da Nang Anti-Infiltration System (DAIS), a physical barrier. The DAIS was huge: "a 12,000 meter semicircle centered on the DaNang airfield whose radius was the maximum range of the enemy's 122mm and 140mm rockets. The project . . . was to consist of a 500 meter wide cleared belt of land containing two parallel barbed wire fences, concertina wire entanglements, 23 observation towers, and minefields which would halt or at least delay enemy infiltrators."[554]

The marines worked on the barrier for years, tying up scarce combat maneuver infantry battalions as work crews. However, about forty marine, naval, and army engineer battalions in I Corps during that time period were not doing much of anything.

By the beginning of June 1969, the barrier effort was floundering. Marine General Simpson went on record with strident warnings: "Unless radical improvements are made the DaNang Barrier will prove to be ineffectual in countering infiltration into the DaNang Vital Area."[555]

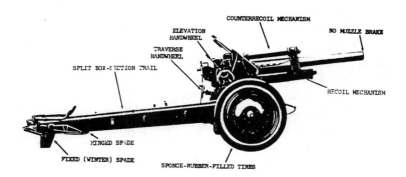

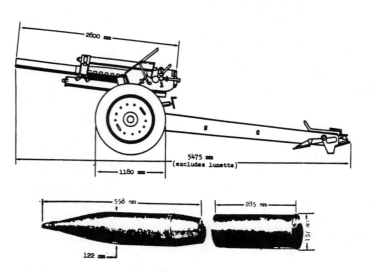

122 mm Frag-HE Round

The barrier was already falling down, with brush eighteen feet high growing in its "cleared strips."

"Marine, ARVN, and Korean engineers had cleared the land, and had finished laying barbed wire, minefields and over 100 line sensors. . . Divided responsibility, poor site planning, and the lack of manpower, material, and a well-coordinated fire support plan continued to prevent completion of the system."[556]

Although three marine infantry battalions were assigned to work on the barrier in late 1969, that didn't fix it. Barrier construction efforts only wasted ever more combat manpower while service troops and millions of South Vietnamese peasants lay idle.

Medium and Heavy NVA Artillery

Many different NVA artillery weapons were used in standoff attacks against the allies. However, five NVA indirect fire weapons were used far more than others including:

- 120mm heavy mortar.
- 122mm howitzer.
- 122mm field gun.
- 130mm field gun.
- 152mm gun-howitzer.

Of the five weapons, only the 120mm heavy mortar was consistently used against the allies *inside of* South Vietnam during the Second Indochina War.

The weight of the heavy mortar means that the reds usually didn't move it much. They usually fired 120mm heavy mortars from positions located in the DMZ, Laos or Cambodia.

One of the few occasions when a 120mm mortar was intended for use within South Vietnam, was aborted by a U.S. Special Forces patrol. That patrol killed an NVA mortar survey team which was preceding the arrival of a

NVA 120mm Heavy Mortar

Weight/lbs: 606	Number of Animal Packloads Required: 3
Range: 5700 meters	

Target neutralization coverage in Hectares (10,000 square meters/2.47 acres).
Target type/length of fire, for a 120mm heavy mortar battery

	Personnel in the Open		Personnel under Cover	
Time	4 minutes	5 minutes	10 minutes	15 minutes
Hectares	15	1	2	2

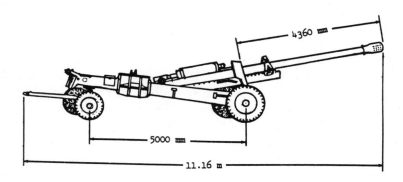

(No photograph of ammunition available)

two-tube 120mm mortar battery in order to check firing data and prepare firing positions. What was found on the bodies of the five man NVA team revealed a lot of information about how the NVA carried out 120mm mortar standoff attacks: "In a tin on the shoulders of the third body down was an instrument that Freeman at once recognized as a universal mortar sight, of Chinese make. In the rucksack on the second body were a compass and binoculars. Beside the fourth body was a cloth sack containing a quadrant.

"It was the find on the lieutenant's corpse which tied in these pieces of loot to events almost ready to unfold. In his pack was a manual, along with a firing table for the 120mm mortar. There was also a memorandum, reading that the unit should be ready to attack not later than 1600 on 19 May. A hand-drawn map, neatly and accurately drafted, showed mortar firing positions, ammo supply points, observation points and the trail network winding between the mountains and the riverbank opposite Vinh Thanh. With the firing table were azimuths, ranges and coordinates, all with reference to that same target The church steeple in Vinh Thanh—of possible use as an OP—was marked for destruction.

"One more go at the other rucksacks . . . yielded another find. Besides a battery roster and a notebook carried by one of the squad leaders, which gave the strength of the unit, the names and job positions in a two-tube battery with fifteen round per gun."[557] (There were about 23 men in the battery).

The green berets who killed the red mortar unit knew something else about the 120mm mortar battery. "With a one-twenty mortar, it will not be VC."[558] Only NVA regulars employed heavier artillery in standoff attacks.

American and allied forces didn't have to fear standoff attacks by enemy long range artillery unless they were deployed along the DMZ or within ten to fifteen kilometers of the Laotian or Cambodian borders. Troops located in those areas were frequently barraged with long range shell fire.

The reds poured thousands of indirect fire rounds across the DMZ. The Americans frequently found themselves outranged by enemy artillery.

NVA Artillery Weapons

Weapon	122mm howitzer	122mm gun	130mm gun	152mm gun-howitzer
Range	11.8km	21.9km	26.7km	17.2km

U.S. Artillery Weapons

Weapon	105mm howitzer	155mm howitzer	8inch howitzer	175mm gun
Range	11km	14.6km	16.8km	32.8km

In most artillery duels American 105mm and 155mm howitzers would try to fight NVA 122mm and 130mm guns. They were outranged and inevitably beaten. The U.S. military committed few 8 inch howitzers and 175m guns to the Vietnam War and they were hesitant to deploy them in forward locations. As a result, 175mm guns, the only American artillery piece capable of outranging NVA guns, was rarely decisive in artillery duels. There were too few of them and they were not pushed forward aggressively.

The Americans, having complete control of the air, at least over South Vietnam, tried to use their air forces against red artillery. The communists were quite effective at avoiding American air bombardment against their artillery. They protected their batteries with a massive flak umbrella, dug the artillery pieces into bomb-proof caves and shelters and camouflaged them.

During the Khe Sanh battle, the enemy revealed some of his artillery protection practices: "a big square hole opened. It was a big bamboo mat that had fallen off to the side from this string of bombs when the overpressure blew stuff around. And sticking out of this hole was a 130mm gun. Apparently what they were doing was rolling the gun out, firing a round or two, and then rolling it back in, putting this cover back on top and being relatively impervious to aerial observation . . . out in Laos . . . probably seven or eight kilometers beyond the Vietnamese border.

"North Vietnamese had emplaced those guns not in a battery position, but in single gun positions on the gun-target line, so that in order to hit Khe Sanh they only had to adjust for range, not for deflection. And once they cranked in that range adjustment for each gun, which adjustment would remain more or less constant since Khe Sanh wasn't going to move, they could fire in battery fire, even when the guns were not emplaced in a battery position . . . they had emplaced their guns at about 500-meter intervals, with the rear guns probably close to max range, which is 27,000 meters for the 130mm field gun—and then forward from there."[559]

The NVA heavier artillery was used mostly for standoff attacks during the Second Indochina War, not as fire support for offensives.

Mines and Booby Traps

In April 1970 a tired U.S. Marine patrol decided to rest on a paddy dike near Da Nang. Assuming that the dry ground was safe, the unit machine gunner sat down. Suddenly the air was rent with an earthsplitting explosion as an NVA mine detonated with terrifying lethal force, "all portions of the marine's body from the middle of his stomach on down, were completely blown off and he was killed instantly."[560]

As standoff weapons, mines and booby traps were nearly perfect. They killed allied troops at a distance and kept on killing long after the people who laid them were gone. Booby traps and mines function like standoff artillery:

"Booby traps and mines, however, fulfill the same function. Even when used en masse, as at the Battle of El Alamein, they cannot by themselves deny an area to the enemy, for unprotected minefields and booby traps can be removed by engineers. *Rather, they function like artillery in that by their very presence they harass and interdict the enemy.* In the battlefield, mines are primarily used in static defense positions, for it requires time to plant and remove them."[561]

Over fifty percent of all American casualties during the Vietnam War were caused by NVA mines and booby traps.

"In the Vietnam War, the Americans again encountered boobytrap warfare, only more intense than had been experienced in the Second World War. Over 50% of American losses in that war were caused by mines and booby traps. The Viet Cong and North Vietnamese found out, much to their delight, that over half of the devices they planted were eventually detonated."[562]

Defensive or security units, dug into static, stationary positions, suffer relatively greater losses from mines and booby traps. Nearly fifty percent of the 1st Marine Division's casualties, for example, were caused by NVA mines and booby traps.

Mines consisted of hidden, emplaced explosives which could be detonated either by the victims or by the enemy, as victims moved into proximity to the mine. The latter weapon was called a command-detonated mine and could be detonated by a hidden NVA soldier watching the mined location until a target arrived. Emplaced mines were ignited by the victim stepping on them or otherwise triggering them. Mines could either explode upward or be emplaced as directional mines, aimed to explode in a certain direction.

Booby traps consisted of mines which were not just buried in the ground or along the side of a trail; some element of their placement was deceptive. An innocent looking pistol rigged to explode when it was picked up qualified as a booby trap, not a mine. "Booby traps are, . . . generally only employed in areas the defender does not intend to occupy. His own troops could fall prey to them, since they cannot be mapped and marked as minefields are."[563]

American troops in Vietnam called any man-made primitive trap, such as a punji stake pit, a booby trap. In addition they broadened the definition to include explosives detonated by trip wires and even pressure release devices, which would only qualify as booby traps if they were rigged in some way other than simply burying them in the ground.

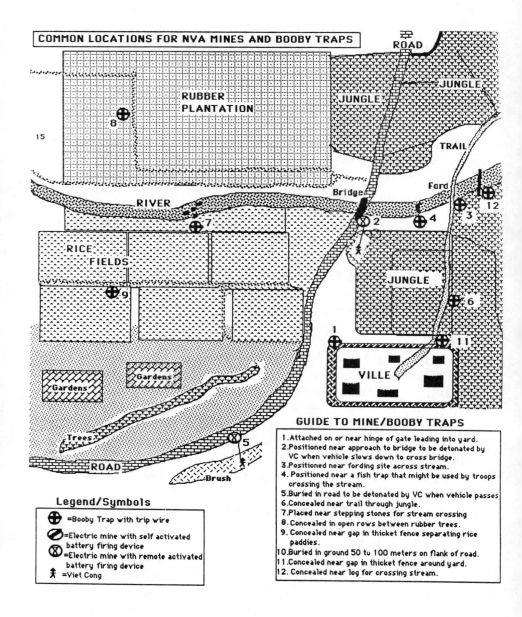

COMMON LOCATIONS FOR NVA MINES AND BOOBY TRAPS

RUBBER PLANTATION

JUNGLE

JUNGLE

ROAD

TRAIL

Ford

Bridge

RIVER

RICE FIELDS

JUNGLE

Gardens

Gardens

Trees

ROAD

Brush

VILLE

GUIDE TO MINE/BOOBY TRAPS

1. Attached on or near hinge of gate leading into yard.
2. Positioned near approach to bridge to be detonated by VC when vehicle slows down to cross bridge.
3. Positioned near fording site across stream.
4. Positioned near a fish trap that might be used by troops crossing the stream.
5. Buried in road to be detonated by VC when vehicle passes
6. Concealed near trail through jungle.
7. Placed near stepping stones for stream crossing
8. Concealed in open rows between rubber trees.
9. Concealed near gap in thicket fence separating rice paddies.
10. Buried in ground 50 to 100 meters on flank of road.
11. Concealed near gap in thicket fence around yard.
12. Concealed near log for crossing stream.

Legend/Symbols

⊕ =Booby Trap with trip wire

⊘ =Electric mine with self activated battery firing device

⊗ =Electric mine with remote activated battery firing device

🚶 =Viet Cong

336

NVA mines were laid everywhere around American bases. In addition to mines and booby traps already laid, the reds would rapidly lay new fields along the route of advancing American troops while they were still moving. Frequently red minelayers came in behind moving American units and mined their return route too. "it was not uncommon for one of our patrols to go out and in the space of four hours find as many as five or six booby traps . . . We have found as many as 15 boobytraps in . . . 45 minutes."[564]

Aggressive units who fought within enemy controlled areas encountered few mines and booby traps there. Mining and booby trapping trails in the communist controlled interior of South Vietnam interfered with NVA mobility. In fact, when NVA main force units moved into an area, mines were usually cleared from trails so that the NVA could move fast: "You can always tell when a main force unit has moved into some place like the Arizona or Dodge City, which is notoriously bad for boobytraps, because all the boobytraps disappear for about three days."[565]

Chu Luc mining and booby trap efforts served systematic tactical purposes. They were emplaced to cause casualties to the enemy, distract attention from caches, headquarters and hideouts, restrict and channel enemy movements, impede pursuit, protect flanks, supplement defensive systems and protect NVA installations and bases.

Frequently the reds moved their explosive devices in response to the movement of American sweeps and patrols. Or they might lure American troops into a mined kill zone and then rapidly ring the unit with mine and booby trap fields.

Civilians were conscripted as mine and booby trap installers by the NVA. The civilians worked in teams, observing American operations around the U.S. bases and mining the area accordingly.

Small paper signs with crude drawings of explosions warned enemy troops that an area was mined. They also marked the trail with combinations of sticks and stones to warn friendly communists and peasants. (See Chapter 5)

NVA explosive devices were buried or attached to something on, or near, trails and roads used by American troops. In addition, the reds mined dikes, potential defensive positions, landing zones and areas suitable for observation posts. They would booby trap anything, including the corpse of a child. On Hamburger Hill the reds placed a command-detonated Chinese claymore mine in a knapsack on top of the body of a dead American soldier.

The communist method of mining was "never predictable. They usually have an area boobytrapped for a while, and then just leave the area alone, if all the booby traps are found. And they won't touch this area again, possibly for about a month or two months, until everyone gets lax . . . then all of a sudden they'll put 'em back out to catch people off guard."[566]

The maze of mines and boobytraps around American installations caused severe psychological problems among local American troops. "Whenever they took a step outside of their perimeter, the only thing (the American troops) could think of was boobytraps . . . And it really put them in a bind as far as getting the job done."[567]

American infantry was given no real help in detecting and clearing mines, and even if they were given some mine detection training, they understood that the training was inadequate. Infantrymen correctly believed that mine detection and removal should have been left up to professional engineers, who were always suspiciously absent.

The American infantry in Vietnam was nearly immobilized, slowing their movements to a fearful gut-wrenching crawl. They avoided walking on trails, paths and more trafficable avenues: "It may be a little hard on the individual marine, but he will find it a lot safer to walk in rice paddies where the water may be up to his hips or even . . . his chest."[568] So they plowed through the mud and gunk, weighed down with "bullet proof" flak jackets, helmets and gear weighing up to one hundred pounds, in scorching, 100 degree Fahrenheit sun.

The pitiful grunts tried everything to stay alive. They paid the peasants protection money to turn in, or refrain from laying or detonating mines. They watched the peasants and tried to walk where they did. (American generals wouldn't allow the herding of enemy prisoners, or livestock, in front of U.S. patrols.) To lessen casualties from mines, American units spread out fifteen to twenty meters apart. They reduced unit offensive power in favor of survivability.

Probe sticks, long thin bamboo or other light material, were used to prod the ground ahead. The grass and dirt was skimmed for trip wires, lumps, or anything suspicious. Fatigued point men were relieved every fifteen minutes.

Reduced patrolling, and night patrolling, saved a few lives: "The VCI would put on boobytraps in the day, ahead of us, and they'd bring them in at night so that their people could get out and roam at large. So we took advantage of their concept by moving at night with them and avoiding the boobytraps. Then we'd stop during the day and stay out. The kids and the VCI would watch us, and we just wouldn't move into a position where they could lay some boobytraps either in front of us or behind us."[569] Such tactics by American troops were both innovative and rare. American soldiery feared the darkness and few of their leaders could come up with such imaginative solutions.

Very few mine detectors were issued to the combat troops. Mine detecting dogs were also in short supply. The military's technocratic elite seemed to

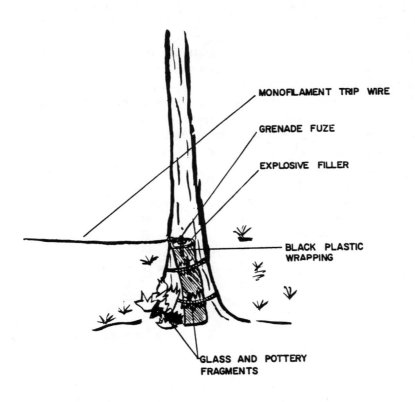

MONOFILAMENT TRIP WIRE

GRENADE FUZE

EXPLOSIVE FILLER

BLACK PLASTIC
WRAPPING

GLASS AND POTTERY
FRAGMENTS

VC LOCALLY MANUFACTURED EXPLOSIVE ITEM.

have a blind spot about solving the mine and booby trap problem. The engineer officer corps, resistant to a mine warfare role and offensive combat duty, exacerbated the problem.

Most of the tons of mines and booby traps used against U.S. troops were supplied to the enemy by the Americans themselves. Through indiscriminate bombing and artillery bombardment, U.S. troops dumped over two hundred and fifty million bombs and shells on South Vietnam. Two to ten percent of that amount failed to explode. Over two million artillery shells and millions of American grenades, rockets, mines, mortar shells, booby traps, and M79 rounds lay ready to explode, all over South Vietnam.

The reds recovered and reused hundreds of tons of American explosives. Those explosives were the lethal side effect of indiscriminate bombing and shelling. In addition, Americans were always losing explosives, especially M26 fragmentation grenades which, not being carried in grenade pouches, fell off in the bush. Over seventy-five percent of the boobytraps encountered by the U.S. 1st Marine Division were made from M26 fragmentation grenades.

A lot of American explosives and ammunition were stolen too. In June 1970 one U.S. Marine battalion spent $380.00 purchasing from the local South Vietnamese peasants:

- 44 M26 grenades.
- 11 containers of C4 explosive.
- 13 81mm mortar rounds.

- 69 Chinese communist grenades.
- 44 105mm artillery shells.
- 19 60mm mortar rounds[570]

From April to September 1967, one U.S. 4th Infantry Division battalion "compiled some interesting statistics:

- One hundred and seventy-two boobytraps were located; of these, 35 were found the hard way—we had 32 men killed and 70 wounded . . . 75 percent of our casualties during this period resulted from enemy mines and booby traps.
- Twenty-four of the enemy's boobytraps were homemade explosive devices constructed from discarded U.S. C-ration cans.
- Thirty five enemy boobytraps used captured U.S. hand grenades.
- Four enemy boobytraps used captured U.S. claymores; five used U.S. M16 antipersonnel mines; 12 used 155mm artillery rounds; eight used 250 pound bombs rigged as booby traps; seven were boobytrapped 105mm howitzer shells; six were boobytrapped 81mm mortar rounds; four were boobytrapped 5 inch U.S. naval gun shells; and some 18 other homemade

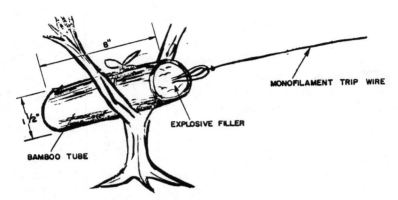

MINE TIED IN CROTCH OF BUSH RIGHT OFF OF TRAIL AND
MARKED WITH BROKEN SAPLING APPROXIMATLY 3 FEET IN
FRONT OF MINE.

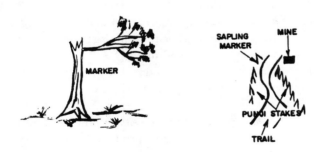

VC LOCALLY MANUFACTURED EXPLOSIVE ITEM.

explosive devices used powder from U.S. artillery shells and other miscellaneous material.

- During a two week period in September 1967 . . . (on) Highway 1, ten enemy antitank mines were discovered on the road. Most of these had been rigged for electrical detonation by using parts of U.S. AN/PRC-25 batteries.

"Policing the immediate battlefield and campsite was not enough. We found a large number of dud bombs and artillery shells in our areas of operation, and in the same time frame mentioned above, we located and destroyed seventy six 250 pound bombs, two 500 pound bombs, 50 CBU bomblets, and 189 artillery and mortar shells."[571]

The reds lost a few men during their extensive recovery of American explosives and ordnance, but in most cases such losses were negligible. One NVA recovery method is described as follows:

"The guerrillas were known to dig such shells out of the soil and unscrew their detonating fuses. They would cut the shell in half with a hacksaw to remove the TNT or other explosive 'filler.' Knowing that a blast rather than heat detonates the explosive, the guerrillas would liquefy the TNT by cooking it over a fire and then pour it into Coca Cola cans salvaged from an American dump. Finally the cans were capped and topped with pull-string detonators to form deadly hand grenades or satchel charges. On other occasions the guerrillas would leave the dud American shell intact and merely replace the dud fuse with a new trip wire fuse or pressure fuse and set the shell in a strategic location as a booby trap or land mine."[572]

The Americans never took proper ordnance counter measures against communist recovery of dud shells on any relevant scale. They could have introduced large amounts of complicated fuses, like the M36, that would explode when its magnetic field was interrupted by a steel or non-beryllium metal. All shell fuses could also have been booby trapped to detonate if it they were unscrewed improperly.

Engineer Clearance of Mines and Booby Traps

Trained engineer troops were required to breach mine and boobytrap fields: "Specialist troops could usually breach a minefield and mark the location of the mines and neutralize them at a rate of 50 meters an hour, in a patch, one to seven meters wide."[573]

There were dozens of allied engineer battalions available in Vietnam for mine and booby trap clearance. Yet, in spite of the fact that their mission was "close combat engineer support," they preferred construction roles. In the I

SOME METHODS OF EMPLOYING IMPROVISED MINES.

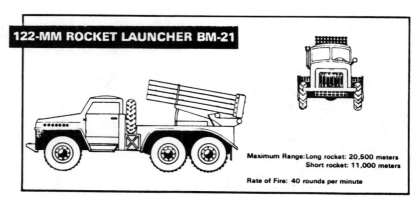

122-MM ROCKET LAUNCHER BM-21

Maximum Range: Long rocket: 20,500 meters
Short rocket: 11,000 meters

Rate of Fire: 40 rounds per minute

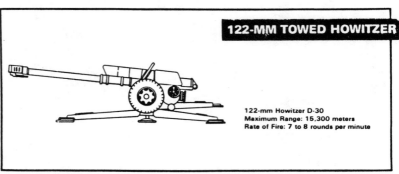

122-MM TOWED HOWITZER

122-mm Howitzer D-30
Maximum Range: 15,300 meters
Rate of Fire: 7 to 8 rounds per minute

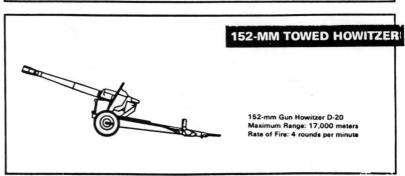

152-MM TOWED HOWITZER

152-mm Gun Howitzer D-20
Maximum Range: 17,000 meters
Rate of Fire: 4 rounds per minute

Corps area there were so many Army, Marine and Navy engineer battalions that they were falling all over themselves. Marine Colonel Nicholas Canzona described the engineer situation in I Corps: "I never saw so many engineers in all my life working in a given area, and . . . I don't think I've ever seen so much attention and confusion as to who is supposed to do what and why."[574]

One thing the engineers were sure of, they were not interested in mine clearing. U.S. engineer units invariably deployed only a small number of their hundreds of engineer companies on combat mine and booby trap clearing. Even then, they stuck to the roads where they had a clear view and could use electric mine detectors. Perhaps American engineer troops and officers remembered the predictable losses suffered by engineer troops breaching minefields in earlier wars: "For a one meter wide path (through a minefield), one man would be lost every two hours. For a seven meter wide path, losses were four times that."[575]

Mine and Booby Trap Warfare Norms

- A trained engineer can completely remove and disarm a mine in five minutes.
- Booby traps take twice as long to remove, on the average.
- An experienced specialist can lay between four and sixteen mines an hour.
- Two anti-personnel mines per meter of frontage usually cost attacking units 20% casualties.
- Four mines per meter of frontage usually cause 30% casualties.
- Casualties are increased among attacking units by 2.5% for each additional mine laid, above four mines, per meter.

Engineer land clearing efforts involved using bulldozers to clear wide strips, while being protected by the infantry, of course. They stayed away from enemy fortified areas and tunnel systems too. Instead of forming engineer battalions into mine clearing parties, assault pioneer units and tunnel rat companies, they were allowed to endlessly overbuild roads and installations.

Under great pressure to do something about the mines and booby traps, the engineers finally acted. They formed land mine and booby trap schools where they put a few infantrymen through brief, inadequate three day-maximum, courses of orientation to mines and booby traps.

It takes months to develop mine clearing ability. A few melodramatic explosives and dozens of firecracker booby trap experiences hardly prepare infantry to protect themselves from standoff mine and booby trap systems.

The 1st Marine Engineer Battalion's Land Mine Warfare School at Camp Faulkner, with its "intensive" three day course, was an ironic joke. Running a few marines along a few booby trap lines was not enough. Neither was telling them," Charlie will mine everything and usually does. While in the field there's no substitute for alertness, caution and a suspicious attitude."[576] The same might be said about the absence of combat engineers in infantry patrols.

SOME METHODS OF EMPLOYING SMALL EXPLOSIVE ITEMS

PART III.
Order of Battle

CHAPTER 16

NVA Order of Battle: 1965–68

During the years 1965 through 1968, the Chu Luc grew into the most effective veteran army in Asia. As the tempo of the war increased and allied troops rallied to the defense of South Vietnam, the communist army only got stronger. It gained sustenance from enemies who, in the name of logistics and attrition, madly slung more and more dud rounds and supplies in all directions.

The size of the NVA was doubled and then tripled during the Second Indochina War, as its troop units were formed and hardened in the crucible of battle.

NVA Order of Battle in South Vietnam: 1965

In late 1964, the 325th NVA Infantry Division with the 9th, 32nd, and 101st Infantry Regiments moved into South Vietnam's Central Highlands region. The 325th concentrated on preparing fortifications and battlefields in the II Corps border area.[577]

At the same time, NVA units all over South Vietnam were formed into mobile battalions and regiments. Rearming with a superior family of Soviet small arms was begun in all Viet Cong main force units.

Soon NVA regimental and battalion attacks began. In December 1964, two NVA regiments attacked an ARVN post at Binh Ga in III Corps.

In May 1965, the 1st Viet Cong Regiment with the 40th, 60th and 90th Infantry Battalions was carrying out offensive operations in I Corps' Quang Ngai Province. The regiment was reinforced with two batteries of 75mm pack howitzers, an antiaircraft company, several local force Viet Cong companies, and some special action squads.

In August 1965, I Corps' 1st Viet Cong Infantry Regiment mauled a U.S. Marine Corps unit during Operation Starlight. In October 1965, it was reinforced in the Que Son Valley, with the 195th (aka 9th) NVA Antiaircraft Battalion, detached from the 308th NVA Division. In November 1965, the 1st VC Regiment began overrunning ARVN posts around the Que Son Valley War Zone. In December 1965, the 70th VC Battalion, attached to the now brigade-sized 1st VC Regiment, mauled an ARVN ranger battalion near the Que Son War Zone.[578]

In April 1965, the 2nd Viet Cong Infantry Regiment with the 93rd, 95th and 97th Viet Cong Battalions was fighting ARVN troops in II Corps' Binh Dinh War Zone. Elements of the 2nd VC Regiment attacked an ARVN marine battalion in the Bong Son area of Binh Dihn. Further north in Binh Dinh Province, near An Khe, the 2nd VC Regiment mauled a battalion of the U.S. 101st Airborne Division.[579]

During the fall of 1965 the NVA formed four new divisions within South Vietnam:

- 2nd NVA Infantry Division in I Corps. Two NVA regiments, the 3rd and 21st, infiltrated into the Que Son War Zone (Quang Tin and Quang Ngai Provinces) where they joined the 1st Viet Cong Regiment to form the division.
- 3rd NVA Infantry Division in II Corps. Two NVA regiments, the 18th and 22nd infiltrated into the Binh Dinh War Zone where they joined the 2nd Viet Cong Regiment to form the division.
- 5th and 9th NVA Infantry Divisions in III Corps. The 9th NVA Division was formed with the 271st, 272nd and 273rd VC/NVA Regiments. The 5th NVA Division was formed with the 274th and 275th VC/NVA Regiments.

At the same time a division-sized front, "X Front," was maneuvered into the border area of II Corps. That front controlled the 32nd, 33rd, and 66th NVA Infantry Regiments and several supporting battalions. Its mission was to carry out the Tay Nguyen (Western Plateau) Campaign as part of the NVA 1965–66 Dong Xuan (Winter-Spring) Campaign. The Dong Xuan Campaign was supposed to be a series of NVA area control and shakedown operations occurring in the area between the DMZ in the north, and Pleiku City in the south.

The first major operation of the Tay Nguyen Campaign was aimed at U.S. Special Forces CIDG camps in Kontum and Pleiku Provinces. Then the X Front assaulted Plei Me. The campaign was climaxed by several battles with the U.S. 1st Cavalry Division in the Ia Drang Valley near the Chu Pong War Zone. For a while the unit controlling the 32nd, 33rd and 66th NVA Regiments in II Corps was called the 1st NVA Division.[580]

NVA Order of Battle in 1966

American military intelligence estimated that five NVA Divisions were near enough to invade I Corps in 1966. The estimated strength of those divisions was as follows:

- 304th NVA Division—9800 infantry.
- 320th NVA Division—7400 infantry.
- 324B NVA Division—9500 infantry.
- 325th NVA Division—5500 infantry.
- 325C NVA Division—5500 infantry (may have been the same as 325).[581]

According to American General Williamson: "During 1966 . . . Giap sent 15 new regiments (5 divisions totaling 58,000 men) to the South."[582]

In January 1966, the 810th VC Main Force Battalion went into operation near I Corps' Phu Bai. In the same month a marine landing force believed that it had encountered the following NVA units thirty miles northeast of Duc Pho:

- 18th and 95th NVA Regiments.
- 2nd VC Regiment.
- 38th Independent VC Battalion.
- Binh Son Transportation Battalion (250 NVA troops and 1,000 press-ganged South Viet laborers).[583]

In February, the marines launched Operation New York against the 810th VC Battalion still operating near Hue/Phu Bai. In March, the marines encountered the 802nd VC Battalion dug into fortified villages north of Hue at Ap Chinh An. That battalion, along with the 804th VC Battalion, was part of the 1st VC Provisional Regiment headquartered in the Co Bi/Thanh Tan area fifteen miles west of Hue.[584]

In March 1966, the entire 95th NVA Regiment of the 325th NVA Division seized the A Shau Valley from U.S. Special Forces indigenous troops. The reds began converting the valley into the infamous A Shau War Zone.

Around April 1966, the ARVN I Corps command mutinied against Saigon. The 324B NVA Division sought to exploit that mutiny by moving south out of the DMZ into Quang Tri Province. In March 1966, the 1st VC Regiment also moved south out of the Que Son War Zone to attack allied outposts near An Hoa.[585]

By June 1966, the 2nd (aka 620th) NVA Infantry Division with the 1st VC, 3rd NVA and 21st NVA Regiments controlled the Que Son Valley. At the same time, the following VC/NVA units, subordinate to the Chu Luc's northern subregion, Tri Thien Hue Military Region Headquarters, were encountered in northern I Corps:

- 7th and 8th VC Battalions, along the southern bank of the Thach Han River forty miles northwest of Hue.
- 6th NVA Regiment with the 806th, 808th and 812th Battalions, thirty miles northwest of Hue along the south bank of the Thach Han River.
- 1st Viet Cong Mobile Regiment with the 800th, 802nd, and 804th VC Battalions, ten miles northwest of Hue at Co Bi Thanh Tan.
- 95th NVA Regiment with three battalions, twenty-five miles southwest of Hue.
- 810th VC Battalion, twenty-five miles southeast of Hue.[586]

In July 1966 it was discovered that the 90th NVA Infantry Regiment was infiltrating Quang Tri Province through the Ngan Valley. That regiment, along with the 803rd and 812th Regiments, made up the 324B NVA Division. Those two regiments were detected south of the DMZ, near the Rockpile, in August, 1966.[587]

By 1966, Quang Ngai Province was swarming with Viet Cong: "four local force battalions and eleven companies of VC were the forces primarily responsible for harassing the area under government control. The 48th Local Force (LF) Battalion became the principal enemy force in Son Tinh District, although it also operated in the Batangan area to the north as well as to the south of the Song Tra Khuc."[588]

There was not much activity in II Corps in early 1966. The 95th NVA Regiment engaged ROK (Republic of Korea) and American 101st Airborne troops near coastal Qui Nhon. The 3rd Viet Cong Main Force Regiment conducted offensive operations out of the mountainous region west and north of coastal Tuy Hoa. The 3rd NVA Division sought to secure Binh Dinh War Zone's Bong Son area. The 24th NVA Regiment engaged elements of the U.S. 101st Airborne near Kontum.

In April 1966, the U.S. launched Operation Attleboro in III Corps against the base areas of the 9th NVA Division. The 9th NVA counterattacked, and fought over 100 engagements during a two month period, which the NVA referred to as the Tay Ninh Campaign.

In May 1966, the 5th NVA Division, with the 274th and 275th VC/NVA Regiments and the D445 VC Battalion, consolidated its May Tao Mountain, Dinh Hills, Long Hai Hills and Hat Dich strongholds in Phuoc Tuy Province. The 5th NVA Division controlled over 5,000 men including:

- 274th VC/NVA Regiment - 1650 men.
- 275th VC/NVA Regiment - 1500 men.
- D445 VC Battalion - 400 men.
- Four district companies - 400 men.
- 400–600 local village guerrillas.[589]

The 5th Division's NVA Military Region 1 soon controlled all of northern Phuoc Tuy.

Throughout 1966, the 165th NVA Infantry Regiment operated out of III Corps' Ho Bo Woods near Saigon, along with the nearby D800 VC Battalion. Near Loc Ninh and Route 13 in War Zone C were the 271st, 272nd, and 273rd NVA Infantry Regiments of the 9th NVA Division. In November 1966, the 70th VC Guards Regiment and the 101st NVA Regiment engaged American troops near III Corps' Suoi Ca.

By mid 1966, "the estimated strength of the Viet Cong in the IV Corps . . . was 82,545 men. Of these 19,270 were combat troops; 1,290 were support troops; 50,765 were local part-time guerrillas; and 11,220 were working as political cadre. At the time, no North Vietnam Army forces were reported in the IV Corps Tactical Zone . . . organized military forces in the IV Corps . . . consisted of three regimental headquarters, 28 battalions (8 of which were in regiments), 69 separate companies, and 11 separate platoons."[590]

Viet Cong battalions identified in IV Corps: July 1966, by Province

- Long An-5th Battalion of the Nhabe Regiment.
- Dinh Tuong-DT1 Regiment, with the 261st, 263rd, and 514th VC Battalions
- Kien Hoa-516th and 518th.
- Sa Dec-306th.
- Vinh Binh-307th.
- Vinh Long-857th.
- Taydo-Phong Dinh-303rd Regiment.
- Kien Giang-504th.
- Minh-Chuong Thien-309th, D2.
- Bac Lieu-320th, 716th.

In October 1966, the 261st and 262nd NVA Infantry Regiments attempted to infiltrate the IV Corps by sampan. They were traveling in nearly a hundred sampans down the My Tho River when detected by U.S. Navy river patrol boats of River Section 531. During the ensuing battle, those two NVA regiments were destroyed before they could escape from the My Tho River.[591]

NVA Order of Battle in 1967

According to General Williamson, the NVA force within South Vietnam grew again in 1967. "This force controls 9 division headquarters. 34 regimental headquarters, 152 combat battalion and about 200 separate companies."[592]

The effective strength of each VC/NVA battalion was approximately 320 men, each company approximately 100 men and each platoon contained approximately thirty men. The equivalent of fifteen NVA/VC divisions were operating in South Vietnam in 1967. "By 1967 the North Vietnamese had assumed the bulk of the fighting in the Central Highlands and near the demilitarized zone. Another 40,000 soldiers are in Laos-15,000 acting as cadre for the Pathet Lao troops and 25,000 working on the Ho Chi Minh Trail—and some 35,000 to 40,000 have been operating in and around the demilitarized zone."[593]

The Chu Luc command structure in 1967 became more complicated. COSVN (Central Office South Vietnam) still controlled all of III and IV corps, but the I and II corps areas were organized into several command echelons.

North Vietnam's Military Region 5 controlled two groups of forces too:

1. Two NVA infantry divisions.

    a. The 2nd NVA Infantry Division, which operated in I Corps' Quang Ngai and Quang Tin Provinces.

    b. The 3rd NVA Division, which operated in II Corps' Binh Dinh Province. In some cases the 3rd Division would travel north into I Corps or west into II Corps' Kontum Province, but not very often.

2. The B-3 Front, headquartered in the Triborder War Zone, and controlling the 1st and 10th NVA Divisions, along with several independent regiments, B-3 Front units operated in Kontum, Pleiku and Dar Lac Provinces.

North Vietnam's Military Region 4 also controlled two groups of forces:

1. Tri Thien Hue Military Region, the I Corps coastal area near Hue.

2. Four NVA divisions North of the DMZ: 304th, 320th, 324B (refitting in early 1967), and 325C. The 325C Division was the strategic reserve for NVA Military Region 4.

NVA units began pouring into I Corps, which they recognized as weakly held by several division equivalents of timid U.S. Marines and two reinforced ARVN infantry divisions. Five new communist troop bivouacs and two way stations on routes from Sanctuary Base Area 606 into I Corps' Quang Tri Province were identified early in the year.

The 5th and 6th NVA Infantry Regiments' Stronghold Base Area 101 was identified in the rugged hills of Hai Lang Forest, south of Quang Tri, in mid-1967. The 6th NVA, and the 810th and 814th VC Battalions were identified north of Hue near the long-time communist "Street Without Joy" stronghold. The 716th NVA Infantry Regiment was detected in southern Quang Tri.

Reconnaissance units of the 324B and 341st NVA Divisions were detected in Quang Tri Province in early 1967. In February 1967, the 812th NVA Regiment of the 324B NVA Infantry Division began fighting U.S. marines near Cam Lo. In April, the 325C NVA Division, controlling the 66th and 101D Regiments, was identified near Khe Sahn. Throughout the rest of the year the 324B Division's 90th and 812th Regiments fought U.S. marines in the Con Thien area.

At the same time, the 2nd NVA Division began offensive operations out of I Corps' Que Son War Zone with its 3rd and 21st NVA Regiments. Its 2nd VC Regiment was operating in Quang Ngai Province. In February 1967, "The 2d NVA Division and supporting battalions moved south from Quang Tin Province to Quang Ngai Province. This move appeared related to movement of other subordinate units at the turn of the year in preparation for a proposed dry season offensive in Quang Ngai."[594]

Also in February 1967, the enemy first used rocket barrages in South

Vietnam. "On 27 February, NVA forces attacked Da Nang Airbase with 140mm rockets, the first known use of large tactical rockets by the enemy in South Vietnam. The Da Nang attack preceded rocket attacks on Camp Carroll in Quang Tri Province on 6 and 12 March and another attack on Da Nang on 15 March. . .

"The rockets employed in the attack against Camp Carroll were 107mm Communist copies of the U.S. 4.5 inch barrage rocket with a range of 5,000 meters. The 140mm Soviet rocket used at Da Nang had a range of almost 9,000 meters."[595]

By June 1967, the small 2nd NVA Division was pinning down the entire U.S. 1st Marine Division, nine U.S. Army battalions of Task Force Oregon and four ROK Marine battalions. That huge allied force was dug in along the coast in massive fortified enclaves.

By the end of 1967 the following NVA units were identified in I Corps:

- DMZ-341st NVA Division, of unknown strength.
- Quang Tri Province: (10,800 combatants) 324B NVA Division (90th and 812th Regiments); 325C NVA Division (9th, 29th and 95th Regiments); 5th NVA Regiment, twenty-seven NVA independent battalions and four independent companies.
- Thua Thien Province: Northern Front Headquarters (3,650 combatants) five NVA regiments, four independent NVA battalions, four independent companies.
- Quang Nam Province: (2,950 combatants) 368B Artillery Regiment (rocket), four independent NVA battalions, four independent NVA companies.
- Quang Tin Province: (6,100 combatants) 2nd NVA Division (1st VC, 3rd NVA and 21st NVA Regiments), three independent NVA battalions, seven independent NVA companies.
- Quang Ngai Province: (3,650 combatants) Headquarters Military Region 5, 2nd VC Main Force Regiment, six independent NVA battalions, nine independent NVA companies.[596]

Quang Ngai Province was riddled with VC/NVA units, "During February and March the 1st VC Regiment moved southwest of Quang Ngai City and in April the 21st NVA Regiment was deployed to Quang Tin. After this . . . enemy man force/local force battalions operated in increasing numbers in Son Tinh District in 1967. The 409th Sapper Battalion began operating in the northern portion of the district in January, augmenting the 48th LF Battalion. Toward the end of 1967, these two battalions were joined by the 81st and 85th LF Battalions.

"Prior to the 1968 Tet Offensive (1/68), the VC formed two regiments in Quang Ngai Province by consolidating main and local force battalions. The 401st NVA Regiment was formed from main forces and infiltration packets, and three of the prominent LF battalions in the area, the 38th, 48th and 81st Battalions were consolidated to form the 328th VC Regiment."[597]

Most of the battles fought in II Corps in 1967, were fought along the coast in Binh Dinh War Zone or near the Triborder War Zone along the Cambodian frontier. The 3rd NVA Division with its 2nd VC, 18th NVA and 22nd NVA Regiments was assisted during its defense of coastal Binh Dinh by the E28 and E210 VC Battalions. These units fought the U.S. 1st Cavalry Division in Binh Dinh War Zone for control of six strongholds: Bong Son Plains, Cay Giep Mountains, Kim Son Valley, Nui Mieu Mountains, Suoi Ca Valley and Phu Cat Mountains.

Near the Triborder War Zone, the 1st NVA Division with the 32nd, 66th and 95B NVA Regiments drove the U.S. 4th Infantry Division out of the border area. Soon the 1st NVA controlled a wide border strip from the Triborder War Zone to south of the Ia Drang Valley and Chu Pong Mountain War Zone.

The 24th and 174th NVA Regiments caused heavy casualties among allied troops operating near II Corps' mountainous Dak To area in mid 1967. During October 1967, the 1st NVA Division concentrated in a huge rectangular bridgehead in the mountains on all sides of the Dak To area with five NVA regiments: 24th, 32nd, 66th and 174th Infantry and 40th Artillery.

The NVA's Military Region 4 in III Corps' Thanh Dien Forest/Iron Triangle Stronghold areas, controlled its own 1st and 7th VC Battalions in January 1967. Also operating nearby were the 165th NVA Regiment (2nd, 3rd, and 8th Battalions), the 680th VC Training Regiment, and the 272nd VC/NVA Regiment.

When the U.S. Army launched its corps-sized Operations Cedar Falls and Junction City in early 1967, the 9th NVA Infantry Division commanded the four communist regiments which resisted the American incursions. During the time that the Americans attempted to gain control of War Zone C and the Iron Triangle, 9th NVA Division subordinate units attacked continuously. During the first three months of 1967, the 101st NVA, the 272nd VC/NVA and 273rd VC/NVA Regiments attacked American troops at Prek Lok, Ap Bau Bang and numerous other locations.[598]

In March 1967, the 271st VC/NVA Regiment and the 70th Guards VC

Regiment attacked the U.S. 1st Battalion of the 26th Infantry Regiment in War Zone C. At the same time the 272nd and 273rd Regiments attacked two U.S. battalions at Landing Zone Gold near Suoi Tre in War Zone C.

In October 1967, the 9th NVA Division's 273rd VC/NVA Regiment struck at Loc Ninh. At the same time the 88th NVA Regiment attacked III Corps' Song Be in Phuoc Long Province.

In December 1967, the 271st and 272nd VC/NVA Regiments attacked American Fire Support Base Burt in War Zone C. Then they moved to the Phu Loi area where they joined the Phu Loi VC Battalion in pinning the U.S. 1st Infantry Division in its base camps.

Around Cu Chi the F-100 Sapper Battalion and the Cu Chi VC Battalion kept the U.S. 25th Infantry Division pinned to its base. These continuous attacks first halted, then drove out, the Americans from the communist III Corps War Zone and stronghold areas.

In southern III Corps, near Vung Tau, the 5th NVA Infantry Division held sway: "The VC Province (or Local Force) Battalion, D445, was normally based, in accordance with its intermediary role, in one of a number of long used bases. The Main Force Headquarters (HQ 5 VC Division) with its logistics units were in May Tao mountains, from which they could control and support the operations of their combat forces in Phuoc Tuy and neighboring provinces, and at the same time be well placed for support from the large base area of War Zone D."[599]

In 1967, the 275th VC/NVA Regiment was removed from the vicinity of Phuoc Tuy. A new local force battalion made up of NVA troops and the D440 VC Battalion, was formed in Phuoc Tuy at the same time.

COSVN's principal armored force in III Corps was code named Unit 16. During late 1967, that unit trained selected Bo Dai in the operation of captured ARVN armored vehicles. That training was carried out in preparation for the forthcoming Tet Offensive.

In late 1966, no allied forces were operating in the northern IV Corps area controlled by the 261st and 263rd Viet Cong Main Force Battalions (regional) and the 514th VC Main Force Battalion (provincial). The 1st, 7th and 8th Viet Cong Battalions were also active in the IV Corps in early 1967. Most of the offensive action undertaken by these battalions was small scale and reactive throughout 1966. None of the battalions fought a major battle in 1966 or early 1967.

However the power of the Chu Luc in the Delta area was both consolidated and growing:

"The sixteen (Delta) provinces form a Region governed by a Viet Cong civilian-military committee. The Committee exercises direct control over two regiments, three battalions each—the DT-1 Regiment based fifty miles south of Saigon, and the D-2 Regiment based in the southernmost U Minh forest along the Gulf of Siam. The regiments do not function as integrated units; assignments are addressed to individual battalions. These six so-called 'main force' battalions are the Viet Cong elite. Wherever they go—and they can go anywhere in the Region—local units provide food and lodging.

"Province. The Viet Cong 'provincial mobile' battalion, at the next level of command, operates only in its home province at the discretion of the provincial civilian-military committee.

"District. The Viet Cong district committee directs a multiplatoon District Concentrated Unit (DCU) of some forty to one hundred men. The DCU's primary missions are road interdiction, harassment of government outposts and offices, and security; When district officials move, the DCU screens; when district officials stop for meetings or propaganda lectures, the DCU sets up a floating perimeter.

"Village. The village committee musters a squad of from six to twenty men who fabricate grenade traps and pointed bamboo 'punji' stakes, provide security for couriers and village political officers, and sometimes fire on small government outposts.

"The whole system is geared for quick small unit thrusts. Toward this end, battalions are split up into independently operating companies, though they occasionally mass for an attack on a major outpost. That occasion . . . is extremely rare. Even the main force battalions, the elite units, seldom strike in battalion strength. For instance in Vinh Long province, in the heart of the delta, where an estimated 6000 Viet Cong are operating, including one provincial battalion and one main force battalion, *the year 1967 produced only one battalion-size engagement.* During the same period, 1024 'incidents' were recorded, most of them roadblocks, assassinations, minings, ambushes and attacks on small outposts . . . Hundreds, probably thousands, of more subtle enemy actions went unrecorded in Vinh Long."[600]

The 506th VC Battalion engaged allied troops at Rach Kin in IV Corps' Long An Province in early 1967. In Dinh Tuong Province, the 261st, 263rd and 514th VC Battalions began to concentrate in response to greater allied activity in the province.

In September-October 1967, the Chu Luc initiated Phase One of its Winter-Spring Campaign of 1967–68. Utilizing the Coordinated Fighting Method, NVA Regiments attacked in three locations: I Corps' Con Thien (September-October 1967) where the 812th NVA Regiment attacked marine positions; III Corps' Loc Ninh (October 1967) where the 273rd VC/NVA Regiment attacked U.S. Army units; and II Corps' Dak To (November 1967) where the 1st NVA Division fought a corps size allied force.

At Dak To the battlefield had been prepared in fortified mountain bastions months in advance. Four NVA Regiments of the 1st NVA Division occupied fortified areas center in the following locales:

* 24th NVA Regiment—Hill 1416, northeast of Dak To.
* 32nd NVA Regiment—Hill 1338, southeast of Dak To.
* 66th NVA Regiment—Hill 823, south of Dak To.
* 174th NVA Regiment—Hill 875, southwest of Dak To.

When the NVA regiments finally withdrew from the Dak To area, they left both the U.S. 4th Infantry Division and 173rd Airborne Brigade seriously depleted.

Phase Two of the campaign consisted of the 1968 Tet Offensive I, which lasted from January to March, 1968. That offensive involved NVA initiated combat in thirty-two of South Vietnam's major population centers.

MACV Estimate of Enemy Battalion Strength: March, 1968

Location	North Vietnamese	Viet Cong
I Corps	77 battalions	18 battalions
II Corps	55 battalions	18 battalions
III Corps	26 battalions	50 battalions
IV Corps	———	34 battalions
TOTAL	158 NVA battalions	120 VC battalions[601]

NVA Order of Battle-1968

"In March 1968, enemy strength throughout South Vietnam was estimated to be approximately 263,200 men. Of this total about 55,900 were Viet Cong (VC) combat forces, 87,400 were North Vietnamese Army (NVA) combat troops, and 69,100 were guerrillas, with the remaining 50,800 comprising administrative personnel."[602]

By early 1968, the NVA had concentrated four infantry divisions across the DMZ from northwestern Quang Tri and in the Khe Sahn area:

* 304th NVA Division—9,800 men.
* 320th NVA Division—7,400 men.

LOCATIONS: SELECTED NVA DIVISIONS & REGIMENTS: 1965-68

1965
I Corps: 2nd Div (3, 21 Rgts); 1st VC Rgt
II Corps: 3rd Div (18, 22 Rgts); 1st Div (32, 33, 66 Rgts);2nd
            VC Rgt
III Corps: 5th Div (274, 275 Rgts); 9th Div (271, 272, 273
            Rgts)
IV Corps: VC Dong Thap Rgt; VC Q763 Rgt

1966
I Corps: 2nd Div (1VC, 3, 21 Rgts); 324B Div (90, 803, 812
            Rgts); 1st VC Mobile Rgt, 1st Prov Rgt, 2nd Rgt,
            6th Rgt, 18th Rgt, 45th Rgt
II Corps: 3rd Div (2VC, 18,11 Rgts); 1st Div (32, 33, 66
            Rgts); 24th Rgt, 95th Rgt
III Corps: 5th Div. (274, 275, Rgts); 9th Div (271, 272, 273
            Rgts); 70th VC Guards Rgt; 101st Rgt; 165th Rgt
IV Corps: Nhabe VC Rgt; DT1 VC Rgt; 303 Rgt
North Vietnam: 304th Div; 320th Div; 324B Div; 325th Div; 325 C Div

1967
I Corps: 2nd Div (1VC, 3, 21 Rgts); 324B Div (90, 812 Rgts);
            325C Div (66, 101D Rgts); 325C (8, 29, 95) aka?; 5th
            Rgt; 6th Rgt; 328 VC Rgt; 401st Rgt; 761st Rgt
II Corps: 3rd Div (18, 22 Rgts); 1st Div (32, 33, 66 Rgts);
            1st Div (24, 32, 66 Rgts); 174th Rgt; 40th Arty Rgt
III Corps: 5th Div (274, 275 Rgts); 9th Div (101, 272, 273
            Rgts); 88th Rgt; 165 Rgt; 271st Rgt; 275th Rgt;
            680th VC Rgt
IV Corps: Nhabe VC Rgt; DT1 VC Rgt; 303 Rgt
North Vietnam: 304th Div; 320th Div

1968
I Corps: 2nd Div (1VC, 3, 21 Rgts); 324 B Div (90, 812 Rgts);
            325C Div (66, 95, 101D Rgts); 304th Div (66 Rgt);
            308th Div (31, 36, 38 Rgts) 4th Rgt; 5th Rgt; 6th
            Rgt; 24th Rgt; 90th Rgt; 803rd Rgt; 368B Arty Rgt;
            88th Rgt; 102nd Rgt; 141st Rgt
II Corps: 3rd Div (18, 22 Rgts); 10th Div (24, 32, 66 Rgts);
174th Rgt; 33rd Rgt; 95th Rgt; 40th Arty Rgt
III Corps: 5th Div (174, 275 Rgts); 9th Div (271, 272, 273
            Rgts); 1st Div (32, 33, 66 Rgts); 88th Rgt; 165th
            Rgt; 101st Rgt; 274th Rgt; VC Dong Nai Rgt
IV Corps: Nhabe VC Rgt; DT1 VC Rgt; 303 Rgt
Laos: 312th Div, 316th Div, 766th Rgt
North Vietnam: 320th Div

NOTE: All units NVA Infantry unless otherwise noted.

- 324B NVA Division—9,500 men.
- 325C NVA Division—7,400 men.[603]

Four regiments of the 304th and 325C Divisions, the 66th, 95th, 101st(?) and 101D NVA Regiments, were identified as part of the force surrounding the reinforced U.S. 26th Marine Regiment at Khe Sahn. Yet the 26th Marines were confused about the difference between the 101st and 101D Regiments, as the following excerpt from their After Action Report indicates:

"On January 21, the enemy was generally disposed with the 95th Regiment (325C Division) to the north and west, occupying the high ground opposite the 881S/861 complex. The 4th Battalion was located with the regimental headquarters, the 6th battalion was in the vicinity of Hill 881N, and the 5th Battalion was east of that position to, and south, along the Rao Quan River Valley. The 101st Regiment was believed to be headquartered with a battalion in the vicinity of Lang Hoan Tap. A second battalion was along the Dong Dang ridgeline. A third battalion was in the vicinity of Co Put and along Route 9 north of Lang Vei. One battalion from the 304th Division may have alternatiely held this site.

"Following the Battle of Khe Sahn Village (January 20), the 66th Regiment, 304th Division, was identified from documents. Except for the positions on Hill 471, which may have been alternately occupied with elements of the 101D Regiment, 325C Division, elements of the 304th Division generally remained south of route 9."[604]

As the Tet Offensive began, the 803rd NVA Infantry Regiment was dug into a line of fortified hamlets just south of the DMZ and above the north bank of the Cua Viet River. The 812th's defenses were sited to interdict river traffic.

The 368B Artillery Regiment unleashed thirty 122mm rockets on Da Nang on January 2, 1968. According to marine General Robertson, "Commencing 29 January 1968, enemy forces have made repeated attempts to occupy the city of DaNang and to destroy or control installations in the DaNang vital area. Employed in these attacks were the 2d NVA Division, the 402d Sapper Battalion, four independent infantry battalions, one rocket artillery regiment and local guerrilla forces."[605]

Every province in I Corps was swamped with communist units. In Quang Ngai Province, for example, "enemy strength was estimated to be between 10,000 and 14,000 men of which 2,000–4,000 were regular forces, 3,000–5,000 were guerrillas, and 5,000 were assigned to administrative units."[606]

The massive assault against most of South Vietnam's population centers which began near the end of January 1968, as the Tet Offensive, involved many VC and NVA units. Their order of battle is recounted in another chapter.

In February 1968, elements of the recently refitted 2nd NVA Division began moving from Laos into South Vietnam along the French-built Route 14. A small American force moved into a border base camp near Kham Duc where it was defeated by the forward elements of that unit in March and April 1968. By August 1968, the 2nd NVA Division was operating near coastal Tam Ky with all three of its regiments.

In April 1968, elements of the 320th NVA Division engaged U.S. Marine forces near Dong Ha. Soon thereafter the reds launched Mini-Tet in the I Corps area as 119 rocket and mortar attacks swept the length and breadth of South Vietnam.

In January 1968, the 31st NVA Regiment had been detected in western Quang Nam Province. But by Mini-Tet, the situation had clarified and the following new units were discovered in I Corps:

- 308th NVA Division with the 31st, 36th and 38th NVA Regiments fighting U.S. marines near An Hoa in southern I Corps.
- 141st NVA Regiment on Go Noi Island west of Hoi An.

U.S. Marine intelligence units, confused by NVA deception, erroneously identified the 308th NVA Division as south of Khe Sanh in late May, 1968: "By the end of May it was obvious that the 308th NVA Division, fresh from Hanoi, with two regiments, the 88th and 102d, had moved south of Khe Sanh and a major attack was in the making. (The 304th NVA Division, badly battered, had been withdrawn to the north for refurbishing; this was not immediately known.)"[607]

In June 1968, the 308th NVA Division was supposedly engaged in the Vietnam Salient, south of Khe Sanh. Supposedly the 88th and 102nd NVA Regiments were destroyed there at that time.

According to U.S. Marine sources, in July 1968 the 36th and 38th NVA Regiments of the 308th NVA Division were fighting marines south of the Ky Lam-Thu Bon River near the Que Son War Zone. In August 1968, the 21st and 38th NVA Regiments were fighting near Tam Ky south of Da Nang.

Located within the huge Stronghold Base Area 112 complex near the periphery of the Que Son War Zone were numerous enemy units: "Among the units identified were the two main command elements which controlled NVA and VC activities within Quang Nam, Quang Tin, and Quang Ngai Provinces: Front 4 headquarters and Headquarters Military Region 5. Attached and directly subordinate to the two headquarters elements, and also located within the base area were the 21st Regiment, 2d NVA Division, 220th Transport Regiment, Q81st (Deux Xuan) and Q83rd (Dai Loc) Local Force Battalions, and 2d Battalion, 141st NVA Regiment. Reinforcing the estimated 3,500 enemy troops were another 6,000 located just outside the base area in the Que Son Mountains and on Goi Noi Island to the east."[608]

In the III Corps area, four NVA Divisions, the 1st, 5th, 7th and 9th, began to concentrate north and west of Saigon.

In April 1968, the 165th NVA Regiment was based in III Corps' Catcher's Mitt Stronghold along the Song Be River north of Tan Uyen and Binh My, and twenty miles northeast of Lai Khe. In May 1968, the 141st NVA Regiment (the same number as another NVA Regiment operating simultaneously in I Corps) was also operating north of Saigon.

In August 1968, a third round of Tet Offensives was launched by the 5th and 9th NVA Infantry Divisions in III Corps' Tay Ninh Province. The following NVA units participated in that offensive:

- 5th NVA Division with the 33rd, 174th and 275th NVA Regiments and one antiaircraft battalion.
- 9th NVA Division with the 271st, 272nd and 273rd NVA Regiments and one antiaircraft battalion.
- Corps troops consisting of the 88th NVA Regiment and several Viet Cong battalions.

The NVA corps-sized unit fought over fifteen skirmishes and battles during an eleven day period. They fought the 1st Brigade of the U.S. 25th Infantry Division and retired back into their war zones when the American airpower advantage became overwhelming.

In November 1968, the Long An Viet Cong Battalion and the 12th NVA Rocket Battalion were operating to the south of Saigon in Long An Province and also along the Vam Co Dong River.

In the IV Corps zone, confusion concerning the NVA order of battle was pervasive. An example of that order of battle muddle occurred in IV Corps Long An Province: "intelligence briefers in December 1968 emphasized their arguments about a Viet Cong collapse by citing low strength figures for Viet Cong battalions operating in Vinh Long; 306th Battalion, 200 men; 308th, 200 men; 312th, 200 men; D857a, 125 men; D857b, 150 men; 509th, 150 men. The strength figures certainly were low. The trouble was that this analysis included one battalion that had been created specifically for the Tet Offensive (308th) and two battalions that had been formed since the Tet Offensive. Though the number of men per Viet Cong battalion had dropped, the number of battalions had doubled since mid 1967."[609]

CHAPTER 17

NVA Order of Battle II: 1969–73

In 1969, the NVA fielded approximately fifty-two regiments and 352 combat maneuver battalions in South Vietnam. Most of the enemy buildup continued to occur in the I Corps area which the Chu Luc seemed to control by 1969, regardless of the presence there of nearly half of all the allied combat troops stationed in Vietnam. "Within the boundaries of I Corps, the Demilitarized Zone, and contiguous North Vietnamese and Laotian border regions were 123 North Vietnamese Army (NVA) and 18 Viet Cong (VC) combat and support battalions composed of close to 89,000 enemy troops . . . 42,700 were North Vietnamese Army regulars while 6,500 were Viet Cong main and local force unit members."[610]

Five different enemy headquarters directed enemy operations in the I Corps area. They controlled troops in the following locations:

- B-5 Front: along the DMZ.
- 7th Front: Quang Tri Province.
- Tri Thien/Hue Military Region: Quang Tri and Thua Thien provinces.
- 4th Front: Quang Nam and Quang Tin Provinces.
- Military Region 5: Quang Ngai Province.

There was some confusion among allied intelligence, since the NVA command structure was not based on geographical location. However, the U.S. Marines thought that all five of the above listed headquarters were subordinate to COSVN, a communist Front headquarters, located in III Corps' Tay Ninh Province.

Certain NVA units were subordinate to specific headquarters in January 1969. For example:

- B-5 Front Headquarters: (DMZ) 138th, 270th, 84th, 31st, 27th, and 126th Naval Sapper NVA Regiments. The 320th NVA Division with the 48th, 52nd and 64th NVA Regiments.
- 7th Front: (Central Quang Tri Province) 812th NVA Regiment and the 308th NVA Division in the Vietnam Salient with the 88th and 102nd NVA Regiments.
- Tri-Thien/Hue: (A Shau Valley War Zone) 4th, 5th, 6th, 9th and 29th NVA Regiments, along with 11A and 11B NVA Counter-reconnaissance Companies; (Base Area 114) 803rd NVA Regiment; (Da Krong War Zone) 65th Artillery Regiment and 83rd Engineer Regiment. Tri-Thien/Hue also controlled Stronghold Base Areas 101 and 114, being serviced by Sanctuary Border Bases 607 and 611.
- 4th Front: (Quang Nam) and the 2nd NVA Division Headquarters, (Que Son War Zone and Stronghold Base Area 112) 21st, 31st Independent, 141st, 36th and 38th NVA Infantry Regiments, 1st VC Infantry Regiment, 68B and 368B Rocket Artillery Regiments. Serviced by Sanctuary Border Base Area 614.
- Military Region 5 Headquarters: (Quang Tin and Quang Ngai provinces) 3rd NVA Infantry Regiment. (Chu Lai) 3rd NVA Division Headquarters with the 2nd VC, 22nd, 31st and 401st VC Sapper Infantry Regiments. Military Region 5 controlled Stronghold Base Areas 117, 119, 121 and 124, and was serviced by Sanctuary Border Base Area 614.

In February 1969, the 141st NVA Regiment made a three-pronged thrust into the Da Nang Vital Area. The 1st Marine Division defending that area was able to blunt the thrusts.[611]

The kaleidoscope of changing Chu Luc troop units continued to pulsate, even as their numbers continued to increase: "By March 1969, there were five NVA regiments and two VC regiments in Quang Tri and Thua Thien provinces, the equivalent of twenty-four VC and NVA battalions in Quang Nam province, and twelve VC and NVA battalions in the southern provinces of Quang Tin and Quang Ngai."[612]

In April 1969, the 27th and 36th NVA Regiments, defending bunker complexes, fought allied troops in the Vietnam Salient. The Vietnam Salient Stronghold was located on the Laotian border, about twenty-five kilometers south of Khe Sahn and fifteen kilometers west of the Da Krong Valley.

In May 1969, the 7th U.S. Marine Regiment engaged the 31st and 141st

NVA Regiments near the Que Son War Zone. The two enemy regiments were located about thirty kilometers southwest of Da Nang.

Located in nearby Dodge City and Go Noi Island Strongholds in May 1969 were the following communist units:

- 36th NVA Infantry Regiment.
- Elements of the disbanded 38th NVA Infantry Regiment.
- District II Da Nang Force composed of the T-89th Sapper, D-3 Sapper and R-20th VC Battalions.

In June 1969, the 304th NVA Division was fighting U.S. Marines in western Quang Tin province. The 57th Regiment of the 304th Division engaged marine units south of Route 9.

By late June 1969, the following NVA units were consistently active in western Quang Tri near the DMZ:

- 9th, 24th, 27th and 31st NVA Infantry Regiments.
- 84th Artillery (Rocket) Regiment.

In July and August 1969, the 2nd NVA Division was fighting in the Que Son War Zone and near the An Hoa Stronghold area. The 3rd NVA and 1st VC Regiments fought U.S. troops in the Hiep Duc region and near the Nui Chom Mountains. In August 1969, the 5th U.S. Marine Regiment encountered the 90th NVA Regiment (7th, 8th and 9th Battalions) and the 1st Battalion, 368B Artillery Regiment, in the Arizona Stronghold area southwest of Da Nang.

In May 1969, the 9th and 29th NVA Regiments defended the A Shau Valley against the U.S. 101st Airborne Division. The 29th NVA Regiment fought the Battle of Hamburger Hill.

In late December 1969, the 36th NVA Regiment was encountered in the Que Son Valley War Zone.

In III Corps, the 33rd NVA Regiment and the D440 Battalion moved south from Long Khan Province into the Binh Ba District of Phuoc Tuy Province. Operations of the Australian Task Force sometimes forced the 33rd to withdraw into Long Khan, but it always returned.

The III Corps area around Saigon was teeming with NVA troops in 1969. The U.S. 1st Cavalry Division conducted spoiling attacks into III Corps' War Zones C and D to interrupt movements toward Saigon by the 1st, 5th, 7th and 9th NVA Infantry Divisions. Many new VC and NVA units sprung up all over III Corps. For example, about thirty battalions of "Viet Cong" troops were deployed within thirty kilometers of Tan Son Nhut Air Base outside of Saigon in January 1969.

VC/NVA Units Deployed Near Tan Son Nhut: January, 1969

1st VC Main Force Battalion—150 men
2nd VC Main Force Battalion—200 men
Gia Dinh Sapper Battalion—250 men
8th VC Artillery Battalion—270 men
Cu Long Regiment—950 men
6th Local Force Battalion of the Cu Long Regiment—300 men
308th Local Force Battalion of the Ch Long Regiment—300 men
12th VC Local Force Battalion—100 men
2nd Independence Main Force VC Battalion—250 men
265th Main Force Battalion—150 men
506th Main Force Battalion—250 men
Dong Phu Main Force Battalion—300 men
3rd Artillery Battalion—150 men
D6 Heavy Weapons Battalion—180 men
Doan 10 Sapper Battalion—180 men
Thu Duc Regiment—800 men
Dong Nai Regiment—1400 men
K2 Battalion of the Dong Nai Regiment—250 men
208th Artillery Regiment—650 men.[613]

NVA Order of Battle in 1970

The North Vietnamese Army stationed within South Vietnam by early 1970, was organized into eight division headquarters, fifty-seven regiments, 271 combat battalions and fifty-eight combat support units.

"Communist units operating in South Vietnam (in 1970) were equipped with weapons made in Russia, Red China and other communist countries. These included the AK-47 assault rifle, the RPD machine gun, the RPG grenade launcher, the 12.7mm and 14.5mm machine guns . . . Communist forces used extensively 107mm and 122mm rockets. In addition, their units were equipped with 75mm, 82mm and 107mm recoilless rifles and Chinese made 60mm, 82mm and 120mm mortars. . . . sapper units were equipped with the K-6 pistol with collapsible stock which could be used as a sub-machine gun. In 1969, communist units began to receive such modern signal equipment as the Russian TA-57 telephone set and R-105 radio set and the Chinese B-600 radio set."[614]

The NVA sorted out their command structure again in 1970. COSVN was given command of all communist troops in II, III and IV Corps, while I Corps was broken down into the following command echelons:

- B-5 Front commanded all troops along the DMZ.
- Military Region Tri Thien/Hue commanded Quang Tri and Thua Thien Provinces.
- Military Region 5 commanded the rest of I Corps.
- Front 4, subordinate to controlled Quang Nam Province.

NVA Front 4, threatening Da Nang, was commanded by Major General Nguyen Chanh Binh. General Binh used several designations for his head-quarters, including Front 4, Group 44 and Quang Da Special Zone Unit. He also utilized three tactical headquarters, or wings, to direct his field opera-tions:

- Northern Wing: Operating in the Hai Van area.
- Central Wing: Operating west of Dan Nang.
- Southern Wing: Operating in the Que Son War Zone area. This unit had disbanded its 36th NVA Regiment to reinforce "Viet Cong" units fighting within U.S. Marine "pacification areas."

In early 1970, General Binh's Front 4 commanded sixteen NVA infantry battalions totaling 13,000 men. In addition, he controlled two rocket artillery battalions, and numerous guerrilla forces.

High point attacks were launched as offensive surges within I Corps in January, April–May, and August–October, 1970. During such offensive surges or "high point" attacks, rocket, mortar and sapper assaults predomi-nated. The NVA main force continued to recruit personnel, seize tribute and plunder, and extend area control while avoiding major battles.

"Small detachments of NVA and VC regulars moved continually throughout the 1st Marine Division's TAOR (Tactical Area of Operational Responsibility). Enemy rocket and mortar teams positioned themselves for attacks, and local VC planted mines and booby traps. While these combat actions were carried on, replacements, medical units, and supply parties upon whom depended the enemy's elaborate and flexible logistics system, operated continuously. According to allied estimates, about 90 percent of the

LOCATIONS: SELECTED NVA DIVISIONS & REGIMENTS: 1969-70

1969

DMZ: 320th Div (48, 52, 64 Rgts); 27th Rgt; 31st Rgt; 84th Rgt; 126th Naval Sapper Rgt; 138th Rgt; 270th Rgt

I Corps: 2nd Div (1VC, 21 Rgts); 308th Div (88, 102 Rgts); 3rd Div (2VC, 18, 22 Rgts); 4th Rgt; 5th Rgt; 6th Rgt; 9th Rgt; 27th Rgt; 29th Rgt; 36th Rgt; 38th Rgt; 141st Rgt; 803rd Rgt; 812th Rgt; 83rd Eng Rgt; 65th Arty Rgt; 68B Arty Rgt; 368 Arty Rgt; 401st VC Sapper

II Corps: 3rd Div (18, 22 Rgts); 10th Div (24, 32, 66 Rgts); 174th Rgt; 33rd Rgt; 95th Rgt; 40th Arty Rgt

III Corps: 5th Div (174, 275 Rgts); 9th Div (271, 272, 273 Rgts); 1st Div (32, 33, 66 Rgts); 7th Div (141, 165, 209, Rgts); 88th Rgt; 165th Rgt; 101st Rgt; 208th Arty Rgt; Cu Long VC Rgt; Thu Duc VC Rgt; Dong Nai VC Rgt; 274th Rgt

IV Corps: Nhabe VC Rgt; DT1 VC Rgt; 303 Rgt

Laos: 312th Div, 316th Div, 148th Rgt; 174th Rgt

1970

DMZ: 320th Div (48, 52, 64 Rgts); 27th Rgt; 31st Rgt; 84th Rgt; 126th Naval Sapper Rgt; 138th Rgt; 270th Rgt

I Corps: 2nd Div (1VC, 21 Rgts); 308th Div (88, 102 Rgts); 3rd Div (2 VC, 18, 22 Rgts) 324B Div (29, 812 Rgts); 4th Rgt; 5th Rgt; 6th Rgt; 9th Rgt; 27th Rgt; 29th Rgt; 36th Rgt; 38th Rgt; 141st Rgt; 803rd Rgt; 83rd Eng Rgt; 65 Arty Rgt; 68B Arty Rgt; 368th Arty Rgt; 401st VC Sapper Rgt

II Corps: 3rd Div (18, 22 Rgts) 10th Div (24, 32, 66 Rgts; 174th Rgt; 28th Rgt; 33rd Rgt; 95th Rgt; 40th Arty Rgt

III Corps: 5th Div (33, 274, 275 Rgts) or (6, 174, 275 Rgts); 9th Div (271, 272, 95 Rgts); 1st Div (52, 101, Rgts); 7th Div (141, 165, 209 Rgts); 88th Rgt; 165th Rgt; 101st Rgt; 208th Arty Rgt; Cu Long VC Rgt; Thu Duc VC Rgt; Dong Nai VC Rgt; 274th Rgt

IV Corps: D2 Rgt; Nhabe VC Rgt; DT1 VC Rgt; 303 Rgt

Laos: 986th Div (9.19, 29 Rgts); 2nd Div (1, 3 Rgts); 304th, 308th, 316th, 320th Divs; 66th Rgt; 141st Rgt

Cambodia: 1st, 5th, 7th, 9th, C40 Divs; 205th Rgt; 207th Rgt; 69th Arty Rgt

NOTE: All units NVA Infantry unless otherwise noted.

LOCATIONS: SELECTED NVA DIVISIONS & REGIMENTS: 1971-72

1971

DMZ: 320th Div (48, 52, 64 Rgts); 27th Rgt; 31st Rgt; 84th Rgt; 126th Naval Sapper Rgt; 138th Rgt; 270th Rgt; 164th Arty Rgt; 246th Rgt

I Corps: 2nd Div (1st VC, 21 Rgts); 308th Div (88, 102 Rgts); 3rd Div (2 VC, 18, 22 Rgts); 324B Div (29, 812 Rgts); 304th Div (9, 24B, 66 Rgts); 4th Rgt; 5th Rgt; 6th Rgt; 9th Rgt; 27th Rgt; 29th Rgt; 36th Rgt; 38th Rgt; 141 Rgt; 803rd Rgt; 83rd Eng Rgt;65th, 68B, 368th Arty Rgts; 401st VC Sapper

II Corps: 3rd Div (18, 22 Rgts); 10th Div (24, 32, 66 Rgts); 174th Rgt; 28th Rgt; 33rd Rgt; 95th Rgt; 40th Arty Rgt

III Corps: 5th Div (33, 274, 275 Rgts) or (6, 174, 275 Rgts); 9th Div (271, 2721, 95 Rgts); 1st Div (52, 101 Rgts); 7th Div (141, 165, 209 Rgts); 88th Rgt; 165th Rgt; 101st Rgt; 208th Arty Rgt; Cu Long VC Rgt; Thu Duc VC Rgt; Dong Nai VC Rgt; 274th Rgt

IV Corps: D2 Rgt; Nhabe VC Rgt; DT1 VC Rgt; 303 Rgt

Laos: 986th Div (9.19, 29 Rgts); 2nd Div (1,3,141 Rgts); 324B Div (29, 803, 812, 675 Arty Rgts); 308th Div (36, 88, 102 Rgts); 304th, 316th, 320th Divs; 66th Rgt; 141st Rgt; 203rd Armored Rgt

Cambodia: 1st, 5th, 7th, 9th and C40 Divs; 205th Rgt; 207th Rgt; 69th Arty Rgt

1972

DMZ: 320th Div (48, 52, 64 Rgts); 304th Div (9, 29, 66, 68 Arty Rgts); 308th Div (36, 88, 102 Rgts); B5 (31, 270, 246 Rgts; 126 Naval Sapper Rgt; 38 Arty Rgt, 84 Arty Rgt; 203, 204, 205 Armored Rgts); 138th Rgt; 164 Arty Rgt; 27th Rgt;84th Rgt

I Corps: 2nd Div (1VC, 21 Rgts); 308th Div (88, 102 Rgts); 3rd Div (2VC, 18, 22 Rgts); 324 Div (29, 803, 812 Rgts); 304th Div (9, 24B, 66 Rgts); 325th Div (18, 995, 101 Rgts); 711th Div; 4th Rgt; 5th Rgt; 6th Rgt; 9th Rgt; 27th Rgt; 29th Rgt; 36th Rgt; 38th Rgt; 141st Rgt; 803rd Rgt; 83rd Eng Rgt; 65th Arty Rgt; 68B Arty Rgt; 368th Arty Rgt; 401st VC Sapper

II Corps: 3rd Div (18, 22 Rgts); 10th Div (24, 32, 66 Rgts); 174th Rgt; 986th Div (9.19, 29 Rgts); 28th Rgt; 33rd Rgt; 95th Rgt; 40th Arty Rgt

III Corps: 9th Div (271, 272, 95 Rgts); 7th Div (141, 165, 209 Rgts); 88th Rgt; 165th Rgt; 101st Rgt; 208th Arty Rgt; Cu Long VC Rgt; Thu Duc VC Rgt; Dong Nai VC Rgt; 274th Rgt

IV Corps: 1st Div (52, 101 Rgts); 5th Div (33, 274, 275 Rgts) or (6, 174, 275 Rgts); D2 Rgt; Nhabe VC Rgt; DT1 VC Rgt; 303 Rgt

Cambodia: C40 Div; 205th Rgt; 207th Rgt; 69th Arty Rgt

NOTE: All units NVA Infantry unless otherwise noted.

enemy's arms and ammunition in Quang Nam Province, 30 percent of his food, and about 25 percent of his other supplies in early 1970 were trucked down the Ho Chi Minh Trail (See: J. W. McCoy, *Secrets of the Ho Chi Minh Trail*.) from North Vietnam and then moved by porters into mountain base areas 20–30 miles south and southwest of Da Nang. These base areas also harbored camps, training installations, and headquarters. The rest of the enemy's supplies, including most of the food and material for booby traps, came from the populated lowlands, where it was procured by the Viet Cong infrastructure through purchase, contribution, or forced requisition and then cached for movement to the base areas.

"Within Quang Nam Province, most enemy supplies traveled on the backs of porters. These porters were members of transport battalions and sometimes regular frontline troops, reinforced when necessary with civilians conscripted in VC controlled hamlets. They customarily operated in teams of three to ten persons each carrying a 30-to-70 pound pack. Usually protected by armed escorts and moving at night or through covering terrain, the supply parties often followed rivers or streams in and out of the mountains. The waterways also allowed them to move rockets and other heavy equipment by sampan."[615]

The U.S. Marines in Quang Nam, who claimed they were accomplishing more with their "pacification efforts among the populace," never seemed able or willing to attack the vulnerable enemy supply system. The marines were too busy trying to defend themselves.

Approximately forty NVA infantry and eleven support battalions massed around the DMZ in early 1970. Sixteen more infantry and four support battalions were massed near Da Nang in Quang Nam. The total enemy troops in I Corps was approximately 78,000 men: "According to allied intelligence, the Communists' order of battle included 49,000 North Vietnamese Army (NVA) regulars, perhaps 6,000 main force Viet Cong (VC), over 12,000 VC guerrillas, and 11,000 supply and administrative personnel."[616]

By now the American military, beaten back into fortified bases where it had languished for years, was eager to retreat out of South Vietnam. To complement their real attitude, American generals devised the "One War" concept which was a pretense at keeping the enemy main forces away from the populated areas. That mission was supposedly accomplished by defending allied bases located near population centers, while avoiding any offensive action. In the meantime, NVA troops swarmed throughout the countryside and entered the defended enclaves at will.

There was widespread confusion among U.S. Marine officers regarding both their mission and accomplishments. Following is a quotation from one of those officers which revealed a distorted view of NVA maneuvers in South Vietnam in 1970: "most of the fighting prior to Tet was with large scale NVA units that had been up in I Corps, and III MAF (U.S. Marine High Command in I Corps) had borne the brunt of a lot of this. And I think there was an unspoken attitude up there that this was the war, in I Corps. Well I found that this was not the case. And of course later on when the NVA gave up, to a certain extent, their large scale attempts to infiltrate through the DMZ, and we saw the appearance of NVA divisions that had fought up in I Corps down in the highlands in II Corps and even over in western III Corps. As the war shifted, and it did necessarily when the NVA started bringing large formations down to II and III Corps, there was less pressure from main force units up in I Corps . . . I'm not saying this as criticism of anybody. It's a natural reaction. Everybody is concerned for his own area, and naturally he's concerned with his own war."[617] Many U.S. military officers in Vietnam had no understanding of current situational realities.

I Corps' 3rd U.S. Marine Division had pulled out of Vietnam in 1969. The 1st U.S. Marine Division remained behind, huddled in its huge fortified belts surrounding one town, Da Nang.

ARVN troops carried out all offensive action in 1970. In March 1970, ARVN troops skirmished with the V-25 Viet Cong Battalion and the T-89th Viet Cong Sapper Battalion near Hoi An.

In early 1970, the 66th Regiment of the 304th NVA Division moved into the Ba Long area, northwest of I Corps' Thua Thien Province. At the same time the 29th NVA Regiment of the 324B NVA Division reinfiltrated into western Thua Thien Province. Further north, the 812th Regiment of the 324B Division reinfiltrated into southwest Quang Tri Province.

In December 1970, allied intelligence detected the following NVA troop strength in Laotian sanctuary bases near I Corps:

- The 812th Regiment, 324B NVA Division was located in the Laotian Salient west of Quang Tri Province.
- The 9th and 141st Separate NVA Infantry Regiments were operating in lower Laos under control of the NVA's Southern Laotian Front. The 141st NVA Regiment was earmarked to return to Quang Nam after refitting.
- The 2nd NVA Division, with its 1st and 3rd Regiments, was refitting north of Sanctuary Base Area 612. After refitting it was supposed to return to I Corps' Quang Tin and Quang Ngai Provinces.
- Eight regimental-sized "Binh Tram" military stations west of Quang Tri had been reinforced with twenty antiaircraft battalions.

In II Corps, the NVA 28th Infantry and 40th Artillery Regiments withdrew into the Triborder War Zone for refitting after an unsuccessful assault upon an allied border camp in Kontum Province. The 24th NVA Regiment worked to upgrade its fortifications/logistics network during 1970.

The 66th NVA Regiment, now subordinate to the 2nd NVA Division and B-3 Front, withdrew to Sanctuary Base Area 609 for refitting. In the coastal area of II Corps the 22nd Regiment of the 3rd NVA Division returned to the Binh Dinh War Zone from I Corps' Quang Ngai Province.

In southern III Corps, the D445 "VC" Battalion, made up of NVA regulars, withdrew from operations in Phuoc Tuy Province. The 5th NVA Division had moved its headquarters out of Phuoc Tuy in 1969 into the area north of Saigon where, in 1970, it controlled the 33rd, 274th and 275th NVA Regiments. However, one source claimed that the 5th NVA Division commanded the 175th, 275th and 6th NVA Regiments in 1970.

The 5th NVA Division held most of its units in Cambodia or the Bo Duc and Bu Dop areas north of Binh Long Province, South Vietnam. Its 33rd NVA Regiment was detached to the Binh Tuy-Long Khan area.

The 7th (aka CT-7) NVA Division with the 11th, 165th and 209th NVA Infantry Regiments operated within Cambodia and South Vietnam during 1970. The 7th also briefly maneuvered in South Vietnam, east of War Zone C and north of Binh Long Province.

The 9th NVA Division, with the 271st, 272nd and 95th NVA Infantry Regiments operated in Cambodia, near Phnom Penh, and South Vietnam throughout 1970. In Vietnam, the 9th NVA (aka CT-9) deployed its elements from the Dog's Head to the Angel's Wings sanctuary areas.

The 1st NVA Division, with the 52nd and 101st NVA Infantry Regiments, deployed southwest of Phnom Penh in Cambodia during 1970. It also periodically raided into South Vietnam's IV Corps, due south of its Cambodian operational area.

In Cambodia, the NVA also deployed the 510th, 511th and 512th NVA Infantry Battalions, and the 69th Artillery Regimental Headquarters in 1970. Cambodian sources identified the following deployment of NVA troops in Cambodia in 1970:

"1. The 1st NVA Division, operating in the south and southeast of Phnom Penh.

2. The 5th, 7th, and 9th NVA Divisions, located east of the Mekong in areas north and east known as their sanctuaries. Note that the 9th Division often placed its units west of the Mekong for certain periods.

3. An additional division of VC/NVA forces, called the C40 Division,

operating in the area north and northwest of Tonle Sap Lake (may have included Khmer Cong elements).

4. A large base known as the B3 Base, established in the triborder region of Cambodia, Laos and Vietnam."[618]

In IV Corps, the 273rd Regiment of the 9th NVA Division was transformed into the D2 Regiment and moved into the U Minh area. Communist activity also increased in the Seven Mountains area of Chau Doc Province.

In April 1970, COSVN began reshuffling its troops to avoid ARVN offensive efforts against the Cambodian sanctuary bases. The 271st Regiment of the 9th Division moved to the Bo Ba Tay area. In addition, the 165th Regiment of the 7th Division was withdrawn westward leaving behind its 1st Battalion. That unit defended part of the Cambodian border sanctuary areas, along with the 50th Rear Security Unit and the 250th Rehabilitation Unit.

In May 1970, the 9th NVA Infantry Division occupied the Chup Plantation area northeast of Kompong Cham, Cambodia. Then the 9th began standoff attacks and infantry probes against the city. Kampong Cham's airfield was closed by shelling and the 9th Division blocked the city's Mekong River communications line to Phnom Penh. During ARVN efforts to relieve Kompong Cham, they clashed with the 9th Division's 272nd Regiment.

In October 1970, the NVA formed the 70th Front in Laos. That corps headquarters was to command all red troops fighting in the Route 9 Campaign. The Route 9 Campaign was the NVA counteroffensive which was scheduled to occur when ARVN Operation Lam Son 719 invaded the Route 9-Tchepone, Laos area in early 1971. The 70th Front was supposed to command the 304th, 308th and 320th NVA Divisions, several artillery regiments, several antiaircraft regiments, an armored regiment and numerous supporting units during the Route 9 Campaign.

NVA Order of Battle in 1971

In early 1971, the B-5 Front in the DMZ area commanded a variety of different forces with specific missions:

- 27th, 207th and 246th NVA Infantry Regiments and several artillery battalions were deployed to defend the DMZ area.
- 33rd Sapper Battalion and 126th Naval Sapper Regiment launched attacks within the DMZ area, along Route 9 and in the Cua Viet area.
- 270th Infantry and 164th Artillery NVA Regiments defended the DMZ coast and Vinh Linh area.

The 320th NVA Division had deployed its regiments widely in early 1971. Its 48th Regiment was in Laotian Sanctuary Base 604, the 64th was building roads in Quang Binh Province and the 52nd was located west of the DMZ.

The 9th and 66th Regiments of the 304th NVA Division had returned to North Vietnam. The 304th left behind its 24B Regiment west of Khe Sahn.

The Tri Thien Hue Military Region around Hue, South Vietnam controlled the 4th, 5th and 6th NVA Regiments and several sapper battalions. The sapper battalions raided allied bases and interdicted Route 1 along the coast.

In Laotian Sanctuary Base 611, west of Thua Thien, the 324B NVA Division lay poised. The 324B NVA Division controlled the 29th, 803rd, and 812th Infantry Regiments, and the 675th Artillery Regiment.

There were also many other communist combat troops deployed in the two Laotian military regions closest to South Vietnam's I Corps. In northern Laos there were 16,000 NVA and 17,000 Pathet Lao troops in early 1971.

Communist Troops in Laos Military Regions 3 and 4
1/1971

Troop Types	MR 3	MR 4
NVA Battalions	13	17
Pathet Lao Battalions	20	21
Total NVA	5,000 men	7,000 men
Total Pathet Lao	5,000 men	4,000 men
Total Logistics Personnel	32,000 men	10,000 men
Number of Binh Trams	18	6
Total:	33 Inf. battalions	38 Inf. battalions
	18 Binh Trams	6 Binh Trams

By February 1971, the 24B Regiment of the 304th NVA Division infiltrated western Quang Tri. It was soon joined there by advance elements of the 9th and 66th Regiments.

Also in February 1971, the following units of the 70th Front began to concentrate against ARVN Operation Lam Son 719, north and south of Route 9, and east of Tchepone, Laos:

- 2nd NVA (Yellow Star) Division with its 1st, 3rd, 141st Infantry Regiments and 14th Air Defense Battalion.
- 304th NVA Division's 24B Infantry Regiment.

- 324B NVA Division's 675th Artillery Regiment and 29th and 812th Infantry Regiments.
- 308th NVA Division's 36th, 88th and 102nd Infantry Regiments.
- 320th NVA Division's 64th Infantry Regiment.
- Binh Tram 41's 75th Engineer Battalion and 4th Air Defense Battalion.

By late March, 1971 the following NVA units had joined the units listed above and the Route 9 Campaign.

- An unknown infantry regiment of the 304th NVA Division.
- 324B NVA Division's 803rd Infantry Regiment.
- 202nd NVA Armored Regiment.
- Binh Trams: 7, 27, 32, 33, and 34.[619]

As the units of the 70th Front defeated Lam Son 719 and drove it back into South Vietnam, the NVA initiated other operations. In April 1971, the 39th NVA Regiment launched the NVA's 1971 Laotian Offensive by driving into southern Laos' Saravane.

In the fall of 1971, ARVN intelligence reported the buildup of NVA troops opposite the II Corps area. Supposedly the B-3 Front, in the Triborder War Zone, was assembling three divisions and an armored regiment for a "Winter-Spring" Campaign. Those units included:

- 2nd NVA Infantry Division.
- 3rd NVA ("Gold Star," aka NT-3) Infantry Division.
- 320th NVA Infantry Division.
- 203rd NVA Armored Regiment.

The campaign was supposed to begin in January 1972.

In III Corps, the 33rd NVA Regiment from Long Khan Province had joined the 274th VC/NVA Regiment and the D445 VC Battalion in Phuoc Tuy Province. All of the red units in that area were under strength:

- 33rd NVA Regiment: 1,221 men.
- 274th VC/NVA Regiment: 1,030 men.
- D445 VC Battalion: 190 men.

In addition there were 370 main force Viet Cong and 246 provincial force VC soldiers in Phuoc Tuy Province.

NVA Order of Battle 1972

In 1972, the NVA controlled 123 combat regiments and 646 maneuver battalions. That was the equivalent of fifty-four infantry divisions of twelve battalions each.

The communists launched their Easter Offensive (see Chapter 21) in early 1972. In South Vietnam's I Corps they committed their forces as follows:

NVA Units Attacking Across the DMZ 1-3/1972

Division	Regiments
304th	9th Infantry, 24th Infantry, 66th Infantry, 68th Artillery
308th	36th Infantry, 88th Infantry, 102nd Infantry
B-5 Front	126th Sapper, 31st Infantry, 207th Infantry, 246th Infantry, 84th Artillery (Rocket), 38th artillery, 203rd Armor, 204th Armor, 205th Armor

NVA Units Attacking From The A Shau Valley 1-3/1972

Division	Regiments
324th	29th Infantry, 803rd Infantry, 812th Infantry,
Independent	5th Infantry, 6th Infantry

NVA Second Echelon Reinforcing Units April-May 1972

Division	Operations
320th	This division conducted follow on attacks at Cam
48B Infantry Regiment	Lo, La Vang and Hai Lang.
64B Infantry Regiment	
325th	
18th Infantry Regiment	Participated in attack on Quang Tri City: 4/72
995th Infantry Regiment	Infiltrated 7/72.
101st Infantry Regiment	Fought at Ouang Tri 7-9/72

From January to March 1972, the 5th NVA Division was operating out of Cambodian Sanctuary Base 712 near Snoul. The 7th and 9th NVA Divisions were located in Cambodia's Dambe and Chup Plantations. In late March

1972 the 9th NVA Division began moving toward South Vietnam's Tay Ninh Province.

In April 1972, an NVA task force was still operating in III Corps' Phuoc Tuy Province. That 3,000 man force was composed of the 33rd NVA Regiment, the 274th VC Regiment and the D445 VC Battalion. In May, 192 attacks upon the provincial town of Dat Do, by the 33rd NVA Regiment, left the town in ruins.

By the end of 1972, NVA Group 559, in charge of the Ho Chi Minh Trail logistics corridor, controlled forty-five regimental-sized Binh Trams (literally "military stations"). Each Binh Tram logistics unit was a combined force of infantry, antiaircraft, engineers, transportation, depot facilities and administrative troops. Group 559 set up five Rear Services Divisions to control those Binh Trams:

- Division 571.
- Division 472.
- Division 473.
- Division 471.
- Division 470.

In the wake of the 1972 Easter Offensive, the NVA sent most of its forces into South Vietnam. With a total strength of 300,000 men, the Chu Luc then had in South Vietnam fourteen regular infantry divisions, thirty separate infantry regiments (ten more division equivalents) and numerous sapper, artillery, armored and antiaircraft regiments.

NVA Divisional Distribution 12/1972

SVN Military Region	NVA Divisions
1: DMZ Area	304, 308, 312, 320, 324B
1: South of Hai Van Pass	711, *NT-2
2:	NT-3, F-10, 968
3:	CT-7, *CT-9
4:	1. CT-5

Source: ARVN Intelligence, Note: *NT.CT. & F = ARVN designator codes

NVA Main Forces, Ceasefire Period, After 12/72

Military Region	DIVISIONS			REGIMENTS				
	Infantry	Arty	Flak	Infantry (Separate)	Sapper	Arty	Armor	Flak
MR 1	7	1		6	3	6	2	12
MR 2	3			5	1	2	1	
MR 3	2	1		8	2	2	1	
MR 4	2							
TOTAL 14		1	1	30	6	10	4	12

It is obvious that the NVA was a conventional army, but the above tables provide more conclusive evidence. The NVA host in South Vietnam in 1972 exhibited the following force distribution:

- Combat Forces: 57%
- Service Forces: 29%
- Guerrilla/Infrastructure: 14%

NVA Order of Battle in 1973

NVA Strength Ceasefire Period, After 12/72

Military Region	Combat Units	Rear Service Units & Administrative	Guerrillas & Infrastructure	TOTAL
MR 1	79,450	35,240	5,928	120,618
MR 2	31,200	18,500	11,017	60,717
MR 3	27,300	17,315	10,730	55,345
MR 4	29,050	14,065	13,325	56,440
TOTAL	167,000	85,120 men	41,000 men	293,120 men[620]

NVA Troops in South Vietnam's MR 1
1/73(71,350 troops) (150) = Number of men in unit

NVA B-5 Front, Quang Tri Province (47,200 troops)

Divisions: *325th* (5,000) Regts: 18,95,101; *320B* (3,500) Regts: 48B, 64B; *312th* (6,000) Regts: 141, 165, 209; *304th* (5,000) Regts: 9, 24B, 66.
Regiments, Infantry and Sapper: 27B 81,000); 31st (500); 126th Naval Sapper Group (500); 270B (1,000); DMZ Sapper Group (5 Bns, 1500).
Regiments, Armor: 202d (4Bns, 1500); 203d (4 Bns, 1500)
Regiments, Artillery: 45th (1,000); 58th (1,000); 68th (1,000); 84th (1,000); 164th (1,000); 166th (500).
Misc. Bns: 15th Sapper (150); 47th Inf (300); 75th AAA (150).

NVA Military Region Tri Thien (8,600 troops)

324B Division (Thua Thien-5,000) Regts: 29,803,812.
Regts, Inf (Thua Thien) 5th (1,000; 6th (1,000)
675B Arty Regt (Quang Tri-500)
Misc Bns (Thua Thien): 7th Sapper (200); 11th Recon (200); 35th Rocket (200); 582d Inf (300); Phu Loc Inf (200).

NVA Front-7, Quang Tri Province (750 troops)

Battalions: 808th Inf (250); 810th Sapper (250); 814th Inf (250).

NVA Troops in South Vietnam's MR 1
1/73(71,350 troops) (150) = Number of men in unit *(continued)*

NVA MR5, Quang Nam & Ouang Tin Provinces (9,800 troops)
Divisions: *711th* (3,500), Regts: 31,38,270; *2d* (4,000) Regts: 1,52,141.
Regts, Sapper: 45th (550); 5th (1,000)
572d Tank/Artillery Group (500).
Misc. Bns. (Quang Tin): 32 (Recon (150); 120th VC Montagnard Inf.
(100).

NVA Front-4 (3,300 troops)
Quang Nam, Misc. Bns: 1st NVA Inf (200); 2d NVA Inf (150); 42d VC
Recon (150); 80th NVA Inf (150); 83rd NVA Inf (150); 86th NVA Inf
(150); 89th NVA Sapper (200); 91st NVA Sapper (200); 471st NVA
Sapper (150); 575th NVA Arty (250); 577th NVA Arty (250).

Quang Tin, Inf Bns: 11th NVA (150); 70th NVA (150); 72d NVA (150);
74th VC (150).

Quang Ngai, Misc Bns: 38th NVA Inf (150); NVA Inf (150); 70th VC
Sapper (150); 107th NVA Rocket (100); 145th VC Inf. (150).

Separate Combat Platoons, All MR 1 (1,700)

NVA Troops in South Vietnam's MR 2
1/73 (25,550 troops)

NVA B-3 Front (12,350 troops)
Divisions: *320th* (3,000) Regts: 48,64; 10th (3,800) Regts: 28, 66, 95B.
Regiments: 24C Inf (800); 40th Arty (1,100); 400th Sapper (800).
Misc Bns: 2d NVA Inf (200); 5th NVA Inf (200); 28th NVA Recon (250);
297B
NVA Armor (200); 631st NVA Inf (250); Unknown Arty (200).

Knotum (P) Bns: 304th NVA Inf (250); 406th NVA Sapper (150).

Gia Lai(P) Bns: 2d NVA Inf (250); 45th VC Inf (150); 67th VC Inf (200);
408th VC Sapper (200).

Dar lac (P) Bns: 301st NVA Inf (200); 401st NVA Sapper (200).

NVA MR 5 (6,800 troops)

NVA Troops in South Vietnam's MR 2
1/73 (25,550 troops)

NVA B-3 Front (12,350 troops) (continued)

3d Division (3,500) Regts: 2,12,21.
405th NVA Sapper Bn. (150).

Binh Dinh (P) NVA Inf Bns: 50th (200); 53d (200); 53d, (150); 54th (200); 55th (200); 56th (200).

Phu Yen (P)NVA Bns: 9th Inf (150); 13th Inf (150); 14th Sapper (150); 96th Inf (150).

Khanh Hoa(P) Bns: 7th NVA Sapper (200); 12th NVA Inf (200); 407th NVA Sapper (200); 460th NVA Inf (200); 470th NVA Inf (200); 480th NVA Inf (200); Khanh Hoa VC Sapper (200).

VC MR 6 (1.250 troops)

Misc Bns: 130th NVA Arty (150); 186th NVA Inf(200); 240th NVA Inf (150); 481st VC Inf (200); 482d VC Inf (150); 810th NVA Inf (250); 840th NVA Inf (150).

VC MR 10
251st VC Inf Bn (150).

NVA Troops in South Vietnam's MR 3
1/73 (24,600 troops)

All Under COSVN Command
Divisions: *7th* (4,100) **Regts:** 141,165,209; *9th* (4,100) **Regts:** 95C,271,272.
Regts.
Inf: 201st (00); 205th (1,200); 271st (1,200); 101st (1,100); 33rd (1,200); 274th (900)
429th Sapper Command Headquarters (400); **29th Sapper Regt** (600); **Sapper Battalions:** 7, 8, 9, 10, 11, 12, 16 (1,400).
Separate Sapper Bns, NVA: 89th (150); 268th (150); 4th (150) 6th (150); 7th (150); 211th (150).
Separate Sapper Bns, Viet Cong: 10th (100); 12th (150).
Armor Bns: 3rd (200); 5th (200)
Artillery Bns: 35th Bn, 96th Arty Regt, NVA (250); 2d NVA (150); 74A NVA Rocket (150); 3d NVA (150); 8th VC (150); 74B NVA Rocket (150).

NVA Troops in South Vietnam's MR3
1/73 (24,600 troops) *(continued)*

Inf Bns, VC: 168th (150); 368th (150); 1st Tay Ninh (150); 6th (150); 20th (150); 445th (150); 9th (150); 269th (150); 508th (150).
Inf Bns, NVA: 14th (200); 1st (250); 2d (100); 4th (150) 267th (250); 506th (150).

Separate Combat Platoons, all MR 3 (2,800).

NVA Troops in South Vietnam's MR 4
1/73 (27,050 troops)

COSVN (11,700 troops)
Divisions: *1st* (3,400) Regts: 44 Sapper, 52, 101D; *6th* (2,300) Regts: 24, 207th; *5th* (3,900) Regts: 275,6,174.
Regts, Inf: Z-15 (900); Z-18 (700)
Artillery Bns: Bn/96th NVA Arty Regt (250); Bn/208th NVA Arty Regt 8250).

VC MR 2 (3,800 troops)
DT-1 Regt (600)
Misc Bns: 504th NVA Inf (200); 207th Sapper (100); 309th VC Arty (150).
NVA Sapper Bns: 267B (100); 281st (200).
VC Inf Bns: 209th (100); 268C (150); 271st (150); 278th (150); 279th (200); 295th (300); 310th (200); 512th (300); 516A (200); 516B (150); 590th (150); 502d (200); 514C (200).

VC MR 3 (5,750 troops)
Regiments: VC D-1 (600); NVA D-2 (900); VC D-3 (1,000); NVA 18B (900); NVA 95th (900).
962d NVA Inf Bn (100).
VC Sapper Bns: 2012D (150); 2014th (150).
VC Artillery Bns: 2311th (100); 2315th (100).
VC Inf Bns: Tay Do(100); U Minh 10th (250); U Minh 2d (100); 764th (150); 501st (150); 857th (100).
Separate Combat Platoons. All MR 4 (5,800)[621]

NVA Troops in South Vietnam January, 1973

Chu Luc Troops	MR 1	MR 2	MR 3	MR 4	Total
In Thousands	96	42	41	40	219
Combat Troops	71	25	25	27	148
*NVS Regulars	68	19	20	16	123
*Viet Cong	3	6	5	11	25
Service Troops	25	17	16	13	71
*NVA Regulars	19	9	5	1	34
*Viet Cong	6	8	11	12	37
Number of Divisions	8	3	2	3	16
Regimental HQ	54	11	13	16	94
Battalion HQ	195	73	77	79	424[622]

A Brief History and Organization: NVA Regular Divisions 1965–72

Division	Regiments	History
1st NVA Div.	44th Sapper, 52, 101D	Operated in II Corps area until after Tet 1968, then III Corps/Cambodia & IVC. Aka 630 Front & 32 1965–66: 88NVA, 174NVA, 40 NVA Art.
2nd	1, 52Vc, 141	Operated in I Corps area until 1971, then II Corps 1965–66: 1 VC, 3 NVA, 21 NVA 1966: 90 NVA, 141 NVA 1971: 1 NVA, 31 NVA, 141 NVA
3 Division	2, 12, 21	II Corps 1965–75. aka 610 NVA 1965–68: 2VC, 18 NVA, 22 NVA 1973: 33 NVA, 274 NVA
4th	D1 VC, 18B NVA, 95A NVA	IV Corps, 1974
5th	E6, 174, 205, 275	III Corps 1965–72. IV Corps 1973 1966: 274 VC, 275 VC 1967: 88 NVA, 101 NVA, 33 NVA, 84 Artv

A Brief History and Organization: NVA Regular Divisions 1965–72 (*continued*)

Division	Regiments	History
6th	DT1 VC.24 NVA, 207 NVA	IV Crops, 1973
7th	141,165,209	III Corps 1966–75 1965: 141 NVA. 165 NVA. 320 NVA
8th	Z15.Z18	IV Corps. 1974
9th	95C,271,272	III Corps 1965–75 1965–66: 271.272.273 VC/NVA.70 VC.101 NVA
10th 28, 66, 95B	II Corps, 1966–74	
304th	9,24B,66	I Corps and DMA 1965–74
308th	36,88,102	I Corps and DMZ 1965–74 1968: 31NVA, 36NVA, 38NVA
312th	141,165,209	Laos 1965–72
316th	—	Laos 1965–72
320th 320B	48,64	I Corps and DMA 1965–74 1964: 32, 95.101 NVA
324B	29,803,812	I Corps and DMZ 1965–74
325th	18,95,101	I Corps and DMZ 1965–74
711th	31,38,270	I Corps 1970–73 1971-572 Armored Artillery Regt.
968th	9,19,29	Laos. 1968–75 SVN 1975
75 Artillery	?	North Vietnam 1973
25 Engineer	?	I Corps 1973
25 Sapper	?	I Corps 1972, aka 27 Sapper
305 Sapper	?	North Vietnam 1965, aka 305 Airborne
477 Antiaircraft	?	North Vietnam, 1972, aka 377 Flak Div.
B-3 Front:	28, 66, 95B, 40 Artillery	II Corps 1965–74
B-5 Front:	27B, 31, 246, 270B, 38 Arty, 84 Artillery	DMZ 1965–74

A Brief History and Organization: NVA Regular
Divisions 1965–72 *(continued)*

Division	Regiments	History
Mil.Reg. 3:	D1 VC,D2 VC,D3 VC, 18B NVA,95 NVA	IV Corps
Mil. Reg. 2:	DT1 VC,86 NVA	IV Corps
Mil. Reg. Tri Thien Hue:	4NVA, 5NVA, 6NVA	I Corps
Indep.Regts:	24NVA. 101NVA. 271NVA	I & III Corps

PART IV.

Operations

CHAPTER 18

NVA Division Operations I

In April 1965, the 273rd Infantry Regiment of the 9th Viet Cong Infantry Division moved through War Zone C to jump-off positions near the South Vietnamese town of Song Be. The Regiment attacked the Song Be airfield, was caught in the open by American airpower, and driven back into the jungle. In what was the first NVA division sized operation of the Second Indochina War, the other two regiments of the 9th NVA Division got a toehold in Song Be, but were soon forced to retreat with the 273rd.

The next target was Dong Xoai and its U.S. Special Forces compound. While the 272nd Regiment attacked the town, the 271st and 273rd Regiments set ambushes along avenues of approach, hoping to destroy any rescue forces. Once again allied airpower drove off the 9th NVA Division.

In November 1965, the U.S. 1st Infantry Division and the ARVN 5th Infantry Division attacked the 9th Division's 271st and 273rd Regiments north of Lai Khe, along Highway 13. After six hours of aggressive fighting the 9th VC Division was driven off by allied helicopters.[623]

Also in 1965, another NVA Division force fought the allies at Plei Me and in the Ia Drang Valley. In the first part of that offensive the reds also tried the lure and ambush tactic.

In late 1965, the newly formed 3rd NVA Division again engaged the U.S. 1st Cavalry Division on Binh Dinh Province's coastal Bong Son Plains. There the 3rd NVA Division deployed its 2nd VC, 18th NVA and 22nd NVA regiments in a broad offensive arc attempting to decimate the ARVN 22nd Infantry Division.

Operating out of their bases in the Kim Son and An Lao Strongholds, the

18th and 22nd NVA Regiments maneuvered battalion size stabs against the ARVN division. When the 1st Cavalry and its heavy preponderance of airpower arrived, the two NVA regiments beat a hasty retreat.

After the initial beginnings of NVA division level combat, the art form seemed to languish. The Tet general offensive of 1968, in which a large number of separate battalions and regiments fought independently throughout South Vietnam, seemed to catalyze some metamorphosis. The NVA division-size battle was suddenly reborn in mid-1968, but first there was the bloodletting of the independent battalion and regimental battle, carried out on an unprecedented scale.

In the later phases of the 1968 Tet Offensive, the Chu Luc unleashed sustained divisional assaults. Divisional and multi-divisional offensives would continue throughout the next two years. In one campaign after another the NVA would ultimately drive all allied troops into coastal enclaves or defensive positions around Saigon and a few lesser cities. From that time forward the initiative was in the hands of the Chu Luc. From January 30, 1968 the reds won the war!

The Assault on Saigon: Tet 1968

On the morning of January 31, 1968 the 1st and 2nd VC Battalions seized part of the ARVN Joint General Staff compound in Saigon. Simultaneously, nine other NVA battalions struck throughout the Saigon-Cholon area. Included in that force were the: 3rd Di An, 4th Thu Duc, 5th Nha Be, 6th, 267th, 269th, 506th, and 508th Local Force VC Battalions, the 2nd Independent G.Mon Battalion and the C-10 Sapper Battalion. Those troops were part of a three-division (5th, 7th, and 9th NVA/VC Infantry Divisions), thirty-six-battalion, NVA effort to seize Saigon.

At the same time, more than six NVA regiments attacked throughout the Saigon area. The various communist attacks were distributed as follows:

- 275th VC Regiment and the U-1 VC Local Force Battalion attacked Long Binh supply base near Saigon.
- 274th VC Regiment attacked Bien Hoa Air Base.
- 238th VC LF Battalion struck III ARVN Corps Headquarters.
- 275th VC Regiment blocked Highway 1 north of Saigon.
- 271st VC Regiment, along with the 267th and D16 VC Battalions, hit Tan Son Nhut Air Base near Saigon.
- 101st NVA Regiment struck the ARVN depot complex at GO Vap near Saigon.

- 273rd VC Regiment blocked 1st U.S. Infantry Division reinforcing efforts north of Saigon.

The reds attacked from the north, south, east, and west. It was an amazing demonstration of military art and it almost worked. By the end of March, the huge red force had been driven from Saigon, but not before scaring the allied high command so badly that they relinquished the initiative to the Chu Luc.

Orchestrated to coincide with the assault on Saigon, urban areas were struck by the Chu Luc all over South Vietnam. The following urban areas were attacked by the Chu Luc units indicated:

- Da Nang: 2nd NVA Division spearheaded by the 402nd Sapper Battalion.
- Quang Tri: 812th NVA Regiment (K4, K5, K6 Battalions), along with the 10th VC Sapper and 814th VC Battalions.
- Tuy Hoa: 95th NVA Regiment.
- Ban Me Thuot: 33rd NVA Regiment and 301E VC LF Battalion.
- Pleiku: 15H Local Force and 40th Sapper Battalions.
- Kontum: 24th NVA Regiment, 304th VC Battalion and 406th Sapper Battalion.
- Phan Thiet: 482nd VC Local Force and 804th Main Force Battalions.
- Dalat: 145th and 186th VC Battalions.
- Song Be: 211th and 212th VC Infiltration Groups.
- My Tho: 261st, 263rd and 14th VC Battalions.
- Truc Giang: 516th and 518th VC Battalions.
- Vinh Long City: 306th, 308th and 857th VC Battalions.
- Khe Sahn: 304th (66th and 101st NVA Regiments) and 325C NVA Divisions. 95th (4th, 5th, 6th Battalions) and 101D NVA Regiments and the Van An Rocket Artillery Regiment.
- Hue: 4th NVA, 5th NVA, 6th NVA, 24th NVA, 90th NVA, 812th NVA, 803rd NVA Regiments; 810th VC Battalion, and 12th and Co Be Sapper Battalions.

To prove that they had not been defeated during the Tet Offensive, the NVA launched a Phase II Offensive in May 1968. It unfolded as follows:

- *First Surge* (May 5, 1968): VC Dong Nai Regiment and two VC battalions hit northeast Saigon. 272nd VC Regiment and 267nd VC Battalion hit west Saigon. Two Viet Cong battalions then attacked south Saigon.
- *Second Surge* (May 25, 1968) The same units attacked from the same

direction again with one exception. The Quyet Thang Viet Cong Regiment joined the attack against northeast Saigon.[624]

The Tet Attack on Hue

On the eve of the Tet Offensive it seemed that the number of allied combat battalions was nearly the same as the number of opposing communist battalions in I Corps.

However, more factors than the relative number of opposing battalions determined the pre-Tet correlation of forces in I Corps. The allied army was on the defensive, a configuration which entailed distinct advantages in itself. In addition, U.S. battalions, which were two to three times as large as NVA battalions, had a theoretical firepower edge of about 50% over the communists. Those factors increased the allied strength of approximately 96 battalion equivalents. Allied airpower increased the allied combat edge by at least another 30%.

Airpower, added to other force multipliers, increased the allied battalion firepower equivalent in I Corps to that of 125 NVA/VC battalions. Thus the allied defenders enjoyed at least a "2-to-1" advantage over the attackers. Most western military manuals claim that attackers require at least a 3-to-1 advantage over defenders in order to be assured of victory. Therefore it seemed that the reds had little hope of winning any victories in I Corps.

In late January 1968, the 324B NVA Infantry Division moved into the Song Bo River area near Hue. The division deployed its 90th, 803rd and 812th NVA Regiments to secure its supply dumps near Hue, then being held by two division equivalents of NVA troops. Nearby, the immediate rear base of the NVA Front command, masquerading as the 6th NVA Regiment and controlling sixteen to twenty battalions, was in the La Chu Woods held by the 29th NVA Regiment, with its 7th and 9th Infantry Battalions, of the 325C NVA Infantry Division. That regiment had recently infiltrated all the way from the Khe Sahn area.

On January 31, 1968 nine NVA battalions struck Hue from three directions, driving toward the Imperial Palace. That reinforced division sized force, supposedly the 6th NVA Regiment, had 196 specified targets or objectives and controlled the following forces in the first wave:

Communist versus allied battalions, I Corps 12/67

NVA = 46 battalions	US = 38 battalions
VC = 19 battalions	ARVN = 35 battalions
	Korean = 4 battalions
Total = 65 battalions	= 77 battalions[625]

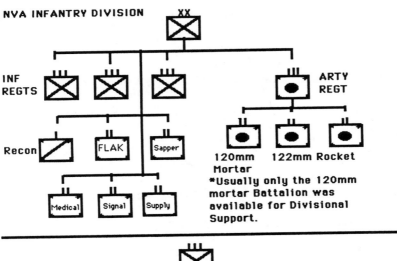

NVA INFANTRY DIVISION

INF REGTS

Recon   FLAK   Sapper

ARTY REGT

120mm Mortar   122mm   Rocket

Medical   Signal   Supply

*Usually only the 120mm mortar Battalion was available for Divisional Support.

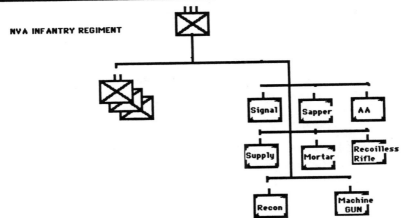

NVA INFANTRY REGIMENT

Signal   Sapper   AA

Supply   Mortar   Recoilless Rifle

Recon   Machine GUN

- 6th NVA Regiment (800th, 802nd, 806th Battalions); 4th NVA Regiment (K4B, K4C, 804th Battalions); 810th VC, 12th Sapper and Co Be Sapper Battalions.
- At least two 81/82mm mortar battalions, one 120mm mortar battalion, and one 122mm or 140mm rocket battalion

Within a few days of the NVA first wave's seizure of Hue, the following NVA forces reinforced the Hue Front:

- 5th NVA Regiment (416th Battalion).
- 90th NVA Regiment of the 324B NVA Infantry Division (with the 7th and 9th Battalions).
- 24th NVA Regiment (with the 4th and 6th Battalions) fresh from the attack on Kontum.[626]

By March 1968, the Hue Front was driven from Hue and retreated into the A Shau Valley from whence it came. However, fighting in the outskirts of Hue against the 324B and 325C NVA Divisions continued into June, 1968.

Soviet Maneuver Form Influences

In spite of their repetitive use of the ambush lure tactic at division level, the Chu Luc was already grappling, by 1968, with new division maneuver schemes, heavily influenced by the Soviets. The two primary forms of Soviet maneuver, the *Okhvat,* flanking maneuver, and the *Obkhod,* envelopment maneuver, as well as combinations of the two maneuvers, were highly valued by NVA commanders.

Soviet Divisional Maneuver Forms

- *Okhvat:* The flanking maneuver focuses upon relatively shallow penetration of the enemy flanks and rear. The maneuver is initiated through "gaps" in enemy battle formations identified by reconnaissance probes.
- *Obkhod:* The envelopment maneuver is deeper and requires the enemy to turn and fight in a new direction. It could be launched without a requirement for fire support coordination against both enemy formational gaps and open flanks.[627]

From 1966 forward, one objective of the Chu Luc would be to employ its divisional units in order to achieve one or both of the Soviet maneuver forms. Although the Chu Luc was not able to execute that array before the Easter

Offensive of 1972, NVA divisional commanders began to school themselves in Soviet-style maneuver applications.

The Forward Detachment

The advance, or forward, detachment is also a Soviet military maneuver art form. Its Chu Luc application rquired the shaping of subordinate NVA units as facilitative organisms charged with complementing, protecting and preserving the power and maneuver scheme of attacking North Vietnamese infantry divisions. Calling them leading, or independent forces, the NVA usually deployed two or more infantry battalions or regiments in the role of advance detachments.

NVA leading forces, or advance detachments, acted in relation to the maneuver of the division they spearheaded. Leading forces were assigned a variety of missions, including:

- Launching leading attacks which engaged the enemy along the primary divisional assault route and/or inflicted casualties, freezing him in place.
- Executing diversionary attacks in order to draw enemy forces and/or attention away from the main effort.
- Replacing divisional units as temporary attachments.
- Conducting covering movements and anti-recon screens.
- Seizing key objectives in front of the advancing division.
- Conducting withdrawals as a rear guard.
- Disrupting enemy forces in front of the main force by cutting lines of communication.

The main purpose of NVA advance detachments was to preserve the integrity of the primary strike force. That mission sometimes required the absorption of enemy counterforce efforts and resultant casualties. Preservation of NVA assault division striking power maintained the primary striking force as an intact cohesive unit, along the route of main effort.

The NVA considered it very important to continue attacking for as long as possible. Advance detachments, combined with some reinforcement by divisional regiments, facilitated sustained operations. However, during the period of 1968–71, the Chu Luc frequently misused their echeloning and dissipated their divisional attacks by employing their regiments in sequential assaults. Although such methods enabled the reds to maintain fresh assaulting forces, they allowed the allies to defend against each regiment in turn. Thus many pre-1972 NVA divisional and multi-divisional attacks degenerated into a piecemeal commitment of regiments. Such deployment invariably led to defeat in detail.

Advance detachments were used to seize objectives and strike enemy units in order to facilitate friendly maneuver. That mission might require assigning one or more of several tasks.

Advance Detachment Missions

- Break through an enemy covering force.
- Attack enemy reserves.
- Conduct operational pursuit of the enemy.
- Strike enemy flanks and rear.
- Seize important terrain, such as defiles and river crossing points, to facilitate maneuver.
- Seize important facilities such as headquarters, communications centers, airfields, and POL storage facilities.
- Destroy enemy supplies and equipment including: artillery, aircraft, ammunition dumps or key logistics nodules.
- Delay enemy air-amphibious landings, or ground incursions.
- Detect, isolate and destroy enemy special troops.
- Decapitate enemy forces by killing leadership (Blossoming Lotus).
- Divert the enemy's attention and/or reserves by attacking.
- Destroy enemy security screens.
- Spearhead an attack.
- Probe for enemy gaps or breach points.

Leading units gave depth to the NVA battlefield by giving Chu Luc commanders forward reach. By striking the enemy from several directions, while a main effort force approached from two or more directions, a partial paralysis could occur within the enemy array.

Advance detachments could fight independently if the main effort force was diverted. Although their overall mission was to create and sustain favorable conditions for the main effort, forward detachments represented offensive power themselves. If the situation required it, advance detachments could be converted into units with offensive thrust missions.

Unit missions determined individual advance detachment organization and strength. That mission also defined the time, depth and duration of unit commitment.

There were five types of NVA Advance Detachments: Reconnaissance, Diversionary, Raiding, Forward and Turning. Reconnaissance detachments were charged with reconnoitering enemy forces and terrain immediately in front of the advancing division. They moved just ahead of the main assault unit and could deliver immediate warning of important changes on the battlefield.

Diversionary detachments had the mission of deceiving the enemy as to the friendly forces direction of main effort and intentions. In addition, they had a special missions character that might require them to destroy important enemy command, communications or other objectives within the enemy's deep rear. They were sometimes utilized to influence enemy operational and strategic planning by spreading false rumors and panic while leaving misleading indicators in the enemy rear. At the same time, they secured any available enemy operational or strategic intelligence data.

Raiding detachments could also divert enemy attention. They struck objectives that threatened the mission of the main effort, or in the enemy rear. They sought to disorganize the tactical-operational rear of the enemy by spreading panic at that level. They were usually dispatched to destroy enemy forces and/or objectives, but not to hold them.

Forward detachments faciliated the scheme of maneuver for a larger force. They captured key heights, passes, and other objectives in the enemy rear. Their missions usually required them to hold what they seized until relieved by the main effort.

Turning detachments were charged with disrupting enemy defenses by attacking from unexpected directions. They might infiltrate enemy lines and then strike from the rear. Or they might maneuver through theoretically impassable terrain to hit an enemy weak spot. They sought to force an enemy reaction out of proportion to the size of the Turning Detachment.

Five Types of Offensive Advance Detachments

Reconnaissance		Diversionary Raiding		Forward	Turning
Organization level	Front.div. rgt	Front	Front. div. rgt	Front. div. rgt*	Div. rgt. bn
Strength	Company to Regiment	Squad to Company	Battalion to Regiment	Battalion to Regiment	Company to Battalion
Depth in enemy rear	15-90km	50-150km	15-40km	5-60km	5-30km
Duration of action	Unlimitd	Unlimited	Up to 2 days	Up to 1 day	Up to 1 day
Main Body arty support	No	No	Frequently	yes	Rarely
Reunite with *main body*	No	No	Yes	Yes	Yes

Source: Rand Document DS 1873; Legend: *Div = division, rgt = regiment, bn = battalion

The 320th NVA Infantry Division at Dai Do

By April 1968, most NVA divisions were practicing the new division maneuvers. For whatever reason, however, few communist divisions demonstrated much knowledge of the maneuver, or even executed it properly.

When elements of the 320th NVA Infantry Division engaged two U.S. Marine battalions in I Corps' Dai Do, near the DMZ, the reds fought their battle in an attrition oriented manner. Ten companies of the 320th's 48th and 52nd Regiments, about 1,000 men, had moved as advance detachment to screening positions in front of the division, along Quang Tri Province's Cua Viet River. This effort was part of Tet II, a new enemy operational and strategic level offensive which struck in every one of South Vietnam's four Corps areas. Besides proving that the, only three months' previous, Tet Offensive had not hurt the Chu Luc, Tet II marked the second phase of the enemy's new divisional maneuver schemes.

The ten advance detachment companies of the 48th and 52nd NVA Regiments had infiltrated south along the Jones Creek Infiltration Route from the DMZ in late February and early March 1968. Their infiltration had

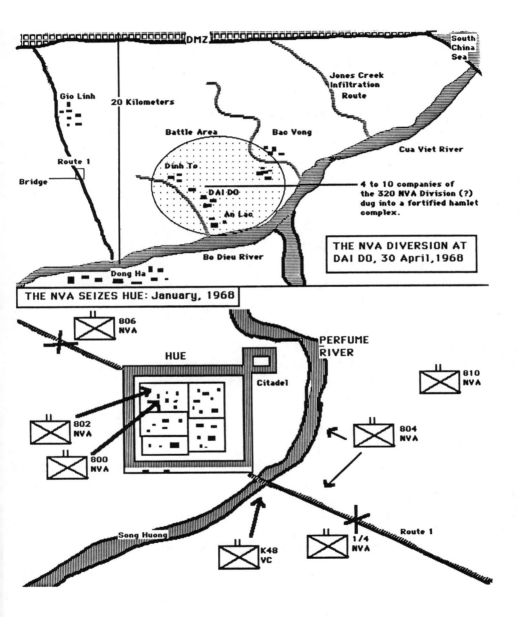

THE NVA DIVERSION AT DAI DO, 30 April, 1968

4 to 10 companies of the 320 NVA Division (?) dug into a fortified hamlet complex.

THE NVA SEIZES HUE: January, 1968

placed them about fifteen miles inside South Vietnam, in a string of abandoned hamlets near the intersection of the Cua Viet and Bo Dieu Rivers.

The reds took time to fortify the abandoned hamlets of Thuong Do, An
Lac, Dong Huan, Dinh To and Dai Do. Fortification of those hamlets was
enhanced by the presence of thick vegetation, hedgerows, and banana and
palmetto trees in the area.

On April 30, 1968 the NVA troops began interdiction operations, attacking a navy patrol boat in the Cua Viet River. They fired on the naval craft
from a V shaped string of abandoned hamlets. Those hamlets were located
two and one-half kilometers northeast of the U.S. Marine base at Dong Ha,
thirteen kilometers west of the Gulf of Tonkin and thirteen kilometers south
of the DMZ. The red forward detachment, or screening force, in Dong Ha
would have had to cross several obstacles to get to Dong Ha, including a
river, an open coastal plain and a major highway. None of those open spaces
offered much in the way of covered or concealed avenues of approach.

A U.S. Marine rifle company was dispatched to reconnoiter the NVA
fortified area. Soon the marine rifle company, depending mainly on massive
naval, air and artillery bombardment support, began fighting through the
NVA bunkers, spider holes and trenchlines, seizing the hamlet of Dong
Huan. Then the predictable buildup of American fire support began, as the
marines began their usual method of feeding troops into battle piecemeal.
The NVA troops were not very aggressive and recoiled before the massive
bombardment.

The next morning, instead of that night, marine fire support destroyed
NVA troops massing for a counterattack. Then the marines attacked Dai Do
hamlet where they encountered strong defensive works:

"The bunkers were A-frame in design, constructed of concrete and heavy
bamboo, 8 to 10 inches thick. Layered with rice mats, dirt and straw, they
were surprisingly impervious to collapse from heavy vehicles, such as tanks,
The bunkers were connected by tunnels and interlocking fields of fire that
were so well camouflaged the attacking Marines were unaware of their
presence until almost on top of them.

"Another obstacle encountered . . . was the barbed wire strung around the
enemy enclaves. Razor sharp, the taut metal cable would whip in every
direction if cut, causing serious injury."[628]

The marine attack bogged down as enemy counterattacks hit them in their
rear. It was then that the battalion commander learned that he was facing ten
to twelve companies of the 320th NVA Division. Highly given to exaggeration, the marines soon claimed that "one marine battalion was taking on the
whole NVA division."[629] If the reds had used similar criteria they could have

reported to Hanoi, "a few companies of Bo Dai took on the whole 3rd Marine Amphibious Force."

Red outflanking counterattacks nearly destroyed the marines, who were saved again and again by fire support. The fact that the NVA units utilized very little of the fire support which could have been provided by numerous NVA 130mm gun, rocket, or mortar batteries then hidden in the nearby DMZ, indicated that the Chu Luc force was not fighting a major battle.

Yet, after the reds withdrew a few miles, the marines began crowing about "a major defeat of the 320th NVA Division."[630] Supposedly "the 320th NVA Division was attacking south towards Dong Ha and then on to Quang Tri City ten miles further south." Amazingly, "one heroic marine battalion stopped the offensive, killed over 1500 red troops, and drove the communists out of the area."[631] The claims of marine success were exaggerated. What was probably closer to the truth was quite different. Actually the dug-in NVA advance detachment was of unknown size. It could have consisted of three to six NVA companies, 600 men, deployed in the hamlet string.

The NVA companies were bombarded and forced back by a reinforced marine battalion *and* an ARVN mechanized battalion of the 2nd ARVN Regiment. At least three 12.7 mm heavy antiaircraft machineguns were spotted during the battle. Such weapons were found in an NVA regiment's antiaircraft company, but that doesn't mean that a whole regiment was on the scene. There were no signs that the action was related to an offensive by the 320th NVA Division. In fact, there was no real evidence that the troops engaged represented any sizable percentage of the 320th NVA Division. The enemy casualty figures, for example, were grossly exaggerated.

Supposedly, the "beaten and ineffective 320 NVA Division launched yet another desperate assault against Dong Ha, only twenty two days later."[632] On May 25, 1968 one communist battalion, supposedly from the 320th Division, was encountered six miles northeast of Dong Ha at Nhi Ha. It was even further from Dong Ha than Dai Do. However, Nhi Ha was located along the Jones Creek Infiltration Route. That infiltration route north of Dai Do, was an important supply artery habitually utilized by all red troops operating in the area.

One author, depending on highly colored marine accounts for his facts, depicted that NVA battalion's presence as "another (attempted) strike at the Marine Combat Support Base of Dong Ha."[633] He described the short skirmish, after which fifteen enemy bodies were discovered, with great exaggeration. He finished his side bar by proclaiming: "The 'Magnificent Bastards' had done it again. The 320th NVA Division, at least temporarily, was rendered 'combat ineffective.'" How could an engagement against one battalion, from a division controlling twenty battalions, render that division "combat ineffective?"[634]

It is also obvious that the 320th NVA Division was not engaged in any attempt to take Dong Ha in 1968. More than one battalion would have been needed for that mission.

Marine Brigadier General William Weise, whose career was helped by his command of the U.S. Marine battalion at Dai Do, very carefully avoided claiming that the 320th NVA was interrupted on its way to attack Dong Ha. He only characterized that interpretation as a possibility. General Weise indicated that he really didn't understand why elements of the 320th NVA fought at Dai Do: "What was the 320th Division trying to do? Why was it in the Dai Do area? I can't be sure . . . We may never know for certain. But if the 320th Division *had* planned to attack Dong Ha . . . then BLT 2/4 had conducted a successful . . . spoiling attack."[635]

However, General Wiese didn't hesitate to exaggerate when he wrote: "How badly was the 320th NVA Division hurt at Dai Do? I'm not sure, but much of its fighting effectiveness was destroyed."[636] The evidence, including General Weise's own words, do not substantiate such claims. He gave as substantiation that the two allied battalions were facing major elements of the 320th NVA Division the following evidence: "We had taken prisoners from two of its (320th NVA Division) four regiments. One of them told us that there were 12 NVA companies in the village of Dai Do alone . . . I believed the prisoner's story."[637]

There is no reason to believe the uncorroborated testimony of one enemy prisoner. Besides, Dai Do was a hamlet, not a village. It was physically impossible, and militarily incredible, to presume that twelve to sixteen hundred NVA could, or would, squeeze into one hamlet, which could accommodate one battalion at most. Such behavior violated the Chu Luc battle doctrine, the famous NVA common sense, and the physical capability of available space.

Even if the U.S. Marines had gleefully counted the corpses of two full NVA regiments after the battle, a total of 3,600 to 5,000 men, they could not claim that such destruction had destroyed the 320th's "fighting effectiveness." The division could have fought on with its other two full-strength regiments. The madcap exaggeration engaged in by many, supposedly responsible, Vietnam-era U.S. military commanders was quite common.

What is known for certain is that the enemy troops defending the seven hamlets around Dai Do were not properly led. Since the hamlets were arranged in a V shape with two flanking hamlets, the reds should have fought a withdrawing battle along both arms of the V, toward their bases to the northwest. That in effect is what they did. However, the red commander needlessly sacrificed troops by massing them in the open: "large numbers of enemy troops in the open fields northwest of Dai Do. We called in air, artillery, and mortar fire."[638]

In addition there was evidence that the NVA trenchlines were dug improperly, without zig zags: "Several times Echo marines gained the flank of trench lines and placed killing, enfilade fire on large numbers of NVA soldiers who remained to die in their positions."[639]

The marine battalion had also been poorly handled. It attacked straight ahead, right into the enemy defensive works. The marines failed to notice the opportunity to cut off the enemy force from its line of retreat. That failure cost the marines a lot of unnecessary casualties.

When the 1st Battalion, 3rd Marines arrived to relieve the 2/4 on May 3, after the reds had already pulled out, they found: "BLT 2/4 had four rifle companies with 1 officer and 40 marines each at the perimeter at Dai Do."[640] Enough 2/4 Battalion marines were left to form one rifle company, out of a battalion which contained over 1,000 men when at full strength.

At the beginning of the battle, the 2/4 Battalion controlled: four rifle companies, an 81mm mortar platoon, a 4.2 inch (107mm) mortar battery, a recon platoon, a tank platoon, an engineer platoon, a 105mm howitzer battery, an amphibian tractor platoon and a headquarters and service company. The prescribed strength of a marine rifle company was over two hundred men in May, 1968.

The enemy force was poorly placed for the actions which the marines claimed it intended. The NVA were hemmed into a U shaped configuration with streams on its immediate flanks and a major river to its front. On the NVA's deep left flank was the South China Sea coast (10 to 12 kilometer away). On its deep right flank was Highway 1 (3 kilometers away).

Why didn't the Marines close the bottleneck between Nhi Ha Hamlet and the Highway 1 bridge, already guarded by a U.S. Marine rifle company, and then drive south into the enemy rear? Naval river craft, along with troops deployed opposite the enemy units along the Bo Dieu River, could have sealed the southern area.

CHAPTER 19

NVA Division Operations II

The Tet Offensive, which began in late January 1968, was part of a two-year Chu Luc offensive effort extending into 1970. That offensive effort would feature the deployment of NVA corps-sized forces practicing the new divisional maneuver methods.

One NVA division was used in the central DMZ area to prepare for that future operational level effort. From the DMZ north of the U.S. Marine outpost at the Rockpile, westward toward the area north of Cam Lo, the 320th NVA Division established its suzerainty.

The 320th NVA Division Prepares a Bridgehead

Around February 1968, the 320th probably began preparing its deployment area for an offensiv stab into north central Quang Tri Province. That effort had two preliminary components:

1. A diversionary detachment of two to three battalions masquerading as elements of the 320th's 48th and 52nd Regiments was dispatched to the Dai Do area. Those diversionary units initiated combat two and one-half kilometers from Dong Ha in April and May, 1968. Dai Do drew marine attention and reserves away from the central DMZ.
2. Stockpiling and fortification of several invasion routes was intensified.

The intention of the 320th NVA Division was to establish a well-fortified war zone bridgehead, encompassing the area from the central DMZ to Route 9, in 1968. That bridgehead would serve as a fortified base and maneuver

hinge for massive influx of red troops to be introduced into the area south of
the DMZ in 1969.[641]

The 320th spread its three regiments in a forward screening deployment to
shield intensified construction of the new central DMZ bridgehead area. Its
regiments were deployed as follows:

- 64th NVA Regiment (6th, 7th, and 8th Battalions): north of Cam Lo. The
  marines thought that this regiment "anchored the (320th) Division's
  eastern flank (capable of) attacking south via the Mutter's Ridge area with a
  three part mission which included the interdiction of Route 9, the initiation of ambush and counter-sweep operations south of Route 9 as well as
  attacks upon the Cam Lo and Mai Loc resettlement areas."[642] The marines
  were wrong. Route 9 was not important at that time.
- 52nd NVA Regiment: "in a wide arc extending from the Razorback area to
  the Nui Tia Pong Massif, thereby flanking Route 9 as it curved around the
  marine base at the Rockpile."[643]
- 48th NVA Regiment: In division reserve, the 48th was deployed northwest
  of the Razorback area. From there it covered the division's west flank, and
  participating in construction activities.

Relying upon an in-place maze of infiltration routes and fortified areas, the
320th set about stockpiling supplies and fortifying the bridgehead. Way
stations, a night's march apart, facilitated an increasing cache and fortification effort. Throughout early- and mid-1968, huge numbers of civilian
laborers and porters worked in the 320th's zone.

East of Mutter's Ridge, the reds constructed Route 1022 South, plunging
due south, straight out of North Vietnam. The road followed the Ben Hai
River eastward, crossed over underwater bridges, then ran due south several
kilometers into South Vietnam. Civilian conscript labor reinforced the road
with logs so that it could withstand the pressure of heavy artillery tractors.

Many explosions were set off in the area as the land was cleared, never
alerting the allied forces hiding in their coastal enclaves miles away. Along
the route were huge construction base camps, with their large caches of TNT,
which such a major roadbuilding effort required. Naturally, painstaking
camouflage, against aerial surveillance, masked the effort.

Route 1022 South crossed the Ben Hai River at three different locations by
underwater bridges. When the marines drew near to the road, they heard
artillery prime movers withdrawing heavy artillery back across those bridges.
Near the southern end of the road in South Vietnam, positions for 152mm
gun howitzers, 85mm guns and numerous protective antiaircraft guns were

dug. The fortified NVA gun pits were sited to fire toward both Cam Lo and Thon Son Lam. Hundreds of rounds of 152mm ammunition were also cached in the area.

Soviet artillery prime movers, including the Soviet Medium Tracked Artillery Tractor ATS-26, were used to move the artillery pieces into position for firing. A prime mover unit stood ready to move the guns back out again whenever necessary.

The solidly constructed NVA gun pit artillery positions, afforded protection from anything but a direct hit: "The depth of the gun pits was seven feet and the two 8-foot wide entrances were obliqued at a 30 degree angle. An underground bunker was located outboard from the gun pit and afforded protection for the crew. Opposite the crew bunker was a small ammunition storage area with a capacity for 8–10 rounds."[644]

Enough artillery positions were dug in the area to support at least two artillery battalions. A truck park was established nearby also. Numerous caches, in packages of 250 to 450 rounds of 152mm howitzer, 85mm gun and antiaircraft ammunition, were also hidden in the area. Around the artillery areas, the enemy also stockpiled food, rockets and weapons.

Southwest of Con Thien, the 64th NVA Regiment screened another series of fortified stockpile areas. Although rolling, open terrain to the east constricted their operations and movements, the communists had constructed hundreds of stocked bunkers in the area and along the floor of the Cam Lo River Valley.

Around, and on, Mutter's Ridge were dozens of well-constructed NVA storage bunkers. Marines later found many of the enemy prepared sites "down the southern slopes of Mutter's Ridge, numerous new platoon and company size bunker complexes were found, each complex leading to a more sophisticated one farther south along the slopes.

"The most significant finds were a storage area for an enemy supply battalion and what appeared to be a regimental command post. The supply cache included over 1500 82mm mortar rounds, 119 RPG rounds, 15,000 AK-47 rounds and 1600 rounds of 12.7 ammunition.

"The complex contained messhalls, kitchens, and 60mm and 82mm mortar pits. A Chinese field phone communications system and extensive ammunition storage bunkers were also found. Four hundred pounds of captured TNT were required to destroy the ammunition and the bunkers."[645]

The 64th NVA Infantry Regiment fought delaying actions against U.S. Marine troops who entered its screening areas in August and September 1968. The 8th Battalion of the 64th Regiment fought the marines on Mount

Kho Xa. The 7th Battalion of the 64th Regiment fought the marines north of Mutter's Ridge.

In September 1968, elements of the 48th NVA Regiment reinforced the spread-out 52nd NVA Regiment, defending the withdrawal of NVA supplies north of Mutter's Ridge. U.S. Marine patrols discovered numerous supply dumps and other facilities in the area. Many red supply dumps were located along the ridges and peaks of nearby Nui Tia Pong and Nui Ba Lao Mountains. The marines "uncovered over 55,000 pounds of rice, 11,000 pounds of salt, 4,000 pounds of TNT, 3,400 82mm mortar rounds, and 390,000 rounds of AK-47 ammunition."[646]

Nearby, another huge NVA supply dump and headquarters complex was discovered which included "a regimental supply area located along a high narrow ridge, this cache include over 10,000 82mm mortar rounds; 13,000 Chinese Communist hand grenades; plus 3,000 anti-personnel mines and hundreds of 122mm, 140mm and 107mm rockets."[647]

The jubilant marines, crowing about "defeating the 320th NVA Division and driving it back into North Vietnam," missed the point. The huge complex, under construction for months and years, under their very nose, meant that the days of the marines in I Corps were closely numbered. The huge dump areas, protected by the 320th NVA Division, were intended as support areas for an army, an army that was preparing to occupy all of northern Quang Tri Province.

The marines poured on the airpower and drove hard to "kill NVA." But even they were a little confused about the situation: "The enemy's continued use of delaying tactics (very limited objective attacks, small unit ambushes employing claymore mines, harassing mortar fire) indicated that the 320th Division was attempting to gain time in order to escape north."[648] The marines were right that time, but they interpreted the reasons wrongly. The 320th was not beaten and in headlong retreat. it withdrew because it knew four things:

1. By withdrawing it avoided annihilation by B-52 bombardment.
2. The marines had discovered only a portion of the fortified bridgehead redoubt.
3. The marines would pull out quickly and the 320th could roll back in, even quicker.
4. The creation of the huge central bridgehead redoubt south of the DMZ would not be prevented by the U.S. marines.

The reds were right, too. By mid-1969, the marines didn't dare venture into the area in battalion strength, any more: "By march 1969 there were five NVA regiments and two VC regiments in Quang Tri and Thug Thien provinces . . . All the (NVA) . . . were very young. Clothes khaki, weapons well kept. Some kids probably 14–16, fought bravely. Very fair complexion and features more regular than our ARVN soldiers. There is not a hill west of Con Thien and in particular approaching the DMZ that is not occupied by the (NVA). They can be seen in the hundreds everywhere. . . The hills in the (south of the) DMZ are well fortified and bunkers and personnel are easily seen. Much Russian material in the area. NVA food consists of rice, baked hard with granulated sugar, not bad eating. Tinned meat, fish. Rucksacks in good conditions."[649]

The 1968 Tet Third Phase Offensive in III Corps

By August 1968 the communists had already conducted two Tet offensives and then launched number three. Yet it is doubtful if the Third Tet Offensive was really an offensive; it might have been a diversion. That's what U.S. Headquarters in Saigon thought.

The very intimidated U.S. high command was busy stacking three concentric circles of U.S. and ARVN battalions around Saigon in a desperate attempt to keep the reds out. Huddling terrified in their air conditioned condos at Disneyland East, MACV commanders were not looking at the situation with the coolness under fire demanded of combat "frontline" generals.

Another factor which contaminated Vietnam war leadership was the reporting resorted to by the losing U.S. high command. Besides exaggerating body counts and disguising their own casualty figures, U.S. commanders began falsifying combat after-action reports during the war.

Since the war, pro-military writers have used those falsified reports to write slanted stories about the Vietnam War. Now practically every book on the Vietnam War is full of distortions.

Some of America's best Vietnam combat officers were lieutenant colonels such as David Hackworth and others who left or were forced out of the service because they were frankly critical of its corrupt amateurism and deceits. Colonel Hackworth in his revealing tome, *About Face,* revealed numerous deceits carried out during the Vietnam War by American officers intent upon falsifying records so that posterity would reward malfeasance. One example of that self-serving military deceit was the document entitled *"History of the Battle of Thank Phu, 11-12 March 1969."* According to Colonel Hackworth, a participant in the battle, their after-action report was: "the quintessential false report. The absolute, ultimate snow job . . . the perfect hoax; the faker outfaking the fakers . . . a bogus, zero-defect report that was being used as a bona fide teaching aid in Vietnam, in the U.S., and God only knew where else."[650]

One account of the Tet III Offensive, *The Infantry Brigade in Combat,*[651] may also include some self-serving material. Several marked red flags dot its pages with clues to either exaggeration or outright deception. The report covers the eleven-day offensive which supposedly pitted the reinforced 5th and 9th NVA Infantry Divisions against an understrength brigade of the U.S. 25th Infantry Division. Supposedly the NVA "enemy launched thirteen attacks of battalion and/or regimental strength against the units of the 1st Brigade", (U.S. 25th Infantry Division).[652]

All enemy casualty figures were calculated by the Americans as "estimates of dead and two times that for wounded." The reason? "the 1st Brigade CO ordered his units to respect . . . and to honor the enemy dead by not violating their graves with exhumation in order to count their bodies . . . the 1st Brigade's units were permitted to estimate . . . enemy casualties in a given operation and cautioned to be very conservative in such estimates."[653] Careers were also riding on those body counts!

Another dead giveaway of the self-serving and exaggerated nature of American after-action reports was the widespread use of self-praising adjectives. For example, instead of stating "the task force withdrew," military chroniclers would write, "the task force skillfully effected its withdrawal."

Even more blatantly self-serving were such statements as, "The defeat of the enemy ambush was largely due to the professionalism and fighting spirit of the 1st Brigade."[654] How could military writers claim that American units were professional when they rotated back home every twelve months, and to the rear constantly. Seventy-five percent of the 1st Brigade's rifle platoons in 1968 were commanded by young sergeants with less than two years' total military service, and only a few months' sporadic combat experience? Where is the professionalism there?

The NVA Situation: Tet III

Supposedly the 1st Brigade, 25th Infantry Division defeated an enemy force in eleven days of battle near II Corps' Tay Ninh City. That force was supposedly composed of two NVA divisions, plus one NVA regiment, two antiaircraft battalions and two Viet Cong infantry battalions. According to U.S. reports, the order of battle of the operational level NVA command which fought in Tay Ninh from 17 to 27 August 1968 was impressive.

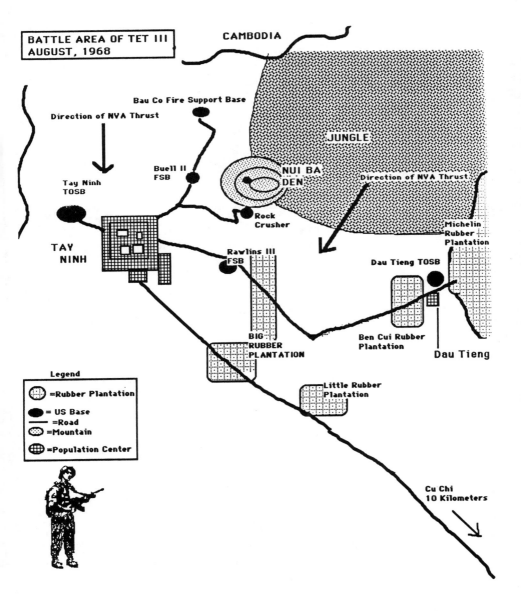

BATTLE AREA OF TET III
AUGUST, 1968

CAMBODIA

JUNGLE

Bau Co Fire Support Base

Direction of NVA Thrust

Buell II
FSB

NUI BA
DEN

Direction of NVA Thrust

Tay Ninh
TOSB

Rock
Crusher

Michelin
Rubber
Plantation

TAY
NINH

Rawlins III
FSB

Dau Tieng TOSB

BIG
RUBBER
PLANTATION

Ben Cui Rubber
Plantation

Dau Tieng

Legend

⊙ =Rubber Plantation
● = US Base
—— =Road
◎ =Mountain
⊞ =Population Center

Little Rubber
Plantation

Cu Chi
10 Kilometers

413

5th NVA Infantry Division Tay Ninh area: Aug. 1968

- 271st Infantry Regiment
- 272nd Infantry Regiment
- 273rd infantry Regiment
- 1 NVA antiaircraft battalion attached

9th NVA Infantry Division Tay Ninh area: Aug. 1968

- 33rd NVA Infantry Regiment
- 174th NVA Infantry Regiment
- 275th NVA Infantry Regiment
- 1 NVA antiaircraft battalion attached

NVA Leading Detachment Unit Tay Ninh area: August 68

- 88th NVA Infantry Regiment
- 2 Viet Cong Infantry battalions (each with five rifle companies) attached

The first noticeable potential error in the U.S. Army's official report is found in the above listed order of battle. During the Vietnam War, the 9th NVA always commanded the 271st, 272nd and 273rd Regiments and the 5th NVA usually commanded the 33rd, 274th and 275th Regiments. What are the real facts here?

According to the military, NVA infantry regiments participating in Tet III "had an estimated strength of two thousand four hundred officers and men (approximately eight hundred men per battalion)."[655] Each unidentified antiaircraft battalion had an "estimated strength of two hundred personnel." Those figures mean that the reds outnumbered the U.S. 1st Brigade eight to one.

Is it even probable that the reds were content to forego the advantage of such numerical superiority, preferring to conduct sequential, piecemeal attacks for eleven days? Such behavior violates NVA doctrine, their emphasis upon mass, and common sense. What is closer to the truth is that the enemy probably conducted eleven days of diversionary assaults by five or six NVA battalions, two Viet Cong battalions and two antiaircraft companies.

The primary probable intent of those attacks was to demonstrate that the NVA was still vigorous and in control of the initiative. In addition, the Chu Luc was probably conducting a diversion. They were probably also testing

American reaction to a series of attacks contesting U.S. control of Tay Ninh Province.

If the reds were conducting a full scale offensive, their forces would have probably attacked simultaneously in several areas of the front. NVA forces were appropriately deployed in the area for deep battle maneuvering.

One such force was the 88th NVA Regiment, located north of the Michelin Plantation, and on the American right flank during the battle. The 88th could have been intended as a rear blocking or outflanking force against the U.S. main supply route, South Vietnamese Route 22. But the 88th stayed put during the battle and never moved close enough to constitute a threat.

There were indications that the enemy was also practicing the deployment of forward detachments: "1st Brigade forces frequently contacted enemy platoon and company sized units . . . in the jungles close to 1st Brigade bases in the TAOR."[656] The Americans thought that the NVA troops were reconnaissance and battlefield preparation troops intent on building forward assembly areas for the attack. Such measures were unnecessary. The reds had controlled the area for several decades and already had numerous fortified bases, assembly areas, and tunnel systems hidden in nearly every area terrain feature which offered cover and concealment.

The reds had all the advantages of terrain too, since their main routes and camps were hidden in the jungled area. They also controlled Tay Ninh's Nui Ba Den, or Mountain of the Black Virgin. From that mountain, the only one in Tay Ninh, they could observe all of Tay Ninh Province and every movement made by the Americans in their nearby base camps. The mountain contained an important NVA headquarters and was probably defended by two infantry battalions. The Americans thought the cost of assaulting the red cave position was too high. There was, however, an American communications facility, defended by a weak rifle company, located on the top of the mountain during the eleven day battle.

The Black Virgin Mountain also looked down on the NVA's primary north-south infiltration route. Oxcart and porter convoys made daily runs from Cambodia through War Zone C and on through Ben Cui and Michelin Rubber Plantation. Only the rubber plantations controlling the infiltration routes were strongly defended by the reds during Tet III.

The American Situation: Tet III

The 1st Brigade, 25th Infantry Division was under strength and out on a limb in August 1968. The other two brigades of the 25th Division were dug in at Cu Chi and defending Saigon, along with nearly all other American units in III Corps.

The 1st Brigade was responsible for defending the main supply route to Tay Ninh City and seven U.S. bases located in its TAOR. It was further hamstrung by its military organization and inappropriate battle methods. According to Colonel Duke Wolf:

"The ROAD organizational concept (followed by the 1st Brigade) tends to burden maneuver battalions with logistical functions which distracts the attention of the leadership of the battalion from its primary tactical functions. Such logistical functions could be better handled at the next higher level (brigade), as had been previously done by the regiment for its organic battalions and attached units. Also the "battalion trains" and "brigade trains" of the ROAD logistical concepts have proved to be impractical even in peacetime maneuvers in Europe, because they require excellent long range communications and complex coordination between the separate battalions, the brigades and division, and because they violate the cardinal principle of logistics for combat: 'the impetus of supply is from the rear areas to the front lines. In effect, the ROAD logistical concept is just the opposite: 'if the front line combat maneuver battalions are not logistically supported they have not supplied themselves.' Essentially it reverses the cardinal principle of logistics by saying "the impetus of supply is from the front to the rear!' "

"Further the ROAD organizational concept tends to diffuse the 'unity of command' and the 'tactical integrity' of the combat maneuver battalions. The frequent shifting of units from one brigade to another does not permit higher or lower commanders to get to know each other and build personal confidence in one another."[657]

1st Bde/25th Division Bases near Tay Ninh, 1968

- **Tay Ninh Base:** An airfield and logistics complex of 4,000 service troops and one 105mm Philippine artillery battery.
- **Dau Tieng Base:** A supply base located on the right flank of the brigade TAOR covering Michelin Plantation. The base contained two artillery batteries, one mechanized battalion and service troops.
- **Bau Co Fire Support Base (FSB):** The most exposed American FSB, inside the edge of War Zone C. It contained four 175mm guns.
- **Buell II FSB:** Near Bau FSB this base contained one battery of 155mm howitzers (self-propelled) and one battery of 105mm howitzers (towed).
- **Rawlins III FSB:** East of Tay Ninh, contained one battery of 105mm howitzers.

- **Nui Ba Den Signal Facility:** atop Black Virgin Mountain.
- **Rock Crusher Site:** 588th Engineer Battalion site at the foot of Nui Ba Den.

The Americans had too many bases in their TAOR, as usual. NVA attacks against the 1st Brigade base complex were not concentrated against the two rather isolated bases, Bau Co FSB and Dau Tieng Base. Instead the attacks were distributed at various locations in a pattern that suggested diversion rather than major offensive intent.

NVA Attack Profile Tet III

- Seven battalion/regimental attacks against American bases. All of them in the triangle of bases nearest Tay Ninh City.
- Six attacks dedicated to defending the red rubber plantation bases or cutting the American main supply route, Route 22.

None of the NVA attacks used either the ambush lure scenario or strong forward detachments spearheading division assaults. The red attacks were probably harassing and diversionary actions. In addition, the attacks against the Americans were conducted in a piecemeal, sequential manner. That clear violation of the NVA prime maneuver principle of simultaneity was uncharacteristic of NVA operations.

The communists fought savagely in the vicinity of their rubber plantation base areas, which were bisected by American supply routes. Road cutting ambushes were regular features of the war, whatever else was going on.

As for American allegations that major regimental attacks were undertaken by the 273rd, 33rd, 174th and 275th NVA Regiments, they were probably incorrect. Battalion or multi-company attacks might have occurred with the intention of confusing American Order of Battle analysts with spurious unit identification data. There is little evidence that any of the four above listed regiments participated in regimental sized attacks. If they had, they would have made more progress. Neither is the allegation substantiated that two entire battalions of the 275th NVA Regiment blocked Route 26 on August 20th.

Supposedly, six platoons of the weak U.S. 2/27 Infantry Battalion staged a "trip wire" ambush of the 275th NVA Infantry Regiment "marching in a column of battalions,"[658] westward along Route 13 on the night of 17 August, 1968. The reds never marched down a road within a few miles of an enemy base without proper advance guards. It doesn't make sense that they would present such a huge target for instant allied air bombardment either.

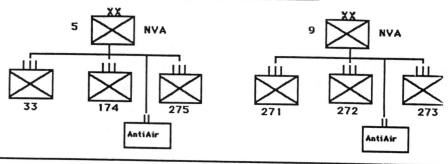

The 5th and 9th NVA Divisions, III Corps, August, 1968

5 NVA
XX

33
174
275
AntiAir

9 NVA
XX

271
272
273
AntiAir

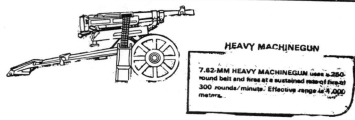

HEAVY MACHINEGUN

7.62-MM HEAVY MACHINEGUN uses a 250-round belt and fires at a sustained rate of fire of 300 rounds/minute. Effective range is 1,000 meters.

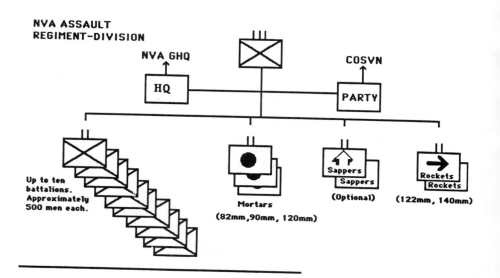

NVA ASSAULT
REGIMENT–DIVISION

NVA GHQ

HQ

COSVN

PARTY

Up to ten
battalions.
Approximately
500 men each.

Mortars
(82mm, 90mm, 120mm)

Sappers
Sappers

(Optional)

Rockets
Rockets

(122mm, 140mm)

The sparse American forces available to defend the 1st Brigade TAOR were hardly supermen. They were greatly dispersed and possessed little striking power. Their superiors at Headquarters 25th Infantry Division decided that the enemy action around Tay Ninh City was diversionary and refused to reinforce the 1st Brigade.

When asked what they needed, the 1st Brigade requested two more infantry battalions and another fire base. They believed more is better!

On the tenth day of the battle, 25th Division Headquarters actually removed three battalions from 1st Brigade control. By August 26, 1968 the 1st Brigade, 25th Division controlled one rifle battalion, one mechanized infantry battalion and four batteries of artillery, for a total of eight companies.

The 1st Brigade was constantly observed from the slopes of Nui Ba Den and by major enemy recon elements in the area. The Americans' movements, habits and plans were open books. They were deployed and functioned defensively trying to protect their bases and supply routes, nothing more. During the eleven-day period of Tet III, the 1st Brigade's only three offensive actions were reactions to enemy initiatives. It doesn't make sense to claim they outmaneuvered forces eight times their size.

US Forces: 1/25th U.S. Infantry Division: Tay Ninh TAOR:8/68

- **Armored task force:** Three M-113 recon platoons and three tank platoons with 160 Armored Personnel Carriers and fifteen M-48 tanks. Wrongly deployed as road security and for nighttime defense of four fire bases.
- **Four "leg" infantry companies from two battalions,** The two other battalion companies were pinned down defending a FSB and as a reaction force. Usually deployed as picket lines across potential enemy avenues of approach to the Tay Ninh Supply Base. Helicopter assets, capable of lifting one of those companies without heavy weapons, were available every other day.
- **Six mechanized infantry companies.** The brigade's main reaction force.

About eighty percent of the U.S. 1st Brigade was deployed in defense of Tay Ninh City. They also had one mechanized infantry battalion stationed on the right flank, at the second largest supply base, Dau Tieng.

The Americans only moved in the daylight, rapidly retreating into their fortified bases at night. Since the terrain was rather open throughout the

TAOR, and the Americans stuck to the roads, the NVA had no trouble monitoring American movements. Every day the Americans habitually sent armored patrols along the roads bounded by the Michelin and Ben Cui Rubber Plantations.

The American artillery fired numerous nightly "H&I" (harassing and interdicting) missions, wasting 4,000 artillery rounds every twenty-four hours of an average, "moderate enemy contact," day. Such usage rates required constant resupply convoy traffic along the U.S. main supply route from Cu Chi to Tay Ninh. Those convoys offered many opportunities for decisive communist military action, if the reds had wanted to attack in force.

The 1st Brigade demonstrated, by its manner of combat, every fallacy and misguided concept plaguing the American military. The brigade's worst mistake was its dependence on task force organization. "Task Forcing" required a constant shuffling of troop units into temporary groupings, as if they were interchangeable assembly line parts. The Americans called it "breeding flexibility." Actually such measures bred inflexibility and centralized control.

When a Viet Cong battalion ambushed a 1st Brigade supply convoy on August 26, the 1st Brigade commander took direct command of the local gaggle of American task force units immobilized by lack of initiative. Bypassing the "task force commander," he directly controlled small unit movements from a helicopter overhead. Thus, young American combat leaders were presented with the spectacle of a "full bird" colonel minutely directing the movements of several M-113 APCs, and sometimes single vehicles. The brigade commander also directed platoon fires, a company-size attack, and several direct frontal assaults against an entrenched enemy. His unspectacular abuse of the chain of command, made necessary by his own "flexible task force" organization, resulted in another American defeat.

Even the tank battalion ostensibly available to the 1st Brigade had been "task forced" and "detached" to death. Two of its three tank companies, and one of its remaining three tank platoons, had been assigned to other American units in other provinces. American generals didn't understand the importance of keeping tank units together as massed striking forces. To them, tanks were mobile pillboxes for defending roads and FSBs.

When the eleven-day Tet III offensive was over, the NVA broke contact. Their sporadic, sequential attacks had borne none of the earmarks of NVA divisional or multi-divisional offensives. In fact, the battle area was far too small for the type of operational level maneuver which the reds were capable of executing.

Why would the NVA tie up most of its III Corps strike force skirmishing with a depleted American brigade? If the communists had intended to destroy that brigade, they would have behaved differently.

The Americans claimed to have defeated a corps-sized NVA unit with twelve infantry companies, one armor company and a few artillery batteries. Eight thousand allied troops, 5,500 of whom were support troops, supposedly defeated 16,000 NVA front line combat troops. Did they really do it?

Tet 69

In December 1968, the Chu Luc was supposedly massing for another Tet Offensive. Four NVA divisions were supposedly preparing their III Corps battlefield for another assault on Saigon.

Planned Tet 69 NVA Divisional Offensives Toward Saigon

1st Phase: 1st, 7th, and 9th NVA Divisions prepare the battlefield.
The 5th NVA Division moves down the Adams Road/Song Be Corridor Infiltration Route to attack positions near Bien Hoa-Long Binh.
2nd Phase: 5th NVA Division poised to attack from the east.
1st, 7th and 9th NVA Divisions maneuver into attack positions.
3rd Phase: 1st Division attempts to draw allied troops into War Zone C.
4th Phase: 5th NVA Division strikes from the east. 7th NVA Division strikes down the Saigon Corridor Infiltration Route from the north. 9th NVA Division strikes out of the Angels' Wings from the west.

In December 1968, the 9th NVA Division attempted to move out of the Angel's Wings area, while the 5th NVA Division moved south in War Zone D. The 1st and 7th NVA Divisions maneuvered into deployment areas north of the Michelin Plantation.

In February 1969, elements of the 5th NVA Division attacked the Bien Hoa Air Base. Another of the 5th's offensive prongs struck Dau Tieng Supply Base near the Michelin Plantation.

The 1st NVA Division then attacked American fire bases in War Zone C. Throughout February 1969, the 1st NVA Division's 95C and 101D NVA Regiments continually attacked American fire bases.

In March 1969, The 9th NVA Division was engaged east of the Angel's Wings area. In the meantime, the 7th NVA Division was attacking near the Michelin Plantation.

By May 1969, the 5th NVA Division had vanished into War Zone D. The

1st and 9th NVA Divisions moved toward each other in a pincers movement against Tay Ninh City. The 7th NVA Division lay dormant along the Saigon Corridor.

Suddenly the offensive effort halted. By the end of May 1969, all enemy divisions began withdrawing. [659]

The American High Command, entrenched in the layered defense of Saigon, told a skewed version of what had happened. Its account claimed that the four NVA infantry divisions approaching Saigon were outmaneuvered during several months of campaigning by the reinforced 1st U.S. Cavalry Division. Supposedly the 1st Cavs' spoiling attacks, supported by brigades of reinforcements from the Saigon Front and many B-52 strikes, stopped the red divisions and drove them back into their lairs. Once again there seems to be some discrepancy regarding the facts.

NVA troop movements were continuous from December 1968 through May 1969. However, they did not bear the earmarks of a concerted four-divisional North Vietnamese "Army Offensive." Only two NVA regiments, the 101D and 95C, attacked American bases whenever a prospect of victory seemed apparent.

Most red units in III Corps seemed to be functioning as covering battalions. They maneuvered against 1st Cavalry Division RIFs (Reconnaissance in Force) as if they were screening their base areas and infiltration routes.

Throughout early 1969, the NVA also brought Saigon under increasing attack by rockets. Soon a Saigon rocket belt appeared just outside the American FEBA (Forward Edge of the Battle Area) around Saigon.

In 1969, the communists were building up for an invasion of South Vietnam and merely wanted to keep the allies on the defensive. They pretended to continue launching major Tet type offensives, depending upon the American military establishment to exaggerate their efforts. Such exaggerations began to paralyze the minds of American commanders. NVA maneuvers were more in the nature of probes, raids and diversions directed toward producing a "Maginot Line" defensive syndrome within the allied leadership. It worked, too!

CHAPTER 20

NVA Cambodian and Laotian Campaigning

The North Vietnamese used punitive military expeditions to control two nominally sovereign nations subordinate to the communists, Cambodia and Laos. Like other colonial powers, the reds sponsored armies of puppet troops in each nation. In Laos they sponsored the Pathet Leo, in Cambodia the Khmer Rouge.

The aristocratic dictators of Laos and Cambodia, the usual allies of communism, were loyal to the North Vietnamese and provided a false national base. That base consisted of a hierarchy of communist stages mainly employed for the creation of puppet troops, nothing more. However, the people of each country, distinct from the ruling elite of each nation, owed no loyalty to the North Vietnamese. The hostility of the Cambodian and Laotian people expressed itself as armed resistance to communist domination. As a result, the Chu Luc had to stage numerous pacification campaigns within both nations from 1965 through 1975. In effect, the NVA carried out a protracted counterinsurgency campaign in each country. The troops which fought against Cambodian and Laotian patriots included a combination of NVA regulars and puppet troops.

NVA Operations in Cambodia

Using its puppet troops, the adroit subversion of covert operatives, as well as the cunning cooperation of the ruler of Cambodia, the NVA had little trouble dealing with anticommunist/anticolonialist elements within Cambodia. In fact, the communists were hardly threatened for the first five years of their occupation of that country.

In 1970, with five NVA infantry divisions (1st, 5th, 7th, 9th and C40) and several independent regiments camped there, the situation changed in Cambodia. The Cambodian people were fed up. They threw out their corrupt Prince Sihanouk and changed their nation into a representative anticommunist democracy.[660]

The Chu Luc decided to use its Cambodian puppet troops, various independent regiments, and the 9th NVA Division to crush the fledgling regime. Soon the reds were dealing with three military problems:

1. The protection of their numerous Ho Chi Minh Sanctuary bases within Cambodia.
2. Cambodian resistance to their rule.
3. Allied forces attacking westward from South Vietnam.

The problem facing the communists was somewhat relieved by the presence of the huge Chu Luc army already stationed within Cambodia. Every red base in that country already supported its own independent garrison. For example, the 267th and 269th NVA Battalions guarded Cambodian Santuary Base Areas 706 and 367. Three NVA battalions secured the Parrot's Beak/ Angel's Wings base area.

The 9th NVA Division, reinforced with independent NVA regiments and Khmer troops, carried out a simultaneous mission from its base at Chup Plantation. The 9th defended against South Vietnamese incursions along Route 7 with about one third of its forces. The remainder of that reinforced division attacked the Cambodian Army which was trying to eject the reds.

Assisting the 9th NVA Division defense was the 1st NVA Division. The 1st NVA was deployed near the Cambodian coast, north of South Vietnam's IV Corps, securing communist port facilities and Cambodian Route 4. It also dealt with South Vietnamese incursions from the IV Corps area.

In August 1970 the Cambodian government sent twelve battalions against the NVA in Operation Chenla I. Cambodian forces attacked along Route 6 and Route 7 toward the Chamkar Andong Plantation, which was held by three NVA regiments. Flanking counterattacks by the 9th NVA Division thwarted the Cambodian effort.

The North Vietnamese also used their special forces against freedom fighters in occupied Cambodia. On the night of 21 January 1971, a 100-man company of North Vietnamese commandos attacked the Cambodian Air Force Base at Pochentong west of the capital, Phnom Penh. That attack destroyed all the aircraft on the field, including every MIG fighter belonging to Cambodia.

In April 1971 the Cambodians launched Operation Chenla II in another attempt to reopen Route 6 all the way to Kompong Thom. Red bases at Chamkar Andong and Chamkar Leu Plantations, along Route 21 paralleling Route 6, directly threatened the operation.[661]

On the night of 26 October 1971, communist units attacked the right flank of Cambodian forces spread out along Route 6. According to Cambodian Brigadier General Hou Hang Sin, the communist assault developed into a disaster for the Cambodians: "the 9th NVA Division, reinforced by the 205th and 207th NVA regional regiments, launched a general attack against our static defense positions . . . the FANK (Cambodian Army) 376th Battalion . . . was completely overrun in a single blow . . . Simultaneously with the above attack, the enemy was able to encircle and isolate Rumlong . . . The bridge at Spean Dek . . . was blown by the enemy on the same night . . . (the) enemy used toxic gas shells (in another attack) . . . the (NVA) enemy, expert in this type of warfare, dug deep trenches in which their drugged and chained soldiers waited to strike us, all of which was synchronized with the fire of heavy weapons located in the Chamkar Andong Plantation, and directed by observers located everywhere. We found it impossible to carry out effective counter battery fire."[662]

The communists had hit the strung-out divisional size column of Cambodian troops in an area north of Rumlong, where Route 6 ran through a series of flat, open, water-logged rice fields. The reds acted with great dash, rapidly cutting the Cambodian column into several sections. The bridge which connected the Cambodian force to its base, was also destroyed during the red attack.

The battle lasted several days and resulted in the total annihilation of the Cambodian unit. Ten battalions of Cambodian personnel were destroyed along with another ten battalions worth of equipment. It was a major debacle.

By 1972, the NVA had converted the two main Cambodian archaeological sites, the Angor Wat and Angor Thom temple complexes, into communist sanctuary bases, cantonment areas and logistics centers. The communists set up defense lines running along the periphery of the archaeological sites, destroying many historical treasures. A January 1972 Cambodian Army effort to take back their national shrine was defeated.

In March 1972, the communists bombarded Prey Veng City and Neak Luong with 122mm rocket, recoilless rifle, and mortar fire. A South Vietnamese army incursion, Toan Thang VIII, threw back the NVA siege.

In late March, NVA troops began attacking near Kompong Trach. The Cambodian capital of Phnom Penh was brought under increasing bombardment by rocket and mortar fire. Floating mines were used to interdict Cambodian shipping and many Cambodian airfields were barraged with continuous standoff attacks.

During the years 1972 to 1974, the NVA intensified its Khmerization policy within Cambodia. Numerous new Khmer Rouge troop units were formed, including regiments and divisions. "Khmer Cong" units joined the fighting everywhere, relieving NVA troops for intensified operations within South Vietnam. Khmer commandos began hitting Cambodian headquarters and airfields. Alerting the world press, communist propagandists began calling the NVA's Cambodian suppression campaign a "civil war."

During the 1972 to 1974 period, the initiative passed from the Cambodian Army to the NVA and their puppet troops. The Cambodian Army became a defensive entity, obsessed with protecting its lines of communications, capital and centers of population. That strategy was foisted off on the Cambodians by defense-minded American advisers.

In early 1972, elements of the 1st NVA Division on its way to South Vietnam's IV Corps, fought Cambodian and ARVN troops near Kompong Trach. At the same time, a battalion of NVA sappers hit Phnom Penh's Monivong Bridge, electric power station and Caltex storage facility.

On April 30, 1972 Kompong Trach fell to the communists. Ambushes of Cambodian Army forces occurred all around Phnom Penh, as standoff bombardment was constantly directed at the capital city.

In August 1972 an NVA armored battalion, attacking out of the NVA Chup Plantation Base, secured part of Route 1 by surrounding five Cambodian Army battalions. In that same month, a combined NVA and puppet troop regiment, the 203rd NVA/Khmer Rouge Infantry Regiment, captured Phnom Bakheng Mountain overlooking Siem Reap's airfield. That capture interdicted Cambodian supply efforts in the area.

The Cambodian Army depended too much upon U.S. military advisers. As a result they became addicted to air support, helicopters, frontal attacks and firebase defense. The more flexible NVA forces outmaneuvered the Cambodians, using captured American riot control gas whenever possible.

In October 1972, another NVA sapper company infiltrated into Phnom Penh and set a vehicle park ablaze. Standoff attacks were directed against ammunition and logistics dumps in the area.

Also in early October, the NVA 1st Infantry Division attacked from south of Takeo. In short order red troops overran Kirivong, Tun Loap, Nui O Mountain, Kompong Chrey, Lovea, and Koh Andet. The Cambodian Army

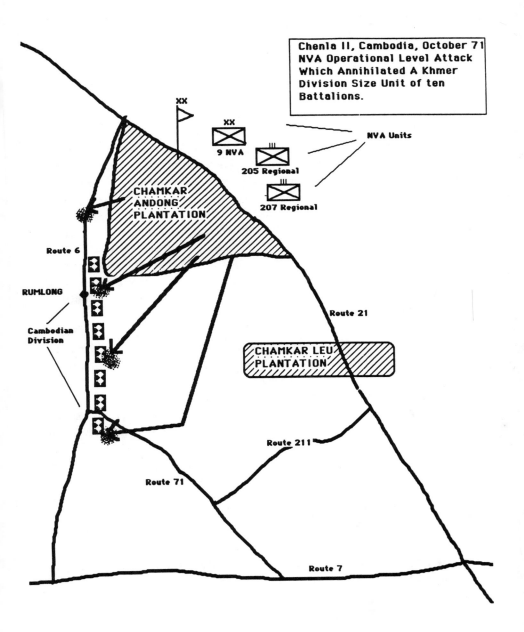

Chenla II, Cambodia, October 71 NVA Operational Level Attack Which Annihilated A Khmer Division Size Unit of ten Battalions.

NVA Units

9 NVA

205 Regional

207 Regional

CHAMKAR ANDONG PLANTATION

Route 6

RUMLONG

Cambodian Division

CHAMKAR LEU PLANTATION

Route 21

Route 211

Route 71

Route 7

was reduced to using helicopters to lift Cambodian battalions all over the country in reaction to NVA road cutting, standoff bombardment and probing attacks.

In late 1972, 7,000 NVA and puppet troops attacked Kompong Thom. Once again the Cambodian Army reacted like Pavlov's high tech dog. American helicopters and aircraft were, of course, involved in the counterattack.

In early 1973, three Khmer Rouge regiments gained control of the Mekong River supply line. As before, Cambodian Army troops with American air support strove to "contain" the enemy. The Cambodian effort showed all the earmarks of eventual defeat. Intensified communist initiatives along Route 1 and the Mekong continued to destroy Cambodian battalions in spite of B-52 strikes against red bases.

By late 1973, the Cambodians had lots of helicopters, 105mm howitzers, armored personnel carriers, an American-trained parachute brigade, special forces detachments and American air support. In other words, they were doomed to defeat. The reds made mincemeat of the typically clumsy American-inspired Cambodian airmobile operations. Unrelenting NVA pressure by a few elite Chu Luc regiments, and many puppet units, continued to destroy Cambodian battalions.

In January 1974, two communist regiments began to move toward Phnom Penh. American-style Cambodian infantry brigades began to concentrate for defense of their capital. Numerous squadrons of M-113 armored personnel carriers, an American supplied fleet of river defense craft (PBRs), and other technological gadgetry was fielded by the desperate Cambodians.

Most of the Cambodian Army was bogged down defending the last few cities under their control. The countryside belonged to the foot-mobile communist forces.[663]

Strong U.S. State Department pressure forced the Cambodian government in July, 1974, to began appealing to the reds for peace talks. The American pattern of diplomatic and military reactivity in Cambodia was an exact copy of the behavior displayed in South Vietnam. The repetition of ruinous behavior patterns, carried out in spite of their proven bankruptcy, is an uncanny and unsettling aspect of the American linear approach to war and diplomacy. U.S. diplomats and generals seem to have an unbelievable inability to adapt.

In April 1975, the Cambodian 1st, 2nd, 3rd, 7th, and 15th Infantry Divisions, along with the FANK (Cambodian Army) Parachute Brigade, were surrounded in the Phnom Penh area. The red army which surrounded them, only slightly larger than the opposing government forces, began to close in.

Under American pressure, Marshal Lon Nol, the Cambodian premier, was forced to leave the country. The Cambodian nation surrendered. Soon a red-sponsored genocide, in which three million Cambodians perished, would begin.

NVA Campaigning in Laos

During years 1960 to 1975, many North Vietnamese units moved through Laos constantly. Many more defended the huge NVA supply bases there. From the early sixties, several NVA division sized units also attempted to pacify Laos in a full scale counterinsurgency war.

The NVA divided Laos into three operational areas: Northern Laos, the Plain of Jars and Laotian land bordering China and North Vietnam; Central Laos, the panhandle region of Laos which included most of the Ho Chi Minh Trail sanctuary bases; and Southern Laos, which included the Bolovens Plateau and the Cambodian border.

Chu Luc combat units were permanently assigned to each area of Laos during most of the Second Indochina War. NVA artillery and tank regiments and battalions, such as the 202nd NVA Tank and the 675th Artillery Regiments, were deployed all over Laos by 1966.

Locations of Permanently Assigned Main NVA Units: Laos

Northern Laos:	316th and 312th Infantry Divisions. 766th Infantry Regiment.
Central Laos:	9th–13th independent NVA infantry battalions.
Southern Laos:	968th Infantry Division with the 19th and 29th Regiments. Also temporary assignments of the 9th, 141 and 39th. (Separate) Infantry Regiments.

By 1970 there were large numbers of independent NVA and Pathet Lao battalions garrisoning Laos. In addition, forty regimental size Binh Trams (logistics/engineer/defense units) were also functioning there. Usually eighty percent of the Binh Trams were deployed in Central Laos and twenty percent in Southern Laos. Many of the Binh Trams were powerful units. For example, the eight Binh Trams stationed in the area just west of South Vietnam's Quang Tri Province controlled twenty antiaircraft battalions in 1970.[664]

Independent Communist Battalions: Laos, 1970

Northern Laos:	40 NVA Battalions and 48 Pathet Lao Battalions.
Central Laos:	13 NVA Battalions and 20 Pathet Lao Battalions.
Southern Laos:	17 NVA Battalions and 21 Pathet Lao Battalions.[665]

In addition to permanently assigned combat troops operating within Laos, there were also numerous units passing through the Ho Chi Minh Trail or stationed temporarily in Laos. Such units were especially prevalent in the panhandle region opposite South Vietnam's I and II Corps zones.

"Mission C," the North Vietnamese designation for combat in Laos, was a familiar role to many North Vietnamese units.[666] However, the 316th NVA Infantry Division and the 968th NVA Division Group specialized in fighting on the Laotian front.

NVA units cooperated with numerous battalions of Pathet Lao puppet troops against the Laotian people. The North Vietnamese seized whatever they wanted from the Laotians, forcing many Laotian citizens into service as slave laborers.

Certain areas within Laos were reserved exclusively for NVA troops: "There were no Lao—we were all Vietnamese. We were separated into squads for the work. On Route 7, Battalions 2 and 3 worked on the roads. This is Route 7, which leads to Phou Kout and on which a lot of Vietnamese troops came into Laos. I was told that we had a lot of troops in Phou Kout, so we had to work hard and pave the way for them."[667]

As the Laotian people tried to fight back, the NVA intensified their control efforts. The North Vietnamese Politburo decided that "special NVA shock troops would be sent (into Laos) to soften up"[668] anticommunist resistance. Dac Cong commandos, which the North Vietnamese called their "answer to American B-52s,"[669] and regular NVA infantry easily defeated the relentless Laotian insurgents in battle after battle.

In essence, North Vietnamese troops were used to guarantee communist imperial power in Laos: "The NVA maintains a strategic capability that permits it to mount coordinated attacks throughout Laos. Demonstrations of that capability . . . were the attacks, in late 1967 and early 1968, on Nam Back in the northern mountains, in the region of Paksane in the center, and near Saravane in the south as well as the Plain of Jars offensives of mid-1969 and early 1970 . . . the . . . NVA campaign of 1967–68 . . . gained . . . territory in North and South Laos; the . . . thrust of 1969 . . . resulted in reoccupation of the Plain of Jars and, in early 1970, the ouster of the forces of General Vang Pao from the Plain by a combined North Vietnamese/Pathet Lao assault despite U.S. air support, including the use of B-52s."[670]

In Laos the reds played by the bizarre set of rules so staunchly defended by the U.S. State Department. That corrupt adolescent game was another manifestation of American diplomatic dogmatism: "Although the 1962 Geneva Accords have been repeatedly violated, the DRV (North Viet reds) sees advantage in their being preserved. If Hanoi were to disregard the terms of the treaty openly (?) by invading large areas of RLG (Laotian government) controlled territory, the constraints on its enemies would be lifted and the war might well be widened, forcing the (reds) to spend scarce resources that it would rather commit to achieving victory in South Vietnam."[671]

Who were they kidding? The U.S. State Department of course.

In 1962, the Chu Luc began officially sending military advisory missions into Laos. Doan (Group) 959 Headquarters in North Vietnam controlled a Group 959 Headquarters in Laos. That headquarters coordinated political action with every provincial command committee, military and political, within Laos.

Group 959 assigned ten to fifteen North Vietnamese communist political-administrative cadres (leaders) to each province in Laos. Those political cadres formed command committees along with representatives from the two NVA Military Regions controlling Laos.

By 1968, there were 40,000 NVA permanently assigned to Laos. That force included service troops and advisory military missions. It did not include assigned mobile forces or NVA regular units bivouaced in Laos.

Each NVA military mission to Laos was commanded by a North Vietnamese Military Region headquartered in North Vietnam. For example:

- The Northwest Military Region, Son La, North Vietnam controlled six northern Laotian provinces.
- The 4th Military Region, Vinh, North Vietnam controlled six central and southern Laotian provinces.

The NVA Military Region Headquarters coordinated their efforts with various Pathet Lao puppet troops headquarters and the supreme Pathet Lao LPLA Headquarters at Sam Neua, Laos. The Sam Neua HQ commanded all twelve Pathet Lao controlled provinces.

The Houa Khong Provincial Headquarters for Military Affairs, subordinate to the Northwest Military Region, commanded all NVA advisers to the Pathet Lao Houa Khong Provincial Command. The Pathet Lao Houa Khong Provincial Headquarters commanded the 408th Pathet Lao Battalion, the 51st and 53rd Independent Pathet Lao Companies and four district Pathet Lao Companies.[672]

Five NVA advisers served the 408th Battalion. Each independent Pathet Lao company had two NVA advisers and each district company had one.

At the NVA Houa Khong Provincial Headquarters the reds stationed three North Vietnamese Army companies:

1. The C-1 "Independence Company of Volunteers": 125 men strong.
2. The C-2 "Independent Company of Volunteers": 125 men strong.
3. The C-90 Transport Company: 47 men strong.[673]

Into each Laotian province the communist Military Region Headquarters established a provincial headquarters and three subordinate commands:

1. NVA military advisers to the Pathet Lao.
2. Three companies of NVA infantry, of one hundred to one hundred twenty-five men each. Those companies were called "volunteer forces" for "reasons of morale."
3. NVA "mobile forces" assigned from North Vietnam and transferred throughout Laos, as required.[674]

NVA Advisory/Pacification Troops: Pathet Lao Provinces

- 24 NVA Infantry Companies
- 12 NVA Transport Companies
- NVA Advisory units[675]

Every Pathet Lao battalion was assigned one military and one political advisor and an NVA battalion staff of five men. Monthly, the NVA advisors used their 15-watt radio to report to their Military Region Headquarters.

An NVA adviser to the 408th Pathet Lao Battalion once described one of the operations he led. After first conducting a reconnaissance, sand table exercise and rehearsal, the NVA adviser devised a plan for attacking the "enemy post" within Laos:

"We would use one company of infantrymen. The company would divide into two groups: one would advance to the main gate, while the other would follow to support it . . . The preparations took about three days . . . On February 18, 1966 we launched our operation against the Phieng Luong outpost . . .

"At 3 AM of the 19th, the first group advanced . . . When the sentry flashed his light on us, he was killed instantly by the advance squad which

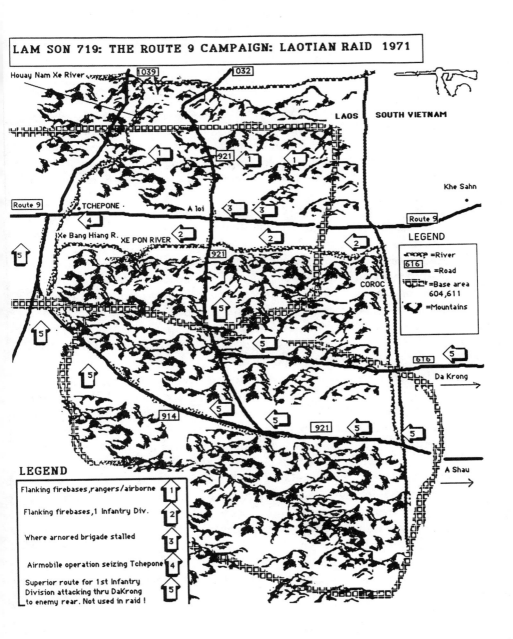

LAM SON 719: THE ROUTE 9 CAMPAIGN: LAOTIAN RAID 1971

Houay Nam Xe River | 1039 | | 032

LAOS   SOUTH VIETNAM

Khe Sanh

Route 9   TCHEPONE · | 921   A loi   Route 9

Xe Bang Hiang R.   XE PON RIVER   921   COROC   LEGEND

=River
| 616 | =Road
=Base area 604,611
=Mountains

| 914 | 921   616   Da Krong

A Shau

LEGEND

Flanking firebases, rangers/airborne **1**

Flanking firebases, 1 Infantry Div. **2**

Where armored brigade stalled **3**

Airmobile operation seizing Tchepone **4**

Superior route for 1st Infantry Division attacking thru DaKrong to enemy rear. Not used in raid ! **5** took possession of the bunker. A second squad followed and stormed the post using a B40 rocket to burn a number of buildings . . . The enemy was caught by surprise . . . it took more than two hours of fighting in the trenches and blockhouses to complete the occupation of the post . . . We captured one 60mm mortar, one DK 57mm Recoilless Rifle, one bazooka 90, 2 submachine guns, a number of rifles and a quantity of military uniforms and equipment."[676]

NVA regular units were engaged in constant warfare against Laotian anticommunists. Every year, the 316th NVA Infantry Division marched across Route 7 to attack anticommunist forces. It usually dispersed its troops into small detachments for counterinsurgency operations. However, in 1969 the 316th began using tanks and captured 175mm artillery in the Plain of Jars area.

By early 1969, the North Vietnamese permanently assigned troop presence in Laos had increased to: 34,000 combat troops, 18,000 support troops, 13,000 road building troops and 6,000 advisers to the Pathet Lao.

Also in early 1969, an NVA supply dump was discovered near the Plain of Jars: "a chance combination of sun and shadow outlined a freshly dug trench. It gave away the position of an interconnected series of ditches and trenches which the North Vietnamese had laboriously worked upon until they reached the edge of the plain itself. The network had been dug to house 175mm cannons and 120mm rockets, also being brought forward on tracked vehicles . . . directed a bombing strike on the ditch . . . The stored ammo cooked off for a day and a night at the rate of eighty explosions a minute."[677]

In March 1969 the NVA used the 148th and 174th NVA Infantry Regiments to take Na Khang, Laos. They were supported by 23mm, 37mm and 57mm antiaircraft guns.

In mid 1969 a huge NVA supply dump was captured in northern Laos, which contained over 7,500 tons of booty: "Rows of captured Russian tanks, which the enemy had abandoned after locking their turrets . . . whole batteries of 85mm guns, trucks with their tanks full of gasoline, and cases of Soviet sniper rifles still in their original cosmoline."[678]

After the 316th NVA Division was mauled by American airpower, it was replaced by the 312th NVA Division. The 312th lost over a regiment of infantry to American air strikes by October, 1969. In December 1969, however, a replenished 312th NVA Division, accustomed to avoiding American airpower, attacked across the Plain of Jars. It was supported by 85mm and 122mm artillery.

In March 1970, the NVA 9th Infantry Regiment was sent to Laos. The

9th attempted to capture anticommunist insurgency operational bases on the Plateau de Bolovens.

In the mid-1970s, the 968th NVA Group began operations in Laos. Supported by tanks and artillery, the 968th Group commanded the 9th, 19th and 29th Independent NVA Infantry Regiments for operations in central Laos. It was later joined by the 39th Independent NVA Infantry Regiment.[679]

In October 1970 the NVA began preparing for the forthcoming ARVN Operation Lam Son 719 in southern Laos. To prepare for their counteroperation, the "Route 9 Campaign," the reds created the 70th Front. The 70th Front would command five infantry divisions including the 304th, 308th and 320th NVA Infantry divisions, along with several antiaircraft regiment regiments and the 202nd NVA Armored Regiment. In late October 1970 units subordinate to the 70th Front began moving into the Tchepone, Laos area.

NVA 70th Front Units: 1971 Route 9 Campaign

- 2 NVA Infantry Division with its 1, 31 and 141 Infantry Regiments.
- 304 NVA Infantry Division with its 9, 24B and 66 Infantry Regiments
- 308 NVA Infantry Division with its 36, 88 and 102 Infantry Regiments.
- 320 NVA Infantry Division with its 48, 52, and 64 Infantry Regiments.
- 324B NVA Division with its 29, 803 and 812 Infantry Regiments and 675 Artillery Regiment, temporarily garrisoned in Sanctuary Base Area 611.
- 202 NVA Armored Regiment.
- 27, 33, 34, and 41 Binh Tram Regiments (logistics)[680]

In a masterpiece of troop concentration, the reds began reinforcing their two regiments near the Route 9 Campaign battle area in February, 1971. They had rapidly increased that number to seventeen regiments, not counting antiaircraft regiments, by late March 1971.

Although troops of the 70th Front easily defeated the ARVN incursion, reinforcements were nearby if needed. At that time, the NVA high command controlled thirty-eight NVA security battalions and fifty-seven Pathet Lao security battalions in North Laos alone.

The 9th NVA Regiment occupied Laotian Route 23, west of Paksong, in mid-1971. In September 1971 an attack by two American-trained Laotian battalions surprised and defeated the NVA regiment. "The NVA bunkers and fighting positions were well fortified, heavily manned and sited in depth along Route 23 west of Paksong and the advancing Neutralist battalions met strong resistance. But cut-off from the rear by GM-32 and BI-7, and under heavy air and artillery attack, the NVA 9th Regiment had to pull out of its Paksong defenses and to avoid annihilation or capture, break into small groups and withdraw through the forest."[681]

In March 1972 seven NVA divisions were fighting Laotian irregulars in Laos. In their attack near Saravane they fought against an allied firebase on the Bolovens Plateau manned by a thousand Thai mercenaries.

The NVA had secured most of Laos by late 1970.

CHAPTER 21

1972 Easter Offensive

Ominous warnings began to filter into South Vietnam's II Corps intelligence organizations in the fall of 1971. The reds were preparing another "Winter-Spring" campaign for the approaching dry season. NVA B-3 Front Headquarters in the Triborder Zone began moving advance detachments forward as allied generals worried about another enemy threat to cut South Vietnam in two.[682]

The intelligence reports identified what was to become a familiar pattern of communist offensives in II Corps. A main communist force would drive through northwestern Kontum, annihilating allied border camps, as it struck for the cities of Pleiku and Kontum. In the ARVN rear the NVA division in Binh Dinh would attack toward the enemy main force. The intelligence reports claimed that the red offensive would begin in late January or early February of 1972, and would unfold in several phases.

Attacking from the border area the NVA B-3 Front would send forward the 320th and 2nd NVA Divisions along with the 203rd NVA Armored Regiment. Attacking from "behind" the ARVN front would be the 3rd NVA Division (also known as NT-3 and "Gold Star Division") moving westward out of Binh Dinh Province.

Captured documents and agent reports secured all over South Vietnam began to form a pointed mosaic during the last six months of 1971. The reds were planning a major offensive throughout all of South Vietnam which they called the Nguyen Hue Campaign.[683]

The Nguyen Hue Campaign's Strategic Design

Rumor has it that the Nguyen Hue Campaign was the last major NVA offensive led by that old communist warlord General Vo Nguyen Giap. He meant to take all of South Vietnam in a multi-pronged offensive calculated to draw ARVN forces in all directions, dissipate American air cover and defeat the South Vietnamese Army in detail.

By the beginning of 1972, most of the allied forces who had been defeated by North Vietnam during the seven previous years were gone. Only two U.S. brigades and one Korean division remained in South Vietnam. General Giap knew that the allied units would either flee out of South Vietnam or remain motionless in their fortified bases when the Chu Luc struck. Only American air power slightly worried Giap.

Giap planned to launch a four-pronged offensive which would secure more real estate and population for North Vietnam while spreading ARVN forces into dissipated fragments. Without massed troops, the South Vietnamese could hardly stand up to the hard-fighting North Vietnamese.

General Giap conceived of his Easter Offensive as being composed of a series of phases. Each sequential phase was interdependent with the others in the scheme.

Giap's Nguyen Hue Offensive Phases

- **Phase I:** Border battles at Loc Ninh, Dak To and the DMZ, Giap's favorite areas, would draw ARVN forces into meatgrinder battles near the NVA supply bases and sanctuaries.
- **Phase II:** Infiltrated forward detachment regiments would move into threatening deployments near Saigon, Hue and on the Binh Dinh coast of II Corps.
- **Phase III:** I Corps falls to the NVA and troops are rushed into II Corps which also falls. Saigon is struck by six to nine close-in advanced regiments.
- **Phase IV:** I and II Corps are consolidated and the full force of the NVA is turned against Saigon.[684]

Huge levies of North Vietnamese teenagers were drafted into the inflated NVA ground force. Hundreds of Soviet ships disgorged mountains of military equipment. Hundreds of tanks and artillery pieces were moved with tens of thousands of troops along the Ho Chi Minh Trail southward. Yet the allies, bereft of loyal, rational and competent intelligence resources, were surprised!

The reds committed their entire army outside of their home country. Yet

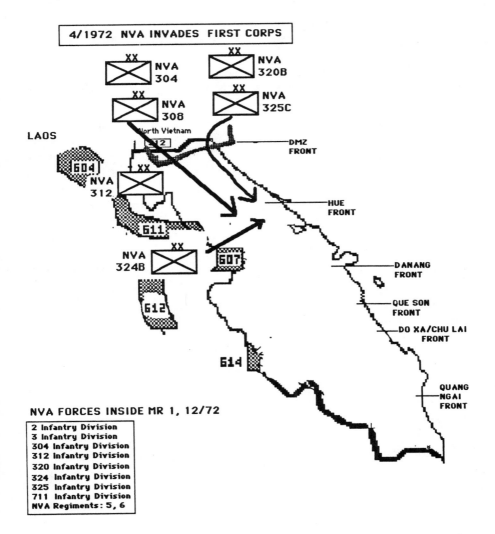

4/1972 NVA INVADES FIRST CORPS

NVA 304

NVA 320B

NVA 308

NVA 325C

LAOS

North Vietnam

2

DMZ FRONT

604

NVA 312

HUE FRONT

611

NVA 324B

607

DANANG FRONT

QUE SON FRONT

612

DO XA/CHU LAI FRONT

614

QUANG NGAI FRONT

NVA FORCES INSIDE MR 1, 12/72

2 Infantry Division
3 Infantry Division
304 Infantry Division
312 Infantry Division
320 Infantry Division
324 Infantry Division
325 Infantry Division
711 Infantry Division
NVA Regiments: 5, 6

the allies struck at neither their ground supply lines, nor invaded North Vietnam! Only Linebacker II, a short but effective demonstration of the power of American aerial bombardment, accomplished much.

Sure the ARVN fought back and the traitors in I and II Corps were cashiered, but the South Vietnamese never adopted a total war footing. There was too much corruption and weakness in the South Vietnamese hierarchy. That corruption and weakness was caused by South Vietnamese mimicking of American procedures and habitual mind sets!

The Chu Luc had continuously increased the size of their army. From 149 combat battalions at the end of 1969, the NVA doubled the number of its troop units.

General Giap planned to commit the entire North Vietnamese Army to what the allies called the Easter Offensive: fourteen infantry divisions, twenty-six separate infantry regiments and three armored regiments. Only two units were not committed, the 316th Division fighting in Laos, and a small corps-size reserve retained in North Vietnam. In spite of the losses incurred during the Easter Offensive, the Chu Luc expanded to 285 battalions by the end of 1972.

Most NVA troops were retrained in the conventional offensive methods to be used in the Easter Offensive. Many North Vietnamese tank crews had graduated from the Soviet Armor School in Odessa in late 1971. They would be fighting in units made up of T-54 and T-55 tanks fitted with 100mm guns. Those 100mm guns had more penetrating power than the most powerful American model in Vietnam, the M48, with its 90mm gun. Reinforced artillery and flak units were also upgraded by Soviet advisers within North Vietnam.

The first prong of the communist assault would be a four division invasion across the DMZ into I Corps. It would be complemented by a flanking attack by two additional divisions out of the A Shau Valley War Zone, from whence came two divisions during the Tet offensives.

In the II Corps zone, an NVA corps would strike eastward out of the Triborder zone to seize Kontum and drive on to the South China Sea coast. It would be reinforced by another NVA division striking out of coastal Binh Dinh War Zone.

Giap's prong number three was to be a reinforced three division attack on III Corps' An Loc. From there the assault would continue on to Saigon.

In the IV Corps area, red troops planned to do more maneuvering than fighting. They would tie down ARVN forces in the area while seizing as much real estate as possible.[685]

The Easter Offensive in I Corps

The Chu Luc stacked its forces in several echelons for the conquest of I Corps. The NVA B-5 Front would control the battle.

The first communist asset in the battle consisted of ARVN traitors in command positions at the South Vietnamese I Corps, 3rd ARVN Infantry Division and regimental levels. Those traitors could be counted upon to sabotage the South Vietnamese effort by both overt and covert action, in the short and long term.

For the first strike in March 1972 the Chu Luc would invade I Corps with three divisions and eleven independent regiments. Striking across the DMZ would be a powerful communist assault corps practicing forward detachment tactics. It was composed of:

- 304th NVA Infantry Division with the 9th, 24th and 66th Infantry Regiments and the 68th Artillery Regiment.
- 308th NVA Division with the 36th, 88th and 102nd (aka 162th) Infantry Regiments.
- B-5 Front Independent Forces: 126th Sapper Regiment (aka 126th Infantry Regiment), 31st, 270th (aka 27th) and 246th Infantry Regiments; 203rd, 204th and 205th Armored Regiments, 84th (Rocket) and 38th Artillery Regiments.

A flanking corps would debouch from the A Shau Valley, striking the ARVN deep left flank. It was composed of:

- 324B NVA Division with the 29th, 803rd and 812th Infantry Regiments.
- Independent Forces: 5th and 6th NVA Infantry Regiments.

The 304th NVA Infantry Division, along with B-5 Front independent regiments, would drive due south in the main attack. Attacking from the NVA right flank would be the 308th NVA Division enveloping Quang Tri City, about ten kilometers south of the Cua Viet River.

The 324B NVA Division and two independent regiments were attacking Hue further south. Their deep flank assault threatened to cut off the 3rd ARVN Infantry Division.

Available in April through May 1972 would be the 320th NVA Division with its 48B and 64B Infantry Regiments fighting in Quang Tri Province. In late April, elements of the 325th NVA Division would join the offensive and by July, 1972, all three of 320th's regiments (18th, 95th and 101st Infantry Regiments) would be committed against Quang Tri City.[686]

The ARVN in I Corps: 1972

Most of that communist host would initially fall upon the corps-sized 3rd ARVN Infantry Division. The 3rd was a huge division commanded by the mediocre General Vu Van Giai, who may have been a deep cover communist agent. The 3rd Infantry Division was initially composed of the 2nd, 56th and 57th Infantry Regiments, an armored cavalry battalion and an artillery regiment.

The 2nd Infantry Regiment, taken from the 1st ARVN Infantry Division, was a good veteran regiment. Two other infantry battalions and the armored cavalry squadron were also composed of veterans, as was the division staff.

American influence was strong in the 3rd ARVN Division. Naive American advisers tried to call the 3rd the "ring of steel" division.[687] The 3rd was deployed in a ruinous American pattern of eighteen fire support bases and five larger "combat bases" in I Corps' northern Quang Tri Province. That defensive configuration dissipated the division's power.

On March 30, General Giai did something that could only be considered a traitorous act by hard-core military professionals. However, he was dealing with amateurs, so he got away with it.

"On 30 March, the 56th and 2nd Regiments began the scheduled rotation of their respective Tactical Areas of Responsibility . . . Late in March information was obtained by the South Vietnamese JGS that 29 March was to be D-Day of an NVA general offensive . . . General Giai . . . did not comply with the JGS alert or alter his planned rotation . . . his two . . . regiments began their exchange of tactical areas . . . Tactical command posts (CPs) were vacated, unit radios shut down, antennas dismantled and placed aboard jeeps and six-by-six trucks . . . the 3d ARVN Division literally went non-tactical for the duration of the rotation and was temporarily unable to perform as a viable fighting force . . . It is incomprehensible that a military leader, in daily contact with an enemy growing stronger daily and who has been alerted of an impending attack, would attempt to execute an intradivision relief of lines and then . . . fly to Saigon for the holiday weekend."[688]

The reds struck while the South Vietnamese were in the midst of their rotation and immediately routed the ARVN Regiments. "Two of the 3rd Division's infantry regiments were in the process of exchanging positions and moving towards FSB Carroll and Charlie 2, when thousands of artillery rounds struck the exposed troops causing instant death and chaos."[689]

As Marine Colonel G. H. Turley explained it: "This would not be the first situation where South Vietnamese combat units were subjected to a military disadvantage because of the possibility of covert sympathy for the North Vietnamese enemy at the highest levels of government or their own military leadership."[690]

In front of their advance detachments the Chu Luc infiltrated artillery forward observers (FO) teams, "By the morning of the 31st, the NVA artillery forward observer teams had infiltrated between the ARVN fire bases into positions on the north side of the Cam Lo-Cua Viet River. From these hidden locations, they began to direct accurate artillery fire on to vehicle traffic moving east and west along Route 9."[691]

Periodic barrages of fire from 122mm and 130mm artillery began to impact in the ARVN rear areas.

In the meantime, General Giai had panicked, suddenly evacuating his command post at Ai Tu and running south toward Quang Tri City. "Radios were left on and simply abandoned; maps and classified materials lay where last used and were unguarded . . . complete bedlam."[692]

Files and office equipment were abandoned as ARVN officers scrambled for safety. The 3rd Division's American Advisory Team 155 also panicked and began to "haul ass," abandoning: "twenty-two machine guns, three 81mm mortars, eleven ANPRC-77 radios, a telephone switchboard and numerous other items."[693] Later, American B-52s bombed the numerous abandoned ARVN firebases.

NVA artillery had a devastating effect upon the ARVN defenders who cringed before it. "the NVA was following the Soviet practice of emplacing artillery just outside the range of U.S. 105mm and 155mm howitzers. With careful planning, the attackers had located their guns just outside the 10,500 meter maximum range of the 105mm howitzers and the 14,800 meter range of the 155mm howitzers. Then by exploiting the 27,500 meter range of the Soviet 130mm guns, the North Vietnamese were able to attack the fire bases with little threat from ARVN counterbattery fire. Only the U.S. made 175mm gun had sufficient range to counter the NVA's massive artillery attacks. However, the four 175mm guns at Camp Carroll and the four located at Dong Ha, failed to respond effectively. Each time the 175mm batteries would fire, the NVA would counter with a heavier barrage. ARVN cannoneers, frightened by the incoming rounds, abandoned their guns to seek safety, permitting the NVA to win the artillery duel."[694]

On April 2, 1972 another act of officer treachery rocked the 3rd ARVN Division. Lieutenant Colonel Pham Van Dinh, commander of the ARVN 56th Infantry Regiment and a deep cover red agent, surrendered his com-

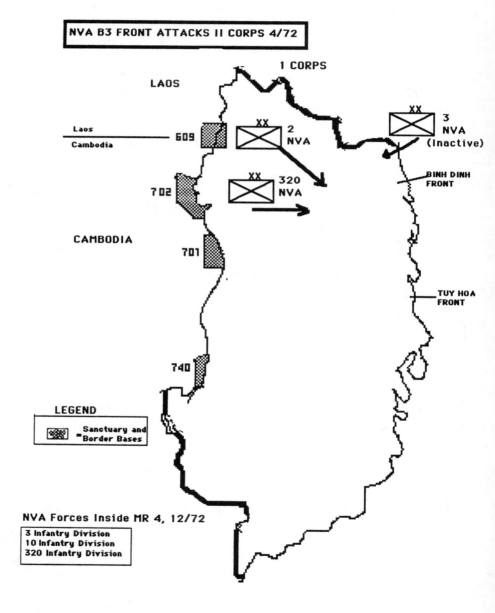

NVA B3 FRONT ATTACKS II CORPS 4/72

1 CORPS

LAOS

Laos
─────────────
Cambodia

609

XX
2
NVA

XX
3
NVA
(Inactive)

BINH DINH
FRONT

702

XX
320
NVA

CAMBODIA

701

TUY HOA
FRONT

740

LEGEND

= Sanctuary and
Border Bases

NVA Forces Inside MR 4, 12/72

3 Infantry Division
10 Infantry Division
320 Infantry Division

444

mand without a fight. According to an American adviser on the scene: "Colonel Dinh . . . told us he was going to surrender Camp Carroll . . . offered me the choice of surrendering . . . He said that we . . . could hide among his troops when they went out the gate to surrender to the North Vietnamese and once we were outside the perimeter, we could fall down in the grass and crawl away."[695]

The American advisers' reaction was strange, too: "Camper extended his right hand to his counterpart and they shook hands. He wished Dinh well."[696] Then Dinh revealed the reason for not killing the Americans outright, he wanted to cling to his cover: "He (Dinh) asked me not to tell General Giai that he was surrendering."[697]

The red agent Dinh then surrendered over 2,000 ARVN troops of the 56th Infantry Regiment, five batteries of artillery (including important 175mm guns) and several huge supply dumps to the reds. The following day, April 3, 1972 Dinh identified himself as a communist agent as he broadcast propaganda on communist Radio Hanoi. "I have returned to the National Liberation Front . . . ARVN troops return to the NLF . . . the American-Thieu gang is going to lose the war . . . refuse combat orders . . . you must not fight the NLF . . . save your life."[698]

When the 308th NVA Division and three leading regiments struck the 3rd's spread out defenders the ARVN defensive array folded like a house of cards. By April 2, 1972 the reds had reached the Cua Viet-Cam Lo River line having seized thirteen "fire bases," a "combat base," and fifteen artillery pieces.

Suddenly the Chu Luc had compressed the 3rd ARVN Division into a breast-shaped salient with its nipple end twenty-five miles from the coast. The breast itself was fifteen miles deep from Dong Ha to Fire Base Nancy, located ten miles south of Quang Tri City.

Bearing down on the strategic Dong Ha bridge was the mass of red troops, preceded by an armored regiment. Defending the bridge was one timid ARVN armored battalion which soon panicked and fled, leaving behind a brave ARVN marine battalion to defend the bridge. That battalion held long enough for an American adviser to blow the bridge in the face of NVA T-54, T-55 and PT-76 tank companies. In the meantime the 57th ARVN Regiment broke and streamed south in panic.

General Lam, commander of all ARVN troops in I Corps, was both incompetent and a suspected NVA deep agent. Lam's sabotage of the ARVN effort began to become strongly apparent during the Lam Son 719 Campaign of 1971. His "errors" were just subtle enough to be viewed, by amateurs, as either mistakes or misguided thinking, a frequent refuge of traitors. He was a favorite of the Americans.[699]

General Lam was a prototypical American-style general. He was heavy on administration and the good life, and very light on military arts. When given an order by Saigon, he simply passed it on, verbatim, to his subordinates. If his troops "got in a jam," he depended upon the Americans, and the expending of greater resources, to solve the problem. Lam preferred defending bases with his artillery fragmented into two-gun batteries and scattered in numerous locations. He also tended to reinforce failure the same way American generals did. Lam didn't hesitate to commit his troops piecemeal to reinforce defense lines either.

Even as the evidence of General Giai's incompetence began to mushroom, General Lam reinforced the 3rd ARVN Division. By April 2, 1972 the 3rd had the 147th Marine Brigade and the 1st Armored Brigade attached. By April 10, 1972 the 258th Marine Brigade and four multi-battalion ranger groups had also been added to General Giai's command. His span of control became unmanageable, with ten major regimental formations and an M48 tank battalion under his command.

On April 9, after the ARVN line had been driven in another fifteen kilometers, General Lam was quite optimistic. He decided to counterattack, naming his counteroffensive Operation Quang Trung 729. ARVN commanders at regimental and brigade level began arguing among themselves and the counterattack fell apart. Then another ARVN officer's operational sabotage occurred:

"On his own initiative (ARVN officers hardly ever demonstrated initiative, unless it served the enemy), the 1st Armor Brigade commander directed his 20th Tank Squadron (M-48 tanks) on the Cua Viet line to pull back south . . . as soon as they saw the tanks move south, ARVN troops were gripped with panic, broke ranks and streamed along . . . the Cua Viet defense (along an unfordable river) . . . had been abandoned. It was virtually handed to the enemy on a platter."[700] By April 23, 3rd ARVN Division was defending a pocket around Quang Tri City.

Attacks by the 324B NVA Division out of the A Shua Valley cut Route 1 and isolated the 3rd ARVN Infantry Division in Quang Tri Province. General Giai sent an armored cavalry battalion south which failed to break through.

On April 28, the 1st ARVN Armor Brigade broke and streamed south. Its commander was also a suspected red agent.

Now as the reds closed in around the pocket of ARVN troops south of Quang Tri City, the corps commander, General Lam, added to the confusion.

He issued a string of hyperactive, contradictory orders which served to immobilize the remaining ARVN troops.

On April 29, an inventory of South Vietnamese army troops available for the defense of Quang Tri was logged as follows:

"20th Tanks: Eighteen M48A3 tanks operational. . .
57th Regiment: Approximately 1400 men. . .
4th Rangers: Approximately eighty men. . .
5th Rangers: Approximately 600 men. . .
13th and 17th Cavalry Squadrons: Two thirds of combat vehicles still operational."[701]

On April 30, the ARVN 147th Marine Brigade fled south out of the Quang Tri City area as the ARVN defense lines collapsed. American helicopters rescued the 3rd Division commander who was fleeing south in an armored personnel carrier.

By the evening of April 30, 1972 the NVA controlled all of Quang Tri Province and sent several spearheads into neighboring Thua Thien Province. They were seeking a linkup with NVA forces which had already cut Route 1. Hue City was the next target as two NVA corps groupings converged upon it.

ARVN Defense Of II Corps

In 1971 General Ngo Dzu, ARVN II Corps commander, began reconnoitering the area east of NVA Sanctuary Base 609 and the Triborder War Zone. Infiltration corridors leading from the Triborder and the Plei Trap Valley, fifty-five kilometers west of Kontum City, were scouted by area reconnaissance troops. Signs of an enemy offensive buildup were soon detected. Enemy tank units, along with 122mm and 130mm artillery, were discovered in the border area. The 320th NVA Infantry Division was also found there.

General Dzu, who was not a traitor to his country, ordered Colonel Le Duc Dat to reinforce his 22nd ARVN Infantry Division in the Tan Cahn-Dak To area. The 47th ARVN Regiment and the 19th ARVN Armored Cavalry Battalion moved in, joining the 42nd ARVN Regiment already dug in near the junction of Routes 1 and 512. As B-52 bombers futilely bombed suspected enemy buildup areas, the 2nd ARVN Airborne Brigade occupied a string of fire support bases on Rocket Ridge.[702]

By February 8, 1972 the preparations for a red offensive were completed.

The ARVN high command expected the reds to make their main effort in the Central Highlands, perhaps limiting their offensive to the II Corps area.

Across the border in Cambodia, the NVA B-3 Front lined up its forces for an enveloping attack north and south of Dak To. On the northern flank the 320th NVA Infantry Division, with the 64th and 48th Infantry Regiments and the 203rd Tank Regiment, deployed. To the south of the 320th Division, the B-3 Front deployed the following units:

- 2 NVA Infantry Division with the 1st, 52nd and 141st Infantry Regiments.
- B-3 Front Independent Regiments including the 28th, 66th and 95B Infantry Regiments, and the 40th Artillery Regiment.[703]

In mid-March, 1972 the B-3 Front struck the South Vietnamese along Rocket Ridge and near Ben Het where most of the available ARVN armored units were stupidly dug in as mobile pillboxes a la the American style. From the 10th to 19th of April, the 2nd ARVN Airborne Brigade fought desperately to hold Rocket Ridge. By April 23, Tan Canh and Dak To were surrounded by North Vietnamese forces with Soviet Sagger antitank missiles added to their infantry antitank weaponry. Those Saggers destroyed most of the ARVN M41 tanks dug in around Tan Canh.

On April 24, a column of NVA T-54 tanks bypassed Dak To and hit Tan Canh as part of a combined arms assault. The ARVN troops panicked and fled. Then Dak To, five kilometers to the west, was hit by an NVA combined arms assault spearheaded by tanks. By that evening, the 22nd ARVN Infantry Division was routed. Its scattered fragments fled through the jungle, leaving Dak To and Tan Canh to the red victors. The NVA then spent a few days inventorying their captured loot which included "twenty three 105mm howitzers, seven 155mm howitzers, a number of M41 tanks and about 15,000 rounds of artillery ammunition."[704]

On April 25, ARVN forces abandoned Rocket Ridge and retreated toward Kontum City, now defended by the 23rd ARVN Division commanded by the capable Colonel Ly Tong Ba. Colonel Ba set about training his troops in antitank warfare since the South Vietnamese now knew that the 203rd NVA Tank Regiment was spearheading the NVA offensive. The U.S. 1st Combat Aerial TOW Team (antitank) arrived by mid-May to help fight the enemy armor.

On May 14, the reds hit Kontum with four infantry regiments and part of their armored regiment. The first Chu Luc assault was repulsed with the aid of American airpower.

THE 1972 EASTER OFFENSIVE

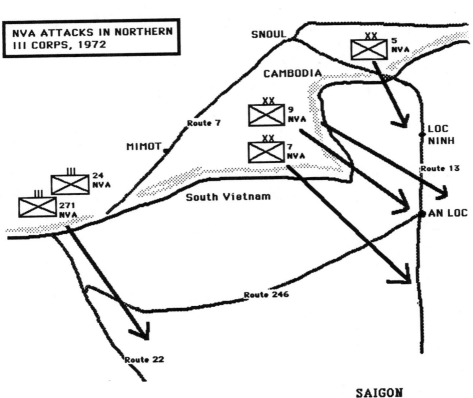

NVA ATTACKS IN NORTHERN III CORPS, 1972

SNOUL

CAMBODIA

5 NVA

LOC NINH

9 NVA

7 NVA

Route 7

MIMOT

24 NVA

Route 13

271 NVA

South Vietnam

AN LOC

Route 246

Route 22

SAIGON

On the 26th of May, the 320th NVA Division attacked along Route 14 due south toward the west side of Kontum. Its forces included the 48th and 64th Regiments and the 28th Regiment from the B-3 Front, as well as armored units. The ARVN 44th and 45th Infantry Regiments defended against the 320th NVA Division.

The 2nd NVA Division outflanked Kontum, striking it from due north with the 1st Regiment, and from due south with the 141st Regiment which had crossed the Dak Bla River. 2nd NVA Division troops seized two bridgeheads in Kontum. In the north they drove the 53rd ARVN Regiment back. In the south, they defeated a scratch ARVN regiment defending Kontum's southern outskirts.

At that point American airpower, including B-52s, intervened on a massive scale. The ARVN 8th Armored Cavalry Squadron reinforced Kontum's defenders, forcing the reds to begin to withdraw on May 31, 1972.

However, violent skirmishing continued with red advance detachments who had cut the roads around Kontum. That stranglehold wasn't broken until June 19. Then fresh ARVN armored cavalry units began to drive the enemy westward.

The 3rd NVA Division in Binh Dinh remained dormant during the offensive. With its 2nd, 12th and 31st Infantry Regiments, it moved northward to a location contiguous to the border with I Corps, near coastal Route 1.

ARVN Defense of III Corps

ARVN III Corps' intelligence assets detected NVA troop movements in February and March, 1972. The 9th NVA Infantry Division moved into the Fishhook (Base Area 708) in March with its 272nd Regiment. Then the 9th Division's 95C Regiment disappeared.

Rumors circulated that the 7th and 9th NVA Divisions, currently training their troops in urban warfare, might cooperate in a future offensive action. Captured communist recon troops revealed an NVA plan to attack through Tay Ninh City toward Binh Long. To protect that area, ARVN III Corps Headquarters "activated Task Force 52 composed of two infantry battalions of the 52d Regiment, 18 Division and two artillery sections (105mm and 155mm) and deployed it at a fire support base on Interprovincial Route LTL-17, two kilometers west of QL-13 and 15 kilometers north of An Loc."[705]

Transfixed with the assault on I Corps, ARVN headquarters in Saigon was surprised when a new NVA offensive was opened in III Corps. Red troops began driving southeastward on April 2, 1972. The 24th NVA Regiment (Separate), reinforced with tanks, hit the Lac Long FSB thirty-five kilometers northwest of Tay Ninh City. Lac Long was defended by one ARVN battalion. The reds overran the base by mid-day. Following closely behind the 24th NVA was the 271st NVA Infantry Regiment. Suddenly two NVA regiments were poised along Route 22.

As the South Vietnamese looked worriedly to the west, an NVA corps continued to maneuver into assault positions in the north. In Cambodian Sanctuary Base 712, a few miles north of Loc Ninh, an NVA north assault force assembled. It was composed of:

- 5th NVA Division with its 174th, 205th and 275th Infantry Regiments.
- Supporting the 5th Division was the 203rd Tank Regiment (it had the same number as another tank regiment in II Corps), the 208th Rocket Regiment, the 42nd Artillery Regiment and the 271st Antiaircraft Regiment.

The 5th NVA Division's mission was to drive down Route 13 to seize Loc Ninh. Then, after flanking attacks were launched by the 7th and 9th NVA divisions, to move off Route 13 to the east enveloping An Loc.

On the west flank of Route 13, due west of An Loc, lay Sanctuary Border Base 708, where another NVA assault force was assembling. It was deployed as follows:

- 9th NVA Division with its 95C, 101st and 272nd Infantry Regiments supported by the 202nd NVA Tank Regiment.
- 7th NVA Division with its 141st, 165th and 209th Infantry Regiments.

The mission of the 9th NVA Division was to move west, hitting An Loc from the west and north, while the 5th Division struck it from the east. Simultaneously the 7th NVA Division was to cut Route 13 south of An Loc, at Binh Long.

Now the South Vietnamese were threatened from two directions. Two northern NVA offensive prongs were made more dangerous by two NVA regiments which threatened the ARVN right flank along Route 22.

South of Saigon, the NVA deployed a divisional size force with no apparent mission. The 33rd and 274th NVA Infantry Regiments, along with the 74th NVA Artillery Regiment, were probably poised to attack Saigon from the south once the NVA divisions attacking north of An Loc reached the

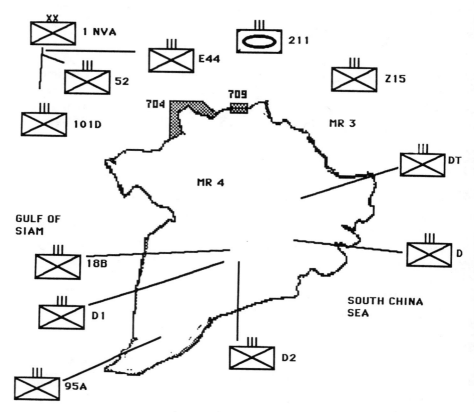

NVA REGIMENTAL DISPOSITIONS MR 4, APRIL, 1972

CAMBODIA

1 NVA

211

52

E44

Z15

704

709

MR 3

101D

MR 4

DT

GULF OF
SIAM

18B

D

D1

SOUTH CHINA
SEA

95A

D2

NVA FORCES INSIDE MR 4,2/72

1st Infantry Division(44,52,101D Rgts)
5th Infantry Division
6th Infantry Division
NVA Regiments: 18B, 95A
VC Regiments: D1, D2, D3

452

outskirts of Saigon. Also available to the southwest of Saigon, were the 86th NVA and the DT1 Viet Cong Regiments.

On April 4th and 5th, the 5th NVA Division penetrated Loc Ninh, spearheaded by a tank battalion. As Loc Ninh was overrun, retreating ARVN defenders were ambushed south of the town. On April 7th, 5th NVA Division troops took Quan Loi airfield north of An Loc as red spearheads neared the outskirts of An Loc.

Both the 5th and 9th NVA Divisions then stalled outside of An Loc. They were experiencing severe logistics problems, having consumed all of their area supply caches, and they were reeling from B-52 aerial bombardment.

The NVA's week's pause outside of An Loc enabled the South Vietnamese to bring in the 21st Infantry Division, which began to attack northward toward An Loc. In the meantime, the 7th NVA Division and elements of the 9th NVA Division, was battling ARVN troops along Route 13 south of An Loc.

In late April, the 21st ARVN Division engaged the 101st Regiment of the 9th NVA Division and the 165th and 209th Regiments of the 7th NVA Division. Five kilometers north of Tau O the ARVN 32d Regiment was stalled in front of a huge NVA blocking position: "the reinforced 209th Regiment of the 7th NVA Division whose fortified blocking positions, arranged in depth, held the ARVN 32d Regiment effectively in check . . . A blocking position called "Chot," generally an A-shaped underground shelter arranged in a horseshoe configuration with multiple outlets was assigned to each company. Every three days, the platoon which manned the position was rotated so that the enemy continually enjoyed a supply of fresh troops. These positions were organized into large triangular patterns called "Kieng" (tri-pods) which provided mutual protection and support. The entire network was laid along the railroad which paralleled Route QL-13, and centered on the deep swamps of the Tau O stream. The network was connected to a rubber plantation to the west by a communication trench.

"Armed mostly with B-40 and B-41 rocket launchers, enemy troops from their seemingly indestructible positions stopped the 21st Division's advance for 38 consecutive days. Despite extensive use of B-52s, tactical air, and artillery, the 32d was unable to dislodge the enemy from this area. This stalemate continued until the enemy pulled out the 209th Regiment for his second attempt to capture An Loc."[706]

The ARVN 21st Division set up a FSB for artillery support at Tan Khai, ten kilometers south of An Loc on Route 13. The 141st Regiment of the 7th NVA Division began attacking that base on May 20 and was continually repulsed throughout June.

Finally, massive B-52 strikes all over the NVA units and their rear areas began to tell. By May 14, 1972 the siege of An Loc was broken and the communist enemy reeled back toward Cambodia in defeat.

ARVN Defense of IV Corps

In early March 1972, the 1st NVA Infantry Division with its E44 Sapper Regiment and 52nd and 101D Infantry Regiments, was deployed in Kampot Province, Cambodia. It was poised to invade South Vietnam's IV Corps. To its right flank was the 211th NVA Armored Regiment and the Z15 NVA Infantry Regiment, north of Kien Tuong Province.

Inside the IV Corps, communist troops were deployed as follows:

- 18B and 95A NVA Infantry Regiments in the U Minh area.
- D1 and D2 Viet Cong Regiments southwest of Chuong Thien Province.
- D3 Viet Cong Regiment scattered between Vinh Long and Vinh Binh Provinces.
- Dong Thap 1 Viet Cong Regiment located south of Route 14 in Dinh Tuong Province.

In mid-march communist units began moving throughout IV Corps. By April 1, 1972 they were deployed as follows:

- 95A NVA Regiment: An Xuyen Province, moving eastward.
- 18B NVA, D1 Viet Cong and D2 Viet Cong Regiments: Chuong Thien Province, moving eastward.
- D3 Viet Cong Regiment: Vinh Binh Province.
- Dong Thap 1 Viet Cong Regiment: Dinh Tuong Province.
- 1st NVA Division moving toward the South Vietnamese border.

The two remaining ARVN divisions in IV Corps, the 7th and 9th Infantry Divisions, were panicked by the reds' maneuvers. Massive air strikes began to hit the 1st NVA Division as any hope of a major NVA offensive in IV Corps was bombed into stagnation.

The Situation as of December 1972

American airpower saved South Vietnam from total defeat, yet NVA conventional units were not driven back into Laos and Cambodia. They now garrisoned huge tracts of land in every one of South Vietnam's corps areas.

The South Vietnamese military did try to strike back at the communists in

NVA Control In I Corps, 12/72

Units	Provincial Location	ARVN Defenders
304,312,320,325 NVA Divisions 27, 31 NVA Regiments	Quang Tri	Marine & Airborne Divs
324 NVA Division 5,6 NVA Regiments	Thua Thien	1st Infantry Div
711 NVA Division (3,38,270 NVA Rgts)	Quang Tin	2nd Infantry Rgt.
2 NVA Division	Quang Ngai	2nd Infantry Div(-)[707]

their newly secured South Vietnamese real estate: "two South Vietnamese marine brigades . . . (assaulted the) coast of Quang Tri Province . . . (in) December, 1972. . . . (They were) opposed by elements of the NVA 325th Division, principally the 101st Regiment and the 48th Regiment of the 320th Division, both regiments supported by the 164th Artillery Regiment of the B-5 Front. The 164th was equipped with Soviet 130mm field guns.

"Between the 101st Regiment operating along the coast, and Quang Tri City, the NVA employed the 27th and 31st Regiments of the B-5 Front, as well as the 18th Regiment, 325th Division. The practice of assigning the same numerical designation to more than one unit was not unusual in the NVA. The 101st Regiment, 325th Division, was distinct from the 101st Regiment that operated in Tay Ninh and Hau Nghia Provinces under the control of the Central Office for South Vietnam (COSVN)."[708]

Just before the ceasefire became effective, the disgraced ARVN 3rd Infantry Division, defending the DaNang area, like the U.S. Marines before then, fought some skirmishes with the 711th NVA. ARVN commanders falsely claimed a great victory over the 711th: "the 3d Infantry Division clashed violently with the NVA 711th Division and inflicted serious losses. . . . (leaving) . . . the 711th Division nearly paralyzed."[709]

NVA Control In II Corps, 12/72

Units	Provincial Location	ARVN Defenders
10 NVA Division (28, 66, 95B NVA Rgts)	Kontum	44 infantry Rgt.
320 NVA Division	Pleiku	23 Infantry Div(-)
3 NVA Division	Binh Dinh	22 infantry Div.[710]

NVA Control In III Corps, 12/72

Units	Provincial Location	ARVN Defenders
272 NVA Regiment	Phuoc Long	9 Infantry Rgt.
95 and 272 NVA Regiments	Binh Long	——
7th NVA Division 205 and 101 NVA Regiments	Binh Duong	5 Infantry Div.
271 NVA Regiment	Hau Nghia	25 Infantry Div.
274 NVA Regiment	Bien Hoa	——
33 NVA Regiment	Long Khan	18 Infantry Div.[711]

NVA Control In IV Corps, 12/72

Units	Provincial Location	ARVN Defenders
1st NVA Division	Kien Giang	44 STZ
18B and 95A NVA Regts. D2 Viet Cong Regiment	Chuong Thien	21 Infantry Div.
D1 Viet Cong Regiment	Phong Dinh	——
D3 Viet Cong Regiment	Vinh Long	9 Infantry Div.
6 NVA Division (DT1 Viet Cong and 86 NVA Rgts)	Dinh Tuong	7 Infantry Div.
5 NVA Division (ZT1 Infantry and 74 Artillery Rgts)	Kien Tuong	—— [712]

What Really Defeated the NVA During the Easter Offensive

The American air force broke the red will to drive on to victory during the Easter Offensive. At the tactical level many communist troops were killed by aerial bombardment, but the bombing alone could not have saved South Vietnam. Linebacker II, a strategic aerial bombardment of North Vietnam, caused the reds to cease their aggression.

According to military expert Sir Robert Thompson, if the Americans had not lost their nerve and ceased bombing they would have won the war:

"In my view, on December 30, 1972, after eleven days of those B-52 attacks on the Hanoi area, you had won the war. It was all over! They had fired 1,242 SAMs; they had none left, and what would come in overland from China would be a mere trickle. They and their whole rear base at that point were at your mercy. They would have taken any terms. And that is why, of course, you actually got a peace agreement in January, which you had not been able to get in October."[713]

Then the peace was lost at the negotiating table again. Decadent establishment elites caved in before the blandishments of a beaten, yet bravely arrogant foe. If the North Vietnamese had negotiated with tough, intelligent adversaries loyal to the best interests of America and South Vietnam, the reds would have been outmaneuvered. Yet diplomatic weaklings "pissed it all away!"

Are these statements merely exaggerations? Were the reds really hurt by the bombing? Enough to cave in? Is that possible? Consider the evidence:

"The Hanoi/Haiphong area was the obvious focus of the bombing effort. In the fields of logistics, communications, electric power and air bases, most of the lucrative targets were centered within ten or fifteen miles of those two cities. Transportation related targets and military supplies had high priority.

"A brief assessment showed the following results: the entire railroad complex of North Vietnam was severely crippled—to include damage to 383 rail cars, fourteen steam locomotives, 191 storage warehouse buildings, and two railroad bridges. The important railroad yard in downtown Hanoi was struck and badly damaged by laser-guided bombs. (This yard had been used by the North Vietnamese for years as a sanctuary, since they were able to bring railroad cars into the "off limits" middle of Hanoi. We had only been allowed to attack it once or twice during the whole war, and then it was quickly repaired.) The railroad shops and the warehouse area were also hit with laser-guided bombs, all of which went directly into the target area. The railroad yard at Gia Lam, two miles across the river from Hanoi and jammed at the time with loaded rail cars, was hit hard and extensively damaged. The Haiphong railroad siding was fairly well broken up and interdicted almost completely. The Kinh No complex, where the railroad from Thai Nguyen, and the northwest railroad come together to serve as the largest logistics grouping in North Vietnam, was well cleaned out. It was being used to assemble and redistribute cargo and contained many large warehouses packed with military supplies. The Yen Vien military complex and the Kep railroad yard were also hit heavily, and the Hanoi railroad highway bridge over the Rapides Canal interdicted.

"In addition, nine major supply storage areas—seven in the Hanoi area and two near Haiphong—were struck with excellent results. Vehicle repair facilities (the North Vietnamese used trucks by the thousands) received considerable damage, as did the nine port and waterway targets on the strike list. Furthermore, the electric power grid of North Vietnam was sharply compromised by the combined effect of the Hanoi power plant being hit by smart bombs . . . the Hanoi transformer station being rendered inoperative, and the Viet Tri thermal power plant and two other big power plants (one at Uong Bi and one just northwest of Hanoi) all being successfully struck. The main control buildings of the Hanoi radio communications center (where the transmitters were located) were also damaged. Finally, ten airfields, mostly around the Hanoi area, were struck in order to ensure that aircraft operations from these fields would be interdicted, and a number of surface to air missile sites were put out of commission. Most importantly, all of this damage was done in eleven days of concentrated attacks. There was no respite for the North Vietnamese—the shock effect was tremendous."[714]

For once there was no sabotage of American airpower by traitors. Aerial bombardment had worked.

America could have beaten North Vietnam in 1967 and 1968 if American ground forces had known how to fight a maneuver war. By 1972, the Chu Luc had such fantastic ground military power that any force on earth would have had a hard time beating the reds.

By 1972, the NVA was strong enough to whip the U.S. and South Vietnam combined, on the ground. The only hope for victory was a weapon never properly used before, airpower. If American air attacks had been continued for two months, hitting every dam, port, road and enemy military installation, the reds would have streamed home, starving. Then their divisions could have been obliterated on the roadways.

But the courage to fight such a war was missing from the American ruling elite. They did not identify with the more than 50,000 American war dead and the hundreds of thousands of Americans maimed by the war. As a result, the North Vietnamese have still not been paid back!

CHAPTER 22

1975 Conquest of South Vietnam

After the so-called ceasefire following the 1972 Easter Offensive, the communists had another agreement to abuse. They continued their expansionistic aggression within South Vietnam.

"At the time the standstill ceasefire was announced, military forces of both sides were supposed to stay where they were. The area under effective enemy control and the fuzzy contested zone in between ran from the DMZ where it included the northern half of Quang Tri Province, southward along the Truong Son Mountain range to almost all mountainous areas of MR-1, and MR-2 and northern MR-3 (MR = Military Region, the new name for corps zones). The remaining consisted of "dents" scattered throughout GVN controlled territory, which figuratively looked like spots on a leopard skin . . . Laos and Cambodia, meanwhile, remained the sanctuaries where the enemy enjoyed absolute freedom of action."[715]

Some historians have referred to the period from January 1973 to April 1975 as the Third Indochina War. However, the name doesn't fit. The last North Vietnamese war against the free people of South Vietnam should be called the Second Indochina Continuation War.

The NVA began its campaigning in 1973 from deep bridgeheads within South Vietnam. Those bridgeheads, combined with the buildup of the Ho Chi Minh Trail East within South Vietnam, facilitated rapid NVA troop movements. Now the increasingly motorized, yet essentially foot-mobile, red army began to make even more spectacular achievements in the maneuver war realm.

461

Rebuilding the North Vietnamese Army

The Easter Offensive which had raged throughout 1972 had exhausted many NVA units. They had to be replenished and restored to first class fighting condition in 1973. Increased aid poured in from China and Russia until over 2.8 million metric tons were received in 1973. In 1974, the supply tonnage received by North Vietnam reached 3.5 million metric tons. The logistics buildup was in keeping with the Chu Luc requirement that logistics be organized prior to offensive action.

Such a deluge of supplies required increased logistic efforts at the frontline level. Five logistics groups subordinate to MR 559 carried out logistics functions in service to the NVA field army.

NVA Logistics Groups Service Areas

- Group 470: Triborder War Zone and mountain provinces of South Vietnam.
- Group 471: From the Triborder Zone north, including the A Shau Valley.
- Group 473: From north of the A Shau Valley War Zone to south of Khe Sahn and west to Laos' Muong Nong region.
- Group 472: Southern Laos.
- Group 571: Southern North Vietnam and northern Laos

Chu Luc logistics groups began to increase and streamline their nearly fifty subordinate Binh Tram regiments in 1973. Seven Binh Trams were converted to antiaircraft, infantry or engineer regiments.

In March, 1973 the NVA initiated a transportation offensive for moving huge amounts of supplies down the Ho Chi Minh Trail. Long truck and tank columns ran south, bumper to bumper. Some truck convoys included over 300 trucks. The number of NVA tanks deployed within South Vietnam rose to over 655, or the equivalent of twenty Soviet type tank battalions. The transportation offensive also rapidly increased the number of NVA artillery pieces to over 430, enough to form thirty-four (12 gun) artillery battalions. Most of those artillery pieces were 122mm and 130mm guns which far outranged ARVN's 105mm and 155mm howitzers.

NVA logistics units also moved many new communist, mostly Soviet, weapons systems into South Vietnam in 1973–74, including "the tank launched Scissors Bridge (MT-54 and MT-34) and the armored personnel carrier BTR-152 series; . . . airborne assault guns, ASU-75; the Soviet light artillery tractor, M2; the 152mm gun-howitzer, D20; the 100mm antitank gun T12 . . . the T-60 medium tank and SA-7s mounted in groups."[716]

By early 1973, after twenty-five years of effort, the NVA controlled a huge international army of over three million men and women. A large part of that army consisted of poorly equipped, but well trained militia units within North Vietnam.

One provincial infantry regiment was maintained as an internal reserve in each of North Vietnam's seventeen provinces. Also employed as an internal defense force was an over 1.6 million peasant militia force. A huge regional elite force had been selected from the best militia units and was being formed into over twenty battalions within North Vietnam by late 1972.

Imperial North Vietnamese regular forces were distributed, in January 1973, as follows: 290,000 in North Vietnam, 70,000 in Laos, 25,000 in Cambodia and over 185,000 in South Vietnam. The communist nation thus became a garrison state whose main preoccupation was war!

NVA Strength in South Vietnam, January 1973

Force Category	MR 1	MR 2	MR 3	MR 4	TOTAL
Divisions	8*	3	4	3	18
Regimental HQ*	54	11	13	16	94
Battalion HQ*	195	73	77	79	424[717]

*includes an air defense division. *includes independent regiments/battalions

Separate NVA Regiments, January 1973

Category	MR 1	MR 2	MR 3	MR 4	TOTAL
Infantry	6	5	8	11	30
Sapper	3	1	2	——	6
Artillery	6	2	2	——	10
Armor	2	1	1	—	4
Antiaircraft	12	4	6	——	22
Total	29	13	19	11	72[718]

NVA Antiaircraft Units in North Vietnam, Jan. 1973

Air Defense Divs	Surface to Air Missile (SAM) Regts	Automatic Weapons Regts*
9	10	30

Note: *Divs = Divisions, ᴛs = Regiments

The NVA eighteen-division force of 1973, which included one artillery, one sapper and one antiaircraft division, was opposed by only thirteen ARVN divisions. In addition, the reds fielded sixty-two separate regiments and 140 separate battalions of infantry, sapper, reconnaissance, tank and artillery troops.

The Chu Luc usually retained five training divisions inside North Vietnam: 304B, 320B, 330th, 338th and 350th NVA Infantry Divisions. In early 1973, the 338th Division was converted to a combat infantry division. The 341st Division was reactivated as a combat division in southern North Vietnam. In Laos, the 968th NVA Infantry Division was redesignated as a general reserve division. The 316th NVA Infantry Division was withdrawn from Laos, equipped with over 2,000 vehicles and commenced training in motorized operations. It joined the 308B NVA Division already stationed in North Vietnam.

The 377th Air Defense Division was deployed in South Vietnam, joining numerous NVA antiaircraft units already stationed there. The 263rd Surface to Air Missile (SAM) Regiment, equipped with SA-2 missiles, was moved to Khe Sahn in Quang Tri Province, in early 1973. The regiment contained one support battalion and four firing battalions. Each firing battalion launched from one firing site with four to six launchers.[719]

There were already ten NVA antiaircraft regiments operating in South Vietnam's Quang Tri Province in late 1972. In early 1973, the 671st, 673rd, 675th and 679th Antiaircraft Regiments, located in Quang Tri Province, were greatly reinforced. By the end of April 1973, there were thirteen antiaircraft regiments in Quang Tri, with two others already deployed to Laos. "These antiaircraft regiments were equipped with cannon ranging from the automatic 20mm to 100mm. They also had 12.7mm and 14.5mm antiaircraft machine guns, and many of their 57mm cannon were radar controlled. Furthermore they had the SA-7 'Strella' Soviet hand-held, heat-seeking missile, and early in 1973 evidence began to accumulate that at least some of the SA-7s were an improved version."[720]

In the rest of South Vietnam there were ten more NVA antiaircraft regiments in January 1973. New communist antiaircraft weapons began to take their toll. In March and April 1973 Strella missiles destroyed six GVN aircraft in the air.

The North Vietnamese Air Force grew to over 300 aircraft. That force included over 200 jets, sixty propeller planes and forty helicopters.

The 308th, 312th and and 320th (aka 320B) NVA Infantry Divisions, which had been mauled during the Easter Offensive fighting, returned to

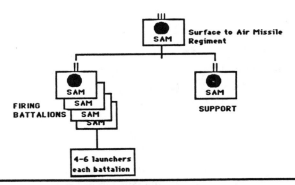

Surface to Air Missile Regiment

FIRING BATTALIONS

SAM
SAM
SAM
SAM

SAM **SUPPORT**

4-6 launchers each battalion

S-60, 57-MM ANTIAIRCRAFT GUN. This gun can be used against armored vehicles as well as low-flying aircraft. It has a maximum horizontal range of 12,000 meters and a tactical antiaircraft range of 6,000 meters with off-carriage and 4,000 meters with on-carriage fire control. It can be elevated from -72 mils to +1,500 mils; traversed 6,400 mils; and has a cyclic rate of fire of 105 to 120 rounds per minute. A twin version is mounted on the self-propelled ZSU-57-2.

ZPU-4, 14.5-MM MACHINEGUN. The ZPU-4 is a towed, four-barrel, 14.5-mm machinegun that uses a four-wheeled carriage that must be lowered onto stabilizing jacks for firing. It has a range of 1.4 kilometers against aircraft and 2.5 kilometers against ground targets. This optically directed weapon has a rate of fire of 2,200 to 2,400 rounds per minute.

465

North Vietnam in early 1973. They were slated for complete restoration and overhauling.

In South Vietnam's Quang Tin Province (MR 1) near Hiep Duc the 711th NVA Infantry Division was supported by the 572nd Armored Artillery Regiment composed of a battalion each of tanks, artillery and antiaircraft weapons. In early 1973 that regiment was used to form three regiments, one each of artillery, tanks and antiaircraft.

Near Saigon (MR 3) and in the Delta (MR 4) four new NVA infantry divisions were activated: the 3rd NVA Infantry Division (33rd and 274th Infantry Regiments) in MR 3; and the 4th (D1, 18B and 95A Infantry Regiments), 6th (24th, DT1 and 207th Infantry Regiments) and 8th (Z15th and Z18th Infantry Regiments) NVA Infantry Divisions in MR 4.

COSVN also added several new units to its order of battle, including the 26th Armor Brigade, the 75th Artillery Division, the 477th Antiaircraft Division, the 25th Engineer Division and the 25th Sapper Division. By mid-1973, COSVN began to function like an army group headquarters.

The 1973–74 Dry Season Campaign

Several overlapping campaigns were conducted by the communists during the last two years before Saigon fell. The North Vietnamese continued to seize real estate and populations all over South Vietnam, in a general "land grab" campaign which overlapped other localized or regional campaigns.

The Dry Season Campaign of 1973–74 was carried out under the leadership of NVA Colonel General Tran Van Tra, the military commander of the Central Office of South Vietnam (COSVN) which controlled all communist troops in South Vietnam's III and IV Corps. The COSVN theater of war, also called the B-2 Front, included two thirds of South Vietnam's population and stretched from Dar Lac Province in the Central Highlands periphery to the jungled tip of Cau Mau Peninsula. It included more than half of South Vietnam's land mass.

General Tra's intention was to expand Chu Luc control of the countryside in South Vietnam's IV Corps. He used the 7th and 9th NVA Divisions to occupy the three ARVN infantry divisions around Saigon: the 5th, 18th and 25th. He sent the 5th NVA Division into the Mekong to force the ARVN 7th, 9th and 21st divisions stationed there to fight a big unit war at division level. That meant that the countryside would be open to greater organization and control by the reds.[721]

After some setbacks to Tra's efforts to control regional rice production, the NVA began to make noticeable gains by June 1973. Communist recruitment of South Vietnamese into the NVA guerrilla army accelerated as more Delta resources began to slip from ARVN control.

By the last months of 1973, Tra's combination of guerrillas and regular forces were fighting another Rice Harvest Campaign. This time they were beating ARVN. COSVN began predicting the fall of South Vietnam by 1975 or 1976. By December 1974, 500 of the 3,300 Government of Vietnam (GVN) outposts in the Delta had fallen to Tra's forces and for the first time an entire GVN province, Phuoc Long, was clearly communist.

Tra's campaign had made use of Sun Tzu's offensive combination of *cheng* or normal direct force and *ch'i* or extraordinary, indirect force: "Tra used the main force divisions in War Zone C and War Zone D as normal forces to fix and distract Saigon forces and to engage ARVN's strongest divisions, whereas the local and guerrilla forces (reinforced by some main forces) acted as the extraordinary forces to gain their strategic objective in the Mekong Delta. Judging by the deployment of ARVN units, it seems that Saigon thought the reverse was true."[722]

Other NVA Operations in 1973

Usually the NVA operated the same in every GVN Military Region. During the Landgrab 73 Campaign, communist main force units made over fifty attacks throughout South Vietnam to fix ARVN main forces in their bases. At the same time, smaller NVA units penetrated the hamlet level, gaining control and seizing resources and manpower.

ARVN troops in MR 1 endured relatively fewer assaults. The reds were frantically building the new Truong Son East road network just beyond the mountains.

In MR 2, the NVA conducted relentless attacks against ARVN border camps such as Dak Pek, Mang Buk, Pateau Gi and Tieu A Tar. As each fell, it was lost forever, as ARVN drew back in alarm.

In May 1973, the 320th NVA Division moved its 64th and 48th Regiments into positions north and south of MR 2's Thanh Giao area. In northern Binh Dinh War Zone, the 3rd NVA Division had lost a lot of men during its landgrab efforts in early 1973. By mid-1973 its 2nd and 21st Regiments, with an average battalion strength of below 200 men, were withdrawn to the Hoa An District west of the An Lao River for refitting. The 12th NVA Infantry Regiment was located in Binh Dinh's Tam Quan District.

In addition, the 10th NVA Division with three regiments was located in MR 2. An additional four separate NVA regiments and forty understrength battalions, continuously pushed Vietcom controlled borders outward throughout II Corps.

NVA L SHAPED ANTIAIRCRAFT, OR FLAK, TRAP.

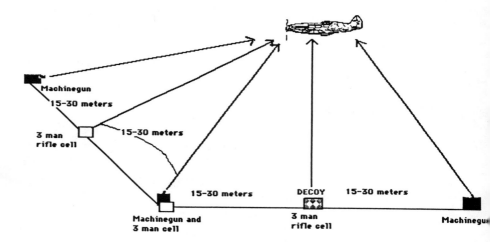

The L shaped antiaircraft or Flak trap, featured three machinegun
positions and three rifle cells. One cell would be designated as a decoy.
The decoy would fire at an enemy aircraft and draw it into the triangular
kill zone where three heavy or antiaircraft machineguns would be sited.
NVA riflemen and machinegunners practiced synchronized firing in this
position.

In August through September 1973, four NVA regiments engaged ARVN troops in the Central Highlands. Ten miles west of Kontum, along the new border of red controlled Kontum province, the 42nd, 44th and 53rd ARVN Regiments attacked the 28th and 66th NVA Regiments, driving them back across the Krong Poko River. Ten miles south of that battle area, two ARVN regiments drove elements of the 95B NVA Regiment back westward. Forty miles due west of Pleiku, the 26th NVA Infantry Regiment attacked the 80th ARVN Ranger Battalion at Plei Djereng.

By October 1973, four ARVN regiments had driven NVA troops out of their bridgeheads over the Krong Poko. However, the 320th NVA Division, along with its 28th Regiment and the 26th NVA Regiment, had advanced to within twenty-five miles of Pleiku along a fifteen mile front. There the reds faced six ARVN regiments, controlled by the 22nd ARVN Infantry Division.

In MR 3, a small NVA offensive was launched near the Cambodian border. The reinforced 271st NVA Infantry Regiment attacked Dak Song but was forced out in a counterattack by the 44th ARVN Regiment. The reinforced 205th NVA Regiment, supported by the 208th NVA Artillery Regiment, then struck south thirty miles driving ARVN forces before it all the way to Kien Duc, where ARVN defenses held.

In the fall of 1973, the NVA reconstituted its strategic reserve and concentrated it in North Vietnam's Thanh Hoa Province between Hanoi and Vinh. The I NVA Corps was formed there with the 308th, 312th and 320B Divisions. The II NVA Strategic Reserve Corps was then formed with the 308B, 341st and 316th Divisions.

In the end of 1973, the 968th NVA Division moved its 9th and 19th Regiments into MR 2. Simultaneously two new NVA corps headquarters were formed in MR 1 and one new one was formed in MR 3.

NVA Operations in 1974

South Vietnamese forces attempted to seize the initiative in MR 3 in early 1974. Their target was sixty-mile-long salient into South Vietnam. That salient, the sixteen-mile-wide Svany Rieng Province of Cambodia, included the Parrot's Beak Sanctuary Base only thirty miles west of Saigon.

In early February 1974, three ARVN regiments struck northward out of IV Corps. Their Tri Phap Operation struck the Chu Luc's Z15 and Z18 NVA Regiments, and sent them reeling. The 5th NVA Infantry Division tried to rescue the two regiments but was also driven northward.

For awhile the 5th Division was a North Vietnamese fire brigade: "The NVA 5th Division was perhaps the most versatile of all communist divisions;

at least it was called upon to perform missions of extreme diversity. In the Nguyen Hue offensive of 1972, it participated in the Binh Long campaign, and after suffering heavy casualties in the jungles and plantations around An Loc, invaded the paddies and swamps of the Mekong Delta. Forced to withdraw, it sent elements to relieve the battered NVA forces in the forests of Quang Du. In early 1974, it pulled these units back to bases in Tay Ninh and dispatched some battalions back to the delta to try to save disintegrating defenses in the Tri Phap (Kien Tuong Province). This mission failed in the face of powerful ARVN attacks, and COSVN ordered the division to assemble forces in southern Svay Rieng. From here, generally centered on Chi Phu, it could direct forces against southern Tay Ninh, Hau Nghia and Kien Tuong. In early February an advance element of division headquarters began moving toward the Angel's Wing from Tay Ninh, and by mid-March it was established there east of Chi Phu."[723] COSVN probably knew that the ARVN forces would soon launch an attack in that region.

In late March 1974, the 5th NVA Division began to maneuver its 6th and 174th Regiments offensively. Two battalions of the 6th NVA Regiment struck the ARVN post at Duc Hue which was defended by the 83rd Ranger Battalion. Although driven off in several assaults, the 6th Regiment was reinforced with a local sapper battalion and besieged the camp. The battle raged into April.

ARVN Lieutenant General Pham Quoc Thuan, MR3 commander, decided to attack into Svay Rieng with eighteen battalions. Keeping his American advisers in the dark, General Thuan struck at suspected 5th NVA Division locations with forty-five air sorties on April 27 and 28.

As ARVN troops began sweeping toward Svey Rieng, the 5th NVA Division launched an attack with its 275th Regiment and 25th Sapper Battalion on Long Khot. Long Khot was an ARVN base on the other side of the Svay Rieng salient. In their attack the reds deployed a squadron of captured American armored personnel carriers (M-113), 122mm howitzers, 105mm howitzers, AT-3, antitank missiles and SA-7 antiaircraft missiles. ARVN's 3rd Air Division flew over 100 combat sorties against the new threat.

On April 29th, four mechanized ARVN columns (Task Forces 315, 318, 322 and 310) plunged westward fifteen kilometers into eastern Svay Rieng. Then the columns wheeled southward toward the 5th NVA Division's logistics installations and its E6 and 174th Regiments. In the meantime two new MR 4 ARVN task forces struck the red troops who had invested Long Khot, driving the 275th NVA Regiment back.

Upon order, all units of the 5th NVA Division then broke contact and

Soviet T-54/55 Tanks : This 35.9 ton tank mounted a 100mm D-10T gun and two 7.62mm PKT machineguns. It had a range of 310 miles (500km) at a maximum speed of 30mph, with a four man crew. An NVA tank battalion usually included thirty one tanks organized into three tank companies.

NVA Tank Battalion
31 tanks

10 tanks each

NVA Tank Regiment
65-100 tanks

22-31 tanks

TYPICAL NVA TANK BATTALION MANEUVER FORMATION

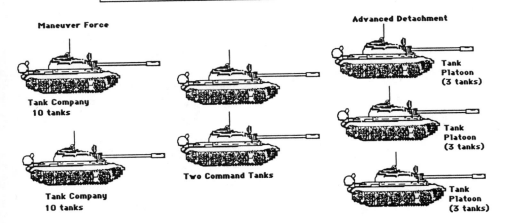

Maneuver Force

Tank Company
10 tanks

Tank Company
10 tanks

Two Command Tanks

Advanced Detachment

Tank Platoon
(3 tanks)

Tank Platoon
(3 tanks)

Tank Platoon
(3 tanks)

retreated westward and northward into Cambodia. The ARVN task forces ground to a halt to police the battlefield where they found a few truckloads of spoils. That was the last major offensive ever launched by ARVN. On May 2, 1974 an era ended.

In early 1974, the NVA began stockpiling 33,000 tons of food, fuel, ammunition and other supplies in their forward depots near the forthcoming battlefields where the final offensive would be waged. Hundreds of thousands of new communist loyalists organized themselves as supply transporters, road repairers and rear security units. The North Vietnamese had made the decision to conquer South Vietnam in 1975:

"In October 1974 the Political Bureau and Central Military Party Committee of North Vietnam held a conference to hear its General Staff present its strategic combat plan. According to General (Van Tien) Dung one of the first problems raised was the question, 'Would the United States be able to send its troops back to the south if we launched large scale battles that would lead to the collapse of (South Vietnam)?' Their conclusion was that 'the internal contradictions within the U.S. . . . had intensified.'[724] The NVA did not think the U.S. would try to save South Vietnam again.

The Truong Son Corridor East, or new Route 14, was nearing completion all the way down the western spine of South Vietnam. Two new fuel pipeline systems were also built in South Vietnam, one crossing the DMZ and terminating in MR 1's Quang Nam Province. The other led through Laos, along the Cambodian border and then eastward into MR 3's Quang Duc Province. Both pipelines were carrying diesel fuel for tanks and trucks.

In May 1974, Dak Pek district town in Kontum Province was seized by the NVA. Major elements of the 304th NVA Division and the 29th Regiment of the 342B Division attacked Thuong Duc district town in Quang Nam in July 1974.

In the summer and fall of 1974, the communists hit MR 3 with fifteen major strategic raids. In May 1974, the 95C and 272nd NVA Regiments launched a two-pronged attack into the Iron Triangle. The 95C Regiment attacked eastward toward Ben Cat and the 272d Regiment attacked southeastward toward Phu Cuong. Both attacks were halted by ARVN counterattacks.

In May through September 1974, twenty strategic raids were launched by the NVA in MR 1 and MR 2. Most of those raids struck near the coastal area. In August 1974, the 324B NVA Division attacked northward out of its MR 1 Ruong Ruong Stronghold toward Hue. Ten miles north of Ruong Ruong the 6th, 271st, 803rd, and 812th NVA Regiments encountered the ARVN 1st Division's front line west of Route 1. The NVA attack bogged down in that area.

The Ho Chi Minh Offensive of 1975

Still worried about possible U.S. intervention, the NVA decided to test American reactions. In December 1974 the NVA 301st Corps, with its 3rd and 7th NVA Divisions, attacked the provincial capital of Phuoc Binh in northern MR 3. When the first South Vietnamese provincial capital to fall since the 1972 ceasefire was seized by NVA forces with scarcely a whimper from the Americans, on January 6, 1975, the reds knew "the game was in the bag." There would be no American counterattack!

The annihilation of South Vietnam began on March 8, 1975 as NVA units moved into position along Routes 19, 14 and 21 in MR 2. Suddenly the Chu Luc pounced, as the 95B and 3rd NVA Division cut Route 19 between Pleiku and coastal Qui Nhon. The 9th NVA Division then cut Route 14 north of Ban Me Thuot and elements of the 320th Division cut Route 21 east of that city.

While all that was going on, the 10th, 320th and 316th NVA Divisions closed in on ARVN's 53rd Infantry Regiment defending Ban Me Thuot. An advance detachment of two NVA infantry battalions had infiltrated Ban Me Thuot before the attack began. The advance detachment was combined with a deep strike unit to take the center of Ban Me Thuot and then execute a Blossoming Lotus technique. General Dung described the scheme of maneuver:

"We would use a relatively strong, coordinated assault force of regimental size (advance detachment), not set in place in the positions from which the attack would be launched, but assembled at a distance and moved in, bypassing the enemy's outer defense perimeter positions, and unexpectedly striking deep within the town. This assault force would coordinate its attack with sapper and infantry units that had been stationed there secretly ahead of time (infiltrated shock troops), immediately wipe out the command nerve centers (command decapitation) and other crucial positions, and only when the springboard positions inside were firmly under control, strike out from the town (Blossoming Lotus) to wipe out the isolated posts."[725]

Suddenly several NVA tank spearheads plunged into Ban Me Thuot, aiming directly at the two airfields and important command communications centers. The town was seized in record time.

When the ARVN counterattacks began, the Chu Luc was ready: "As we had foreseen, the 45th Regiment of Saigon's 23rd Division had been brought from Pleiku by helicopter and set down east of Ban Me Thuot, in the Phuoc An area, where we had already deployed our troops to wipe them out. Another key battle in the Tay Nguyen was about to begin."[726]

On March 14, GVN President Thieu ordered an evacuation from MR 2's

NVA CLOSES IN ON THE SOUTH VIETNAMESE 1975

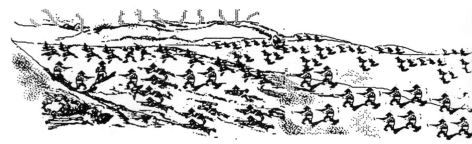

NVA INVESTS SAIGON 4/1975

303	=Stronghold
▨	=Sanctuary and Border Bases

MR 2

SOUTH VIETNAM   MR 3

CAMBODIA

NVA III CORPS

NVA I CORPS

NVA IV CORPS

NVA 232 FORCE

SAIGON

NVA II CORPS

MR 4

NVA DELTA FORCES

Central Highlands. ARVN troops predictably panicked and the NVA began a mad pursuit. By March 31, 1975 the reds controlled all of MR 2. They had already seized all of MR 1 by attacking from their bridgeheads south of the DMZ on March 25, 1975.

In the meantime, the 6th and 7th NVA Divisions attacked near Saigon in MR 3 at Xuan Loc. Xuan Loc was defended by the ARVN 18th Infantry Division which fought the finest defensive battle of the war, adding glory to the name of at least one ARVN unit. The ARVN 5th, 18th, 22nd and 25th Infantry Divisions along with the 6th, 8th and 9th Ranger Regiments and the 468th Marine Brigade guarded Saigon in April 1975.

An NVA army group of 23 infantry divisions soon drew up around Saigon. They were deployed as follows:

- I Corps: 312th, 308th and 338th NVA Infantry Divisions.
- II Corps: 3rd (Binh Dinh), 304th, 324th and 325th NVA Divisions.
- III Corps: 10th, 316th and 320th NVA Divisions.
- IV Corps: 6th, 7th and 341st NVA Divisions.
- 232 Force: 3rd (IV Corps), 5th, 8th and 9th NVA Divisions.

Six more NVA Divisions from the Delta and the strategic reserve, including the 1st NVA Division, lay poised near Saigon. In addition, six sapper regiments prepared for deep penetration operations inside the Saigon defenses.

Missions of the Five NVA Assault Corps

- *I Corps:* Attacking from the north, seize the ARVN Joint General Staff Headquarters near Tan Son Nhut Air Base.
- *II Corps:* Attacking from the southeast, seize Saigon's port facilities and eastern Saigon.
- *III Corps:* Seize Tan Son Nhut airport from the northwest.
- *IV Corps:* Seize Bien Hoa air base and the Dong Ngai bridges by attacking from the northeast.
- *232 Force:* Attacking from the west, secure the Saigon Defense Command and National Police Headquarters [727]

When the NVA IV Corps attacked, it was bogged down, as the rough-fighting 18th ARVN Division held the 6th and 7th NVA Divisions at bay. Most of the ARVN general reserve was then thrown into the Xuan Loc battle. On April 18th, the 341st NVA Division flanked Xuan Loc and cut its supply lines to Saigon. On the 20th of April, retreating ARVN troops were de-

■ PT-76 Series

The PT-76 is a 14-ton amphibious reconnaissance tank with a twin water jet-propulsion system. Its chassis is used in over eight other vehicle series. The PT-76 is 7.6m (25 ft) long (including the gun tube), 3.1m (10 ft) wide, and 2.2m (7½ ft) tall.

Primary Weapon
**76-mm stabilized main gun firing kinetic energy APC and chemical energy HEAT ammunition.
Basic load 40 rounds.
The PT-76 Model 1 has a multi-slotted muzzle brake; Model 2 has a double-baffle muzzle brake and a bore evacuator.**

Secondary Armament
**7.62-mm coaxially-mounted machinegun.
Basic load 1,000 rounds.**

Mobility
**Operating range 260 km.
Road speed 44 kmph, water speed 10 kmph.
Maximum grade is 76% (38° slope).
Can cross a 2.7m (9 ft) trench and climb a 1.2m (3½ ft) vertical obstacle.
Maximum tilt in water while swimming is 18°.**

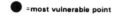

● =most vulnerable point

How to Defeat
The PT-76 is thin-skinned; artillery can disable it. Fire LAW or 40-mm HEDP (high explosive dual purpose) rounds at its flanks to defeat it. When the PT-76 is hull-down, fire at its center of mass.

stroyed by ambushes along that route. Then the NVA IV Corps seized Bien Hoa and Long Binh.

In fifty-five days the Chu Luc had defeated the following ARVN ground forces:

- 190 infantry, airborne, ranger and marine battalions.
- 75 105mm, 155mm, and 175mm artillery battalions.
- 40 engineer battalions.
- 16 signal battalions.
- 12 military police battalions.
- 4 antiaircraft battalions.[728]

Twenty-five division equivalents of ARVN infantry, supported by twenty regiments of artillery, were defeated by a force that didn't outnumber them by more than two to one.

The South Vietnamese Army was trained by Americans for twenty years to fight just such a conventional defensive war. Yet, they lost it in fifty-five days. Why? Because American military doctrine, training, equipment, weapons and technological anti-warrior mentality is counterproductive and unsuitable for war-fighting!

By the end of April, South Vietnam had fallen. The destruction of South Vietnam seemed to be the only possible outcome after it had become so corrupted by American technological and material depravity. As so often happens, a decadent regime was destroyed by a more virile, inhuman and barbaric system. Thus millions of people were enslaved because of the simple fact that free countries sometimes spawn impotent and unimaginative governments led by lazy elitists.

The peculiarly American form of materialistically anti-military foreign policy, displayed during the Vietnam War, should be closely studied. South Vietnam was an American microcosm. Its defeat was an American defeat.

CHAPTER 23

Sino-Vietnamese War

After South Vietnam was wiped from the face of the earth, a brave new communist order descended over Indochina. The Vietnamese communists had it all now, all of Vietnam, the two puppet states of Cambodia and Laos, as well as plans for seizing even greater power in Asia. But first, all anti-communist opposition had to be mopped up. Leaving Cambodia to be administered by the Khmer Rouge's four divisions and three regiments, the Viets went about their own pacification and re-education campaigns.

The Cambodian Khmer Rouge had been seduced, trained, and inspired by their Viet masters. Now their leader, Pol Pot, and his small army, instead of starving and whittling away at their own people in the typical communist long-term program, sought quicker results.

"It was discovered that Pol Pot and his Khmer Rouge supporters had literally *murdered nearly half of the country* (estimated to be 7.3 million) in the four year period they had been in power. Even today mass graves are still being discovered. The slain included practically all the professional, administrative, and educated classes, as well as merchants, shopkeepers, skilled and semiskilled workers. Pol Pot had emptied all the cities and towns, decreeing that all should return to the villages to live at a primitive peasant level, and all Western machinery, goods and gadgets, such as automobiles, typewriters, radios, telephones, television sets and electrical appliances, should be destroyed. Schools and hospitals were stripped and left empty, and the country was left essentially without medical or educational facilities."[729]

Where were those citizens of the world who so piously decried the Nazi/Jewish holocaust? Were the lives of millions of Cambodians less important?

Since Pol Pot had killed every Cambodian capable of administration, the Vietnamese would take over everything. But there was a problem. The murderous Khmer Rouge dictator, Pol Pot, resisted total Vietnamese take-over of his nation. He fought back!

On December 27, 1978 twelve Vietnamese Communist divisions invaded Cambodia. Other nations of Asia protested even as the NVA destroyed Pol Pot's army and set up a new puppet government called the People's Republic of Kampuchea.[730]

The Chinese Military's Bastard Son

The Chinese have always viewed Indochina with concern. It is a natural invasion route into southern China.

Chinese blood pressure began to rise as a new Vietnamese aggressor nation, led by ruthless killers, grasped for control of Indochina and Southeast Asia.

Ironically, the Chinese had created the Vietnamese Communist military machine, the Chu Luc. Many Chinese communist military ideas, organizational devices, methods and tactics were directly absorbed into the Chu Luc military doctrine, with little or no modification. Certain basic maxims of Chinese communist (ChiCom) military art were reflected by Vietcom military operations. The Chinese military had fathered a bastard son.

There were numerous similarities between Chinese and Vietnamese military art. The most famous Chu Luc military catch phrase was, "One Slow-Four Fasts." The Chinese communist concept of offensive action is also exemplified by a "One Slow-Four Fasts," catch phrase.

The One Slow portion of the Chinese version refers to the commander's responsibility for careful evaluation, planning, and inspection prior to an attack. The Four Fasts portion of the phrase, relates to speed in execution of the attack:

1. Speed in preparation, including reconnaissance.
2. Speed in the advance, to flank or encircle the enemy.
3. Speed in exploitation of gains, to prevent enemy regrouping.
4. Speed in pursuit, to overtake and destroy a retreating enemy.

Another Chinese catch phrase, "One Point-Two Sides," describes a second ChiCom concept of offensive action. It is a maneuver technique of launching a number of separate attacks against one objective. It is not the same as an envelopment, because the Chinese coordinated attacks are made by separate units which have deployed prior to battle.

1. "One Point" means to concentrate overwhelmingly superior strength against an enemy weak point or gap.
2. "Two Sides" means that two or more assaults are necessary in any attack, in order to deceive the enemy as to the main effort. It does not mean that the attack is limited to only two sides.

Individual strongpoints in a defensive zone are isolated and reduced by the ChiCom divide-and-destroy tactical method. The Chinese believe that no defensive system can be equally strong everywhere. So they try to locate enemy weak points, or gaps, by infantry probes and reconnaissance. Then a deep penetration through the gap is made. Operations rolling out through that captured gap area permit subsequent attacks upon the flank and rear of adjacent strongpoints. This concept was the father of NVA power raid and narrow front assault techniques.[731]

The Chinese Communists Go on the Warpath

The Chinese Communist Army moved thirty-one divisions (330,000 men, ten percent of their total army) and 1,200 tanks to the Vietnamese border. Those forces were subordinate to the ChiCom Southern Front, an army group. However, the Chinese forces committed against Vietnam were organized for conquest of only a portion of Vietnam.

The ChiComs used neither their air force nor navy during their invasion of Vietnam. Therefore it was easy to zero in on what the Chinese ground army could do. After all, the Chinese Army was a power so feared by the American armed forces and ruling establishment, that they refused to fight the Second Indochina War properly. Fear of the Chinese army prevented the Americans from consistently bombing the North Vietnamese properly, from invading red sanctuaries, raiding and invading North Vietnam and really trying to win. How formidable were those fearsome ChiCom hordes which had inspired so much terror?

Actually the Chinese were not that formidable. Their armed forces had seen no full-scale war since 1954. Their overall commander of the Southern Front, General Hsu Shihyu was seventy-three years old and his primary subordinates were in their seventies. General Shihyu was a close political associate of Deng Xiaoping, the ChiCom dictator. General Yang Dezhi,

The Chinese Southern Front Against the Vietnamese: 1975

Eastern Wing: Commended by General Xu Shiyu
41st Army; 42nd Army; 43rd Army; 54th Army; 55th Army; 1st Division-artillery. 70th Division—antiaircraft.

Western Wing: Commanded by General Yang Dezhi
12th Army; 13th Army; 14th Army; 43rd Army; 49th Army;
4th Division—Artillery. 65th Division—antiaircraft.

Air Force: Commanded by General Zhang Tingfa (958 aircraft)
MIG-21s: 28; MIG-19s: 560; MIG-17s: 98; F-9s; 120; Other planes: 142
The Southern Front Air Force was deployed in fifteen air bases near the frontier.

Navy: South Sea Fleet (693 shps)
Destroyers: 2 (missile); Escort destroyers: 4 (missile)
Submarines: 20; Patrol Boats (missile): 27; Other boats: 604[732]

commander of the Western Wing, was a veteran mountain fighter from the Korean War.

In planning for the offensive the Chinese considered several situational imperatives:

1. To cover their rear against a Soviet attack.
2. To attack when Vietnam was vulnerable.
3. To obtain some propaganda support from other nations in the world.

General Li Desheng set up a special military force to defend the Sino-Soviet frontier. Those forces were placed on a war footing and 300,000 Chinese civilians were evacuated from the border zone. The Chinese calculated that the Soviets were unlikely to intervene in the war in any case. Such an intervention would jeopardize their SALT II negotiations being carried out against the Carter administration.

Before the assault on Vietnam, Chinese Premier Deng toured America loudly denouncing Vietnamese imperialism and threatening to "teach them a lesson." When he returned to China the world's media had the impression that Chinese punitive action enjoyed American acquiescence.

China had been supplying Vietnam with fifty percent of its oil. When the Vietcom invaded Cambodia, that oil supply was cut off. China's invasion was

T-54 MEDIUM TANK

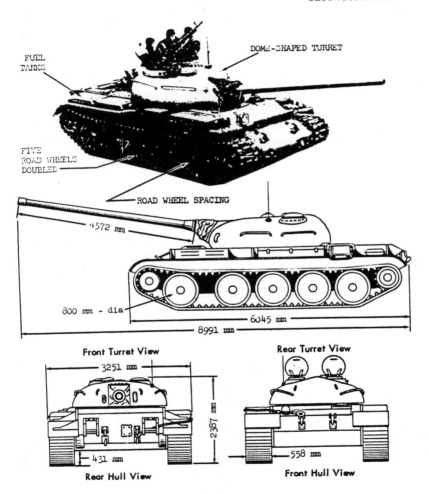

FUEL TANKS

DOME-SHAPED TURRET

FIVE ROAD WHEELS DOUBLED

ROAD WHEEL SPACING

4572 mm

800 mm - dia

6045 mm

8991 mm

Front Turret View

3251 mm

2387 mm

431 mm

Rear Hull View

Rear Turret View

558 mm

Front Hull View

timed to catch Hanoi with low oil reserves. It was also timed to strike at Hanoi while most of the Vietcom Army, sixteen to eighteen divisions, was committed in Cambodia.

The Chinese "armies" which invaded Vietnam were actually corps of three to four infantry divisions each, although each corps did have several tank battalions attached. All the Chinese troops committed to the Vietnam invasion were regulars. In many cases, however, Chinese divisions were made up of regiments from several other divisions. The Chinese were trying to "blood" as many of their units as they could.

Elements from nearly fifty Chinese divisions were identified in Vietnam, although there were never that many complete divisions inside the Vietnamese border. Along the border areas, the Chinese also organized a huge militia force: "They were organized into 102 battalions and several hundred companies, including a mortar company, a heavy machine gun company, an antiaircraft company, a medical company, a road repairing company, a transportation company, donkey-horse transportation units, and other logistics units."[733]

Although the Chinese were experts at orchestrating nonmotorized logistics, their logistics effort during the Vietnam invasion was awkward. They were used to relying on a combination of trucks, human porters, horses and other pack animals for supply portage. A modern army, as the Chu Luc proved, can do very well with such logistics. Neither were inadequate modern communications nor other seeming problems a real handicap to the Chinese. They had maneuvered for fifty years without such niceties.

Yet the Chinese army group confronting Vietnam was equipped with modern weapons, too. Its inventory included: T-62 and T-59 tanks; 122mm and 152mm artillery; 107mm and 140mm multiple rocket launchers; modern antiaircraft guns and SAM missiles.

The Chinese had sent many advisers and troop units to help the Vietcom during the Indochina wars. They knew that the Vietcom had Soviet advisers, modern equipment and veteran, victorious troops. They knew that the Vietnamese had fortified the border areas near China and dug in a 120,000 man border security force to defend the mountainous border zone in depth.

Every Vietnamese/Chinese border mountain pass, frontier town and ridgeline was riddled with successive Vietcom tunneled fortifications, bunkers, minefields, barbed wire and mantraps. Machine guns with grazing and overlapping fields of fire were sited to cover the front in depth. In addition, the area was zeroed in and pre-registered by many supporting mortar and artillery units. The Vietcom even circulated propaganda that their border security force was armed with "laser death rays,"[734] which they were supposedly testing for their Soviet comrades.

The Chinese initially moved up fifteen infantry and three artillery divisions into staging areas along the Vietnamese border. On the Western wing (command post in Mengzi), contiguous to the Laotian border, three axes of advance were selected. On the Eastern wing (command post in Nanning), flanked on the east by the South China Sea, three axes of advance were also selected.

The Three Western Axes of Chinese Advance

- Lai Chau, on the right, southward along Highway 1 to Hanoi. (42nd Infantry Division spearheading the 14th Army)
- Lao Cai, in the center, southward down the Red River Valley. (13th Army)
- Ha Giang, on the left, southward along Highway 2 to Hanoi (11th Army)

The Three Eastern Axes of Chinese Advance

- Mon Kai, on the right, along the South China Seacoast toward Hanoi. (165th Infantry Division spearheading the 55th Army)
- Friendship Pass toward Dong Dang and Lang Son, in the center. (42nd Army)
- Cao Bang, on the right, a shallow diversionary, flank-covering penetration advancing toward Dong Khe. (41st Army)

Only eight Chinese infantry divisions were to be deployed in the first wave, with seven more in the second echelon. Three artillery divisions were assigned to support the first wave attacks. Sixteen more infantry divisions were held in dispersed Army (corps-sized) packets to exploit Vietnamese weak points.

The Chinese were well aware that they would have to fight through a strong crust of Vietnamese border defenses in depth. After that, their troop columns would enter flatlands where they would be exposed to strong Vietnamese aerial and artillery bombardment. When the flatlands of North Vietnam were reached, the Chinese would have to use their air force and obscuring smoke screens if they hoped to advance major units forward.

The northwestern mountainous areas of Laos and the rugged terrain along the Laotian-Vietnamese border offered strong possible invasion routes and potential long-term base areas for a Chinese army group. The Chinese had garrisoned northern Laos for twenty years and built roads there. The vegetative cover and trail network along the Laotian border was perfect for Chinese foot-mobile operations. If the Chinese had fought from that region,

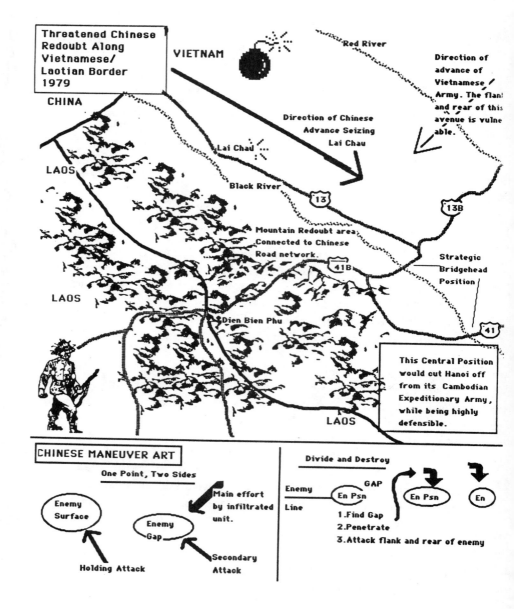

Threatened Chinese Redoubt Along Vietnamese/ Laotian Border 1979

VIETNAM

CHINA

Red River

Direction of advance of Vietnamese Army. The flank and rear of this avenue is vulnerable.

Direction of Chinese Advance Seizing Lai Chau

Lai Chau

LAOS

Black River

13

13B

Mountain Redoubt area Connected to Chinese Road network.

41B

Strategic Bridgehead Position

LAOS

Dien Bien Phu

41

This Central Position would cut Hanoi off from its Cambodian Expeditionary Army, while being highly defensible.

LAOS

CHINESE MANEUVER ART

One Point, Two Sides

Enemy Surface

Main effort by infiltrated unit.

Enemy Gap

Holding Attack

Secondary Attack

Divide and Destroy

GAP

Enemy Line

En Psn

En Psn

En

1. Find Gap
2. Penetrate
3. Attack flank and rear of enemy

they would have been fighting from a Napoleonic central position, the occupation of which would have split and jeopardized the strength and ultimate survival of the Vietnamese nation.

The Chinese Army had compiled a wealth of intelligence data on Laos and the border regions of Vietnam. Thousands of Chinese combat troops had served there during the Second Indochina War. Many Chinese-built roads traversed Northern Laos.

Dien Bien Phu Valley, with the ill-fated former French base located nearby, was a key Vietnamese communications center. It could be controlled from Chinese mountain redoubts, even while the Chinese spread their base areas and road networks south, north and east.

Advantages of the Laotian Border Central Position

1. Chinese occupation of the area would have cut off from Hanoi the Vietnamese Cambodian Army Group, more than half the total Vietnamese army.
2. It offered good cover and strong fortifications.
3. An occupying army could move rapidly within the area using internal lines.
4. It was easily supplied from China.
5. It threatened both Hanoi and Vietnam's Cambodian and Laotian allies.
6. Any Vietnamese approach from the northwest, east or southwest would be exposed to Chinese flanking attacks.
7. The base area exploited Chinese strengths and resources already located in the area.

Chinese occupation of the Laotian central position would have exposed the Vietnamese Army to defeat in detail. If pressure was kept on Hanoi while another Chinese army group plunged south to Cambodia, the Vietnamese would have been in a quandry.

NVA Forces Affected by a Laotian Central Position

- Cambodian Army Group: Eighteen infantry divisions.
- Deployed in Laos and South Vietnam: Ten infantry divisions.
- Deployed around Hanoi: Twelve infantry divisions.
- Units tied down in pacification/internal security roles: Ten infantry divisions.

However, in spite of the best wishes of professional western warriors yearning to study the results of a major protracted Sino-Vietnamese foot-mobile war, the Chinese had more limited objectives in mind. They would effect shallow penetrations of the border area, kill and capture Vietnamese, devastate the countryside, and then withdraw.

The Vietnamese Prepare for an Invasion

The Vietnamese knew that the Chinese were coming. They backed up their border security force with five regional infantry divisions: 325D, 334D, 337D, 338D, and 346D. In addition, they also sent the 241R Infantry Regiment toward the border. Two regular infantry divisions, the 3D and 346D, later moved up into supporting range of the Lang Son area.

The supreme Vietnamese commander, Vo Nguyen Giap, also deployed a strong defense force around Hanoi. Five regular Chu Luc infantry divisions were part of that force, including: 308D, 320D, 329D, 386D and 431D. Four supporting brigades rounded out the Hanoi defense force: 45B Artillery, 329B Engineer, 202B Armor, and 241B Antiaircraft. Also emplaced around the capital were dozens of batteries of ultramodern antiaircraft artillery and surface to air missiles.[735]

Three hundred Vietnamese aircraft, their entire air force, could be committed to the war within a week. Only seventy MIG-21 aircraft in the Vietnamese inventory were considered superior to Chinese aircraft. The Hanoi's navy, although equipped with the latest U.S. ships and boats (captured during the Second Indochina War) was no match for the Chinese Navy.

Giap's strategy was simple. He would bleed and slow down the invading forces in the mountains. Then he would destroy them in the flatlands with his artillery and better-equipped regulars. He had one major worry, however. If the Chinese Army moved along his left flank into Laos and the rugged terrain along the Laotian-Vietnamese border, he would be in trouble. Then the Chinese would force him to either move troops out of Hanoi to drive the invaders out of the border are, or suffer the inconvenience of Hanoi being cut off from its main army group in Cambodia.

The Chinese Invasion

The Chinese wanted to spill some Vietnamese blood. Besides their invasion of Cambodia, the Vietnamese had begun persecuting the "Hoa," people of Chinese stock who had lived within Vietnam for generations. The Vietcom seized Hoa property and wealth, ejecting them from Vietnam.[736]

In 1978, China had demonstrated its displeasure with such actions by

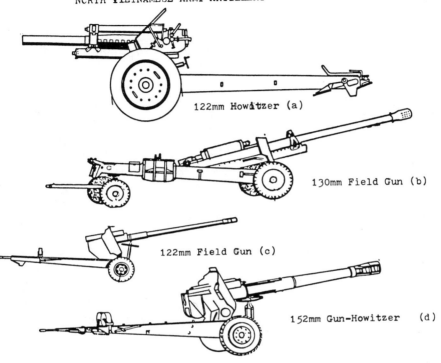

122mm Howitzer (a)

130mm Field Gun (b)

122mm Field Gun (c)

152mm Gun-Howitzer (d)

	✳	WEAPON	RANGE	NORMAL DISTANCE BEHIND FEBA (KM) OFFENSE	DEFENSE	RATE OF FIRE (RD/MIN)
		120-mm MORTAR	5,700 meters	0.5	1	15
b	✳	130-mm FIELD GUN	27,000 meters	5	9	5 to 6
a	✳	122-mm HOWITZER	15,300 meters	3	4	6 to 8
	✳	122-mm GUN	15,300 meters	3	4	4 to 6
b	✳	130-mm FIELD GUN	27,000 meters	5	9	5 to 6
	✳	152-mm GUN/HOWITZER	17,000 meters	4	5	5
d	✳	152-mm SP GUN/HOWITZER	17,300 meters	4	5	4 to 6
		122-mm MRL BM-21	20,500 meters	5	5	40 RDS/10 MIN (Rate/reload time)
		122-mm MRL RM-70	20,500 meters	5	5	40 RDS/5 MIN (Rate/reload time)
		FROG-7	11 to 70 kilometers	18	23	1 RD/20 MIN

✳Highest probability for employment in Direct-Fire role.

staging border incidents. In a letter to the United Nations, the Vietnamese denounced China as war mongers and guilty of "583 armed encroachments"[737] on the Vietnamese border. When the Chinese occupied some strategic hills in Cao Loc district of Long Son Province, Hanoi screamed in rage, demanding immediate withdrawal of "occupationist troops." Hanoi accused the Chinese of "dangerous and premeditated steps by the authorities in their criminal hostility toward Vietnam."[738]

On January 30, 1979 Chinese advance detachments began raiding the Vietnamese border. In another propaganda message the Vietnamese communists declared: "By invading Vietnam, they have thrown off the revolutionary mask under which they hide, to collude with the imperialists. They have become a dangerous and direct enemy of the whole socialist system and of the movement for national independence, democracy and peace in Asia and the world."[739]

When the Chinese invaded Vietnam on February 17, 1979, they immediately called on Vietnam for peaceful negotiations. Radio Hanoi replied: "What is to be negotiated when the Chinese troops are trampling our soil? This is tantamount to a robber whetting his knife to compel the houseowner to negotiate the haul."[740]

The Chinese began their invasion with a flurry of diversionary attacks all along the border. Advance detachments then plunged forward, seizing defiles and passes. Following closely were Chinese divisional columns, who advanced behind heavy artillery barrages. The Chinese necessarily broke their units down into battalion battle groups for mountain fighting.

Fighting as mountain troops, Chinese columns slashed forward according to the "granular principle." They thrust forward along whatever avenues of approach were available, paying no attention to their flanks.

Although tanks and artillery supported every invading column, the Chinese also employed every light infantry tactic imaginable. They employed "the tactics and methods of fire wave and human wave, tunnel search and dynamite detonation, mine explosion, surprise attacks, encirclement and other forms of guerrilla warfare."[741] For example, the Chinese used water buffaloes to touch off booby traps and mines.

Pushing hard, the Chinese crossed the Red River and drew near Lao Cai. By the end of the month they had taken the Vietnamese cities of Lao Cai, Ha Giang and Dong Dang. The Viets resisted strongly at Cao Bang, Lang Son and Mon Kai, making two small counterattacks into Chinese territory. At Dong Dang in Lang Son Province, the Chinese defeated Hanoi's regular army "Flying Tiger Regiment."[742]

Fighting under orders to advance no more than fifty kilometers inside

Vietnam, the Chinese took two days to fight their way through the mountain passes. As they slowly advanced, being careful to destroy Viet tunnels and fortifications as they moved, they periodically paused for troop reinforcement. In that way, the Chinese consistently leap-frogged fresh troops into their spearhead force.

One biased source who reported on the fighting during the invasion used Vietnamese sources to conclude that the Chinese "relied upon sheer numbers . . . to force their way forward in massed charges . . . The frontier passes were taken by frontal assaults, by sheer hard fighting, with whole battalions, moving as a single solid human mass. Charges were regulated by bugle calls. When the buglers became priority targets for the Vietnamese snipers and were killed, hopeless confusion ensued.

"Advances were made with callous disregard for casualties. The Chinese troops gamely and blindly battled forward."[743]

There is little evidence to substantiate such claims. While it is true that the Chinese did fight awkwardly, even the Viets credited them with fighting a maneuver battle at all levels. What's the rub about buglers and "primitive communications means?" If it works, it's good! Besides, killing a few buglers hardly inconveniences a maneuver army. On the other hand, killing a few radio operators immobilizes American army and marine units.

As they advanced, several Chinese battalion equivalents were destroyed, but they wiped out even more Viets as well as seven missile bases. By February 26, Hanoi was deploying regular army formations including tanks and artillery against the Chinese.

Vietnamese General Giap became alarmed as the Chinese pushed deeper into Vietnam. He despatched several regular army divisions forward to Lang Son, led by the 308th Division of Dien Bien Phu fame. Hanoi's leader began to prepare for evacuation, as the 3,000 Soviet advisers within North Vietnam were asked for greater contribution to the war effort.

A climatic battle at Lang Son began to develop. There ten Chinese divisions met an equal number of Vietnamese divisions dug in on Hills 417, 473, 556, 568, 608 and 800. Nearby Khua Ma Son Mountain was heavily fortified too, with six major Viet strongpoints dug into it.

Lang Son itself was turned into a Viet fortified camp with "extensive tunnel works, including a road wide enough for several vehicles to drive along abreast and an assembly hall for political meetings and entertainment."[744]

In wide enveloping attacks, the Chinese cut all roads leading into Lang Son. Then major attacks began on February 27, hitting the defended hill complex, as "heavy casualties were reported on both sides. Thousands of corpses scattered along Highway 1A (southwest of Lang Son on the road to Hanoi)."[745]

By March 2, the Chinese took all of the hills around Lang Son except the key Khua Ma Son Mountain redoubt. On March 3, 1979 a Chinese combined arms (tank-infantry-artillery) attack rolled over Hill 303 in ten minutes. Then the attacking Chinese columns swept up Khau Ma Son Mountain.

"After fierce exchanges of fire power, mine explosions and tunnel destruction, the six Vietnamese firing positions on the mountain were destroyed one after another. Lang Son was captured."[746]

During their invasion, the Chinese had mauled the Vietnamese 320D and 308th Divisions at Lao Cai. They almost destroyed the 304th Viet Division at Lang Son. At Dong Da they did destroy the 3D Vietnamese Division. No Chinese divisions were destroyed by the Viets, although several were severely mauled.

On March 5, 1979 the Chinese began withdrawing from Vietnam. As they left, the Chinese destroyed everything they couldn't take with them in a fashion reminiscent of Ghengis Khan's Mongols. The Chinese scorched earth policy rendered ineffective many Vietnamese bridges, roads, irrigation canals and buildings, without resorting to indiscriminate bombing and shelling.

The Chinese razed 320 villages in the six Vietnamese provinces they occupied, as well as the three provincial capitals of Lao Kai, Lang Son and Mon Kai. The Viets would not soon forget the Chinese visit.

"Everywhere bridges have been blown up and roads have been mined and destroyed.

"The hospitals in Lao Cai, Lang Son and Cao Bang were demolished. In all three towns . . . everything lies in ruins and all is silent. About 80% of the buildings were destroyed.

"Not a single electric power pole remains standing in or around the three towns . . . There is a water shortage through the region and electricity has been cut off.

"Nearby villages also lie in ruins."[747]

As the Chinese withdrew, General Giap called for total mobilization of the Vietnamese people. He screamed invectives aimed at influencing naive western observers. His anti-Chinese statements included: "(The Chinese leaders are) war criminals more cruel than Hitler . . . (waging) undeclared war against our country and trampling under foot all norms of international law and the basic principles of relations between independent and sovereign nations . . . the Chinese aggressors should know that despite their vast country and large population, they are not strong; though great in number, are weak."[748]

NVA T55 TANK

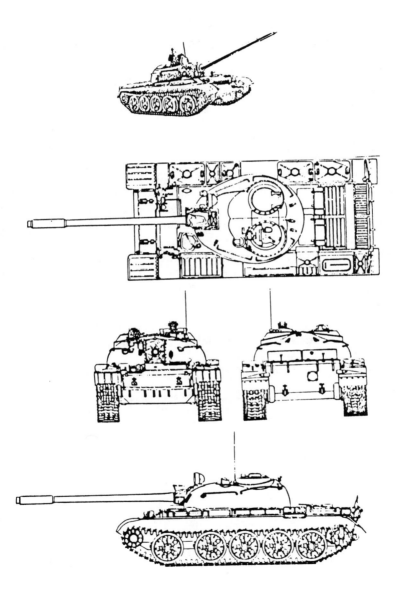

"From generation to generation, we have on many occasions risen up to fight and defeat the northern feudalist aggressors (China) to preserve our independence and sovereignty . . . Our nation can be proud that our country, the Dai Viet, vanquished the most ferocious Yuan invaders in the 13th century . . . The Beijing reactionary clique has started a large-scale war in an attempt to annex our country and enslave our people . . . In this historic confrontation between civilization and barbarity . . . the Vietnamese people will certainly win."[749]

The Sino-Vietnamese War is shrouded in deception, lies and the fog which exists because the west has no viable human asset intelligence gathering capability. Anything reported about any communist activity is possibly untrue. America and the west know nothing of communist intentions. The, communist-provided, final total of war losses on both sides could fall into the category of disinformation.

After the Chinese left Vietnam, at the end of the thirty day war, Hanoi accused China of: "terrible destruction, plunder and atrocities against the civilian population. Chinese soldiers . . . sacked villages and towns, carried off clothes, household utensils, valuable equipment, tens of thousands of tons of rice, agricultural machines and a large number of cattle . . . destroyed power plants, communication facilities, eighty-one industrial enterprises built with foreign aid, burnt down houses, hospitals, schools and destroyed 80,000 hectares of crops."[750]

For the first time, one communist nation had fought another with the weapons of modern war. Did that war offer evidence which reinforced rational humanity's hope that eventually communism would begin to consume itself?

Sino-Vietnamese War Losses: February–March 1971

Category	Chinese	Vietnamese
Killed	26,000	30,000
Wounded	37–52,000	32–60,000
Prisoners of war	260	1,638
Tanks, armored vehicles	420	185
Heavy mortars and guns	66	200
Missile sites	0	6

CHAPTER 24

Chu Luc Triumphant

In 1975, Saigon fell and the curtain rang down on Southeast Asia. The communists had won another war. Suddenly a new military colossus stood dominant over four nations. The Democratic Republic of Vietnam had become the most dangerous military power in Southeast Asia.

The North Vietnamese Army had transformed the Hanoi regime into an international power, holding suzerainty over dozens of ethnic groups. Hundreds of thousands of those diverse subjects were soon confined in concentration camps.

"Since April 1975 well over one million Vietnamese have been incarcerated in the 'Bamboo Gulag,' a network of more than 150 re-education camps and prisons . . . it is estimated that at least 600,000 Vietnamese remain in detention throughout the country. 'The re-education program is vital to the regime's security,' writes Nguyen Van Canh (deputy dean of the Faculty of Law at the University of Saigon until 1975) . . . Among the prisoners are former South Vietnamese military officers and government officials; writers, journalists and poets; doctors and lawyers; educators, students and religious leaders."[751]

"All prisoners are forced to . . . 'confess' their alleged misdeeds, . . . clear old minefields . . . (experience) torture . . . and other brutal forms of punishment . . . Disease is rampant. . . . and (the prisoners suffer) severe malnutrition and starvation . . . the death rate in the camps is high."[752] "the communist regime has refused to permit the Red Cross to visit the camps, . . . a visit by Amnesty International resulted in a report of terrible human rights violations."[753]

On March 4, 1985, "NBC's 'Today Show' aired Jon Alpert's incredibly insensitive interview of a former South Vietnamese major in a model 're-education' camp near Saigon. Alpert . . . put the major in the position of either having to lie about the treatment of the prisoners, sending a false message to the outside world, or telling the truth, knowing that he would be tortured by his jailers if he did."[754]

According to Truong Nhu Tang, a founder of South Vietnam's "National Liberation Front," and a defector to the West: "To help pay its debts to the Soviet Union, the Vietnamese government recently agreed to export 500,000 'guest workers' for Siberian slave labor."[755] Tang "estimates that most of these slaves come from the reeducation camps and jails for political prisoners."[756]

Thanks to the Chu Luc, red Vietnam emerged as a true regional power, because it possessed a first class army which threatened the security of all Asia. That threat was manifested by newly-won communist control of major ports and bases along the very strategic China Sea.

The red liberation of Indochina began to disappoint the world when it revealed itself to be nothing more than a prelude to mass murder. Yet, the communist bloodbath should have been expected. Curzio Malaparte had described the pathologies which dominated the minds of communist populaces during World War II: ". . . there is nothing either human or inhuman of which . . . (the communist) people is incapable. . . . a people who hate God in themselves, and who hate themselves . . . in their fellow human beings . . . Death, to the (godless) communist, is a smooth, compact, windowless wall. It is cold, hermetically-sealed sleep. It is a void—a vacuum . . . this mixture of sadism and masochism, . . . nihilism, . . . utter hopelessness . . ."[757]

A New Red Army, Navy, and Air Force

As victors in the Second Indochina War, the Vietnamese communists had gained a mass of spoils unbelievable and fantastic even by western standards. Their booty included nuclear reactors, mounds of gold bullion, hundreds of warehouses filled with supplies, and thousands of miles of brand new all-weather roads. Millions of dollars in newly minted American currency was also seized.

Indochina's new communist landlords had acquired hundreds of huge, city-sized cantonments and base areas, over one hundred new airfields, dozens of new port facilities, numerous electrical and other fuel plants, and many large fuel depots. That largesse was worth tens of billions of American taxpayer dollars.[758]

American intelligence documents, easily secured by the advancing reds, laid bare the last remaining U.S. secrets. The North Vietnamese captured over thirty super-secret code machines. Hundreds of U.S. code books, and top secret material sufficient to fill dozens of warehouses, were soon being read by agents from every communist controlled nation. South Vietnamese intelligence assets, abandoned as the Americans fled in panic, also provided the reds with secret information: "What some of the Vietnamese officers had in their heads was more important (to the Communists) than the hardware. They had the education and skill to recreate equipment that they had studied or worked on, or even to build it from diagrams that we had given to them."[759]

Being wise investors, the reds plowed their new found wealth back into the force that made it all possible, the Chu Luc. Hanoi was given a military force multiplied by ten. The Chu Luc had seized enough supplies and equipment to form a modern army, navy, air force and helicopter force. Suddenly, the red military was stronger than ever before.

The birth of a new Vietnamese armed force would have been aborted if the American military, corrupted by amateurism and timidity, had only been more professional. The U.S. military, leaving a wealth of spoils behind, failed to scuttle ships, demolish aircraft and airfields, contaminate supplies, blow up supply dumps, or destroy port and other facilities. The Americans left no scorched earth, no desert of destruction, and no jungle of booby traps to hinder the victorious communist energy. The reds received their American war loot and logistics windfall in pristine condition!

The new red army was soon re-equipped with a vast arsenal of captured American weaponry, including:

- 791,000 M16 Rifles
- 47,000 M79 grenade launchers
- 63,000 light antitank weapons
- 857,580 other assorted rifles and carbines
- Untold numbers of heavy machine guns and recoilless rifles.[760]
- 90,000 .45 caliber pistols
- 50,000 M60 machine guns
- 12,000 mortars

That haul of infantry weapons was sufficient to equip a million-man army with a complete family of crew-served and individual weapons.

If the red army needed to communicate, they could talk on 48,000 captured tactical radios. To haul it all around they had seized a massive fleet of 42,000 trucks.

For artillery support, the reds could now field ten or fifteen artillery divisions equipped with the finest, mint condition American artillery pieces, including:

- Eighty 175mm self-propelled cannon. (four battalion equivalents)
- 250 155mm cannon. (8 battalion equivalents)
- 1,000 105mm cannon. (33 battalion equivalents)
- Hundreds of antiaircraft guns.[761]

In fact, the Vietnamese added five new artillery divisions to their order of battle after the Vietnam War.

If the Chu Luc wanted to form an armored army of six to ten tank and mechanized divisions, they could. The reds captured all the brand new mechanized equipment they needed, including:

- 300 M41 tanks. (enough to form ten battalion equivalents)
- 250 M48 tanks. (enough to form eight battalion equivalents)
- 1200 armored personnel carriers. (enough to form eight battalion equivalents)
- Over a thousand armored cars and other armored fighting vehicles.[762]

What about close air support and airmobility? The North Vietnamese armed forces had few helicopters and other aircraft during the Second Indochina War. Now the Chu Luc could be airmobile too. The reds had captured the wherewithal to form a couple of airmobile divisions:

- 430 Huey helicopters.
- 36 CH-47 medium helicopters.
- A large number of other airmobile division choppers.[763]

With the modern aircraft captured on dozens of abandoned South Vietnamese airfields, the reds could also transport, air deliver and support a couple of paratroop divisions. The new communist air force was a modern and well balanced force. Its inventory now included the latest tactical support, reconnaissance and transport aircraft. The huge fleet of confiscated U.S. aircraft included:

- 73 F-5 jet fighter/interceptors.
- 36 A-1 ground attack planes.
- Ten C-130 transports.
- 40 C-119 transports.

- 40 C-7 transports.
- 36 C-47 cargo aircraft.
- 22 T41 training aircraft.
- 144 T34 training jets.
- Hundreds of reconnaissance and light aircraft.[764]

Suddenly the Vietnamese navy had all the equipment and facilities necessary to become a major seagoing power. In fact, the reds had captured sufficient equipment and supplies to form two navies, one ocean-going and one riverine. The new Vietnamese ocean-going navy's inventory was composed of 940 captured ships of various sizes and types. In addition, a complete naval infrastructure with four or five world class ports, stood ready to serve the communist regime. Among the many U.S. Navy ships captured (Why weren't they scuttled?) were:

- 18 LCUs.
- 5 LSMs.
- 3 501-1145 LSTs.
- 1 Barnegat-class Frigate.
- 2 Admirable-class Corvettes.
- 19 PGM 59/71.[765]

As a regional power, the communists had to control the many Indochinese waterways. For that purpose the Chu Luc could now field a three-division riverine force and several river "fleets." For their new river navy the reds had seized the most modern American equipment available, including:

- 27 river patrol craft (RPC).
- 26 Coast Guard patrol boats (WPB).
- 107 Swift inshore patrol boats.
- 84 assault support patrol boats.
- 293 PBR river patrol boats.
- 42 monitors, MK5 (1969 model).
- 22 monitors, modified LCM6.
- 100 armored troop carriers, modified LCM6.
- Eight command and control boats (CCB).[766]

Enough amphibious craft and equipment were included in the massive naval booty for the Vietnamese to organize three new marine, or naval infantry, divisions too.

Naturally the huge new multi-service communist military machine needed supplies, spare parts, maintenance and other facilities. In dozens of locations throughout South Vietnam, the reds had seized huge supply dumps, vast military bases, and numerous radar and communications installations. They were the proud owners of billions of dollars worth of sophisticated military and personal supplies. Thousands of American-trained South Vietnamese technicians stood ready to keep it all running.

Over 130,000 tons of American ammunition were seized by the conquerors. That haul averaged out to more than four pounds of ammo for every Vietnamese man, woman and child. The value? Over $5 billion!

The conquest of South Vietnam enabled the communist army to be increased to:

- 1 armored division.
- 28 infantry divisions.
- 3 marine, or naval infantry divisions.
- 2 artillery divisions.
- 1 antiaircraft division.
- 1 engineer division.
- 5 independent armored regiments.
- 15 independent motorized infantry regiments.
- 35 independent artillery regiments.
- 50 independent antiaircraft regiments.
- 25 SAM (surface to air missile) antiaircraft regiments.
- 15 independent engineer regiments.[767]

This massive Vietnamese Army of one hundred division equivalents dwarfed the U.S. Army and Marine corps combined. Its force was further multiplied by a superior maneuver war fighting doctrine and a mass of veteran officers and men. The Vietnamese Communist Army was now larger and more powerful than the Imperial Japanese Army of World War II. A new "Greater South East Asia Co-Prosperity Sphere" had begun!

The New Age of Vietnamese Imperialism

The new Vietnamese empire "(relies) on a native communist elite that can build and operate a tolerable imitation of the Leninist state with a pervasive bureaucratic control over all spheres of public life."[768]

By the 1980s, the Vietnamese had deployed over fifty combat infantry and marine divisions in Indochina. They had put four divisions in Laos, eighteen in Cambodia, twelve in South Vietnam, and nineteen divisions, including

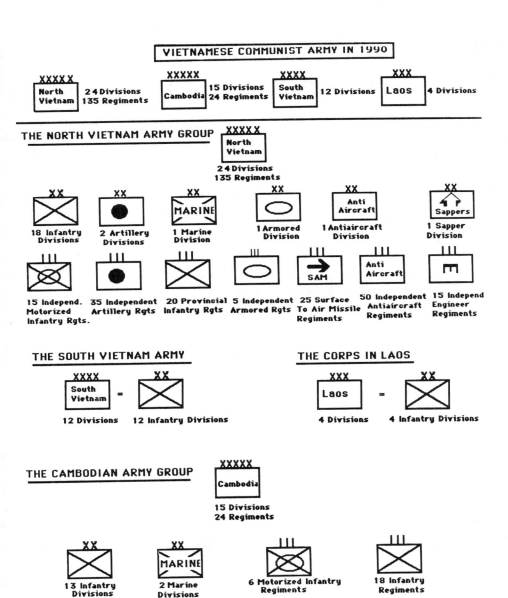

VIETNAMESE COMMUNIST ARMY IN 1990

North Vietnam — 24 Divisions, 135 Regiments
Cambodia — 15 Divisions, 24 Regiments
South Vietnam — 12 Divisions
Laos — 4 Divisions

THE NORTH VIETNAM ARMY GROUP

North Vietnam
24 Divisions
135 Regiments

18 Infantry Divisions
2 Artillery Divisions
1 Marine Division
1 Armored Division
1 Antiaircraft Division
1 Sapper Division

15 Independ. Motorized Infantry Rgts.
35 Independent Artillery Rgts
20 Provincial Infantry Rgts
5 Independent Armored Rgts
25 Surface To Air Missile Regiments
50 Independent Antiaircraft Regiments
15 Independ Engineer Regiments

THE SOUTH VIETNAM ARMY

South Vietnam =
12 Divisions   12 Infantry Divisions

THE CORPS IN LAOS

Laos =
4 Divisions   4 Infantry Divisions

THE CAMBODIAN ARMY GROUP

Cambodia
15 Divisions
24 Regiments

13 Infantry Divisions
2 Marine Divisions
6 Motorized Infantry Regiments
18 Infantry Regiments

501

five corps headquarters, on the Chinese/Vietnamese border, and around Hanoi. Each of Vietnam's 500 districts was insructed to recruit and train a division of self-defense militia infantry to fight at the village level. Vietnam became the most militarized nation in the world. The Vietnamese Communist Army found itself able to challenge and defeat any power, or alliance of powers, in Asia!

Yet, for all of their loot and massive military power, the new red state is not a paradise. In 1985, with a per capita annual income of only $160, Vietnam still ranked as one of the world's twenty poorest countries. Its currency on the openly traded 'black market' drew only a small fraction of its official value, and hyper-inflation was especially disastrous to its urban population. A dozen eggs, for example, represented almost two weeks' wages for an average Hanoi government worker, and a tube of toothpaste the equivalent of three months'.[769] "The average (Vietnamese) worker earns 160 dong ($18 at the official rate) a month and must make do with a monthly ration of cereal (13kg), meat (2kg), fish (2kg) and sugar (1kg) . . . It would take . . . several years to buy one of the Viettronics color television sets assembled at a onetime Sanyo plant in Bien Hoa."[770]

Evidence exists which may substantiate that some American MIAs (Missing in Action) are still alive.[771] That evidence is sketchy and hard to verify. Sometimes, the U.S. Government inadvertently reveals part of what appears to be a cover-up.[772]

Elements within the U.S. government now want to send foreign aid to the Vietnamese, suspected holders of still-living American POWs.[773] Some claim that, "America could benefit economically from commerce with the new markets available within the Vietnamese Empire." However, their wishcraft is contradicted by the facts. According to Donald K. Emmerson of the University of Wisconsin's Center for Southeast Asia Studies: "The raw materials and cheap labor offered by Vietnam are more readily available elsewhere; the quality of Vietnamese manufactured goods is too poor to compete among U.S. buyers; and Vietnamese incomes are too low to purchase U.S. goods. And in any event, whatever Vietnamese market may exist is peanuts in comparison with the markets that already exist in capitalist countries of East and Southeast Asia, let along the potential market of China."[774]

Loss of Strategic Bases

Into the newly conquered base and port facilities of South Vietnam, soon streamed ships and aircraft bearing thousands of Soviet, Warsaw Pact and Cuban technicians and advisors. A Soviet naval infantry battalion was immediately dispatched to Cam Rahn Bay as a security force for the new Soviet strategic air and naval base there. Soviet transport and combat aviation units also occupied South Vietnam's ten major jet air bases.

The loss of the strategic base at Cam Rahn Bay is a major defeat for American power in the Pacific. Close to the straits of Malacca, Lombok and Sunda, the base enables Soviet and Vietnamese long-range air fleets and navies to threaten strategic shipping. That threat has skewed the international correlation of military forces toward an eventual communist victory.

Now the Soviet military behemoth is within striking distance of U.S. naval and air bases in the Philippines, which will soon fall under Soviet control in any case. China has been outflanked and targets in South China, formerly out of range of Soviet Far Eastern Air Forces, can now be hit.

America's allies in Asia now quake before the Soviet power umbrella. Soon America will be totally driven from the Pacific, already earmarked to become a communist ocean.

American sea and air lines of communication through the Pacific and Indian Oceans to the Asiatic landmass, are now vulnerable to Soviet strike forces. Soviet air and naval power is now in range of Alaskan oil fields and supply lines, the Aleutian Islands, and U.S. territory in the Pacific. No longer is the Soviet port of Vladivostok in danger of being sealed off in a crisis.

Cam Ranh Bay gives Moscow a year-round warm port 2,200 miles closer to the Indian Ocean than Vladivostok, and 3,800 miles closer than the Soviet port of Petropavlosk. This geographical advantage enables the Soviets to more adroitly deploy their surface, sub-surface, and air forces into the Indian Ocean and South China Sea. Now "the Soviets will certainly be in a position to deny transit along the oil routes to anyone—including the once-mighty Seventh (U.S.) Fleet. To ask the people of East Asia not to heed the new masters of their lifelines is to ask too much."[775]

The forward staging base of Cam Ranh Bay, South Vietnam, shortens Soviet logistics lines, reduces fuel consumption, saves engine wear and extends the core life of nuclear submarines. The base is also a staging base for reconnaissance flights. Now the range of Soviet aerial reconnaissance has been extended to the southern coast of Australia.

Soviet missile weapons are now within easy striking range of American bases throughout Asia as well as all Southeast Asian capitals. Thanks to their new Vietnamese bases, the Soviets are now able to employ all of their naval ships and weaponry in the Pacific, including: VSTOL carriers, TU-142 "Bear F" long-range antisubmarine warfare aircraft, TU-16 "Badger" medium range bombers and TU-95 "Bear D" reconnaissance aircraft.

"Today 25 to 35 Soviet naval vessels are stationed at Cam Rahn, including four to six submarines and five to ten surface combat vessels, and all are serviced by a large floating dry dock. There are over 7,000 Soviet military personnel in Vietnam. The Soviet Union has also stationed there eight of its approximately 125 Bear (TU-95) strategic bombers, and since 1984, 16 of its 240 Badger (TU-16) medium range fighter bombers. As one military specialist pointed out, this is a notable development since it represents 'the only Russian strike aircraft deployed anywhere in the world beyond Soviet borders.'

"For the Soviets, Cam Rahn and Da Nang represent the culmination of long held ambitions for unencumbered year round facilities in the Pacific. In 1945, these ambitions led to Stalin's demands at Yalta for 'extraterritorial' naval rights from China (at Darien and Port Arthur), an arrangement that Mao was later required to renew. When he brought it to an end in 1955, Moscow began an unsuccessful search for alternatives, first in Indonesia, then in Cambodia and probably North Korea, and not long ago a Soviet 'rental' offer was reportedly made to the Republic of Maldives. The achievement of this goal in Vietnam is a development of major strategic importance, as Brezhnev underlined when the Kremlin hierarchy welcomed Hanoi's treaty signing delegation in 1978 and hailed Vietnam as 'this important outpost for peace and socialism in Southeast Asia.'

"the important point is that these new Soviet facilities are less than 800 miles from the Philippines . . . the South China Sea . . . (is) no longer an 'American lake'."[776]

Cam Ranh Bay is now the largest Soviet naval base outside of the USSR. Constructed by the American Navy and its civilian subcontractors, the base "is being further expanded, even though it already has six floating docks, seven piers, an airfield and a fuel depot with storage capacity for 1.4 million litres of fuel. Some twenty-five to thirty warships, including submarines, generally operate from Cam Rahn Bay. For some time now, a 15,000 ton Madina class missile support ship has also been stationed there. Stationed at the base airfield are usually about 14 MiG-23 Flogger G fighters, three TU-95 maritime reconnaissance aircraft, three TU-142 Bear F ASW aircraft and 16 TU-16 Badger G bombers armed with AS-2 and AS-6 missiles.

"The Soviets are also expanding their second Vietnamese base, at DaNang, where accommodations for 1,000 men was recently completed. Located on Ngu Naha Mountain (Monkey Mountain) is a modern communications monitoring station. The naval base at Kampong Son and the airfield at Phnom Penh in Cambodia are also available for use by the Soviet Navy and Air Force respectively.

"Those bases in Indo-China are of great strategic significance to the Soviets, since forces operating from them can control not only the Strait of Malacca, the eastern port of entry into the Indian Ocean, but also the Pacific sealanes out as far as the Philippines. Transit voyages between ships' home ports and these bases are made easier by the fact that vessels of the Pacific Fleet can also use the North Korean port of Nampo in an emergency.

"In the Indian Ocean the Russians have set up a comprehensive network of mooring buoys used as rendezvous points for warships and replenishment vessels."[777]

Over 6,000 Soviet advisors and several thousand East European and Cuban advisers now serve in Vietnam. Over 500 more Cuban advisors assist the Vietnamese in their efforts to "pacify" Laos and Cambodia.

The Dominos Are Falling

According to the Domino Theory, the loss of South Vietnam would be followed by the loss of Laos, Cambodia, Thailand and the rest of Southeast Asia. The "Domino Theory" has now become a reality! Laos and Cambodia have fallen to the Chu Luc . . . Thailand and Malaysia are under attack.

"In 1978 Vietnamese troops occupied and have now fortified the hitherto unquestionably Malaysian island of Amboyna, lying just south of the disputed Spratley islands . . . The implicit Soviet naval menace not only deters Malaysian military action to retake Amboyna, . . . it also threatens the major trade routes to Hong Kong, Japan, Taiwan and China."[778]

For the past decade, Vietnamese troops have been skirmishing along and crossing over the Thai border, "tank-led Vietnamese troops reached the Thai border (in 1978) . . . Thai officials have described the continuing flood of refugees from Laos, Cambodia, and Vietnam . . . as a strategy by Hanoi that is designed to destabilize and lay the groundwork for subversion."[779] In the meantime, red subversion eats at Thailand from within.

Vietnamese subversion had immediate success in Thailand, "between 1973 and 1976, . . . Thailand had five weak civilian governments . . . leading to degeneration of law and order and (power grabbing) . . . by communist front organizations."[780] In 1976, the Thai government closed all U.S. bases there.

The red inspired coup which toppled Thai Prime Minister Thanin and his Cabinet on October 20, 1977 was a devastating defeat to world anti-communism. In announcing the coup, the Revolutionary Council "criticized Thanin for the *excessive nature of his anti-communism,* his failure to improve the investment climate . . . and his *unwillingness to negotiate with the neighboring states of Vietnam, Laos and Kampuchea.* The . . . (Thai) constitution . . . was abrogated with the promise that a new, *more liberal* constitution will be drafted."[781]

In the late 1970s, the 75th PAVN (People's Army of Vietnam) Infantry Division established four permanent base camps just east of the Thailand border. Those bases are used as staging areas for a crack regimental-size *Dac Cong,* sapper/commando unit.

During the first three years of red Vietnamese border incursions, the Thais followed "American tutors, floundering around in the jungle on aimless 'search and destroy' missions."[782] Soon the Thais realized that the survival of their freedom was in a state of jeopardy unredeemable by incompetent American military assistance.

As part of their militaristic maneuvering the Vietnamese communists have built their own version of the Berlin Wall. "By mid-May 1983 the Vietnamese completed construction of a landmined and bamboo-spike-studded trench, six meters wide and 25 kilometers long, in Kampuchea near the Thai border. Apparently designed as both an antipersonnel and an antitank barrier, the trench begins about 12 miles south of Aranyaprathet and runs in a northeasterly direction."[783]

"From November 1984 to March 1985, Vietnamese troops conducted a successful dry season offensive against base camps near the Thai border that Khmer resistance groups had developed in the early 1980s. The offensive resulted in the complete demolition of the camps."[784]

In mid-1987 Vietnamese surrogates, the Laotians, seized seventy kilometers of Thai territory and dug in on Hills 1428, 1370 and 1146. "At its peak the incident involved nearly a division of troops plus support units on each side. Thailand . . . losses were close to 400 dead and 1,100 injured."[785]

The Laotians easily defeated the Thai troops sent against them who "had never conducted an exercise above battalion level."[786] The Thais had been following American doctrinal guidance with emphasis on small unit operations. As a result, "only one Thai division, the 7th Infantry, even has the divisional support command (which the Americans have told the Thais is absolutely required) . . . for divisional operations."[787]

The Thais also discovered that their ultra modern high-tech U.S. aircraft were unsuitable for ground support in jungle terrain. The American-trained Thais also ran out of ammunition during the three month long campaign and had to be resupplied by Red China.

On February 17, 1989 the victorious Laotians signed a cease-fire accord with the defeated Thais. Thailand's new Prime Minister pledged to provide money, manpower and technology to Laos in order to help develop Laotian natural resources.

Such are the wages of defeat by the Chu Luc and their puppets!

The Vietnamese Occupation of Cambodia

Since 1978, the Vietnamese Communist Army has occupied Cambodia with many divisions of combat troops. In addition, the Chu Luc is carrying out a clever subversive program of far-reaching significance within Cambodia.[788]

In 1983, "Vietnamese forces in Kampuchea . . . disarmed the entire 286th Division of the PRK (Cambodian puppet army) based in Oddar Meanchey, and arrested its commander and senior officers."[789] Under suspicion, the Vietnamese-sponsored army, the Army of the People's Republic of Kampuchea (PRK), deployed six divisions along the Cambodian border in 1988. Since PRK units remain unreliable, necessitating frequent reorganization and disciplinary measures, reliable Vietnamese units watch them closely from their immediate rear.

However, the Vietnamese and their puppet troops cannot hold the roughly 8,000 Khmer villages, in spite of the size of their huge occupation army. A flourishing resistance army, carrying out strategic guerrilla war against the pro-Vietnamese regime, has been active in Cambodia throughout the 1980s. The Viet reds call their battles against that freedom fighter army a "civil war."

The Vietnamese have repeatedly attacked border refugee camps which they claim are hideouts for their enemies. In January 1983 "some 4,000 Vietnamese troops, supported by light artillery and tanks, attacked the Nong Chan refugee camp just inside the northwestern Kampuchean border. During this operation there were heavy fire exchanges between Thai and Vietnamese troops. On 31 March 1983 . . . about 1000 Vietnamese troops, augmented by about 600 PRK 'people's volunteers,' attacked the refugee settlements of Phnom Chat and Chamkar Kor, aided by artillery, rocket and Soviet T-54 tank fire . . . the Vietnamese attacks again . . . resulted in 'spillovers' of Vietnamese artillery and mortar shells falling into adjacent Thai territory."[790] Such attacks continued throughout 1983.

In August 1984, "Two PAVN regiments were badly bloodied in an abortive frontal assault on the KPNLF's (Cambodian Resistance Group) GHQ at Ampil and a country wide . . . guerrilla offensive struck at several Viet-held provincial capitals, marking the first serious blow to Vietnam control in the country."[791]

As part of a cunning deception program, numerous Vietnamese troops have disguised themselves as PRK troops. Such units are scattered throughout Cambodia, in platoon, company, battalion, regiment and division sized formations, stiffening the PRK.

In addition, the reds are trying to "Khmerize" their military. The Vietcom leadership encourages their troops and cadre to learn the Khmer language, marry Khmer females and adopt the cultural trappings of Khmer citizenry.

The most clever red deception of all is based upon a special military organization formed by the Vietnamese. That organization, set up in a cell structure like any other communist subversive unit, seeks to support "sleepers" lurking deep within Khmer society. The sleeper agents will remain behind if the Viets are driven from Cambodia. Their mission will be to lead an internal communist insurgency: "They constitute an underground organization outside the framework of (ordinary Vietnamese) settlers. Their presence is based on the idea that within twenty years, the current leadership of Democratic Kampuchea will be gone, that there will be no more leadership for the Kampuchean people's (anti-communist) struggle. The (goals of the) Vietnamese-led Indochina Federation will be realized (with the help of the sleepers) at that time."[792]

To fool the gullible and sympathetic western media, Vietnamese troop units are adopting low profiles. In 1988, for example, the 7701st Vietnamese Infantry Regiment moved from Kompong Thom into the camouflage of a nearby forest.

The Vietnamese communist army has scattered four general and regional headquarters throughout Cambodia. In 1988, those headquarters controlled three types of Vietnamese occupation forces:

- Provincial regiments: Eighteen three-battalion regiments permanently assigned to occupy eighteen Cambodian provinces.
- Mobile regiments: Six three-battalion regiments which move around Cambodia as needed.
- Mobile divisions: Fifteen three-regiment divisions that can operate anywhere within Cambodia.

In spite of their vast military power, the communists have not been able to exterminate the Khmer resistance, "it is likely that the size of the combined resistance now numbers 60,000–70,000, and its growth is testified to by actions Vietnam has taken recently to reduce its activities.

"Even in late 1985, months after Vietnam's destruction of the coalition's base camps near the Thai border, occasional attacks were still taking place

Communist Vietnamese Units: Cambodia, 1988

Provincial Regiments (Separate): 5501, 5502, 5503, 5504, 7701, 7702, 7703, 7704, 7705, 7706, 7707, 7708, 9902, 9903, 9905, 9907.

Mobile Regiments (Separate): 5, 6, 7, 14, 117, and 196.

Mobile Divisions: 2, 4, 9, 8 (aka* 984), 950, N25, 155 Marine, 101 Marine, 310, 315, 57 (aka 307), 72 (aka 302), 75 (aka 5), 59 (aka 309), 330 (aka 90), and 868.

Note: *aka = also known as. The assigning of various numbers and names for the same units is standard Vietnamese communist deception practice.[793]

within 15 miles of Phnom Penh, deep in the interior of Cambodia . . . a Western reporter wrote . . . 'trains and buses from the Battambang area arrive in Phnom Penh with armored guards aboard, no bridge or village . . . was unguarded . . . after midnight intersections and major roads are patrolled by Vietnamese troops."[794]

The Chu Luc in Central America: 1980–1991

In 1980, Le Duan, the former executive secretary of the Vietnamese Communist Party publicly committed the Vietnamese to the support of communist insurgency in El Salvador. Since then, the Chu Luc has been publicly supporting communist insurgencies in Central America. The Vietnamese, along with the Nicaraguans, have provided leadership, advice, training and thousands of captured American weapons. Chu Luc advisers have been primarily responsible for the development of El Salvador's most combat-effective communist military force, the 7500 man Farabundo Marti National Liberation Front (FMLN).[795]

The Vietnamese Army has provided much sapper type training to communist insurgent cadres including: "instruction for FMLN leaders at the politico-military level and specialized mine warfare and commando/special forces (sapper) training at the tactical level."[796]

In 1988, the American Public Broadcasting System aired exclusive footage of Chu Luc trained FMLN troops: "While standing in formation, six of the approximately 40 team members stand out because they are covered from head to toe in black camouflage paint. These six members are the team's sappers, vested with the responsibility of conducting the actual infiltration of a compound and severing the perimeter wire. The other members in formation represent support and assault team personnel . . . All carry M-16 and CAR-15 rifles."[797]

Using guidebooks printed in Hanoi, El Salvadorian guerrillas also copy NVA mine warfare methods. Forty-five to eighty percent of anti-communist military casualties in El Salvador are currently caused by mines.[798]

The FMLN executed fifteen spectacular military raids from 1981 through 1989. Those raids were military clones of NVA power raid, close assault operations. Five of the raids hit lines of government communications and electrical power centers. The other ten raids were decapitation operations directed against military headquarters and command centers.[799]

The FMLN communists also seem to be aping two NVA fighting methods: "the coordinated fighting method . . . a medium-size attack against a relatively important target, an enemy battalion headquarters, for instance. The essence of its success lies in its being perfectly planned and flawlessly executed. The target is destroyed with *surgical precision* [Author's note: Why do American writers like this term so much?], and the impact on the enemy is not military so much as psychological. The second tactic . . . the independent fighting method . . . sometimes called the gnat swarm technique. This involves mounting dozens of daily small-scale actions, no single one being important but cumulatively raising the enemy's anxiety level and destroying his self confidence."[800]

The ultimate irony in El Salvador is that Chu Luc-led guerrillas are beating American-led government forces, with each side practicing the same methods used in the Second Indochina War. The American generals who are repeating the bankrupt tactics which lost them the Vietnam War, are both derelict in their duty and guilty of mindless dogmatism.

General Phillip B. Davidson has described the well-known and never-ending American military incompetence with ominous clarity: "Sad to say, we cannot counter revolutionary war even now (1988)—our defeat in Vietnam has taught us nothing . . . The United States does not understand low-intensity conflict nor does it display the capability to adequately defend against it."[801] American military incompetence remains uncorrected while the Chu Luc continues to triumph.

The Indochinese dominos have fallen! Will the next dominos fall on our doorstep?

APPENDIX

POMZ-2 Antipersonnel Stake Mine

The PDMZ-2 uses an iron fragmentation body (like a hand grenade) with five rows of fragments. The top of the mine is threaded to receive a pull fuze. The mines are normally laid in clusters of at least four mines fitted with trip wires.

Characteristics:

> Weight—1.7 kg
> Diameter—66mm
> Height w/fuse—111mm
> Main charge—TNT
>   Weight—75 g
> Operating force—1.0 kg
> Bootytrapping—Improvised

OZM-3 Bounding Antipersonnel Mine

The OZM-3 can be detonated electronically or mechanically. The electronic fuzing allows the mine to be command detonated. Mechanical fuzing is done through the use of pull fuzes, although other types, such as pressure and pull-tension release models, can be used. Of further note is the fact that the OZM-3 does not have inner and outer mine cases. On firing, the base of the mine case blows through while the rest of it bounds. The height of the explosion is determined by a tethering wire.

Characteristics:

> Weight—3.0 kg
> Diameter—75mm
> Height—120mm
> Main charge—TNT
>   Weight—75 g
> Operating force—0.22 kg when equipped
>   with pull fuze
> Boobytrapping—Improvised

TMD-B Wooden Antitank Mine

The TMD-K is of simple wooden construction with the boards either nailed together or fastened by tongue-and-groove joints. There are three pressure boards on the cover, with the center board hinged to permit insertion of the fuze. When the mine is armed, the hinged pressure board is held shut by a wooden locking bar. The main charge normally consists of two waterproof, paper-wrapped blocks of pressed amatol, dynammon, or ammonite. The TMD-B, which may either be factory or field manufactured, employs the MV-5 pressure fuze and the MD-2 detonator. Because these mines are not waterproof, they are not suitable for permanent-type minefields.

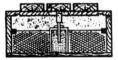

Characteristics:

> Weight—7.7 kg
> Length—320mm
> Width—280mm
> Height—140mm
> Main Charge—Varies
>   Weight—5-6.7 kg
> Operating Force—200 kg
> Boobytrapping—Improvised

TMK-2 Charged Mine

The TMK-2 consists of a double-truncated, conical-shaped mine body with the shaped charge placed in the lower half. The mine is fitted with an adjustable-length, tilt-rod fuze which is fitted into a holder on the side of the mine. The effectiveness of the mine results from the shaped charge (HEAT) which produces a penetrating jet in the same manner as shaped demolition charges. It is designed to attack the belly of the tank where the armor is thinnest.

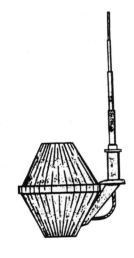

13 LB CEMENT

BASKET

**DIRECTIONAL
(CLAYMORE TYPE)**

CEMENT TURTLE

SHAPED CHARGE

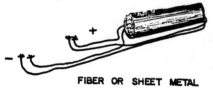

FIBER OR SHEET METAL

SOME VC LOCALLY MANUFACTURED MINES.

Footnotes

Chapter 1: Chu Luc Maneuver Fighting Methods

1. Sir Basil H. Liddell Hart, *Strategy of the Indirect Approach,* (New York: Praeger, 1954).
2. Sun Tzu, *The Art of War,* Edited and Translated by Samuel B. Griffith. (London: Oxford University Press, 1963).
3. Sir Basil H. Liddell Hart, *The Memoirs of Captain Liddell Hart,* (London: Cassell, 1965).
4. *Ibid.*
5. *National Security Memorandum 1* "The Situation In Vietnam" (December 1968).
6. Wilbur H. Morrison, *The Elephant and the Tiger,* (New York, Hippocrene, 1990).
7. Martin Von Creveld, *Command In War,* (Cambridge, Mass: Harvard University Press, 1985).
8. J. B. Berger, *Military Communications: A Test For Technoogy,* (Washington, D.C.: Center of Military History, 1986).
9. Vo Hguyen Giap, *The Military Art of Peoples War,* (New York, Monthly Review Press 1970), p. 47.
10. John Le Hockey, *Strategic and Operational Military Deception,* (Washington, D.C.: Department of the Navy, 1989).
11. Anderson, M., Arnsten, M. and Averch, H., *Insurgent Organization and Operations: A Case Study of the Viet Cong in the Delta, 1964–66,* (Santa Monica, CA: The Rand Corporation, August, 1961), p. 106
12. *Ibid.,* p. 108.
13. D.W.P. Elliott, M. Elliott, *Documents of an Elite Viet Cong Delta Unit: The Demolitions Platoon of the 514th Battalion—Part Three: Military Organizations and Activities,* (Santa Monica, CA: The Rand Corporation, May 1969).
14. *Ibid.,* p. 59.
15. M. Gurtov, *The War In The Delta: Views From Three Viet Cong Battalions,* Santa Monica, CA: The Rand Corporation, September 1967.
16. *Ibid.,* p. 22.
17. *Ibid.,* p. 23.
18. *Soviet Army Operations,* (Arlington Hall Station, Arlington, VA: U.S. Army Intelligence Threat Analysis Center, 1978), p. 77.
19. Lubenow, Larry R., "Rag-Tag No More." *Infantry,* September–October, 1966, p. 39.
20. Anderson, *op. cit.,* p. 157.
21. Anderson, *op. cit.,* p. 159.

515

22. Anderson, *op. cit.*, p. 159.
23. Elliott, *op. cit.*, p. 66.
24. S.L.A. Marshall, *Vietnam: Three Battles,* (New York: DeCapo Press, 1971), p. 53.
25. *Ibid.*, p. 144.
26. *Ibid.*
27. S.L.A. Marshall, *West to Cambodia,* (New York: Cowles, 1968), p. 88.
28. Samuel Zaffiri, *Hamburger Hill,* (Novato, CA: Presidio, 1988), p. 121.
29. Tom Mangold and John Penycate, *The Tunnels of Cu Chi,* New York: Random House, 1985), p. 88.
30. Marshall, *Vietnam Three Battles, op. cit.*, p. 122.
31. Marshall, *Vietnam Three Battles, op. cit.*, p. 108.
32. Mangold, *op. cit.*, pp. 124–30.
33. Marshall, *Vietnam: Three Battles, op. cit.*, pp. 222–24.
34. Marshall, *West to Cambodia, op. cit.*, pp. 88–89.
35. Marshall, *Vietnam: Three Battles, op. cit.*, p. 219.
36. Marshall, *Vietnam: Three Battles, op. cit.*, p. 72.
37. Marshall, *West to Cambodia, op. cit.*, p. 89.
38. Marshall, *Vietnam: Three Battles, op. cit.*, p. 118.
39. Marshall, *Vietnam: Three Battles, op. cit.*, p. 105.
40. Marshall, *loc. cit.*
41. Zaffiri, *op. cit.*, p. 252.
42. Mangold, *op. cit.*, p. 237.
43. Zaffiri, *op. cit.*, pp. 270–71.
44. Albert N. Garland, ed. *A Distant Challenge,* (New York: Jove, 1985), p. 96.
45. S.L.A. Marshall, *Ambush,* (Nashville, TN: Battery Press, 1969), p.
46. Garland, *op. cit.*, p. 59.
47. Marshall, *Vietnam: Three Battles, op. cit.*, p. 145.
48. Robert J. O'Neill, *Vietnam Task,* (Melbourne, Australia: Cassell, 1968), pp. 53–4.
49. Curzio Malparte, *The Volga Rises In Europe,* (London: Alvin Redman Ltd., 1975), p. 270.

Chapter 2: Chu Luc Military Organization

50. Robert J. O'Neill, *General Giap,* New York: Praeger, 1969, p. 74.
51. *Ibid.*, p. 75.
52. *Ibid.*, p. 87
53. J.J. McCuren, *The Art of Counter-Revolutionary Warfare,* Harrisburg, PA: Stackpole, 1966, p. 263.
54. Bernard B. Fall, *Street Without Joy,* 1967, Harrisburg, PA: Stackpole, pp. 269–70.
55. Bernard B. Fall, *Hell In A Very Small Place,* (New York: J. B. Lippincott Co., 1967) pp. 486–7.
56. *Ibid.*, pp. 126–28.
57. Anderson, *op. cit.*, p. 15.
58. J. D. Coleman, *Pleiku,* (New York: St. Martin's Press, 1988), pp. 56–57.
59. L. P. Holliday, R. M. Gurfield, *Viet Cong Logistics,* Santa Monica, CA: The Rand Corporation, June, 1968), p. 47.
60. Anderson, *op. cit.*, p. 57.
61. Holliday, *loc. cit.*
62. Holliday, *op. cit.*, p. 14.
63. *Ibid.*
64. *Ibid.*

65. Anderson, *op. cit.*, p. 57.
66. Holiday, *op. cit.*, p. 4.
67. Anderson, *loc. cit.*
68. Berger, *op. cit.*, p. 374.
69. Holliday, *op. cit.*, p. 56.
70. Coleman, *op. cit.*, p. 56.
71. Coleman, *op. cit.*, p. 171.
72. Holliday, *op. cit.*, p. 100.
73. Holliday, *op. cit.*, p. 101.
74. Holliday, *op. cit.*, p. 102.
75. Albert N. Garland, *Infantry In Vietnam*, (Fort Benning, GA: Infantry Magazine Press, 1967), pp. 357–363.
76. Keiith W. Noland, *Death Valley*, (Novato, CA: Presidio, 1987), p. 62.
77. Anderson, *op. cit.*, p. 15.
78. Holliday, *op. cit.*, p. 99.
79. Holliday, *op. cit.*, p. 74.
80. Anderson, *op. cit.*, p. 11.
81. Holliday, *op. cit.*, p. 53.
82. Shelby Stanton, "The 273rd Viet Cong Regiment," *Vietnam Magazine*, (Spring 1989), pp. 10, 65–66.
83. Anderson, *op. cit.*, p. 139.
84. Anderson, *op. cit.*, p. 139–40.
85. Anderson, *loc. cit.*
86. Anderson, *loc. cit.*
87. Anderson, *op. cit.*, p. 140.
88. Anderson, *op. cit.*, p. 139–40.
89. Anderson, *op. cit.*, p. 140.
90. Anderson, *op. cit.*, p. 139.
91. Anderson, *op. cit.*, p. 140.
92. Stanton, *op. cit.*, p. 10.
93. Stanton, *loc. cit.*

Chapter 3: Chu Luc Logistics

94. J. W. McCoy, *Secrets of the Ho Chi Minh Trail*, (Unpublished 1990, manuscript).
95. O'Neill, *op. cit.*, p. 82.
96. D. M. O. Miller, "Logistics Support In Revolutionary Warfare," *British Army Review*, April, 1975, p. 10.
97. Holliday, *op. cit.*, p. 4.
98. Holliday, *op. cit.*, p. 5.
99. Holliday, *op. cit.*, p. 7.
100. Holliday, *loc. cit.*
101. Holliday, *op. cit.*, pp. 49–50.
102. Holliday, *op. cit.*, p. 49.
103. S. L. A. Marshall, *Ambush and Bird*, (Garden City, New York: Nelson Doubleday, Inc., 1968), p. 210.
104. Holliday, *op. cit.*, p. 73.
105. Anderson, *op. cit.*, p. 53.
106. Holliday, *op. cit.*, p. 8.
107. Holliday, *op. cit.*, p. 52.
108. Holliday, *op. cit.*, p. 54.

109. Holliday, *loc. cit.*
110. Holliday, *loc. cit.*
111. Anderson, *op. cit.*, p. 76.
112. Holliday, *op. cit.*, p. 75.
113. Holliday, *op. cit.*, p. 48.
114. Holliday, *op. cit.*, p. 49.
115. Holliday, *op. cit.*, p. 50.
116. Holliday, *op. cit.*, p. 5.
117. Holliday, *op. cit.*, p. 9.
118. Holliday, *op. cit.*, p. 48.
119. Holliday, *loc. cit.*
120. Holliday, *op. cit.*, p. 73.
121. Holliday, *op. cit.*, p. 78.
122. Holliday, *loc. cit.*
123. Holliday, *loc. cit.*
124. Holliday, *op. cit.*, p. 76.
125. Holliday, *op. cit.*, p. 126.
126. Holliday, *op. cit.*, p. 127.
127. Holliday, *op. cit.*, p. 36.
128. Larry R. Lubenow, "Rag-Tag No More," *Infantry Magazine*, September-October, 1966, p. 36.
129. Holliday, *op. cit.*, p. 128.
130. Holliday, *op. cit.*, pp. 130–1.
131. Holliday, *op. cit.*, pp. 129–30.
132. Holliday, *op. cit.*, p. 130.
133. Nigel Calder, *The Green Machines*, (New York: Putnam's Sons, 1986), p. 192
134. Holliday, op. cit., pp. 19–20.
135. Frank Frost, *Australia's War In Vietnam*, (Sydney, Australia: Allen and Universe, 1987).
136. Berger, *op. cit.*, p. 281.
137. Miller, *op. cit.*, p. 6.
138. Miller, *loc. cit.*
139. Miller, *op. cit.*, p. 7.

Chapter 4: Command, Control and Resupply

140. Van Creveld, *op. cit.*, p. 46.
141. Van Creveld, *op. cit.*, p. 56.
142. Van Creveld, *op. cit.*, pp. 70–75.
143. Van Creveld, *op. cit.*, p. 70.
144. Van Creveld, *op. cit.*, p. 75.
145. Van Creveld, *op. cit.*, p. 87.
146. Van Creveld, *op. cit.*, p. 88.
147. M. Gurtov, *Viet Cong Cadres and the Cadre System: A Study of the Main and Local Forces*, (Santa Monica: CA: The Rand Corporation, December, 1967), p. 37.
148. *Ibid.*
149. Gurtov, *Viet Cong Cadres, op. cit.*, p. 38.
150. Anderson, *op. cit.*, p. 39.
151. Anderson, *op. cit.*, p. 115.
152. Anderson, *op. cit.*, p. 8.
153. Gurtov, *op. cit.*, p. 23.

154. Berger, *op. cit.*, pp. 376–81.
155. Berger, *op. cit.*, p. 377.
156. Berger, *op. cit.*, p. 381.
157. *Ibid.*
158. R. E. Appleman, *Ridgeway Duels For Korea*, (College Station, Texas: Texas A&M University Press, 1990), p. 82.
159. Holliday, *op. cit.*, p. 36.
160. Holliday, *op. cit.*, p. 36.
161. Holliday, *op. cit.*, p. 25.
162. Holliday, *op. cit.*, p. 37.
163. Marshall, *op. cit.*, p. 212.
164. Holliday, *op. cit.*, pp. 22–23.
165. Holliday, *op. cit.*, p. 37.
166. Holliday, *op. cit.*, p. 34.
167. *Ibid.*
168. Marshall, *op. cit.*, p. 212.
169. Holliday, *op. cit.*, p. 45.
170. Holliday, *op. cit.*, p. 42.
171. Holliday, *op. cit.*, p. 45.
172. Holliday, *op. cit.*, p. 46.
173. Holliday, *op. cit.*, p. 102.
174. *Ibid.*
175. Holliday, *op. cit.*, p. 103.

Chapter 5: Unit B-36: NVA Intelligence and Security

176. J. Schlight, *Second Indochina War Symposium*, (Arlie, VA; Center of Military History, 1986), pp. 113–14.
177. Schlight, *op. cit.*, p. 115.
178. Robert A. Liston, *The Pueblo Surrender*, (New York: M. Evans and Co., 1988), p. 221.
179. T. B. Allen and N. Polmar, *Merchants of Treason*, (New York: Dell Publishing, 1988).
180. G. A. Comas, *U.S. Marines In Vietnam: Vietnamization and Redeployment*, Washington, D.C.: History & Museums Division, HQ, USMC), p. 256.
181. David Hackworth, *About Face*, (New York: Simon and Schuster, 1989), p. 723.
182. Allen, *op. cit.*, p. 27.
183. John Barron, *Breaking The Ring*, (New York, Avon: 1988), p. 210.
184. *Ibid.*
185. Barron, *op. cit.*, pp. 210–11.
186. *loc. cit.*
187. Allen, *op. cit.*, p. 424.
188. Donard Jameson, "Trends in Soviet Covert Action," *Colloquium on Counterintelligence*, April 24–26, 1980, pp. 173–5.
189. Allen, *op. cit.*, p. 425.
190. Herbert Roberstein, "Soviet Intelligence in the United States," *Colloquium on Counterintelligence*, April 24–26, 1980, p. 184.
191. Alan Dawson, "Saigon Regime Riddled with Viet Cong Before Its Fall," *Washington Star*, September 9, 1975, p. A3.
192. Edgar O'Ballance, *The Wars In Vietnam*. (New York: Hippocrene, 1981), pp. 144–145.
193. Ernest Volkman, *Warriors of the Night*, (New York: William Morrow and Co., 1985), p. 256.

194. Volkman, *op. cit.*, pp. 253–257.
195. Volkman, *op. cit.*, pp. 256–257.
196. Volkman, *op. cit.*, p. 260.
197. Shelby Stanton, *Green Berets At War,* (Novato, CA: Presidio, 1985), pp. 185–6, 190, 261, 268.
198. Hoang Ngoc Lung, *Intelligence,* (Washington, D.C.: U.S. Army Center of Military History, 1982), p. 217.
199. *Ibid.*
200. Lung, *op. cit.*, p. 217.
201. Volkman, *op. cit.*, p. 259.
202. Lung, *op. cit.*, p. 195.
203. *Ibid.*
204. Lung, *op. cit.*, pp. 195–198.
205. R. P. Fox, *Air Base Defense In The Republic of Vietnam 1961–73,* (Washington, D.C.: Office of Air Force History, 1979), p. 32.
206. Lung, *op. cit.*, pp. 204–07.
207. *Ibid.*
208. Fox, *op. cit.*, p. 35.
209. *Ibid.*
210. Fox, *op. cit.*, p. 33.
211. *Ibid.*
212. Lung, *op. cit.*, p. 222.
213. Lung, *op. cit.*, p. 223.
214. *Ibid.*
215. Volkman, *op. cit.*, p. 257.
216. Lung, *op. cit.*, p. 226.
217. Fox, *op. cit.*, p. 33.
218. Fox, *op. cit.*, p. 34.
219. Fox, *op. cit.*, p. 35.
220. *Ibid.*
221. Lung, *op. cit.*, p. 206.
222. Lung, *op. cit.*, p. 214.
223. Lung, *op. cit.*, p. 215.
224. Fox, *op. cit.*, p. 228.
225. Lung, *op. cit.*, p. 207.
226. Lung, *op. cit.*, p. 198.
227. Elizabeth Bentley, *Out of Bondage,* (New York: Ivy Books, 1988), p. 13.
228. Bruce E. Jones, *War Without Windows,* (New York: Vanguard Press, 1987), p. 228.
229. J. S. McChristian, *The Role of Military Intelligence,* Washington, D.C.: Department of the Army, Vietnam Studies, 1974), p. 30.
230. Lung, *op. cit.*, p. 215.
231. Comas, *op. cit.*, p. 258.
232. Liston, *op. cit.*, p. 220.
233. Liston, *op. cit.*, p. 222.
234. Berger, *op. cit.*, p. 395.
235. MACV, *Counterinsurgency Lessons Learned No. 64, Imitative Communications Deception,* September 15, 1967, p. 3.

Chapter 6: Chu Luc Reconnaissance

236. Lung, *op. cit.*, p. 208.
237. Billy J. Biberstein, *A Monograph of 2Lieutenant Nguyen Van Thong, Platoon Leader,*

Reconnaissance Company, 320th Regiment, 1st NVA Division (USARV: 13th Military History Detachment, undated), p. 5.
    238. Biberstein, *op. cit.*, p. 7.
    239. Anderson, *op. cit.*, p. 11.
    240. Lung, *op. cit.*, p. 205.
    241. William E. Le Gro, *Vietnam: From Cease-Fire to Capitulation*, (Washington, D.C.: U.S. Army Center of Military History, 1981), pp. 29–30.
    242. Lung, *op. cit.*, p. 209.
    243. Fox, *op. cit.*, p. 36.
    244. Lung, *op. cit.*, p. 209.
    245. *Ibid.*
    246. *Ibid.*
    247. Lung, *op. cit.*, pp. 209–210.
    248. Biberstein, *op. cit.*, p. 8.
    249. Fox, *op. cit.*, p. 39.
    250. Biberstein, *op. cit.*, p. 9.
    251. Anderson, *op. cit.*, pp. 103–04.
    252. Eric Hammel, *Khe Sahn*, (New York: Crown Publishers, 1989), p. 25.
    253. Fox, *op. cit.*, p. 37.
    254. Anderson, *op. cit.*, p. 105.
    255. Anderson, *op. cit.*, p. 103.
    256. Fox, *op. cit.*, p. 38.
    257. *Ibid.*
    258. Anderson, *op. cit.*, p. 105.
    259. *Ibid.*
    260. Anderson, *op. cit.*, p. 106.
    261. Fox, *op. cit.*, p. 38.
    262. Nolan, *op. cit.*, p. 63.
    263. Fox, *op. cit.*, p. 40.
    264. *Ibid.*
    265. Berger, *op. cit.*, p. 406.
    266. Berger, *op. cit.*, p. 404.
    267. Lung, *op. cit.*, p. 205.
    268. *Ibid.*
    269. Berger, *op. cit.*, p. 405.
    270. Fox, *op. cit.*, p. 39.
    271. Berger, *op. cit.*, p. 402.
    272. *Ibid*, pp. 402–3.
    273. Berger, *op. cit.*, p. 405.
    274. Don Ericson and John L. Rotundo, *Charlie Rangers*, (New York: Ivy Books, 1989), p. 218.
    275. Ray W. Stubbe, *Aarugha: FMFRP12-21*, (Washington, D.C.: U.S. Marine Corps Office of Military History, 1989), p. 306.
    276. Michael Lee Lanning, *Inside the LRRPS*, (New York: Ivy Books, 1988), p. 170.

Chapter 7: Mobility, Nomading and Security

    277. J. M. Van Dyke, *North Vietnam's Strategy For Survival*, (Palo Alto, CA: Pacific Books, 1972), p. 36.
    278. O'Neill, *Giap, op cit.*, p. 51.
    279. O'Neill, *Giap, op. cit.*, p. 54.
    280. O'Neill, *Giap, op. cit.*, p. 52.

281. O'Neill, *Giap, op. cit.*, p. 54.
282. O'Neill, *Giap, op. cit.*, pp. 141–42.
283. *Ibid.*
284. *Ibid.*
285. *Ibid.*
286. Bernard B. Fall, *Street Without Joy*, (Harrisburg, PA: The Stackpole Co., 1967), pp. 275–76.
287. J. J. Chodes, *The Myth of American Military Power*, (Boston: Branden Press, 1972), p. 198.
288. Marshall, *Vietnam: Three Battles, op. cit.*, p. 30.
289. Holliday, *op. cit.*, p. 151.
290. *Ibid.*
291. Marshall, *Bird, op. cit.*, p. 210.
292. Marshall, *Bird, op. cit.*, p. 212.
293. Marshall, *Bird, op. cit.*, p. 210.
294. Anderson, *op. cit.*, p. 60.
295. Anderson, *op. cit.*, p. 89.
296. Anderson, *op. cit.*, pp. 73–75.
297. Anderson, *op. cit.*, p. 75.
298. Anderson, *op. cit.*, p. 69.
299. Anderson, *op. cit.*, p. 73.
300. Anderson, *op. cit.*, p. 85.
301. Anderson, *op. cit.*, p. 86.

Chapter 8: Chu Luc Offensive Maneuvers

302. Wayne Babb, "The Bridge," *Marine Corps Gazette,* June, 1971, p. 19.
303. Babb, *op. cit.*, p. 20.
304. Babb, *op. cit.*, p. 21.
305. O'Neill, *Giap, op. cit.*, p. 140.
306. O'Neill, *Giap, op. cit.*, p. 148.
307. O'Neill, *Giap, op. cit.*, p. 84.
308. Anderson, *op. cit.*, p. 114.
309. Anderson, *op. cit.*, p. 116.
310. Anderson, *op. cit.*, p. 117.
311. Ibid.
312. Anderson, *op. cit.*, p. 119.
313. Anderson, *op. cit.*, p. 122.
314. Ibid.
315. Anderson, *op. cit.*, p. 123.
316. *Ibid.*
317. *Ibid.*
318. Marshall, *Ambush, op. cit.*, p. 171.
319. Anderson, *op. cit.*, p. 124.
320. George Wilson, *Mud Soldiers*, (New York: Charles Scribner & Son., 1989), pp. 23–4.
321. Anderson, *op. cit.*, p. 104.
322. Anderson, *op. cit.*, p. 106.
323. Anderson, *op. cit.*, p. 107.
324. Anderson, *op. cit.*, p. 109.
325. *Ibid.*
326. Anderson, *op. cit.*, p. 107.

327. Anderson, *op. cit.*, p. 110.
328. Anderson, *op. cit.*, p. 107.
329. Anderson, *op. cit.*, p. 110.

Chapter 9: NVA Defensive Maneuvers

330. David H. Hackworth, "Hedgerows of Vietnam," *Infantry Magazine*, May-June 1967, p. 6.
331. Hackworth, *op. cit.*, p. 3.
333. Garland, *op. cit.*, p. 63.
334. Hackworth, *op. cit.*, p. 5.
335. Hackworth, *op. cit.*, p. 4.
336. Marshall, *Vietnam: Three Battles, op. cit.*, p. 169.
337. Hackworth, *op. cit.*, p. 3.
338. Marshall, *Vietnam: Three Battles, op. cit.*, p. 121.
339. Marshall, *Vietnam: Three Battles, op. cit.*, p. 80.
340. Hackworth, *op. cit.*, p. 5.
341. Chodes, *op. cit.*, p. 77.
342. Garland, *op. cit.*, pp. 55–56.
343. Marshall, *Bird,* op. cit.
344. Anderson, *op. cit.*, p. 99.
345. Anderson, *op. cit.*, pp. 98–99.
346. *Ibid.*
347. Anderson, *op. cit.*, p. 97.
348. Anderson, *op. cit.*, p. 98.
349. Anderson, *op. cit.*, p. 100.
350. Military Assistance Advisory Group, Vietnam, HQ, U.S. Army Section, *Lessons Learned No. 57: Fortified Village*, February 1967.
351. Anderson, *op. cit.*, p. 98.
352. Anderson, *op. cit.*, p. 97.
353. Anderson, *op. cit.*, pp. 100–01.
354. Hackworth, *op. cit.*, p. 5.
355. Anderson, *op. cit.*, p. 94.
356. *Ibid.*
357. Anderson, *op. cit.*, p. 90.
358. Anderson, *op. cit.*, p. 92.
359. Anderson, *op. cit.*, p. 93.
360. Coleman, *op. cit.*, pp. 110–11.
361. *Soviet Army Operations, op. cit.*, p. 171.
362. J. C. Studt, "Battalions in the Attack," *Marine Corps Gazette*, February, 1977, p. 44.
363. Charles K. Breslauer, "Battle of the Northern Arizona," *Marine Corps Gazette*, January, 1977, p. 55.
364. *Ibid,* p. 48.
365. *Ibid,* p. 49.
366. Jack Schlumlinson, *An Expanding War: 1966,* (Washington, D.C.: History and Museums Division, HQ USMC), p. 128.
367. *Ibid.*
368. Keith W. Nolan, *Battle For Hue: Tet 1968,* (New York: Dell 1983), p. 203.
369. *Ibid,* p. 111.
370. *Ibid,* p. 83.
371. *Ibid,* p. 90.

372. *Ibid*, p. 116.
373. *Ibid*.
374. *Ibid*, pp. 204–205.

Chapter 10: Chu Luc Strike Tactics

375. Marshall, *Battles In The Monsoon, op. cit.*, p. 206.
376. Hackworth, *About Face, op. cit.*, p. 522.
377. SLA Marshall, *Vietnam Primer*, (Sims, Arkansas: Lancer Militaria, 1979), p. 55.
378. Biberstein, *op. cit.*, p. 9.
379. D.W.P. Elliott and W. A. Stewart, *Pacification and the Viet Cong System in Ding Tuong: 1966*, (Santa Monica, CA: The Rand Corporation, January, 1969).
380. Stephen B. Patrick, "Confined Arms," *Strategy and Tactics, No. 46*, September-October, 1944, p. 39.
381. Nolan, *op. cit.*, p. 222.
382. Rod Paschal, *The Defeat of Imperial Germany*, (Chapel Hill, N.C.: Algonquin Books, 1989), p. 133.
383. Paschal, *op. cit.*, p. 143.
384. Marshall, *West to Cambodia, op. cit.*, p. IX.
385. S.L.A. Marshall, *Vietnam Primer, op. cit.* pp. 36–37.
386. Anderson, *op. cit.*, p. 92.
387. Patrick, *op. cit.*, p. 35.
388. Patrick, *op. cit.*, p. 38.
389. Johnnie M. Clark, *Guns Up*, (New York: Ballantine Books, 1984), pp. 13, 66.
390. Coleman, *op. cit.*, p. 57.
391. J. Meyer, "Machine Guns," *Marine Corps Gazette*, September, 1973, p. 19.
392. Donn A. Starry, *Mounted Combat In Vietnam*, Washington, D.C., 1978), p. 47.
393. *Ibid*.
394. Anonymous Interview With Vietnam Veteran: "Story Told All Over The Nam."
395. David Hackworth, "Target Acquisition," *Military Review*, April, 1968, pp. 73–77.
396. Elliott and Stewart, *op. cit.*, pp. 61–62.
397. Elliott and Stewart, *op. cit.*, p. 10.
398. Elliott and Stewart, *op. cit.*, p. 63.
399. Elliott and Stewart, *op. cit.*, p. 66.
400. Elliott and Stewart, *op. cit.*, p. 67.
401. Elliott and Stewart, *op. cit.*, p. 64.
402. *Ibid*.
403. *Ibid*.
404. Elliott and Stewart, *op. cit.*, p. 63.
405. Anderson, *op. cit.*, p. 92.
406. E. S. Martin, *Reaching The Other Side*, (New York: Crown Publishers, 1978), p. 182.
407. *Ibid.*, p. 171.
408. Ngo Quang Tuong, *The Easter Offensive of 1972*, (Washington, D.C.: U.S. Army Center of Military History, 1980), p. 132.
409. C. R. Smith, *High Mobility and Standdown: 1969*, (Washington, D.C.: History and Museums Division, HQ, USMC), p. 195.
410. John Kireges, "Viet Cong Triangle Formation," *Infantry Magazine*, May, 1968, p. 57.
411. U.S. Army Infantry School, *Vietnam Information Booklet*, November, 1967, p. 67.
412. Anderson, *op. cit.*, p. 75.

Chapter 11: Close Assault Breakthrough Operations

413. Stanton, *op. cit.*, pp. 139–40.
414. Robert Pison, *The End of the Line*, (New York: Ballantine Books, 1982), pp. 94–6.
415. *Vietnam Information Booklet*, *op. cit.*, pp. 51–2.
416. Anderson, *op. cit.*, p. 110.
417. *Ibid.*
418. Headquarters U.S. Continental Army Command, *Vietnam Operations Lessons Learned*, (Fort Monroe, VA. March, 1966), p. 16.
419. Fox, *op. cit.*, p. 51.
420. Fox, *loc., cit.*, p. 51.
421. Hammel, *op. cit.*, p. 57–58.
422. Hammel, *op. cit.*, p. 185.
423. Marshall, *Bird, op. cit.*, pp. 217–21.
424. Marshall, *Bird, op. cit.*, p. 212.
425. Marshall, *Bird, op. cit.*, pp. 215–16.
426. Marshall, *Bird, op. cit.*, p. 329.
427. Marshall, *Bird, loc. cit.*
428. Marshall, *Bird, op. cit.*, p. 216.
429. Marshall, *Bird, op. cit.*, pp. 245, 252.
430. Marshall, *Bird, op. cit.*, p. 261.
431. Marshall, *Bird, op. cit.*, p. 329.
432. Marshall, *Vietnam: Three Battles, op. cit.*, p. 15.
433. Marshall, *Vietnam: Three Battles, op. cit.*, p. 20.
434. Marshall, *Vietnam: Three Battles, op. cit.*, p. 169.

Chapter 12: Chu Luc Ambush

435. G. J. Telfer, *Fighting the North Vietnamese: 1967*, (Washington, D.C.: History and Museums Division, HQ, USMC), pp. 11–13.
436. *Ibid.*
437. Anderson, *op. cit.*, p. 118.
438. James R. Desmukes, "After Action Report: VC Ambush," *Infantry Magazine*, April, 1967, p. 40.
439. "The Viet Cong," Monthly Intelligence Test, *82d Airborne Division*, August 28, 1966, p. 2.
440. Ibid.
441. *VC Ambush Tacticx*, MACV Intelligence Study, January 1967.
442. *Ibid.*
443. *Ibid.*
444. Anderson, *op. cit.*, pp. 109–10.
445. Anderson, *op. cit.*, p. 118.
446. Anderson, *op. cit.*, p. 117.
447. Anderson, *op. cit.*, pp. 117–18.
448. Coleman, *op. cit.*, pp. 54–5.
449. Coleman, *op. cit.*, pp. 70–85.
450. Coleman, *op. cit.*, pp. 231–34.
451. Coleman, *op. cit.*, pp. 238.
452. George C. Herring, *America's Longest War*, (New York: Wiley Coleman, 1979), pp. 319–22.
453. Coleman, *op. cit.*, p. 242.
454. Coleman, *op. cit.*, p. 248–49.

455. Marshall, *West to Cambodia, op. cit.,* pp. 124–27.

Chapter 13: Chu Luc Sappers

456. Fox, *op. cit.,* p. 46.
457. Jack Shulimson, *The Landing And The Buildup, 1965,* Washington, D.C.: History and Museums Division, HQ, USMC), pp. 99–100.
458. *Ibid,* p. 131.
459. Babb, *op. cit.,* pp. 19–21, Garland, *op. cit.,* p. 192.
460. Keith W. Nolan, *Into Laos,* (Novata, CA: Presidio, 1986), pp. 334–35.
461. *CE 469,* U.S. Military Assistance Command Vietnam, 1969, p. 19. Ngoc Lung, *Strategy and Tactics,* (Washington, D.C., U.S. Army Center for Military History, 1980), p. 95.
462. OSI CIM, South Vietnam, *Sapper Tactics and Threat Against the USAF,* April 6, 1971, p. 5.
463. Anderson, *op. cit.,* p. 163.
464. Fox, *op. cit.,* p. 46.
465. *Ibid.*
466. Fox, *op. cit.,* p. 46–7.
467. Anderson, *op. cit.,* p. 14.
468. Anderson, *op. cit.,* p. 163–4.
469. Study 69–10, *VC/NVA Sapper Tactics* (CICIV, October 23, 1969).
470. Fox, *op. cit.,* p. 47.
471. Lung, *op. cit.,* p. 96.
472. Lung, *op. cit.,* p. 97.
473. Lung, *op. cit.,* p. 98.
474. *Ibid.*
475. Lung, *op. cit.,* pp. 98–9.
476. John G. Nettles, *The Bridge At Dong Ha,* (Annapolis, MD: Naval Institute Press, 1989), pp. 99–100.
477. Zaffiri, *op. cit.,* pp. 188–91.
478. Fox, *op. cit.,* p. 49.
479. Fox, *op. cit.,* p. 50.
480. Zaffiri, *op. cit.,* pp. 119–24.
481. Garland, *op. cit.,* p. 192.
482. *CE 1-69,* U.S. Military Assistance Command Vietnam 1969, p. 1.
483. Fox, *op. cit.,* p. 38.
484. Gary J. Pieringer, "Countering The Sappers," *Field Artillery,* August 1988, p. 8.
485. Le Gro, *op. cit.,* pp. 29–30.
486. Lung, *Strategy and Tactics, op. cit.,* p. 97.
497. Nguyen Ding Hinh, *Vietnamization and The Cease Fire,* (Washington, D.C.: U.S. Army Center of Military History, 1980), p. 347.
488. Lung, *op. cit.,* p. 100.
489. Hinh, *op. cit.,* pp. 347–51.
490. Hinh, *op. cit.,* p. 352.
491. *Ibid.*
492. *Ibid.*

Chapter 14: Hilltop Maneuvers

493. Shelby L. Stanton, *The Rise and Fall of an American Army,* (Navato, CA.: Presidio, 1985), pp. 112, 122, 156.

494. Stanton, *op. cit.*, pp. 111, 156, 165–6.
495. Stanton, *Ibid.*, pp. 166–67.
496. Stanton, *Ibid.*, pp. 168.
497. Stanton, *Ibid.*, p. 169.
498. Stanton, *Ibid.*, p. 171.
499. T. Maitland, *A Contagion of War*, (Boston: Boston Publishing, 1983), pp. 167–9.
500. Stanton, *op. cit.*, p. 174.
501. *Fourth Infantry Division in Vietnam*, 1967, p. 171.
502. F. Clifton Berry, *Sky Soldiers*, (New York: Bantam Books, 1987), p. 90.
503. Berry, *op. cit.*, p. 93.
504. Shelby L. Stanton, *Anatomy of a Division*, (Novato, CA.: Presidio, 1987), pp. 120–27.
505. Maitland, *op. cit.*, p. 169.
506. Stanton, *op. cit.*, p. 174.
507. Stanton, *op. cit.*, p. 175. Berry, *op. cit.*, p. 97.
508. Stanton, *op. cit.*, p. 176.
509. Berry, *op. cit.*, pp. 114–15.
510. Berry, *op. cit.*, p. 124.
511. Berry, *op. cit.*, p. 120.
512. Jones, *op. cit.*, p. 131.
513. *Ibid.*
514. Zaffiri, *op. cit.*, pp. 78, 83, 131, 271.
515. Zaffiri, *op. cit.*, p. 272.
516. Zaffiri, *op. cit.*, p. 244.
517. Zaffiri, *op. cit.*, p. 272.
518. Zaffiri, *op. cit.*, p. 280.
519. Zaffiri, *op. cit.*, p. 161.
520. Zaffiri, *op. cit.*, p. 283.
521. Zaffiri, *op. cit.*, p. 277.
522. Zaffiri, *op. cit.*, p. 205.
523. Zaffiri, *op. cit.*, p. 243.
524. Zaffiri, *op. cit.*, p. 166.
525. Zaffiri, *op. cit.*, p. 188.
526. Zaffiri, *op. cit.*, p. 167.
527. Zaffiri, *op. cit.*, p. 173.
528. Zaffiri, *op. cit.*, p. 175.
529. Zaffiri, *op. cit.*, p. 203.
530. Zaffurum *op. cit.*, p. 183.
531. Zaffiri, *op. cit.*, p. 151.
532. Zaffiri, *op. cit.*, pp. 232–33.
533. Zaffiri, *op. cit.*, p. 251.
534. Zaffiri, *op. cit.*, p. 278.
535. Zaffiri, *op. cit.*, p. 275.
536. *Ibid.*

Chapter 15: Standoff Attacks

537. Fox, *op. cit.*, p. 41.
538. Fox, *op. cit.*, p. 42.
539. S. L. A. Marshall, *Battles In The Monsoon* (New York: Warner, 1989), p. 249.
540. Hammel, *op. cit.*, pp. 57–8.

541. Fox, *op. cit.*, p. 43.
542. Fox, *op. cit.*, pp. 42–5.
543. Richard D. Camp, *Lima-6*, (New York: Atheneum, 1989), pp. 38–41.
544. Fox, *op. cit.*, p. 42.
545. Hammel, *op. cit.*, p. 17.
546. Fox, *op. cit.*, pp. 44–5.
547. Fox, *op. cit.*, p. 45.
548. Telfer, *op. cit.*, p. 223.
549. Smith, *op. cit.*, pp. 201–02. G. A. Comas, *Vietnaminzation and Redeployment 1970–71* (Washington, D.C.: Museums and History Division, HQ, USMC), pp. 23–8.
550. Smith, *op. cit.*, p. 174.
551. Comas, *op. cit.*, p. 27.
552. *Ibid.*
553. *Ibid.*
554. Smith, *op. cit.*, p. 201.
555. *Ibid.*
556. *Ibid.*
557. Marshall, *Battles in the Monsoon, op. cit.*, pp. 22–23.
558. *Ibid.* p. 23.
559. Hammel, *op. cit.*, p. 322.
560. Comas, *op. cit.*, p. 263.
561. Patrick, *op. cit.*, p. 30.
562. *Ibid.*
563. *Ibid.*
564. Comas, *op. cit.*, p. 263.
565. *Ibid.*
566. *Ibid.*
567. Comas, *op. cit.*, p. 264.
568. *Ibid.*
569. Comas, *op. cit.*, p. 266.
570. Comas, *op. cit.*, p. 264.
571. Garland, *op. cit.*, p. 71.
572. Martin, *op. cit.*, p. 182.
573. Patrick, *op. cit.*, p. 30.
574. Comas, *op. cit.*, p. 324.
575. Patrick, *op. cit.*, p. 30.
576. Comas, *op. cit.*, p. 267.

Chapter 16: Chu Luc Order of Battle I

577. Phillip B. Davidson, *Vietnam at War*, (Novato, CA: Presidio, 1988), p. 29.
578. Shulimson, *Expanding War, op. cit.*, p. 103.
579. Stanton, *The Rise and Fall, op. cit.*, pp. 49–52.
580. Stanton, *The Rise and Fall, op. cit.*, p. 111.
581. Jones, *op. cit.*, p. 143.
582. Williamson, *op. cit.*, p. 354.
583. Shulimson, *Expanding War, op. cit.*, p. 23.
584. Shulimson, *Expanding War, op. cit.*, p. 84.
585. Shulimson, *Expanding War, op. cit.*, p. 120.
586. Shulimson, *Expanding War, op. cit.*, p. 17.
587. Shulimson, *Expanding War, op. cit.*, p. 163.

588. W. R. Peers, *Report of the DA Review of the Preliminary Investigation into the My Lai Incident*, (Washington, D.C.: Department of the Army), p. 3-1.

589. O'Neill, *Vietnam Task*, *op. cit.*, p. 117.

590. W. B. Fulton, *Riverine Operations*, (Washington, D.C.: Department of the Army), 1973.

591. Thomas J. Cutler, *Brown Water, Black Berets*, (Annapolis, MD: Naval institute Press, 1988), pp. 200–02.

592. Williamson, *op. cit.*, p. 382.

593. Van Dyke, *op. cit.*, p. 120.

594. Telfer, *op. cit.*, p. 8.

595. Telfer, *op. cit.*, p. 77.

596. Telfer, *op. cit.*, pp. 258–59.

597. W. R. Peers, *Report of the DA Review of the Preliminary Investigation into the My Lai Incident, Vol. I, The Report of Investigation, Department of the Army*, March 14, 1970, pp. 3-2.

598. Stanton, *Rise and Fall of An American Army*, *op. cit.*, pp. 148–51.

599. Frost, *op. cit.*, p. 87.

600. Harvey Meyerson, *Vinh Long*, (Boston: Houghton Mifflin Company, 1970), p. 93.

601. Peers, *op. cit.*, p. 3-1.

602. *Ibid.*

603. Jones, *op. cit.*, p. 143.

604. Hammel, *op. cit.*, p. 153.

605. Telfer, *op. cit.*, p. 251.

606. Peers, *op. cit.*, p. 3-1.

607. Smith, *op. cit.*, pp. 63–4.

608. Smith, *op. cit.*, p. 83.

609. Meyerson, *op. cit.*, pp. 192–3.

Chapter 17: Chu Luc Order of Battle II

610. Smith, *op. cit.*, p. 6.

611. Smith, *op. cit.*, pp. 99–100.

612. Smith, *op. cit.*, pp. 193–201.

613. Fox, *op. cit.*, p. 224.

614. Lung, *op. cit.*, p. 187.

615. Comas, *Vietnamization and Redeployment*, *op. cit.*, p. 26.

616. Comas, *op. cit.*, p. 5.

617. Smith, *op. cit.*, p. 318.

618. Sak Suisakhan, *The Khmer Republic At War and The Final Collapse*, (Washington D.C.: U.S. Army Center of Military History, 1980), pp. 28–9.

619. Nguyen Duy Hinh, *Lam Son 719*, (Washington D.C.: U.S. Army Center of Military History, 1979), p. 112.

620. Le Gro, *op. cit.*, p. 153.

621. Le Gro, *op. cit.*, pp. 29–39.

622. Le Gro, *op. cit.*, p. 28.

Chapter 18: NVA Divisional Doctrine I

623. Stanton, *273rd VC Regiment*, *op. cit.* p. 66.

624. Hoang Ngoc Lung, *The General Offensive of 1968–69*, (Washington, D.C.: U.S. Army Center of Military History, 1980), p. 96.

625. John Hill, "Tet Offensive, 1968," *Conflict,* October 20, 1973.

626. Nolan, *Hue, op. cit.,* p. 56.

627. *Soviet Army Operations,* Washington, D.C.: Department of the Army, April, 1978, p. 3–10.

628. Michael D. Harkins, "Magnificent Pressure Exerted," *Vietnam,* Summer, 1989, p. 47.

629. *Ibid.,* p. 42.

630. William Weise, "Memories of Dai Do," *Marine Corps Gazette,* September 1987, p. 55.

631. Harkins, *op. cit.,* p. 49.

632. Harkins, *op. cit.,* p. 47.

633. *Ibid.*

634. *Ibid.*

635. Weise, *op. cit.,* p. 55.

636. *Ibid.*

637. Weise, *op. cit.,* p. 50.

638. Weise, *op. cit.,* p. 53.

639. Weise, *op. cit.,* p. 50.

640. Weise, *op. cit.,* p. 54.

Chapter 19: NVA Divisional Operations II

641. Raymond G. Davis, "Defeat of the 320th NVA Division," *Marine Corps Gazette,* Vol. 53, #3 (March, 1969), pp. 22–3.

642. *Ibid.,* p. 24.

643. *Ibid.*

644. *Ibid.,* p. 28.

645. *Ibid.,* p. 23.

646. *Ibid.,* p. 26.

647. *Ibid.*

648. *Ibid.,* p. 27.

649. Ian McNeill, *The Team,* (London: Secker and Warburg, 1984), p. 156.

650. Hackworth, *About Face, op. cit.,* p. 676.

651. Duquesne A. Wolf., *The Infantry Brigade in Combat,* (Manhattan, Kansas: Sunflower University Press, 1984).

652. *Ibid.,* p., 12.

653. *Ibid.,* p. 14.

654. *Ibid.,* p. 34.

655. *Ibid.,* p. 14.

656. *Ibid.,* pp. 9–10.

657. *Ibid.,* p. 40.

658. *Ibid.,* p. 13.

659. Stanton, *Rise and Fall of An American Army, op. cit.,* pp. 287–8. Stanton, Shelby, *Anatomy of a Division, op. cit.,* pp. 160–1.

Chapter 20: NVA Campaigns: Cambodia and Laos

660. Bruce Palmer, *The Twenty Five Year War,* (New York: Simon and Schuster, 1984), pp. 98–99.

661. Sutsakhan, *op. cit.,* pp. 72–73.

662. *Ibid.,* pp. 74–77.

663. *Ibid.,* pp. 139–44.

664. Hinh, *op. cit.,* pp. 21–24.

665. *Ibid.*

666. P. F. Langer and J. J. Zasloaf, *North Vietnam and The Pathet Lao*, (Cambridge, MA: Harvard University Press, 1970), pp. 158.

667. *Ibid.*

668. *Ibid.*

669. *Ibid.*, p. 159.

670. *Ibid.*, p. 161.

671. *Ibid.*, p. 163.

672. *Ibid.*, pp. 113–14.

673. *Ibid.*, p. 114.

674. *Ibid.*, pp. 110–16.

675. *Ibid.*

676. *Ibid.*, p. 147.

677. Christopher Robbins, *The Ravens*, (New York: Crown Publishing). p. 141.

678. *Ibid.*, p. 19311

679. Hinh, *op. cit.*, pp. 19–25, 78.

680. Soutchag Vongsavanh, *RLG Military Operations and Activities In the Laotian Panhandle*, (Washington D.C.: U.S. Army Center of Military History, 1981), p. 58.

681. *Ibid.*, p. 65.

Chapter 21: The Nguyen Hue/Easter Offensive: 1972

682. Ngo Q. Truong, *The Easter Offensive of 1972*, (Washington, D.C.: U.S. Army Center of Military History, 1980), p. 81.

683. *Ibid.*, p. 82.

684. John Prodos, "Year of the Rat: Vietnam, 1972," *Strategy and Tactics*, Spring–Summer, 1973, pp. 13–18.

685. *Ibid.*

683. CNA Study #1035, *Defense of Hue and Quang Tri City: The 1972 NVN Invasion of MR-1.*

687. G. H. Turley, *The Easter Offensive, Vietnam, 1972*, (Novato, CA: Presidio Press, 1985), p. 92.

688. *Ibid.*, p. 46.

689. *Ibid.*, p. 46.

690. *Ibid.*, p. 32.

691. *Ibid.*, p. 93.

692. *Ibid.*, p. 99.

693. *Ibid.*, p. 100.

694. *Ibid.*, p. 65.

695. *Ibid.*, p. 144.

696. *Ibid.*, p. 145.

697. *Ibid.*, p. 145.

698. *Ibid.*, p. 274.

699. *Ibid.*, pp. 23–29.

700. *Ibid.*, p. 230.

701. *Ibid.*, p. 234.

702. Ngo Quang Truong, *The Easter Offensive of 1972*, (Washington, D.C.: U.S. Army Center of Military History 1972), pp. 82–3.

703. MACV Historical Study: *The Nguyen-Hue Offensive.*

704. Starry, *op. cit.*, p. 214.

705. Truong, *op. cit.*, p. 112.

706. Lung, *op. cit.*, pp. 132–33.

707. Le Gro, *op. cit.*, p. 7.

708. Le Gro, *op. cit.*, p. 49.

709. Truon, *op. cit.*, p. 133.

710. Le Gro, *op. cit.*, p. 10.

711. Le Gro, *op. cit.*, p. 12.

712. Le Gro, *op. cit.*, p. 14.

713. U.S.G. Sharp, *Strategy For Defeat*, (San Rafael, CA: Presidio Press, 1978), p. 255.

714. *Ibid.*, pp. 252–54.

Chapter 22: Chu Luc Conquest of South Vietnam

715. Nguyen Duy Hinh, *Vietnamization and the Cease Fire*, (Washington, D.C.: U.S. Army Center for Military History, 1979), p. 32.

716. C. V. Vien, *The Final Collapse*, (Washington, D.C.: U.S. Army Center for Military History, 1985, pp. 34–5.

717. Le Gro, *op. cit.*, p. 28.

718. Dinh, *op. cit.*, p. 152.

719. Le Gro, *op. cit.*, p. 40.

720. *Ibid.*

721. Hung P. Nguyen, "Communist Offensive Strategy and the Defense of South Vietnam," *Parameters*, Vol XIV, No. 4, p. 9.

722. *Ibid.*, pp. 9–10.

723. Le Gro, *op. cit.*, pp. 92–93.

724. Vien, *op. cit.*, p. 121.

725. Van Tien Dung, *Our Great Spring Victory*, (New York: Monthly Review Press, 1977), pp. 45–46.

726. Dung, *op. cit.*, p. 79.

727. Williams E. Depuy, "Our Experience in Vietnam: Will We Be Beneficiaries Or Victims?," *Army*, July, 1987, p. 2–11.

728. Le Gro, *op. cit.*, pp. 3–280.

Chapter 23: The Chinese Army Versus The NVA

729. J. Smith, "The Sino-Vietnamese War," *Marine Corps Gazette*, March, 1981, p. 41.

730. Michael Leifer, *Cambodia: The Search For Security*, (New York: F. A. Praeger, 1967).

731. *Handbook On The Chinese Communist Army*, (Washington, D.C.: Headquarters, Department of the Army, 1960), pp. 23–25.

732. King C. Chen, *China's War Against Vietnam: 1979*, (Stanford, CA: Hoover Institute Press, 1987), p. 12.

733. *Ibid.*, p. 212.

734. *Ibid.*, p. 107.

735. *Ibid.*, p. 103.

736. J. Smith, "The Sino-Vietnamese War," *Marine Corps Gazette*, March, 1981, p. 41.

737. *Ibid.*

738. Herman Ray, *China's Vietnam War*, New Delhi, India: Radiant Publisher, 1983), p. 95.

739. *Ibid.*, p. 98.

740. Ray, *op. cit.*, p. 99.

741. King C. Chen, "China's War Against Vietnam," *Journal of East Asian Affairs*, Vol. 3 (Fall–Spring–Summer), 1983, p. 17.

742. *Ibid.*, p. 18.
743. Smith, *op. cit.*, p. 44.
744. Chen, *op. cit.*, p. 111.
745. Chen, *op. cit.*, p. 110.
746. Chen, *op. cit.*, p. 111.
747. Chen, *op. cit.*, p. 114.
748. Ray, *op. cit.*, p. 101.
749. Ray, *op. cit.*, pp. 101–02.
750. Chen, *Journal of East Asian Affairs*, p. 26.

Chapter 24: The Chu Luc Triumphant

751. Editor, "The Basket Case of Southeast Asia," *The New American*, February 2, 1987, p. 8.
752. *Ibid.*
753. Reed Irvine, "Lost In The Killing Fields," *Aim Report*, Vol. XIV-6, March 8, 1985, p. 2.
754. Reed Irvine, "Homage To Hanoi", *Aim Report*, Vol. XIV-10, May 8, 1985, p. 2.
755. Al Santoli, "Why Viet Cong Fee," *Parade*, July 11, 1982, page 4.
756. *Ibid.*, p. 5.
757. Malparte, *op. cit.*, p. 272.
758. H. J. Kaplan, "Remembering Vietnam," *Commentary*, December, 1987, p. 29. Interview with former Ambassador to South Vietnam, Graham Martin, 1986.
759. Leston, *op. cit.*, p. 23.
760. Bruce Palmer, *The Twenty Five Year War*, (Lexington, KY: University Press of Lexington, 1984), pp. 222–223 "Intelligence Watch," *Reserve*, May–June–July, 1977, p. 32.
761. *Ibid.*
762. *Ibid.*
763. *Ibid.*
764. *Ibid.*
765. Cutler, *op. cit.*, p. 352.
766. *Ibid.*
767. *The Military Balance*, 1979–80, pp. 464–65.
768. Edward N. Luttwak, *The Grand Strategy of the Soviet Union*, (New York: St. Martin's Press, 1983).
769. Bernard K. Gordon, "The Third Indochina Conflict," *Foreign Affairs*, p. 67.
770. "When Will The Peace Begin?" *Time*, April 25, 1983, p. 83.
771. C. J. Patterson and G. L. Tippin, *The Heroes Who Fell From Grace*, (Canton, OH: Daring Books, 1985). James Rosenthal, "The Myth of the Last Pows," *The New Republic*, July 1, 1985, p. 16.
772. *The New American, op. cit.*, p. 29.
773. Anonymous interview with active duty U.S. Army officer in Washington, D.C., 1987.
774. George Black, "Republican Overtures to Hanoi," *The Nation*, June 4, 1988, p. 793.
775. Angelo M. Codevilla, "Is There Still a Soviet Threat?" *Commentary*, November, 1988, p. 26.
776. Gordon, *op. cit.*, pp. 80–81.; O'Ballance, *op. cit.*, pp. 225–226.
777. Peter Weiss, "Soviet Ambitions In The Far East," *International Defense Review*, December, 1986, pp. 82–83.
778. *The Military Balance, op. cit.*, p. 464.
779. *Ibid.*

780. Slade, *op. cit.*, p. 25.

781. Stephen Young and William Bradley, *Thailand: Domino By Default,* (Athens OH: Ohio University Center for International Studies, 1978), p. 57.

782. Stuart Slade, "How Thais Burnt the Books and Beat the Guerillas," *International Security and Coin (Supplement to International Defense Review,* October, 1989), p. 22.

783. Justus M. Van Der Kroef, "Kampuchea: Southeast Asia's Flashpoint", *Paramaters,* Vol. XIII, No. 1, p. 64.

784. Gordon, *op. cit.,* pp. 71–73.

785. Edmond Dantes, "The Royal Thai Army and Its Problems," *International Defense Review,* July, 1989, p. 923.

786. *Ibid.*

787. *Ibid.*

788. Son Sen, "No More Revolutionary Ideals," *International Defense Review,* July, 1989, p. 920.

789. Justus M. Van Der Kroef, "Kampuchea: Southeast Asia's Flashpoint," *Paramaters,* Vol. XIII, No. 1, p. 62.

790. *Ibid.*

791. Mike Winchester, "Plays Change: The Game's The Same," *Soldier of Fortune,* February, 1985, p. 43.

792. Sen, *op. cit.,* p. 919.

793. *Ibid.,* p. 921.

794. Sen, *op. cit.,* p. 922.

795. Victor M. Rosello, "Vietnam's Support to El Salvador's FMLN," *Military Review,* January, 1990, pp. 71–3.

796. *Ibid.,* p. 74.

797. *Ibid.*

798. *Ibid.,* p. 72.

799. *Ibid.,* p. 72.

800. Douglas Pike, *PAVN: People's Army of Vietnam,* (Navato, CA: Presidio Press, 1986), p. 221.

801. Phillip B. Davidson, *Vietnam At War,* (Novato, CA: Presidio Press, 1988), p. 730.

Index

535